HONG KONG

114°20'E
MIRS BAY
Ping Chau
CROOKED HARBOUR
Crooked Island
Crescent Island
DOUBLE HAVEN
Double Island
Port Island
Grass Island
NORTH CHANNEL
MIDDLE CHANNEL
TOLO CHANNEL
LONG HARBOUR
Plover Cove Reservoir
TAI PO
TOLO HARBOUR
SHA TIN
SAI KUNG
MA ON SHAN
Kau Sai Chau
High Island Reservoir
HIGH ISLAND
TAI LONG WAN
SHARP PEAK
PORT SHELTER
ROCKY HARBOUR
TSEUNG KWAN O
KOWLOON PEAK
LION ROCK
Sharp Island
Jin Island
Town Island
Hole Island
Bluff Island
Basalt Island
Shelter Island
HIGH JUNK PEAK
Tai Au Mun
Fat Tong Chau
Ninepin Group
Tung Lung Chau
KONG ISLAND
SHEK O
D'AGUILAR PEAK
STANLEY
TAI TAM WAN
Middle Island
Round Island
Beaufort Island
Po Toi Islands
Sung Kong
Waglan Island
Po Toi
LEGEND
Built-up Area
Cultivation
Country Park
Main Road
Tunnel
Secondary Road
Railway
Light Railway
Contour (vertical interval 100 metres with supplementary contour at 50 metres)
Sea depth in metres
CHINA
Beijing
Nanjing
Shanghai
Chongqing
Fuzhou
Guangzhou
MACAU
HONG KONG
TAIWAN
EAST CHINA SEA
SOUTH CHINA SEA
PACIFIC OCEAN
PHILIPPINES
MALAYSIA
SINGAPORE
INDONESIA
22°30'N
22°20'
22°10'N
10 12 14 km

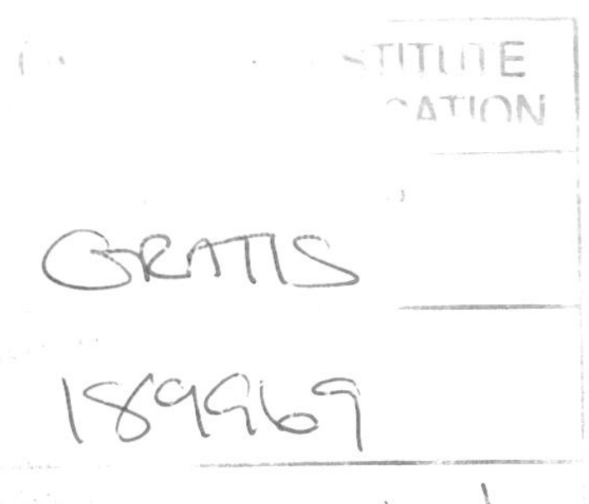

HONG KONG *1994*

Editor: Renu Daryanani
Government Information Services

Designers: Everett Lee
Liu Chiu-tsan
Government Information Services

Photography: Stone Chiang, Augustine Chu, David Ho, Au-yeung Yiu-man and other staff photographers. Other photographs by arrangement with Neil Pryde Ltd, South China Morning Post, Chinese University of Hong Kong and The Hong Kong University of Science and Technology

Special Contributor: Sir David Ford (Chapter 1)

Statistical Sources: Census and Statistics Department

The editor acknowledges all contributors and sources.

Code No.: F30019400E0 (ISBN 962-02-0139-6)

Price: HK$60.00 US$26.00 UK £ 19.00

Cover: *Central Plaza, Asia's tallest building, stands out in the constantly changing skyline of Hong Kong Island.*

Frontispiece: *Hong Kong and its environs in 1846, as seen from the Anchorage by Lieutenant I. G. Heath RN, of HMS Iris.*
(Reproduced with the permission of the Hydrographer of the Navy.)

CONTENTS

ILLUSTRATIONS

END-PAPER MAPS

APPENDICES

When dollars are quoted in this report, they are, unless otherwise stated, Hong Kong dollars. Since October 17, 1983, the Hong Kong dollar has been linked to the US dollar, through an arrangement in the note-issue mechanism, at a fixed rate of HK$7.80 = US$1.

*   *   *

Some figures in the text are estimated; actual figures appear in the appendices.

CALENDAR OF EVENTS IN 1993

1.1 Twenty-one people are trampled to death during crowd revelry at Lan Kwai Fong, Central, where thousands gathered to welcome in the New Year. The Governor, the Right Honourable Christoper Patten, orders an immediate inquiry and appoints a High Court judge to recommend ways to prevent similar tragedies.

12.1 The government announces that the Bank of China will become the third note-issuing bank in Hong Kong in May 1994.

13.1 A motion to withdraw the government's political reform proposals is defeated in the Legislative Council.

Cathay Pacific flight attendants strike over a staff deployment and pay adjustment dispute. Air traffic during the Lunar New Year is seriously disrupted before the strike is called off on January 30.

15.1 The Governor opens the $400 million Island East Refuse Transfer Station, part of a multi-billion dollar long-term waste management strategy.

21.1 A Compendium of Proposals on the 1994–95 elections is published. It includes 65 written submissions received since October 7, 1992, when the Governor announced proposals on constitutional development.

28.1 Chief Secretary, Sir David Ford, heads a delegation to promote Hong Kong at the World Economic Forum at Davos, Switzerland.

1.2 A $2.6 billion contract is signed for the West Kowloon Reclamation, one of the major projects in the Airport Core Programme.

4.2 A Provisional Governing Council is appointed to prepare for the formal establishment of a new institute of education, the Hong Kong Institute of Education.

19.2 Legislative Councillors elect fellow member, Mr John Swaine, as President of the council.

24.2 Hong Kong signs a new air services agreement with Sri Lanka.

25.2 The government approves a package of measures, recommended by the Education Commission Report No. 5, for improving the quality of education in primary and secondary schools.

26.2 An $856 million contract is awarded for the construction of the Cheung Ching Tunnel on the Tsing Yi Island section of Route 3, a key element in the Airport Core Programme's highway network.

27.2 A record price of $9.5 million is paid for the vehicle registration number '2' in a government auction, the proceeds of which are used for charitable purposes.

3.3 Financial Secretary, Mr Hamish Macleod, presents the 1993–94 Budget in the Legislative Council, which provides for real increases of more than seven per cent in recurrent expenditure on social welfare, health and education.

5.3 The Governor leaves for a two-day visit to Japan to meet government officials and business leaders. He also addresses the ninth annual meeting of the United Kingdom–Japan 2000 Group at Awashima, where Hong Kong is featured as a major agenda item for the first time.

12.3 The Electoral Provisions (Miscellaneous Amendments) Bill 1993, which sets out in legislative form various proposals in the constitutional package in the Governor's address to the Legislative Council in October 1992, is published in the Government Gazette.

16.3 The University of Hong Kong, the territory's oldest tertiary institution, celebrates the 80th anniversary of its foundation day.

19.3 A Charter for Youth is introduced, proclaiming principles and ideals for youth development with the aim of giving young people the best possible opportunities in life.

26.3 The Tin Shui Wai new town is opened by the Governor. The first phase of the development covers 169 hectares and will provide homes for some 135 000 people by 1995.

30.3 Hong Kong is ranked sixth in global foreign exchange market activity in a report by the Bank of International Settlements.

31.3 The Governor leaves for a visit to Brussels and London. It is his first visit to Brussels as Governor.

1.4 The Royal Hong Kong Auxiliary Air Force is formally disbanded and succeeded by the Government Flying Service.

The Hong Kong Monetary Authority is formally established, by merging the Office of the Exchange Fund and the Office of the Commissioner of Banking.

2.4 The government publishes a consultative paper on the findings of the Railway Development Study, which presents proposals for the further development of Hong Kong's railway system up to 2011.

16.4 The Council for the AIDS Trust Fund is appointed, to advise on the management and disbursement of a special trust fund to provide assistance to those infected with AIDS and to enhance awareness of AIDS prevention.

22.4 Sino-British talks open in Beijing on the arrangements for the 1994–95 elections in Hong Kong. The talks stretch to 17 sessions, totalling more than 150 hours.

30.4 A $2.27 billion contract is awarded for the construction of the Kwai Chung Viaduct section of Route 3.

2.5 The Governor begins his first visit to the United States as Governor of Hong Kong, during which he meets President Bill Clinton to discuss trade and the economic relationship between Hong Kong and the United States.

Secretary for Security, Mr Alistair Asprey, leaves for a seven-day visit to Vietnam to discuss the return and reintegration of Vietnamese non-refugees.

4.5 Hong Kong signs a mutual recognition agreement on laboratory accreditation with the Netherlands. The agreement, which covers laboratory testing standards, will facilitate the access of exports between the two territories.

7.5 The Sino-British Land Commission holds its 27th meeting to discuss the 1993–94 Land Disposal Programme. The meeting, which is continued on May 11, agrees that 127.8 hectares of land should be made available during the year.

12.5 Former Prime Minister, Baroness Thatcher of Kesteven, arrives in Hong Kong for a two-day visit as guest of the Governor.

18.5 The Royal Navy moves to its new HMS Tamar headquarters on Stonecutters Island.

Legislative Councillor, Mr Stephen Cheong, passes away at the age of 51. Mr Cheong served in the Legislative Council for 12 years.

29.5 Minister of State for Foreign and Commonwealth Affairs with special responsibility for Hong Kong, Mr Alistair Goodlad, arrives in Hong Kong for a four-day visit.

31.5 The government awards a subscription television licence to Wharf Cable Limited.

2.6 A $670 million contract is awarded for the construction of the Route 3 Rambler Channel Bridge, part of the Airport Core Programme highways network.

The first integrated chemical waste treatment facility in the Asia-Pacific region opens on Tsing Yi Island.

Twelve people are killed when a passenger hoist collapses at a construction site in North Point.

4.6 The Sino-British Airport Committee meets in Hong Kong, to continue discussions on the financial arrangements for the new airport projects. Three further meetings are held during the year.

5.6 Secretary for Health and Welfare, Mrs Elizabeth Wong, leads a government delegation to the Ninth International Conference on AIDS in Berlin.

6.6 The last group of 175 recruits of the Royal Hong Kong Regiment (The Volunteers) pass out. The regiment will be disbanded in 1995.

8.6 The government announces arrangements for a new housing scheme to help middle-income families buy their own homes.

11.6 Hong Kong Monetary Authority Chief Executive, Mr Joseph Yam, represents Hong Kong at the annual meeting in London of the Central Bank Governors, hosted by the Bank of England.

21.6 The Sino-British Joint Liaison Group holds its 26th meeting in Hong Kong to discuss arrangements for the smooth transfer of sovereignty over Hong Kong in 1997. The 27th and 28th meetings are held in Beijing and London on September 14 and December 7, respectively.

23.6 A $3.2 billion contract is signed for the West New Territories Landfill, the first of three strategic large-capacity landfills to be developed under Hong Kong's long-term waste management strategy.

30.6 The government announces arrangements for the implementation of the Home Secretary's decision to allow Hong Kong British Dependent Territories Citizens to retain their passports in addition to their British National (Overseas) passport.

1.7 The Governor attends a Cabinet Committee meeting in London to discuss the way forward in the Sino-British talks on the political development in Hong Kong.

The Telecommunications Authority is set up to oversee all aspects of the regulation of telecommunications services in Hong Kong.

5.7 Twenty senior civil servants attend the first seven-week China studies course at Beijing's Qinghua University.

7.7 The 30 000th Vietnamese illegal immigrant returns home under the UNHCR's Voluntary Repatriation Programme.

9.7 Hong Kong becomes the first major city in the world to have a completely digital telephone network.

Secretary of State for Foreign and Commonwealth Affairs, Mr Douglas Hurd, arrives in Hong Kong, after a visit to Beijing.

14.7 A medical services consultative document, 'Towards Better Health', is published, offering various options for health care reform including increased accessibility, more choice, better services, improved efficiency and cost-effectiveness, and simpler administration.

19.7 A $1.27 billion contract is awarded for the construction of the Western Kowloon Expressway North Section.

20.7 The Privy Council makes Orders providing for the implementation of the final phase of the British Nationality Selection Scheme, and for the phased issue of British National (Overseas) passports to British Dependent Territories Citizens before July 1997.

The Ministry of Defence announces plans for the deployment of British Forces in Hong Kong between now and 1997. The garrison will be reduced in stages over this period, as local forces assume responsibility for its former operational tasks.

23.7 The government announces the establishment of the Boundary and Election Commission, an independent body to take charge of electoral matters including the delineation of geographical constituency boundaries.

31.7 The government announces the sale of Overseas Trust Bank, Limited to the Guoco Group Limited for a total consideration of $4,457 million. The sale of the bank, taken over in June 1985, marked the end of the government's efforts to rescue banks in the 1980s.

5.8 A $997 million contract is awarded for the construction of the Western Kowloon Expressway South Section.

Hong Kong's essential services mobilise, in response to a request from the Mayor of Shenzhen, to assist their Guangdong counterparts to fight a major fire at a dangerous goods storage depot at Qingshuihe in Shenzhen.

25.8 Baron Kadoorie of Kowloon in Hong Kong and of the City of Westminster, the first Hong Kong resident to be made a member of the House of Lords, dies at the age of 94.

26.8 The Green Paper on Equal Opportunities for Women and Men is released for public consultation.

A $1.72 billion contract for the first phase of the Central Reclamation is awarded by the Mass Transit Railway Corporation on behalf of the government.

2.9 A $5.7 billion contract for the construction of the Western Harbour Crossing is signed.

3.9 Container Terminal 8, which has the capacity to handle 1.8 million TEUs a year, is officially commissioned.

15.9 Hong Kong and Australia sign a new air services agreement and an agreement for the promotion and protection of investments.

21.9 Mrs Anson Chan, Secretary for the Civil Service, is appointed Chief Secretary to succeed Sir David Ford on November 29. She is the first local, female officer to be appointed to the post.

22.9 Hong Kong and the Guangdong authorities sign a Memorandum of Understanding on emergency co-operation in the event of a nuclear incident at the Daya Bay Nuclear Power Plant.

23.9 A $3.5 billion contract for the Southeast New Territories Landfill is signed.

Central Plaza, the tallest building in Asia and the fourth tallest in the world, dedicates to the people of Hong Kong an innovative time piece — 'Lightime' — located at the top of the 374-metre building.

24.9 Financial Secretary, Mr Hamish Macleod, leaves for the United States to attend the annual meetings of the International Monetary Fund and the World Bank.

26.9 Torrential rain accompanying Typhoon Dot causes widespread flooding in the northwest New Territories, affecting an estimated 400 hectares of farmland. More than 300 millimetres of rain falls in 72 hours, twice the average for the whole of September.

30.9 Major proposals for Hong Kong's growth up to the year 2011 are published in a consultative document entitled 'Territorial Development Strategy Review — Development Options'.

1.10 Foreign Secretary, Mr Douglas Hurd, and Chinese Foreign Minister, Mr Qian Qichen, meet in New York to exchange views on issues including those relating to Hong Kong.

4.10 Hong Kong's first female fire-fighters join the ranks of the Fire Services, which also celebrated its 125th anniversary this year.

6.10 The Governor delivers his second policy address in the Legislative Council and outlines the priorities to meet rising public aspirations in the year ahead.

11.10 Minister of State for Foreign and Commonwealth Affairs with special responsibility for Hong Kong, Mr Alastair Goodlad, arrives in Hong Kong for a two-day visit.

15.10 The Central to Mid-Levels Escalators open for public use. The escalator system, measuring about 800 metres in length and climbing about 135 metres in height, is the longest in the world.

16.10 A 12-member delegation of the House of Commons Foreign Affairs Committee arrives in Hong Kong for a four-day visit. The trip is part of the committee's inquiry into relations between the United Kingdom and China in the period up to and beyond 1997.

26.10 Hong Kong enters the Guinness Book of Records for the largest jig-saw puzzle ever assembled. The jig-saw puzzle, measuring 21 936 square metres, was assembled by some 1 500 able and disabled young people to mark the International Day of Disabled Persons.

29.10 The provisional constituency boundaries drawn up by the Boundary and Election Commission for the 1994 District Board elections are gazetted for public consultation.

31.10 Wharf Cable Limited commences broadcasting with eight cable television channels.

4.11 A China Airlines Boeing 747 jetliner from Taipei skids off the airport runway at Kai Tak into Victoria Harbour. Among the 296 passengers and crew on board, 23 passengers sustained minor injuries.

5.11 Heavy rain from Typhoon Ira causes widespread flooding and mudslips, resulting in two deaths, and disruption of water supply to 400 000 residents in Tuen Mun for four days.

10.11 The Governor attends a Cabinet Committee meeting in London to review progress of Sino-British talks held to date on the arrangements for the 1994–95 elections in Hong Kong.

A 'Hong Kong Works' conference organised by the government, in association with the Institute of Directors, is opened in London by Prime Minister, Mr John Major.

14.11 Chief Secretary (Designate), Mrs Anson Chan, launches Hong Kong '93 in Europe — a major trade and economic promotion in Hong Kong's foremost trading partners in continental Europe: Germany, the Netherlands and France.

15.11 Hong Kong and Australia sign an agreement on the surrender of accused and convicted persons that will remain in force after 1997.

17.11 A delegation led by the Secretary for Trade and Industry, Mr Chau Tak-hay, attends the three-day annual ministerial meeting of the Asia-Pacific Economic Co-operation (APEC) in Seattle.

20.11 Financial Secretary, Mr Hamish Macleod, joins world leaders at the first APEC Economic Leaders Meeting in Seattle to discuss future economic development in the region.

22.11 The seventh annual conference of the Asian Association of Open Universities opens in Hong Kong. The conference attracts participants from 30 countries.

30.11 The government announces that it will license three new fixed telecommunications networks, marking an important new stage in the implementation of its pro-competitive telecoms policy.

1.12 The Legislative Council passes a resolution to establish a disaster relief fund to help victims outside Hong Kong. The $50 million fund will allow the territory to respond quickly to international appeals for humanitarian aid.

4.12 A $305.9 million contract is awarded for the supply and installation of a traffic control and surveillance system on the Lantau Fixed Crossing and part of Route 3. The contract forms part of the Airport Core Programme.

9.12 The Hong Kong Academy of Medicine is formally inaugurated.

10.12 The Electoral Provisions (Miscellaneous Amendments) (No. 2) Bill 1993 is gazetted. The Bill deals with the more immediate issues relating to the 1994–95 elections, including a 'single seat, single vote' system for all three tiers of geographical constituency elections; lowering the voting age from 21 to 18 years; abolishing appointed membership in the municipal councils and district boards; and relaxing existing restrictions on Hong Kong residents who are members of the Chinese People's Congresses from running for election and holding office in the Legislative Council, municipal councils and district boards.

The government announces its intention to pursue a compulsory contributory old-age pension scheme. A feasibility study will be undertaken on the subject.

11.12 Phase I of the Cheung Sha Wan wholesale food market — the first building to be completed under the Airport Core Programme — is officially opened. The $504 million market is designed to handle over 370 000 tonnes of fresh foodstuffs yearly.

13.12 A ground-breaking ceremony is held for the new campus of the Open Learning Institute in Ho Man Tin.

17.12 The Housing Authority commemorates the 40th anniversary of Hong Kong's public housing programme which has so far provided homes for three million people, half of Hong Kong's population.

A $519.59 million waterworks contract — part of the North Lantau water supply project — is approved for award under the Airport Core Programme.

29.12 The Tian Tan Buddha, at 26.4 metres the largest outdoor bronze statue of Buddha in the world, is inaugurated at the Po Lin Monastery on Lantau Island. Monks from 13 countries are among the thousands attending the inauguration.

31.12 The Financial Secretary, Mr Hamish Macleod, is made a Knight Commander of the Most Excellent Order of the British Empire in the Queen's New Year honours list.

After a succession of records, the Hang Seng Index closes for the year at 11 888.39 points, up 115.67 per cent from 12 months earlier.

Above: *Promoting Hong Kong business interests was high on the agenda for the Governor, Mr Christopher Patten* **(left),** *seen here with the Prime Minister, Mr John Major, and Lord Young of Graffham* **(centre),** *during a Hong Kong trade conference in London.*

Preceding page: *Her Royal Highness Princess Anne presents a trophy at the Royal Hong Kong Jockey Club racecourse at Happy Valley, during a visit in November.*

Hong Kong, represented by Financial Secretary Mr Hamish Macleod **(second from right),** *was an active participant in the APEC Economic Leaders summit hosted by U.S. President Mr Bill Clinton, in November.* **Pictured from left are:** *Canadian Prime Minister, Mr Jean Chrétien; the President of the People's Republic of China, Mr Jiang Zemin; Mr Clinton; Australian Prime Minister, Mr Paul Keating; the President of the Philippines, Mr Fidel Ramos; Thailand's Prime Minister, Mr Chuan Leekpai; Mr Macleod; and South Korean President, Mr Kim Young Sam.*

The Governor shares a light-hearted moment with U.S. President Mr Bill Clinton, during Mr Patten's first visit to Washington, as Governor, in May.

Baroness Thatcher of Kesteven showed keen interest in recent developments along the northern shore of Hong Kong Island when she toured the Eastern District atop a double-decker tram in May, accompanied by the Governor.

DIEU ET MON DROIT

Above: *The Former U.S. President, Mr George Bush, called on Mr Patten, during his visit to the territory in mid-November.*

Left: *The German Chancellor, Dr Helmut Kohl, leaves Government House after a meeting with the Governor on November 20.*

On her official visit to Europe in November, the Chief Secretary designate, Mrs Anson Chan, called on the President of the Senate of France, Mr René Monory.

1
A RARE ALCHEMY

A personal view by Sir David Ford, KBE, LVO, JP.
Sir David served in Hong Kong for 27 years
and was Chief Secretary from February 1987 to November 1993.
He is now Hong Kong Commissioner in London.

FOR me, *Hong Kong* defines not so much a place as a people, not so much its tightly circumscribed location as the unbounded spirit of its inhabitants.

When I arrived 27 years ago, my reaction was that of most people who see Hong Kong for the first time. I was bowled over by a spectacular natural harbour, around which was arrayed — even then — a no less spectacular architectural achievement. But this soon gave way to a more enduring sense of admiration — for the human enterprise which projected that image across the world, to millions who may never have seen it except in the graphic representation of its unmistakable contours.

The panorama looked compelling enough on a postcard, but it was a label that, on a global dimension, aroused the greater curiosity. '*Made in Hong Kong*' it declared — a simple but telling label, small and modest in its earliest appearance, and then bigger and prouder as, with increasing confidence, year after year it attached itself to product after product.

What was the source of all this abundance of every known variety of manufactured produce for which the world could conceivably find a use? The typical atlas was unhelpful to those who did not know where to start looking. One needed a magnifying glass in the right quadrant.

Finding the location instantly prompted the question. Was it conceivable that an area so small could produce so much? The answer, as the world now knows, because Hong Kong has so magnificently proved the point, is a resounding *yes* — if you have the right people living in it.

What then are the ingredients alloyed in the character of such a people, who have surmounted tiny territorial confines to leave their imprint upon far wider horizons?

Many elements have been identified in the composition. Business acumen, quickness of eye in recognising opportunity, willingness to venture on the outcome, mingled with endurance, determination to succeed against all odds, adaptability to circumstance and, not least, total commitment of physique and intellect to the accomplishment of the principal goal.

Though these characteristics are neither unique nor unprecedented, they have combined here, in the crucible of Hong Kong, to produce a rare alchemy. An alchemy that resists analysis, retaining its properties of toughness and imperishability, however hot the flame.

Hong Kong, when I first saw it, was in crisis. The Cultural Revolution was in full conflagration across the border and had already ignited riots in Hong Kong streets, threatening to engulf this tiny corner of China which history had temporarily vouchsafed to British governance. That it never did so was due as much to the good sense and resolution of the Hong Kong populace as to the steadfastness of our administration and the efforts, behind the scenes in Beijing, to avert the danger.

Crisis — mainly external, mainly arising from causes beyond Hong Kong's control — has never been long absent or far removed from the life of its people. Whether induced by political change, economic circumstance or natural phenomena, the risk factor is inherent in the conditioning of the Hong Kong temperament, as much to be taken into account as the daily meteorological forecast. People who live in a typhoon belt learn to build strong shutters. They know how to contain the damage and, if necessary, to rebuild and start afresh.

Change — dramatic change — was thrust upon Hong Kong soon after it emerged from the Japanese occupation of World War Two. America imposed a trade embargo upon China for intervening in the Korean War, and Hong Kong, which had lived by the China trade, had to seek other means of survival. This it did through rapid industrialisation, to produce just about every product that not only America but any quarter of the world might need, or be induced to buy, even if hitherto ignorant of its existence.

Vivid among my early impressions of Hong Kong were scenes of hastily built flatted factories, erected by the government to house the thousands of little entrepreneurs staking their hard earned and often meagre capital on their ambitions to manufacture better, faster and cheaper than their rivals. A stroll through the streets of San Po Kong or Sham Shui Po meant dodging the lorries, the baling trucks, the handcarts and the jostling, high-spirited labourers who knew what the word 'labour' stood for and were not afraid of it.

Meeting the boss of any of these factories, I would be persuaded that the arrangement was only temporary, that he would soon outgrow these rented premises and move to his own establishment. Meeting his staff, I would sense that their arrangement with *him* was only temporary, that they would soon acquire enough experience and capital to invest in *their* own factories.

Where, I wonder, have they since dispersed? Those bright, those energetic, incurably hopeful men and women with their unquenchable ambitions who typified — and still typify — our population. What fortunes have they made, and possibly lost, and made again?

The spectacle I witnessed then was of apparent chaos, but it worked, and from those tiered factory tenements emerged a prodigious flow of the thermos flasks, hand-painted porcelains, shoes, textiles, torches and plastic flowers which preceded the computers, quality garments, watches, cameras and highly sophisticated electronic components of today.

I quickly grasped the fact that where others spoke of returning home, the Cantonese of Hong Kong spoke of returning to work. The colloquial phrase *faan gung* (返工) has precisely that meaning, placing the emphasis on the epicentre of their existence.

This concentration on the workplace, and on work itself as the very meaning of life, accounts for the appearance of Hong Kong and the manner in which it has evolved. If the concept of 'home' was transposed into the workplace, then that other location where one snatched a few brief hours of rest had to be as close by as possible, to reduce the amount of time taken up in travelling that could be more profitably employed in productivity.

Hence the emergence of what I regard as the most remarkable urban development in the world — remarkable because it has responded to the dictates of the populace, rather than through a random series of arbitrary decisions, as to where to put what. It was a development that took its cue from the early — and in the prevailing force of circumstances, at the time necessarily very expedient — rush to simply cope with the astonishing flood of refugees pouring into Hong Kong in the late forties and early fifties.

Those were the years that saw the growth of the first high-rise — or perhaps, by today's standards, medium-rise — residential blocks, cheek by jowl with industrial areas, where a few square feet of tiered bunk space would suffice for sleeping, so long as one had elbow room to cook and a window from which to thrust the poles of washing.

I well remember how parties of overseas visitors would react with dismay to see whole families crowded into such confines. They had to be educated to the hard facts about Hong Kong's survival; principally, the fact that this was the *only* way in which our administration could provide housing for the thousands of refugees who had fled China to seek freedom and opportunity, for which they considered such basic resettlement was a small price to pay.

That standards of housing have since improved beyond all recognition, that greater affluence has encouraged a taste for more spatial and better quality design, that old resettlement blocks have either disappeared or been extensively renovated, does not alter the underlying priority of proximity. Which, in turn, has dictated a wholly new architectural principle of development on the vertical rather than the horizontal plane, transforming Hong Kong into a multi-storeyed megalopolis where all amenities — shops, schools, recreational parks and transportation systems — are layered for instant and convenient access.

However, containment within the traditional urban areas around the harbour could not be achieved indefinitely. There was a limit to the miracles of hillside engineering, on the steepest of seemingly impossible slopes, that even Hong Kong could not surpass.

And when that limit was reached, one of the greatest tasks the government had to face, back in the late sixties and early seventies, was the challenge of persuading the populace to move to the New Territories. So far from work? So removed from the whole premise of existence?

But it had to be. It had to come. The twin cities of Victoria and Kowloon were straining at the seams. The overspill into Kwun Tong, on the north side of Kowloon Bay, and westwards to Tsuen Wan, had only temporarily allayed the demands for more industrial zones, for more and better housing.

At that time, the last rice fields were dwindling in the backwaters of the New Territories, and agricultural land had been steadily taken over by market gardens. Fishing ports and market towns like Tai Po, Fanling, Sheung Shui and Yuen Long had survived pretty well unchanged for a century or more. I remember that Castle Peak Bay, where the tower blocks of Tuen Mun are now arrayed on reclaimed land, was largely given over to boatyards building those majestic sailing junks which have also long since departed from Hong Kong waters.

One could appreciate why the city dwellers of Hong Kong and Kowloon would look askance at the rusticity of this seldom visited hinterland.

To entice them there, the new satellite towns would have to be the very models of ingenuity, benefiting from the lessons learned in those older urban conurbations. And above all, it was apparent that the chief objective must be proximity — of everyone to everything.

Conspicuous among the first of the satellites, along with Tai Po, Yuen Long and Tuen Mun, was Sha Tin, nestling at the foot of a valley where, seemingly not too long ago, rice had been cultivated for the Emperor in Beijing. Sha Tin became something of a test case, and a major publicity campaign was undertaken by its District Office and the Housing Department to lure its pioneer settlers.

Those due to be rehoused under the resettlement programme provided the — albeit frequently reluctant — spearhead of this emigration, followed in due course by private developers, once it was apparent Sha Tin really *was* fulfilling its promise. And behind these came a wave of business and commercial investors, increasingly convinced that here indeed was an independent, self-contained, fully-serviced township, directly linked by road and rail to the older developed areas just south of the Kowloon foothills.

While architecture and infrastructure served to build the framework of the new town, building the community to inhabit it called for another kind of engineering — social rather than structural. And the government responded to this challenge by developing communal programmes and institutions that would put the pioneer settlers in touch with each other, turning strangers into neighbours and engendering a spirit of shared endeavour that marked the first step towards civic pride.

Sha Tin served as the prototype, not only for other satellites in the New Territories but for architects and town planners from abroad to come and admire. As a major exhibition at the Frankfurt Museum of Architecture demonstrated in November 1993, what has been achieved in Sha Tin is a far cry from the nightmare visions of H.G. Wells and movie maker Fritz Lang when, earlier this century, they respectively conceived their journeys in *The Time Machine* and to the equally grim fantasy of *Metropolis*.

Sha Tin and its successors have shown that it is not only possible to house multitudes, humanely, comfortably and decently, in what might once have been regarded as impossibly confined spaces, but that people will readily *choose* to dwell in such conditions, in order to enjoy the convenience and the accessibility they afford.

What a tribute to the farsightedness, the care, the pride and dedication of the government planners and architects who designed such a showcase for 20th century living! Unsung public servants, operating from small back rooms away from the public spotlight, they too contracted that contagious Hong Kong infection which drives people to give unremittingly of their best. And they exemplified the spirit of a civil service that, I submit, has been crucial to Hong Kong's success.

One story, so frequently retold it has come to be regarded as apocryphal, relates how that whole development plan for the New Territories came about. It tells of a group of senior civil servants who sat around a dinner table back in the sixties, after a typically exhausting day, to pursue, informally, the problem of what could be done about the growing pressure on diminishing land supply around the main harbour. One of them unfurled his napkin and started sketching in the New Territories and its existing, but meagre, centres of population. Somebody else drew a finger from an approximate Kowloon across an imaginary mountain range and *presto*! "Let's take a look at that on paper in the morning."

It may not be true, but one would like it to be true, because it *rings* true.

Which brings me to another change enforced by altered circumstance in the aftermath of World War Two. The *style* of our administration has been transformed beyond recognition. What that style once was is best captured in the charming reminiscence by

Austin Coates, *Myself a Mandarin*, describing days, not so long ago, when a young district officer in the New Territories would have much in common with his counterpart in colonial Africa, who dispensed justice from tent flaps and parleyed with tribal chiefs.

The subsequent influx of refugees, the sheer numbers of people settling in and around the central harbour — and by now, also in the latter-day metropolises spreading in the New Territories — demanded a fresh approach. It was clear that the traditional role of the district officer, with its emphasis on intimate human contact, would be impossible to sustain. Yet the bridge he provided between government and community was so valuable that he could not be allowed to disappear. So he was transplanted into the urban environment, given a larger and considerably more populated 'parish', and provided with an office where his parishioners were free to drop by at any time, to seek assistance or discuss their grievances.

The new system worked, thanks in part to the newly developed mutual aid committees and the traditional *kaifong* associations, through which contact was maintained with all levels of society, but even more to the dedication and resourcefulness of the young administrative officers recruited to its ranks, many of whom now occupy very senior posts in the higher echelons of government.

Their task was infinitely more complex than that of their pastoral predecessors. The districts they served were no longer remote agrarian backwaters but densely populated, increasingly sophisticated communities swelling the ranks of Hong Kong's rapidly expanding middle class. Old style paternalistic administration would be out of place in this new age of awakening expectations.

Accessibility was once again the key to satisfying these expectations. Which meant communication not only at the grassroots level between citizens and civil servants, but between the different kinds of civil servant now emerging to cater to the altered priorities. Hotlines were established between the district officers and the new professionals cropping up in the pages of the government telephone directory — the civil engineers, the architects, the housing managers, the road builders and the *whiz kids* trained overseas in whole new fields of urban planning and administration. The objective of this network was to make the government more responsive and responsible to a people no longer content to ignore the existence of a remote administration so long as it didn't interfere with their freedom to make a living.

Accessibility also called for a rapid response in the full public arena of broadcast radio and television, where public servants were expected to give instant answers to sometimes very complex questions. Some fared better than others, but at least the overall impression was of a government prepared to be called to account for its actions, to explain its policies and to answer its critics.

If at times this engendered an appearance of Hong Kong as one huge debating forum, with people picking up the phone on an impulse to talk on air to the population at large, on any subject under the sun, so much the better. There is no sense of community stronger than that which exists at the village level, and if the spirit of the village debating hall can be transposed into the metropolitan dimension, the fabric of society holds stronger, endures longer and resists the terrible deprecations that have occurred in other cities around the world that have lost their commonalty, their central identity, their shared experience.

Hong Kong has been extremely fortunate to remain one huge, closely integrated, immensely powerful village, a village where things get done in the good old, tried and trusted village style, where people *know* each other at all levels of life, where the proverbial Madam Wong of Wong Tai Sin has as much right to be heard as the Governor. Long may it cling to that most valuable of assets.

Herein also lies the secret of why Hong Kong *functions* so well, and acts so fast, in the stress of crisis, or in its communal response to the needs of others; why it can, not only ride out, but continue to prosper in times of global recession; why it has earned a place in the *Guinness Book of Records* for the generosity of its charitable donations. It is, quite simply, a community endowed not only with brains but with heart, a community which cares and shares precisely the way you would hope to find in the village context.

The phrase 'Hong Kong Inc.' is no glib sobriquet. It accurately defines the corporate behaviour of a highly interactive and integrated society. A society mercifully spared the divisions of class and caste that have bedevilled the efforts of so many other societies to achieve anything like the same unanimity of purpose. Whereas theirs have developed in layers based on social distinctions, long and carefully cultivated, ours is a crucible too much on the boil to permit any such sedimentary process.

In our society, yesterday's hawker can be today's millionaire; and if he over-reaches his cash flow and is forced back to his street stall to begin all over again, nobody will think the worse of him but will admire his courage for trying that hard.

In our society, the carelessly parked Mercedes may be stolen by an enterprising smuggler with a waiting, high horsepower vessel especially tailored to its dimensions. But it is unthinkable that it should be vandalised by the envious and spiteful simply because it represents unattainable wealth.

Unattainable wealth? Not in Hong Kong. So why should the owner of the Rolls Royce be abused when he can be emulated, when his vehicle testifies to his very proper success and symbolises what others are aiming for and merely waiting to achieve?

Whatever its origins, and however free it may be of the barriers that break down and separate other communities, how do you account for the performance of 'Hong Kong Inc.'? How do you get a society to respond with such speed, and with such consensus, to a commonly agreed course of action? Not by imposing the will of an individual or an administration, but by allowing the naturally evolved, in-built machinery of consensus to take its natural course.

It is a formula that has served both the community and its government to good effect over a long period of time; a process of consultation, either through advisory committees or appeals for public comment, embarked upon before major new policies are put in place. Indeed, in the past we often demonstrated our concerns in the collective, corporate response far better than we did as individuals.

As individuals we were, until relatively recently, less articulate — probably because the Chinese traditionally placed common good above individual interest. When I first came to Hong Kong, I was surprised to find there existed no word in the Chinese language that expressed the concept of the individual in terms other than as rebel and renegade.

Happily, in my view, that tradition has disappeared, and a very strong and healthy respect for the individual *within* the social context has flowered and taken firm root. Which is as it should be in a world where human rights are coming increasingly to the fore, when the world is placing greater value on the freedom of the individual as something not to be readily and automatically surrendered to the interests of the majority.

In Hong Kong, we need to balance the public good with the private need, the will of the majority with the protection of the minority. And, happily, there are more and more champions emerging in our midst to defend the latter against the former. One has only to scan the reader's correspondence in a typical newspaper to see how much more freely nowadays the voice of individual reason makes itself heard in columns where once sheer indifference, or absence of opinion, marked the comfortable complacency of the silent majority.

If there is still an area in our society where an element of exclusion persists, where the distinction of 'us' from 'them' survives, it is in the attitude of the public towards its public service.

And here, we have been in danger of forgetting our commonalty of interest. Because it has been fashionable elsewhere to regard civil servants as some kind of pampered, wholly separate species, the trend has been transplanted to Hong Kong, ignoring the reality that civil servants are first and foremost fellow citizens, with the same concerns and aspirations as anyone else. And, by definition, imbued with the identical qualities that make Hong Kong citizens so special.

Of these qualities, I would count ingenuity as especially beneficial to the new administrative style. A quality upon which, as I have already remarked, heavy demands were placed when Hong Kong was inundated with refugees from China in the mid-century. And, again, much later, when we were confronted with a massive influx of illegal immigrants from Vietnam, who were arriving, from the late seventies to the end of the following decade, at the rate of hundreds if not thousands a day, to strain our overburdened resources.

Our ability to cope, to take the strain, to vault every hurdle placed in our path, has sometimes seemed as much a liability as an asset. And no more so than in the case of the Vietnamese boat people. At first, there was an international response to the problem, but when compassion fatigue set in, and the numbers failed to diminish, it became steadily easier to regard Hong Kong's ability to cope as evidence that this too was no more than just another straw on the back of an imperishable camel.

Much the same perception, time and again throughout history, has dogged our endeavours for fair treatment, whether in the form of requests for special recognition of our status as a developing country or in trade negotiations. Our record of achievement *despite* the obstacles has led others to believe we lead some kind of charmed existence, as though we were the economic equivalent of that renowned escape artist Houdini, capable of extricating ourselves from any predicament, however chained, manacled and encumbered.

A very dear friend of mine, born here and totally, irrevocably committed to this little but towering territory, told me how much she hates to hear the word *challenge* go hand in hand with Hong Kong, as though the two were synonymous. "It merely encourages others", she argued, "to inflict impossible demands on us because they think we thrive on them".

She was right of course. But also wrong. Because, although they do not invite challenge, although they would do anything to avert yet another of its obstacles, the people of Hong Kong do *thrive* on adversity. Ask him why, and your typical citizen would shrug. He can't help it. It's in his nature.

This is why I regard myself as fortunate for having been privileged to share the Hong Kong experience. And why I shall forever carry with me the memory, not so much of a place as of a very special people.

2

CONSTITUTION AND ADMINISTRATION

Arrangements for the 1994 and 1995 Elections

THE Governor announced, in his annual policy address in October 1992, a constitutional package to ensure that Hong Kong has a vigorous and effective executive-led government which is accountable to the legislature; to broaden the participation of the community in the conduct of Hong Kong's affairs; and to devise arrangements for the district board elections in 1994 and the Legislative Council and municipal council elections in 1995 which command the confidence and the support of the community. Many of the proposals which aimed to achieve the first two objectives were implemented during 1993.

Regarding the 1994 and 1995 elections, it was proposed that the voting age should be lowered from 21 to 18; that corporate voting be replaced by individual voting in all the present Legislative Council functional constituencies; that every eligible member of Hong Kong's 2.7 million-strong working population be able to vote in one of the nine additional functional constituencies; that a 'single seat, single vote' voting system be adopted for all geographical constituency elections; that all appointed seats in the municipal councils and the district boards be abolished; and an Election Committee drawing all, or most, of its members from the elected district boards be established to elect up to 10 Legislative Council members in 1995.

Government representatives of Britain and the People's Republic of China started discussion in April 1993 on arrangements for the 1994 and 1995 elections. The discussions on the elections for Hong Kong's three-tier system of representative government were held in accordance with the Sino-British Joint Declaration on the Question of Hong Kong, the principle of convergence with the Basic Law of the Hong Kong Special Administrative Region of the People's Republic of China and the relevant agreements and understandings reached between Britain and China.

The British side aimed for arrangements which were fair, open and acceptable to the people of Hong Kong and, at the same time, were within the framework of the Basic Law so that continuity through 1997 could be achieved. Additionally, the British side had made clear that it was essential for the two sides to reach an agreement on the 'through train' arrangement, so that there would be clear and objective criteria for members of the Legislative Council elected in 1995 to remain in the legislature through 1997 for their full four-year term.

In his policy address to the Legislative Council in October 1993, the Governor reported that, conditional on an overall agreement including acceptable arrangements for the 'through train', the British side had offered revised proposals on the arrangements for functional constituencies and the Election Committee. Firstly, the British side had devised a new proposal for the nine new functional constituencies based on organisations and with a total eligible electorate of about one-third of that in the original proposal. Secondly, the British side had put forward proposals for a four-sector Election Committee along the lines set out in the Basic Law for the post-1997 Election Committee, while maintaining the view that all members of the Election Committee should themselves be elected. These alternative proposals were designed to meet known Chinese concerns, while upholding the British side's firm objective of ensuring open and fair elections in Hong Kong.

Despite the 17 rounds of talks held since April, both sides were unable to reach agreement by December on the more straightforward and immediate issues relating to the elections. These immediate issues required legislation by February 1994 if orderly arrangements are to be in place for the 1994 and 1995 elections. To provide slightly more time for the talks to continue on the more difficult issues, draft legislation on the more immediate issues was introduced into the Legislative Council on December 15.

The Electoral Provisions (Miscellaneous Amendments) (No. 2) Bill 1993 covered the lowering of the voting age from 21 to 18 for all three tiers of elections; the adoption of the single-seat, single-vote voting method for the Legislative Council, municipal council and the district board geographical constituency elections; the abolition of appointed district board and municipal council membership; and an increase in the number of elected municipal council seats (from 15 to 32 for the Urban Council and from 12 to 27 for the Regional Council).

As a mark of the British side's sincere wish to continue co-operation with the Chinese, the Bill also contained draft provisions to permit, as proposed by the Chinese side during the talks, Hong Kong residents who were members of Chinese People's Congresses at various levels to serve in the Legislative Council, the municipal councils and the district boards.

General

Hong Kong is administered by the Hong Kong Government, which is headed by the Governor. Under the terms of the Joint Declaration, which entered into force on May 27, 1985, Hong Kong will become, with effect from July 1, 1997, a Special Administrative Region of the People's Republic of China.

The Governor is the representative of the Queen in Hong Kong. He has the ultimate direction of the administration of Hong Kong. An Executive Council offers advice to the Governor on important matters of policy.

At the central level of the three-tier system of representative government, the Legislative Council enacts laws, debates policy issues and controls public expenditure. At the regional level, the two municipal councils — the Urban Council and the Regional Council — provide public health, cultural and recreational services in their respective regions. At the district level, 19 district boards offer advice on the implementation of policies in their districts and provide an effective forum for public consultation.

There are elections on the basis of universal franchise at all the three tiers of representative government: two-thirds of district board members, 38 per cent of Urban

Council members, 33 per cent of Regional Council members, and 30 per cent of Legislative Council members are elected from geographical constituencies.

Constitution

The Letters Patent establish the basic framework of the administration of Hong Kong and, together with the Royal Instructions passed under the Royal Sign Manual and Signet which lay down procedures that must be followed, form the written constitution of Hong Kong.

The Letters Patent create the office of Governor and Commander-in-Chief of Hong Kong, and require him to observe laws and the instructions given to him by the Queen or the Secretary of State. They also deal with the constitution of the Executive and Legislative Councils, the Governor's powers in respect of legislation, disposal of land, the appointment of judges and public officers, pardons, and the tenure of office of Supreme Court and District Court judges.

The Royal Instructions deal with the appointment of members of the Executive and Legislative Councils, the nature of proceedings in the Executive Council, the Governor's responsibility to consult the Executive Council on important policy matters, and his right to act against its advice (a right only exercised once, in 1946). They also deal with the membership of, and election to, the Legislative Council, the nature of proceedings there, and the nature of legislation which may not be passed.

There are various well-established practices which determine the way in which these constitutional arrangements are applied. Hong Kong is governed by consent and through consultation with the community. Although from the constitutional instruments described above, Her Majesty's Government would appear to have substantial control over the way in which Hong Kong is run, in practice the territory largely controls its own affairs and determines its own policies. Similarly, the Governor, by convention, rarely exercises the full extent of his powers.

Role of the Governor

The Governor is appointed by the Queen and derives his authority from the Letters Patent. He has ultimate direction of the administration of Hong Kong and is also the titular Commander-in-Chief of the British Forces stationed in Hong Kong. He makes policy decisions on the advice of the Executive Council, and makes laws by and with the consent of the Legislative Council. As head of the government, he presides at meetings of the Executive Council. The present Governor, the Right Honourable Christopher Patten, assumed office on July 9, 1992, and is the 28th incumbent.

The System of Government

Executive Council

The Executive Council comprises three *ex officio* members — the Chief Secretary, the Financial Secretary and the Attorney General — and 10 other members appointed by the Governor with the approval of the Secretary of State, including one official. The council normally meets once a week, and its proceedings are confidential, although many of its decisions are made public.

The Governor is required by the Royal Instructions to consult the council on all important matters of policy. The Governor in Council — the Governor acting after consulting the Executive Council — is Hong Kong's central and highest executive authority on policy matters. In practice, decisions are arrived at by consensus rather than by division. Members tender their advice in an individual capacity, and the council is collectively responsible for the decisions made by the Governor in Council. Individual non-official members do not hold personal responsibility for given subjects or portfolios. This is a matter for the government.

In addition to policy matters, the Governor in Council determines appeals, petitions and objections under those ordinances which confer a statutory right of appeal. The council also considers all principal legislation before it is introduced into the Legislative Council, and is responsible for making subsidiary legislation under numerous ordinances. The council's advice on matters of policy involving the expenditure of public funds is subject to the approval of the necessary funds by the Finance Committee of the Legislative Council.

Legislative Council

The Legislative Council comprises 60 members. There are three *ex officio* members — the Chief Secretary, the Financial Secretary and the Attorney General — and 57 non-official members. Of the 57 non-official members, 18 are appointed members and 39 are elected members. The appointed members are appointed by the Governor, with the approval of the Secretary of State. Among the elected members, 21 are elected by functional constituencies, each representing an economic, social or professional sector, and 18 elected by direct elections in geographical constituencies which cover the whole territory. The Governor was the President of the Legislative Council until February 19, 1993, when he handed over the presidency to a non-official member elected to that office by all non-official Legislative Councillors.

The chief functions of the Legislative Council are to enact laws, control public expenditure and put questions to the government on matters of public interest. The government is responsible for initiating legislative and public funding proposals to the Legislative Council for consideration.

Legislation is enacted in the form of bills. Most business, including bills, is transacted by way of motions, which are decided by the majority of votes. Private bills, not representing government measures and intended to benefit particular persons, associations or corporate bodies, are introduced from time to time and enacted in the same way. A bill passed by the Legislative Council does not become law until the Governor gives his assent to it. After the Governor's assent, a bill becomes an ordinance without being subject to external approval, although the Queen has reserve powers to disallow an ordinance. The power of disallowance has not been used for many years.

Apart from the enactment of legislation, the business of the council includes two major debates in each legislative session: a wide-ranging debate on government policies which follows the Governor's Address at the opening of the new session of the council in October each year, and the budget debate on financial and economic affairs concerning the annual Appropriation Bill which takes place in March.

Members of the council may also question the government on policy issues for which the government is responsible, either seeking information on such issues or asking for official action on them. Members may request either oral or written answers to the questions asked, and supplementary questions for the purpose of elucidating an answer already given may also be asked.

The council normally meets in public once a week for the transaction of normal council business. In addition, about once a month, the Governor addresses or answers questions from members at a special sitting.

House Committee

The House Committee of the Legislative Council consists of all members of the council other than the President and *ex officio* members. Its chairman and deputy chairman are elected from among its members. The House Committee performs overall co-ordinating and house management functions in respect of the business of the council and its committees. It also considers matters referred to it by these committees.

When the Legislative Council is in session, the House Committee meets every week to discuss the council's proceedings and to undertake preparatory work for meetings of the full council. Regularly on the agenda of these meetings are reports on subsidiary legislation tabled in the council; questions that members intend to put to the government; motions and bills to be debated; and any other matters of public concern or relating to the business of the council.

The House Committee may appoint sub-committees to assist in the consideration of specific subsidiary legislation and issues of public concern. Sittings of the committee and its sub-committees are normally held in public.

Finance Committee

The Finance Committee of the Legislative Council consists of the Chief Secretary as the chairman, the Financial Secretary and 56 non-official members. It scrutinises public expenditure, both at special meetings held in March at which members examine the draft estimates of expenditure for the year ahead, and at regular meetings, held throughout the year, to consider requests which entail changes to the provisions agreed upon by the Legislative Council in the estimates each year, or to note financial implications of new policies. Both the special and regular meetings are held in public. The Finance Committee has two sub-committees: the Establishment Sub-committee and the Public Works Sub-committee, whose meetings are also held in public.

The Establishment Sub-committee consists of 26 members of the Legislative Council, one of whom is the chairman. Representatives of the Secretary for the Civil Service and the Secretary for the Treasury are in attendance. It examines mainly the creation, redeployment and deletion of permanent and supernumerary posts remunerated from the directorate pay scales, and changes to the structure of civil service ranks and grades (including pay scales, new grades and new ranks), and makes recommendations on them to the Finance Committee. It also reports to the Finance Committee on changes in departmental establishments, and on the size and cost of the civil service.

The Public Works Sub-committee consists of 32 members of the Legislative Council, and the Financial Secretary as the chairman. The Secretary for Planning, Environment and Lands; the Secretary for Works; the heads of all works departments and the Environmental Protection Department; and representatives from the Finance Branch are in attendance at all meetings to provide advice. The sub-committee makes recommendations to the Finance Committee in the upgrading of projects to Category A of the public works programme, which indicates their readiness to start, and on changes to the scope and approved estimates of projects already in that category.

Public Accounts Committee

The prime concern of the Public Accounts Committee of the Legislative Council is to see that public expenditure has not been incurred for purposes other than those for which the funds were granted, that full value has been obtained for the sums expended, and that the government has not been faulty or negligent in its conduct of financial affairs.

The committee, established in 1978, is a standing committee consisting of a chairman and six members, none of whom is an *ex officio* member of the council. Its main function is to examine, and report on, the findings of the Director of Audit's reports on the audit of the government's annual statements of account, prepared by the Director of Accounting Services. It also examines, and reports on, matters relating to the performance of the Director of Audit's duties and the exercise of his powers under the Audit Ordinance, and on matters relating to value-for-money audits carried out by the Director of Audit. Value-for-money audits are carried out under a set of guidelines tabled in the Legislative Council in November 1986. These guidelines were agreed upon by the Public Accounts Committee and the Director of Audit, and have been accepted by the government.

The Director of Audit submits two reports to the President of the Legislative Council during the course of the year. The first, tabled in April, relates to value-for-money audits; the second, tabled in November, relates to the audit of the government's annual statements of account and also value-for-money audits. Following the tabling of the reports, the committee holds public hearings and controlling officers for different heads of public expenditure give evidence. The committee's report, based on these hearings, is tabled in the Legislative Council within three months of the submission of the Director of Audit's report to which it relates. The government's response to the committee's reports is contained in the government minute, which describes the measures taken to give effect to the committee's recommendations or reasons why these recommendations cannot be accepted. The government minute is also tabled in the Legislative Council within three months of the submission of the Public Accounts Committee's report.

Committee on Members' Interests

The Committee on Members' Interests, established by a resolution of the Legislative Council in 1991, is a standing committee consisting of a chairman and six members. It examines the arrangements for the compilation, maintenance and accessibility of the Register of Members' Interests. It also considers matters pertaining to the declaration of interests by members and matters of ethics in relation to the conduct of members in their capacity as such, and makes recommendations on matters relating to members' interests. The committee sits in public, unless the chairman otherwise orders in accordance with any decision of the committee.

Bills Committee

After a bill has been introduced into the Legislative Council, it is referred to the House Committee. The House Committee may, as it sees fit, allocate the bill to a Bills Committee for detailed scrutiny.

Any member of the Legislative Council, other than the President and *ex officio* members, may join a Bills Committee. The chairman is elected by the committee from among its members. Government officials and members of the public may be invited to attend such meetings. A Bills Committee may consider the principles and merits of a bill allocated to it for scrutiny, as well as the detailed provisions of the bill. In addition, it may consider any amendments relevant to the bill. A Bills Committee may also appoint sub-committees for the purpose of assisting it in the performance of its functions. Sittings of Bills Committees and their sub-committees are normally held in public.

After a Bills Committee has completed scrutiny of a bill, it makes its reports to the House Committee. A Bills Committee is dissolved on the enactment of the bill it has considered, or as decided by the House Committee.

Panels

The Legislative Council has set up 18 panels to examine and monitor government policy matters.

The panels cover community and New Territories affairs; constitutional development; economic services and public utilities; education; environmental affairs; finance, taxation and monetary affairs; health services; housing; information policy; lands and works; administration of justice and legal services; manpower; public service; recreation and culture; security; trade and industry; transport and welfare services.

Council members, other than the President and *ex officio* members, may join any of the panels. The chairman and deputy chairman of a panel are elected from among its members. Besides meeting among themselves, panel members hold sessions with senior government officials and interest groups to hear their views.

A panel may form sub-committees to study specific issues and to report to it. Sittings of panels and their sub-committees are normally held in public.

Select Committees

The Legislative Council may appoint select committees to consider matters or bills in depth. The purpose is to enable small groups of members to examine complex problems and to report their findings and recommendations to the council. In 1993, no select committee was formed.

OMLEGCO

OMLEGCO stands for the Office of the (non-government) Members of the Legislative Council.

Before October 1992, the office was called OMELCO (Office of the (non-government) Members of the Executive and Legislative Councils), serving, among other things, as a link between the members of the two councils. With the withdrawal of members of the Executive Council, following the separation of the non-government membership of the two bodies, OMLEGCO continues to play a role in facilitating communication between members of the Legislative Council and Executive Council, as well as the community.

Collectively, the non-government members of the Legislative Council play a significant role in the administration of Hong Kong. They scrutinise, process and enact legislation; approve public expenditure; monitor the effectiveness of public administration; and consider complaints and representations from members of the public.

In 1993, OMLEGCO continued with the process of developing a formal committee system for the Legislative Council, to facilitate the efficient transaction of council business. The House Committee, Bills Committees and panels are now formal committees of the council.

Councillors operate a redress system, under which members of the public can make representations on, or seek solutions to, problems arising from government policies, decisions and procedures. Every week, a number of councillors are on duty to oversee the system and to receive representations made by deputations.

A member is also on 'ward duty' for two hours a day, to meet complainants who wish to discuss their complaints with a councillor. Cases received are examined in the light of government policies and procedures. If members consider a complaint to be justified, they will ask the government department concerned to reconsider the decision or to re-examine the procedures that have given rise to the complaint. Where a change in policy or in law is considered necessary, members will make recommendations to the appropriate policy branch in the Government Secretariat. Cases involving matters of policy, or of particular importance, are put to the appropriate Legislative Council policy panels for further consideration by members. Members may also ask questions in the council on the problem itself, or the policy giving rise to it. During the 1992–93 session, more than 2 250 new cases were handled under the Legislative Council Members' Redress System.

Pursuant to the Governor's announcement in October 1992 that the Legislative Council must have clear and separate management of its own affairs, members decided to merge OMLEGCO and the Office of the Clerk to the Legislative Council, to form an independent Legislative Council Secretariat with financial and managerial autonomy. The new secretariat will be put under the management of a statutory Legislative Council Commission. Preparatory work for its establishment is underway. It is envisaged that the commission and the new secretariat will be set up by April 1, 1994.

Urban Council

The Urban Council is a statutory council with responsibilities for the provision of municipal services to almost 3.2 million people in the urban areas. These services include street cleansing, refuse collection, control of environmental hygiene, and ensuring the hygienic handling and preparation of food in restaurants, shops, abattoirs and other places.

The Urban Council is also the authority for the control of hawkers and street traders, although some of this devolves to the police as the council does not have the manpower or finance to shoulder the whole burden.

Within the urban areas, the council provides and manages all public recreation and sporting facilities such as swimming pools, parks, playgrounds, indoor and outdoor stadia, tennis courts, football grounds, squash courts and basketball courts; and promotes a large number of sports at district level. Included among its facilities is the Hong Kong Stadium, which is undergoing redevelopment funded by the Royal Hong Kong Jockey Club. Work will be completed by March 1994 and its seating capacity will increase to 40 000 for major sporting, entertainment and cultural events.

The council manages museums, public libraries and several major cultural venues and multi-purpose facilities, including the City Hall, the Queen Elizabeth Stadium, the Hong Kong Coliseum, the Hong Kong Science Museum and the Museum of Art. The City Hall, opened in 1962, is undergoing a $72 million renovation programme to improve the efficiency and effectiveness of its infrastructure. The renovation work started in July and will take 15 months to complete in phases. The council promotes cultural performances and runs a comprehensive programme of public entertainment throughout the urban areas.

The council consists of 40 members — 15 elected from geographical constituencies, 15 appointed by the Governor and 10 representative members from the urban district boards. It meets in public once a month to pass by-laws and deal with its finances, formal motions and questions on its activities. The routine business of the Urban Council is conducted by the Standing Committee of the whole council, supported by 14 select committees and 26 working groups or sub-committees. All the council's select committees, as well as the Keep Hong Kong Clean Committee, have opened their meetings to the public.

The council's chief executive is the Director of Urban Services, who controls the operations of the Urban Services Department, with its staff of 16 300. The director is charged with carrying out the council's policies and implementing its decisions.

The council is financially autonomous and during 1992–93, spent about $4,033 million on council-controlled activities and projects. It is financed by a share of the rates, which forms the main part of its income, with the balance coming from various licence fees and other charges.

The council has ward offices spread throughout the urban areas, where council members deal with and answer complaints from the public on a wide variety of matters. Members of the public may also make their complaints and views known to the council through the 'Members Duty Roster System'. Under this system, the council members are placed on a duty roster to meet the public, by appointment, twice a week.

Regional Council

The Regional Council is the statutory municipal authority for the New Territories, where some 2.6 million people live. It is responsible for all matters concerning environmental hygiene, public health, sanitation, liquor licensing; and the provision of recreation, sports and cultural facilities and services within its jurisdiction.

The Regional Council consists of 36 members. Twelve are elected from geographical constituencies, nine are elected as representatives of the nine New Territories district boards, and 12 are appointed by the Governor. The remaining three are *ex officio* members, being the chairman and the two vice-chairmen of the Heung Yee Kuk (a statutory advisory body which represents the indigenous population of the New Territories). The chairman and vice-chairman of the council are elected by members among themselves.

The council's policies are implemented by its executive arm, the Regional Services Department, which is headed by the Director of Regional Services and has a staff of about 10 000.

The council is financially autonomous. Its main source of revenue comes from rates collected in the council area, and in 1992–93, this provided about 84 per cent of total revenue. The remainder of its revenue comes from fees and charges, and rental income (mostly rent for market stalls). In 1992–93, total revenue amounted to $2,446 million, while total expenditure came to $2,351 million.

The council meets monthly to deal with policy issues, formal motions and members' questions on its activities. It has four functional select committees, nine geographically-based district committees, and a Liquor Licensing Board. The four select committees deal with finance and administration, capital works, environmental hygiene, and recreation and culture. The district committees deal with and monitor the provision of services, and advise on the management of council facilities in individual districts. The select committees meet monthly, the district committees meet bi-monthly, and the Liquor Licensing Board meets quarterly. All meetings of the council, its various committees and the Liquor Licensing Board are open to the public, unless confidential items are under discussion.

The Regional Council maintains close liaison with the district boards in the New Territories and the Heung Yee Kuk, to ensure that local aspirations and views are taken into account in its deliberations. Four district board members and other personalities are co-opted to each of the district committees of the council, providing an opportunity for the views of district representatives to be taken into account in the planning and provision of services and facilities.

The council is represented on a number of organisations, whose work is closely related to its responsibilities. These organisations include the Council for the Performing Arts, the Sports Development Board, the Hong Kong Arts Centre, the Chung Ying Theatre, the Hong Kong Children's Choir, the Hong Kong Ballet and the Hygiene Services Advisory Committee.

District Administration

District boards are statutory bodies which provide a forum for public consultation and participation in the administration of the districts. For the 1991–94 district board term, there are 19 district boards throughout the territory, with 274 elected members and 140 appointed members. In the New Territories, 27 rural committee chairmen are *ex officio* members of the respective district boards.

The next district board elections will be held in September 1994.

The main function of the district boards, set up in 1982, is to advise the government on a wide range of matters affecting the well-being of the people living and working in the districts. Through their advice, they make an important contribution to the management of district affairs. District boards are also consulted on a wide range of territory-wide issues.

The budgets, responsibilities and functions of district boards were expanded in 1993, to give them greater influence over district matters. For 1993–94, $75 million is being made available to the district boards for the implementation of minor environmental improvement and community involvement projects in the districts. An additional $17 million was provided by the two municipal councils for district boards to undertake minor environmental improvement projects. The responsibilities for managing these funds and for determining the priorities of projects were also assumed by the district boards. In addition, the district boards were given responsibility for overseeing the management of community halls.

As an important service for residents, each district board operates a 'meet-the-public' scheme, under which residents may meet board members face-to-face to express their views on any district problems. The scheme has been well received by the general public, and has proved effective in providing a direct channel for collecting public views on local issues and reflecting them to the government.

In each district, there is a district management committee, chaired by the district officer, comprising representatives of departments providing essential services in the district. It serves as a forum for inter-departmental consultation on district matters, and co-ordinates the provision of public services and facilities to ensure that district needs are met promptly. The committee works closely with the district board and, as far as possible, follows the advice given by the board. To improve communication between the district management committee and the district board, district board chairmen are invited to attend the committee's meetings.

Area committees and mutual aid committees have become an important component of the district administration scheme. They were set up in the early 1970s throughout the territory, in support of the Keep Hong Kong Clean Campaign and Fight Violent Crime Campaign.

Each area committee serves a population of about 40 000 to 50 000, and members are appointed from a wide spectrum of the community.

Mutual aid committees are building-based residents' organisations, established to improve the security, cleanliness and general management of multi-storey buildings.

At present, there are over 120 area committees and 4 100 mutual aid committees. They provide an extensive and effective network of communication between the government and the people at the local grassroots level.

Attached to the district offices are 20 public enquiry service centres, which provide a wide range of free services to members of the public.

These include answering general enquiries on government services; distributing government forms and information materials; administering oaths and declarations for private use; and referring cases under the meet-the-public scheme, Free Legal Advice Scheme and Rent Officer Scheme. During the year, a total of 11 585 645 cases were handled. To strengthen the public enquiry service, a central telephone enquiry centre also operates during office hours.

Links Between the Representative Institutions

The Urban Council and the Regional Council, which cover much the same fields in their respective areas, hold liaison meetings and institute joint ventures such as the Keep Hong Kong Clean Campaign during the year.

The Urban Council and the Regional Council are closely linked to the district boards. Each district board in the urban area has a representative member on the Urban Council. In addition to a similar arrangement between the Regional Council and the district boards in the New Territories, members of the latter are also included in the district committees under the Regional Council. Through these channels, the district boards are consulted on a wide range of council matters affecting their areas.

New Territories district boards maintain a close relationship with the Heung Yee Kuk. Seats are reserved on the district boards for rural committee chairmen, who are also *ex officio* members of the Kuk's executive committee.

The Regional Council also has a formal link with the Heung Yee Kuk, through the *ex officio* membership of the Kuk's chairman and two vice-chairmen on the council.

Starting from the 1991–92 Legislative Council session, the two municipal councils as well as the Heung Yee Kuk became functional constituencies, each returning one member to the Legislative Council.

The Electoral System

Electoral System for the Municipal Councils and District Boards

Elections to the Urban Council, Regional Council and district boards are on a geographical constituency basis and through a broad franchise. Practically everyone who is

21 years-of-age or over, and who is a Hong Kong permanent resident or has ordinarily resided in Hong Kong for the preceding seven years, is eligible to apply for registration as an elector in the constituency in which he lives. An applicant should be ordinarily resident in Hong Kong at the time of application. A statutory registration exercise is conducted between April and June each year, although applications for registration can be made at any time of the year. The 1993 electoral roll carried 1 944 680 names, representing 52.4 per cent of an estimated potential electorate of 3.71 million.

There are 210 constituencies, each with one or two seats, for district board elections, returning 274 district board members. In the 64 constituencies where there are two seats, each elector can cast two votes. For elections to the Urban Council and the Regional Council, there are 15 and 12 single-seat constituencies, respectively. Elections to the district boards and the municipal councils are by simple majority.

An elector may vote only in the constituency in which he has been registered. He may, however, stand for election to the Urban Council, the Regional Council or a district board in any constituency, provided he has been ordinarily resident in Hong Kong for the preceding 10 years and his nomination is supported by 10 electors in that constituency.

Electoral System for the Legislative Council

The electoral system for the Legislative Council comprises both geographical and functional constituencies.

There are nine double-seat geographical constituencies — two on Hong Kong Island, three in Kowloon and four in the New Territories, returning a total of 18 members. Elections for geographical constituencies are by simple majority, and each elector can cast two votes.

There are 15 functional constituencies consisting of 20 electoral divisions, which cover the commercial, industrial, finance and financial services, labour, tourism, real estate and construction, social services, medical and health care, teaching, accountancy, legal, engineering, architectural, surveying and planning, municipal council and rural sectors. They return a total of 21 members (with the labour functional constituency returning two members). A preferential elimination voting system is used for the functional constituencies.

The franchise for Legislative Council geographical constituency elections is the same as for the elections to the district boards and the municipal councils. They use the same electoral roll. For functional constituency elections, the electorate is made up of either individual or corporate electors, or a mixture of both. An individual elector in a functional constituency is also required to be a registered elector for the geographical constituency elections. A corporate elector which wishes to vote at a functional constituency election is required to nominate an authorised representative to vote on its behalf. An authorised representative is not allowed to represent more than one elector in the same functional constituency, and no individual elector or authorised representative is allowed to be registered in more than one functional constituency. In 1993, the electoral roll for functional constituencies carried 70 400 entries, representing 61.7 per cent of an eligible electorate of 114 031.

The qualifications for candidature in geographical constituency elections are the same as in the district board and municipal council elections. In functional constituency elections, a candidate must have, in addition, a substantial connection with the relevant functional constituency in which he stands. Each nomination requires 10 subscribers who are electors in that functional constituency, except for the municipal council functional constituencies which require only five subscribers, due to the small electorate in the constituencies.

Boundary and Election Commission

The three-member Boundary and Election Commission, appointed by the Governor on July 23, is an independent authority established under the Boundary and Election Commission Ordinance. It is responsible for reviewing the geographical constituency boundaries of the Legislative Council, municipal councils and district boards, and making recommendations to the Governor. It is also responsible for overseeing the conduct and supervision of elections, keeping under review the procedure for these elections and the arrangements for registration of electors to ensure that the elections are conducted openly, honestly and fairly. The commission performs its functions through the Registration and Electoral Office, which is staffed by civil servants and headed by a Chief Electoral Officer.

In October, the commission published its provisional recommendations on the 1994 district board constituency boundaries and commenced a 30-day public consultation on these recommendations. The provisional recommendations were drawn up in accordance with the statutory criteria laid down in the Boundary and Election Commission Ordinance which include the population quota, community identities, physical features and development of the relevant areas. On December 30, the commission submitted its recommendations, which took into account the representations received during the public consultation, to the Governor for consideration.

Advisory Committees

The government's network of boards and committees is a distinctive feature of the system of government, which seeks to obtain, through consultation with interested groups in the community, the best possible advice on which to base decisions. Advisory bodies of one kind or another are found in nearly all government departments and quasi-government bodies.

In general, advisory bodies are divided into five categories: statutory bodies which give advice to a head of department (such as the Endangered Species Advisory Board); statutory bodies which give advice to the government (such as the Board of Education); non-statutory bodies which give advice to a head of department (such as the Labour Advisory Board); non-statutory bodies which give advice to the government (such as the Transport Advisory Committee); and committees which are executive in nature (such as the Hong Kong Examinations Authority).

Government officials and members of the public are represented on these committees. About 5 720 members of the public have been appointed to serve on a total of 563 boards and committees, and some serve on more than one of these advisory bodies. These members are appointed in view of their specialist knowledge or expertise, or their record or interest in contributing to community service. Increasing importance has been attached to the contribution they make to the formulation and execution of government policies and, in order to utilise their potential to the full, the composition and effectiveness of these bodies are regularly monitored. Where appropriate, the government broadens the cross-section of representation and encourages an inflow of new ideas through a reasonable turnover of membership.

The Administration

Role of the Chief Secretary

The Chief Secretary is principally responsible to the Governor for the formulation of government policies and their implementation. She is the head of the public service. The Chief Secretary is one of the Governor's principal advisers, along with the Financial Secretary and the Attorney General.

The Chief Secretary exercises direction primarily as head of the Government Secretariat, the central organisation comprising the secretaries of the policy branches and resource branches and their staff. She deputises for the Governor during his absence, and is the Senior Official Member of the Executive and Legislative Councils and chairman of the Finance Committee.

Role of Financial Secretary

The Financial Secretary, who reports directly to the Governor, is responsible for the fiscal and economic policies of the government. He is an *ex officio* member of both the Executive and Legislative Councils. He is, in addition, a member of the Finance Committee of the Legislative Council and chairman of the Public Works Sub-committee of the Finance Committee. As the government official with primary responsibility for Hong Kong's fiscal and economic policies, the Financial Secretary oversees the operations of the Finance, Financial Services, Trade and Industry, Economic Services, and Works Branches of the Government Secretariat, and the new Hong Kong Monetary Authority.

The Financial Secretary is responsible under the Public Finance Ordinance for laying before the legislature each year the government's estimates of revenue and expenditure. In his capacity as an *ex officio* member of the Legislative Council, he delivers a major speech outlining the government's budgetary proposals and moving the adoption of the Appropriation Bill, which gives legal effect to the annual expenditure proposals contained in the budget. He is also responsible under a number of ordinances for carrying out executive duties, such as setting levels of certain charges and remunerations, and overseeing the accounts of certain trust funds and statutory bodies.

Role of the Central Policy Unit

The Central Policy Unit forms part of the Government Secretariat, but it is not a policy branch and does not have responsibility for a defined programme area of its own. Its role is to undertake in-depth examinations of complex policy issues, to analyse options, and to recommend solutions. These issues are assigned to it by the Governor, Chief Secretary and Financial Secretary, and are specified on a case-by-case basis. They are mostly issues of a long-term, strategic nature, or issues which cut across, or fall between, the boundaries of several policy branches or government departments.

Role of the Efficiency Unit

The Efficiency Unit was established in May 1992. The unit reports to the Chief Secretary. Its objective is to pursue the government's commitment to improve services to the community and to achieve openness and accountability by formulating, securing support for and co-ordinating the implementation of a programme of public sector reform.

The Structure of the Administration

The administration of the Hong Kong Government is organised into branches and departments. The branches, each headed by a policy secretary, collectively form the Government Secretariat. There are currently 12 policy branches, and two resource branches concerned with finance and the public service.

The policy branches whose secretaries report directly to the Chief Secretary are: the Home Affairs Branch (known, before October 15, as the City and New Territories Administration); Constitutional Affairs Branch; Education and Manpower Branch; Health and Welfare Branch; Planning, Environment and Lands Branch; Recreation and Culture Branch; Security Branch; and Transport Branch.

The Civil Service Branch, a resource branch, also comes under the aegis of the Chief Secretary.

The policy branches whose secretaries report directly to the Financial Secretary are: Economic Services, Financial Services (known, before April 1, as Monetary Affairs), Trade and Industry, and Works.

The Finance Branch, a resource branch, is also responsible to the Financial Secretary.

There are 76 departments and agencies whose heads are, with certain exceptions, responsible to the branch secretaries for the direction of their departments and the efficient implementation of approved government policy. The exceptions are the Audit Department, whose independence is safeguarded by the Director reporting directly to the President of the Legislative Council; the Independent Commission Against Corruption, whose independence is safeguarded by the Commissioner reporting directly to the Governor; the Judiciary, which is the responsibility of the Chief Justice; and the Legal Department, which is the responsibility of the Attorney General.

To assist in the co-ordination of government policy, there are, under the umbrella of the Chief Secretary's Committee, seven policy groups which bring together branch secretaries in related programme areas. The six which are chaired by the Chief Secretary are: Community Affairs; Constitutional Affairs; Lands, Works, Transport, Housing and Environmental Protection; Public Services; Social Services; and Legal and Security. The Legal Affairs Policy Group is chaired by the Attorney General.

Office of the Commissioner for Administrative Complaints

The Commissioner for Administrative Complaints (COMAC) is an independent authority, established in 1989 to provide citizens with some means through which an independent person outside the public service can investigate, and report on, grievances arising from administrative decisions, acts, recommendations or omissions.

COMAC has jurisdiction over all government departments, except the Royal Hong Kong Police Force and the Independent Commission Against Corruption, for which there are separate systems to deal with complaints from the public. He also has jurisdiction over the Hospital Authority.

In mid-1992, the government undertook a review of the COMAC redress system to identify areas where improvements can be made to strengthen its role as a safeguard against government maladministration. After a three-month public consultation exercise, the government proposed a number of changes to the system. They include replacing the referral system to enable the public to take their complaints directly to the Commissioner, extending the Commissioner's jurisdiction to major statutory bodies, and allowing the Commissioner to publicise investigation reports of public interest, subject to the withholding of the names of the individuals involved in the complaint. To put these recommendations into effect, the Commissioner for Administrative Complaints (Amendment) Bill 1993 was introduced into the Legislative Council on July 21. It is to be scrutinised by a bills committee of the council, to be formed soon.

Between January 1 and December 31, a total of 166 complaints were received by the office. Together with 41 cases carried over from the previous year, there were altogether 201 cases for disposal. During the year, 168 cases were completed. Of these, 88 were investigated and 18 were settled by mediation or informal resolution. Of those cases investigated, 10 (11 per cent) were found to be substantiated in whole and 26 (30 per cent) in part. In 52 cases, (59 per cent), complaints were found to be unsubstantiated.

The areas which attracted substantial numbers of complaints in 1993 related to errors or wrong decisions; followed by delay, negligence or omission; faulty procedures; disparity in treatment or unfairness; rudeness and failure to follow procedures. In terms of complaints by department, the Buildings and Lands Department (which was reorganised into the Buildings Department and the Lands Department on August 1) received the most complaints, followed by the Housing Department, the Inland Revenue Department, the Immigration Department, the Correctional Services Department, the Government Secretariat, the Labour Department and the Marine Department. These departments have much contact with members of the public and are more vulnerable to complaints than the others.

Office of the Director of Audit

The necessity for an audit presence was recognised in the very early days of Hong Kong and the Audit Department is, in fact, one of the oldest departments in the territory. An Auditor-General was first appointed in 1844, only three years after the cession of the territory.

The audit of the accounts of the Hong Kong Government is carried out under the terms of the Audit Ordinance enacted in 1971, which provides for the appointment, security of tenure, duties and powers of the Director of Audit; for the submission of annual statements by the Director of Accounting Services; for the examination and audit of those statements by the Director of Audit; and for the submission of the latter's report on these to the President of the Legislative Council. Certain specific duties relating to the examination, audit, reporting and certification of the government's accounts are prescribed in the ordinance, and wide powers are given to the Director regarding his access to books, documents and records, and the explanations which he may require. In the performance of his duties and the exercise of his powers, the Director is not subject to the direction or control of any other person or authority, and considerable discretion is given to him in the conduct of his inquiries. The Director functions independently of the administration and he is free to report publicly as he sees fit.

Aside from auditing the government's accounts, the Director of Audit also audits the accounts of the Urban Council, the Regional Council, the Vocational Training Council, the Hong Kong Housing Authority, the ex-government hospitals under the Hospital Authority, and more than 50 statutory and non-statutory funds and other public bodies. He reviews, in addition, the financial aspect of the operations of the multifarious government-subvented organisations in Hong Kong.

Government auditing practised in Hong Kong falls into two main categories, termed 'regularity' audit and 'value-for-money' audit, respectively. The regularity audit, which is intended to provide an overall assurance of the general accuracy and propriety of the financial and accounting transactions of the government and other audited bodies, is carried out by means of selective test checks and reviews designed to indicate possible areas of weakness. The audit is designed to ensure, as far as reasonably possible, that the accounts are properly presented or give a true and fair view of the state of affairs, although, with the considerable volume and variety of government revenue and expenditure, it cannot be expected to disclose every accounting error or financial irregularity. Value-for-money audit is carried out according to guidelines tabled in the Legislative Council by the chairman of the Public Accounts Committee in 1986. The audit is intended to provide independent information, advice and assurance about the economy, efficiency and effectiveness with which any branch, department, agency, other public body, public office, or audited organisation has discharged its functions. This involves going beyond the normal accounting records. In line with contemporary developments in both government and commercial auditing elsewhere, it is also becoming increasingly relevant to ascertain whether efficient and economical practices are being followed in pursuing prescribed goals and whether these goals are being achieved.

The Director of Audit's report, after it has been submitted to the President of the Legislative Council and laid before the council, is considered by the Public Accounts Committee. In 1993, the Director submitted two reports. The first report was tabled on April 28, covering the results of value-for-money audits completed, and the second report on November 17, covering the audit certification of the government's accounts for the preceding financial year, as well as the results of value-for-money audits completed.

The Director's reports on the accounts of other public bodies are submitted to the relevant authority, in accordance with the legislation governing the operation of these bodies.

Foreign Relations

The Role of the British Government

Because of Hong Kong's status as a dependent territory, the Secretary of State for Foreign and Commonwealth Affairs is constitutionally responsible to the British Parliament for the actions of the Hong Kong Government and he has authority to give directions to the Governor of Hong Kong. In practice, however, such formal directions have not been issued in living memory, and Hong Kong conducts its affairs with a high degree of autonomy in all domestic matters.

The relationship between London and Hong Kong is essentially one of co-operation. One important task regularly undertaken by the Foreign and Commonwealth Office is to ensure that Hong Kong's interests and views (which are not always identical to those of the United Kingdom) are properly considered within the British Government machinery, particularly when new policies are being formulated by other Whitehall departments.

Hong Kong's foreign relations are constitutionally the direct responsibility of the British Government. The British Government is internationally responsible for ensuring that the Hong Kong Government fulfils its obligations under the many international conventions and agreements which extend to Hong Kong, as well as to the United Kingdom. But in the day-to-day conduct of external affairs, Hong Kong in practice enjoys a considerable degree of autonomy, and full autonomy regarding trade matters. It is a contracting party to the General Agreement on Tariffs and Trade in its own right.

The Role of the Political Adviser

The Political Adviser is a senior member of the British Diplomatic Service, seconded to the Hong Kong Government principally to advise the Governor and the Chief Secretary on international issues, and particularly matters concerning Hong Kong's relations with China. His office is part of the Hong Kong Government.

The Political Adviser's office, in conjunction with the Constitutional Affairs Branch, is closely involved in the work of implementing the Sino-British Joint Declaration on the Question of Hong Kong. In addition, the Political Adviser's office continues to offer advice, and in some cases to co-ordinate action, on many other matters, notably in promoting the wide range of contacts between Hong Kong Government departments and their counterparts in China's Guangdong Province, particularly in the Shenzhen Special Economic Zone. Close and effective cross-border co-operation has developed in diverse areas, including immigration, the fight against crime, anti-smuggling operations, transport, environment issues, customs, the postal services and telecommunications.

The Political Adviser's office is also a communication channel between the Hong Kong Government and foreign and Commonwealth missions in the territory. These missions do, however, deal directly with the relevant departments of the Hong Kong Government in most day-to-day matters.

The Public Service

The Public Service employs about 6.7 per cent of Hong Kong's workforce. It provides staff for all government departments and other units of the administration. As at October 1, 1993, the total strength of the Public Service was 181 295. Nearly 99 per cent are local officers. The service is structured into some 420 grades or job categories in the administrative, professional, technical and manual fields, with about 1 210 ranks or job levels.

Overall responsibility for the management of the Public Service lies with the Civil Service Branch of the Government Secretariat. The branch deals with matters such as appointments, pay and conditions of service, staff management, manpower planning, training and discipline. It is also the focal point for consultation with the principal staff associations. There are five departmental divisions, each responsible for the full range of personnel management matters of a group of departments; and three functional divisions, dealing with service-wide issues such as training, staff relations and pensions. In addition, its General Grades Office is responsible for the overall management of officers in certain categories of general grades.

Recruitment and promotion to the middle and senior ranks of the Public Service are subject to the advice of the Public Service Commission, which is independent of the government. The commission has a full-time chairman and prominent citizens serving as members.

The government is advised on matters relating to pay and conditions of service by four independent bodies. The Standing Committee on Directorate Salaries and Conditions of Service advises on matters affecting directorate officers (the 1 000 or so most senior public servants). The Standing Committee on Judicial Salaries and Conditions of Service advises on matters affecting judicial officers. The Standing Committee on Disciplined Services Salaries and Conditions of Service advises on the salaries and conditions of service of the disciplined services. The Standing Commission on Civil Service Salaries and Conditions of Service advises on matters affecting all other civil servants.

A new civil service housing package, which comprises a Home Financing Scheme, an Accommodation Allowance Scheme and an improved Home Purchase Scheme, was introduced in October 1990. The objective of the housing package is to make more effective use of the resources provided for civil service housing benefits and to encourage home ownership among civil servants. Over 17 000 officers are currently receiving benefits under the schemes.

The government fully recognises the value of regular communication and consultation with staff. There are four central consultative councils — the Senior Civil Service Council, the Model Scale 1 Staff Consultative Council, the Police Force Council and the Disciplined Services Consultative Council. Departmental consultative committees, established in most government departments, constitute an important part of the consultative machinery. In addition, individual members of the Public Service or staff associations have ready access to the departmental or grade management, as well as to the Civil Service Branch. Staff are encouraged to make suggestions to improve the efficiency of the service under the Staff Suggestions Scheme, which was recently revised to enable individual departments to consider and reward valuable suggestions, rather than having all suggestions considered centrally.

In recognition of staff commitment and contributions, long-serving civil servants are granted awards under the Long Service Travel Award Scheme and the Long and Meritorious Service Certificate Scheme. Those with 30 years of meritorious service are also presented with a gold pin. Civil servants with 20 or more years of service on retirement are given a retirement souvenir.

Traditionally, the terms of employment offered to civil servants have been divided into two major categories — overseas and local. Whether an officer should be offered overseas or local terms was determined before he joined the service and could not be altered after the appointment, irrespective of changing circumstances. A review of this policy was conducted with a view to rationalising the position of permanent residents, whose rights are guaranteed by the Bill of Rights, and making provisions for the future as stipulated under the Basic Law. A two-stage approach was adopted.

As an interim measure, overseas agreement officers who are permanent residents of Hong Kong could apply for transfer to local terms for one contract only, subject to certain conditions. These conditions include service need, satisfactory conduct and performance, and physical fitness. However, the Public Officers (Variation of Conditions of Service) (Temporary Provisions) Ordinance, introduced into the Legislative Council as a private member's Bill, suspended the interim measure until April 1994. The ordinance was enacted in December despite opposition by the government.

For the long term, the government has proposed bringing in standardised conditions of service, and defining for the first time who should in future be regarded as 'local'. The objective is to converge with the Basic Law, while still complying with existing laws. A wide-ranging consultation exercise is being conducted and a consolidated proposal will be developed, with the intention of discussing the matter with the Chinese authorities in due course.

Meanwhile, the government is developing its use of manpower planning techniques and practices, to ensure that the Public Service possesses the right mix of officers in terms of numbers, experience, qualifications and skills to achieve its objectives and goals.

Particular care and attention are paid to the selection and grooming of senior government officials.

Public Sector Reform

Public sector reform is a programme of financial and management reforms, aimed at bringing about long-term improvements to the efficiency and management of the public sector, and better service and accountability to the community. The Efficiency Unit was established to serve as a focal point to direct and co-ordinate the efforts of public sector reform.

The government is committed to providing the best service possible to the public. In October 1992, the Governor launched the performance pledge programme, to help engender a culture of service in the public sector. The majority of government departments directly serving the public have already produced performance pledges, informing their customers what services are available, what standards have been set and how those standards are being monitored. Customer liaison groups are in place in some 12 departments under the programme. Some 20 departments are also involving their customers through advisory groups and users' committees. These groups are an important forum to channel customer input on the services provided. The performance pledge programme will be a permanent feature of the public sector. The government will continue to build on the message of serving the community within the Public Service.

In 1993, the government embarked on a practical programme of public sector reform which sees the Civil Service Branch and Finance Branch concentrating more on their strategic roles; and policy branches and departments being given more responsibility over the way in which they manage their activities. This gives the necessary authority to those responsible for the delivery of programmes to do so in the most effective way, channelling available resources to priority activities. Departments now have greater authority in matters such as non-directorate appointments and promotions, leave and passage, and professional training.

The government also introduced a system of programme management, which divides a department's work into its major activities, for monitoring and review purposes. This has placed more emphasis on performance measurement, quality of service, value for money and, not least, accountability. The government has also adopted a more business-like approach to the delivery of services. This has seen an increase in the use of new technology, including office automation, desktop publishing and automated telephone answering systems.

Civil Service Training

The government attaches great importance to the training of civil servants in order to increase efficiency and effectiveness, and to help them meet new challenges. Induction and refresher training is provided by many departments to equip staff with the knowledge and skills to carry out their duties effectively. Where the need arises, staff are also sponsored on overseas training courses or attachments, so that they can keep abreast of the latest developments in their specialised fields.

To meet common departmental needs, the Civil Service Training Centre conducts a wide range of management, language and computer courses, and co-ordinates the management training undertaken by public servants at local and overseas institutes. It also provides advice and assistance to departments in planning and implementing their training programmes.

The China Studies Programme, which aims to provide officers with a better understanding of various aspects of life and government in China, is being strengthened. Seminars and talks are conducted for officers at various levels. Chinese studies courses in China and familiarisation visits to China are also arranged to give officers first-hand experience of the country. Existing management development programmes have also been expanded to include a China dimension.

The programmes offered by the Senior Staff Course Centre play an important role in the training and development offered to senior public servants. The centre emphasises 'learning from doing'. Participants analyse real administrative and organisational problems, and make proposals for improvement.

Government Records Service

The Government Records Service is responsible for the management of government records. It undertakes two different but related programmes: the Records Management Office is responsible for a records management programme to handle records at their current and non-current stages, and the Public Records Office for an archive administration programme to look after the preservation and use of permanent records.

The appropriate management of records affects the efficiency of business in government. It is the responsibility of the Records Management Office to oversee and develop a comprehensive system to manage records effectively and efficiently, from their creation to their 'death' or destruction, when all useful purposes have been served. The aim is to have fewer records to store, better records to use and more economical record management costs to finance.

The Public Records Office is one of the largest local sources of information for historical and other studies relating to Hong Kong.

Language

The official languages of Hong Kong are English and Chinese. The Official Languages Ordinance, enacted in 1974, provides that both languages possess equal status and enjoy equality of use for the purposes of communication between the government or any public officer and members of the public. Correspondence in Chinese from the public is replied to by government departments either in Chinese or in English accompanied by a Chinese version. Major reports and publications of public interest issued by the government are available in both languages. Simultaneous interpretation is provided at meetings of the Legislative Council, Urban Council, Regional Council and other government boards and committees where English and Chinese are used.

A Bilingual Laws Advisory Committee was set up in October 1988 to advise the Governor in Council on, among other things, the authentication of Chinese texts of existing laws which are being translated. Following the declaration of the Chinese version of Chapter 1 of the Laws of Hong Kong, the Interpretation and General Clauses

Ordinance, to be authentic in July 1992, eight more ordinances were declared authentic in 1992–93. Chinese versions of other existing laws are being processed sequentially for authentication. Since April 1989, all new principal legislation has been enacted in both English and Chinese.

Cantonese is the most commonly-spoken dialect in the territory among the local Chinese community, while Putonghua has gained popularity as closer ties with China are developed. English continues to be used not only by the expatriate community, but by a wide cross-section of the local community in commercial, financial and professional circles.

3
THE LEGAL SYSTEM

THE legal system in Hong Kong is firmly based on the rule of law and the independence of the judiciary.

Capital punishment was formally abolished in April and was replaced by the mandatory sentence of life imprisonment for murder, and discretionary maximum sentences of life imprisonment in the case of treason and piracy. Since 1966, all sentences of death had been commuted to imprisonment for life or for determinate terms by exercise of the Royal Prerogative.

The body of local jurisprudence in respect of the Hong Kong Bill of Rights Ordinance continued to grow during the year, almost exclusively in relation to the criminal law. A decision of the Privy Council in May, on appeal from the Hong Kong Court of Appeal, provided guidance on when it may be appropriate to place an onus of proof on an accused person.

The Sino-British Joint Declaration on the Question of Hong Kong and the Basic Law of the Hong Kong Special Administrative Region of the People's Republic of China provide that the present judicial system will be maintained after 1997, except for those changes consequent upon the establishment of the Court of Final Appeal (CFA). At the 20th meeting of the Sino-British Joint Liaison Group in September 1991, the two sides reached agreement in principle on the establishment of the CFA. Action is in hand to establish the CFA before 1997 to replace the Judicial Committee of the Privy Council as Hong Kong's highest appellate body.

Law in Hong Kong

The law of Hong Kong generally follows that of England. The Application of English Law Ordinance declares the extent to which English law is in force in the territory. The ordinance provides that the common law of England and the rules of equity shall be in force in the territory so far as they are applicable to the circumstances of Hong Kong or its inhabitants, subject to such modifications as circumstances may require. The ordinance applies some English Acts, such as the Habeas Corpus Act 1816, to Hong Kong.

The Governor, acting with the advice and consent of the Legislative Council, has plenary powers to enact laws for the peace, order and good government of Hong Kong. Most of the legislation applicable in the territory is, and has been since its earliest days, enacted in the form of ordinances or as subsidiary legislation made under an ordinance.

Until 1989, the laws of Hong Kong were published in a 32-volume compilation known as the *Laws of Hong Kong*. This was updated annually. A new loose-leaf edition of the *Laws of Hong Kong* is in the course of preparation and about 75 per cent of the volumes have been issued. The new edition will be based upon the 1989 revised edition, as amended by laws taking effect since then and will be updated continuously. In addition, all new laws are published in the *Hong Kong Government Gazette*.

The Attorney General's Chambers are responsible for drafting new legislation in both Chinese and English, and translating existing legislation into Chinese. Both the Chinese and English texts are authentic versions of the laws. The first bilingual ordinance was enacted on April 13, 1989. Since then, all new principal legislation has been enacted bilingually. In October 1988, the government set up the Bilingual Laws Advisory Committee, to advise on the publication of Chinese texts of existing ordinances. The committee examines Chinese texts prepared by the Law Drafting Division of the Attorney General's Chambers, and then recommends the Governor-in-Council declare these approved texts an authentic version of the laws. The first Chinese text of existing legislation was declared authentic in July 1992. Some 520 ordinances remain to be translated or authenticated.

United Kingdom legislation may be applied to Hong Kong either directly or by order of Her Majesty-in-Council under the legislation. In addition, the power of Her Majesty to make all such laws, as may appear necessary, for the peace, order and good government of the territory is expressly reserved by Article IX of the Letters Patent. In practice, the exercise of these powers is largely confined to matters which have a bearing on Hong Kong's international position. For example, the Multilateral Investment Guarantee Agency (Overseas Territory) Order 1988 is an Order-in-Council implementing in Hong Kong a treaty to which the United Kingdom is a party.

To ensure that by 1997, Hong Kong will possess a comprehensive body of law which owes its authority to the legislature of Hong Kong, it is necessary to replace such United Kingdom legislation, which applies to Hong Kong, by local legislation on the same topics. The Hong Kong legislature has been empowered under the Hong Kong Act 1985 to repeal or amend any enactment so far as it is part of the law of Hong Kong, and to make laws having extra-territorial operation, if the enactment relates to civil aviation, merchant shipping, or admiralty jurisdiction or is required in order to give effect to an international agreement which applies to Hong Kong. Legislation has already been enacted to localise laws in the fields of admiralty jurisdiction, marine pollution and merchant shipping, and work in other areas is in progress.

A Localisation and Adaptation of Laws Unit has been established in the Attorney General's Chambers. The unit's role is to give legal advice on the localisation of United Kingdom legislation which presently applies to Hong Kong. It also advises on the adaptation of the laws of Hong Kong to ensure compatibility with the Basic Law of the Hong Kong Special Administrative Region, which was promulgated in April 1990. A review by policy branches of all ordinances within their spheres of responsibilities has been undertaken and, where necessary, drafting instructions will be prepared with a view to appropriate amendments being effective before July 1, 1997.

Human Rights

Since 1976, the International Covenant on Civil and Political Rights (ICCPR) and the International Covenant on Economic, Social and Cultural Rights (ICESCR) have been extended to Hong Kong. The Sino-British Joint Declaration guarantees that the provisions of the two covenants, as applied to Hong Kong, shall remain in force after 1997.

Until recently, the provisions of the ICCPR, like those of the ICESCR, were implemented in Hong Kong through a combination of common law, legislation and administrative measures. In view of the strong support in the community for the embodiment of basic civil and political rights in a justiciable Bill of Rights, the Hong Kong Bill of Rights Ordinance was enacted in June 1991. The ordinance gives effect in local law to the provisions of the ICCPR as applied to Hong Kong.

To complement the protection afforded by the Bill of Rights, the Letters Patent for Hong Kong have been amended, to ensure that no law can be made in Hong Kong which restricts the rights and freedoms enjoyed in Hong Kong in a manner which is inconsistent with the ICCPR as applied to the territory. The amendment came into operation at the same time as the Bill of Rights Ordinance.

The Judiciary

The Chief Justice of Hong Kong is head of the judiciary. He is assisted in his administrative duties by the Registrar, seven Deputy Registrars and one Assistant Registrar of the Supreme Court. The Assistant Registrar is designated Chief Magistrate. Recruitment is underway for a Judiciary Administrator to take over from the Registrar the responsibility for assisting the Chief Justice in the overall administration of the judiciary. The new Judiciary Administrator is expected to be in post next year. The Registrar and Deputy Registrars will then be free to concentrate on their judicial and quasi-judicial duties.

The judiciary operates on the principle, fundamental to the common law system, of complete independence from the executive and legislative branches of government. This applies equally whether a dispute is between the government and an individual, or whether it involves private citizens or corporate bodies.

The most senior court in Hong Kong is presently the Supreme Court, comprising the Court of Appeal and the High Court. Sitting in the Supreme Court, in addition to the Chief Justice, are nine Justices of Appeal and 22 High Court Judges. The Registrar and Deputy Registrars also have jurisdiction as Masters of the Supreme Court in civil trials in the High Court. The jurisdiction of the High Court is unlimited in both civil and criminal matters. The Court of Appeal, the highest court in Hong Kong, hears both civil and criminal appeals from the High Court and from the District Court. Further appeal lies to the Judicial Committee of the Privy Council in London; however, this is infrequent, as leave to appeal is granted only on stringent conditions.

High Court Judges usually sit alone when trying civil matters, although there is a rarely-used provision for jury trials in certain cases, including defamation. For criminal trials, they sit with a jury of seven, or nine on special direction of the judge. The issue of guilt is determined by the jury, which must have a majority of at least five to two, except with charges attracting a death sentence, when unanimity is required.

The District Court has both civil and criminal jurisdiction. Its civil jurisdiction is limited to disputes involving a value up to $120,000, and its criminal jurisdiction provides for sentences up to seven years' imprisonment. Its judges sit without a jury and may try the more serious cases, the principal exceptions being cases alleging murder, manslaughter and rape, which are reserved for trial by the High Court. There are 29 Judges of the District Court.

The Magistrates' Courts try annually some 90 per cent of all the cases heard in the territory. There are 71 professional magistrates sitting in 10 magistracies, two of which are on Hong Kong Island, four in Kowloon and four in the New Territories.

Magistrates have a purely criminal jurisdiction covering a wide range of offences. Professional magistrates are generally empowered to impose sentences of up to two years' imprisonment and fines of up to $10,000; however, under a number of statutes, they are empowered to impose higher fines. Professional magistrates also try cases in the Juvenile Court, which has jurisdiction in charges against children and young persons aged up to 16 years, except in cases involving homicide.

In addition to the professional magistrates, there are 11 Special Magistrates, who are not legally qualified. They handle routine cases, such as littering and minor traffic offences, and their powers of sentencing are limited to fining up to $20,000. They are all Cantonese-speaking and usually conduct their cases in that language.

In addition to the principal courts of civil and criminal jurisdiction, there are five specialised tribunals. The Coroner's Court handles inquiries into unusual circumstances causing death. The Small Claims Tribunal hears civil claims of up to a limit of $15,000. The Labour Tribunal hears individual civil claims arising from contracts of employment. The Lands Tribunal has jurisdiction in matters of rating and valuation, and in assessing compensation when land is resumed by the government or reduced in value by development. The Obscene Articles Tribunal has jurisdiction to determine whether or not an article is obscene, and to classify it into statutory categories of acceptability or otherwise.

The Small Claims and Labour Tribunals provide the public with inexpensive recourse to litigation, as their proceedings are informally conducted and professional representation is not permitted.

The official language of the court is English in the Court of Appeal, the High Court and the District Court; in the other courts and tribunals, the court may use Chinese. Whichever language is used, a party or witness in any court in Hong Kong may use Chinese or English or any other language permitted by the court.

It is the government's policy to move towards greater use of Chinese in the courts. A working party, headed by a Justice of Appeal, is looking into the issue.

The government attaches great importance to judicial efficiency. To strengthen the administrative structure of the judiciary, the Working Party on Judiciary Administration was formed in October. Chaired by the Chief Justice, this high-level working party comprises members of the judiciary, the legal profession and the public. It is conducting a thorough review of existing administrative systems to determine how and where improvements can be made.

Three Court Users Committees were appointed by the Chief Justice during the year to advise on matters of concern to users of the courts. The Criminal Court Users Committee, the Civil Court Users Committee and the Tribunal Court Users Committee will look at all matters of practice and procedure, administration of the courts as well as the facilities provided in court buildings.

Arbitration and Alternative Dispute Resolution

Arbitration has been a popular method of dispute resolution in Hong Kong for some time. It is governed by the Arbitration Ordinance, which has two distinct regimes — a domestic regime based on English law and an international regime which includes the UNCITRAL Model Law, the model law adopted by the United Nations Commission on International Trade Law. Arbitral awards made in Hong Kong can be enforced in more than 80 other jurisdictions which are signatories to the New York Convention on the Recognition and Enforcement of Foreign Arbitral Awards.

The Hong Kong International Arbitration Centre (HKIAC) was established in 1985, to act as an independent and impartial focus for the development of all forms of dispute resolution in Hong Kong and Southeast Asia. The HKIAC provides information on dispute resolution and arbitrations both in Hong Kong and overseas. It operates panels of international and local arbitrators, and maintains lists of mediators. The HKIAC premises, situated at 1 Arbuthnot Road, have purpose-built hearing rooms and full support facilities. The number of cases involving the HKIAC has substantially increased in recent years. It is anticipated, given the increasing popularity of arbitration and mediation as a means of dispute resolution, that there will be a further increase in such cases in the future.

The Attorney General

The Attorney General is the Governor's legal adviser. The Royal Instructions provide for him to be an *ex officio* member of both the Executive Council and the Legislative Council. He is chairman of the Law Reform Commission of Hong Kong, and a member of the Judicial Services Commission, and the Operations Review and Complaints committees of the Independent Commission Against Corruption.

All government departments requiring legal advice receive it from the Attorney General. He is the representative of the Crown in all actions brought by, or against, the Crown. He is also responsible for the drafting of all legislation.

The Attorney General is responsible for all prosecutions in Hong Kong. It is his responsibility to decide whether or not a prosecution should be instituted in any particular case, and, if so, to institute and conduct the prosecution.

The Attorney General is chairman of the Legal Affairs Policy Group, one of several policy bodies established under the umbrella of the Chief Secretary's Committee, to bring together branch secretaries in related programme areas. The group plays an important co-ordinating role in legal policy matters, decision-making and allocation of responsibility for legislative initiatives which have a substantial legal policy content. Often, the group will call upon the Attorney General to take responsibility, as sponsor and spokesman, for legislative proposals to be submitted to the Executive and Legislative Councils.

The Attorney General's Chambers have six divisions, five of which are headed by a Law Officer to whom the Attorney General delegates certain of his powers and responsibilities. The remaining division deals with administrative matters concerning the chambers.

The Civil Division, headed by the Crown Solicitor, provides legal advice to the government on civil law and conducts civil litigation, arbitration and mediation, on behalf of the government.

The International Law Division, headed by the Law Officer (International Law), deals with all external legal matters arising out of the Sino-British Joint Declaration and other international agreements, and advises upon questions of international law.

The Law Drafting Division, headed by the Law Draftsman, is responsible for drafting all legislation, including subsidiary legislation, in Chinese and English, and assists in steering legislation through the Executive and Legislative Councils.

The Solicitor General heads the Legal Policy Division, which includes the Law Reform Commission Secretariat. The division services the professional needs of the Attorney General, and provides legal input on a wide variety of topics being considered by the government.

The Prosecutions Division is headed by the Crown Prosecutor, who is commonly known as the Director of Public Prosecutions. Counsel from this division conduct the prosecution in the majority of High Court and District Court trials, and often appear before magistrates when an important point of law is involved. The division also provides legal advice to the police and other government departments responsible for prosecuting offences.

Law Reform Commission

The Law Reform Commission was appointed by the Governor in Council to consider and report on such topics as may be referred to it by the Attorney General or Chief Justice. Its membership includes Legislative Councillors, academic and practising lawyers, and prominent members of the community.

Since its establishment in 1980, the commission has published 23 reports covering subjects as diverse as commercial arbitration, homosexuality, bail, sale of goods and supply of services, and illegitimacy. The recommendations in 11 of its reports have been implemented, either in whole or in part. The other reports are still under consideration.

The commission is currently considering references on evidence in civil actions, fraud, privacy, codification of the criminal law, guardianship and custody, insolvency, description of flats on sale, and interpretation of statutes.

Registrar General

The office of the Registrar General was established in 1949 by the Registrar General (Establishment) Ordinance. Prior to its re-organisation, the Registrar General's Department included what are now the Intellectual Property Department, the Office of the Commissioner of Insurance, the Official Trustee and the Official Solicitor (both in the Legal Aid Department), the Official Receiver's Office, the Legal Advisory and Conveyancing Office of the Lands Department, the Land Registry, the Companies Registry and the Money Lenders Registry.

On May 1, the re-organisation of the Registrar General's Department was completed, with the establishment in the final phase of the new Land Registry and the new Companies Registry as separate departments of the government. The Land Registry operates a land registration service under the provisions of the Land Registration Ordinance, and a registry of owners corporations under the Building Management Ordinance. The Companies Registry administers the provisions of the Companies Ordinance and a number of related ordinances, and includes the Money Lenders Registry, which regulates money lenders under the Money Lenders Ordinance.

On August 1, the Land Registry and the Companies Registry were the first departments of the government to be operated on the basis of their own separate trading funds, established by resolution of the Legislative Council under the provisions of the Trading Funds Ordinance. The establishment of these trading funds represents a new initiative designed to enable certain government agencies to improve and meet increasing demand for the services they provide to the public.

Director of Intellectual Property

The Director of Intellectual Property was established in 1990 as a statutory office by the Director of Intellectual Property (Establishment) Ordinance, to take over from the Registrar General the statutory offices of Registrar of Trade Marks and Registrar of Patents. The Intellectual Property Department includes the Trade Marks and Patents Registries, which provide and administer a system of trade mark and patents registration and protection under the provisions of the Trade Marks Ordinance and Registration of Patents Ordinance. The department is also responsible for other forms of intellectual property protection, and will serve as a focal point for the further development of Hong Kong's intellectual property regime.

The Legal Profession

There are around 2 700 solicitors and 425 local law firms in Hong Kong. In addition, there are around 30 foreign law firms which advise on foreign law.

The Law Society is the governing body for solicitors. It has wide responsibilities for maintaining professional and ethical standards, and for considering complaints against solicitors.

There are around 500 barristers in Hong Kong.

The Bar Committee is the governing body for barristers. The conduct and etiquette of the Bar are governed by the Code of Conduct for the Bar of Hong Kong.

Legal Aid, Advice and Assistance

Hong Kong has developed, over the years, a comprehensive system of legal aid, advice and assistance, funded by the government through the Legal Aid Department and the Duty Lawyer Service. The latter is administered by the Law Society and the Bar Association.

Legal Aid

The Legal Aid Department provides assistance in legal representation to persons in both civil and criminal cases heard in the District Court, the High Court, the Court of Appeal in Hong Kong and also, the Judicial Committee of the Privy Council in England. An applicant is required to satisfy the Director of Legal Aid of his financial eligibility (the means test) and of the justification for legal action (the merits test).

Under the means test, a person whose disposable financial resources, including both income and capital, do not exceed $120,000 is eligible for legal aid. In calculating an applicant's disposable financial resources, the value of his owner-occupied home, tax payments and contributions to retirement schemes, in addition to various allowances for the support of himself and his dependants, are deducted. In criminal cases, the Director of Legal Aid has a discretion to grant legal aid to an applicant who fails the means test, if it is in the interests of justice to do so.

Legal aid is granted to a successful applicant either free of charge or upon payment of a graduated contribution, depending on his disposable financial resources. The Director of Legal Aid will assign his case either to a private lawyer or to one of the department's own lawyers in its Litigation Division.

Legal Aid in Civil Cases

In civil cases, apart from financial eligibility, an applicant must satisfy the Director of Legal Aid, under the merits test, that he has reasonable grounds for taking or defending a court action, and that it is reasonable to grant aid in the circumstances of the case. Legal aid is available for a wide range of civil proceedings, including traffic and industrial accident claims, employees' compensation, immigration matters, professional negligence, employment and family law disputes, and landlord and tenant matters. An applicant who is refused legal aid, either because he fails the means or merits test, may appeal against such refusal to the Registrar of the Supreme Court or, in Privy Council cases, to a committee of review. The department's total expenditure for 1993 was $88 million in civil cases. During the year, 19 653 applications were received, out of which 6 627 were granted legal aid and $269 million was recovered for the aided persons.

The Director of Legal Aid also operates a Supplementary Legal Aid Scheme for people whose resources exceed the financial limits under the ordinary legal aid scheme, but are not sufficient to meet the high costs of conducting litigation on a private basis. The scheme is available for claims in the High Court, the Court of Appeal, and certain claims in the District Court for damages and compensation for personal injuries. An applicant with financial resources exceeding $120,000, but not exceeding $280,000, is eligible. The scheme is self-financing, funded by contributions from damages or compensation recovered. A successful litigant is required to pay back to the scheme 10 –12.5 per cent of the damages he recovers. The total expenditure of the scheme in 1993 was $5 million. A total of 78 applications were received, out of which 52 were granted legal aid.

An independent counselling agency, the Hong Kong Catholic Marriage Advisory Council, funded by the Royal Hong Kong Jockey Club, provides counselling services to legal aid applicants in family problems in the department's Kowloon branch office.

Legal Aid in Criminal Cases

In criminal cases, legal aid is available for representation in proceedings in the Supreme Court and District Court, in the Magistrates' Courts (where the prosecution is seeking committal of a defendant to the High Court for trial), in appeals from the Magistrates' Courts, and appeals to the Court of Appeal and to the Privy Council.

For appeals against conviction for murder, the grant of legal aid is mandatory to ensure that all relevant matters are placed before the court by the appellant's legal representative. For all other criminal appeals, legal aid will be given, subject to financial eligibility, if the Director of Legal Aid is satisfied that there are arguable grounds of appeal.

With effect from July 1992, an amendment to the Legal Aid in Criminal Cases Rules was introduced, to provide the Director with discretion to grant legal aid to an applicant charged with a criminal offence even if his disposable financial resources exceed the limit of $120,000, if the Director is satisfied that it is in the interests of justice to do so. The great majority of persons charged with criminal offences have therefore become eligible for the grant of legal aid.

The total expenditure on legal costs on criminal cases for 1993 was $108 million. During the year, 2 925 applicants were granted legal aid out of 4 656 applications received.

The Official Solicitor

Following the entry into force of the Official Solicitor Ordinance in August 1991, the Director of Legal Aid was appointed the first Official Solicitor, and a separate office, with a senior lawyer and support staff, was established to represent persons under legal disability in court proceedings in Hong Kong. Since its inauguration and up to July 1993, the Official

Solicitor received a total of 157 such requests in receivership, unclaimed estates, adoption, guardianship, and other cases. The Official Solicitor assigned less than 10 per cent of the cases to private legal practitioners for litigation, and litigated the balance herself.

Duty Lawyer Service

The Duty Lawyer Service was, until August 17, 1993, known as the Law Society Legal Advice and Duty Lawyer Schemes. It operates the Legal Advice Scheme, which provides legal advice; the Duty Lawyer Scheme, which provides legal representation; and the Tel Law Scheme, which provides legal information over the telephone.

The service is jointly managed and administered by the Law Society and the Bar Association of Hong Kong. It is funded by the government and the subvention in 1993–94 was approximately $57 million.

The Legal Advice Scheme was set up in 1978 to provide to members of the public free advice, without means testing, at five advice centres located in the District Offices. Members of the public can make appointments to see the volunteer lawyers through one of the 120 referral agencies, which include all District Offices, Caritas Services Centres and the Social Welfare Department. There are approximately 450 lawyers in the scheme. A total of 3 057 people were given legal advice during the year.

The Duty Lawyer Scheme was introduced in 1979. It initially provided free legal representation to defendants charged with one of six 'scheduled' offences in three magistracies. This was subsequently extended to nine 'scheduled' offences in 1981 and covered all magistracies in 1983. Upon the enactment of the Bill of Rights Ordinance in 1991, the scheme was expanded to offer representation to virtually all defendants charged in the magistracies who cannot afford private representation.

The scheme also assigns barristers and solicitors, on a roster basis, to advise defendants facing extradition, to monitor the one-way viewer in police identification parades and to represent hawkers upon their appeals to the Governor in Council.

Applicants are subject to a simple means test, with the financial eligibility limit set at a gross annual income of $90,000. The Administrator of the Duty Lawyer Service has a discretion to grant legal representation to defendants whose gross annual income exceeds the specified financial eligibility limit. An applicant is also subject to a merits test, based on the 'interest of justice' principle in accordance with the Bill of Rights Ordinance. The prime consideration is whether the defendant is in jeopardy of losing his liberty or whether a substantial question of law is involved.

In 1993, there were approximately 710 remunerated barristers and solicitors on the duty lawyer roster. A total of 35 413 defendants facing charges received advice and representation at trial under the Duty Lawyer Scheme.

The Tel Law Scheme was introduced in 1984 as a free telephone enquiry service. It provides members of the public with basic taped legal information, in both English and Chinese, on the legal aspects of everyday problems. The tapes covers aspects of matrimonial, landlord and tenant, criminal, financial, employment, environmental and administrative law. The tapes are constantly updated, and new tapes are added when a new subject is identified as being of interest to the public. During the year, Tel Law handled over 47 611 calls.

4

Implementation of the Sino-British Joint Declaration

The Sino-British Joint Declaration on the Question of Hong Kong was signed by the British and Chinese Governments on December 19, 1984. Under the terms of the agreement, on July 1, 1997, the British Government will restore Hong Kong to the People's Republic of China and Hong Kong will become a Special Administrative Region (SAR) of China, enjoying a high degree of autonomy. Also, the capitalist system and life-style of Hong Kong will remain unchanged for 50 years.

To ensure effective implementation of its provisions, the Joint Declaration provided for the establishment of the Sino-British Joint Liaison Group (JLG) and the Sino-British Land Commission.

The Sino-British Joint Liaison Group

The functions of the JLG are to conduct consultations on the implementation of the Joint Declaration, to discuss matters relating to the smooth transfer of government in 1997, and to exchange information and conduct consultations on such subjects as may be agreed by the two sides. It is an organ for liaison, with no role in the administration of Hong Kong.

The JLG comprises a senior representative and four other members on each side. It held its first meeting in July 1985. Since July 1988, it has taken Hong Kong as its principal base. Both sides have established offices in the territory and their respective senior representatives are resident in Hong Kong. The JLG holds plenary sessions at least once every year in Beijing and London, besides Hong Kong.

During the year, the JLG held three plenary sessions in June, September and December, the last one being its 28th meeting. It also held expert talks on a number of issues. While some limited progress was made, the overall progress was slow.

Matters discussed included defence lands, major franchises and contracts extending beyond 1997, right of abode, travel documents, international rights and obligations, air services agreements, and localisation and adaptation of laws.

Defence Lands

During the plenary sessions and talks at expert level, the JLG further discussed the future of lands in Hong Kong presently used for defence purposes. The objective was to agree on a package which would satisfy both the reasonable defence requirements of the Chinese Government after 1997 and the need to release land for the socio-economic development of Hong Kong.

Franchises and Contracts Extending Beyond 1997

The JLG discussed a number of major franchises and contracts extending beyond 1997. Agreement was reached on the Scheme of Control Agreement with the Hong Kong Electric Company Limited and Hong Kong Electric Holdings Limited; the West New Territories Landfill; the Southeast New Territories Landfill; and the subscription television licence.

Right of Abode

The JLG continued to discuss the alignment of the provisions on right of abode in the Immigration Ordinance with those in the Basic Law. It also discussed the questions of right of abode for persons not of Chinese race, and for children born outside Hong Kong to Hong Kong permanent residents.

Travel Documents

The JLG agreed on the transitional arrangements for the issue of Hong Kong re-entry permits. So far, the JLG has reached agreement on transitional arrangements for nearly all existing travel and identity documents.

International Rights and Obligations

The Sub-Group on International Rights and Obligations was formally established under the JLG in July 1986, to examine and discuss the continued application after 1997 of international rights and obligations affecting Hong Kong. The sub-group, based in Hong Kong, reports its conclusions to the JLG.

During the year, the JLG reached agreement on the continued application to Hong Kong of 12 international treaties. So far, the two sides have reached agreement on the continued application of about half of the approximately 200 multilateral treaties which currently apply to Hong Kong. These include agreements on Hong Kong's continued participation in some 30 international organisations, including the General Agreement on Tariffs and Trade (GATT), the Asian Development Bank, the Economic and Social Commission for Asia and the Pacific (ESCAP) and the International Maritime Organisation.

Air Services Agreements

In order to maintain Hong Kong's status as an international civil aviation centre after 1997, there is an on-going air services agreements (ASAs) separation programme, under which provisions involving Hong Kong in United Kingdom ASAs are separated into discrete Hong Kong ASAs. Two ASAs were signed in 1993. To date, Hong Kong has signed 10 ASAs, with the Netherlands, Switzerland, Canada, Brunei, France, New Zealand, Malaysia, Sri Lanka, Brazil and Australia.

Localisation and Adaptation of Laws

The Joint Declaration provides that after the establishment of the SAR, the laws previously in force in Hong Kong shall be maintained, except for those that contravene the Basic Law, and subject to any amendment by the legislature of the SAR.

Nearly 300 United Kingdom laws which currently apply to Hong Kong will cease to have effect in the territory after June 30, 1997. Apart from 80 that will not be needed after 1997, the rest have to be 'localised', that is, replaced by legislation enacted in Hong Kong

Ten years in construction, the Tian Tan Buddha — the world's largest, outdoor, bronze image of Buddha — drew thousands of devotees to the Po Lin Monastery on Lantau Island to witness the inauguration of the statue at the year's end.

A milestone was reached in September, when Mrs Anson Chan **(above),** *became the first local, female officer appointed to the top civil service post of Chief Secretary.*

Right, and opposite page: *As Chief Secretary (designate), Mrs Chan had a hectic schedule of engagements in November, leading Hong Kong '93 — the biggest promotion ever staged by Hong Kong in Europe.*

Visitors to the University of Hong Kong's Expo 2001 exhibition **(above),** *caught an exciting glimpse of the territory's future.*

Right: *The shape of things to come held onlookers spellbound at the Transport Department's prize-winning pavilion.*

Top: *Thirty years ago, the vision behind the Chinese University of Hong Kong was just beginning to change the landscape at Ma Liu Shui.*

Above: *Today, the Chinese University of Hong Kong is firmly established in the life of the community, as it celebrates its 30th anniversary.*

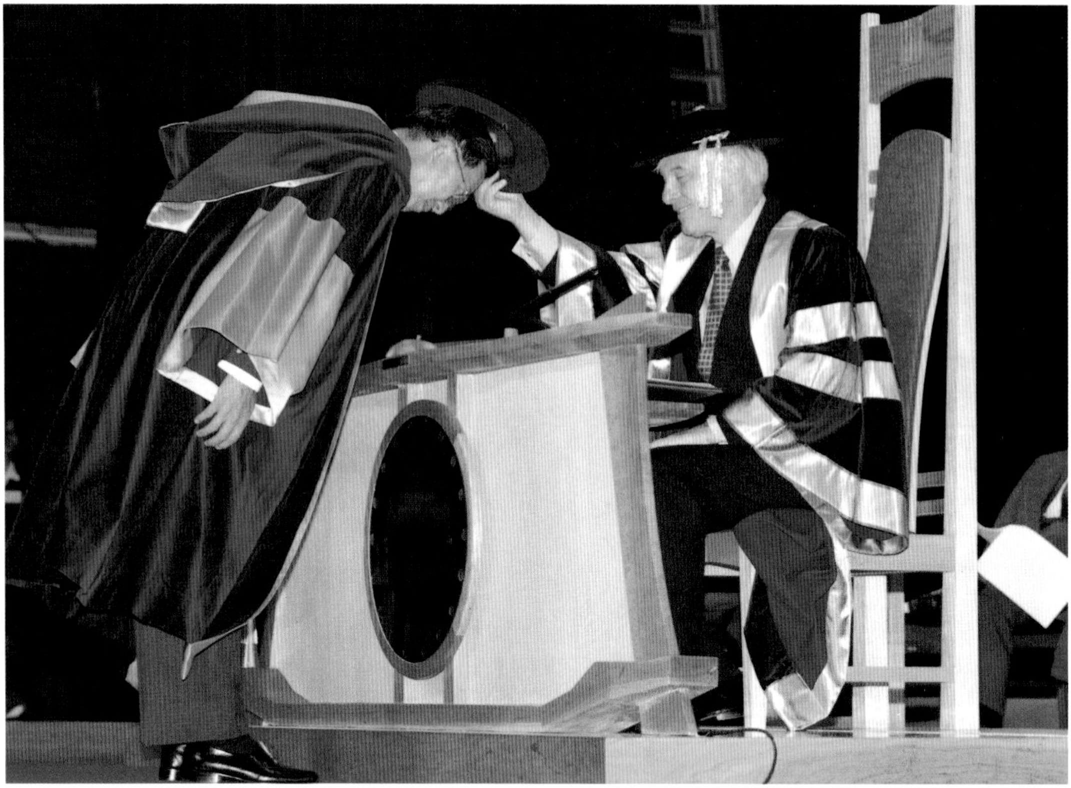

Opportunities in education continue to grow. In 1993, the Governor officiated at the first congregation of the Open Learning Institute of Hong Kong **(above)**; *while* **(right)**, *the Hong Kong University of Science and Technology began its third year of operation.*

Above: *Television viewers gained a wider choice of channels, when Wharf Cable Ltd. introduced the territory's first subscription television service on October 31.*

Left: *Public transport scored a world 'first', with the opening of the escalator service between Central District and the Mid-Levels. In addition to the convenience, it's free of charge.*

Top: *Teamwork and determination were rewarded with an entry in the Guinness Book of Records, when some 1 500 able and disabled young people produced the largest jig-saw puzzle ever assembled, to mark the International Day of Disabled Persons.*

Above: *Champagne corks popped at the Stock Exchange of Hong Kong on December 10, when the Hang Seng Index soared through the mythical 10 000-point barrier. After a succession of records, the Index closed the year at 11 888.39 points.*

in order to survive July 1, 1997. The JLG has so far agreed on the localisation of some 30 United Kingdom enactments.

The laws of Hong Kong also need to be reviewed and, if necessary, 'adapted' to ensure their compatibility with the Basic Law, so that they can continue to be in force.

During the year, both sides continued to exchange views on the localisation and adaptation of laws.

Land Commission

The Sino-British Land Commission was established in 1985 in accordance with Annex III to the Joint Declaration. Its function is to conduct consultations on the implementation of the provisions of Annex III on land leases and other related matters. It holds meetings in Hong Kong.

During 1993, the Land Commission held two formal meetings. The two sides agreed to make available, during the 1993–94 financial year, a total of about 127.8 hectares of land. This included 45.59 hectares for the development of the Black Point Power Station. Discussions continue on the land grant for Container Terminal 9, construction of which has to commence as soon as possible to meet the growing demand for container handling capacity.

Under the terms of the Joint Declaration, premium income obtained by the Hong Kong Government from land transactions is, after the deduction of the cost of land production, to be shared equally between the Hong Kong Government and the future SAR Government. The Hong Kong Government's share of premium income is put into the Capital Works Reserve Fund for financing public works and land development. The future SAR Government's share is held in a trust fund, called the Hong Kong Special Administrative Region Government Land Fund, established by the Chinese side of the Land Commission. The fund is managed under the direction and advice of an investment committee, which includes prominent bankers in Hong Kong, as well as a monetary expert from the Hong Kong Government. Over $44,232 million, representing the future SAR Government's share of premium income for the period May 27, 1985 to December 31, 1993, has been transferred to the fund.

The Basic Law

The Joint Declaration provides that the basic policies of the People's Republic of China regarding Hong Kong will be stipulated in a Basic Law of the Hong Kong SAR by China's National People's Congress (NPC). The Basic Law Drafting Committee and Basic Law Consultative Committee were established in 1985 to undertake the drafting of the Basic Law and to canvass public views on the drafts of the Basic Law. The first draft was published in April 1988 and the second draft in February 1989. The Basic Law was promulgated in April 1990 by the NPC, together with the designs for the flag and emblem of the SAR. It will come into effect on July 1, 1997.

Like the Joint Declaration, the Basic Law provides that the SAR will enjoy a high degree of autonomy and that the capitalist system and way of life shall remain unchanged for 50 years after July 1, 1997. It also prescribes the systems to be practised in the SAR.

5
THE ECONOMY

THE Hong Kong economy maintained a steady growth in 1993. The gross domestic product (GDP) grew by 5.5 per cent in real terms, with increases of 5.4 per cent in the first half of the year and 5.6 per cent in the second half. The corresponding growth rate in 1992 was 5.3 per cent.

Locally, consumer spending continued to register solid increases.

Investment in building and construction strengthened, supported by the acceleration in activity in the public sector.

However, investment in machinery and equipment consolidated, following the large increases in the previous years.

Externally, re-exports continued to perform strongly. The growth rate was, however, less rapid in the fourth quarter, affected by the slack demand in the major overseas markets. Many of these re-exports were products of outward processing arrangements involving Hong Kong companies and manufacturing entities in China. Domestic exports, after showing virtually no change in the first quarter, slackened further in the ensuing three quarters.

In line with the steady economic growth, the labour market tightened slightly in the second half after a temporary easing earlier in the year. The seasonally adjusted unemployment rate was 2.3 per cent in the first half of 1993, while in the second half it was two per cent. Labour resources continued to shift from manufacturing to the services sector, induced by the on-going structural transformation of Hong Kong into a more service-oriented economy. Average earnings in the major sectors showed further significant increases.

Apart from temporary relapses in some months due to volatile movements in the prices of certain essential foodstuffs, consumer price inflation was generally on a moderating trend during 1993. The inflationary pressures were largely generated domestically, rather than imported.

The rate of increase in the Consumer Price Index (A) for the year as a whole was 8.5 per cent, appreciably lower than the 12 per cent recorded in 1991 and 9.4 per cent recorded in 1992.

The GDP deflator, as a broad measure of overall inflation in the economy, also moderated, from 10.1 per cent in 1992 to 7.8 per cent in 1993. The rate of increase in the domestic demand deflator was consistently lower than that in the GDP deflator, and it decelerated from 6.6 per cent in 1992 to 5.7 per cent in 1993.

Structure and Development of the Economy

Due to its limited natural resources, Hong Kong has to depend on imports for virtually all its needs, including food and other consumer goods, raw materials, capital goods, fuel and even water. It must, therefore, export on a sufficient scale to generate foreign exchange earnings to pay for these imports, and the volume of exports must continue to grow if the population is to enjoy a rising standard of living.

The externally-oriented nature of the economy can be seen from the fact that in 1993, the total value of visible trade (comprising domestic exports, re-exports and imports) amounted to 250 per cent of the GDP. If the value of imports and exports of services is also included, this ratio becomes 282 per cent. Between 1983 and 1993, Hong Kong's total exports grew at an average annual rate of 17 per cent in real terms, which was roughly twice the growth rate of world trade. The corresponding average annual increase was 16 per cent for imports. With a gross value of $2,119 billion in overall visible trade in 1993, Hong Kong ranks 10th among the world's trading economies.

Contributions of the Various Economic Sectors

The relative importance of the various economic sectors can be assessed in terms of their contributions to the GDP and to total employment.

Primary production (comprising agriculture and fisheries, mining and quarrying) is small in terms of its contributions to both the GDP and employment.

Within secondary production (comprising manufacturing; the supply of electricity, gas and water; and construction), manufacturing still accounts for the largest share in terms of both the GDP and employment. The contribution of the manufacturing sector to the GDP declined steadily from 31 per cent in 1970 to 21 per cent in 1982. It then increased to 23 per cent in 1983 and to 24 per cent in 1984, before stabilising at around 22 per cent during the period 1985 to 1987. It fell again to about 13 per cent in 1992, reflecting partly the continued expansion of the services sector and the progressive relocation of manufacturing processes across the border. The share of the construction sector in the GDP increased from four per cent in 1970 to eight per cent in 1981. It then declined to seven per cent in 1982 and six per cent in 1983, before settling at about five per cent during the period 1984 to 1992.

The contribution of the tertiary services sector as a whole (comprising the wholesale, retail and import/export trades; restaurants and hotels; transport, storage and communications; finance, insurance, real estate and business services; and community, social and personal services) to the GDP increased from 60 per cent in 1970 to 65 per cent in 1982. It fell to around 62–64 per cent during the period 1983 to 1986, before rising steadily to 76 per cent in 1992.

The most notable change in employment since the early 1970s was the continuous decline in the share of the manufacturing sector in total employment, from 47 per cent in 1971 to 41 per cent in 1981, and further to 22 per cent in 1993. On the other hand, the share of the tertiary services sector as a whole in total employment increased from 41 per cent in 1971 to 47 per cent in 1981, and further to 69 per cent in 1993.

The Manufacturing Sector

Although Hong Kong's domestic exports are concentrated in a number of major product groups, there has been continuous upgrading of quality and diversification of items within these groups. The pressures of protectionism and growing competition from other economies have resulted in local manufacturers intensifying their efforts to diversify, not only products but markets. A major proportion of Hong Kong's manufacturing output is eventually exported. During the period 1984 to 1993, the volume of domestic exports grew at an average of 5.1 per cent *per annum*, notwithstanding the restructuring in the manufacturing sector and decline in employment.

Manufacturing firms in Hong Kong must be flexible and adaptable to cope with the frequent changes in demand patterns and to maintain their external competitiveness. The existence of a large number of small establishments, providing an extensive local sub-contracting system, has greatly facilitated the necessary changes in production and helped to increase the flexibility of the manufacturing sector. Moreover, increasing use has been made of the outward processing facilities in China for handling the relatively labour-intensive production processes. Because of land and space constraints, the territory's manufacturing industries usually operate in multi-storey factory buildings, resulting in concentration in the production of light manufactures.

Over the past 30 years, many industries have emerged and grown, the most notable being plastics and electronics. The textiles and clothing industries remain prominent, despite their continuous decline in relative importance. Other industries of importance include fabricated metal products, electrical appliances, watches and clocks, toys, jewellery, and printing and publishing.

Of particular note is the significant upgrading in labour productivity within the manufacturing sector over the years. During the period 1973 to 1991, the value of net output by the manufacturing sector grew at an average annual rate of 14 per cent, while manufacturing employment fell at an average annual rate of one per cent. Even after taking into account the effect of price increases on the output value, a significant improvement in labour productivity was evident.

The most significant change occurred in the textiles industry. The share of this industry in the net output of manufacturing declined from 27 per cent in 1973 to 15 per cent in 1991, while its share in manufacturing employment fell from 21 per cent to 15 per cent. Set against this decline was the expansion of the electrical appliances and electronics, and watches and clocks industries. Between 1973 and 1991, their shares in the net output of manufacturing increased from nine per cent to 12 per cent, and from one per cent to two per cent, respectively.

Market diversification over the years has been the combined result of initiatives taken by local manufacturers and exporters, and promotion efforts supported by the government. Over the past five years, China's share of Hong Kong's total domestic exports has been increasing steadily, and in 1993, overtook the United States of America to become the territory's largest market. The shares of domestic exports to a number of countries in the Asia-Pacific region have also risen. In 1993, Singapore became the fourth largest market for Hong Kong's domestic exports. The territory has, in addition, diversified into other new markets, including countries in the Middle East, Eastern Europe, Latin America and Africa.

The Services Sector

Over the past decades, the rapid growth in external trade has not only enabled Hong Kong to build up a strong manufacturing base, it has also provided the underlying conditions for the services sector to flourish and diversify. Of particular note has been the rapid growth and development in finance and business services, including banking, insurance, real estate, and a wide range of other professional services.

Entrepôt trade re-emerged prominently in the late 1970s, as China embarked on its 'open door' policies to facilitate its modernisation programmes. Rapid economic growth in the Asia-Pacific region over the past decade provided an added stimulus. Hong Kong, with its strategic location and well-established transport and communications network, was in a favourable position to take advantage of these opportunities. Trading and other economic links between Hong Kong and the region in general, and China in particular, increased rapidly. Re-export trade thus showed a significant increase, with an average annual growth rate of 26.6 per cent in real terms during 1984 to 1993.

Over the years, Hong Kong has developed an efficient wholesale and retail network to cater for the growing consumption needs of a more affluent population. Supermarkets, large department stores, convenience stores and modern shopping centres have become increasingly popular. This development has been reinforced by the rapid growth in tourism. Restaurants and hotels have also experienced a substantial increase in business. With higher household incomes, there has been a growing demand for services of a better quality and services in the community, social and recreational fields have also grown substantially.

Analysed by sectors, the contribution to the GDP of the wholesale, retail and import/export trades, restaurants and hotels varied between 19 and 21 per cent from 1970 to 1983, before rising to 27 per cent in 1992. The contribution to the GDP of the transport, storage and communications group was stable at around seven to eight per cent, before rising to nine per cent for the period 1987 to 1991, and further to 10 per cent in 1992. The contribution of finance, insurance, real estate and business services to the GDP experienced considerable fluctuations. It rose from 15 per cent in 1970 to 24 per cent in 1981, but fell back to 16 per cent in 1984, mainly reflecting the slump in the property market. It rose steadily in the following years, to 24 per cent in 1992.

Within the services sector, the most notable increase in employment was in the wholesale, retail and import/export trades, restaurants and hotels field. The largest employer in the services sector, its share of the total employed workforce rose from 16 per cent in 1971 to 19 per cent in 1981 and further, to 28 per cent, in 1993. This was followed by finance, insurance, real estate and business services, where the employment share rose from three per cent in 1971 to five per cent in 1981 and further, to nine per cent, in 1993.

Between 1983 and 1993, exports of services rose at an average annual rate of nine per cent in real terms, while imports of services were higher at 10 per cent *per annum*. The major components of Hong Kong's trade in services are shipping, civil aviation, tourism and various financial services. The shares of transportation services in total exports and total imports of services were 45 per cent and 33 per cent, respectively, in 1992. Travel services accounted for 35 per cent of the total value of exports of services and 46 per cent of the total value of imports of services. The corresponding shares for financial and banking services in total exports and total imports of services were six per cent and three per cent, respectively.

Increasing Economic Links between Hong Kong and China

Since the adoption of 'open door' policies by China in late 1978, Hong Kong's economic relations with China have undergone rapid growth and development. The two are each other's major trading partners.

In 1993, the total value of visible trade between Hong Kong and China amounted to $740 billion, representing an increase of 18 per cent over 1992. This rapid growth reflected partly the buoyant economic conditions in China and partly the sustained growth in outward processing trade.

China was the largest market for Hong Kong's domestic exports during the year, accounting for 28 per cent of the total. China was also the largest market for, as well as the largest supplier of, Hong Kong's re-exports. About 88 per cent of the goods re-exported through Hong Kong were destined for, or originated from, China.

In addition to trade in goods, Hong Kong also serves as an important service centre for China generally and South China in particular. This includes the provision of infrastructural facilities such as the use of the port and airport, as well as institutional support such as financial and related business services. This is evidenced, among other things, by the increasing importance of Hong Kong as a centre for entrepôt, trans-shipment and other supporting activities involving China.

Hong Kong has always been a convenient gateway to China for business and tourism. In 1993, 23 million trips to China were made by Hong Kong residents, and another 1.9 million trips to China were made by foreign visitors through Hong Kong. These represented increases of eight per cent and 10 per cent, respectively, over 1992.

Besides visible and invisible trade, Hong Kong is also the most important source of external investment in China, accounting for about two-thirds of the total. While Hong Kong's direct investment in China has been concentrated in light manufacturing industries, investment in hotels and tourist-related facilities, property and infrastructure has also been increasing. As can be expected, Guangdong Province occupies an important position in this respect. It has been estimated that, in Guangdong, more than three million people are working for Hong Kong companies, either through joint ventures or in tasks commissioned by Hong Kong companies in the form of outward processing arrangements and compensation trade. This, in effect, provides Hong Kong with a substantial production base.

Concurrently, China has also been investing heavily in Hong Kong. Its investment ranges from traditional activities such as banking, importing and exporting, wholesaling and retailing, and transportation and warehousing to newer areas such as property development, provision of financial services, manufacturing and involvement in infrastructural projects.

Increasing financial links between Hong Kong and China are reflected by the rapid growth in financial transactions with China in recent years. The Bank of China Group is now the second largest banking group in Hong Kong, after the Hongkong Bank Group. The latter group is among the best-represented foreign banks in China; others include the Bank of East Asia and the Standard Chartered Bank.

Hong Kong is a major funding centre for China. Most of China's fund-raising activities in the territory have taken the form of syndicated loans. Although in some cases Hong Kong is not the direct source of funds, it serves as a window through which China can gain access to external borrowings. These loans are mostly for financing China's own economic development, but some are used by China-interest companies in Hong Kong to finance their investment activities in the territory or abroad. In addition to syndicated loans, China-interest banks and other enterprises have been making greater use of negotiable certificates of deposit, bonds, commercial paper and the issue of shares to raise funds. A major development in 1993 was the listing of the shares of six of China's state-owned enterprises on the Hong Kong Stock Exchange.

The prospects for further development of economic and financial links between Hong Kong and China continue to be good, given the firm foundation which has been established over the years as well as the broadened 'open door' policies and accelerated economic reforms in China.

The Economy in 1993

External Trade

Reflecting the on-going structural shift of domestic exports to re-exports, re-exports grew further — by 19 per cent in value terms in 1993 over the level for the previous year. With an estimated one per cent decrease in prices, there was a 20 per cent increase in real terms. The corresponding growth rates in 1992 were 29 per cent and 28 per cent, respectively.

China remained the largest source of, as well as the largest market for, Hong Kong's re-exports. Supported mainly by the expansion of outward processing activities across the border, re-exports involving China (in both directions) continued to rise rapidly. Re-exports not involving China showed only a marginal increase. The other major re-export markets were the United States of America, Germany, Japan, Taiwan and the United Kingdom. The major suppliers of Hong Kong's re-exports, apart from China, were Japan, Taiwan, the USA, and the Republic of Korea.

Analysed by end-use categories, Hong Kong's re-exports comprised mostly consumer goods, and raw materials and semi-manufactured goods, which represented 54 per cent and 26 per cent, respectively, of the total value of re-exports. Re-exports of footwear, clothing, telecommunications and sound recording and reproducing equipment, textile fabrics, and electrical machinery and appliances showed faster increases than re-exports of other commodity items.

The value of domestic exports fell by five per cent in 1993 over 1992. As prices were relatively static in 1993, there was a five per cent decline in real terms. This compared with an increase of one per cent in value terms or virtually no growth in real terms in 1992. On a year-on-year comparison, domestic exports recorded virtually no change in real terms in the first quarter of 1993, but fell by seven per cent, five per cent and seven per cent in the following three quarters, respectively.

Domestic exports to China were up by three per cent in real terms in 1993 — a much slower growth rate than the 14 per cent increase recorded in 1992. A large proportion of these domestic exports were related to outward processing arrangements commissioned by Hong Kong companies. Domestic exports to the USA, Germany, the United Kingdom and Japan declined, by nine per cent, 11 per cent, 10 per cent and 13 per cent, respectively, in real terms in 1993. On the other hand, domestic exports to a number of economies in the Asia-Pacific region continued to rise considerably.

Analysed by major product categories, domestic exports of metal manufactures recorded the fastest growth, up by four per cent in real terms. This was followed by domestic exports of electronic components, up by three per cent. Conversely, domestic exports of textiles, metal ores and scrap, clothing, watches and clocks, and electrical appliances fell, by one per cent, four per cent, eight per cent, 15 per cent and 20 per cent, respectively, in real terms.

Imports grew by 12 per cent in value terms, or by about 13 per cent in real terms, in 1993. This compared with an increase of 23 per cent in value terms, or 22 per cent in real terms, in 1992. The major sources of Hong Kong's imports were China, Japan, Taiwan, the USA, the Republic of Korea and Singapore. The slower growth in imports in 1993 was largely attributable to the less rapid rise in re-exports and the more moderate increase in imports retained for local use.

Retained imports increased by only three per cent in value terms, or by about four per cent in real terms. Among the various end-use categories, retained imports of consumer goods, food, capital goods and raw materials and semi-manufactured goods increased by about 10 per cent, two per cent, one per cent and one per cent, respectively, in real terms. But retained imports of fuels fell by nine per cent in real terms.

With the value of total exports (domestic exports plus re-exports) smaller than that of imports, a visible trade deficit of $26 billion, equivalent to 2.5 per cent of the total value of imports, was recorded in 1993. This compared with a deficit of $30 billion, equivalent to 3.2 per cent of the total value of imports, recorded in 1992. As the prices of total exports declined at a slower rate than those of imports in 1993, the terms of trade showed a small improvement.

Domestic Demand

Domestic demand recorded further solid growth of five per cent in real terms in 1993, following a 10 per cent growth in 1992. Against the background of full employment and rising real incomes, private consumption expenditure registered a further significant increase of seven per cent during the year, having risen by eight per cent in 1992. Government consumption expenditure, on the other hand, recorded only a modest increase of two per cent (in national accounts terms). Investment demand, measured in terms of gross domestic fixed capital formation, grew by five per cent in real terms in 1993, following a 10 per cent increase in 1992. Among its major components, expenditure on building and construction recovered significantly to register an increase of 14 per cent in real terms in 1993, following virtually no growth in 1992. The pick-up was mainly attributable to the acceleration in work on a number of major infrastructural projects in the public sector. Expenditure on machinery and equipment consolidated, however, registering an increase of six per cent in real terms in 1993, compared with 22 per cent in 1992.

The Labour Market

The labour market tightened slightly in the latter part of 1993, after a temporary easing earlier in the year. In the fourth quarter, the seasonally-adjusted unemployment rate was two per cent, the same as that in the third quarter but 0.1 of a percentage point lower than that in the same quarter in 1992. The under-employment rate, at 1.5 per cent, was 0.2 of a percentage point higher than that in the third quarter and 0.5 of a percentage point lower than that in the same quarter in 1992.

Continuing the shift to the services sector, employment in the manufacturing sector decreased by 11 per cent from the level of a year earlier to 508 100 in September 1993, with vacancies also declining markedly by 26 per cent over the same period to 14 100. Offsetting this, employment in the services sector as a whole increased by six per cent to 1 722 900, and vacancies also rose, by three per cent to 55 800. In the services sector, employment in the wholesale, retail and import and export trades increased by eight per cent; that in finance, insurance, real estate and business services by nine per cent; and that in water transport, air transport and services allied to transport by seven per cent, but employment in restaurants and hotels fell by two per cent. On building and construction sites, employment decreased by 18 per cent. However, for the building and construction industry as a whole, employment of site and non-site workers taken together showed a smaller decline of five per cent.

The generally tight labour market conditions continued to boost labour incomes. Comparing September 1993 with September 1992, average earnings in all major economic sectors, in terms of payroll per person engaged, continued to show significant increases in money terms. Average earnings in the wholesale, retail and import and export trades recorded the fastest increase, up by 14 per cent in money terms between September 1992 and September 1993. This was followed by finance, insurance, real estate and business services, up by 13 per cent; restaurants and hotels, up by 12 per cent; and manufacturing, up by 10 per cent. After adjusting for inflation, the increases in real terms for these sectors were six per cent, five per cent, three per cent and two per cent, respectively. Earnings in transport, storage and communications recorded a more moderate increase of eight per cent in money terms, giving virtually no change in real terms.

The Property Market

After a brief consolidation in the first quarter of 1993, trading in the residential property market picked up markedly, along with a price upsurge, in the second quarter. Market sentiment was boosted by the success of a number of pre-completion sales exercises by the major developers, and the resumption of the Sino-British talks on Hong Kong's constitutional development and on financing arrangements for the new airport. Trading remained active during most of the third quarter with flat prices rising further. But activity contracted somewhat towards the end of the quarter. Notwithstanding a sustained low mortgage rate, reduced affordability following the large price increases and the tightening of mortgage lending by the major banks during the third quarter had set in to dampen demand. The market turned quieter during most of the fourth quarter as flat prices softened slightly. But trading activity revived again towards the end of the year, stimulated this time by the price fetched in the auction of a residential site in Kowloon Tong in mid-December, which was substantially above expectations. Meanwhile, the rental market for residential property was on a steady course, with rentals showing a less rapid increase than sale prices. The average rental yield for residential flats thus fell further in 1993.

In the market for shopping space, demand remained firm due to the rapid increase in visitor arrivals and the steady growth in spending by local residents. Sale prices and rentals for shop premises continued to rise significantly. For office space, rentals were on a general uptrend due to a sustained growth in end-user demand as the economy became more and more service-oriented. Trading in office strata in prime office premises also attracted considerable investment interest, and prices rose significantly. The market for industrial property, however, remained soft. Prices and rentals for conventional flatted factory space were generally static. But the market for modern industrial premises designed also for ancillary office use fared better, with prices and rentals picking up continuously.

The response to the various government land auctions conducted in 1993 was generally good.

Inflation

Consumer price inflation, as measured by the Consumer Price Index (A), or CPI(A), moderated to 8.5 per cent in 1993, from 9.4 per cent in 1992. The CPI(B), Hang Seng CPI and Composite CPI showed broadly similar trends. They rose by an average of 8.7 per cent, 9.5 per cent and 8.8 per cent, respectively, in 1993, compared with increases of 9.6 per cent, 9.8 per cent and 9.6 per cent, respectively, in 1992.

The year-on-year rate of increase in the CPI(A) decelerated from 9.4 per cent in the fourth quarter of 1992 to 8.8 per cent in the first quarter of 1993 and further to 8.2 per cent in the second and third quarters. In the fourth quarter, it edged higher to 8.7 per cent, largely reflecting the volatility in the prices of certain fresh food items amidst changing weather conditions. In December, the year-on-year rate of increase in the CPI(A), CPI(B), Hang Seng CPI and Composite CPI stood at 8.6 per cent, 8.5 per cent, 10.2 per cent and nine per cent, respectively.

Among the various components of the Consumer Price Index (A), the cost of housing continued to show the fastest increase, up by an average of 12.6 per cent in 1993 over 1992. This was followed by price increases for alcoholic drinks and tobacco (10.5 per cent), and miscellaneous services (9.5 per cent). These three components together accounted for 48 per cent of the overall increase in the index. Comparing the first half of the year with the second half, however, the rates of increase in their prices were generally on a moderating trend.

The prices for durable goods, fuel and light, miscellaneous goods and food increased at a much slower rate, by an average of two per cent, four per cent, seven per cent and seven per cent, respectively. As faster price increases were generally recorded for items with a larger local input, inflationary pressures were mostly generated domestically rather than imported.

Economic Policy and Public Finances

Economic Policy

Economic policy in Hong Kong is to a large extent dictated, and constrained, by the special circumstances of the economy. Owing to its small size and open nature, the economy is vulnerable to external factors, and government actions designed to offset unfavourable external influences are of limited effectiveness. Moreover, the government considers that, except where social considerations are over-riding, the allocation of resources in the economy is best left to market forces, with minimal government intervention in the private sector.

This basically free-enterprise, market-disciplined system has continued to contribute to Hong Kong's economic success. A relatively simple tax structure, with low tax rates, provides a good incentive for workers to work and for entrepreneurs to invest. Both workers and entrepreneurs are highly motivated. The primary role of the government is to provide the necessary infrastructure and a sound legal and administrative framework conducive to economic growth and prosperity.

Structure of Government Accounts

In accounting terms, the public sector is taken to include the Hong Kong Government itself, the Hong Kong Housing Authority, the Urban Council and the Regional Council.

Government grants and subventions to institutions in the private or quasi-private sectors are included, but expenditure by organisations in which the government has only equity (such as the Mass Transit Railway Corporation and Kowloon-Canton Railway Corporation), is excluded.

The government controls its finances through a series of fund accounts. The General Revenue Account is the main account for day-to-day departmental expenditure and revenue collection. Four other funds exist mainly to finance capital investment and expenditure, and government loans. They are the Capital Works Reserve Fund, Capital Investment Fund, Loan Fund and Lotteries Fund.

The Capital Works Reserve Fund finances the public works programme, land acquisitions, capital subventions, major systems and equipment items and computerisation. On May 27, 1985, when the Sino-British Joint Declaration on the Question of Hong Kong came into effect, the fund was restructured to enable the premium income obtained from land transactions to be accounted for in accordance with the arrangements in Annex III to the Joint Declaration. The income of the fund is derived mainly from land premia and appropriations from the General Revenue Account.

The Capital Investment Fund finances the government's capital investments in public bodies, such as equity injection in the Mass Transit Railway Corporation, capital investments in the Hong Kong Housing Authority and advances to the Provisional Airport Authority. Its income is derived mainly from dividends and interest on investments and appropriations from the General Revenue Account.

The Loan Fund finances government loan schemes such as housing loans and student loans. Its income is mainly derived from loan repayments, interest on loans and appropriations from the General Revenue Account.

The Lotteries Fund finances social welfare services through grants and loans. Its regular source of income is derived mainly from the sharing of the proceeds of Mark Six lotteries.

Management of the Budget

The government manages its finances against the background of a rolling five-year, medium-range forecast of expenditure and revenue. This models the consolidated financial position of the General Revenue Account and of all the funds except the Lotteries Fund.

The most important principle underlying the government's management of public expenditure is that the growth rate of public expenditure should, over a period, be close to that of the gross domestic product.

The budget presented by the Financial Secretary to the Legislative Council each year is developed against the background of the medium-range forecast, to ensure that full regard is given to these principles and to longer-term trends in the economy.

Public Expenditure

Public expenditure in 1992–93 was $123.5 billion. The government itself accounted for $105 billion, excluding equity injections in the Mass Transit Railway Corporation, the Hong Kong Housing Authority, the Provisional Airport Authority and other bodies. The growth rate over the preceding year was 13.9 per cent in nominal terms or 3.7 per cent in real terms. Some $31.1 billion or 25.2 per cent of the public expenditure in 1992–93 was of a capital nature. An analysis of expenditure by function is at Appendix 8.

Public expenditure has been around 15 to 17 per cent of the gross domestic product since 1987–88. It is estimated that this will rise to about 19 per cent in 1993–94. The growth rate of public expenditure is compared with the rate of economic growth at Appendix 9.

Total government revenue in 1992–93 came to $132.8 billion. The consolidated cash surplus was $22 billion, including net borrowings of $2.5 billion. Details of revenue by source and of expenditure by component for 1992–93 and 1993–94 (estimated) are at Appendix 10.

The draft estimates of expenditure on the General Revenue Account are presented by the Financial Secretary to the Legislative Council when he delivers his annual budget speech. In the Appropriation Bill introduced into the council at the same time, the administration seeks appropriation of the total estimated expenditure on the General Revenue Account.

The estimates of expenditure contain details of the estimated recurrent and capital expenditures of all government departments, including estimates of payments to be made to subvented organisations and estimates of transfers to be made to the statutory funds. They also provide for the repayment of public debt.

With the exception of only five years (1974–75, 1982–83, 1983–84, 1984–85 and 1990–91), the General Revenue Account has shown a surplus of income over expenditure at the end of each year for the past 20 years. The accumulated net surpluses on the General Revenue Account and on the Funds, together, form the government's fiscal reserves. These are available to meet any calls on the government's contingent liabilities and ensure that it is able to cope with any short-term fluctuations in expenditure relative to revenue.

The Urban Council and Regional Council, which operate through the Urban Services Department and Regional Services Department, respectively, are financially autonomous. They draw up their own budgets and expenditure priorities. The expenditures of the two councils are financed mainly from a fixed percentage of the rates from property in the Urban Council area (Hong Kong, Kowloon and New Kowloon) and in the Regional Council area (New Territories). Additional income is derived from fees and charges for the services the councils provide.

The Hong Kong Housing Authority, operating through the Housing Department, is also financially autonomous. Its income is derived mainly from flat sales and rents. If the authority's cash flow is inadequate to meet the construction costs of new estates, it may request an injection of capital by the government. The authority is provided with land on concessionary terms for the construction of public rental housing. Part of the authority's recurrent expenditure, for activities such as clearances and squatter control, is financed from the General Revenue Account. The authority is also responsible for carrying out a programme of squatter area improvements, which are funded from the Capital Works Reserve Fund.

Revenue Sources

Hong Kong's tax system is simple and relatively inexpensive to administer. Tax rates are low. The principal direct taxes are salaries tax and profits tax. Important indirect taxes include rates on property, stamp duty on property and stock market transactions, betting duty and duties on certain specified commodities. The government accords a high priority to curbing tax avoidance and evasion. (For a compilation of the major sources of revenue, see Appendix 11.)

The Inland Revenue Department is responsible for the collection of over 50 per cent of total revenue, including earnings and profits tax, stamp duty, betting duty, estate duty and hotel accommodation tax. Revenue from these sources are collectively described as internal revenue.

Earnings and profits tax, which alone accounted for about 39 per cent of total revenue in 1992–93, is levied under the Inland Revenue Ordinance. Persons liable to this tax may be assessed on three separate and distinct sources of income: business profits, salaries and income from property.

Profits tax is charged only on net profits arising in Hong Kong, or derived from a trade, profession or business carried on in Hong Kong. Profits of unincorporated businesses are currently taxed at 15 per cent and profits of corporations are taxed at 17.5 per cent. Tax is payable on the actual profits for the year of assessment.

Profits tax is paid initially on the basis of profits made in the year preceding the year of assessment and is subsequently adjusted according to profits actually made in the assessment year. Generally, all expenses incurred in the production of assessable profits are deductible. There is no withholding tax on dividends paid by corporations and dividends received from corporations are exempt from profits tax. In 1992–93, the government received some $32 billion in profits tax, amounting to about 24 per cent of the total revenue.

Salaries tax is charged on emoluments arising in, or derived from, Hong Kong. The basis of assessment and method of payment are similar to the system for profits tax. Tax payable is calculated on a sliding scale, which progresses from two per cent to 17 per cent on the first segments of net income (that is, income after deduction of allowances) of $20,000, to nine per cent and 17 per cent on the second and third segments of $30,000 each, respectively, and then to 25 per cent on remaining net income. No one, however, pays more than 15 per cent of their total income. The earnings of husbands and wives are reported and assessed separately. However, where either spouse has allowances that exceed his or her income, or when separate assessments would result in an increase in salaries tax payable by the couple, they may elect to be assessed jointly. Salaries tax contributed some $20 billion, or 15 per cent of total revenue, in 1992–93.

Owners of land or buildings in Hong Kong are charged property tax at the standard rate of 15 per cent for the actual rent received, less an allowance of 20 per cent for repairs and maintenance. There is a system of provisional payment of tax similar to that for profits tax and salaries tax. Property owned by a corporation carrying on a business in Hong Kong is exempt from property tax (but profits derived from ownership are chargeable to profits tax). Receipts from property tax totalled $1.3 billion in 1992–93.

The Stamp Duty Ordinance imposes fixed and *ad valorem* duties on different classes of documents relating to assignments of immovable property, leases and share transfers. The revenue from stamp duties accounted for about 10 per cent of total revenue, or $13 billion, in 1992–93.

Betting duty is imposed on bets at the Royal Hong Kong Jockey Club and on the proceeds of Mark Six lotteries — the only legal forms of betting in Hong Kong. The duty now accounts for about six per cent of total revenue.

The rate of duty is 11.5 per cent or 17.5 per cent of the amount of the bet, depending on the type of bet placed, and 30 per cent on the proceeds of lotteries. The yield in 1992–93 totalled some $8 billion.

Other taxes collected by the Inland Revenue Department include estate duty, imposed on estates valued at over $5 million at levels ranging from six per cent to a maximum of 18 per cent, and hotel accommodation tax of five per cent, imposed on expenditure on accommodation by guests in hotels and guest-houses.

The Customs and Excise Department is responsible for collecting and protecting duty revenue. The Dutiable Commodities Ordinance imposes controls on the import, export, manufacture, sale and storage of dutiable items. In 1992–93, $7.2 billion was collected in duties, accounting for about six per cent of total revenue. Duties are levied on four groups of commodities — hydrocarbon oils, alcoholic liquor, methyl alcohol and tobacco.

Duties are imposed irrespective of whether the product concerned is locally manufactured or imported. There is no discrimination on the grounds of geographic origin.

A comprehensive review of the Dutiable Commodities Ordinance is presently being undertaken to update terminology and streamline administrative procedures.

The Rating and Valuation Department is responsible for assessing and collecting rates, which are levied on landed property at a fixed percentage of its rateable value. The revenue raised helps finance the various public services provided by the Urban Council and Regional Council, besides providing a stable and reliable revenue stream for the government.

The rateable value is an estimate of the annual rent at which a property might be expected to be let, as at a designated date, and general revaluations are conducted at intervals to keep rateable values up-to-date. During the year, the department prepared new lists of rateable values to take effect on April 1, 1994. These rateable values reflect rental values at July 1, 1993.

The percentage charge is fixed annually by the Legislative Council in accordance with the financial requirements of the government, the Urban Council and the Regional Council. The percentage charge for the year 1993–94 was fixed at 5.5 per cent. Of this amount, three per cent of the revenue collected from Hong Kong Island and Kowloon was credited to the Urban Council and 3.75 per cent collected from the New Territories went to the Regional Council. The remainder, amounting to $4.4 billion, was credited to the government's General Revenue Account.

The government derives significant amounts of revenue from a number of other sources. Fees and charges for services provided by government departments generated a total of about $8 billion in 1992–93. The government's general policy is that the cost of the service provided should be fully covered by the level of relevant fees or charges. Certain essential services are, however, subsidised by the government or provided free.

A further $7.2 billion was generated by government-operated public utilities. The most important of these, in revenue terms, are water supplies, postal services and the airport. Significant sums also accrued to general revenue from the tax imposed for the registration of motor vehicles under the Motor Vehicles (First Registration Tax) Ordinance. This revenue, amounting to approximately $4.9 billion, was collected by the Commissioner for Transport.

In addition, some $8.9 billion, or about seven per cent of the total revenue of the year, was generated by land transactions. Following the implementation of Annex III of the Joint Declaration, revenue from land transactions decided upon before the coming into force of the Joint Declaration, and from those conferring a benefit that expires on or before June 30, 1997 (amounting to some $300 million in 1992–93), was credited to the general revenue. All revenue from other land transactions is credited to the suspense account of the Capital Works Reserve Fund, pending sharing with the future Hong Kong Special Administrative Region Government. The sharing arrangement in 1992–93 resulted in $8.6 billion being transferred to the works account of the Capital Works Reserve Fund and $7.6 million to the future Hong Kong Special Administrative Region Government's account.

A further sum of some $1.1 billion was received in the same year by way of royalties and concessions. These are paid by certain major companies holding franchises, such as the Cross Harbour Tunnel Company Limited and television broadcasters, as well as holders of concessions to operate taxis and petrol stations.

The government's revenue sources provide for a stable and fairly broad-based tax system, which is able to ensure that adequate funds are available for the implementation of its medium-term expenditure programmes, as well as the maintenance of adequate fiscal reserves.

6
FINANCIAL AND MONETARY AFFAIRS

HONG KONG'S financial sector comprises an integrated network of institutions and markets which, under various forms of regulation, provide a wide range of products and services to local and international customers and investors.

Some 513 authorised institutions from about 40 countries conduct business under the Banking Ordinance and the presence of 81 of the world's top 100 banks has helped promote the territory as an international financial centre.

The external assets of the banking sector were ranked the fourth largest in the world and the forex turnover was the sixth largest in 1993.

Hong Kong also has the second largest stock market in Asia outside Japan. During the year under review, the Hang Seng Index reached a succession of new records, closing 115.67 per cent higher at 11 888.39 points on December 31. It was also the year when 'H' shares of state-owned enterprises of the People's Republic of China were first listed on the local exchange.

In January, the government announced that the Bank of China will become the third note-issuing bank in Hong Kong in 1994.

On April 1, the Hong Kong Monetary Authority was set up to oversee monetary and reserves management and banking supervision.

During the year, the Hong Kong Government also successfully sold the Overseas Trust Bank to a subsidiary of the Guoco Group Limited for a total consideration of $4,457 million. The Overseas Trust Bank was taken over by the government in June 1985. It was the last government-owned bank returned to the private sector.

Financial Institutions

Hong Kong maintains a three-tier system of deposit-taking institutions — licensed banks, restricted licence banks and deposit-taking companies, which are collectively called authorised institutions.

Banking licences are granted at the discretion of the Governor in Council, in accordance with the provisions of the Banking Ordinance. In September 1992, the Governor in Council made a number of changes to the criteria for bank licence applications as part of a regular review of such criteria. In the case of a local applicant incorporated in Hong Kong, the criterion that it should be predominantly beneficially owned by Hong Kong interests has been broadened to enable close association and identification with the territory to be taken into consideration. Apart from the then prevailing requirements of a paid-up capital of at least $150 million and a minimum trading period of 10 years as an authorised institution, an applicant has to also satisfy minimum requirements on assets (net of contra items) and public deposits. The latter two requirements were increased to $4,000 million and $3,000 million, respectively. In the case of a bank incorporated outside Hong Kong applying to establish a branch in the territory, the asset size requirement (net of contra items) was increased to US$16,000 million. A licence may still be granted in exceptional circumstances, however, if the bank is of exceptionally high standing or if banks from its country of incorporation are under-represented in Hong Kong. The criterion dealing with home country supervision has also been changed to the effect that the home supervisor must demonstrate the necessary capabilities for meeting the minimum standards for supervision of international banks published by the Basle Committee of Supervisors in June 1992. In general, there should be some acceptable form of reciprocity in an overseas applicant's home country to banks from Hong Kong.

At the end of 1993, there were 172 licensed banks in Hong Kong, 32 of which were locally incorporated. They maintained a total of 1 605 offices. In addition, there were 142 representative offices of foreign banks. The total deposit liabilities of all the licensed banks to customers at the end of the year was $1,676 billion. (For details, see Appendix 12.)

Only licensed banks may operate current or savings accounts. They may also accept deposits of any size and any maturity from the public. The interest rate rules of the Hong Kong Association of Banks (of which all licensed banks are required, under their licensing conditions, to be members) result in the setting of maximum rates payable on bank deposits of original maturities of up to 15 months less a day, with the exception of deposits of $500,000 or above, for which banks may compete freely.

Restricted banking licences are granted at the discretion of the Financial Secretary. Companies are required to have a minimum issued and paid-up capital of $100 million and to meet certain criteria regarding ownership, general standing and quality of management. If incorporated overseas, the applicants must also be subject to adequate home supervision. Restricted licence banks may take deposits of any maturity from the public, but in amounts of not less than $500,000. There are no restrictions on the interest rates they may offer. At the end of 1993, there were 57 restricted licence banks and their total deposit liabilities to customers was $29 billion.

Restricted licence banks may use the word 'bank' in describing their business in promotional literature and advertisements, but this must be qualified by adjectives such as 'restricted licence', 'merchant', 'investment' or 'wholesale'. To avoid confusion with licensed banks, descriptions such as 'retail' or 'commercial' are not allowed. Overseas banks seeking authorisation as restricted licence banks may operate in branch or subsidiary form. If in branch form, they may use their registered name even if it includes the word 'bank' or a derivative, but in this case it must be qualified prominently by the words 'restricted licence bank' in immediate conjunction.

The authority to register deposit-taking companies rests with the Hong Kong Monetary Authority. In addition to certain basic criteria, registration will be granted only to companies which are more than 50 per cent owned by a bank. Deposit-taking companies are required to have a minimum paid-up capital of $25 million. They are restricted to taking deposits of not less than $100,000, with a term to maturity of at least three months. At the end of 1993, there were 142 deposit-taking companies, and their total deposit liability to customers was $17 billion.

Apart from deposit-taking, conventional lending and foreign exchange dealing, banks and deposit-taking companies in Hong Kong are increasingly diversifying into other financial services, including the securities business, fund management and the provision of investment advice.

The government's sale of the Overseas Trust Bank to a subsidiary of the Guoco Group Limited in 1993 marked the end of the government's efforts to rescue banks in the 1980s. The Exchange Fund was involved in the rescue of seven banks in the 1980s, either by direct government acquisition or by provision of assistance in acquisitions by third parties. These rescues were carried out to maintain the stability of Hong Kong's banking sector and monetary system during a critical period. The latest estimate of the total net costs of the seven rescues amounted to $3.8 billion (about 3.6 per cent of the accumulated earnings and 1.3 per cent of the total assets of the Exchange Fund as at the end of 1992).

Dealers in securities, investment advisers, commodity dealers and commodity-trading advisers and their representatives are required to be registered with the Securities and Futures Commission. To obtain registration, they must comply with the requirements (including the 'fit and proper' test) stipulated in the Securities Ordinance, the Commodities Trading Ordinance and the Securities and Futures Commission Ordinance. At the end of 1993, there were 10 840 registered persons. Of the 355 registered corporate securities dealers, 177 were from overseas. Of the 117 commodities dealers, 50 were from overseas.

Only members of the Stock Exchange of Hong Kong Limited are permitted to trade on the stock exchange. At the end of the year, the stock exchange had 579 corporate and individual members. Only shareholders who have applied for and been granted membership of the Hong Kong Futures Exchange Limited can trade on the Futures Exchange. At the end of 1993, the Futures Exchange had 107 members.

Under the Insurance Companies Ordinance, insurance companies are authorised by the Insurance Authority to transact business in Hong Kong. At the end of 1993, there were 229 authorised companies. Of these, 125 were overseas companies from 27 countries.

Financial Markets

Hong Kong has a mature and active foreign exchange market, which forms an integral part of the corresponding global market. The link with other major overseas centres enables foreign exchange dealing to continue 24 hours-a-day around the world. With an average daily turnover of around US$61 billion in April 1992, Hong Kong is among the largest markets in Asia, along with Tokyo and Singapore. Besides the Hong Kong dollar, most major currencies are actively traded in the territory, including the US dollar, Deutschemark, Yen, Sterling, Swiss franc, Australian dollar and Canadian dollar. As a market in foreign exchange, Hong Kong is favoured for many reasons, including an advantageous time zone location, a large volume of trade and other external transactions, the presence of a large number of international banks with experience in foreign exchange transactions, the absence of exchange controls and a highly advanced telecommunications system.

Equally well established and active is the interbank money market, which had an average daily turnover of $111 billion in December 1993. Wholesale Hong Kong dollar deposits and foreign currency deposits (mainly in US dollars) are traded both among authorised institutions in Hong Kong, and between local and overseas institutions. The interbank money market is mainly for short-term money — with maturities ranging from overnight to 12 months, for both Hong Kong dollars and US dollars. The traditional lenders of Hong Kong dollars in the market tend to be the locally-incorporated banks, while the major borrowers are those foreign banks without a strong Hong Kong dollar deposit base. As an indication of the size of the market, at the end of 1993, Hong Kong dollar interbank liabilities accounted for 30 per cent of the total Hong Kong dollar liabilities of the banking sector and foreign currency interbank liabilities accounted for 76 per cent of total foreign currency liabilities of the banking sector.

The launch of the Exchange Fund Bills programme in March 1990 has invigorated the local capital markets. Commencing with the weekly issue of 91-day bills, the programme was expanded to include fortnightly issues of 182-day bills in October 1990 and issues of 364-day bills every four weeks in February 1991. The bills are issued in paperless form for the account of the Exchange Fund and are used as a monetary market instrument. They are available in minimum denominations of $500,000 and are issued on a discount basis by tenders which are open to recognised dealers selected from institutions authorised under the Banking Ordinance. To promote secondary market activity, 28 market makers and 102 recognised dealers had been appointed by the end of 1993. The market makers are obliged to quote two-way yields for the bills during normal money market trading hours. At the end of the year, outstanding issues of 91-day, 182-day and 364-day bills amounted to $15.6 billion, $6.2 billion and $4.4 billion, respectively.

Following the establishment of the Hong Kong Monetary Authority (HKMA) on April 1, 1993, the two-year Exchange Fund Notes were first issued in May. They will phase out outstanding two-year government bonds by early 1995. The notes' proceeds are credited to the Exchange Fund, instead of the Capital Works Reserve Fund as in the case of government bonds. To help further develop Hong Kong's debt market, the HKMA launched in October the first quarterly issue of three-year Exchange Fund Notes. This has provided a reliable benchmark for three-year money. The outstanding Exchange Fund Notes and government bonds amounted to $5.4 billion at the year's end. As with the Exchange Fund Bills programme, both recognised dealers and market makers have been appointed under the Exchange Fund Notes programme. The notes are available in minimum denominations of $50,000. They are similarly issued in paperless form through tenders.

The local capital markets are an important source of finance for corporate borrowers. The two main types of negotiable debt instruments traded in the market are certificates of deposit issued by authorised institutions and commercial paper issued by other organisations and companies. Although the majority of issuers are locally-based institutions, a number of non-resident institutions have also come in to tap the local capital markets in recent years. Among the multilateral agencies active in this area in 1993 was the International Finance Corporation (IFC), which issued Hong Kong dollar bonds of $500 million in February. The Asian Development Bank (ADB) issued 30 billion Yen worth of Dragon-yen bonds in March, which were placed simultaneously in Hong Kong, Singapore and Taipei. In May, the Nordic Investment Bank (NIB) also issued US$250 million five-year Dragon bonds which were placed in Hong Kong, London and Singapore. In August and September, the IFC launched two further Hong Kong dollar bond issues of $750 million and $500 million, respectively. In September, the ADB launched its second Hong Kong dollar bonds programme to raise $1 billion. In November, the NIB launched its first Hong Kong dollar issue of $500 million, and the World Bank launched a $1 billion issue which was priced with reference to the benchmark established in October by the three-year Exchange Fund Notes. All these issues were well received by the market.

To promote and facilitate the development of the Hong Kong dollar debt market, the HKMA launched the Central Moneymarkets Unit (CMU) Service in December, with clearing operations to commence on January 31, 1994. The CMU Service, run by the HKMA, performs the role of a central custodian and clearing agent for Hong Kong dollar debt instruments issued by private sector borrowers. It handles debt instruments which are either immobilised or dematerialised, and the transfer of title is effected by computer book entry. The CMU Service offers an efficient, safe and convenient clearing system, which will go a long way towards reducing transaction costs and settlement risk.

The stock market also serves as an important source of capital. In 1993, after the signing of a Memorandum of Regulatory Co-operation by the regulatory authorities and stock exchanges of Hong Kong and the People's Republic of China, 'H' shares of six state-owned enterprises of China were listed on the local stock exchange.

At the end of the year, 477 public companies were listed on the Stock Exchange of Hong Kong Limited.

With a total market capitalisation of $2,975 billion, the Hong Kong stock market was ranked sixth in the world, after the United States of America, Japan, the United Kingdom, Germany and France.

The Hong Kong Futures Exchange Limited successfully launched the first traded options contract in Hong Kong. Since they commenced trading in March, Hang Seng Index options have been well-received by investors. Meanwhile, the futures exchange continues to offer futures contracts in the Hang Seng Index and Sub-Indices, interbank interest rates and gold.

The Chinese Gold and Silver Exchange Society operates one of the largest gold bullion markets in the world. Gold traded through the society is of 99 per cent fineness, weighed in taels (one tael equals approximately 1.2 troy ounces) and quoted in Hong Kong dollars. Prices closely follow those in the other major gold markets in London, Zurich and New York.

There is another active gold market in Hong Kong, in which the main participants are banks, major international bullion houses and gold trading companies. It is commonly known as the Loco-London gold market, with prices quoted in US dollars per troy ounce of gold of 99.95 per cent fineness and with delivery in London. Trading in this market has expanded in recent years.

Regulation of the Financial Sector

The government has consistently worked towards providing a favourable environment in the financial sector, with adequate regulation to ensure, as far as possible, sound business standards and confidence in the institutional framework, but without unnecessary impediments of a bureaucratic or fiscal nature.

The authority for the prudential supervision of banks, restricted licence banks and deposit-taking companies is vested in the HKMA. Its authority is derived from the Banking Ordinance, the provisions of which relate to the supervision of authorised institutions, in order to provide a measure of protection to depositors and to promote the general stability and effective operation of the banking system.

The HKMA has broadened its approach to supervision, which was previously reliant on on-site examinations. Such examinations are still an integral part of the supervisory process, but are supplemented by off-site reviews and prudential meetings with authorised institutions. Off-site reviews involve the analysis of regular statistical returns, and accounting and other management information supplied by institutions with a view to assessing their performance and compliance with the Banking Ordinance. Such reviews are followed by interviews with the senior management of institutions, at which the business, prospects and potential areas of concern of institutions are discussed. This broader approach to supervision has enhanced the HKMA's ability to identify potential areas of concern, which can be followed up by on-site examinations.

As an international financial centre, Hong Kong's banking supervisory policies are in line with international standards, especially those recommended by the Basle Committee on Banking Supervision. In 1992, the Basle Committee issued a set of minimum standards that the G-10 countries have agreed to apply in the supervision of international banking groups and their cross-border establishments. These standards are designed to provide greater assurance that no international bank can operate without being subject to effective consolidated supervision. To ensure compliance with these standards, Hong Kong added them to its bank licensing criteria in September 1992. In the case of a foreign applicant, its home supervisor must have established, or be working to establish, the necessary capabilities to meet the minimum standards.

In February 1993, the same requirement was added to the licensing criteria for restricted licence banks and deposit-taking companies.

The Basle Committee issued another paper in 1992 setting out a number of proposals on the supervision of liquidity for consideration by banking supervisors worldwide. In the light of these proposals, the HKMA carried out a review of its own regime on the supervision of liquidity. A working group on liquidity, comprising representatives nominated by the Hong Kong Association of Banks and the Hong Kong Association of Restricted Licence Banks and Deposit-taking Companies, was established to consider the proposals put forward by the HKMA. Two consultation papers, setting out the details of a proposed new approach towards the supervision of liquidity, were issued in April and July, respectively, for comment by the banking industry. Under the proposed new approach, the adequacy of an institution's liquidity would be assessed having regard to six factors: liquidity ratio, maturity mismatch profile, ability to borrow in the interbank market, intra-group transactions, loan to deposit ratio, and diversity and stability of deposit base. After extensive consultation, the proposal was found acceptable by the market. The HKMA plans to implement the new regime in June 1994.

Due to the rapid rise in property prices and speculation in the property market, the government issued in 1991 a number of warnings about the need for greater prudence in residential mortgage lending. In November that year, a number of leading institutions responded to these warnings by lowering their loan-to-value ratio for residential mortgages to 70 per cent, which then quickly became an industry norm. Since then, the HKMA has worked to ensure that the guideline is observed by all authorised institutions. The HKMA conducts a monthly survey on the residential mortgage lending of a sample of 33 institutions, which together account for about 94 per cent of such lending in Hong Kong, to monitor the possible impact of the guideline on the residential property market and on the mortgage business of institutions.

In response to a series of large over-subscriptions to new share issues, the HKMA established a working group in February to assess implications on the monetary and banking systems. The working group concluded that the monetary and banking systems have been able to cope well with the large over-subscriptions. However, it was not entirely clear that individual institutions had adequately understood and fully managed the risks arising from the financing of the subscriptions to new share issues. As a result, the working group made a number of recommendations which aimed to prevent institutions from over-exposing themselves to such risks. The recommendations include a requirement that institutions should apply a margin requirement of not less than 10 per cent to all their lending for subscriptions of new share issues. This margin requirement should apply to all customers generally, including brokers related to the lending institution. The working group also recommended that the receiving bank of application monies should, when it recycles monies to the interbank market, adhere to the normal credit limits it has assigned to individual banks, which should not be exceeded, unless exceptional circumstances apply, subject to a maximum credit limit of not more than 25 per cent of the capital base of the receiving bank or of its parent bank, as appropriate.

Hong Kong is a member of the Financial Action Task Force, with a mandate of encouraging international efforts in the fight against drug money-laundering. Its system to prevent money-laundering conforms to international standards. To help combat money-laundering, a guideline on the prevention of the criminal use of the banking system for the purposes of money-laundering was issued in 1989 by the then Commissioner of Banking. This guideline was revised in 1993, in the light of the new anti-money-laundering initiatives taken by the international community. It spells out clearly the HKMA's expectations of the internal policies and procedures which institutions should adopt to guard against money-laundering.

The Commissioner of Insurance and the Securities and Futures Commission (SFC) have also taken initiatives separately to ensure that the insurance and securities and futures industries, respectively, take appropriate measures to guard against money-laundering. This included the issue in December of a guideline by the Commissioner of Insurance and the plan for legislative changes by the SFC to enable it to require appropriate actions to be taken by market players.

The SFC, which was established in 1989 in response to the weakness in Hong Kong's financial markets at the time of the October 1987 world stock market crash, exercises prudential supervision of the securities, financial investment and commodities futures industry in Hong Kong. It administers the Securities and Futures Commission Ordinance, the Securities Ordinance, the Protection of Investors Ordinance, the Commodities Trading Ordinance, the Stock Exchanges Unification Ordinance, the Commodities Exchanges (Prohibition) Ordinance, the Securities (Clearing Houses) Ordinance, the Securities (Disclosure of Interests) Ordinance, the Securities (Insider Dealing) Ordinance and part of the Companies Ordinance in so far as it relates to prospectuses and purchases by a company of its own shares. The commission will take on additional regulatory responsibilities when the Leveraged Foreign Exchange Trading Bill comes into effect.

The Securities Ordinance and the Stock Exchanges Unification Ordinance, together with the Securities and Futures Commission Ordinance, provide a framework within which dealings in securities are conducted and the Stock Exchange operates, enabling trading in securities to be regulated. They require the registration of dealers, dealing partnerships, investment advisers and other intermediaries. They also provide for the investigation of suspected malpractices in securities transactions and the maintenance of a compensation fund to compensate clients of defaulting brokers.

The Protection of Investors Ordinance prohibits the use of fraudulent or reckless means to induce investors to buy or sell securities, or to induce them to take part in any investment arrangement in respect of property other than securities (the latter being controlled by the Securities Ordinance). It regulates the issue of publications relating to such investments by prohibiting any advertisement inviting investors to invest without the advertisement first being submitted to the commission for authorisation.

The Commodities Trading Ordinance, together with the Securities and Futures Commission Ordinance, provides a regulatory framework within which the Futures Exchange operates and dealers, commodity trading advisers and representatives conduct their business. It includes provisions for the registration of dealers and their representatives and the maintenance of a compensation fund to compensate clients of defaulting commodity dealers.

The Securities (Clearing Houses) Ordinance provides for the recognition of a clearing house and approval of clearing house rules by the Securities and Futures Commission, and makes certain exceptions to insolvency law in relation to a clearing house and its role in guaranteeing the settlement of market transactions.

Two important components of the regulatory framework in Hong Kong are the Securities (Insider Dealing) Ordinance and the Securities (Disclosure of Interests) Ordinance, which were brought into operation in September 1991. The Securities (Insider Dealing) Ordinance provides much stricter penalties for insider dealing than those previously applicable. The Securities (Disclosure of Interests) Ordinance requires that company shareholders with 10 per cent or more of the voting shares of a listed company disclose their interests and dealings publicly and that directors and executives disclose certain dealings.

The Leveraged Foreign Exchange Trading Bill, when enacted, will add a new component to the regulatory framework. The Bill provides for the regulation, by the Securities and Futures Commission, of the retail end of leveraged foreign exchange trading where an investor buys or sells spot currency by putting up a small percentage of the full value of the contract, settlement being made with reference to differences in exchange rates rather than actual delivery. Leveraged foreign exchange traders and their representatives will be required to be licensed under the proposed framework. The Bill also provides for the investigation of suspected trading malpractices, supplemented by rules governing arbitration, conduct of business, maintenance of financial resources, accounts and audit, contract notes and appeal procedures.

The Office of the Commissioner of Insurance exercises prudential supervision of the insurance industry in Hong Kong. It administers the Insurance Companies Ordinance which brings all classes of insurance business under a comprehensive system of regulation and control by the Commissioner of Insurance (Insurance Authority). The conduct of insurance business in or from Hong Kong is restricted to authorised companies, to Lloyd's members and to certain underwriters approved by the Governor in Council. All new applications for authorisation are subject to careful scrutiny by the Insurance Authority, to ensure that only insurers of good repute, who meet all the criteria of the ordinance, are admitted. The ordinance stipulates minimum share capital and solvency requirements for all authorised insurers and requires them to submit financial statements and other relevant information to the authority annually. It provides that any person who is not considered by the authority to be a fit and proper person to be associated with an authorised insurance company cannot acquire a position of influence in relation to such a company. It also empowers the authority to intervene in the conduct of the business of insurance companies in certain circumstances. Where the authority has cause for concern, it may take remedial or precautionary measures to safeguard the interests of policy-holders and claimants, including the limitation of premium income, the restriction of new business, the placing of assets in custody and petitioning for the winding-up of the company involved.

Self-regulatory measures to strengthen professional discipline in the insurance market have been formulated by the insurance industry, after consultation with the government. The measures involved the adoption by the industry in 1989 of two Statements of Insurance Practice governing the writing of insurance contracts for long-term and general insurance business, and the establishment in February 1990 of an Insurance Claims Complaints Bureau, which provides an independent avenue for resolving claims disputes arising from personal insurance policies. Enabling legislation is to be introduced to support the self-regulatory system under which no person shall be allowed to act as an insurance intermediary unless he is a registered insurance agent or an authorised insurance broker. The self-regulatory system will benefit Hong Kong as a developing international insurance centre.

The Occupational Retirement Schemes Ordinance, providing a registration system for voluntarily established occupational retirement schemes, was brought into force on October 15, 1993. The Commissioner of Insurance was appointed the Registrar of Occupational Retirement Schemes to take on the responsibility for the regulation of private sector retirement schemes. The objective of the ordinance is to provide greater certainty that retirement scheme benefits promised to employees will be paid when they fall due. The ordinance requires all schemes operating in, or from, Hong Kong to be either registered with, or exempted by, the Registrar. All registered schemes are required to comply with certain basic requirements. These include requirements on asset separation (the assets of a scheme must be kept separate and distinct from the assets of the employer or the administrator); independent trusteeship (there should be at least one independent trustee who must not be the relevant employer himself, his employee or associate); restricted investments (prohibiting any loan to the employer of the scheme or his associate out of the scheme's assets, and any excessive investment in the business undertaking of the employer); funding (the assets of the scheme must be sufficient to meet its aggregate vested liability); independent audit and actuarial reviews; and submissions of annual financial statements to the Registrar. There are also requirements for disclosure of information, concerning the operation of the scheme, to its members.

Under the ordinance, existing retirement schemes are required to apply for registration or exemption, before October 15, 1995. It is estimated that there are about 25 000 retirement schemes currently in operation in Hong Kong.

The Securities and Futures Commission

The Securities and Futures Commission (SFC) was established on May 1, 1989, following the enactment of the Securities and Futures Commission Ordinance, which represented a first important phase in the overhaul of securities legislation in Hong Kong and the implementation of some of the major recommendations made by the Securities Review Committee in May 1988.

The ordinance transfers to the SFC the functions of the former Securities Commission, the Commodities Trading Commission and the Office of the Commissioner for Securities and Commodities Trading. It provides a general regulatory framework for the securities and futures industries, leaving certain elements to be covered by regulations, administrative procedures and guidelines developed by the commission.

The SFC was established as an autonomous statutory body outside the civil service. It has 10 directors (half of them executive), who are appointed by the Governor. Each year the commission must present to the Financial Secretary a report and an audited statement of its accounts, which are laid before the Legislative Council.

The commission seeks advice on policy matters from its advisory committee, whose 12 independent members are appointed by the Governor and are broadly representative of market participants and relevant professions. Decisions of the SFC relating to matters concerning the registration of persons and intervention in their business are subject to appeal to the Securities and Futures Appeals Panel.

The SFC is funded largely by the market and partly by the government, although no funding was sought from the latter in 1993. Market contribution is in the form of fees and charges for specific services and functions performed (on a cost recovery basis), plus a statutory levy on transactions recorded on the stock and futures exchanges. Its annual budget in 1993 was about $180 million. On December 31, 1993, the SFC had an establishment of 222.

In its first four years of operation, the SFC has taken steps to develop a detailed framework of securities regulation that brings Hong Kong in line with internationally-accepted standards of market regulation and practice. As part of this exercise, it has issued revised versions of the Code on Unit Trusts and Mutual Funds and the Code on Take-overs and Mergers. The revised versions bring the codes in line with the increasingly sophisticated investment environment and incorporate a number of features designed to deal with situations which are unique to Hong Kong. Two new codes (the Code on Investment-Linked Assurance and Pooled Retirement Funds and the Code on Immigration-Linked Investment Schemes) have also been issued, enhancing the level of protection for investors of these funds within the framework of the Protection of Investors Ordinance.

The SFC has been encouraging the development of more efficient equity trading systems and a greater variety of securities and futures products. It has been working closely with the stock exchange on the phased implementation of an Automatic Order Matching and Execution System (AMS) since November 1993, under which orders are entered into the screen-based trading system and executed automatically when the buy and sell prices match. The AMS enhances the trading capacity and efficiency of the stock market and enables the instant capture and dissemination of market data, which will contribute to greater market integrity and transparency.

Implementation of the AMS will facilitate the introduction of the short-selling of stocks on January 3, 1994. A sound regulatory structure has been developed to allow such short-selling through registered members of the stock exchange. Initially, 21 shares will be eligible for short-selling. These shares are the largest Hang Seng Index constituent stocks, a significant proportion of which are in the hands of the public.

In May, the Hong Kong Securities Clearing Company successfully completed the phased admission of listed securities into the Central Clearing and Settlement System (CCASS). This is an automated book-entry system that handles the settlement of securities among brokers. The system was tested by the sharp increase in turnover during the last quarter of 1993 and proved capable and efficient in handling the large volume of transactions.

Both the stock exchange and futures exchange finalised codes of conduct for their members in 1993. In addition, the SFC will introduce a code of conduct that applies to all other persons registered under the Securities Ordinance and the Commodities Trading Ordinance in 1994. All these codes are based on the principles developed by the International Organisation of Securities Commissions, of which Hong Kong is a member.

The SFC is also rationalising and updating Hong Kong's securities and futures legislation into a coherent, well-organised and user-friendly corpus of securities law.

Transaction costs of securities trading decreased further during the year under review. The stamp duty and statutory levy were reduced from 0.2 per cent and 0.025 per cent to 0.15 per cent and 0.02 per cent, respectively, on the value of each purchase and sale of securities. The special levy on stock and futures transactions, which was introduced in 1987 to help repay the Lifeboat Loan made available after the market crash, was suspended with effect from August 16.

Hong Kong as an International Financial Centre

The favourable geographical position of Hong Kong, which provides a bridge in the time gap between North America and Europe, together with strong links with China and other economies in Southeast Asia and excellent communications with the rest of the world, have helped the territory to develop into an important international financial centre. The absence of any restrictions on capital flows into and out of the territory is also an important factor.

Foreign banks in Hong Kong tend to be the premier banks in their countries of incorporation and this is illustrated by the fact that 81 of the top 100 banks in the world in 1993 have operations in the territory. In addition, many merchant banks or investment banks of world standing operate in Hong Kong. A substantial proportion of the transactions in the banking sector are international in nature: more than 60 per cent of the sector's aggregate assets and liabilities are external, spreading over more than 100 countries. The financial markets, particularly in foreign exchange and gold, form an integral part of the corresponding global markets. Moreover, Hong Kong serves as an important centre for the intermediation of international flows of savings and investment, particularly through the syndication of loans and international fund management. International investors play a significant and increasing role in the territory, and Hong Kong investment overseas is also believed to be considerable.

The Financial Scene

In respect of the liquidation of the Bank of Credit and Commerce (Hong Kong) Limited (BCCHK), two further dividends of 10 per cent and seven per cent were declared in April and October, respectively, to creditors with claims of over $100,000. This brought the total to 58 per cent, following the first payment of 41 per cent in September 1992 to creditors who were not covered by the court-sanctioned Scheme of Arrangement. Recovery of assets will continue and further dividend payment is expected.

During the year under review, the exchange rate of the Hong Kong dollar against the US dollar remained stable under the linked exchange rate system. Local interest rates remained at low levels, consistent with the interest rates in the United States of America. Hong Kong dollar deposits and loans recorded solid growth.

The market exchange rate of the Hong Kong dollar against the US dollar moved within a narrow range of HK$7.722 and HK$7.761 to US$1. In May, it strengthened briefly to around HK$7.722. An inflow of overseas funds into the buoyant stock market and the firming up of interbank interest rates associated with new share issues contributed to the strengthening. In late June, it weakened once to an intra-day low of about HK$7.78, partly due to a rumour on the repatriation of funds to China to defend the exchange rate of the Renminbi. It then quickly rebounded to around HK$7.75 towards the end of June. During the fourth quarter, there was a strong inflow of overseas funds into the local stock market. As a result, the exchange rate of the Hong Kong dollar strengthened slightly, closing the year at HK$7.726 to US$1.

The marco-adjustment stabilisation programme of China, introduced in July, seemed to have little impact on the Hong Kong monetary sector. There was no clear sign of significant net outflow of funds to China, as evidenced by the stable Hong Kong dollar market exchange rate.

Under the linked exchange rate system, the overall exchange value of the Hong Kong dollar, as measured by the effective exchange rate index, is influenced predominantly by the movements of the US dollar against other major currencies. During most of the year, the US dollar appreciated against the major European currencies, as a result of the narrowing of the interest rate differential between the US dollar and the European currencies and the volatility in the exchange rates of some of the currencies under the Exchange Rate Mechanism. On the other hand, the US dollar weakened against the Japanese Yen in the face of the persistent trade surplus in favour of Japan. This trend was, however, reversed in the fourth quarter in view of the improved performance of the US economy. Largely reflecting these movements, the effective exchange rate index of the Hong Kong dollar edged up from 114.2 at the end of December 1992 to 115.3 in early February and then eased to 111.5 towards the end of April. It fluctuated around the range of 112–113 during the third quarter before edging up during the fourth quarter to close the year at 114.3. (For details, see Appendix 13.)

Partly affected by the strong funding demand around the Lunar New Year, the three-month Hong Kong interbank offered rate (HIBOR) generally stayed above the corresponding Euro-dollar deposit rate in January and firmed up further in mid-February under the influence of large share flotation exercises. Subsequent to a liquidity injection into the banking system by the Hong Kong Monetary Authority, the differential between the three-month HIBOR and the corresponding Euro-dollar rate narrowed towards the end of February. The two rates moved closely together between March and June but HIBOR was slightly higher than the corresponding Euro-dollar rate in July, again due to some share flotation exercises. Since July, the three-month HIBOR has eased slightly, drifting marginally below the corresponding Euro-dollar rates in October and the first half of November, but firming towards the end of the year due to share flotation exercises as well as year-end tightness in interbank liquidity. For 1993 as a whole, the average interest rate differential (in terms of three-month rates) was 0.15 of a percentage point, about the same as the corresponding 0.13 percentage point recorded in 1992.

During the year, deposit rates administered by the Hong Kong Association of Banks remained unchanged. At the year's end, the savings deposit rate was 1.5 per cent while the three-month and 12-month deposit rates were 2.75 per cent and 3.75 per cent, respectively. The best lending rate stood at 6.5 per cent.

Hong Kong dollar deposits grew by 25.5 per cent during 1993, higher than the growth rate of 13.2 per cent in 1992. This was also higher than the growth in gross domestic product in money terms, at around 15 per cent. The acceleration in the growth of Hong Kong dollar deposits, particularly during the fourth quarter, was due to the inflow of funds. Foreign currency deposits increased by 5.5 per cent in 1993, compared to the 6.3 per cent increase recorded in 1992. Taken together, total customer deposits (in all currencies) increased by 14.6 per cent in 1993, compared with 9.3 per cent in 1992. The relative share of Hong Kong dollar deposits to total deposits rose to 49.8 per cent at the year's end, from 45.5 per cent a year earlier.

Hong Kong dollar M1, M2 and M3 rose by 20.8 per cent, 26.9 per cent and 25.2 per cent, respectively, in 1993. The corresponding increases for total M1, M2 and M3 were 20.6 per cent, 16 per cent and 15.6 per cent, respectively. (For details, see Appendix 14.)

Hong Kong dollar loans recorded a growth of 17.9 per cent in 1993, while foreign currency loans increased by 14.6 per cent. Analysed by major categories, loans for use in Hong Kong (including those for trade financing) increased by 17.7 per cent. Growth in residential mortgage loans increased from 13.6 per cent in 1992 to 19.5 per cent in 1993. Following a moderate growth of 2.3 per cent in the first quarter, the growth rate accelerated to 6.1 per cent and 7.7 per cent in the second and third quarters, respectively, as trading in the residential property market, in particular the luxury flats sector, revived, alongside a more bullish sentiment. In response to this, banks tightened their lending policy by reducing the maximum loan-to-valuation ratio of luxury flats from 70 per cent to 60 per cent in July. The growth in residential mortgage loans slowed in the fourth quarter to 2.2 per cent. Loans for trade financing recorded a significant increase of 15.7 per cent during 1993, largely reflecting the pick-up in trade activities. Loans to other major sectors, including wholesale and retail trades, building, construction, property development and investment, transport, manufacturing and financial concerns, all recorded some increases during the year.

Turning to the financial markets, the expansion in the government borrowing programme facilitated the further development of the local capital markets. The two-year Government Bond programme was being replaced by the two-year Exchange Fund Note programme, starting from May. The Exchange Fund bills and notes continued to receive favourable market response, with tenders invariably several times over-subscribed. At the end of the year, the yields for the bills were around 35 to 45 basis points below the corresponding Hong Kong interbank offered rate, while the yields for the three-year Exchange Fund notes were around 20 basis points above the corresponding US Treasury bonds. Daily turnover of the bills and bonds, taken together, in the secondary market averaged $15.3 billion, or 48 per cent of the total amount of bills, notes and bonds outstanding, at $31.7 billion, at the year's end.

New issue activity in respect of other debt instruments remained relatively moderate as equity funds were raised through the buoyant stock market. A total of 125 new issues of negotiable certificates of deposit were launched during 1993, of which 87 were denominated in Hong Kong dollars. Of these 87 issues, 57 were arranged on fixed-rate terms and the remaining 30 on floating-rate terms. At the end of the year, the outstanding value of Hong Kong dollar-denominated negotiable certificates of deposit amounted to $33.5 billion, compared with $26.9 billion a year earlier; 54 per cent of these were held outside the local banking sector.

Of the 20 new issues of commercial paper and other debt instruments reported to the Securities and Futures Commission during 1993, eight were denominated in Hong Kong dollars.

The local stock market was very buoyant in 1993. Favourable corporate results helped push the Hang Seng Index up to new records throughout the year. Stimulated by an influx of overseas funds in the fourth quarter, the Hang Seng Index saw a remarkable advance from October when the strong momentum was supported by heavy turnover. The Index rose to a record high of 11 959.06 on December 30, before closing the year at 11 888.39 — 115.67 per cent higher than the level recorded at the end of 1992. Although most Asian stock markets also reported outstanding gains during the year, the performance of the Hong Kong stock market ranked second in the region and also second among the top 15 major stock markets in the world. Average daily turnover in the local stock market also rose substantially to $4.9 billion in 1993, compared with $2.8 billion in 1992.

The number of newly-listed companies was 68, raising a total of $28.9 billion. Among these newly-listed companies, six were state-owned enterprises of the People's Republic of China. They attracted particular market attention. The listing of these enterprises in Hong Kong was one of the most important market development initiatives in recent years. The six enterprises, which together raised a total of $8.1 billion, were among the nine selected by Chinese authorities in early 1992 to apply for a listing in Hong Kong.

In addition to new share issues, funds were tapped through rights issues ($9.3 billion) and private placements ($35 billion).

The Hong Kong Futures Exchange launched options contracts on Hang Seng Index futures on March 5. The instrument was well-received by market practitioners and was traded actively, with the highest turnover of 6 147 contracts being recorded on October 15. Trading in Hang Seng Index futures was also buoyant. The average daily turnover increased considerably to 9 597 contracts in 1993, with a post-1987 crash high of 26 288 contracts reported on November 24, compared with the daily average of 4 347 contracts in the preceding year. Hang Seng Sub-Index futures were, however, unable to share a similar level of activities, while the trading of gold futures and interest rate futures remained inactive.

The price of Loco-London gold moved between US$325 to US$409 in 1993. Partly attributable to the buying wave from Japanese investors due to the weak US dollar and the concerns of inflationary pressure in the United States of America, the price of gold rose from US$333 per troy ounce at the end of 1992 to US$408.80 per troy ounce in early August. It then fell to around US$342.70 per troy ounce, but rebounded to US$391 per troy ounce at the end of the year.

The price of gold at the Chinese Gold and Silver Exchange Society exhibited similar movement. At the end of the year, gold cost HK$3,592 per tael. Turnover on the exchange totalled 25 million taels in 1993.

The number of unit trusts and mutual funds decreased slightly to 895 at the year's end, from 900 a year earlier. Of the 112 newly-authorised funds approved by the Securities and Futures Commission during the year, many were invested in the emerging markets of Asia and Latin America, including two funds (making a total of 12) invested in China. Among the different types of funds, Asian equity and warrant funds recorded the best performance in terms of investment return.

Companies Registry

On May 1, the Companies Registry became an independent department, following the dissolution of the Registrar General's Department of which it was formerly a constituent division. The registry is headed by the Registrar of Companies.

On August 1, the registry became one of the first two government departments to be operated on a trading fund basis. As a trading-funded department, the registry is allowed to retain a proportion of its revenue, rather than paying this over to general revenue. Although it is required to balance its income and expenditure, it will be in a far better position to deploy its resources flexibly, in order to react to changing demands for its services. With the financial freedom of a trading fund, the registry will be in a better position to improve its services.

The registry's main functions and responsibilities include the incorporation and registration of companies; the administration and enforcement of the Companies Ordinance and a number of other ordinances (including the Trustee Ordinance as this relates to trust companies, the Registered Trustees Incorporation Ordinance and the Limited Partnerships Ordinance); the registration of documents required to be lodged by registered companies; and the provision of facilities for the search of company records.

The Companies Ordinance is subject to continual review and improvement, subject to the advice of the Standing Committee on Company Law Reform. The committee was established in 1984 and its secretary is a senior legal officer of the Companies Registry. Its main task is to ensure that Hong Kong's company laws meet the up-to-date needs of government and the business community. In January, the Companies (Amendment) Ordinance 1993 was enacted and came into operation on July 1. It enables the Registrar of Companies to strike off a company which has for two consecutive years failed to forward to the Registrar its annual return. It also allows a company by special resolution to authorise its directors to change its status to that of a 'dormant' company, after which it will be exempted from fulfilling certain requirements of the ordinance while it remains dormant.

On incorporation under the Companies Ordinance, a local company pays a registration fee of $1,300, plus $6 for every $1,000 of nominal capital. In 1993, 61 831 new companies were incorporated — 3 721 more than in 1992. The nominal capital of new companies registered totalled $7,622 million. Of the new companies registered, 309 had a nominal share capital of $5 million or more. During the year, 12 108 companies increased their nominal capital by amounts totalling $57,005 million. At the end of the year, there were 415 911 local companies on the register, compared with 358 129 in 1992.

Companies incorporated overseas are required to register certain documents with the registry, within one month of establishing a place of business in the territory. A registration fee of $650 and some incidental filing fees are payable in such cases. During 1993, 498 of these were registered. At the end of the year, 3 544 companies were registered from 73 countries, including 694 from the United States of America, 373 from the United Kingdom and 318 from Japan.

During 1993, the Companies Registry continued to explore ways and means of improving its services, in consultation with the Efficiency Unit of the Government

Secretariat. The Efficiency Unit undertook an overall operations review of the registry which covered a wide range of areas. At present, the registry is able to complete the incorporation of a local company in seven working days and complete the registration of a charge in 10.5 to 14 working days. The registry aims to further improve its services by streamlining its practices and procedures, and through better staff deployment, office automation and computerisation. Preparatory work for computerising the control book and document index of incoming documents was at an advanced stage and the project is expected to be functional in mid-1994. During 1994, it is intended to provide a computerised directors' index for listed companies, subject to the enactment of the relevant enabling legislation by the Legislative Council. In the longer-term, the registry intends to provide remote search facilities for its main professional customers. The possibility of storing corporate data on optical disks rather than microfilm will also be examined.

Money Lenders

Under the Money Lenders Ordinance, anyone wishing to carry on business as a money lender must apply to a licensing court for a licence. The ordinance does not apply to banks and deposit-taking companies authorised under the Banking Ordinance.

Any application for a licence is, in the first instance, submitted to the Registrar of Companies as Registrar of Money Lenders. A copy is also sent to the Commissioner of Police, who may object to the application. The application is advertised, and any member of the public who has an interest in the matter also has the right to object. During the year, 645 applications were received and 624 licences were granted. At the end of 1993, there were 610 licensed money lenders.

The ordinance provides severe penalties for a number of statutory offences, such as carrying on an unlicensed money-lending business. It also provides that any loan made by an unlicensed money lender shall not be recoverable by court action. With certain exceptions (primarily authorised institutions under the Banking Ordinance), any person, whether a licensed money lender or not, who lends or offers to lend money at an interest rate exceeding 60 per cent per annum commits an offence. Any agreement for the repayment of any such loan, or security given in respect of such a loan, is unenforceable.

Bankruptcies and Compulsory Winding-up

The Official Receiver's office administers the estates of individual bankrupts and companies ordered to be compulsorily wound up by the courts.

Once a receiving order is made against the property of an individual bankrupt, or a winding-up order is made against a company by the courts, the Official Receiver becomes the interim receiver or provisional liquidator, respectively.

In cases where the assets of an estate are not likely to exceed $200,000 in value, the Official Receiver applies to the courts for a summary procedure order and is appointed trustee or liquidator. In other cases, a meeting of creditors in bankruptcy, or of creditors and contributories in compulsory liquidations, is held to decide whether the Official Receiver, or another person from the private sector, should be appointed trustee or liquidator. If a debtor makes a proposal for a composition in satisfaction of his debts or a proposal for a scheme of arrangement of his affairs, he will not be adjudged bankrupt if the proposal is accepted by his creditors and the court. As in past years, the Official Receiver was appointed trustee or liquidator in most cases.

The work of the Official Receiver where he acts as trustee or liquidator includes the investigation of the affairs of the bankrupt or the wound-up company, the realisation of assets and the distribution of dividends to creditors. The Official Receiver also prosecutes certain offences set out in the Companies and Bankruptcy Ordinances. In addition, he supervises the work of outside liquidators and trustees.

During the year, staff adapted smoothly to handling cases under the new 'overall case management' system introduced in June 1992. Efficiency, productivity and accountability have improved in the Official Receiver's office. This has resulted in increases in the amount of dividends declared and payable, book debts recovered and in the number of bankruptcy and winding-up cases completed. There has also been an increase in the number of summonses issued and the amount of fines awarded by the courts for failure to file statements of affairs in liquidations.

During the year, the courts made 329 receiving orders and 408 winding-up orders, an increase of 15.7 per cent over the previous year. The assets realised by the Official Receiver during 1993 amounted to $157.4 million, while $179.38 million in dividends were paid to creditors in 251 insolvency cases. A total of 66 convictions were obtained and the total amount of fines imposed by the courts was $326,458.

Establishment of the Hong Kong Monetary Authority

To maintain the continuity and professionalism in Hong Kong's monetary and reserves management and banking supervision, in a way which commands the confidence of the people of Hong Kong and the international financial community, the Hong Kong Monetary Authority (HKMA) was established in April by merging the Office of the Exchange Fund with the Office of the Commissioner of Banking. The Exchange Fund (Amendment) Ordinance 1992, providing for the establishment of the HKMA, was enacted on December 10, 1992 and came into operation on April 1, 1993.

The HKMA is responsible for the development and execution of monetary policy; maintenance of exchange rate and monetary stability; the development of the debt market in Hong Kong; promoting the efficiency, integrity and development of payment and settlement arrangements; managing the assets of the Exchange Fund; prudential supervision of authorised institutions under the Banking Ordinance; and formulating policies relating to banking supervision. These functions are now carried out by its four departments: the Monetary Management Department, Reserves Management Department, Banking Policy Department and Banking Supervision Department. A fifth, the External Department, will be set up in 1994 to develop contacts and co-operation with other central banks and multilateral financial institutions, strengthen the HKMA's research capabilities and monitor international monetary developments.

The HKMA is an integral part of the government, but is able to employ staff on different terms to those of the civil service to attract personnel of the right calibre, experience and expertise. The staff and operating costs of the HKMA are charged directly to the Exchange Fund, instead of the general revenue.

The HKMA is accountable to the Financial Secretary, who is advised by the Exchange Fund Advisory Committee on matters relating to the control of the Exchange Fund. The involvement of the committee in monetary and investment matters has become much stronger. It functions very much like a management board, and advises the Financial Secretary on the annual budget of the HKMA.

Monetary Policy

A linked exchange rate system was introduced on October 17, 1983, after a period of much instability in the exchange rate of the Hong Kong dollar. Under the system, certificates of indebtedness (CIs) issued by the Exchange Fund, which the two note-issuing banks are required to hold as cover for the issue of Hong Kong dollar notes, are issued and redeemed against payments in US dollars at a fixed exchange rate of HK$7.80 to US$1. In practice, therefore, any increase in note circulation is matched by a US dollar payment to the Exchange Fund, and any decrease in note circulation is matched by a US dollar payment from the Exchange Fund. The two note-issuing banks in turn extend this fixed exchange rate to their note transactions with all other banks in Hong Kong. In the foreign exchange market, the exchange rate of the Hong Kong dollar continues to be determined by forces of supply and demand. Against the fixed exchange rate for the issue and redemption of CIs, the market exchange rate stays close to the rate of HK$7.80 to US$1. In the last few years, the Hong Kong dollar has stayed on the strong side of the link. As a result, some banks have levied charges on large cash deposits to avoid the exchange rate loss on banknote transactions. Discussions are being held with the note-issuing banks on a new arrangement under which all banknote transactions among banks will be for Hong Kong dollar value. This arrangement will make cash-handling charges unnecessary. Exchange rate stability will not be adversely affected. Hong Kong dollar banknotes will continue to be 100 per cent backed by US dollars at the fixed rate of HK$7.80 to US$1. Note-issuing banks will continue to place US dollars with the Exchange Fund in order to acquire the CIs necessary for backing the banknotes they issue.

With the adoption of the linked rate system, the exchange rate is no longer a variable in the economy's adjustment process. Interest rates, the money supply and the level of economic activity over time adjust automatically to balance of payments pressures. If there is an outflow of money, caused, for example, by a tendency for the balance of payments to be in deficit, there will be a contraction in the money supply and higher interest rates. These will induce an inflow of funds to offset the original outflow arising from the balance of payments deficit while reducing domestic demand and imports and enhancing export competitiveness, contributing to restoring the external balance. Alternatively, if there is an inflow of money, caused, for example, by a tendency for the balance of payments to be in surplus, there will be an expansion in the money supply and lower interest rates. These will, on the one hand, induce outflow of funds and, on the other hand, increase domestic demand and imports and erode export competitiveness, again restoring the external balance.

When there is a tendency for the Hong Kong dollar to weaken relative to the US dollar, Hong Kong dollar interest rates will rise relative to US dollar interest rates. They may rise to a level where the interest rate gap between the Hong Kong dollar and the US dollar is large enough to stem or reverse the outflow from the Hong Kong dollar. Similarly, when there is a tendency for the Hong Kong dollar to strengthen relative to the US dollar, Hong Kong dollar interest rates will fall relative to US dollar interest rates. They may fall to a level where the interest rate gap between the Hong Kong dollar and the US dollar is large enough to stem or reverse the inflow into the Hong Kong dollar. From the monetary policy point of view, it is sometimes desirable to expedite this adjustment process in order that the economy is not unduly disrupted by speculative flows of funds aimed at manipulating the value of the Hong Kong dollar. To ensure that the interest rate gap is large enough to produce the corrective inflows or outflows, there is no limit on how low or high interest rates can move.

The lower limit for interest rates was eliminated when the Hong Kong Association of Banks, after consultation with the Financial Secretary, introduced in January 1988 revised interest rate rules, under which banks may impose deposit charges (negative interest rates) on large Hong Kong dollar credit balances maintained by their customers, if the need arises. The revised rules provided a tool to deter speculation on a revaluation of the Hong Kong dollar, which emerged in late 1987 and continued in early 1988. In practice, however, there has been no need to impose the deposit charges, as the mere threat of their imposition has been effective in deterring speculation.

The upper limit for interest rates was removed in July 1988, when the Money Lenders Ordinance was amended to exempt all authorised institutions under the Banking Ordinance from the restriction of lending money at an effective interest rate exceeding 60 per cent per annum.

To enable the government, through the use of the Exchange Fund, to exercise more effective influence over liquidity and interest rates in the interbank market and so assist it in maintaining exchange rate stability within the framework of the linked exchange rate system, accounting arrangements were entered into in mid-July 1988 between the Exchange Fund and the Hongkong and Shanghai Banking Corporation Limited (HSBC) as the management bank of the clearing house of the Hong Kong Association of Banks. Under these arrangements, the HSBC maintains a Hong Kong dollar account with the Exchange Fund. The government uses the account at its discretion to effect settlement of its Hong Kong dollar transactions with the HSBC or with other banks. The HSBC is required to ensure that the net clearing balance (NCB) of the rest of the banking system does not exceed its balance in the account and that the NCB is not in debit; otherwise, it will have to pay interest to the Exchange Fund.

Consequently, the Exchange Fund effectively became the ultimate provider of liquidity in the interbank market, a role which was previously performed by the HSBC. Through its borrowing of Hong Kong dollars in the interbank market, or selling foreign currencies for Hong Kong dollars in the foreign exchange market, the fund is able to reduce the supply of Hong Kong dollars and so raise interest rates in the interbank market, in this way offsetting a weakening of the exchange rate of the Hong Kong dollar against the US dollar. Similarly, it may increase interbank liquidity and lower interest rates by taking action in the opposite direction, offsetting a strengthening of the exchange rate.

Under these accounting arrangements, the government can also influence monetary conditions in the interbank market through its buying or selling of Hong Kong dollar financial assets of acceptable quality. For this purpose, the government has developed a programme for the issue of short-term paper for the account of the Exchange Fund (the Exchange Fund bills). The bills are designed to complement the accounting arrangements by providing the Exchange Fund with an additional instrument for conducting money market operations.

In June 1992, the Liquidity Adjustment Facility was introduced to assist banks in making late adjustments to their liquidity positions. The bid rate (for taking overnight deposits from banks) and offer rate (for lending overnight money to banks) are set having regard to the level of interest rate appropriate for maintaining exchange rate stability. These rates provide an additional tool for the government to influence the movements of the interbank interest rates.

Exchange Fund

The Hong Kong Government's Exchange Fund was established by the Currency Ordinance of 1935 (later renamed the Exchange Fund Ordinance). Since its inception, the fund has held the backing to the note issue. In 1976, its role was expanded, with the assets of the Coinage Security Fund (which held the backing for coins issued by the government) as well as the bulk of foreign currency assets held in the government's General Revenue Account, being transferred to the fund. On December 31, 1978, the Coinage Security Fund was merged with the Exchange Fund.

In 1976, the government began to transfer the fiscal reserves of its General Revenue Account (apart from the working balances) to the fund. This arrangement was introduced to avoid fiscal reserves having to bear the exchange risk arising from investments in foreign currency assets and to centralise the management of the government's financial assets. The fiscal reserves are not permanently appropriated for the use of the Exchange Fund. They are repaid to the General Revenue Account when they are required to meet the obligations of the general revenue. The bulk of the government's financial assets are, therefore, with the fund, which holds its assets mainly in the form of bank deposits in certain foreign currencies and in Hong Kong dollars, and marketable interest-bearing instruments in foreign currencies.

The principal activity of the Exchange Fund on a day-to-day basis is management of these assets. Its statutory role as defined in the Exchange Fund Ordinance is to influence the exchange value of the Hong Kong dollar and it intervenes, when necessary, in the local money market or foreign currency markets to maintain stability. The functions of the fund were extended on the enactment of the Exchange Fund (Amendment) Ordinance 1992 by introducing a secondary and subsidiary role of maintaining the stability and integrity of the monetary and financial systems.

In the past, the management of the fund was passive, characterised by a conservative approach with a preference for a high degree of liquidity and for short-term investments. Both the overall size of the fund, and the greater emphasis on the long-term stability and strength of Hong Kong's financial system, now enable the management of the Exchange Fund to have a longer-term outlook. The HKMA has upgraded and modernised its management of the Exchange Fund. Strategies more appropriate to a long-term fund, such as a benchmark approach and a greater use of the long-term capital markets, have been adopted. The range of currencies and instruments used has been increased, including, for the first time, investments in traded equities for a part of the Exchange Fund. The resources allocated to the management of the fund have also been increased fivefold. The HKMA has placed great emphasis on establishing links with other market participants. The aim is for openness and co-operation with the markets, with a view to developing good working relationships to enable the markets to play their part in assisting in the modernisation of the management of the fund.

Another function related to the Exchange Fund is the supply of notes and coins to the banking system. Bank notes (currently of $10, $20, $50, $100, $500 and $1,000 denominations) are issued by the Hongkong and Shanghai Banking Corporation Limited and Standard Chartered Bank. Apart from a very small fiduciary issue, which is backed by gilt-edged securities, the note-issuing banks may only issue currency notes against holdings of certificates of indebtedness issued by the fund. Legislative amendments were passed in July to make the Bank of China the third note-issuing bank. The Bank of China intends to commence issuing banknotes in May 1994.

These non-interest-bearing Certificates of Indebtedness are issued or redeemed as the amount of notes in circulation rises or falls. The fund bears the costs of maintaining the note issue (apart from the proportion of the costs relating to the fiduciary issue) and the net profits of the note issue accrue to the fund.

Coins of $5, $2, $1, 50 cents, 20 cents and 10 cents denominations, and currency notes of one-cent denomination, are issued by the government. New $5 and $2 coins depicting the bauhinia flower have been issued since January, while the existing coins are being gradually withdrawn. New $1, 50 cents and 20 cents coins were circulated in October. The total currency in circulation at the end of 1993, with details of its composition, is shown at Appendix 14.

As at December 31, 1992, total assets of the fund stood at $287 billion, of which foreign currency assets amounted to US$35 billion. Accumulated earnings of the fund amounted to $107 billion. The financial position of the fund for the six years 1987–92 is shown at Appendix 14A.

7
INDUSTRY AND TRADE

HONG KONG's total exports continued to register double-digit growth in 1993, increasing by 13 per cent from the previous year.

Re-exports recorded a significant 19 per cent rise, as the territory's role as an entrepôt for China dominated external trade. The gross total value of re-exports was $823,224 million.

Domestic exports continued to be affected by the ongoing structural shift in the composition of Hong Kong's exports from domestic exports to re-exports and registered a five per cent decrease, totalling $223,027 million in value.

Imports rose by 12 per cent to $1,072,597 million.

Total merchandise trade amounted to $2,118,847 million, up 13 per cent from 1992.

Despite the recessionary economic climate in some of the territory's major markets, the manufacturing industry in general performed well during the year. Hong Kong also reinforced its growing role as a major service and sourcing centre for the Asian region.

Other highlights of the year in the trade and industry sectors included the setting up of the Hong Kong Industrial Technology Centre Corporation and the Hong Kong Applied R&D Fund Company Limited to promote new technologies.

Trade and Industrial Policies

Hong Kong's trade policy seeks to promote a free, open and stable multilateral trading system; to safeguard Hong Kong's rights and fulfil its obligations under multilateral and bilateral trade or trade-related agreements; and to secure, maintain and improve access for Hong Kong's exports.

The role of the government is to facilitate industrial and trade activities within the framework of a free market. It neither protects nor subsidises manufacturers. It recognises, however, a responsibility to provide an acceptable industrial infrastructure, particularly in terms of land and manpower, and to make available services which enable industry to become more competitive through productivity growth, quality improvement and product innovation. It also encourages technology transfer through an inward investment promotion programme.

Industrial policies are kept under review by the Trade and Industry Branch of the Government Secretariat, which acts on the advice of the Industry and Technology Development Council (ITDC), the government's advisory body on all major industry and technology-related matters. The ITDC chairman is a non-official and its members include prominent industrialists and businessmen, academics, representatives of major industry and trade organisations, and government officials. The council is assisted by a network of committees in its work. Productivity, product innovation and quality improvement services are mainly provided by the Industry Department and the Hong Kong Productivity Council. The Industry Department also promotes inward investment in Hong Kong's manufacturing industries and is responsible for monitoring the provision of an efficient infrastructure within which industry can operate successfully.

On the external relations front, Hong Kong joined the Asia-Pacific Economic Co-operation (APEC) and the Pacific Economic Co-operation Council (PECC) in 1991. APEC is an inter-governmental economic forum inaugurated in 1989. Its main objectives are to strengthen the multilateral trading system, to assess prospects for and obstacles to increased trade and investment flows within the Asia-Pacific region and to identify a range of practical common economic interests. PECC is a non-governmental organisation, comprising tripartite membership drawn from academia and business and public sectors, seeking to develop closer co-operation on trade and economic policy issues within the Asia-Pacific region.

Hong Kong's continuing success as a leading manufacturing and commercial centre is due to a simple tax structure and low tax rates, a versatile and industrious workforce, an aggressive and innovative managerial class, efficient transport facilities, a fine harbour, excellent international communications, and the government's firm commitment to free trade and free enterprise.

Faced with increasing competition from low-cost economies in the region, rising labour costs at home, and demand in its major export markets for ever-higher standards of quality, Hong Kong's manufacturers can no longer compete in the territory's major export markets on price and speed of response alone. Manufacturers are moving decisively away from labour-intensive production into the manufacture of high value-added products which can compete on quality. In this respect, the Hong Kong Productivity Council continued to feature in the past year as the government's principal agent in helping the manufacturing sector improve its productivity and move up the value-added ladder. With its expertise in different disciplines, the council offers diversified services, including management consultancies, training programmes and technological support services.

The government, which supports this restructuring, implements a comprehensive programme to develop the territory's existing quality infrastructure and encourage greater use of quality assurance in manufacturing through a Quality Awareness Campaign. In addition, the Hong Kong Quality Assurance Agency has been established to provide third-party assessment of the quality management systems of companies according to the ISO 9000 standards, and to award ISO 9000 certification to companies that meet the necessary standards. These activities have helped enhance the quality of Hong Kong's products and services.

Science and Technology

Science and technology are transforming the way that business is conducted in all areas of economic activity. To ensure that the territory could respond to the rapidly changing technological environment and to underline the vital connection between industry and technology, the former Industry Development Board and the Committee on Science and Technology were replaced by the Industry and Technology Development Council (ITDC) in early 1992.

With its expanded terms of reference and a more focussed and co-ordinated approach, the council is better placed to advise the government in this area. A proposal was being drawn up at the end of the year to provide the ITDC with a budget of more than $900 million over the next four years to support industry. A Technology Committee advises on technology issues with relevance to Hong Kong's industrial and economic development, and the Technology Review Board gives advice on the directions for technology development on the basis of global technology trends.

Hong Kong has a skilled workforce, ready access to information and technology from overseas, and a sound infrastructure to take advantage of opportunities in technology-based industries. The government is investing substantially in infrastructure to support the use and development of technology in Hong Kong. The key elements of this infrastructure include the provision of education and training in science and technology; the provision of land at development cost to high technology industries; the provision of services and facilities to help manufacturers acquire new technologies; the provision of funding support to applied research and development in industry; and the promotion of technology transfer through inward investment.

On June 1, the Hong Kong Industrial Technology Centre Corporation was established to facilitate the promotion of technological innovation and the application of new technologies in local industries. Among other things, the centre acts as an incubator for technology-based companies that are starting up.

A study commissioned by the Industry Department in 1992 made recommendations to upgrade Hong Kong's technology infrastructure, including the establishment of a science park. The department is now planning to commission a further study to examine the feasibility of implementing these recommendations.

In December 1991, the Finance Committee of the Legislative Council approved $200 million from the Capital Investment Fund as up-front capital for an applied research and development (R&D) scheme. The objective of the scheme is to increase the currently limited volume of applied R&D activity in Hong Kong by providing government funding as a catalyst. The longer-term objective is to improve the technological capability and competitiveness of local industry, in this way helping to sustain Hong Kong's economic growth. A private company named the Hong Kong Applied R&D Fund Company Limited was established in February to administer the scheme. The company is wholly owned by the government, with a board of directors comprising mainly non-officials with a wide spectrum of expertise. Under the scheme, funding support of up to half the cost of a single applied R&D project, or a total of $10 million for a single company or organisation, can be granted. Funding support can either take the form of a loan or equity participation, or a combination of both. Companies incorporated under the Companies Ordinance and statutory bodies undertaking applied R&D locally are eligible to apply.

External Trade

Hong Kong is the world's 10th largest trading entity in terms of the value of its merchandise trade.

With total exports valued at $1,046,251 million and imports at $1,072,597 million, the territory recorded a trade deficit of $26,346 million in 1993.

Its largest trading partner is China, followed by the United States of America and Japan. Appendices 15 and 16 provide summary statistics of external trade.

Imports

Hong Kong is almost entirely dependent on imported resources to meet the needs of its population of six million and its diverse industries. In 1993, imports of consumer goods, valued at $461,195 million, constituted 43 per cent of total imports. The major consumer goods imported were: clothing ($90,526 million); radios, television receivers, gramophones, records, amplifiers and tape recorders ($51,284 million); footwear ($42,482 million); baby carriages, toys, games and sporting goods ($36,429 million); and travel goods, handbags and similar containers ($21,013 million).

Imports of raw materials and semi-manufactured goods totalled $355,355 million, representing 33 per cent of total imports. The principal items imported were transistors, diodes, semi-conductors and integrated circuits ($55,847 million); woven fabrics of man-made fibres ($29,349 million); plastic materials ($28,467 million); iron and steel ($22,407 million); woven cotton fabrics ($15,231 million); and watch and clock movements, cases and parts ($15,204 million).

Imports of capital goods amounted to $202,880 million, or 19 per cent of total imports. They consisted mainly of electrical machinery ($26,819 million); transport equipment ($21,912 million); office machines ($17,743 million); scientific, medical, optical, measuring and controlling instruments and apparatus ($7,689 million); and textile machinery ($7,069 million).

Imports of foodstuffs were valued at $44,986 million, representing four per cent of total imports. The principal imported food items were fish and fish preparations ($10,426 million); fruit ($6,878 million); meat and meat preparations ($5,665 million); and vegetables ($4,228 million).

Mineral fuels, lubricants and related materials worth some $18,668 million were imported in 1993, representing one per cent of total imports.

China and Japan were principal suppliers of imports, providing 38 per cent and 17 per cent, respectively, of the total. China alone supplied 28 per cent of Hong Kong's imported foodstuffs. Taiwan ranked third as a supplier of imports, providing nine per cent, followed by the United States of America, the Republic of Korea, Singapore, Germany and the United Kingdom.

Exports

Clothing remained the largest component of domestic exports, valued at $71,857 million or 32 per cent of the total. Exports of miscellaneous manufactured articles, consisting mainly of jewellery, goldsmiths' and silversmiths' wares, plastic toys and dolls, and plastic articles, were valued at $11,751 million, representing 5.3 per cent of domestic exports. Exports of office machines and automatic data-processing equipment, valued at $17,619 million, contributed another eight per cent. Electrical machinery, apparatus and appliances mainly for household use, transistors and diodes amounted to $11,232 million or five per cent of the total. Photographic apparatus, equipment and supplies, optical goods, and watches and clocks were valued at $16,096 million or 7.2 per cent of the total. Other important exports included textiles (7.3 per cent) as well as telecommunications and sound recording and reproducing apparatus and equipment (six per cent).

The direction and level of Hong Kong's export trade is much influenced by economic conditions and commercial policies in major overseas markets. In 1993, 43 per cent of all domestic exports went to the USA and the European Community. The largest markets were the USA ($58,987 million or 26 per cent of the total); China ($64,239 million or 28 per cent); Germany ($14,430 million or 6.2 per cent); and the United Kingdom ($10,771 million or 4.8 per cent). Domestic exports to Japan and Singapore increased to $9,603 million and $11,447 million, respectively. Other important markets were Taiwan, Canada, the Netherlands and France.

Re-exports

Re-exports showed a very significant increase in 1993 primarily because of China's significant economic development and the continued growing importance of Hong Kong as an entrepôt for China. The gross total value of Hong Kong's re-exports accounted for 79 per cent of the combined total of domestic exports and re-exports. Principal commodities re-exported were miscellaneous manufactured articles ($109,460 million); clothing ($89,842 million); textiles ($70,476 million); telecommunications and sound recording and reproducing apparatus and equipment ($72,981 million); electrical machinery, apparatus and appliances ($69,262 million); as well as footwear ($47,891 million). The main origins of these re-exports were China, Japan, Taiwan, the USA and the Republic of Korea. The largest re-export markets were China, the USA, Japan, Germany and Taiwan.

The Industrial Scene

Hong Kong enjoys a worldwide reputation as a producer and exporter of manufactured consumer goods. Although the territory has a thriving construction industry and, as a major trading economy, has developed ship-building, ship repair and aircraft engineering industries, light manufacturing industries predominate. About 80 per cent of Hong Kong's manufactured products are exported, and clothing, electronic products, textiles, watches and clocks, and plastic products have for many years accounted for the bulk of this output. The major markets in 1993 for Hong Kong's manufactured exports, worth $223,027 million, were China (28.4 per cent), the United States of America (27 per cent), Germany (6.3 per cent), Singapore (5.1 per cent) and the United Kingdom (4.8 per cent).

Manufacturing developed on a large scale in Hong Kong in the 1950s. The territory's limited space precluded the development of heavy or land-intensive industries; its manufacturing industries were characterised by small-scale firms, mostly operating from premises in multi-storey buildings and manufacturing light consumer goods for export.

For many years, manufacturing was both the territory's largest employer and its most important economic sector. However, it lost this dominating position in the 1980s. Employment in the manufacturing sector fell from 904 709 in 1984 (41.7 per cent of total employment) to 508 133 (20.5 per cent) in 1993. Its contribution to the Gross Domestic Product (GDP) fell from 24.1 per cent in 1984 to 13.2 per cent in 1992. Over this period, manufacturers took advantage of China's open door policy to shift labour-intensive jobs into China, to reap the benefits of the lower land and labour costs there. Manufacturing is now the territory's second largest employer, and made the fourth largest contribution to the GDP after wholesale, retail and import/export trades, restaurants and hotels; financing, insurance, real estate and business services; and community, social and personal services in 1992.

There were 39 238 manufacturing establishments in Hong Kong in 1993, of which 34 383 employed fewer than 20 persons, and 37 415 fewer than 50 persons. The remaining 1 823 establishments accounted for about half of Hong Kong's total manufacturing employment.

Many smaller establishments are linked with larger factories through an efficient and flexible sub-contracting network, which has enabled Hong Kong's manufacturing sector to respond swiftly to changes in external demand.

Clothing

The clothing industry, including the manufacture of wearing apparel, knit outerwear and knit underwear, is the largest employer and export-earner in the manufacturing sector. In 1993, it employed 166 401 workers (33 per cent of total manufacturing employment) and earned $71,857 million in exports (32 per cent of Hong Kong's total domestic exports). Hong Kong is one of the world's leading suppliers of clothing, and produces a wide variety of products from simple accessories to expensive and high-quality fashion wear.

Electronics

The electronics industry, including the manufacture of electronic watches and clocks, and electronic toys, is the second largest employer and export-earner. In 1993, it employed 53 591 workers (11 per cent of total manufacturing employment), and earned $57,333 million in exports (25.7 per cent of total domestic exports). The industry produces a wide range of sophisticated and high quality products and components, including television sets, hi-fi equipment, electronic dictionaries, calculators, wired and cordless telephones, modems, microcomputers, computer memory systems, facsimile machines, talk-back toys, watches, multi-layer printed circuit boards, electronic modules, liquid crystal displays, quartz crystals and semi-conductor devices, and surface-mounted devices.

Textiles

The textiles industry, excluding the manufacture of knit outerwear and knit underwear, is the third largest export-earner. It comprises four main sectors: spinning, weaving, knitted fabrics manufacturing and finishing. Textiles finishing, including bleaching, dyeing and printing, is the largest among the four sectors. In 1993, the industry employed 44 182 workers (nine per cent of total manufacturing employment), and earned $16,180 million in exports (7.3 per cent of total domestic exports). On top of its role as an exporter, the textiles industry is a major supplier of yarns and fabrics of various fibres and blends (mostly cotton) to local clothing manufacturers, who are actually the textiles sector's largest customer.

Watches and Clocks

The watches and clocks industry is the fourth largest export-earner. In 1993, the industry employed 17 287 workers (three per cent of total manufacturing employment), and earned $13,161 million in exports (5.9 per cent of total domestic exports). Besides complete electronic and mechanical watches and clocks, the industry also produces high quality components and accessories.

Plastics

During the year under review, the plastic products industry employed 27 516 workers (five per cent of total manufacturing employment), and earned $5,869 million in exports (2.6 per cent of total domestic exports). Major export items included toys, containers, travel goods, handbags, packing bags and household articles.

Printing

The printing industry has grown significantly in the past two decades. Most manufacturing industries in Hong Kong produce mainly for export, but the majority of the output of the printing industry is for local consumption. In addition to printing books, newspapers and periodicals, the industry supports other manufacturing industries by providing packaging printing services. In 1993, the industry employed 40 918 workers (eight per cent of total manufacturing employment) and earned $4,447 million in exports (two per cent of total domestic exports).

Other Industries

Other important light manufacturing industries include jewellery, metal products, toys, food and beverages, industrial machinery, household electrical appliances and photographic and optical goods. The development of the metal products and industrial machinery industries has enabled Hong Kong to produce sophisticated parts and components, and other semi-manufactures of high quality. This has benefited the manufacturing sector in general as the quality of finished products depends heavily on the capability of the linkage industries which service them.

Hong Kong's shipyards provide a competitive repair service and build a variety of vessels. Several large ship-building and repair yards on Tsing Yi Island provide services to the shipping industry, and construct and service oil rigs. Hong Kong's aircraft engineering industry has a high international reputation and provides extensive maintenance and repair services. Facilities are available for the complete overhaul of airframes and engines for many types of aircraft.

Overseas Investment in Manufacturing

There were 472 manufacturing companies in Hong Kong with overseas investment at the end of 1992. The total value of direct overseas investment was $37,279 million. The 472 companies employed 72 148 workers (12.8 per cent of total manufacturing employment) and accounted for 23 per cent of Hong Kong's total domestic exports. The main sources of investment were Japan (33 per cent), the United States of America (27 per cent), China (11 per cent), and the United Kingdom (five per cent). More than three-fifths of this investment was concentrated in four industries: electronics (31 per cent), electrical products (11 per cent), textiles and clothing (11 per cent) and food and beverages (seven per cent).

Documentation of Imports and Exports

As a free port, Hong Kong keeps its import and export licensing requirements to a minimum. A wide range of products do not need licences to enter or leave the territory. Where licences or notifications are required, they are intended to achieve two main objectives. Firstly, they help Hong Kong to fulfil its international obligations to restrain exports of textile products and to monitor the flow of these products into Hong Kong. Secondly, they are imposed on health, safety, environmental, security or anti-smuggling grounds. Items covered include strategic commodities, reserved commodities (namely, rice, frozen meat and frozen poultry), pharmaceutical products and medicines, pesticides, left-hand drive vehicles and ozone-depleting substances.

Hong Kong maintains a certification of origin system that enables the origin of goods which Hong Kong exports to be established. The Trade Department administers this system and issues certificates of origin where required. Five other organisations have been designated by the government to issue certificates of origin. They are the Hong Kong General Chamber of Commerce, the Federation of Hong Kong Industries, the Indian Chamber of Commerce Hong Kong, the Chinese Manufacturers' Association of Hong Kong and the Chinese General Chamber of Commerce.

Electronic Data Interchange

Hong Kong's use of electronic data interchange has expanded considerably during the past few years. Electronic data interchange, the computer-to-computer exchange of business information in a standard format, is one of the techniques being implemented worldwide in an attempt to curb the amount of paperwork involved in business and to improve efficiency.

The government is keen to encourage this trend to maintain Hong Kong's competitiveness in international markets. A particularly important area is the processing of statutory trade documents. Following a joint study with Tradelink Electronic Document Services Limited (a group of 11 leading trade-related organisations in Hong Kong), the government has taken a substantial shareholding in the company. Tradelink will fund and manage a Community Electronic Trading Service. The service will act as the electronic gateway between the trading community and the relevant government departments, checking and validating electronic submissions before passing them on for approval.

Both Tradelink and the government are now installing the computer systems required. The current plan is to commence joint testing by the middle of 1994, with a launch of the service in 1995. The scope of the initial service will cover the lodging of trade declarations and applications for export licences for textiles and clothing shipped under quota. The service will bring about a significant increase in the number of companies using electronic data interchange and will help generate more demand for other electronic trading services.

In the interests of compatibility, the government has agreed that the United Nations Electronic Data Interchange for Administration, Commerce and Transport, a standard language developed by the United Nations for electronic trading, will be adopted for government transactions wherever applicable.

The Industry Department

One of the main tasks of the Industry Department is to carry out regular studies of Hong Kong's main manufacturing industries, with the aim of enabling the government to identify constraints on their efficiency and assess where support is needed. In 1993, a techno-economic and market research study on the electronics industry was conducted, while another on the metals and light engineering industries was completed. The department also conducts annual surveys on overseas investment in Hong Kong's manufacturing industries and on the establishment of regional representation by overseas companies in Hong Kong.

The department provides information on industrial support services available to manufacturers through its Industrial Extension Service (IES), and encourages manufacturers to upgrade their operations by making use of these services. In 1993, a total of 288 visits were made by IES engineers, and 236 referrals were made to organisations which could help to solve the problems encountered by the manufacturers concerned. IES engineers dealt with the problems themselves in a number of other cases.

Another major responsibility of the Industry Department is to monitor the availability of land and trained manpower for industry. Industrial land is normally sold by public auction or tender. Land can be sold under special terms where industries are land and capital-intensive, or use advanced technology, and where their presence is considered to be economically desirable.

During the year, the government put up for sale by auction or tender eight pieces of industrial land with a total area of 32 033 square metres. About 311 000 square metres of flatted factory space were completed by private developers.

Meanwhile, the two industrial estates in Tai Po and Yuen Long, managed by the Hong Kong Industrial Estates Corporation, will be joined by a third industrial estate at Tseung Kwan O in 1994.

Technical education and industrial training are provided in two technical colleges, seven technical institutes and three industrial training centres run by the Vocational Training Council. In addition, the Clothing Industry Training Authority runs two training centres. Technological training at higher levels is mainly provided in Hong Kong's two polytechnics and three universities.

In June 1993, the government injected an additional capital sum of $50 million into the New Technology Training Scheme, on top of the original $55 million. The scheme was launched in June 1992 and is administered by the Vocational Training Council. It provides financial assistance to employers to train, either locally or overseas, their technologists and managers in new technologies strategically important for the industrial and economic development of Hong Kong. The number of training places and the level of training grants have since increased.

During the year, the department played an active role in assisting local manufacturers to comply with environmental measures. A consultancy study on support to industry on environmental matters, commissioned by the department in 1992, was completed in June 1993. The study assessed the operational and financial effects of current and planned environmental legislation and measures on manufacturing in Hong Kong. It recommended a package of support measures designed to help manufacturers improve their competitiveness while moving towards compliance with environmental controls. The department, together with other interested parties, is now planning the implementation of these support measures.

In February, the department published an update to the booklet entitled *A Guide to Pollution Control Legislation Affecting Manufacturing Industries.* The guide provides basic information to manufacturers on environmental legislation and where technical advice can be obtained.

Promoting inward investment in Hong Kong's manufacturing industries is another important area of the department's work. The department provides information and assistance to potential overseas investors in Hong Kong and through overseas Industrial Promotion Units based in Tokyo, San Francisco, New York, Toronto, Brussels and London. Much of the recent manufacturing investment has been from multinationals at the forefront of technological development, and this has helped raise technology and skill levels in the local manufacturing sector.

The department is also increasingly involved in the promotion of the wider application of quality assurance in the manufacturing sector. It has developed a range of services to assist manufacturers to improve the quality of their products. Its Standards and

Calibration Laboratory holds Hong Kong's official standards of measurement and provides a calibration service to manufacturers to enable them to meet measurement standards required for their products. The laboratory has measurement capabilities for a wide range of electrical, temperature, mechanical, pressure, volume and humidity measurements. A new laboratory is being built to provide a force calibration service for the construction industry.

The department's Product Standards Information Bureau provides advice and information to manufacturers on both national and international standards affecting their products. The bureau also maintains a reference library of the national standards issued by Hong Kong's trading partners and the international standards published by the International Organisation for Standardisation (ISO) and the International Electrotechnical Commission (IEC). To improve the storage and retrieval of product standards information, a direct computer link with the databases of overseas standards institutions and a computerised information retrieval system have been established.

The department also operates the Hong Kong Laboratory Accreditation Scheme (HOKLAS), designed to improve the standard of testing and management in Hong Kong's laboratories and to provide official recognition for those assessed as competent. HOKLAS has so far accredited 47 laboratories for testing such items as toys, textiles, electrical and electronic goods, food and construction materials. Several laboratories are accredited in the environmental testing field. A number of mutual recognition agreements have been concluded with overseas laboratory accreditation schemes, including the National Measurement Accreditation Service of the United Kingdom, the National Association of Testing Authorities of Australia, the American Association for Laboratory Accreditation, the Testing Laboratory Registration Council of New Zealand and the Dutch Accreditation Board for Calibration Laboratories, Test Laboratories and Inspection Bodies. Under these agreements, Hong Kong products should not be required to undergo further testing in these countries if they have already been tested and issued with a HOKLAS-endorsed test report in Hong Kong.

Since March 1990, the department has been running a Quality Awareness Campaign. The basic message, disseminated through seminars and workshops, and through a range of promotional literature, is that investment in quality is profitable. Since Hong Kong's economy is heavily dependent on exports, higher quality in production will increase its competitiveness in the market place. The campaign is part of a wider quality improvement programme aimed at encouraging more manufacturers to adopt quality assurance in their companies. The other components of the programme include strengthening the department's existing range of quality services and developing a quality management certification scheme.

Under the certification scheme, government recognition is conferred on companies which adopt quality management systems conforming to the international standard ISO 9000. An independent subvented organisation, the Hong Kong Quality Assurance Agency (HKQAA), was established in 1990 to audit factories for the award of certificates. Response to the scheme has been very enthusiastic, involving both manufacturing and service sector companies. The HKQAA signed a Memorandum of Understanding with the British Standards Institution (Quality Assurance) in June. Under this agreement, companies in Hong Kong can be awarded ISO 9000 certificates both from the HKQAA and the British Standards Institution (Quality Assurance), with the auditing being carried out in Hong Kong by the HKQAA. Similarly, the arrangement applies to British companies in the United Kingdom audited by the British institution.

The Governor's Award for Industry, established in 1989, recognises and encourages excellence in different aspects of industrial performance. The annual award scheme was broadened in scope from two award categories to six award categories in 1992. Different organisations are responsible for arranging annual competitions in each of these categories. The Federation of Hong Kong Industries is responsible for the consumer product design category; the Chinese Manufacturers' Association of Hong Kong for the machinery and equipment design category; the Hong Kong Productivity Council for the productivity category; the Industry Department for the quality category; the Private Sector Committee on the Environment for the environmental performance category; and the Hong Kong Trade Development Council for the export marketing category. Award presentations are made personally by the Governor.

Hong Kong Industrial Technology Centre Corporation

The Hong Kong Industrial Technology Centre Corporation (HKITCC) was established on June 1 by statute, to facilitate the promotion of technological innovation and application of new technologies in Hong Kong industry. It replaced the Provisional Hong Kong Industrial Technology Centre Company Limited, which was formed in May 1990 to undertake groundwork for the statutory corporation. The HKITCC aims to fulfil its mission through three primary functions: the incubation and accommodation of technology-based businesses; the provision of technology transfer services; and the provision of product design and development, and support services.

The HKITCC is governed by a board of directors, consisting of a chairman appointed by the Governor and 11 directors appointed by the Financial Secretary. It is committed to creating innovative synergy within its technology centre. It will do this by identifying and championing the creation of new businesses, tracking technology trends and business opportunities, assisting partnership formations, and encouraging investment in technology enterprises. The HKITCC is required to conduct its business according to prudent commercial principles.

The government has provided a grant of $250 million and committed another $188 million as an interest-bearing loan to meet the initial expenses of setting up the technology centre. A site of about 5 600 square metres at the junction of Tat Chee Avenue and Fa Po Street in Kowloon Tong was granted for the construction of the centre.

Construction of the building to house the technology centre commenced in August 1992, and should be completed by mid-1994. The building will have a total area of 22 000 square metres. Upon its completion, the HKITCC is expected to gradually become financially self-sufficient, with income from rent. Pending its completion, the HKITCC leased space in the Hong Kong Productivity Council Building in October 1991, and has already started providing some services.

The HKITCC introduced a pilot 'incubation programme' in early 1992. Six technology-based companies have been recruited under the programme. They have been provided with a range of infrastructure and support services, including help with business planning and development, communications, marketing and access to laboratory facilities at higher educational institutes. Other business centre services such as conference facilities, accounting and secretariat services are also available on site.

The HKITCC's support services in the transfer of technology locally and internationally are an additional benefit to its tenants. The HKITCC sponsors and organises technology transfer and innovative technology seminars. It intends to establish links with tertiary institutions and industrial support organisations to facilitate technology transfer among companies in the programme and local industry. Through its technology transfer support services, the HKITCC assists tenants by brokering and licensing technology, and by providing referrals for research, design and development contract services.

Hong Kong Productivity Council

There was a growing demand during the year for the Hong Kong Productivity Council's (HKPC) consultancy and technical support services.

The HKPC was established by statute in 1967 to promote increased productivity in Hong Kong industry. It is financed by an annual government subvention and by fees earned from its services. The council consists of a chairman and 22 members appointed by the Governor. Its membership is drawn from the management, labour, academic and professional fields and from the government.

The HKPC has about 500 staff members with expertise in a wide range of disciplines. It provides a variety of training programmes, industrial and management consultancies and technical support services using resources available in its 17 operational divisions: computer services, electronics services, automation services, quality and management, computer-aided design services, chemical and metallurgical, manufacturing engineering, textiles and apparel, business management services, training, environmental management, information services, human resources, development and administration, public relations, marketing and accounting.

During the year, the council undertook 1 208 consultancy projects, covering, among other items, feasibility studies, production management, new plant projects, environmental management, quality management, product design and development, and industrial automation services.

To facilitate the transition to high value-added production, the HKPC invited local companies to join consortia to share the design and development costs of new products. Three consortium projects were completed successfully. These involved 30 local companies in the design and development of a notebook computer, a 900-megahertz indoor cordless telephone, and a palmtop computer with the most advanced application-specific integrated circuit (ASIC) ever developed in Hong Kong.

The HKPC put together a consortium of eight local companies to transfer 3D laser stereolithography (SLA) technology from the United States of America. The SLA machine facilitates rapid prototyping, and is crucial for Hong Kong's manufacturing sector in keeping abreast of competition in the area of marketing and product design.

The HKPC organised 693 training courses for 13 980 participants, covering management and supervisory techniques, advanced programming and electronic data processing, and a range of technology programmes for various industries. In-plant courses continued to be popular and 134 programmes were organised during the year to meet the specific training needs of individual companies.

Twelve overseas study missions were organised for local industrialists to gain first-hand information on the latest technology and management techniques practised in various

Renowned for their swift reponse to international fashion currents, Hong Kong's garment makers rely heavily on an efficient and flexible network of support industries, such as zipper manufacturers.

Sailmaking for the leading edge of international yacht racing and windsurfing has become one of the territory's most exciting industrial success stories.

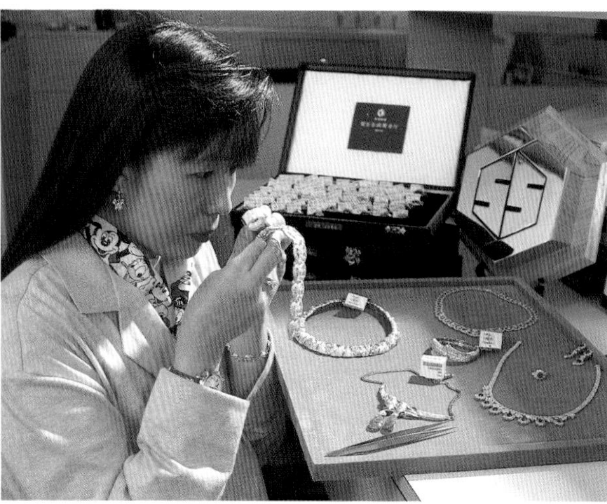

Long-established as an important light industry, Hong Kong's skilled jewellers and goldsmiths create beautiful adornments for the world market.

On top of its role as an exporter, the textile industry is a major supplier of thread, yarn and fabric to local clothing manufacturers.

Combining modern equipment and traditional themes, an artist **(right)** *transforms panes of glass into works of art.*

Careful market research ensures the territory's fashion accessories are totally in step with the new season's apparel.

High-quality ceramics claim an exclusive niche among the wide range of home decorating and furnishing lines which carry the label 'Made in Hong Kong'.

areas, including quality control, human resources development, precision sheet-metal stamping, and mould and die technology.

To meet the increasing demand from institutions and companies for HKPC services in the Pearl River Delta area of China, the HKPC has established a Guangzhou Liaison Office in addition to its Shenzhen Liaison Desk. The office was officially opened in November. Its main function is to strengthen the capabilities of the HKPC by using specialist resources in China, which are not available in Hong Kong, and sub-contracting work to them to reduce costs. It also acts as a marketing agent for HKPC services and co-ordinates HKPC projects in the region.

The HKPC is the government's agent for the Asian Productivity Organisation (APO). During the year, under the sponsorship of the APO, the HKPC hosted two APO programmes — a seminar on total quality management and a symposium on the management of innovations and technology development strategies.

The HKPC Building in Kowloon Tong houses all the council's operations under a single roof. It contains a display area, an auditorium, a technical reference library, electronic data processing facilities, and a computer-aided design service centre. There are also laboratories for surface mount technology, radio frequency and digital communications, photo-chemical machining, metal finishing and industrial chemistry, environmental management, sheet-metal processing, precision machining and die-casting. The building also houses a mould and die technology centre and a 3D-stereolithography technology centre.

Hong Kong Industrial Estates Corporation

The Hong Kong Industrial Estates Corporation is responsible for developing and managing industrial estates in Hong Kong. It offers developed land, at cost, on its industrial estates to companies with new or improved processes and products which cannot operate in multi-storey factory buildings. The corporation has two industrial estates in the New Territories — at Tai Po and Yuen Long — and a third is being constructed at Tseung Kwan O. The industrial estates are fully serviced with roads, drains, sewers, electricity and water. Companies on the estates design and construct their own factory premises to meet their specific requirements. They are required to adopt appropriate environmental protection measures to meet current standards.

Over 100 factories were operating in the Tai Po and Yuen Long estates and more were being built at the end of the year. On the Tai Po estate, which has 73 hectares of industrial land, only one vacant site of about 0.9 hectare, reserved for a high-technology industry, remained. The Yuen Long estate has 67 hectares of land in total, of which 16.5 hectares were still available for leasing. The land premia stood at $1,900 per square metre for Tai Po and $1,600 for Yuen Long.

Construction of the third industrial estate at Tseung Kwan O began in August 1991. The first phase, with 20 hectares of serviced sites, will be available by early 1994. A total of 68 hectares of industrial land will be provided by 1996. The new industrial estate is only three kilometres from the centre of Tseung Kwan O new town. Waterfront sites and berthing facilities will be available for ocean-going ships.

The corporation's estates are held under leases from the government which extend to the year 2047. The corporation also grants sites to 2047, enabling investors to plan up to the middle of the next century with certainty.

External Commercial Relations

Hong Kong possesses full autonomy in the conduct of its external commercial relations. The Governor is entrusted with executive authority to conduct external relations on behalf of Hong Kong, namely, to conclude and implement trade agreements, whether bilateral or multilateral, with states, regions and international organisations and to conduct all other aspects of external commercial relations.

Hong Kong is a contracting party to the General Agreement on Tariffs and Trade (GATT), the basic aim of which is to liberalise world trade and ensure the conduct of trade in a non-discriminatory and stable manner. The Hong Kong Government pursues a free trade policy, and the success of the policy is evidenced by the steady rise in the value and sophistication of Hong Kong's exports in recent years. Within the context of the free trade policy, Hong Kong's commercial relations are designed to ensure that Hong Kong's trading rights in overseas markets are protected and its international obligations are fulfilled.

GATT is the cornerstone of Hong Kong's external trade relations, while the Multi-Fibre Arrangement (MFA), which aims at the orderly development and expansion of international trade in textiles, provides the framework within which Hong Kong negotiates bilateral restraint agreements with textile importing countries.

GATT

Given the externally-orientated and open nature of its economy, Hong Kong contributes to, and relies on, the healthy functioning of the multilateral trading system. Hong Kong has, therefore, always been a staunch supporter of GATT and the free trade principle it espouses. Hong Kong participated in GATT activities for many years as a British dependent territory, before becoming a separate contracting party in 1986. This status, which underlines Hong Kong's autonomy in the conduct of its external commercial relations, will extend beyond 1997.

During the year, Hong Kong continued to participate actively and constructively in the extended Uruguay Round (UR) of multilateral trade negotiations which were finally concluded on December 15 — over seven years after the negotiations were launched in 1986. The package of Uruguay Round Agreements, known as the Final Act, covers a wide range of subjects. Apart from traditional subjects such as tariff reductions on goods, it also includes new areas such as trade in services, trade-related intellectual property rights and trade-related investment measures; a review of GATT disciplines; the creation of a new institution — the World Trade Organisation — to replace the existing GATT structure; and the phasing out of the Multi-Fibre Arrangement (MFA) which provides a legal basis for discriminatory quota restrictions in the area of textiles and clothing.

In overall terms, Hong Kong stands to gain from the successful conclusion of the Round which will strengthen and boost confidence in the most-favoured-nation-based multilateral trading system. It is intended that at a ministerial meeting to be held in April 1994 in Morocco, ministers of GATT UR participants will sign and authenticate the UR agreement and agree on certain implementation details.

Hong Kong continued to work closely with other exporters of textiles and clothing in the International Textiles and Clothing Bureau to press for the integration of the textiles sector into the GATT. Hong Kong has played a pivotal role in forging a consensus on the recent short extension of the MFA, aimed at bridging the gap between the expiry of the MFA and the implementation of a UR agreement.

Textiles

Bilateral agreements negotiated under the MFA govern Hong Kong's textiles exports to Austria, Canada, the European Economic Community (EEC), Finland, Norway and the United States of America.

During the year, representatives of the governments of Hong Kong and the United States of America met to discuss bilateral and international co-operation to control and eliminate illegal trans-shipments of textiles. Both governments agreed to continue their mutual efforts to address the matter.

The bilateral textiles agreement with Canada expired at the end of 1993. In October, Hong Kong and Canada agreed to extend the agreement for two years up to the end of 1995.

Both the bilateral textiles agreements with Finland and Norway expired in December. Consultations with Finland in September resulted in a new Hong Kong/Finland textiles agreement extending the current agreement for a maximum of two years from January 1994 to December 1995. Following consultations with Norway in October, Hong Kong secured a new Hong Kong/Norway textiles agreement, also extending the current agreement for a maximum of two years from January 1994 to December 1995. The new agreements represent improvements in market access over the previous agreements. They will be automatically terminated upon the entry into force of the Uruguay Round agreement on textiles and clothing.

Non-textiles Issues

Anti-dumping investigations against Hong Kong companies in respect of 3.5-inch magnetic floppy disks, initiated by the European Community (EC) in September 1992, are still in progress. The Hong Kong Government considers that there is insufficient evidence of dumping, injury and link between the two for initiation of investigation, and submitted two representations during the year to the EC, seeking termination of the anti-dumping proceedings.

The relatively uncertain developments in trade relations between the United States of America and China continued to cast a shadow over Hong Kong's economic well-being. The areas of concern include, among other matters, the uncertainty of the renewal of China's Most Favoured Nation (MFN) trading status and the trade sanctions against China on the latter's alleged missile-related technology transfer to third countries. On May 28, 1993, China's MFN trading status in the USA was renewed for another year by an Executive Order of the President, Mr Bill Clinton. The order provides that in 1994, the US Secretary of State shall not recommend extension to the President unless he determines that the extension will substantially promote the freedom of emigration and China is complying with the 1992 China/USA agreement concerning prison labour. The Hong Kong Government and the private sector will continue to emphasise to the United States administration and members of Congress the adverse effect on Hong Kong's economy of the withdrawal of China's MFN status, or imposition of conditions on its renewal.

In August 1992, the South Korean authorities initiated an anti-dumping investigation against Hong Kong companies in respect of phosphoric acid originating from China and re-exported from Hong Kong. Final anti-dumping duties on the goods in question were imposed for a period of three years with effect from February 20, 1993.

In September 1992, the Australian authorities initiated an anti-dumping proceeding against Hong Kong companies in respect of disposable plastic cutlery. The Australian authorities completed the investigation in July 1993 and decided not to impose anti-dumping duties against the territory, as there was no evidence that exports from Hong Kong had resulted in material injury to their local industry.

In March 1993, the South Korean authorities initiated another anti-dumping investigation against Hong Kong companies in respect of sodium carbonate originating from China and re-exported from Hong Kong. Final anti-dumping duties on the goods in question were imposed for a period of three years with effect from December 31.

In November 1993, the Australian authorities initiated an anti-dumping inquiry against Hong Kong companies in respect of clear float glass. The case is under investigation.

Trade Department

The Trade Department is responsible for Hong Kong's commercial relations with foreign governments. It implements trade policy and agreements, and conducts import and export licensing and origin certification. On matters of policy affecting trade, the Director-General of Trade takes advice from the Trade Advisory Board and the Textiles Advisory Board, both of which are appointed by the Governor and chaired by the Secretary for Trade and Industry.

The department consists of five divisions, three of which deal with bilateral commercial relations with Hong Kong's trading partners in different geographical areas. Their work includes the conduct of trade negotiations and the implementation of textiles agreements, as well as the collection and dissemination of information on developments which may affect Hong Kong's external trade, especially those relating to trade policies and measures adopted in its major markets. One of these divisions has, in addition, responsibility for regional economic co-operation, and also the computerisation of the department's licensing systems and the introduction of electronic data interchange. The fourth division deals with the multilateral aspects of Hong Kong's external commercial relations, such as its participation in the GATT and in the MFA. The fifth division is responsible for the textiles export control system, common services, origin certification, the import and export licensing of commodities other than textiles, and the rice control scheme.

The department's work is assisted by eight overseas Hong Kong Government offices administered by the Trade and Industry Branch.

Hong Kong Representation Overseas

The Trade and Industry Branch oversees Hong Kong Economic and Trade Offices in Geneva, Brussels, Washington, New York, San Francisco, Toronto and Tokyo, mainly to safeguard and advance Hong Kong's economic and commercial interests overseas. The Hong Kong Government Office in London also promotes the territory's economy. (Address details are at Appendix 6.)

The Geneva Office represents Hong Kong as a contracting party to the GATT. The office participates in the regular activities of the GATT, as well as in the ongoing multilateral trade negotiations, generally known as the Uruguay Round, which were launched in September 1986. It is also responsible for Hong Kong's commercial relations with Switzerland.

The Brussels Office represents and promotes Hong Kong's economic, commercial and public relations interests to the European Commission and the member states of the European Community (other than the United Kingdom), and to Turkey, the Czech Republic, the Slovak Republic, Hungary, Poland, and other Central and Eastern European countries. With effect from July 1, it also took over responsibility for Hong Kong's commercial relations with Austria and the Nordic countries (Finland, Norway and Sweden).

The London Office is responsible for Hong Kong's commercial relations with the United Kingdom. Moreover, it is also responsible for monitoring the economic and political developments in the United Kingdom that are of interest to Hong Kong, for promoting the territory's interests, enhancing understanding of Hong Kong affairs and promoting Hong Kong's image in the United Kingdom. In this connection, the office maintains close liaison with the business and commercial sectors, politicians and the media in the United Kingdom.

The Washington, New York and San Francisco Offices closely monitor economic and trade developments, proposed legislation and other matters in the United States that might affect Hong Kong's economic and trading interests in general.

The Toronto Office has a similar role in Canada, while the Tokyo Office conducts similar activities in Japan.

Participation in International Organisations

As an integral part of the Asian-Pacific economy and an important regional services centre, Hong Kong has a role to play and a contribution to make in regional economic co-operation.

The territory's economic links with the region have been expanding. In 1992, some 80 per cent of Hong Kong's total external trade was accounted for by the other 14 member economies of the Asia-Pacific Economic Co-operation (APEC).

During the year, Hong Kong participated actively in the work of the APEC, culminating in the fifth APEC Ministerial Meeting held from November 17 to 19 in Seattle. The Financial Secretary represented Hong Kong at the APEC Economic Leaders Conference held on November 20 to discuss strategic economic and trade issues affecting the region.

The Hong Kong Committee of the Pacific Economic Co-operation Council (PECC), set up in March 1990 to advise on Hong Kong's participation in, and co-ordinate the territory's input to, the PECC process, continued to participate actively in the various task forces. The 10th general meeting of the PECC will be held from March 23 to 25, 1994 in Kuala Lumpur.

Hong Kong Trade Development Council

The Hong Kong Trade Development Council (TDC) was set up by statute in 1966 to promote and expand the territory's trade. As the international marketing arm for the territory's manufacturers and traders, it plays a vanguard role in opening new or difficult markets for Hong Kong companies.

Through a network of 37 branch offices in 26 countries, the TDC also generates international awareness of business opportunities in Hong Kong, and the territory's advantages as a gateway to markets throughout Asia.

The council's chairman is appointed by the Governor. Its 18 council members include representatives of major trade associations, leading businessmen and industrialists, as well as two senior government officials.

To ensure the wide range of trade services offered by the TDC are useful and supported, the council receives extensive input from manufacturers and traders. Its seven specialised Industry Advisory Committees, with a total membership of more than 200, advise on services and promotional strategies.

Over the past 27 years, the TDC has developed a computer database of about 55 000 local manufacturers and trading firms, and 240 000 overseas importers, categorised according to product and market. This databank is the cornerstone of the council's Trade Enquiry Service, and is invaluable to companies who need to build their own network of overseas contacts. The TDC matches Hong Kong companies with buyers, sellers and agents from around the world, and processes over 300 000 trade enquiries globally each year. Enquiries arrive around-the-clock by telephone, facsimile, letter and personal attendance at the head office, overseas offices and the datashop service centres located in Hong Kong's prime commercial and industrial areas.

Overseas trade promotional projects organised by the TDC are designed to help Hong Kong companies expand their business in existing markets or to make inroads into emerging ones. In 1993, the TDC took more than 2 600 of the territory's companies to the frontline of markets, from Buenos Aires to Beijing, from Moscow to Basel and Hanoi. Nearly $12 billion worth of business orders were taken, and participating firms reported more than 70 000 new business contacts.

The TDC also plays an important role in promoting Hong Kong as the trade fair capital of Asia, organising 16 fairs each year, many of which are the largest of their kind in the region. These include Hong Kong Fashion Week, the Hong Kong Toys and Games Fair, the Hong Kong International Jewellery Show, the Hong Kong Electronics Fair and the Hong Kong Book Fair.

In early 1993, the government agreed to pursue further a TDC proposal to build an extension to the Hong Kong Convention and Exhibition Centre (HKCEC), which is presently operating at near-capacity. The extension will more than double the size of the existing facility, placing Hong Kong firmly on the world map as the trade fair and conference capital of Asia.

The council has a special commitment towards developing China's burgeoning consumer market for Hong Kong companies and their products. This is achieved through special promotions of Hong Kong products, mounted in large mainland department stores to promote the territory's brand names. Under the TDC banner, Hong Kong companies also participate in mainland trade fairs and high-level business seminars in China.

More recently, the council has added to its China programme by staging trade fairs in Shenzhen. Four events were launched in the past two years — the International Machinery and Industrial Supplies Fair, the Joint Venture Products Exhibition, the International Fashion and Accessories Fair, and the International Toys and Gifts Fair. To support this increasingly active programme, the council opened a new branch office in Shenzhen during the year, in addition to its existing network in Guangzhou, Beijing and Shanghai.

Closer to home, another important role of the TDC is to encourage Hong Kong manufacturers to upgrade local products, so they can retain and improve their competitive edge in world markets. Spearheading this initiative is the TDC Design Gallery, which displayed the work of more than 50 local designers and 70 Hong Kong brand names in 1993. Set up as a showcase for the best of Hong Kong design, the prime location of the store in the HKCEC complex gives it wide international exposure, with a steady flow of buyers passing through during major trade fairs and many sourcing enquiries referred to manufacturers and designers. Additionally, the TDC's organisation of the export marketing category in the Governor's Award for Industry serves to heighten awareness of the importance of export marketing strategies.

To promote a positive environment for Hong Kong's trade, the TDC initiates and maintains high-level contacts with business leaders, economic policy-makers and media around the world. It receives almost 500 incoming missions from international markets each year, and advances bilateral ties with both new and long-standing trade partners through influential bodies such as the Hong Kong/Japan Business Co-operation Committee. A special initiative of the TDC in the United States of America is Operation Pacific Bridge, a highly-focussed programme aimed at helping US companies access the China market by using Hong Kong as a springboard. In 1993, the council again partnered the Geneva-based World Economic Forum in organising the second Europe/East Asia Economic Forum at the HKCEC.

The TDC produces updated information on markets, including trade statistics, market surveys and product reports as well as market and industry profiles, import regulations and procedures. Its Research Department publishes the monthly *International Market News* and the quarterly *New Market Search*, which focus specifically on emerging markets; and *Trade Developments*, a series of detailed reports on markets around the world. Other publications include *Hong Kong for the Business Visitor*, which is published in seven languages; and 15 product magazines, in English, Chinese and Spanish, with a global circulation of 1.6 million. Titles include *Hong Kong Enterprise*, *Hong Kong Toys*, *Hong Kong Garments and Accessories*, *Hong Kong Apparel*, *Hong Kong Household*, *Hong Kong Electronics*, *Hong Kong Watches and Clocks*, *Hong Kong Gifts and Premiums*, *Hong Kong Optical*, *Hong Kong Jewellery* and *Hong Kong Leather Goods and Bags*.

To help keep overseas traders informed of business developments and opportunities in Hong Kong, the Publicity Services Department publishes *Hong Kong Trader*, a monthly newspaper which reaches leading businessmen in 162 markets around the world.

Hong Kong Export Credit Insurance Corporation

The Hong Kong Export Credit Insurance Corporation (ECIC) helps Hong Kong exporters to minimise risks and expand their markets.

The ECIC is a statutory corporation set up in 1966. It provides insurance protection to exporters against the risk of monetary loss arising from non-payment by their overseas buyers for goods exported and services rendered on credit which are not normally covered by commercial insurers. The government guarantees the payment of all moneys due by the corporation, with the limit for maximum contingent liability arising from its insurance and guarantee operations currently set at $7,500 million.

Under the Hong Kong Export Credit Insurance Corporation Ordinance, the ECIC has a paid-up capital of $20 million provided by the government and is autonomous in day-to-day operations. It is run on a self-sufficient, commercial basis. A 12-member advisory board, comprising prominent members from the business sector and representatives from the government, advises the corporation on the conduct of its business.

In 1992–93, the ECIC insured exports worth $15,652 million and received gross premium income of $91 million. The maximum liability of policies was $6,406 million. The number of claim cases jumped by 30 per cent to 116 and gross claim payments amounted to $35 million. The excess of income over expenditure was $38.42 million.

The ECIC is a member of the International Union of Credit and Investment Insurers (the Berne Union) and has an international network of contacts. It has ready access to confidential and updated economic and market information on other countries, and credit reports on overseas buyers.

The ECIC's services to the exporting community fall into three main categories. The first category is the protection provided by the corporation to indemnify policy-holders for up to 90 per cent of their losses. Besides domestic exports and re-exports, shipments from third countries direct to overseas buyers are also covered. Protection is provided to exporters against non-payment due to buyers' insolvency, default and repudiation, war or civil disturbance and transfer delays. Cover can be extended to outward processing operations against confiscation and non-repatriation of raw materials, work in progress and finished products. For export of capital goods and services sold on medium or long-term credits, the ECIC can provide tailor-made insurance policies.

Second, the ECIC provides credit advisory services to its policy-holders. On request by a policy-holder, the corporation will investigate the prospective buyer's creditworthiness, having regard to the market trading environment and the terms of payment of the proposed transaction, and advise the policy-holder on the amount of credit that can be prudently extended to the overseas buyer.

Third, when a policy-holder encounters payment problems, the ECIC provides a risk management service and advises the policy-holder on possible courses of action, either to prevent or minimise any loss.

During the year, the corporation expanded its links with trade associations, banks and individual exporters. Publicity was stepped up and outreaching activities extended to exporters and manufacturers. A new External Trade Specific Shipment(s) Policy was introduced, providing cover for transactions with a payment period exceeding 180 days. Increased demand for services was met by streamlining procedures and more efficient use of resources. Premium reductions were continued for qualified policy-holders, and service standards formulated prior to the introduction of a performance pledge on April 1.

Other Trade and Industrial Organisations

A number of associations have been established in Hong Kong to represent the interests of industry and commerce. Among the larger, long-established and more influential associations are the Federation of Hong Kong Industries, the Chinese Manufacturers' Association of Hong Kong, the Hong Kong General Chamber of Commerce and the Chinese General Chamber of Commerce. Other important organisations include the Hong Kong Management Association, the Hong Kong Exporters' Association, the American Chamber of Commerce, the Indian Chamber of Commerce, and the Hong Kong Japanese Chamber of Commerce and Industry.

The Federation of Hong Kong Industries is a statutory body, established in 1960 to promote and protect the interests of Hong Kong's manufacturing industry. It offers a wide range of services, covering certificates of origin, the Hong Kong Quality Mark Scheme, a custom-built multi-risks insurance policy, consultancy work on quality assurance, trade marks and copyrights, trade enquiries and economic research.

With a membership spanning all industrial sectors, the federation services the Hong Kong Toys Council, the Chemical and Pharmaceutical Industries Council, the Transport Services Council, the Hong Kong Watch and Clock Council, the Hong Kong Electronics Industry Council, the Hong Kong Plastics Industry Council and the Hong Kong Mould and Die Council. It also runs the annual Young Industrialist Awards of Hong Kong and is responsible for organising the consumer product design award category of the Governor's Award for Industry.

The Chinese Manufacturers' Association of Hong Kong (CMA), established in 1934, is a non-profit-making chamber of commerce and industry. It is also a member of the International Chamber of Commerce. With a membership of over 3 800 industrial and trade establishments, the CMA is authorised by the government to issue certificates of origin. It also provides trade information; handles trade enquiries; organises missions, fairs and exhibitions; and is active in encouraging product development and quality improvement. The CMA Testing and Certification Laboratories provide technical back-up services, including materials and product testing, pre-shipment inspection and technical consultancy services. The CMA also organises various seminars and training courses, and operates two pre-vocational schools to provide technical education and training for more than 2 000 students. The CMA provides scholarships annually to outstanding students of technical colleges and post-secondary institutions. Since 1989, the CMA has been appointed by the government to organise the machinery and equipment design award category of the Governor's Award for Industry.

The Hong Kong General Chamber of Commerce is the oldest internationally-recognised trade association in Hong Kong and is one of the 10 largest chambers of commerce in the world. Founded in 1861, its membership of over 3 600 member companies is representative of every sector of commerce and industry. The chamber organises trade and goodwill missions overseas and receives inbound delegations. It handles trade enquiries and extends assistance to individual visiting businessmen. It is authorised by the government to issue certificates of origin and is the sole local issuing authority for international Association Temporarie Admission Carnets through its nine local certification offices.

Although an independent, autonomous organisation receiving no subvention, the chamber is represented on a wide range of official advisory committees and bodies. The chamber founded and formed the Hong Kong Article Numbering Association, the Hong Kong Coalition of Service Industries and the Hong Kong Franchise Association; and sponsors the Hong Kong Committee of the Pacific Basin Economic Council.

Established in 1900, the Chinese General Chamber of Commerce is an association of local Chinese firms, businessmen and professionals. It has a membership of over 6 000, representing a wide spectrum of trade interests and industries. Apart from providing a variety of services, including certification of origin and organisation of seminars, exhibitions, trade missions and other trade promotional activities, it maintains close links with trade organisations both in Hong Kong and China. Since 1957, it has been authorised by the Chinese Export Commodities Fair authorities to issue invitations on their behalf to local Chinese firms. It has been operating courses for senior government officials of China since 1982, to enable them to better understand the various aspects of Hong Kong's economy.

The Hong Kong Management Association is a professional management organisation, incorporated in 1960 to improve the efficiency and effectiveness of management in Hong Kong. With a membership of over 7 500, it organises some 1 600 training programmes and provides various management services such as translation, recruitment and the organisation of exhibitions.

The Hong Kong Exporters' Association was formed in 1955, and has a membership of 300 export and manufacturing companies. Its objectives are to protect and promote the interests of its members, to disseminate trade information, and to act as a representative body to voice members' concerns and assist in solving any trade problems they may encounter.

Customs and Excise Department

The Trade Controls Branch of the Customs and Excise Department is responsible for the enforcement of Hong Kong's ordinances and regulations relating to trade controls. These include certification of origin, import and export licensing of textiles and strategic commodities, reserved commodities control, verification and assessment of trade declarations, consumer protection, and weights and measures.

During the year, a high level of enforcement was maintained to protect the integrity of Hong Kong's certification and licensing systems, and to fulfil obligations under international trade agreements. In particular, action was stepped up against country of origin fraud and illegal trans-shipments in the textile trade by conducting more physical checks on textile imports and exports and by monitoring consignments, traders and cargo-forwarders suspected of involvement in illegal trans-shipment.

Greater emphasis was placed on the enforcement of consumer protection legislation, particularly the new Toys and Children's Products Safety Ordinance, which came into effect on July 1.

Trade in Endangered Species

The import, export and possession of endangered species of animals and plants, including parts and derivatives, are strictly regulated by the Animals and Plants (Protection of Endangered Species) Ordinance, which gives effect to the Convention on International Trade in Endangered Species of Wild Fauna and Flora (CITES). The licensing policy follows closely the principles of the convention. Commercial trade in highly-endangered species is prohibited, and trade in less endangered species is subject to strict licensing requirements.

The ordinance is administered by the Agriculture and Fisheries Department, and enforced by officers of the department and the Customs and Excise Department through checking at entry points, markets, shops and restaurants, as well as inspection of endangered species shipments. All suspected offences are investigated and prosecutions are instituted if there is evidence of a breach of the ordinance. During 1993, there were 426 seizures and 117 prosecutions under the ordinance.

Government Supplies Department

The Government Supplies Department is the government's central organisation for procurement and supply of stores and equipment required by government departments and certain subvented organisations.

Since 1979, the department has represented the Hong Kong Government as an entity in the Agreement on Government Procurement of the General Agreement on Tariffs and Trade. Under the agreement, except for special requirements, all purchases exceeding Special Drawing Rights 130 000 ($1.37 million in 1993) are widely advertised and open to competitive bidding internationally. All purchases, ranging from simple office sundries to complex computer systems, are made entirely on the basis of the 'best value for money', regardless of the source of supply. Due to its open procurement policy, goods and services are purchased from over 40 countries and some 4 100 registered local and overseas suppliers.

To ensure continuity of supply, the department maintains goods, which are generally required by other departments, in its main stores in Hong Kong and Kowloon and two sub-stores specially established to serve the government's engineering workshops. It also seconds supplies staff to other departments to ensure a professional approach to acquisition and maintenance of stores and equipment.

In 1992–93, the department placed orders of a total value of HK$2,593 million. The major sources of supply were the United States of America, the United Kingdom, China, Germany, Japan and Hong Kong itself. Major items of purchase included computer systems, rations and pharmaceuticals.

In the purchase of goods and equipment, the department always takes into consideration environmental protection factors.

Intellectual Property

The Intellectual Property Department, which includes the Trade Marks and Patents Registries, provides a focal point for the development of the Hong Kong intellectual property regime.

During the year, two consultative documents on proposals for the reform of both the trade marks and patents law, respectively, were issued. In addition, a bill was introduced in the Legislative Council to provide specific statutory protection for the layout-designs (topographies) of integrated circuits in Hong Kong.

Trade Marks and Patents

The Trade Marks Registry is a registry of original registration. Trade marks are registered under the Trade Marks Ordinance, the provisions of which are similar to trade marks legislation in the United Kingdom. Since March 1992, it has been possible to register trade marks for services as well as goods. The registration procedure is laid down in the Trade Marks Rules, and the prescribed forms may be obtained free from the Trade Marks Registry. Every mark, even if it is already registered in another country, must satisfy the requirements of the ordinance before it may be accepted for registration. During 1993, 14 280 applications were received, 12 043 of which were in respect of goods and 2 237 in respect of services. Overall, 8 260 applications, including those made in previous years, were accepted and allowed to be advertised. A total of 5 720 marks were registered in 1993, compared with 5 500 in 1992. The principal origin of applicants was as follows:

USA	1 408	France	321
Hong Kong	1 240	Italy	285
Japan	647	Switzerland	183
UK	347	Taiwan	166
Germany	328	Netherlands	113

The total number of trade marks on the register at December 31, 1993 was 66 670.

The Patents Registry registers patents that have been granted in the United Kingdom and European Patents (United Kingdom). The Registration of Patents Ordinance provides that any grantee of a United Kingdom Patent or European Patent (United Kingdom) may, within five years from the date of its grant, apply to have the patent registered in Hong Kong.

A total of 1 438 patents were registered in Hong Kong during the year, compared with 1 069 in 1992. Registration of a United Kingdom Patent or European Patent (United Kingdom) in Hong Kong confers on the grantee the same privileges and rights as if the patent had been granted in the United Kingdom with an extension to Hong Kong. The privileges and rights run from the commencement of the term of the patent in the United Kingdom, and continue for as long as the patent remains in force there.

Consumer Council

The Consumer Council was set up under the Consumer Council Ordinance in 1974 to protect and promote the interests of consumers of goods and services, as well as purchasers, mortgagors and lessees of immovable property. The council's chairman, vice-chairman and 20 other members are appointed by the Governor to represent a diversity of consumer interests. A Chief Executive heads the 101-strong office, which is divided into five sections: administration; complaints and advice; survey; research; and information and publication.

Since the late 1980s, Hong Kong has evolved from a manufacturing-based to a service-based economy. While a manufacturing-based, export-oriented economy is more attuned to competition in the international markets, a service-based economy is highly susceptible to domestic monopolies and the concentration of market power. This phenomenon is likely to be detrimental to consumer interests. The council has begun to look into the matter in recent years.

This aspect of work was intensified with the Governor, in his 1992 policy address, calling on the council to defend free markets and to help provide consumers with redress against unscrupulous business practices. A market structural analysis, including a study on restrictive trade practices and the behavioural aspects of the market, was underway at the end of the year. Parallel to the main study were five other sectoral studies to ascertain whether a competitive environment is maintained in the financial services, gas supply, supermarket, broadcasting and telecommunications industries. A final report is expected to be completed by mid-1994.

The council has submitted proposals to the government on the tendering of government carparks and the contracting-out arrangements for the management of parking meters. The proposals stressed the need to award the contracts to more than one operator, to promote competition.

The council's efforts to safeguard the interests of property buyers continued. Recommendations to regulate estate agents through legislation and a full licensing system were well-received by the trade and the public, and the matter is under active consideration by the government. Meanwhile, the interest of the local population in the booming Chinese property market induced the council to make several study visits to Guangdong, to obtain first-hand information on the property transaction procedures adopted in the province. A series of articles were published subsequently in the council's monthly magazine, *CHOICE*, and a seminar on the topic was organised in May, offering advice to interested buyers.

The Toys and Children's Products Safety Ordinance came into effect in July, ushering in a new era of consumer protection in product safety. The ordinance came into being after years of advocacy by the council. In addition, preparation of legislation on consumer product safety reached its final stage.

Regulation of insurance agents and brokers by the insurance industry was introduced early in 1993, five years after the council's first call to monitor the industry.

Following the disclosure of a high level of consumer dissatisfaction with the service of bridal salons, operators in the trade heeded the council's call to establish an ethical code of practice.

The government earmarked $10 million for allocation to the council for the establishment of a Consumer Representative Action Fund, to assist groups of consumers to initiate collective legal action against a common defendant whose conduct was detrimental to the consumers. The council commissioned a legal consultancy to formulate the *modus operandi* of the fund.

While taking on new challenges, the council continued its work to improve consumer welfare through handling consumer complaints, providing consumer advice, organising consumer education activities and conducting in-depth studies, tests and survey projects.

During the year, the council received 9 509 complaints and 198 147 enquiries for advice and information at its 16 Consumer Advice Centres throughout the territory. A total of 11 shops were named for engaging in sharp business practices.

The council was also active in promoting consumer awareness on environmental issues. The wastage of resources in the over-packaging of products, the virtues of using recycled paper and the truthfulness of so-called 'green labels' were some of the subjects covered in *CHOICE*.

In November, the council joined forces with the Environmental Protection Department to organise a high-level workshop comprising representatives of major supermarkets and department stores. Armed with the result of a consumer attitude survey on the use of plastic bags, the council continued to persuade the private sector to minimise their use.

Aside from *CHOICE*, which has an average circulation of 45 000 copies, other council publications include a guide to property purchase and to medical and health services.

In safeguarding consumer interests, the council works closely with various government departments and policy branches. It is consulted on major policies affecting consumer interests and is represented on many committees dealing with specific consumer issues and concerns. It is also a council member of the International Organisation of Consumers Union, which is dedicated to the protection and promotion of consumer interests through research, information and educational activities.

Metrication

The government's metrication policy is to promote and facilitate the progressive adoption of the International System of Units (SI) in Hong Kong. The Metrication Ordinance, enacted in 1976, provides for the eventual replacement of non-metric units by SI units in all legislation in the territory. Government departments use metric units exclusively.

A metrication committee, comprising representatives of industry, commerce, management and consumer bodies, and government officials, is the focal point of liaison for all matters concerning metrication. It advises on, and encourages the commercial and industrial sectors to develop, metrication programmes.

During the year, the committee continued to direct its efforts towards the retail sector. Conversion charts calibrated in metric, Chinese and imperial units were installed in some 60 Urban Council and Regional Council public markets under a private-sector sponsored programme. Metric scale demonstration counters were also set up in various outlets of a major supermarket chain to enhance public awareness of the use of metric units, and publicity materials and metric conversion tables were distributed. In conducting these promotional activities, the assistance of members of the Junior Police Call was sought and they were appointed as Metrication Ambassadors in recognition of their voluntary efforts. A variety show on metrication was screened on a Chinese television channel. A territory-wide Chinese essay-writing competition was also organised for primary and secondary school students to increase their awareness of the adoption of metrication in their daily life.

8
EMPLOYMENT

HONG KONG's labour force grew moderately in 1993. In the third quarter, the labour force had grown by 3.7 per cent, compared to the corresponding period of 1992. With a buoyant economy, unemployment and underemployment remained low, at two per cent and 1.3 per cent, respectively, of the labour force.

The territory's employed stood at 2.8 million, of whom 63 per cent were male and 37 per cent female.

Of the employed, 21.1 per cent were engaged in the manufacturing sector and 69.7 per cent in various services sectors — 28.9 in wholesale, retail, import and export trades, restaurants and hotels; 11.2 per cent in transport, storage and communications services; 9.4 per cent in financing, insurance, real estate and business services; and 20.2 per cent in community, social and personal services.

A large number of Hong Kong residents now work in China, following the rapid growth of its economic link with the territory in recent years. According to a recent survey, some 52 400 Hong Kong residents work on the other side of the border.

As an industrialised economy, the vast majority of employment in Hong Kong is found in industrial and commercial establishments. As a result of continual expansion during the past decade, establishments in the services sector now employ three times as many workers as the manufacturing sector. In September, there were 243 303 establishments in the services sector employing 1 722 873 persons, an increase of 6.2 per cent in employment over the corresponding period of 1992. In contrast, there were only 39 238 establishments in the manufacturing sector employing 508 133 persons, a decrease of 11 per cent in employment. With this shift in employment, which underlines the economic restructuring underway in Hong Kong, many manufacturing workers have been displaced from their jobs. A scheme involving the injection of $300 million into an Employees Retraining Fund by the government is being implemented to re-train affected workers.

In terms of employment size, the import and export trade is the largest industry group in the services sector, employing 452 262 persons in September. Other major service industry groups include the retail trade, restaurants, and business services, which have an employment size of 198 199, 187 655, and 127 793 persons, respectively.

Despite declining employment, the clothing industry remains the largest manufacturing industry, employing 166 401 persons in September. Establishments in the electronics and textiles industries are the next two largest groups of employers in manufacturing, employing 53 591 and 44 182 persons, respectively.

Details of the distribution of establishments and employment by industry group are shown at Appendices 17 and 18, respectively.

Wages

Wage rates are calculated on a time basis, either daily or monthly, or on an incentive basis according to the volume of work performed. The average wage rate for all employees, including wage-earners and salaried employees up to the supervisory level, increased by 10.4 per cent in money terms, or by 2.4 per cent in real terms, between September 1992 and September 1993.

At the third quarter of 1993, the average monthly wage for the supervisory, technical, clerical and miscellaneous non-production workers in the wholesale, retail, import and export trades, restaurants and hotels sector was $8,579. This represented an increase of 10.3 per cent over the same period in 1992, or an increase of 2.2 per cent in real terms.

The average wage rate in the manufacturing sector rose by 10 per cent in money terms between September 1992 and September 1993. After allowing for rises in consumer prices, the wage rate increased in real terms by 1.9 per cent during the same period.

In September 1993, 75 per cent of manual workers in the manufacturing sector received a daily wage, including fringe benefits, of $189 or more; and 25 per cent received $297 or more. The overall average daily wage was $266. The overall average monthly rate was $6,780.

Employee Benefits

The Employment Ordinance provides for benefits and entitlements including statutory holidays, annual leave, rest days, maternity leave, sickness allowance, severance payment and long service payment for employees. In addition, some employers provide employees with fringe benefits such as subsidised meals or food allowances, good attendance bonuses, free or subsidised medical treatment, and transport to and from work. Many employees also enjoy a year-end bonus of one month's pay or more under their employment contracts, usually paid just before the Lunar New Year.

In December 1993, the government announced that it would pursue a compulsory, contributory Old-age Pension Scheme, subject to the outcome of a feasibility study advising on the financial and technical aspects of such a scheme; endorsement by the community of proposals resulting from the feasibility study; and consultation with the Chinese Government. The government would also continue to promote voluntary retirement schemes vigorously. At the end of the year, a total of 14 637 private retirement schemes had been approved by the Inland Revenue Department.

Labour Administration and Services

The Labour Department, headed by the Commissioner for Labour, is responsible for implementing labour policies and enforcing labour legislation. These objectives are achieved through the promotion of the safety, health and welfare of the working community, as well as the promotion of harmonious labour relations, safeguarding of the rights and benefits of employees under labour laws, and the provision of free employment services and careers guidance. During 1993, there were 8 041 prosecutions for breaches of ordinances and regulations administered by the department. Fines totalling $22,793,100 were imposed.

Labour Conditions

The employment of children aged under 15 years is prohibited in all industrial undertakings. Children aged 13 and 14 years may be employed in non-industrial establishments, subject to their having completed nine years' education and other conditions which aim to protect their safety, health and welfare. However, the vast majority in this age group is still at school.

Working hours, night work, rest periods and overtime work for women and for young persons aged below 18 years in industrial establishments are strictly regulated by law for their protection.

The Labour Inspectorate of the Labour Department is responsible for monitoring employers' compliance with requirements in the Employment Ordinance relating to the employment of women and young persons, payment of wages, annual leave and statutory holidays, sickness allowance and maternity protection. The ordinance applies to both local and foreign workers.

Labour Legislation

The Commissioner for Labour is the principal adviser to the government on labour affairs. She is responsible for initiating proposals for new labour legislation and amendments to existing laws. The government's policy on labour is to achieve levels of safety, health and welfare for employees in Hong Kong which are broadly equivalent to those provided in neighbouring countries at a similar stage of economic development. This objective has been achieved through a total of 119 legislative enactments in the past decade.

During 1993, 11 pieces of labour legislation were enacted. An amendment to the Protection of Wages on Insolvency Ordinance raised the amount of *ex gratia* payments in respect of arrears of wages and wages in lieu of notice covered by the ordinance. An amendment to the Pneumoconiosis (Compensation) Ordinance provided a new compensation scheme for pneumoconiosis sufferers, offering improved benefits in the form of monthly payments until death. The maximum level of compensation payable under the Employees' Compensation Ordinance was revised, while an amendment to the Factories and Industrial Undertakings Ordinance revised the levels of penalty, to discourage infringement of the ordinance.

Labour Advisory Board

The Labour Advisory Board, a non-statutory body, helps to formulate labour policies and legislation. It has six members representing employers and another six representing employees. The Commissioner for Labour, or her deputy, is the *ex officio* chairman.

To cope with the increasing range and complexity of work and to encourage greater participation by employers and employees, committees have been set up under the board on special subject areas including employment services, industrial safety and health, labour relations, employees' compensation and the implementation of international labour standards. The views of employers and employees are canvassed in the formulation of labour policies through consultation with the board, to provide a progressive yet balanced programme of labour legislation for the benefit of all concerned.

International Labour Standards

A number of international instruments set out labour standards. Among them are the International Labour Conventions of the International Labour Organisation. These conventions set out the standards on matters relating to employment rights, conditions of work, social policy, labour administration, labour relations and social security. The Commissioner for Labour ensures that Hong Kong's obligations under these conventions are observed.

The International Labour Conventions have significant influence on the formulation of labour legislation in the territory. At the end of 1993, Hong Kong applied 49 conventions, which compared favourably with most members of the International Labour Organisation in the region.

Trade Unions

Trade unions must be registered under the Trade Unions Ordinance, which is administered by the Registrar of Trade Unions. Once registered, a trade union becomes a corporate body and enjoys immunity from certain civil suits.

During the year, 22 new unions were registered. At the end of 1993, there were 532 unions, comprising 491 employees' unions, 26 employers' associations and 15 mixed organisations of employees and employers. Their total memberships were about 525 800, 2 600 and 14 500, respectively.

The majority of employees' unions are affiliated to one of the five major local labour organisations registered under the Societies Ordinance. These are the Hong Kong Federation of Trade Unions (89 affiliated unions with about 192 500 members); Hong Kong and Kowloon Trades Union Council (66 affiliated unions with about 30 600 members); Hong Kong Confederation of Trade Unions (27 affiliated unions with about 75 200 members); the Joint Organisation of Unions, Hong Kong (18 affiliated unions with about 9 700 members); and the Federation of Hong Kong and Kowloon Labour Unions (20 affiliated unions with about 21 600 members). The remaining 271 employees' unions have a total membership of about 196 200.

Labour Relations

In 1993, the Labour Relations Division of the Labour Department conciliated in 157 trade disputes (each involving 21 or more workers), which involved 10 work stoppages and a loss of 16 204 working days. The service also dealt with 17 866 claims for wages and other employment-related payments.

A dispute between the Flight Attendants Union and the management of Cathay Pacific Airways Limited over staff deployment and pay adjustment issues developed into a strike in January, which lasted for 17 days and resulted in the loss of 15 000 working days. The strike, which straddled the Lunar New Year holidays, was unusually long in the experience of Hong Kong.

In July, some 170 staff of the China Motor Bus Company Limited were made redundant, following a government decision to grant Citybus Limited a franchise to operate 26 bus routes, to be excised from the existing network of the former bus company. The staff were dissatisfied with the compensation package, the scale of the retrenchment and other arrangements in the execution of the retrenchment exercise. The matter attracted considerable attention from the public.

The Labour Relations Ordinance provides the machinery for special conciliation, voluntary arbitration and boards of inquiry to settle trade disputes which cannot be resolved through ordinary conciliation.

The division endeavours to promote harmonious labour-management relations in the private sector through a variety of activities such as promotional visits and talks to individual establishments, employers' associations and employees' trade unions; organising training courses, seminars and exhibitions; and publishing newsletters, information leaflets and pamphlets on a wide range of labour matters. Four territory-wide seminars on case studies of the Employment Ordinance and one seminar for contractors of the airport core programme were organised in 1993. These seminars attracted some 600 participants.

Two industry-wide committees, comprising representatives from employers' associations, trade unions and the government, have been set up in the catering and construction industries to provide meeting points for relevant parties to discuss labour matters of mutual concern.

The Labour Tribunal

The Labour Tribunal, which is part of the judiciary, provides a quick, inexpensive and informal method of adjudicating various types of disputes between employees and employers.

In 1993, the tribunal heard 4 029 cases involving employees as claimants, and a further 375 cases initiated by employers. More than $54 million was awarded by the presiding officers. Of these cases, 86 per cent were referred by the Labour Relations Division after unsuccessful conciliation attempts.

Protection of Wages on Insolvency Fund

The Protection of Wages on Insolvency Fund is financed by an annual levy of $250 on each business registration certificate. Employees who are owed wages and other termination benefits by their insolvent employers may apply to the fund for *ex gratia* payment. Previously, it covered wages not exceeding $8,000 accrued during a period of four months preceding the date of application, and seven days' wages in lieu of notice, up to $2,000. These two payment limits were revised in February and the respective levels were set at $18,000 and one month's wages, up to $6,000. The fund also covers an applicant's entitlement to severance payment, in full, up to $8,000 (which is the priority claim limit in a winding-up or bankruptcy), plus 50 per cent of his entitlement in excess of $8,000.

During the year, the fund received 7 054 applications and paid out a total of $76.6 million to 6 137 applicants.

Finding Employment

The Employment Services Division provides free placement services to help employers recruit staff, and to assist job-seekers in finding suitable employment. Since 1992, employers wishing to employ foreign workers under the importation of labour schemes must notify the division of vacancies. This requirement ensures that local job-seekers have priority in filling the vacancies.

As a result of economic restructuring in recent years, there is a growing need for local workers to be re-trained so that they can obtain employment in another trade or more senior jobs in the same trade. In 1992, the government established an Employees Retraining Scheme which was financed by a $300 million government grant and a levy imposed on employers of imported workers. Under this scheme, a local employee undergoing re-training is paid a re-training allowance of up to $3,400 each month or

$30 per session for half-day and evening courses. A wide variety of courses were on offer. At the end of 1993, 6 903 persons had completed re-training and 1 901 were undergoing re-training.

In May, an on-the-job training scheme was launched to bridge the gap between employers with unfilled vacancies and re-trainees looking for jobs. Cash reimbursements of training expenses are made to employers providing on-the-job training. The division is responsible for processing applications under the schemes and assisting the re-trainees to find employment. At the end of 1993, 342 firms (331 already gazetted) had joined the scheme, offering a total of 4 217 jobs.

The Selective Placement Division helps disabled persons integrate with the community through open employment. It provides a free employment counselling and placement service for the hearing impaired, sight impaired, physically disabled, mentally retarded and ex-mentally ill.

The division launched a series of activities to promote the employment of the disabled. These included district-based exhibitions, presentation of awards to employers and disabled employees, and talks to interested parties. Quarterly newsletters were published and distributed to some 20 000 employers. Pamphlets promoting the employment of persons with various disabilities were also issued to members of the public. Apart from making regular promotional visits to employers, special campaigns were conducted in selected trades and industries to identify and secure suitable vacancies for disabled job-seekers.

Careers Guidance

The department's Careers Advisory Service promotes careers education by building up a data bank of careers information and organising careers activities for young people.

The service operates two careers information centres, each equipped with a reference library, an audio-visual unit and an enquiry service. It produces written and audio-visual resource materials, including careers pamphlets, job-sheets, slide presentations and films. All these materials are available to the public free of charge.

The service organises a wide range of activities, including seminars, visits to places of work, exhibitions and quiz competitions. In February, it joined hands with the Hong Kong Trade Development Council to stage the Education and Careers Expo '93, which attracted more than 165 000 visitors. More than 136 500 students took part in the 12th Careers Quiz organised by the service in November.

Foreign Workers

The Immigration Department is responsible for controlling the entry of foreign workers. A foreigner may be permitted to work or invest in Hong Kong if he possesses a special skill, knowledge or experience of value to and not readily available in Hong Kong, or if he is in a position to contribute to the economy. To maintain Hong Kong's economic competitiveness, the department applies the policy in a flexible manner. Genuine businessmen and entrepreneurs are welcome to establish a presence in the territory, bringing with them capital and expertise. Qualified professionals, technical staff, administrators and managerial personnel are also admitted with minimum formalities.

During the year, 17 202 professionals and persons with technical, administrative or managerial skills from more than 60 countries were admitted for employment.

To alleviate manpower shortages in certain bottleneck areas, a separate scheme for the importation of skilled workers at the supervisory, technician, and craftsman levels was introduced in 1989. The scheme was extended in 1990 to include experienced operatives. After a review, it was decided in January 1992 that the scheme should be expanded in such a way that the total number of such workers in Hong Kong did not exceed 25 000 at any one time. Discounting those 12 000 workers who came under the previous schemes and whose contracts were still valid, employers were allowed to import 13 000 workers. The Immigration Department, however, received some 5 990 applications from employers, involving a total of 62 300 workers.

In addition, to facilitate the construction of the new airport and related projects, a scheme to import initially 2 000 construction workers was introduced in May 1990. As demand continued to grow, it was decided in January 1993 to expand the scheme so that the number of workers admitted would not exceed 5 500 at any one time. At the end of 1993, 1 885 imported workers were in Hong Kong under this scheme.

Foreign Domestic Helpers

The entry of foreign domestic helpers is subject to the conditions that they have experience in that field of work, that their employers are *bona fide* Hong Kong residents who are prepared to offer reasonable terms of employment including wages and accommodation, and that the employers are willing to provide for the helpers' maintenance in Hong Kong as well as the costs of repatriation to their country of origin.

Measures were introduced in 1993 to improve the service relating to the employment of foreign domestic helpers. In March, the Labour Department abolished the requirement of contract attestation. A one-stop service is now provided by the Immigration Department in processing applications for employment visas and extensions of stay. The number of service locations was increased in June. Helpers and employers can now obtain consultation and conciliation services from 11 offices of the Labour Relations Service.

In the past few years, the demand for foreign domestic helpers has risen steadily. In 1993, there were 120 604 such helpers in Hong Kong, representing an increase of 19.2 per cent compared with 101 182 in 1992. About 87.4 per cent of these domestic helpers were citizens of the Philippines.

Employment Agencies

The Employment Agencies Administration of the Labour Department is responsible for administering Part XII of the Employment Ordinance and the Employment Agency Regulations, which govern the licensing and operation of employment agencies. The department issued 1 061 licences in 1993.

Employment Outside Hong Kong

The External Employment Service is responsible for administering the Contracts for Employment Outside Hong Kong Ordinance to protect the interests of local employees engaged to work outside Hong Kong by foreign employers. All such employment contracts involving manual employees, or non-manual employees with monthly wages not exceeding $20,000, are required to be attested by the Commissioner for Labour. The department attested 67 contracts in 1993.

Industrial Safety

The Factory Inspectorate Division of the Labour Department is responsible for enforcing the Factories and Industrial Undertakings Ordinance and its subsidiary regulations. These regulations provide for the safety and health of workers in factories, restaurants, catering establishments, building and engineering construction sites and other industrial undertakings. Advice and assistance are given to managements on various safety and health aspects, including the adoption of safe working practices and improving factory layouts to achieve a better working environment. The inspectorate also investigates industrial accidents and dangerous incidents.

During the year, two serious industrial accidents occurred. In the first case, the main mast of a tower crane involved in the construction of the Tsing Ma Bridge buckled during a load test. The two operators inside the driving cabinet died. The other accident involved the failure of a passenger hoist installed at a construction site at North Point. The cage of the hoist plunged from the 20th floor, fatally injuring all 12 workers inside. The incidents were thoroughly investigated by the inspectorate in joint efforts with other authorities. The inspectorate also took prompt action to ensure that the construction industry had adopted suitable safety precautionary measures to prevent the recurrence of similar accidents.

The Factories and Industrial Undertakings (Noise at Work) Regulations 1992 came into operation in mid-July. It provides better protection for employees engaged in noisy work processes. The Factories and Industrial Undertakings (Lifting Appliances and Lifting Gear) (Amendment) Regulations were also enacted in July. The regulations have been extended to cover lifting appliances operating at construction sites, and strengthens the regulatory measures in respect of lifting appliances.

To promote self-regulation, the Safety Programme Promotion Unit helped industries to set up in-plant safety committees. During the year, the unit helped contractors working on the new airport projects to set up 25 management and site safety committees. The unit also assisted managements and workers to identify and assess hazards at work, and to devise their safety and health programmes. A three-day workshop on the national implementation of International Labour Conventions was jointly organised with the International Labour Organisation in February. A symposium on construction safety and health management was also organised for the construction industry in April.

The Factory Inspectorate placed much emphasis on regulatory activities in the high-risk areas of factories and construction sites. Special enforcement campaigns were launched to promote machinery safety, fire prevention and construction safety. During these campaigns, 23 655 factories, 341 restaurants and catering establishments and 1 746 construction sites were inspected and 1 483 summonses were taken out. The inspectorate also worked closely with the New Airport Projects Co-ordination Office in setting up various management and working committees to promote safety and health for workers involved in the new airport projects.

The Industrial Safety Training Centre conducted courses for workers, supervisors and managers from various industries. Talks on safety at work were organised for teachers and students of technical institutes, and special talks were arranged with the Education Department as part of the summer job safety promotional activities. The centre also gave safety talks to university and post-secondary students and to various other organisations. In collaboration with the Hong Kong Polytechnic, the centre continued to organise evening courses leading to the award of certificates in industrial safety. It also assisted the

Construction Industry Training Authority in running certificate courses for construction safety officers.

The inspectorate, in conjunction with the Information Services Department, continued its publicity programme for the promotion of industrial safety and health. Four large-scale symposia and conferences were also held on passenger hoist safety, bridge construction safety, scaffolding safety, and chemical safety.

Construction site safety award schemes for the construction industry and the airport core programme were jointly organised by the Labour Department, Housing Department, Marine Department, New Airport Projects Co-ordination Office, Provisional Airport Authority, Mass Transit Railway Corporation, Occupational Safety and Health Council, Hong Kong Construction Association Limited and Hong Kong Construction Industry Employees General Union.

Boiler and Pressure Vessel Safety

The Pressure Equipment Division of the Labour Department administers the Boilers and Pressure Vessels Ordinance and the Gasholders Examination Ordinance, to ensure the safe use and operation of all pressure equipment covered by the two ordinances.

The former ordinance stipulates that pressure equipment, including steam boilers, thermal oil heaters, steam receivers, steam containers, air receivers and pressurised cement tanks mounted on trucks or trailers, must be approved by and registered with the division. The equipment must be inspected periodically by qualified engineers who are on the approved list of appointed examiners. The division also investigates accidents involving pressure equipment.

Under the Gasholders Examination Ordinance, the division approves the design of gasholders and carries out inspections during fabrication and repairs, and subsequently conducts annual inspections.

During the year, the division processed 2 297 equipment registration applications, and inspected 3 584 factories and 5 600 items of pressure equipment. It also continued to assist the Haking Wong Technical Institute and the Occupational Safety and Health Council in organising training courses on the safe operation of pressure equipment.

The Pressure Equipment Advisory Committee advises the Boilers and Pressure Vessels Authority, presently the Commissioner for Labour, on the effective control of pressure equipment. The authority has issued a code of practice for appointed examiners, and guidebooks on the safe operation and maintenance of pressure equipment.

The division also provides technical support and advice to the Director of Fire Services on the approval of pressurised containers and storage installations for compressed gases under the provisions of the Dangerous Goods Ordinance. During the year, the division assisted the approval process of 24 934 cylinders for licensing purposes and made 74 site inspections.

Occupational Health and Hygiene

The Occupational Health Division protects workers against health hazards arising from employment. It provides an advisory service to the government and the public on matters concerning the health of workers and the hygiene of workplaces, and complements the Factory Inspectorate Division in supervising health standards and practices in industry.

The division published a series of booklets and codes of practice on occupational health and prevention of occupational diseases. Its staff carried out an on-going programme of occupational health promotion and educational activities, including delivery of health talks and lectures. With the Occupational Safety and Health Council as its co-organiser, the division also organised a week-long exhibition and a seminar on occupational health in the office environment.

A major responsibility of the division is to investigate notified occupational diseases and potential health hazards reported by the Factory Inspectorate, and to determine preventive measures. Surveys were conducted in various industries and a number of epidemiological studies on health and hygiene conditions were completed. Programmes to monitor various chemicals, dusts and other occupational health hazards were also carried out.

The division carries out medical examinations on persons exposed to ionising radiation, users of compressed-air breathing apparatus, and government employees working in compressed air or engaged in diving or pest control. It also deals with cases of silicosis under the Pneumoconiosis (Compensation) Ordinance. Registered nurses of the division handle medical clearances for employees' compensation cases. Its occupational health officers serve as members of special assessment boards, and of prostheses and surgical appliance boards under the Employees' Compensation Ordinance.

The laboratory of the division, which is a member of the Hong Kong Laboratory Accreditation Scheme, continued to carry out analytical tests on biological samples collected from workers and on other environmental samples taken during site visits.

Occupational Safety and Health Council

The Occupational Safety and Health Council aims to promote a safer and healthier working environment through education and training; promote the use of modern technology; disseminate technical knowledge; provide consultancy services; and encourage co-operation and communication among government and non-government bodies with similar goals.

The council comprises 20 members appointed by the Governor and drawn from employers and employees, academic and professional fields, and the government. It is financed by a levy on the premium of all employees' compensation insurance policies in Hong Kong.

The council has formed four functional committees to deal with administration, finance, publicity, and education and research. It has industry-based committees covering the catering, construction, electronics, metalware, ship-building and ship-repairing, plastics, printing, textiles, and transport and physical distribution industries. The council also established the Chemical Safety and Health Advisory Committee and the Occupational Health Advisory Committee during the year.

In the year under review, the scope and number of the council's training courses expanded significantly as a result of close co-operation with the Labour Department. These jointly-organised training courses focussed mainly on general safety and health training. At the same time, the council continued to organise its own courses for managers and supervisors on safety management techniques; as well as competence programmes on ionising radiation protection, safe handling of asbestos, laser safety, management of dangerous substances and noise assessment. The council co-operated with other institutions in offering safety and health training to safety practitioners. During the year, it successfully organised safety and health training courses for graduate engineers, in conjunction with the Hong Kong Institution of Engineers; and laboratory safety training for laboratory technicians, with the Government Laboratory. There was an increased demand for in-company training programmes, with a total of 5 500 company staff at all levels attending the training courses.

During the year, the council organised 12 seminars which focussed on selected technical topics for professionals and interested members of the public. Research projects were also undertaken to improve occupational safety and health in Hong Kong. The council continued to provide consultancy services on a cost recovery basis.

Campaigns to arouse public interest included the Occupational Safety and Health Week, held in November. There was a significant increase in co-operation with district-based organisations in staging promotional activities.

To fulfil its role in the dissemination of technical information, the council produces safety and health literature, codes of practice and guidebooks, a bi-monthly journal *Green Cross*, safety advice pamphlets, bulletins for individual industries and posters. A comprehensive library on occupational safety and health is open for public use. It houses a wide collection of journals, technical reference books and a database.

The council's occupational safety and health employees' participation scheme continued to offer financial assistance to employees' organisations running safety and health activities. During 1993, 23 employees' organisations received subsidies under the scheme.

Employees' Compensation

The Employees Compensation Division of the Labour Department administers the Employees' Compensation Ordinance and the Pneumoconiosis (Compensation) Ordinance.

The department ensures that injured employees and dependants of deceased employees covered by the Employees' Compensation Ordinance obtain compensation from their employers in respect of occupational diseases, or injuries, or deaths, caused by accidents arising out of, and in the course of, employment. It also ensures that persons covered by the Pneumoconiosis (Compensation) Ordinance obtain speedy compensation from the Pneumoconiosis Compensation Fund, which is financed by a levy imposed on the construction and quarrying industries.

To provide quick financial relief to employees injured at work and to dependants of employees who die as a result of work-related accidents, a loan scheme was set up in July. Under the scheme, an interest-free loan of up to $15,000 is provided for in each eligible employees' compensation case. The Employees' Compensation Assistance Scheme makes payments of statutory compensation and damages, awarded by common law, which are due to an injured employee or dependants of a deceased employee when an employer defaults or an insurer becomes insolvent. It also covers claims from employers failing to obtain indemnity from their insolvent insurers.

Under the two-tier Employees' Compensation Assessment Board system, employees with work-related injuries which are likely to result in permanent incapacity are assessed by the boards at 10 major hospitals in Hong Kong. In 1993, Ordinary Assessment Boards convened 529 sessions and completed assessments of 15 215 cases referred to them by the Commissioner for Labour and 1 274 review cases. Special Assessment Boards convened nine sessions and completed assessments of eight cases referred to them by the Ordinary Assessment Boards and one review case.

A total of 158 pneumoconiosis cases were awarded compensation from the Pneumoconiosis Compensation Fund. The Pneumoconiosis Compensation Fund Board, which was established to administer the fund, also financed research, educational and publicity programmes to enhance awareness of pneumoconiosis and to promote prevention of the disease.

In July, the Pneumoconiosis (Compensation) Ordinance was amended so that compensation is provided in the form of monthly payments until death instead of a lump sum. Pneumoconiosis sufferers who were diagnosed before January 1, 1981, and who are not covered by the ordinance, receive *ex gratia* payments on a quarterly basis from the government.

The Employees' Compensation Ordinance was also amended in July to improve the maximum levels of compensation. The increase will come into effect on January 1, 1994. Other amendments include improving the provisions on compulsory insurance; and expanding the schedule for assessing the degree of loss of earning capacity suffered by an injured employee, and the schedule for occupational diseases.

Telephone Enquiry Service

The General Enquiry Telephone Service of the Labour Department handles enquiries on the Employment Ordinance and its subsidiary regulations, the Protection of Wages on Insolvency Ordinance, the Employees' Compensation Ordinance and matters relating to the employment of foreign domestic helpers.

In April, a computer-operated answering facility was installed to supplement the public enquiry service. The new system provides a round-the-clock service to the public while the staff operators deal with more complicated enquiries during office hours.

During the year, a total of 833 109 calls were handled by the General Enquiry Telephone Service.

9
PRIMARY PRODUCTION

Most of Hong Kong's food supplies are imported—with China supplying about 47 per cent of the territory's total requirements.

Local production enables Hong Kong to maintain some degree of self-sufficiency and helps to stabilise the price and supply of fresh produce. The territory's farmers and fishermen produce about 24 per cent of fresh vegetables, 27 per cent of live poultry, six per cent of live pigs, 12 per cent of freshwater fish and 61 per cent of all live and fresh marine fish consumed. Their produce is highly regarded in the marketplace for its freshness and quality and so tends to fetch higher prices.

Each day, Hong Kong people consume about 950 tonnes of rice, 1 020 tonnes of vegetables, 7 610 pigs, 370 head of cattle, 270 tonnes of poultry, 570 tonnes of fish and 1 700 tonnes of fruit. Based on these figures, they are among the world's highest consumers of protein, according to the United Nations Food and Agriculture Organisation.

The government, as with other sectors of the economy, does not give direct subsidies to the primary industries or seek to protect them from the free operation of market forces. It does, however, provide infrastructural and technical support services to facilitate their development.

The Agriculture and Fisheries Department is the co-ordinator and main provider of these services, which aim to help the primary industries to increase their productivity and efficiency, and take advantage of new market opportunities. The department studies the business efficiency of different industry sectors to establish and update productivity standards and identify areas for improvement.

Local production statistics are given at Appendix 22.

Agricultural Industry

As only about 7.5 per cent of Hong Kong's total land area is suitable for farming, local agriculture is directed towards the production of high quality fresh foods through intensive land use.

The most common crops are vegetables and flowers, although a small quantity of fruit and other high-yield field crops are also grown. About 1 740 hectares of land were under vegetable and flower cultivation in 1993. The value of crop production was about $412 million.

The main vegetable crops grown are white cabbage, flowering cabbage and lettuce. These are cultivated throughout the year, with peak production in the cooler months. Some exotic temperate vegetables, including tomatoes, sweet corn and celery, are also grown. Straw mushrooms are produced using industrial cotton waste as the growing medium.

Common types of flowers such as gladioli, chrysanthemums and ginger lilies are grown throughout the year. A wide range of ornamental plants is produced in the various commercial nurseries. Peach blossom and ornamental citrus are grown specially for the Lunar New Year.

Because there is insufficient land for extensive grazing, pigs and poultry are the principal animals reared for food. Their production is declining though, as the industry adjusts to the progressive implementation of environmental pollution controls under the livestock waste control scheme. Pigs in Hong Kong are mostly crosses of imported breeds. The value of locally-produced pigs in 1993 amounted to $151 million and that of poultry, including chickens, ducks, pigeons and quail, amounted to $478 million.

Agricultural Development

The Agriculture and Fisheries Department conducts investigations and applied research into modern methods of crop and livestock production, and the control and prevention of plant and animal diseases. One of the more important fields of study is pest management without the use of toxic pesticides. New farming techniques, especially those that are less labour-intensive, are evaluated and promoted if found suitable for local development. Experiments to improve quality and yield are conducted. Good quality seeds and breeding stocks of pigs and poultry are produced and made available for commercial propagation.

To help farmers comply with the livestock waste control scheme, the department introduced the rearing of pigs on sawdust litter, a non-polluting and cost-effective pig husbandry technique. The simple technique involves using a special bedding material comprising sawdust and bacterial products in the pig shed to decompose the pig manure *in situ*. Studies have also been conducted on the recycling of spent sawdust litter for horticultural and landscaping use.

Local vegetable growers are encouraged to cultivate premium vegetables including traditional Chinese types, exotic varieties and vegetables produced through organic farming and hydroponics. Technical advice and marketing services are provided by the department.

Agricultural extension officers are assigned to deal with farming problems and to liaise with co-operative societies and rural associations. Vocational training and seminars on special topics of interest and importance are conducted.

Technical assistance is made available to farmers, who are also frequently advised about the proper handling and safe use of pesticides. Visits are arranged for farmers to see government experimental farms and farming projects.

Low interest loans, administered by the department, are available to the agricultural industry from the Kadoorie Agricultural Aid Loan Fund, the J.E. Joseph Trust Fund and the Vegetable Marketing Organisation Loan Fund. At the end of 1993, loans issued since the inception of these funds had reached $298 million, with $293 million having been repaid.

A total of 65 co-operative societies and two federations, with an overall membership of some 10 535 farmers, help to promote agriculture within the farming community. The Director of Agriculture and Fisheries acts as their registrar. His powers and duties include the registration of the co-operative societies and their by-laws, the auditing of accounts and general supervision of operations.

An agricultural land rehabilitation scheme, aimed at returning fallow arable land to efficient cultivation, is being implemented by the department. Infrastructural improvements in irrigation, drainage and farm road access are being effected, and a package of assistance including advance payment of rent, soil improvement and marketing facilities is offered. The satisfactory results of pilot schemes at Cheung Po in Yuen Long and Hok Tau in Fanling have resulted in the extension of the scheme to other suitable areas.

Fishing Industry

Marine fish constitute one of Hong Kong's most important primary products. During the year under review, total production from marine capture and culture fisheries was estimated at about 221 200 tonnes, with a wholesale value of $2,540 million. This represented a decrease of one per cent in weight and an increase of two per cent in value compared with 1992. In weight terms, marine capture contributed 96 per cent towards total production while the remainder came from culture operations.

The Hong Kong fishing fleet, manned by 21 000 fishermen, comprises some 4 500 vessels of which 4 200 are mechanised. It plays a vital role in primary production, catching over 150 species of commercially important fish and supplying over 60 per cent of all marine produce consumed locally. Golden thread, bigeyes, lizard-fish, squid, melon seed, conger pike eels, croakers, hairtail, scads and yellow belly are the most important species landed.

Major fishing methods include trawling, lining, gill-netting and purse-seining. About 60 per cent of the vessels are between 10 and 34 metres in length, comprising mainly trawlers, liners and gill-netters that operate on the continental shelf of the South China Sea between the Gulf of Tonkin and the East China Sea. The remaining 40 per cent of the vessels are less than 10 metres long, consisting primarily of gill-netters, hand-liners, and purse-seiners which operate in shallow coastal waters.

Trawling accounted for 79 per cent, or 172 000 tonnes, of marine fish landed in 1993. The total catch of live and fresh marine fish available for local consumption amounted to 89 300 tonnes, with an estimated wholesale value of $1,080 million.

Marine fish culture is practised within 26 designated fish culture zones, most of which are found around the coast of the eastern New Territories. Fish culture licences are issued by the Agriculture and Fisheries Department. At the year's-end, there were 1 640 licensed mariculturists. Young fish are reared in cages suspended from buoyed rafts. Grouper, seabream and snapper are the most common culture species. This sector supplied 3 010 tonnes of live marine fish valued at $190 million during the year.

Freshwater fish are also cultured. Fish ponds covering 1 330 hectares are located in the New Territories, mostly around Yuen Long. Several different species of carp are cultured in the same pond, each with a different food requirement to maximise utilisation of the nutrients introduced. The land area devoted to fish ponds has gradually declined with the increasing urbanisation of the New Territories. During the year, pond culture yielded 5 760 tonnes, or 12 per cent, of freshwater fish for local consumption.

Fisheries Development

The Agriculture and Fisheries Department conducts a wide spectrum of studies on marine resources, aquaculture and the environmental impact of development activities on fisheries to assist the development of the local fishery industry.

Large-scale development projects involving construction works affecting the foreshore and seabed have an adverse impact on the marine environment and marine resources. To offset these effects, the department, in collaboration with the Swire Marine Laboratory of the University of Hong Kong, is investigating the feasibility of deploying artificial reefs. The first experimental reef, located at Pak Sha O and covering an area of 100 square metres, was deployed in December 1993.

Aquaculture studies are directed towards the development of more efficient culture systems and improved husbandry techniques to increase productivity and minimise the impact on the environment. A moist pellet preparation which substantially reduces pollution due to wastage and leacheate, and increases nutritional value was introduced to mariculturists to replace trash fish as feed. The feasibility of open sea cage culture is being explored with a view to introducing marine fish culture to more exposed coastal waters. Studies on the marine environment are conducted to assess the impact of pollution and red tides on fisheries, particularly mariculture operations, to help the industry minimise production loss.

Fisheries development work includes modernising fishing craft and introducing more efficient fishing gear and navigational aids. A free advisory service on fishing vessel hull design, fishing methods and fishing equipment is available to fishermen, while studies are conducted to assess the suitability of new fishing gear and methods for local application. Training classes in navigation, engineering, radiotelephony, first aid, survival, fire-fighting and the use of ancillary equipment such as radar and weather facsimile equipment, and seminars on safety on board fishing vessels at sea are organised regularly at major fishing ports.

The department also advises local fishermen interested in building steel-hulled fishing vessels and organises sea-fishing endorsement courses to train and qualify them to operate these vessels. In the long-term interest of the fishing industry, the department, in collaboration with the Marine Department and Post Office, is actively involved in the formulation of international and regional standards on fishing vessel safety under the Torremolinos Convention. Standard vessel drawings were prepared for distribution to the industry to cope with the Convention's requirements.

The department administers four loan funds servicing the fishing fleet. The Fisheries Development Loan Fund with $7 million provides long-term capital for the development of improved vessels, gear and equipment. The World Refugee Year Loan Fund, the Fish Marketing Organisation Loan Fund and the Co-operative for American Relief Everywhere Loan Fund, with a total capital of $27.72 million at the end of 1993, are revolving funds which provide shorter-term financing, mainly for recurrent purposes. By December 31, loans issued since the inception of these four funds totalled $257 million, with $233 million having been repaid.

At the end of the year, there were 63 co-operative societies and four federations supported by fisherfolk, with 2 043 members from the fishing community.

Close contact with the community is maintained by liaison with producer associations and fishermen's co-operative societies through seven Fish Marketing Organisation liaison offices at the major fishing ports.

Marketing

Much of the wholesale marketing of primary products, particularly fresh foods, is the responsibility of the Agriculture and Fisheries Department, and the vegetable and fish marketing organisations. In the year under review, 43 per cent of locally-produced vegetables, and 68 per cent of the landed marine fish, were sold through these organisations.

The Vegetable Marketing Organisation operates under the Agricultural Products (Marketing) Ordinance, which also provides for the establishment of a Marketing Advisory Board to advise the Director of Marketing (the Director of Agriculture and Fisheries). It seeks to maximise returns to farmers by minimising marketing costs. The organisation is responsible for transporting locally-produced vegetables from the New Territories to the wholesale market in Kowloon, providing marketing facilities, and supervising sales and financial transactions in the market. Revenue is obtained from a 10 per cent commission on sales. The organisation is non-profit-making and surpluses are ploughed back into the development of marketing services and the farming industries. The organisation provides ancillary services such as the acquisition and sale of agricultural supplies to farmers, and the awarding of secondary and tertiary education scholarships to their children. It also monitors and checks pesticide residue levels in both the imported and locally produced vegetables that it handles, to safeguard public health. During the year, 37 300 tonnes of local vegetables valued at $114 million were sold through the organisation.

The Fish Marketing Organisation operates under the Marine Fish (Marketing) Ordinance, which also provides for the establishment of a Fish Marketing Advisory Board. The ordinance provides for the control of the landing, transport, wholesale marketing, and import and export of marine fish. The organisation operates seven wholesale fish markets. Revenue comes from a commission on the proceeds of sales. Surplus earnings are channelled back into the industry in the form of services such as low-interest loans to fishermen, improvements to the markets, financial support for schools for fishermen's children, and scholarships for secondary and tertiary education.

In 1993, the wholesale fish markets handled 64 000 tonnes of marine fish, crustacea and molluscs which were sold for $573 million. This included 5 360 tonnes of imported marine fish.

The wholesale marketing of imported vegetables, fruit, poultry, eggs, freshwater fish and crustacea takes place at various Agriculture and Fisheries Department wholesale markets throughout the territory.

Facilities in some of these markets have become dilapidated and congested. Unable to cope with the increasing throughput, their marketing activities have spilled onto adjacent areas, causing obstruction, traffic congestion and environmental problems. To improve the situation, a long-term programme has been devised to replace the outdated markets with large modern wholesale market complexes, on Hong Kong Island and in Kowloon, and to centralise the wholesale marketing of fresh foodstuffs. The department has so far completed the first phases of the complexes on Hong Kong Island and the West Kowloon Reclamation. Phase one of the Hong Kong complex, which handles fruit, freshwater fish and eggs, was commissioned in 1991. Phase one of the Kowloon complex was handed over to the department in September 1993. It provides facilities for the wholesale marketing of imported vegetables, freshwater fish and eggs as well as incorporating the Fish Marketing Organisation market for Cheung Sha Wan. Phase two work on the Hong Kong complex, which includes the poultry and imported vegetable markets, is progressing satisfactorily. Preparation is being made for these markets to be commissioned in early 1994. Pending the completion of the second phase of the Kowloon complex and the permanent markets planned for the New Territories, the department continues to operate two temporary wholesale markets—at North District in the New Territories for agricultural products, and at Cheung Sha Wan in Kowloon for poultry.

During the year, the wholesale markets managed by the department handled 180 810 tonnes of local and imported vegetables, 90 660 tonnes of local and imported poultry, 42 240 tonnes of local and imported freshwater fish and fishery products, 129 040 tonnes of imported fruit and 20 590 tonnes of imported fresh and preserved eggs. The total value of the produce amounted to $4,668 million.

Mining and Quarrying

The Mines and Quarries Division of the Geotechnical Engineering Office of the Civil Engineering Department enforces legislation relating to mining, quarrying and explosives, and administers quarrying contracts. It processes mining and prospecting applications and inspects mining and prospecting areas, stone quarries, blasting sites and explosives stores.

Hong Kong used 1.7 million tonnes of sand, aggregates and other rock products in 1993. About half of the territory's demand for aggregates and sand was met locally, with the balance imported from China. Local quarries and stone processing sites are supervised by the division. New contracts for the Shek O and Anderson Road quarries were prepared to facilitate the progressive rehabilitation of these quarry sites within defined time-spans, in return for the granting of rights to the quarry operators to process and sell surplus rock excavated during the course of the rehabilitation. These quarry sites will be rehabilitated by recontouring and extensive planting to blend with the surrounding natural hillsides in accordance with guidelines set down in the Metroplan Landscape Strategy for the Urban Fringe and Coastal Areas. Rehabilitation schemes for the Mount Butler and Lamma Island quarries are currently being arranged. In 1993, there was one kaolin mine operating under a mining lease.

The Mines and Quarries Division manages three government explosives depots, which provide bulk storage facilities for imported as well as locally-manufactured explosives, and undertakes the delivery of explosives from the depots to blasting sites. It also issues shotfirers' blasting certificates.

The largest use of explosives during the year was for site formation works for the new airport project. A new government explosives depot was set up at the airport site on Chek Lap Kok Island to ensure uninterrupted supply for site preparation work. Explosives were also used in Hong Kong for quarrying works, sewerage tunnel construction and seismic surveys. The overall consumption of explosives was 21 700 tonnes.

In 1993, the government promulgated procedures for the controlled use of pyrotechnics in the production of motion pictures, television programmes and theatrical performances. The division is responsible for issuing storage licences and removal permits, and provides technical support to the Recreation and Culture Branch in assessing the suitability of pyrotechnics and pyrotechnicians.

Popular with local residents and tourists, a brilliantly ornate floating restaurant awaits the evening's dinner patrons, in the Shing Mun River, Sha Tin.

Setting high standards in visitor accommodation helps to secure Hong Kong's Number One ranking as Asia's most popular travel destination.

Unforgettable backdrop. Nearly half of all international visitors to Hong Kong make their way to The Peak on Hong Kong Island **(left),** *to admire the view; while* **(below),** *many also have their fortune revealed at Wong Tai Sin Temple.*

Above and right: *Stanley Market is a magnet for intrepid shoppers who are prepared to work a little harder for their bargains.*

Hong Kong thoroughly enjoys its reputation as an exciting tourist destination, where the delights of shopping, dining, and sightseeing can be experienced within a surprisingly compact area.

Pictured, clockwise: *A gold necklace wins approving smiles; Sold. Another suit, and another suitcase; A seafood dinner begins with a guarantee of freshness; Time out for an authentic Chinese lunch is time well spent.*

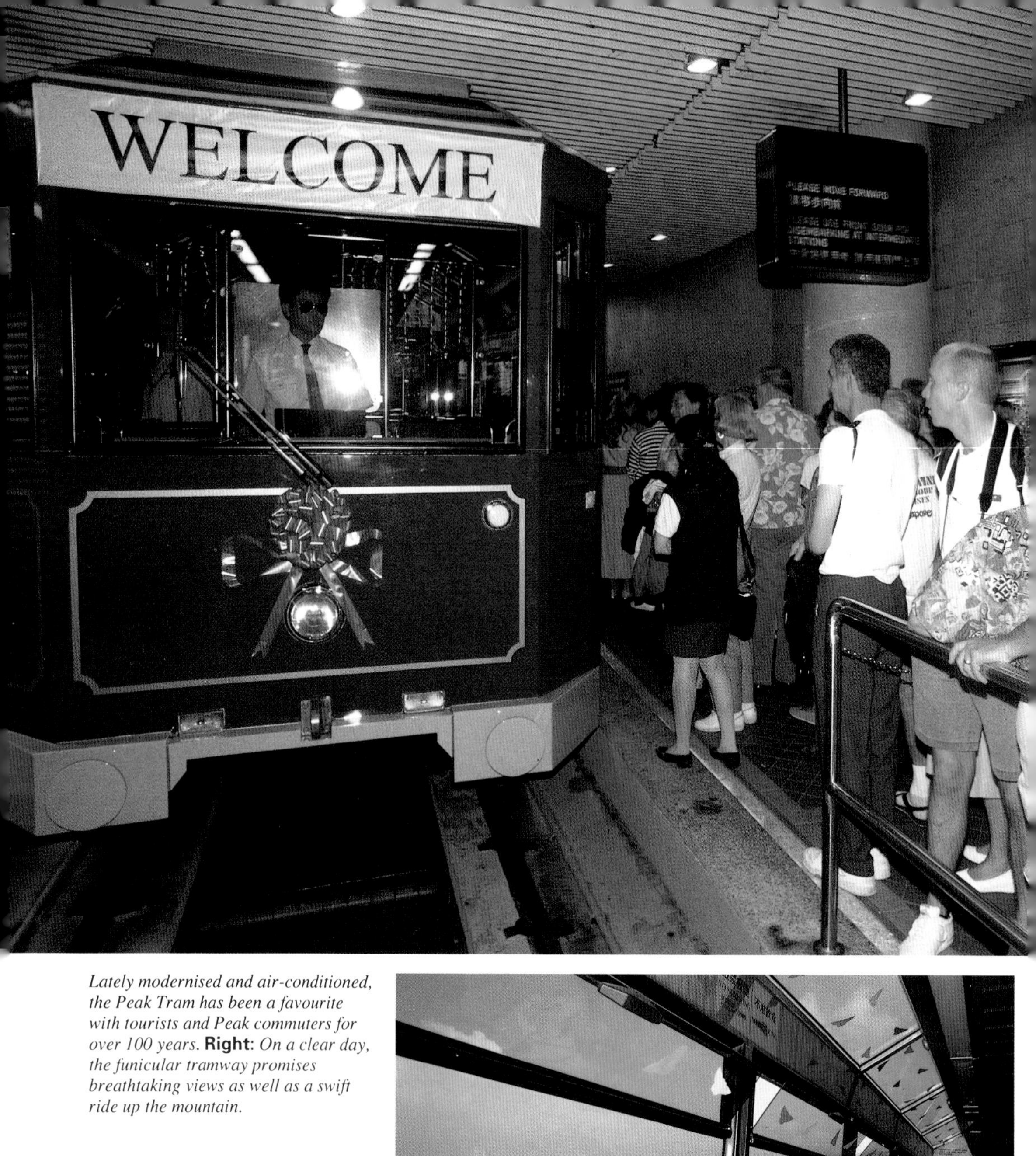

Lately modernised and air-conditioned, the Peak Tram has been a favourite with tourists and Peak commuters for over 100 years. **Right:** *On a clear day, the funicular tramway promises breathtaking views as well as a swift ride up the mountain.*

10
EDUCATION

ABOUT one-fifth of Hong Kong's population was engaged in full-time study, indicating the importance the community attaches to education.

To maintain Hong Kong's position as one of the economic powerhouses of Asia, education continues to be given high priority in the government budget, where it receives a larger share of resources than any other programme except social services.

With targets of provision almost fully achieved at the school level, and with the tertiary expansion programme well on course, attention during the year continued to be focussed on measures to ensure that schools can deliver the quality of education needed to sustain social and economic progress. Major recommendations in the Education Commission's fifth report, for improving the professional development of teachers and the working environment in schools, were accepted as government policy in February.

The Structure of the Education System

Educational opportunities encompass kindergartens, primary schools, secondary schools (including technical and prevocational schools), technical institutes, and tertiary-level institutions. The great majority of places from primary school upwards are provided either free or at highly subsidised rates. All kindergartens are in the private sector. Other areas with strong private support include international schools and schools providing language, computer and business courses.

All children are required by law to be in full-time education between the ages of six and 15 (or completion of Secondary 3, whichever is earlier).

Pre-school education begins for most children in a kindergarten, at the age of three. Primary school begins normally at the age of six, and lasts for six years. At about 12, children progress to a three-year course of junior secondary education in a grammar, technical or prevocational school. After Secondary 3, most stay on for a two-year senior secondary course, leading to the first public examination, the Hong Kong Certificate of Education Examination (HKCEE). Others join full-time craft courses of vocational training; while a small number choose to leave formal education at this point.

Following the HKCEE, students may progress to a two-year sixth form course leading to the Hong Kong Advanced Level Examination (HKALE); to a two or three-year vocational course leading to a certificate or diploma; or to a three-year course of teacher training. Post-HKALE opportunities include a place on a degree or diploma course, or on a course of teacher training normally lasting two years. Those leaving full-time education at the end of the senior secondary or sixth form courses have opportunities for part-time study or vocational training through to degree level.

Most educational establishments are provided in the public sector, but the government directly manages only a small proportion of primary and secondary schools. Most are operated by non-profit-making voluntary organisations receiving public funds under a code of aid. Tertiary institutions are autonomous statutory bodies which (except for the self-funding Open Learning Institute) receive public funds through the University and Polytechnic Grants Committee (UPGC). A comprehensive system of technical education and vocational training is provided, with public funds, by the statutory Vocational Training Council (VTC).

About 1.2 million students, or 20 per cent of the total population, were in full-time education during the year. They attended 1 946 institutions, and were taught by some 55 000 teachers assisted by a large number of support staff. There were some 140 500 candidates for local public examinations, with a further 204 000 candidate entries for 18 overseas examinations.

The Legislative Framework

Any institution offering education to 20 or more students in a day, or to eight or more students at any one time, must operate in accordance with statutory requirements. The operation of schools (including kindergartens, primary and secondary schools, and commercial colleges) is governed by the Education Ordinance, which provides for the registration of schools, teachers and managers, and for attendance by children between the ages of six and 15. The subsidiary Education Regulations cover a wide range of matters including health and safety, fees and charges, and the qualifications of teachers.

The Post-Secondary Colleges Ordinance covers institutions offering post-secondary courses outside the tertiary sector. The Vocational Training Council Ordinance covers technical colleges, technical institutes, industrial training centres, and skills centres for the disabled. Two important bodies with a quality control role have been established under their own ordinances: the Hong Kong Examinations Authority and the Hong Kong Council for Academic Accreditation. The Education Scholarships Fund Ordinance provides for the administration of a large number of scholarships donated by generous members of the public.

The Government's Role

The Secretary for Education and Manpower heads the Education and Manpower Branch of the Government Secretariat. He is responsible for formulating and reviewing education policies, securing funding in the government budget, liaising with the Legislative Council on educational issues, and overseeing the effective implementation of all education programmes.

The Director of Education is responsible for supervising education at kindergarten, primary and secondary levels. He also supervises institutions registered under the Post-Secondary Colleges Ordinance. He directly controls all government schools, the four colleges of education, the Institute of Language in Education and the Curriculum Development Institute.

The main responsibilities of the Education Department relate to the planning and provision of public sector school places; the allocation of these places to pupils; curriculum development, including the development of a target-oriented curriculum and related assessments; professional training for non-graduate teachers; language education for teachers; monitoring teaching standards; and administering the funding of public sector schools and some private institutions. The department also plays an important role in policy development and review.

Other government agencies with a role in education are the Secretariat of the University and Polytechnic Grants Committee, and the Student Financial Assistance Agency.

Community Participation

Members of the community play an important part in the planning, development and management of the education system at all levels — sitting on advisory bodies such as the Education Commission, Board of Education, Curriculum Development Council, UPGC and Research Grants Council; on executive bodies like the VTC, Hong Kong Examinations Authority and Hong Kong Council for Academic Accreditation; on management committees of schools; and on the governing bodies of tertiary institutions.

The Education Commission

The commission advises the government on the development of the education system as a whole in the light of community needs. Its terms of reference are to define overall objectives; to formulate policies and recommend priorities for implementation, having regard to the resources available; to co-ordinate and monitor the planning and development of education at all levels; and to initiate educational research.

The commission has 15 members, of whom 13, including the chairman, are appointed from outside the government to bring a wide range of personal and professional experience to the issues under review. They include the chairmen of the Board of Education, UPGC, VTC and Advisory Committee on Teacher Education and Qualifications. The two government members are the Secretary for Education and Manpower, who is the vice-chairman, and the Director of Education.

In February, the government accepted as policy the recommendations in the commission's fifth report, and implementation proceeded as planned during the year. Three new bodies recommended in the report were set up: the Committee on Home-School Co-operation, the Provisional Governing Council of the Institute of Education, and the Advisory Committee on Teacher Education and Qualifications. Planning proceeded for the setting up of a fourth body, the Council on Professional Conduct in Education.

Having completed five comprehensive reviews of education policy, the commission considered that further wide-ranging reviews would not be needed in the next few years. Instead, the commission selected three topics for in-depth study: education standards, language proficiency, and the funding of schools.

In September, the government published a policy document, *School Education in Hong Kong: a Statement of Aims*, based on a draft issued by the commission for public consultation in 1992. At the same time, plans were announced for monitoring progress in implementing the aims.

The Board of Education

The board is a statutory body appointed to advise the government, through the Director of Education, on educational matters at school level. Its focus is on the implementation of approved policies, and the need for new or modified policies relating to education in schools. Its members include the chairmen of advisory and executive bodies concerned with the school system: the Curriculum Development Council; the Private Schools Review Committee; and advisory committees on home-school co-operation, school guidance and support services, school administration and finance, and school allocation systems. Other members include a representative of the teaching constituency and persons experienced in kindergartens, special schools, school administration, vocational training, tertiary education, business and the professions. Two government officials sit on the board: the Director of Education as the vice-chairman, and the Deputy Secretary for Education and Manpower.

The Curriculum Development Council

The council is appointed by the Governor to advise the government, through the Director of Education, on curriculum matters. Its members include educators, employers and parents.

During the year, the council continued to consolidate syllabus development, conduct research on curriculum issues, develop school-based curricula and help in developing the Target Oriented Curriculum. Curriculum guides, which aim to ensure that subject syllabuses are developed in compatible directions, were produced for each educational level, and were issued to schools.

Curriculum Development Institute

The institute, set up in 1992 as a new division of the Education Department, is staffed by both civil servants and educationists drawn from outside the civil service. This ensures a regular infusion of new ideas to sustain the creativity and innovation needed for good curriculum development, while enabling the institute to draw on the practical experience of its civil service members.

The institute is responsible for developing curricula and helping schools to implement curriculum policies and innovations. It provides a secretariat for the Curriculum Development Council, and conducts research, experimentation and evaluation in curriculum planning. A major part of its work during the year was to develop the Target Oriented Curriculum (TOC), formerly known as the Teaching Targets and Target-Related Assessment. The TOC is a major and long-term curriculum reform, requiring substantial changes in the approach to teaching and assessment, as well as the commitment and co-operation of all educators. A curriculum framework for the TOC was developed; learning targets for Chinese, English and mathematics were identified; a pilot scheme was conducted in 20 primary schools; and reference and resource materials connected with the TOC were issued to schools. The institute also provided advice and assistance to other schools which were evaluating the TOC in 1993–94.

During the year, the institute issued updated curriculum guides and subject syllabuses, and developed resource materials. Circulars on the teaching of different subjects were issued to secondary schools to suggest ways to make learning more pleasurable and effective, and seminars on this topic were held for teachers. Guidelines on school homework were also issued. To find ways to reduce the weight of school bags, the institute held meetings with publishers' associations to see how textbooks could be made smaller and lighter, and guidelines on school bags were issued to schools.

The institute developed and tested new projects including learning programmes, integration of subjects, curricula for the gifted and the less able, and a modular curriculum. It continued to review textbooks and advise schools on their use. It liaised with the Hong Kong Examinations Authority and teacher training institutions on the development and evaluation of the curriculum.

The University and Polytechnic Grants Committee

The UPGC is appointed by the Governor to advise on the development and funding of higher education, and to administer public grants to tertiary institutions. Its membership is comprised of nine overseas academics, five local academics, and three local professionals and businessmen. No government officials sit on the committee, but its secretariat is staffed by civil servants.

Since 1965, when the then University Grants Committee was set up, full-time equivalent student numbers have multiplied more than 12 times, from 4 100 in two universities to more than 51 000 in seven institutions. These (in order of age as a degree-awarding institution) are the University of Hong Kong, the Chinese University of Hong Kong, Hong Kong Polytechnic, Hong Kong Baptist College, City Polytechnic of Hong Kong, Hong Kong University of Science and Technology, and Lingnan College.

The successful achievement of the planned expansion of tertiary education in the period to 1994–95 depends crucially on recruiting and retaining academic staff of the right calibre. The UPGC provides advice and assistance to the institutions, and is closely monitoring the staffing situation. To help train local students for careers in Hong Kong's tertiary sector, the number of places for postgraduate degrees by research is being increased from about 1 300 in 1991–92 to almost 2 800 in 1994–95.

During the year, the UPGC continued to monitor progress towards a revised structure of tertiary education, based on normative three-year degree courses with admission after completion of the two-year sixth form course. It continued to review the development of higher education in the period 1991–2001, and submitted an interim report describing progress in the expansion and restructuring programme to date, and anticipating the 1995–98 triennium and beyond.

The Research Grants Council

The council advises the government, through the UPGC, on the needs of tertiary institutions for academic research and the funding required, and monitors the use of public research grants. It comprises six locally-based academics, five overseas academics and three local professionals and industrialists. Grant applications are considered by three specialist panels comprising mostly local academics, covering physical sciences and engineering, biology and medicine, and humanities and social sciences. An independent network of academic referees provides impartial advice. In 1993–94, the council disbursed $155.6 million in earmarked grants for academic research projects. Spending is planned to increase to $180 million in 1994–95. The council and the British Council jointly sponsored the United Kingdom-Hong Kong Joint Research Scheme, aimed at strengthening existing links between tertiary institutions in Britain and Hong Kong.

The Vocational Training Council

Established under the Vocational Training Council Ordinance and funded by public subvention, the VTC advises the government on measures to ensure a comprehensive system of technical education and industrial training suited to the developing needs of Hong Kong. It administers technical colleges, technical institutes, industrial training centres and skills centres for the disabled. The VTC also administers the statutory apprenticeship scheme. The council's 23 members include industrialists, academics and government officials.

To ensure that the VTC's advice and operations meet the needs of industry and the service sector, the government has appointed, on the council's advice, 20 training boards and eight general committees with members representing those who employ the graduates of VTC training courses. Each training board is responsible for training in one sector of the economy, such as electronics, textiles and insurance; while general committees are concerned with training relevant to several sectors, such as precision tooling, translation and the training of technologists.

During the year, the VTC completed the building of a new technical college on Tsing Yi Island and the conversion of the former Chai Wan Technical Institute into a second technical college. Both colleges offer higher diploma and higher certificate courses transferred from the polytechnics, as part of the government's plans for expanding tertiary education. They admitted their first students in October. Planning started for a new skills centre at Pok Fu Lam, with a tentative completion date of mid-1996.

The Hong Kong Examinations Authority

The authority is an independent, self-funding and non-profit-making statutory body, with members drawn from the teaching profession, tertiary institutions and the business community. Its main role is to operate two local public examinations — the Hong Kong Certificate of Education Examination (HKCEE) and the Hong Kong Advanced Level Examination (HKALE). It also offers proficiency tests in Putonghua, aimed at adults. On behalf of overseas examining bodies, the authority conducts a large number of examinations leading to academic, professional or practical qualifications.

In 1993, 118 500 candidates entered for the HKCEE, and 22 000 for the HKALE. Candidates for overseas examinations totalled 204 000, of whom 62 500 sat for the London Chamber of Commerce and Industry, 45 800 for the Associated Board of the Royal Schools of Music, and 21 100 for the Test of English as a Foreign Language (TOEFL) examinations.

Among the subjects studied by sixth form students were 17 new advanced supplementary subjects, which will be examined for the first time in 1994. These subjects provide students with a broader sixth form curriculum, which includes two core language subjects: Use of English, and Chinese Language and Culture.

The Hong Kong Council for Academic Accreditation

The council has 22 members, including senior academics from Hong Kong and overseas, and local industrialists and business people. Its activities are administered by a small professional secretariat with expertise and experience in higher education and quality assurance.

The council reviews the non-university degree-awarding institutions and their individual courses, to ensure that the degrees they award meet internationally-recognised standards. On average, about 40 review exercises have been conducted yearly, but this number will be reduced as, during the year, the two polytechnics and Baptist College were granted full responsibility for reviewing their own courses. The council maintains a register of over 1 000 local and overseas academics, and other experts, from which members of institutional review and validation teams are drawn.

Other activities are now taking on a larger role, including the provision of advice to the government and other bodies on the standards of overseas institutions and the status of their awards. To be able to give such advice, and to study and contribute to the development of quality assurance processes in higher education, the council makes and maintains contact with relevant organisations around the world. It has stimulated the creation of an international network of such bodies, for which it provides administrative and editorial support. The year saw significant growth in links with accreditation bodies in China.

During the year, advice was given to the Advisory Committee on Teacher Education and Qualifications on the academic quality and professional relevance of teacher education qualifications; to the Provisional Governing Council of the Institute of Education on academic upgrading; and to professional bodies on accreditation procedures. Seminars and professional development workshops were held on quality assurance in higher education.

School Management Committees

Under the Education Ordinance, a non-government school is run by its own management committee. The committee employs staff, and is responsible for the proper education of the pupils and the operation of the school. One of the managers must be registered as the supervisor, whose main role is to be the point of contact between the management committee and the Education Department.

Each aided primary or secondary school is operated, under a letter of agreement, by its sponsoring body, which contributes the full cost of furnishing and equipping the premises, and nominates the first supervisor of the school. In September, a total of 840 schools were in the care of 377 sponsoring bodies, with a sponsoring body operating as many as 72 schools.

In September, the number of schools joining the School Management Initiative (SMI) rose to 127. The SMI started in 1991 as a scheme to give school management committees in the public sector more decision-making power and more flexibility in the use of resources, in return for more formal procedures for planning, implementing and evaluating their activities. During the year, the SMI Advisory Committee produced school administration manuals and other reference materials. A newsletter was sent regularly to school heads and teachers to keep them informed of developments in the SMI. An SMI exhibition in June attracted 1 500 visitors, and four regional exhibitions were subsequently organised.

Governing Bodies of Tertiary Institutions

Each tertiary institution has its own structure of governance, set out in its ordinance. In all cases, the structure includes a governing body (called the court, the council or the board of governors) and a body to regulate academic affairs (called the senate or the academic board). Some institutions operate under three bodies: a governing body, an executive body and a body dealing with academic affairs.

The Governor is empowered by the ordinances to appoint the chairman of each governing body, as well as a prescribed number of members. This ensures that the governing body has a balanced distribution of members from the industrial, commercial and academic fields.

Funding of Education

Approved public spending on education in the 1993–94 financial year amounted to HK$25,298 million, representing 21 per cent of the government's total recurrent expenditure and five per cent of capital expenditure. Public funds cover about 90 per cent of the capital cost of an aided primary or secondary school, and virtually the full cost of tertiary institution campuses; the entire recurrent cost of providing tuition from Primary 1 to Secondary 3; and about 85 per cent of the recurrent cost from Secondary 4 up to degree level. An unknown, but certainly large, additional sum was spent privately on education.

Non-profit-making kindergartens are eligible for rent and rates reimbursements, and needy parents of kindergarten pupils may apply for fee remission. Private primary schools and pupils receive no public funding, on the grounds that there are sufficient places in the public sector; but some private secondary schools receive public funds under two schemes. Under the Direct Subsidy Scheme, a private secondary school meeting a specified standard may receive a recurrent subsidy related to the cost of an aided school place and the fee charged by the school. A secondary school in the Bought Place Scheme, from which the government buys places to make up shortfalls in government and aided school places, is given financial assistance to raise standards.

The site for an aided school is granted to the sponsor by private treaty at a nominal premium, except when it lies within a Housing Authority estate, in which case the school operates under a tenancy agreement between the sponsor and the authority. International schools meeting specified criteria may also be granted land at a nominal premium.

In January, following three years of development work, consultants delivered a linked series of computer models for the financing of education. These financial models were used by planners to assess the resource implications of different policy scenarios, as an aid to policy formulation.

Student Finance

The Student Financial Assistance Agency administers several financial assistance schemes, which ensure, as far as possible, that students are not denied access to education because of a lack of means. The agency also administers a number of scholarships, which are awarded on the basis of academic merit. These schemes are described below.

Student Travel Subsidy

Students aged between 12 and 25 in full-time study up to first degree level are eligible for a subsidy to cover part of their study-related travel expenses. In the 1992–93 academic year, 168 049 students received assistance totalling $137 million.

Textbook Assistance

Primary and junior secondary students who need help to meet the cost of textbooks and stationery may apply for a grant. In 1992–93, 112 524 students received assistance totalling $36.9 million.

Fee Remission

The Senior Secondary Fee Remission Scheme, which relieves secondary students from Secondary 4 upwards of half or all the standard school fee, helps those in need to continue their education without undue financial strain on their families. In 1992–93, 61 360 students were granted fee remission amounting to $94 million.

The Kindergarten Fee Remission Scheme provides assistance to eligible families, ranging from 25 to 100 per cent of the weighted average of fees charged by non-profit-making kindergartens, or the actual fee, whichever is lower. In 1992–93, $35.74 million was granted to 14 410 kindergarten pupils.

Local Student Finance Scheme

Full-time students in UPGC-funded institutions may apply for means-tested assistance under the Local Student Finance Scheme. This provides for loans to meet living expenses and grants to cover tuition fees, academic expenses and student union fees. In 1992–93, 14 168 students received loans totalling $173 million. Of these, 11 475 also received grants totalling $99.4 million. In the 1993–94 academic year, the scheme was extended to students of sub-degree courses transferred from the polytechnics to the VTC's technical colleges and the Prince Philip Dental Hospital.

Student Finance Assistance Scheme

Loans and grants are awarded to eligible full-time students of the colleges of education and Hong Kong Shue Yan College. In 1992–93, 1 448 students received loans totalling $10.8 million. Of these, 1 428 also received grants totalling $7.1 million.

United Kingdom-Hong Kong Joint Funding Scheme

A joint funding arrangement between the governments of the United Kingdom and Hong Kong provides grants and loans, on a means-tested basis, to full-time students on first degree or higher national diploma courses in the United Kingdom. The grant meets the difference between fees for United Kingdom home students and fees for overseas students. In 1992–93, grants of £4.4 million and loans of $33.4 million were made to 1 836 students. With the expansion of tertiary education in Hong Kong, the scheme will be phased out over three years from 1994–95.

United Kingdom-Hong Kong Scholarships Scheme

This scheme aims to help outstanding students from Hong Kong to pursue tertiary education in the United Kingdom. The scholarship fund is contributed equally by the United Kingdom Government and the Royal Hong Kong Jockey Club on behalf of the Hong Kong Government. Nine scholarships were awarded in 1992–93.

Sir Edward Youde Memorial Fund

The fund was established to manage public donations made in memory of the late Governor, Sir Edward Youde, who passed away in service in 1986. The fund promotes education and learning among Hong Kong people, and encourages research. In 1992–93, $7 million was disbursed. Eleven students were awarded fellowships or scholarships for postgraduate or undergraduate study overseas. Locally, 47 postgraduate research students were awarded fellowships; and 80 undergraduate, diploma and certificate students received scholarships. Awards were also made to four students excelling in public examinations, eight disabled students at secondary, post-secondary and tertiary levels, and 615 outstanding senior secondary students nominated by school heads.

Other Scholarships and Assistance Schemes

In addition to the above, there are other scholarships and assistance schemes for school students, endowed by private benefactors. A large number of scholarships are administered by the Education Department under the Education Scholarships Fund Ordinance.

Schools and Kindergartens

Kindergartens

In September, 187 549 children aged three to five years were enrolled in 730 kindergartens, all of which were privately operated. Kindergartens run on a non-profit-making basis are eligible for rent and rates reimbursements, and may be allocated premises in public housing estates. Most kindergartens operate two half-day sessions, but the number of whole-day places is increasing.

The Education Department gives professional advice to kindergarten managers, teachers, parents and the public. It produces curriculum development materials and runs basic training courses, seminars, workshops and exhibitions to help heads and teachers develop their professional skills. It also publishes guidelines to help teachers organise the curriculum and learning activities.

Primary Schools

Primary schooling, beginning at the age of six and lasting six years, has been provided free of tuition fees in all government schools and in nearly all aided schools since 1971. Although enough places are available in the public sector, about 10 per cent of parents prefer to send their children to private primary schools. Admission to Primary 1 in the public sector is processed through a central allocation system, administered by the department. This has helped to eliminate pressure on children caused by intense competition for entry to popular schools.

Most primary schools operate bi-sessionally. The normal class size in public sector schools is 40. Where classes use the activity approach (a less formal and more pupil-oriented approach to teaching now adopted by 266 schools), the class size is 35. In September, the size of public sector Primary 1 classes was reduced by five places, and this reduction in class size will be extended to higher levels a year at a time.

In September, 485 061 children were enrolled in primary schools. A total of six new school buildings were completed during the year to provide for the growing population in the new towns.

A standard primary school consists of 24 classrooms and three special rooms. A new design was introduced in 1990 to provide more accommodation, needed as a result of changes in education policy. It provides 30 classrooms, four special rooms and three remedial teaching rooms — accommodating 60 classes in two half-day sessions or 30 classes in a whole-day school. These premises can be converted into a secondary school, if necessary, by adding a special room block.

Whole-day schooling for all primary students is a long-term goal. In the meantime, any primary school wishing to convert to whole-day operation is allowed to do so if this will not adversely affect the supply of places in the district. New primary schools operate as whole-day schools wherever possible. During the year, 32 half-day primary schools converted to whole-day operation.

All teaching posts in primary schools are in non-graduate ranks. The standard staffing ratio allows for remedial teaching to help slow-learning pupils, and additional teachers are provided where schools need to operate resource classes for pupils requiring special educational help. Staffing ratios are currently being improved. For whole-day classes, a ratio of 1.4 teachers per class was introduced in 1992. For bi-sessional classes, a phased improvement to 1.3 teachers per class began to be implemented in 1993.

Chinese is the language of instruction in most primary schools, with English taught as a second language. In many schools, Putonghua is taught as either a timetabled subject or an after-school activity. A few schools use English as the language of instruction.

The primary school curriculum aims to provide a broad, balanced and general education, appropriate to the age group and the local environment. A core curriculum including Chinese, English, mathematics, social studies, science, health education, music, physical education, and arts and craft is followed by all primary schools, but other learning programmes may be offered on a cross-curricular basis or as separate, optional, subjects. A new core subject — general studies — is being planned, to integrate social studies, health education and primary science. A syllabus for each core subject is prepared by the Curriculum Development Council, and is regularly revised and updated to meet changing educational and community needs.

During the year, an advisory committee on implementation of the Target Oriented Curriculum (TOC) — comprising school principals, teachers, parents, teacher educators and Education Department officials — was set up to advise the Director of Education. Schools began trying out the TOC in some classes on a voluntary basis, with guidance and support from the department. This helped schools to identify operational problems and prepare for full-scale implementation of the TOC.

The class library scheme provides supplementary reading materials to support classroom learning, encourages the habit of leisure reading, and paves the way for effective use of the library in secondary schools. The annual reading award scheme for Primary 5 and Primary 6 pupils attracted 52 000 pupils from 244 primary schools. A booklet containing the winning book reports was issued to all schools.

At the end of the primary course, students are allocated places in government or aided secondary schools, or offered bought places in private schools. The Secondary School Places Allocation system is based on internal school assessments scaled by a centrally-administered academic aptitude test, and on parental choice. For allocation purposes, the territory is divided into 19 school regions. In the 1993 allocation, 86 069 primary pupils took part. Of these, 75 385 (87.58 per cent) were allocated places in government and aided grammar secondary schools, 4 800 (5.58 per cent) in prevocational schools, and 5 884 (6.84 per cent) in private schools in the Bought Place Scheme.

Secondary Schools

In 1978, universal free education was extended to junior secondary classes. The policy for public sector provision after Secondary 3 is broadly to meet the demand for places on senior secondary or vocational courses. In 1993, the number of subsidised Secondary 4 places was equivalent to 85 per cent of the 15-year-old population, with places for a further 10 per cent on full-time craft courses of vocational training. The target for the sixth form is to provide one public sector Secondary 6 place for every three public sector Secondary 4 places two years earlier.

Secondary 3 leavers are selected for a subsidised place in Secondary 4 or for a vocational course according to internal school assessments and parental preference. The selection process aims to enable as many students as possible to progress to Secondary 4 within the same school. In 1993, 75 968 students took part in the process — of whom 64 491 secured Secondary 4 places in the public sector, and 4 384 were admitted to craft courses.

The Secondary 6 admission procedure aims to match applicants with places until all places are filled. In 1993, all of the 23 190 places available were filled.

To meet provision targets, new secondary schools are built and places are bought from private schools. During the year, nine new secondary schools were completed, providing 10 440 places. Most new schools are built to a new standard design introduced in 1990, which provides more teaching space and better facilities.

There are three main types of secondary school: grammar, technical and prevocational.

In 1993, the 403 grammar schools had a total enrolment of 413 319. These offer a five-year secondary course in a broad range of academic, cultural and practical subjects leading to the HKCEE. Most also offer a two-year sixth form course leading to the HKALE.

The 22 technical schools, which prepare students for the HKCEE with an emphasis on technical and commercial subjects, had an enrolment of 21 736. Qualified candidates can continue their studies in the sixth form or in technical institutes.

The 23 prevocational schools, with an enrolment of 20 880, offer an alternative form of secondary education to students with an aptitude for practical and technical subjects. They provide a solid foundation of general knowledge, and a broad introduction to technical and practical education upon which future vocational training may be based. The curriculum in Secondary 1 to 3 consists of about 40 per cent technical and practical subjects, and 60 per cent general subjects. The technical and practical content is reduced to about 30 per cent in Secondary 4 and 5. Students completing prevocational Secondary 3 may enter an approved apprenticeship scheme, or continue studying to Secondary 5 and take the HKCEE. Qualified students can then proceed either to the sixth form, or to a polytechnic or technical institute.

To improve the quality and diversity of education, the Direct Subsidy Scheme was introduced in 1991 to strengthen the private secondary school sector. Private secondary schools meeting specified standards can receive a government subsidy for each eligible student. They are free to decide on their own curriculum, and to set entrance requirements and fee levels. One more school was admitted in September, bringing the number of such schools to 11.

As part of the same policy package, the Bought Place Scheme will be phased out. Schools in the scheme are being helped to raise their standards so that they may, if they wish, apply to join the Direct Subsidy Scheme. Nineteen private schools were operating under contracts with the government which specify improvements in areas such as whole-day operation, class structure, teacher qualifications and school facilities. The contracts will expire in 2001, unless terminated earlier by either party or when a school joins the new subsidy scheme.

Secondary education is divided into two levels: junior secondary and senior secondary. At the junior secondary level — the final stage in the common core curriculum for the nine years of universal education — the aim is to provide a balanced basic education suitable for all students in the age group, whether or not they continue formal education beyond

Secondary 3. The senior secondary curriculum aims to prepare students for education beyond Secondary 5 as well as for employment, and offers a range of subjects from which schools and students may select according to the needs and interests of the individual, school traditions and the facilities available. Most students sit for the HKCEE at the end of Secondary 5.

Teaching syllabuses are prepared by the Curriculum Development Council for all subjects offered at secondary level, while examination syllabuses for senior secondary subjects are prepared by the Hong Kong Examinations Authority. There is close co-ordination between the two bodies, and syllabuses are kept under review and revised as necessary to meet changing needs. During the year, new syllabuses for additional mathematics, and travel and tourism were developed; and the syllabuses for computer literacy, physics, social studies and typewriting were revised. Travel and tourism, which will be examined in the HKCEE in 1995, was introduced as a pilot scheme in 27 grammar, technical and prevocational schools in September.

Since 1992, all sixth form courses last two years and offer students a broader range of subjects at advanced and advanced supplementary (AS) levels. In September, AS-level music was introduced as a new subject, bringing the number of subjects available to 22 at advanced level and 18 at AS-level. Under the Incentive Award Scheme recommended by the Chinese Textbooks Committee, 10 sets of reference books in Chinese, covering five sixth-form subjects, were published in September with government assistance totalling $9.1 million.

To help teachers implement the new sixth form curriculum, and to make them more familiar with syllabuses, teaching approaches and strategies, the Curriculum Development Institute and the Advisory Inspectorate offered short courses and seminars. The institute conducted a seminar for principals and assistant principals on implementing the new curriculum. The department funded in-service teacher education programmes on individual AS-level subjects, mounted by tertiary institutions.

Some important aspects of education are covered on a cross-curricular basis. They include civic education, moral education, sex education and environmental education. Civic and moral education are promoted through learning opportunities in various subjects and in extra-curricular activities. Sex and AIDS education are also integrated into various subjects at primary and secondary levels, with the aim of helping students to understand sex as part of their overall personal and social development. During the year, teaching resources for sex and AIDS education were developed and issued to schools, and a regular newsletter for teachers was published. Leaflets on AIDS were issued to schools, and a booklet, *Facts About AIDS*, was published to help teachers and parents understand the medical, moral and social issues related to the disease. In December, a teaching kit on AIDS was issued to all primary schools, providing teachers with basic information and suggestions on learning activities suitable for primary school students.

Environmental education is promoted through relevant topics and themes in primary social studies and science; and social studies, integrated science, economics and public affairs, geography, biology, physics and chemistry in secondary schools. Extra-curricular activities also help to raise students' environmental interest and awareness.

The school library service promotes good reading habits, cultivates the ability to study independently, and supports teaching and learning in schools. All public sector secondary schools may appoint a teacher-librarian. In March, an exhibition was held on school library support for curriculum implementation in schools. The annual reading award scheme for secondary students attracted 4 100 participants from 218 schools, and a booklet containing the winning book reports was sent to all schools. A newsletter for school librarians is published regularly.

Chinese and English are both used as mediums of instruction in secondary schools. Some schools use Chinese, some use English, while others use both languages. Following recommendations in the Education Commission's fourth report in 1990, a framework is being established for grouping secondary students according to their ability in the two languages. To help school authorities develop a clear policy on their medium of instruction, they were given information on the language abilities of students entering the school in the past few years. To help parents decide on the most appropriate medium of instruction for their children, they were also given information on the child's language ability.

In government and aided secondary schools, the staffing ratio is 1.3 teachers per class in Secondary 1 to 5, and two teachers per class in the sixth form. Additional teachers are available to strengthen language teaching, provide remedial teaching, careers guidance, counselling, extra-curricular activities and library services; and to offer split-class teaching of such subjects as second languages, domestic science, woodwork, metalwork, computer studies, art and design, and music, as well as some sixth form subjects. The ratio of graduate to non-graduate teachers is about 7:3. The pupil to teacher ratio is about 21:1. In government and aided secondary schools, the class structure provides either six classes each in Secondary 1 to 3, four classes each in Secondary 4 and 5, and two classes in each sixth form year; or five classes each in Secondary 1 to 5, and two in each sixth form year.

Extra-Curricular Activities

Extra-curricular activities are an integral part of school life, complementing and enriching formal learning in the classroom. They are usually conducted outside school hours, in the school premises or elsewhere, under the supervision of teachers. The department provides professional guidance and advice to teachers through in-service training programmes and school inspections, and subsidises some activities. Many inter-school activities are organised or co-ordinated by the department. They include the Community Youth Club, the Duke of Edinburgh's Award Scheme, the Lions Club Sister Schools Scheme, the Music Festival, the Schools Drama Festival, the Schools Dance Festival and sports and recreational activities.

The Community Youth Club aims to build a strong community spirit among students through organised activities. Its motto is 'Learn, Be Concerned and Serve'. Its membership, from 1 127 primary and secondary schools, totals about 121 200. Up to June, 54 236 members had gained awards under the club's Merit Award Scheme. A group of 38 outstanding members visited Singapore during the summer holidays.

To mark the club's 15th anniversary, special activities were arranged. A huge poster made by members was recognised by the Guinness Book of Records as the largest poster in the world. The paper used was sent to schools to be converted into cards, and sent to teachers and parents as a gesture of love and respect. A first day postal cover was released at the end of the year to celebrate the anniversary and raise funds for the Community Chest.

Of the 20 operating authorities of the Duke of Edinburgh's Award Scheme in Hong Kong, the department is the largest, with 22 500 members from 190 participating schools.

Over 115 training courses and functions at bronze, silver and gold levels were organised during the year.

The Lions Club Sister Schools Scheme matches ordinary and special schools, to promote social interaction and friendship among students. During the year, 57 ordinary schools and 46 special schools were made sister schools.

In the 1992–93 academic year, the music festival organised by the Hong Kong Schools Music and Speech Association attracted 72 800 participants from 925 schools, while 61 300 took part in the speech festival. The Schools Dance Festival drew entries from 4 078 students in 228 primary, secondary and special schools. The Schools Drama Festival, organised under the guidance of the School Drama Council, encouraged drama productions involving about 8 400 students from 140 schools. Sporting activities organised by the Hong Kong Schools Sports Association and the New Territories Schools Sports Association attracted over 102 000 participants from more than 1 200 schools. The Inter-Primary School Quiz Competition, a joint venture of the Education Department, Radio Television Hong Kong and the City and New Territories Administration, attracted participants from 27 schools.

Special Education

The main policy objective of special education is to integrate the disabled into the community through the co-ordinated efforts of the government and voluntary agencies.

Early identification is an important preventive measure. Screening and assessment services identify special educational needs among school-age children, so that appropriate follow-up and remedial treatment can be given before problems develop into educational handicaps. Under the combined screening programme, all Primary 1 pupils are given hearing and eyesight tests. Teachers are provided with checklists and guides to help them detect children with speech problems and learning difficulties. Children requiring further assessments are given audiological, speech, psychological or educational assessments at special education services centres, or are referred for ophthalmic advice.

Children identified as having special educational needs are integrated into ordinary schools as far as possible. They are placed in special schools only when their handicaps are such that they cannot benefit from the ordinary school programme. There are altogether 62 special schools (including a hospital school) for children who are blind, deaf, physically handicapped, mentally handicapped, maladjusted, socially deprived, unmotivated, or who have severe learning difficulties. Seventeen schools provide residential places. In addition to teachers, special schools are staffed by specialists such as educational psychologists, therapists and social workers.

Special education classes in ordinary schools cater for partially-sighted and partially-hearing children, and children with learning difficulties. Services for children integrated into ordinary classes include remedial support, based either in special centres or special schools; a peripatetic teaching service; and advice for ordinary teachers on how to cope with handicapped students.

In general, special schools and classes follow the ordinary school curriculum, with adaptations or special syllabuses where appropriate to cater for the varied learning needs of the children. The Curriculum Development Council's special education co-ordinating committee, with members from government departments and schools, advises on special educational needs. Special schools give particular attention to daily living skills, and offer extra-curricular activities to enrich the practical life experiences of day and residential pupils.

During the year, a research project on education for the gifted was commissioned, and planning proceeded for a resource centre for gifted children. Various improvements in services for academically less able pupils also began to be implemented.

International Schools

In keeping with Hong Kong's international character, a number of schools offer curricula designed for the needs of a particular cultural or linguistic group.

The English Schools Foundation (ESF) operates nine primary schools (known as junior schools) and five secondary schools for children whose first language is English; and a special education centre for English-speaking pupils with moderate to severe learning difficulties. The education provided is similar in content and method to that available in Britain, and is aimed at British public examinations. To meet the heavy demand for places on Hong Kong Island, one of the secondary schools operated in temporary premises during the year, pending completion of its new building. The ESF receives public grants based on grants paid to local aided schools, and charges fees to meet additional costs.

Other international schools provide education on the American, Canadian, French, Japanese, Swiss-German and Singaporean patterns. In the school year 1993–94, there were 18 such schools operating up to secondary level, 19 at primary level and 27 kindergartens. Some have received help from the Hong Kong Government in the form of favourable land grants and reimbursement of rates, while some are sponsored by their own governments or communities. Others receive assistance from both sources. Four international secondary schools have joined the Direct Subsidy Scheme.

Teacher Education

Four colleges of education offer full-time, pre-service professional training for non-graduate teachers in primary and secondary schools, as well as in-service initial training for primary, secondary and kindergarten teachers. They also offer refresher courses to acquaint serving teachers in primary and secondary schools with modern teaching methods and approaches, and advanced courses of teacher education for non-graduate secondary school teachers of cultural, practical and technical subjects. Full-time pre-service courses last three years for those with HKCEE qualifications, and two years for those with two A-level passes. In October, 2 315 trainees were on full-time courses and 1 910 were on part-time or short courses.

The University of Hong Kong and the Chinese University of Hong Kong offer post-graduate certificate of education courses for graduates who are, or who wish to become, teachers. They also offer short courses for teachers covering areas like curriculum innovation, development of teaching resources, educational psychology, student guidance and counselling, professional development of teachers, and educational administration. Some Bachelor of Education degree programmes are also offered by the two universities.

The Institute of Language in Education (ILE) offers full-time and part-time language-related courses and seminars for serving teachers of Chinese (including Putonghua) and English; conducts policy-focussed research and development work; provides a resource centre for language teachers; publishes a professional journal, books and newsletters; offers consultancy services on languages in education; and organises an annual international conference. During the year, 672 teachers attended full-time ILE courses, and 908 attended part-time courses. Of these, 137 attended a summer immersion programme in the United Kingdom. The annual international conference in December was jointly organised by the ILE, the Department of Curriculum Studies of the University of Hong Kong and the Hong Kong Association for Applied Linguistics. The conference, on the theme of language and learning, attracted over 300 local and overseas scholars, and more than 100 papers were delivered.

The colleges of education and ILE continued to be run by the Education Department, but planning proceeded to merge and upgrade them into a new autonomous Institute of Education, as recommended in the Education Commission's fifth report. In February, the Governor appointed a Provisional Governing Council to prepare for the creation of the institute in 1994. The institute will initially focus on upgrading its courses at pre-degree level, while planning to develop degree programmes.

Support Services

Teaching and learning in schools is reinforced by a wide range of services, mostly provided or supported by the department.

The Advisory Inspectorate advises schools on curriculum implementation, teaching methodology and educational resources; and offers short courses, seminars and workshops for teachers. Its teaching and resource centres offer resources and advice to kindergarten, primary and secondary teachers in the areas of language; mathematics; science; social and cultural subjects; computer education; technical subjects; civic education; religious, ethical and moral education; sex education and kindergarten teaching.

To strengthen the student guidance service in schools, the department encourages a whole-school approach, which emphasises a caring and positive learning environment and the involvement of all staff in solving students' problems. Its Student Guidance Section provides training in student guidance at primary level, enforces compulsory education, and ensures an adequate provision of study room facilities.

Educational television programmes, produced jointly by the department and Radio Television Hong Kong, are transmitted to schools by two local television stations. Syllabus-based programmes for students in Secondary 1 to 3 cover the Chinese and English languages, mathematics, social studies and science. Programmes for pupils in Primary 3 to 6 include health education.

In April, consultants proposed a five-year plan for developing information systems for schools and the department, covering 11 projects. The proposed computer systems will aim to alleviate the administrative workload of schools, enhance the quality of education services, and improve communication between schools and the department.

The Hong Kong Teachers' Centre, set up in 1989 to promote professionalism and a sense of unity among teachers, is supervised by an advisory management committee with wide representation from schools, teacher organisations and educational bodies; and is staffed by the department. During the year, the centre organised, sponsored or hosted over 700 activities with 50 000 participants. It maintains a professional library and publishes news bulletins.

The department's Educational Research Section conducts research, develops tests, evaluates education programmes and monitors educational standards. During the year, the section developed a new series of standardised Hong Kong Attainment Tests for junior secondary levels in the three core subjects of Chinese, English and Mathematics. These tests are administered yearly by primary and secondary schools, so that they can diagnose areas of strength and weakness in these subjects and provide appropriate guidance, counselling and remedial teaching. The results also help the department to monitor standards across years and levels. Research projects conducted by the section included studies into the continuity of curriculum and teaching practices between the various levels of education, the effects of changing the medium of instruction at junior secondary level, and implementation of the new curriculum for Secondary 6 students.

The 19 district education offices, each headed by a senior education officer, provide advice and assistance to schools, teachers, parents and students; and facilitate communication between this group and the department. District education officers attend district board meetings to assist in discussions of educational matters.

The Careers and Guidance Services Section gives advice and information on educational establishments overseas. During the year, 3 477 students went to study in Britain, 2 828 to Canada, 5 025 to the United States of America, and 3 153 to Australia. Exhibitions promoting overseas education were staged by British, Canadian, American and Australian organisations.

Reduced class sizes and improvements in staffing ratios have increased the demand for qualified primary teachers. To increase the supply of such teachers, a new scheme was introduced, as recommended by the Education Commission, to assess non-graduate teacher qualifications obtained outside Hong Kong. The scheme aims to identify a wider pool of potential teachers and to enable suitable applicants, including those whose degrees were not previously recognised, to become qualified non-graduate teachers once their academic and professional competence has been demonstrated. Applications were invited in February and a series of written, oral, listening and practical tests was held in April and May. Nearly 100 candidates passed.

The Students Division of the Hong Kong Government Office in London maintains close contact with Hong Kong students and encourages them to be young ambassadors, promoting Hong Kong in the United Kingdom. During 1992–93, students in Birmingham, Liverpool, Edinburgh, Nottingham, Loughborough, Swansea, Bradford and London organised successful Hong Kong exhibitions and seminars, which were well attended, both by Hong Kong students and by people who have developed an interest in the territory through the goodwill of its students. The division works closely with the Student Financial Assistance Agency in administering the UK-HK Joint Funding Scheme.

Following the Governor's announcement in October 1992 that all government departments providing services directly to the public would make performance pledges, the department quickly began to draw up pledges. The Director of Education announced these at the end of August. Leaflets were distributed to students, parents, teachers and members of the public. The Board of Education began monitoring the department's performance through an educational services liaison sub-committee.

In preparation for launching the pledges, staff received training in customer service skills. A comprehensive review of all forms was carried out, and about half the forms were eliminated. To provide customers with better information, a 24-hour automatic telephone enquiry system was introduced, attracting over 2 500 calls a day during peak periods. The service environment in many offices was improved, and further improvements were planned.

Technical Education and Industrial Training

A comprehensive system of technical education and industrial training offers school-leavers an alternative to further academic study, and helps to prepare them for specific careers. Publicly-funded technical education is provided through the Vocational Training Council (VTC), which operates two technical colleges and seven technical institutes, and provides industrial training for major industrial and service sectors. Two other training authorities operate levy-funded training schemes for the clothing and construction industries.

The manpower needs of each economic sector are identified by regular manpower surveys conducted by the VTC's training boards and general committees. During the year, 11 sectors were surveyed. Based on survey findings, proposals are formulated for new or modified training courses. Other measures adopted by the VTC and its boards and committees, to help employers meet their needs, include assistance with in-house staff training schemes, organisation of out-centre training courses, the New Technology Training Scheme, training seminars and trade tests, and the preparation of job specifications, trade test guidelines, training curricula, and glossaries of common technical terms.

Technical Education

Technical education at the higher technician level is provided by the VTC's two technical colleges. Disciplines cover applied science, business administration, computing and mathematics, construction, design, electrical and electronic engineering, hotel catering and tourism management, manufacturing engineering and mechanical engineering. The colleges offer full-time higher diploma courses, and higher certificate courses on a part-time day-release or evening basis.

In October, the colleges enrolled 1 468 students on 33 full-time courses. The 43 part-time courses attracted 935 day students and 2 541 evening students.

Technical education at technician and craft levels is provided by the VTC's seven technical institutes. Disciplines cover accounting, chemical technology, child care, clothing technology, commercial studies, computing studies, construction, design, electrical engineering, electronic engineering, environmental studies, hairdressing, hotel-keeping and tourism studies, manufacturing engineering, marine engineering and fabrication, mechanical engineering, motor vehicle enginering, printing and textiles.

Courses leading to a recognised qualification are offered at two levels, with several modes of attendance. Courses for craft apprentices, usually Secondary 3 leavers, are offered on a part-time day-release or block-release basis. At technician level, full-time day, part-time day and part-time evening courses are offered, mostly for Secondary 5 leavers. Most technician courses are validated by the United Kingdom's Business and Technology Education Council (BTEC). Upon their completion, students may register for BTEC awards.

In September, the technical institutes offered 315 courses taught by 818 full-time teaching staff and about 740 supporting staff. Evening courses were delivered by 1 913 part-time lecturers. Enrolment in the 1993–94 academic year totalled 9 000 full-time, 15 300 part-time day and 24 400 evening students. In addition, about 7 000 people in employment attended 208 short courses to upgrade their knowledge and skills.

In July, 4 700 full-time, 5 300 part-time day and 8 600 evening students graduated from the technical institutes. The employment of graduates from full-time courses was surveyed during the year. Findings again showed that graduates were readily recruited, and that most found work relevant to the training they had received.

Industrial Training

The VTC's 24 industrial training centres provide basic training and skills upgrading for industrial craftsmen and technicians, and for clerical and supervisory personnel in the service sector. In 1993, over 40 000 trainees attended full-time or part-time courses. Trade tests for serving employees were offered in six industries — building and civil engineering, the automobile and electrical industries, machine shop and metalworking, plastics and printing. Training boards, in conjunction with educational and training institutions, organised out-centre training courses to upgrade or update serving employees.

The Engineering Graduate Training Scheme, administered by the VTC, helps engineering students and graduates complete the professional training which will gain them recognition by the Hong Kong Institution of Engineers or other professional bodies. In 1993, 80 engineering firms took part in the scheme, which provided 295 training places.

The VTC's Management Development Centre conducts research and development projects, and promotes management training. Its projects include work with owner-managers and entrepreneurial firms, development of learning materials, and activities with management trainers and business executives.

The Clothing Industry Training Authority operates two training centres, funded by a levy on the export value of clothing and footwear. In 1993, about 6 000 trainees attended courses. Jointly with the Hong Kong Productivity Centre, the authority also operated a clothing technology demonstration centre, keeping the industry abreast of the latest technology by demonstrating it in a real-life setting. The Construction Industry Training Authority, funded by a levy on the value of construction works exceeding $1 million, operates three training centres, providing about 4 000 training places. Full-time courses are offered for new craftsmen, operatives and supervisors, and part-time upgrading courses are organised for those already working in the construction industry.

Training in New Technologies

The VTC's Precision Tooling Training Centre houses a training unit for precision sheet metal processing, set up in 1990 with financial and expert technical help from the Japan International Co-operation Agency under an agreement between the governments of Hong Kong and Japan. The unit plays an important part in the transfer of precision sheet metal technology to local industries.

The New Technology Training Scheme provides matching grants to companies wishing to help their staff acquire skills in new technologies. Between the scheme's launch in June 1992 and the end of 1993, 49 applications were approved.

Re-training for Local Workers

A statutory Employees Retraining Board was set up in October 1992 to administer an employees' re-training scheme, in which older workers displaced by economic restructuring are reoriented to new jobs and acquire new skills through specially devised programmes. They receive a training allowance of up to $3,400 per month for attending day courses, and $30 per day for evening courses. By the year's end, 6 900 had been re-trained. The scheme is financed by a government injection of $300 million, and by levies paid by employers who import skilled labour from outside Hong Kong. Various agencies, including the VTC, provide re-training courses, and employers are encouraged to offer on-the-job training.

Apprenticeship Schemes

The Apprenticeship Ordinance governs the training of craftsmen and technicians in 42 designated trades. Anyone aged between 14 and 18, who is employed in one of these trades and has not completed an apprenticeship, must enter into a contract with the employer. This must be registered with the Director of Apprenticeship, who is the executive director of the VTC. Contracts in respect of other trades, or for apprentices aged over 18 years, may be registered voluntarily. An apprenticeship normally lasts three to four years, but qualifications earned before the apprenticeship starts, such as completion of a craft foundation course, may lead to exemption from the first year of the apprenticeship.

The Office of the Director of Appenticeship advises and helps employers of apprentices. Inspectors visit workplaces where apprentices are employed, to ensure that training schemes are properly implemented; help to resolve disputes arising from registered contracts; and ensure that apprentices receive the required technical education on courses at the polytechnics or technical institutes. The office also provides a free apprentice placement service to job-seekers interested in apprentice training. In 1993, 4 266 contracts were registered. Of these, 914 were in non-designated trades. The contracts covered 3 664 craft apprentices and 602 technician apprentices. By the year's end, 8 996 apprentices were being trained.

Vocational Training for the Disabled

Six skills centres, three run by the VTC and three by voluntary agencies, prepare disabled people for open employment or mainstream technical education and industrial training. The centres have a capacity of 840 places, of which 358 are residential.

The VTC also provides support services. The vocational assessment service assesses the potential of the disabled person, and helps in selecting a suitable training programme. Internationally-recognised tests are used, as well as work samples designed to match local industrial skill profiles. All mildly mentally disabled school students undergo a one-week vocational assessment in their final school year. An eight-week programme provides an in-depth assessment of more complex cases.

The Technical Aids and Resource Centre designs and makes technical aids for disabled trainees, students and workers to enhance their training, employment prospects and productivity. It also provides information and resource materials on vocational rehabilitation, which are made available to disabled people and professionals in the field.

An inspectorate unit advises skills centres on administration, curriculum, training methods and standards. It also provides guidance and counselling to disabled students in technical institutes and industrial training centres. The unit works closely with the Labour Department's selective placement service, to ensure that training matches the demand for skills in the local employment market. The annual employment survey of disabled students and trainees completing full-time courses in technical institutes and skills centres showed that about 85 per cent either entered open employment, or were enrolled in mainstream technical education courses.

Tertiary Education

Ten years ago, less than five per cent of the 17–20 years age-group could receive tertiary education in Hong Kong. By 1994–95, this figure will increase to 18 per cent, with 14 500 places available for first-year first degree courses.

Degrees up to doctorate level awarded by local institutions are widely-recognised by institutions of higher learning around the world. Academic standards are guaranteed by the appointment of external examiners from prominent overseas universities and colleges. Degree-level courses at non-university institutions have been subject to external validation by the Hong Kong Council for Academic Accreditation on behalf of the UPGC, but in July the government decided that the two polytechnics and Hong Kong Baptist College should assume responsibility for accrediting their own degree-level courses.

The Tertiary Institutions

The oldest tertiary institution is the University of Hong Kong, founded in 1911. Its 9 631 full-time and 2 760 part-time students are enrolled in nine faculties: arts, architecture, dentistry, education, engineering, law, medicine, science, and social sciences.

The Chinese University of Hong Kong was established in 1963 by bringing together three colleges: New Asia College, founded in 1949; Chung Chi College (1951) and United College (1956). A fourth college, Shaw College, was founded in 1986. The university has 9 428 full-time and 2 185 part-time students in seven faculties: arts, business administration, education, engineering, medicine, science and social sciences.

The Hong Kong Polytechnic, established in 1972, offers postgraduate, first degree and sub-degree courses in six faculties: applied science and textiles; business and information systems; communications; construction and land use; engineering; and health and social studies. Concurrent work and study are encouraged by providing part-time and sandwich courses, and the polytechnic has close links with industry, commerce and the community in general. Enrolment in October was 10 192 on full-time and sandwich courses and 12 252 on part-time courses.

Hong Kong Baptist College was founded in 1956 by the Baptist Convention of Hong Kong. In 1983, it was incorporated under its own ordinance and became fully funded by the government. Since 1986, it has been empowered to award degrees, and all courses are now at first degree level or above. It has 3 813 full-time and 1 159 part-time students in five faculties and schools: arts, business, communications, science and social sciences.

The City Polytechnic of Hong Kong, founded in 1984, has 8 452 full-time, 6 545 part-time and 391 sandwich course students. The four faculties of business, humanities and social sciences, law, and science and technology offer first degree courses, postgraduate diplomas and taught master's degrees, as well as Master of Philosophy and Doctor of Philosophy degrees by research. Diploma and higher diploma courses are offered by the College of Higher Vocational Studies through its divisions of commerce, humanities and social sciences, and technology.

The Hong Kong University of Science and Technology was incorporated in 1988 and admitted its first students in October 1991. Three schools — science, engineering, and business and management — offer first and higher degrees. The fourth school, humanities and social sciences, offers higher degree programmes and provides general education to all undergraduates. In October, the university had 3 120 full-time undergraduate students, 450 full-time postgraduate students and 350 part-time postgraduate students. At its first congregation in October, 66 postgraduate students received the first degrees conferred by the university.

The Open Learning Institute of Hong Kong was established in 1989 to provide adults with more opportunities for higher education through open access and distance learning courses. At its first graduation ceremony in November, 161 graduates received Bachelor's degrees. In October, about 15 000 students were enrolled in degree courses in three schools: science and technology, arts and social sciences, and business and administration. The Centre for Continuing and Community Education began offering sub-degree and short courses early in 1993, and 2 400 students enrolled for such courses during the year. The new School of Education plans to launch a Bachelor of Education degree programme for serving primary school teachers, in association with two other local tertiary institutions. The institute is financially self-supporting but, during the year, the government provided a one-off grant of $150 million towards the cost of building a new campus, and another $100 million for course development. Construction of the institute's permanent headquarters in Ho Man Tin began in October.

Lingnan College was founded in 1967 to continue the tradition of Lingnan University. The college was put under the aegis of the UPGC in 1991, and was incorporated as a degree-awarding institution under its own ordinance in 1992. It has three faculties — arts, business, and social sciences — and a general education division. In October, enrolment was 1 718 full-time students, of whom 853 were pursuing honours degree studies and 865 were honours diploma students. Enrolment is planned to increase to 1 900 by 1994. The college is expected to be relocated at a new campus in Tuen Mun by 1995.

Each institution publishes detailed information about admission criteria, courses, staff and other matters in its annual report, calendar and prospectus, obtainable through the institution's information office.

Post-Secondary Colleges

Shue Yan College, registered in 1976 under the Post Secondary Colleges Ordinance, operates a four-year diploma programme. Its faculties of arts, social sciences and commerce include 13 departments, which offer day and evening courses to 2 787 students. The college receives no public funding, but its students may apply for government grants and loans.

Adult Education

Many formal and informal opportunities are available for adults to study in their spare time, either for personal development or to update knowledge and skills relevant to their work. Numerous private schools offer language, business and computer courses. The British Council, Alliance Française, Goethe Institute and Japanese Consulate all offer language courses.

All tertiary institutions, except the Hong Kong University of Science and Technology and Lingnan College, operate extra-mural departments or divisions of continuing education. They offer a large variety of courses, some at degree level, in such areas as languages, translation, business management and professional development for teachers, social workers and others.

The Education Department provides courses of second chance education for adults at primary and secondary level, and courses of personal development at post-secondary level.

Less formal activities, including hobby and fitness classes, are provided in adult education and recreation centres run by the department. During the year, government subventions supported 397 adult education projects organised by 68 voluntary agencies.

The British Council

The aim of the British Council in Hong Kong is to offer British skills and expertise in the key areas of English language teaching and learning, science and technology, and the arts, to meet the challenge of Hong Kong's changing needs into the next century.

English language teaching is one of the council's major programmes in Hong Kong. Through its general and business English courses, distance learning language programmes with Radio Television Hong Kong, summer schools and teacher training courses, the English Language Centre provided English language learning opportunities for over 42 000 Hong Kong residents in 1993. In addition, the council arranged for 62 trainees and 25 lecturers from the colleges of education to visit the United Kingdom for courses jointly funded with the Education and Manpower Branch.

The council provides access to British expertise to help develop local industry through promoting technology transfer. It works closely with the Industry Department and Hong Kong Polytechnic on the provision of post-experience training. The council also works with the government, higher education and other organisations in areas such as the environment, law, planning, education, medicine and nursing — in some cases through joint academic programmes linking Hong Kong and Britain with China. The annual Science Alive lecture series for young people took place at the Hong Kong Science Museum, with the theme of life, science and technology. In 1993, an annual scholarship in environmental science was awarded, co-funded with the Swire Educational Trust and the Aberdeen University Hong Kong Association.

The council's library and information services are open to all Hong Kong residents and cover all aspects of British life and culture, with an emphasis on English literature and English language teaching. The collections include books, magazines, newspapers, videos, CD-ROM, music on CD and audio tapes. The library facilities are computerised and free to students of the council's English Language Centre. Others are charged a nominal annual subscription.

The Educational Counselling Service provides free and impartial advice to students on educational opportunities in Britain. In 1993, 33 000 students used the service.

11 HEALTH

ACCESS to affordable health care for all is the cornerstone of the government's health policy. The comprehensive range of health services available, together with improvements in the standard of living, have fostered a good general level of health in Hong Kong.

Under an extensive development programme, there was continued progress on the planning and improvement of medical facilities, including public hospitals, general out-patient clinics and specialist out-patient services.

The year 1993 saw an increase of 626 hospital beds, bringing the total number of beds to 27 038 — representing 4.6 beds per thousand population.

New medical landmarks appeared with the opening of the Pamela Youde Nethersole Eastern Hospital and the Hong Kong Eye Hospital.

In addition, the go-ahead was given for the construction of a $1.7 billion, 600-bed hospital for North District, to be completed by 1997.

A special fund of $350 million was set up to provide assistance to haemophiliacs infected with HIV through the transfusion of blood products in Hong Kong prior to 1985, to help finance projects to prevent AIDS and provide medical and support services to those with the virus.

A $50 million grant to the Hospital Authority was also announced, to fund research programmes to assess the cost-effectiveness of new technologies and treatment techniques.

Another highlight was the publication of the consultation document, 'Towards Better Health', in July. The document, which seeks to remove any remediable flaws in the health care system, rationalise the financial structure of public health services and offer possible options for change for the better, generated keen public debate.

In the 1993–94 financial year, $13,823 million in funds was allocated to medical and health services in the public sector, including $12,342 million for the Hospital Authority. In addition, subventions totalling $195 million were provided for other medical institutions and organisations. Capital expenditure on new hospitals and related buildings, including equipment and furniture, was about $1,242 million.

The Organisational Framework

The Department of Health is the government's health adviser and the agency for executing health care policies and statutory functions.

It safeguards the health of the community through a comprehensive programme of promotional, preventive, curative and rehabilitation services. These include personal health services such as out-patient clinics, family health and family planning, health education and community health, territory-wide health services for tuberculosis and chest health, social hygiene, child assessment, clinical genetics, dental health, occupational health, public health and special preventive programmes, environmental health, port health, radiation health, drug addiction treatment, pharmaceutical services and hygiene services.

Through collaboration with the private sector and teaching institutions, the department strives to provide a comprehensive range of primary health care services to the community.

The Hospital Authority is an independent statutory body responsible for the management and control of all public hospitals in Hong Kong.

The authority was established in December 1990 to integrate government and government-assisted hospitals with a view to optimising the use of resources, facilitating hospital management reforms and enhancing community participation. A comprehensive range of medical treatment and rehabilitation services is provided to patients through hospitals, specialist clinics and outreaching services operated by the authority. Since 1992, management reforms have been introduced in most public hospitals, with the emphasis on defining clear lines of accountability and greater devolution of responsibilities.

Of the 27 038 hospital beds in Hong Kong, 23 165 are in public hospitals under the Hospital Authority, 2 927 are in private hospitals and 131 in institutions under the Department of Health.

In November, 6 493 doctors were registered with the Hong Kong Medical Council — 2 749 in the public sector and 3 744 in the private sector. The number of nurses registered with the Hong Kong Nursing Board was 33 361.

Health of the Community

The health of the population compares favourably with that of developed countries. The infant mortality rate remains at five per 1 000 live births. The average life expectancy at birth is 81 years for females and 75 years for males.

Cancers, heart diseases and cerebrovascular diseases (strokes) continued to be the leading causes of death during the year, accounting for 30 per cent, 16 per cent and 10 per cent, respectively, of the mortalities in the territory. These diseases generally affect older people. Given the continual ageing of the population, it is anticipated that they will remain prominent in the near future.

Communicable diseases are well under control. In 1993, there were 30 sporadic cases of cholera, 13 being imported cases and 17 local cases. There were 6 537 notifications of tuberculosis, with a notification rate of 110 per 100 000 population. The number of notified hepatitis A cases dropped to 860 compared to 3 626 in 1992.

To protect the population from infectious diseases, children in Hong Kong are immunised against nine infectious diseases at an early age. These are tuberculosis, diphtheria, pertussis, poliomyelitis, tetanus, hepatitis B, measles, mumps and rubella. The average coverage for primary school children is 99 per cent. As a result of the high coverage of immunisation, diphtheria and poliomyelitis have been virtually eradicated from the territory and the incidences of other diseases among children are kept at low levels.

HIV Infection and AIDS

The menace of HIV (Human Immunodeficiency Virus) infection and AIDS (Acquired Immunodeficiency Syndrome) is increasing worldwide, in particular in Asian countries

With no cure for AIDS and no effective vaccine against infection, HIV continues to pose a serious threat.

In 1993, 79 cases of HIV infection were reported, an increase of 11 per cent compared with the previous year. This brought to 416 the total number of such cases reported since the beginning of the surveillance programme in April 1985. Nineteen new patients with AIDS were reported in 1993, giving a cumulative total of 92 patients, of whom 63 have died.

In April, the Finance Committee of the Legislative Council approved the allocation of $350 million to set up a special fund to provide assistance to those infected with HIV, through transfusion of blood or blood products in Hong Kong prior to August 1985. This manifested the government's commitment to respond with speed and compassion to those in need. The AIDS Trust Fund is administered by a council which is appointed by the Governor. The council also gives support to projects which augment the medical and support services provided by the government, and to publicity and public education which aim to enhance awareness of AIDS prevention and to remove discrimination against HIV-infected persons.

The Advisory Council on AIDS also plays a key role. The council operates through three committees — the Committee on Education and Publicity on AIDS, the Scientific Committee on AIDS and the AIDS Services Development Committee. The Committee on Education and Publicity on AIDS helps to promote community involvement in AIDS education; sustain public awareness; co-ordinate the training of intermediaries to provide education and counselling; foster support towards HIV-infected individuals; and co-ordinate activities for target groups such as students, youth, drug abusers, and others practising high-risk behaviour. To achieve these objectives, working groups have been formed under the committee. The Scientific Committee on AIDS is concerned with the technical aspects of the AIDS programme. It concentrates on the production of comprehensive guidelines for the prevention of HIV transmission in health care settings, oversees HIV surveillance programmes, undertakes quality assurance programmes on HIV antibody testing and carries out studies and scientific research projects. The AIDS Services Development Committee was established in 1993 to advise the government on the development of clinical and support services for HIV-infected individuals. Secretarial and operational support to the three committees is provided by the Department of Health.

The department's AIDS Unit provides counselling and medical consultation for persons at risk of HIV infection. Members of the public can use a special telephone hotline (780 2211) to obtain advice in confidence. This service was upgraded by the incorporation of an interactive voice-processing system in April. Other hotlines using pre-recorded messages in Putonghua, Thai, Tagalog and Vietnamese languages became operational in July.

The AIDS Unit regularly arranges talks, exhibitions, seminars and other educational programmes for community groups. Blood tests may be arranged under conditions of complete anonymity. Publicity materials, notably television advertisements, were produced with the support of the Information Services Department.

The Hong Kong AIDS Foundation and AIDS Concern are two non-government organisations which supplement and complement the government's efforts. Activities include counselling, publicity and education, as well as patient support services.

Primary Health Care

Primary health care, which emphasises the promotion of general health and prevention of disease, is recognised worldwide as the most cost-effective means to provide health care services.

The Working Party on Primary Health Care, whose report was endorsed by the government in 1991, made 102 recommendations to improve primary health care services. The key recommendations are being implemented in phases. These include improvements to over 50 general out-patient clinics, the establishment of a well-woman clinic and preventive health programmes for the elderly. A feasibility study for a Clinic Operations Support System, which looked into improvement of the health information system and computerisation of the department's general out-patient clinics, was completed in 1993.

Training in family medicine is a priority area for improvement. Vocational training opportunities were offered in training centres, universities and hospitals. A series of lectures and clinical attachments were arranged for doctors keen to improve the quality of their service by participating in continuing medical education activities.

District Health System

The District Health System, an organisational framework for the delivery of primary health care services, involves the decentralisation of services from the regional to the district level, and public involvement in service planning and health promotion. It attaches importance to the need for efficient co-ordination among the various providers of medical and health services and community participation.

A pilot District Health System programme was initiated in 1992 in Kwun Tong. The six government health institutions in the district were organised into a network for better co-ordination and were administered by a multi-disciplinary district management committee with wide clinic representation. To facilitate co-ordination among the health institutions, other community service providers and the public, a multi-sectoral district health committee was set up with members drawn from the health and other sectors. Its functions include provision of a forum for information exchange and enhancing the role of the community in the identification of health needs.

During 1993, a Healthy Lifestyle campaign was launched at Telford Gardens. A pilot scheme was introduced with the district hospital on joint care for diabetic patients to enhance the interface between primary care and secondary care and to provide better continuity of care for chronic disease patients. A patient liaison group was established to facilitate communications with clinic customers, who also assisted in monitoring the performance pledge of clinics. Another pilot scheme to train volunteers for the district-based diabetic support group involving multi-sectoral collaboration was initiated and is being implemented in phases. Progress towards integration of the general out-patient service and the family health service within the district was made. At the end of the year, an evaluation of the pilot programme was underway.

Hospitals and Development Programmes

Public hospitals provide low-charge services which are easily accessible to the community.

During the year, the demand for hospital services remained high, as reflected by the large number of hospital admissions, and attendances at out-patient and specialist clinics, and accident and emergency departments.

A total of 745 000 patients were treated in public hospitals, while there were 4 622 680 attendances at specialist clinics.

The accident and emergency departments of major public hospitals, which handle cases of acute illness and accident casualties free of charge, saw 1 342 080 attendances — an average of 3 677 per day.

Projects in the hospital development programme progressed satisfactorily.

The 1 620-bed Pamela Youde Nethersole Eastern Hospital in Chai Wan opened in October. At the end of the year, 244 beds were in operation.

The Hong Kong Eye Hospital opened in Mongkok in September and is the first hospital of its kind offering a full range of care and treatment for eye patients in the territory. Reorganised from what was previously the Argyle Street Ophthalmic Centre, it offers specialist ophthalmology services at both the secondary and tertiary referral levels.

The number of beds available at Tuen Mun Hospital, which opened in 1990, increased to 1 175 at the end of the year. The hospital will provide a total of 1 606 beds upon full operation.

The year also saw the reopening of Siu Lam Hospital to provide 300 beds for mentally handicapped patients.

The first cancer centre is being built at the Prince of Wales Hospital to conduct multi-disciplinary cancer research, diagnosis, treatment, counselling and public education.

New or additional services are being progressively introduced at Tuen Mun Hospital, Queen Mary Hospital Extension, Ruttonjee Hospital, Shatin Cheshire Home, Shatin Hospital and Yan Chai Hospital.

Major projects under construction include the extension of the United Christian Hospital, refurbishment and air-conditioning of Queen Elizabeth Hospital, extension and refurbishment of Princess Margaret Hospital, construction of the 618-bed North District Hospital, redevelopment of Haven of Hope Hospital and Castle Peak Hospital, relocation of Nethersole Hospital to Tai Po, extension of the out-patient department of Kwong Wah Hospital, establishment of a geriatric day hospital at Wong Tai Sin Hospital, and construction of the Tai Po Infirmary and Convalescent Hospital.

Clinics

General out-patient services form a vital part of the health care system. The government operates 66 general out-patient clinics. In the more densely-populated areas with higher demand, evening, Sunday and public holiday sessions are also provided. Total attendances came to 10.4 million in 1993. To cater for increasing demand, 10 additional clinic projects have been included in the medical development programme for the next decade.

Mobile dispensaries and floating clinics provide the necessary medical services to remote areas of the New Territories and outlying islands. Other inaccessible areas are visited regularly by the flying doctor service, with the assistance of the Government Flying Service.

Registered medical practitioners belonging to the Estate Doctors' Association run clinics in housing estates to provide a low-cost service for residents. Private medical practitioners continue to attend to the majority of out-patients.

At the end of the year, a total of 89 clinics were operated by various charity organisations registered under the Medical Clinics Ordinance and 139 were registered as exempted clinics.

Performance Pledge

The Department of Health has set performance pledges with the aim of improving the delivery of services to the public and developing a more customer-oriented culture of service. Phase I of the programme covered 15 general out-patient clinics starting from December 1992. Phase II extended the programme to another 13 clinics from August 1993.

Improvements achieved included the use of medical records and patient-held records to enhance continuity of care, shortened waiting times, labelling of all dispensed medicine, a better clinic environment, health education and counselling by nurses.

Family Health

The Family Health Service of the department operates 47 maternal and child health centres, providing a comprehensive health programme for women of child-bearing age and children aged below six years. Ante-natal and post-natal medical consultation, as well as family planning services, are offered to women. Immunisation, child health advice and physical examinations are provided for children. During the year, about 92 per cent of newborn babies attended maternal and child health centres.

Under the Comprehensive Observation Service, children are assessed at different ages for early detection of developmental abnormalities. They are referred to specialist clinics or child assessment centres for further examination, as necessary.

There are four government (and one government-assisted) child assessment centres. These provide comprehensive physical, psychological and social assessment as well as treatment, parental counselling and referrals for the appropriate placement of children in the various institutions and centres run by the government and voluntary agencies. Three more centres have been included in the department's medical development programme.

Health education is an essential component of the Family Health Service. In addition to health talks and counselling on child care at centres, health education for expectant mothers has been extended to public hospitals, with emphasis on the promotion of breast-feeding. A telephone service is available to answer public enquiries.

The government-subvented Family Planning Association of Hong Kong runs 22 birth control clinics, providing services such as pre-marital counselling, contraception, sterilisation, vasectomy and advice on sub-fertility. It also provides health education and publicity on family planning and sex education.

Medical Care for the Elderly

The provision of hospital facilities for acute geriatric cases has been made an urgent priority. The government announced that by 1997, an additional 461 acute beds and day-places would be provided for elderly patients, bringing the total to 1 735.

A network of nursing homes with medical and nursing facilities is also being developed for elderly patients who would otherwise have to remain in hospital or in an infirmary. By 1997, an initial seven nursing homes providing 1 400 beds at a capital cost of about $800 million will be in operation.

In 1994–95, a total of six new specialist medical teams will be formed to provide health care, assessment and rehabilitation services for a total of 55 700 elderly people.

School Health

The School Medical Service Scheme is operated by an independent School Medical Service Board. Participation is voluntary and all students from Primary 1 to Form 3 of the participating schools can join the scheme by paying a token fee of $20 a year. At the end of 1993, more than 335 900 children from 1 114 schools participated in the scheme — representing about 45 per cent of the eligible school population — and about 516 general medical practitioners had enlisted. Since November, a student pays $18 for a consultation at the chosen medical practitioner's office. The government contributes $136 a year for each pupil enrolled and also bears the administrative cost.

A new Student Health Service, with emphasis on health promotion, disease prevention and continuity of care, will replace the existing School Medical Service. Preparations for its implementation are underway.

The school health service also deals with the environmental health and sanitation of school premises, and the control of communicable diseases. School health officers, health nurses and health inspectors make regular inspections of schools to advise on matters concerning the health of children, and organise health education activities and immunisation campaigns.

Port Health

The Port Health Service is the control authority for preventing the entry of quarantinable diseases into Hong Kong by air, land or sea. It enforces the measures stipulated under the Quarantine and Prevention of Disease Ordinance and the International Health Regulations.

A 24-hour health clearance service is provided for all incoming vessels, including those ferrying refugees, and radio pratiques are granted to ships. The service provides vaccination facilities and issues international vaccination certificates. It inspects and supervises the eradication of rats from ships on international voyages and ensures adequate standards of hygiene and sanitation on board vessels or aircraft. The service also provides medical assistance to ships and aircraft within the territory, and gives medical advice to vessels at sea.

The food catering service for international airlines is kept under close surveillance by its health staff, to ensure that food and water supplied to flight kitchens are clean and safe. The hygiene and sanitation of the airport is also covered.

The service regularly exchanges epidemiological information with the World Health Organisation in Geneva and its Western Pacific Regional Office in Manila, as well as with neighbouring countries.

Occupational Health

The Occupational Health Service of the department provides an advisory service to the government and the public on matters concerning the health of workers and the hygiene of workplaces. It also supervises the observance of occupational health standards and practices. The objectives of the service are to maintain and improve the physical and mental well-being of workers, to protect them against any health hazards arising from employment and to help them adjust to their jobs. The emphasis is on occupational disease prevention and health promotion.

In 1993, the service continued to participate in occupational health activities organised to promote public awareness of the importance of health at work. With the assistance of the Occupational Safety and Health Council as a co-organiser, the service also organised a week-long, large-scale exhibition and a seminar on occupational health in the office environment in October.

The Expert Working Group on Occupational Health Services, which was established by the Director of Health in December 1991 to improve the provision of occupational health services in Hong Kong, submitted its report in September 1992. Of its 39 recommendations, some 30 have been implemented or are at various stages of implementation through redeployment of staff, improving work systems and procedures, and mobilising resources from non-government agencies such as the Occupational Safety and Health Council, the universities and the Pneumoconiosis Compensation Fund Board. These recommendations included, among other things, the setting up of an occupational health clinic — the first of its kind — in Kwun Tong. The clinic opened on November 30 to provide the working population with a new specialised service specifically for the consultation, treatment and investigation of work-related diseases.

Dental Services

The School Dental Service aims to promote dental health among primary school children. Services include regular dental examinations, treatment and oral health education. Participation is voluntary at an annual fee of $20 per child. In the 1993–94 school year, 385 938 children from 954 schools participated, representing 80 per cent of the primary school population.

A pilot Youth Dental Care Programme was launched in 1993. It aimed to transfer primary six school-leavers from the existing School Dental Service to a private practice-based dental programme in their secondary school years. The pilot scheme was carried out in Tuen Mun and Yuen Long in collaboration with the Hong Kong Dental Association, involving a target of 9 765 primary six students and over 50 dentists working in the area.

The department's Oral Health Education Unit organises oral health education activities for the community. In February, the unit launched a pilot three-year education programme for 400 000 pre-school children. Plans are also in hand to procure and outfit an education bus for wide dissemination of oral health messages throughout Hong Kong.

A pilot scheme began operating at the Tuen Mun Hospital Dental Unit on August 1 to provide comprehensive dental treatment for patients classified under the special need group.

The Government Dental Service provides emergency treatment for the public at a number of district dental clinics. Dental treatment is also provided for patients in public hospitals and inmates of correctional institutions.

Services for the Mentally Ill and Mentally Handicapped

Medical services for mentally ill persons include treatment in hospitals, outpatient clinics and day hospitals, and outreaching services. The Hospital Authority, in conjunction with various government departments and non-government organisations, provides a comprehensive psychiatric service for the territory. Emphasis is placed on continuity of care and integrating rehabilitation with medical treatment.

At the end of 1993, 3 322 beds were provided in psychiatric hospitals, and 1 157 beds in public psychiatric units of general hospitals. An additional 1 510 beds are being planned for psychiatric patients in public hospitals by the year 2000. Psychiatric patients are treated, as far as possible, in the community. The community work and aftercare units of the psychiatric hospitals provide multi-disciplinary assistance to discharged patients. The community psychiatric nursing service and domiciliary occupational therapy service, in particular, aim to provide continual care and treatment programmes for discharged mental patients in their home settings — in this way assisting in their social readjustment, and educating patients as well as their families on mental health. Three community psychogeriatric teams have been set up to provide designated care and rehabilitation programmes to psychogeriatric patients. There are 11 Community Psychiatric Nursing Service centres. Other complementary rehabilitative services include day-centres, half-way houses, long-stay care homes, vocational training, selective placement and social clubs, run by government departments and non-government organisations.

Severely mentally handicapped persons requiring intensive nursing care and rehabilitation services are cared for at Tuen Mun Hospital (which offers 204 beds), Caritas Medical Centre (300 beds), the Duchess of Kent Children's Hospital (25 beds) and the re-opened Siu Lam Hospital (300 beds).

The Castle Peak Hospital is being redeveloped to provide a better physical environment, as well as medical treatment and rehabilitation, for psychiatric patients.

Support Services

The Pathology Service of the Department of Health provides both clinical and public health laboratory services for government clinics and some public hospitals.

The Forensic Pathology Service, with its forensic laboratory, works closely with the Royal Hong Kong Police on the medical aspects of criminology and other medico-legal work. It also performs investigations in all homicides and coroners' inquests.

The Virus Unit is the central laboratory for the diagnosis and surveillance of viral infections, including HIV infections. It provides laboratory support for the screening, assessment and guidance of vaccination programmes against viral diseases.

The Institute of Immunology undertakes the monitoring and quality control of biological products, including vaccines for use in local health services.

The Central Neonatal Screening Laboratory co-ordinates the laboratory activities of the territory-wide neonatal screening programme on congenital hypothyroidism and glucose-6-phosphate-dehydrogenase deficiency.

The Pharmaceutical Service provides pharmaceutical services to all government clinics. It also deals with the inspection and licensing of pharmaceutical manufacturers and dealers, and the registration and import-export control of pharmaceutical products and medicines. Action is taken against the illegal sale and distribution of pharmaceutical products and medicines. In 1993, there were 75 prosecutions.

Radiation Health

Regular visits are made by the staff of the Radiation Health Unit to medical, commercial and industrial premises to inspect the working conditions of people working with radiation. The unit issues radiation licences to proprietors in accordance with the Radiation Ordinance and Regulations and operates a centralised radiation monitoring service for all occupationally-exposed individuals. It also assists in the Environmental Radiation Monitoring Programme organised by the Royal Observatory to monitor the changes in background radiation levels in Hong Kong.

Community Nursing Service

The Community Nursing Service of the Hospital Authority provides rehabilitative nursing care and treatment to the sick, the elderly infirm and the disabled, in their own homes. The service is provided through a network of eight hospital stations and 40 satellite centres. During the year, 19 439 patients were served and 277 335 home visits were made.

Health Education

The Central Health Education Unit of the Department of Health is responsible for the planning, organisation and promotion of health education activities. In 1993, it focussed on the prevention of communicable diseases such as hepatitis A and diarrhoeal diseases, organ donation, mental health, self-care and prevention of cancer, among other areas.

The theme of the major health education campaign for the year was 'Treasure Life, Prevent Injury'. A series of programmes — including a 24-hour, pre-recorded telephone information service, competitions for students and the public, and health news — was arranged. An exhibition was also held in October.

Special training courses were arranged for students and teachers, notably the 14th Young Health Leaders' Training Course in July. Health talks and presentations were delivered to schools, voluntary agencies, private companies and government departments. Health education materials, such as pamphlets, cassettes, slides, videos and exhibits, were produced for distribution or loan. Selected video titles have been on sale since July.

A new health education centre in Tsuen Wan was opened in August to improve services for the region.

Close liaison is maintained with both government and non-government organisations in promoting health education activities.

Smoking and Health

The Hong Kong Council on Smoking and Health is an independent statutory body, established in 1987 to acquire and disseminate information on the health hazards of using tobacco products, and to advise the government on matters relating to smoking and health. During the year, the council conducted publicity campaigns with particular emphasis on discouraging young people from smoking. Its volunteer anti-smoking ambassadors also travelled around Hong Kong, reminding passengers that smoking has been prohibited in all forms of public transport since 1992.

Following a public consultation exercise, the government announced a package of new anti-smoking proposals in September. These will extend existing requirements for health warnings on cigarette packaging and advertising to cigars and pipe tobacco; prohibit the sale (or giving for the purpose of promotion) of tobacco products to persons under the age of 18; and require all restaurants to display a sign stating whether they have a no-smoking area. Legislation giving effect to these proposals is expected to be introduced in 1994.

Medical Charges

The government is committed to the policy that no one should be denied adequate medical treatment through lack of means. Medical charges remain low, reflecting a substantial subsidy from public funds.

Patients in general wards of public hospitals are charged $43 a day and the fee covers everything from meals, medicine and tests, to surgery or any other treatment required. The charge may be reduced or waived in cases of hardship certified by a medical social worker. A limited number of private beds are provided at major public hospitals with higher maintenance and treatment charges.

The charge for a consultation at general out-patient clinics is $21, while that at specialist clinics is $33. Charges for physiotherapy, occupational therapy and child assessment services are $33 per session. Attendances at geriatric or psychiatric day centres and home visits by community nurses cost $34 per session. These fees may also be waived if warranted.

The charge for injections and dressings in general out-patient clinics is $9, while charges for visits to family planning clinics and methadone clinics remain at $1.

Free medical services continued to be offered at maternal and child health centres, tuberculosis and chest clinics, social hygiene clinics, and accident and emergency departments.

Towards Better Health

The consultation document, 'Towards Better Health', which was published in July, included discussion of various health care reforms. It attracted 494 submissions from the public during the four-month consultation period, which ended in October.

The government, in issuing the document, wished to ensure that the existing policy — that no-one should be denied adequate medical treatment through lack of means — remained paramount. It also wished to ensure that a balance was struck between the provision of services and level of subsidy for these services.

Increased accessibility to health services in the form of reduced waiting times, better services and more choice; simpler administration and improved efficiency were also targets behind the document.

Training of Medical and Health Personnel

Basic training of doctors is provided by the University of Hong Kong and the Chinese University of Hong Kong. Graduates of the two medical schools are awarded degrees which are recognised by the General Medical Council of Great Britain. The medical student intake in 1993 was 165 at the University of Hong Kong and 167 at the Chinese University of Hong Kong.

Under the Licentiate Scheme of the Hong Kong Medical Council, 25 externally-trained doctors passed the local licentiate examination in 1993. After satisfactory completion of an externship programme in public hospitals, they will become registered medical practitioners.

The Hong Kong Academy of Medicine, which is an independent statutory body with the authority to approve, assess and accredit all post-internship medical training, was inaugurated in December.

Basic training for nurses is provided in 16 Hospital Authority nursing schools. Eleven schools provide training programmes for registration and five provide programmes for enrolment. Among the 16 schools, three provide both registration and enrolment programmes. The total number of trainees recruited in 1993 was 1 561, including 1 041 student nurses and 520 pupil nurses. There are also three private nursing schools, which had an intake of 61 student nurses and 111 pupil nurses during the year.

Training in dentistry is available at the University of Hong Kong, which produced its ninth group of 33 graduates in January 1993. Training of dental therapists is provided at the Tang Shiu Kin Dental Therapists Training School.

The departments of diagnostic sciences, rehabilitation sciences and health sciences of the Hong Kong Polytechnic provide training for para-medical and para-dental staff, including radiographers, optometrists, physiotherapists, occupational therapists, medical laboratory technicians and dental technicians. Training for speech therapists and pharmacists is provided by the University of Hong Kong and the Chinese University of Hong Kong. Both universities offer masters degree courses in the training of clinical psychologists. The Sha Tin Technical Institute, of the Technical Education and Industrial Training Department, provides training for dispensers which is complemented by in-service training. There is also in-service training for prosthetists, mould laboratory technicians and therapeutic radiographers in the respective units of public institutions. Where local training is not yet available, government training scholarship programmes are offered. These cover the supply of audiologists, audiological technicians, orthoptists and chiropodists. There are also opportunities for overseas training in specialised areas for medical, nursing, para-medical and para-dental staff.

School of Public Health Nursing

The School of Public Health Nursing, under the Public Health Nursing Division, provides full-time and part-time public health nursing training programmes for the professional development of nurses in the Department of Health. Its main training programme is a nine-month, full-time course which leads to a diploma in public health nursing studies for registered nurses.

The school's new premises at Lam Tin Polyclinic in Kwun Tong were officially opened in January. With its expanded facilities and additional staff, the school will double its yearly student intake of public health nursing students to 60 for the full-time course.

Government Laboratory

The Government Laboratory provides a wide range of chemical testing services to government departments, and other institutions, for the protection of public health. This includes the provision of analytical and advisory services on environmental protection. The laboratory has statutory responsibilities for testing under a number of ordinances and regulations.

During the year, food products were regularly tested for composition, additives, toxic residues and contaminants. Services were rendered to the Department of Health, Urban Services Department and Regional Services Department in cases of food-related complaints and suspected food poisoning.

Pharmaceutical products, for use in hospitals managed by the Hospital Authority and public clinics, were tested for compliance with pharmacopoeia or other specifications. Products intended for use and sale locally were examined for compliance with registration and labelling requirements. Herbal medicines were checked for the presence of synthetic drugs and toxic metals.

A product safety laboratory was set up to undertake testing of toys and children's products for compliance with safety standards and specifications under the Toys and Children's Products Safety Ordinance, which was enacted in November 1992. Before the ordinance came into operation in July 1993, a project was conducted with the Consumer Council to test toys supplied locally.

Examination of a wide range of commodities submitted by the Customs and Excise Department continued. These included dutiable commodities tested for duty assessment purposes, weighing equipment for compliance with the Weights and Measures Ordinance, suspected forged commodities for identification, gold and platinum articles for fineness determination, and jade suspected of being resin-impregnated for differentiation.

The laboratory also provided analytical and advisory services to the Fire Services Department, in relation to the storage, carriage and classification of dangerous goods. A round-the-clock service was available to assist fire services personnel at scenes of emergencies involving hazardous chemicals.

Drug Abuse and Trafficking

The government's policy is to stop the illicit trafficking of drugs into and through Hong Kong; to develop a comprehensive treatment and rehabilitation programme for drug abusers; and to dissuade people, particularly young people, from experimenting with drugs, to eradicate drug abuse from the community.

Data collected by the government's Central Registry of Drug Abuse in 1993, based on 36 000 reports on 17 000 persons, indicated that 91 per cent of drug abusers were male and nine per cent female. Fifty-nine per cent of the reported individuals were aged over 30 years, 27 per cent were in the 21 to 30 bracket and 14 per cent were aged under 21 years.

The most common drug of abuse was heroin, which was used by 93 per cent of the persons reported to the registry. In the case of young persons aged below 21 years, the common drugs of abuse included heroin, cannabis and cough medicines.

A total of 4 000 drug abusers came to the notice of the registry for the first time in 1993. Of the new cases, 83 per cent were male and 17 per cent were female. Most of them, or 73 per cent, were within the age bracket of 16 to 30. The drugs reported to be commonly abused by these new cases were again heroin, cannabis and cough medicines.

Overall Strategy and Co-ordination

The government has a comprehensive anti-drug programme which has achieved considerable success. The programme adopts a four-pronged approach — law enforcement, treatment and rehabilitation, preventive education and publicity, and international co-operation. Effective law enforcement induces abusers to seek treatment voluntarily, as a result of short supply of drugs. Treatment and rehabilitation are undertaken by the government and a number of voluntary agencies which offer a wide range of facilities to meet the different needs of drug abusers from varying backgrounds. The effectiveness of these treatment programmes reduces the demand for illicit drugs. At the same time, the government places great emphasis on preventive education and publicity to heighten public awareness of the drug problem and to promote the advantages of a drug-free lifestyle. Co-operation at the international level, through exchange of information and experience, and joint action against illicit trafficking, enhances the effectiveness of efforts in these areas.

These efforts are co-ordinated by the Action Committee Against Narcotics (ACAN), a non-statutory body which includes both non-official and government members. The committee is the government's advisory body on all anti-drug policies and actions, including those undertaken by non-government agencies. It is serviced by the Narcotics Division, which is headed by the Commissioner for Narcotics.

Legislation and Law Enforcement

The major anti-drug laws are the Dangerous Drugs Ordinance, which prohibits trafficking, possession, unlawful manufacture and consumption of dangerous drugs; the Pharmacy and

Poisons Ordinance, which provides for controls over pharmaceutical products; and the Acetylating Substances (Control) Ordinance, which controls the use of the main precursors in the manufacture of heroin. The Drug Trafficking (Recovery of Proceeds) Ordinance provides for the confiscation of the proceeds of drug trafficking and the countering of drug money-laundering in Hong Kong.

The Royal Hong Kong Police and the Customs and Excise Department seized some 230 kilogrammes of heroin, 590 kilogrammes of cannabis and 20 kilogrammes of cocaine during the year. Following joint operations with overseas law enforcement agencies, a number of international drug trafficking syndicates were neutralised, with substantial quantities of dangerous drugs seized and ringleaders arrested locally and abroad. In 1993, police and customs action resulted in the arrest of 12 100 persons for drug offences.

Treatment and Rehabilitation

The voluntary Methadone Treatment Programme, operated by the Department of Health in 23 clinics, provides both maintenance and detoxification for out-patients. Methadone maintenance aims to reduce or eliminate an abuser's reliance on opiate drugs, while the detoxification programme aims to eliminate dependence on drugs. The programme has proved to be very effective in serving both drug abusers and the community.

The largest voluntary in-patient treatment programme is run by the Society for the Aid and Rehabilitation of Drug Abusers (SARDA), which operates an in-patient treatment centre for up to 380 men on the island of Shek Kwu Chau, and one for up to 39 women at Sha Tin. Linked to these centres are four regional social service centres, five halfway houses, a job skills training laboratory and a clinic which provides pre-admission medical examination, counselling and detoxification services, urine analysis and post-discharge medical care.

A compulsory in-patient treatment programme is operated by the Correctional Services Department under the Drug Addiction Treatment Centres Ordinance. Its drug addiction treatment centres accommodate 784 men on the island of Hei Ling Chau, and 100 women at Tai Lam Chung and Tai Tam Gap. The treatment ranges from two to 12 months, the actual period being determined by the inmate's progress and the likelihood of continued abstinence from drugs following release. All persons discharged are given one year of statutory aftercare.

In 1993, the two voluntary treatment programmes and the Correctional Services Department's compulsory treatment programme admitted 14 200 abusers. On average, 11 000 drug abusers and ex-drug abusers were receiving some form of treatment, rehabilitation or aftercare every day.

The counselling centre, PS33, set up in Tsim Sha Tsui in 1988 to provide counselling and telephone advice for psychotropic substance abusers, handled 144 cases and 1 455 telephone and 'drop-in' enquiries during the year. PS33 is operated by the Hong Kong Christian Service, with financial support from the Social Welfare Department.

Preventive Education and Publicity

The government and the community continued to promote anti-drug preventive education and publicity. The anti-drug publicity campaign in 1993 focussed on encouraging young people to adopt a healthy lifestyle and to say 'no' to all drugs; and reminding them of the legal consequences of drug-related offences. At the same time, parents were reminded of their responsibility to guide their children away from drugs.

Eight district campaigns were held, involving the community through carnivals, variety shows, competitions and exhibitions.

The Narcotics Division's school talk team gave 242 drug education talks to 83 000 students in 226 primary and secondary schools and technical institutes. Starting from September, drug education talks using different approaches were extended to Primary 6 students. Apart from school students, talks were also organised for members of youth organisations, parents, and juvenile offenders at the boys' and girls' homes operated by the Social Welfare Department.

To better equip prospective teachers and social workers for the fight against drug abuse, a series of drug education workshops were organised for students of the four colleges of education and a territory-wide seminar was held for social workers. A seminar for private medical practitioners was also organised to appeal for their support in reporting drug abuse cases.

In support of the annual International Day Against Drug Abuse and Illicit Trafficking, a large-scale exhibition was held in Sha Tin in June. The anti-drug message 'Say NO to Drugs' was also applied as a post mark on all mail for two weeks in June.

The Community Against Drugs Scheme continued to provide encouragement to interest groups to plan and implement their own anti-drug education and publicity projects. Under the scheme, financial support of up to $5,000 is granted for each project. The 75-member ACAN Youth Volunteer Group took part in district campaigns and organised a number of community involvement projects. The ACAN Youth Advisory Group, comprising a cross-section of young people, advised on educational and publicity materials and activities.

The ACAN Drug Abuse Telephone Enquiry Service was enhanced and automated in February, providing information on 12 types of commonly abused substances. Information on treatment facilities was also available. A total of 370 000 calls were received during the year.

International Action

Hong Kong continued to play an active international role, maintaining close links with the United Nations, inter-governmental agencies such as the Financial Action Task Force, Interpol and the Customs Co-operation Council, as well as with individual governments. The territory took part in 34 regional and international meetings and seminars concerned with anti-drug policies, law enforcement, treatment and rehabilitation, and preventive education.

The techniques and methods employed in Hong Kong have made it an important venue for training anti-drug personnel from overseas. During the year, 306 people from 19 countries and international bodies came to the territory on study visits and training courses.

As at the end of the year, bilateral agreements had been concluded with 11 foreign jurisdictions with a view to enhancing international co-operation, particularly with regard to the tracing and confiscation of the proceeds of drug trafficking.

Auxiliary Medical Services

The Auxiliary Medical Services (AMS), formed in 1950, is a disciplined medical civil defence corps. Its primary mission is to provide supplementary resources to augment regular medical and health services in times of natural disasters and emergencies.

The AMS had an establishment of over 5 200 volunteer members at the end of the year. They comprised physicians, nurses, pharmacists, dispensers, radiographers, paramedical personnel, civil servants and laymen in the private sector.

By statutory requirement, the Director of Health is the Commissioner and Unit Controller of the AMS. Assisted by a number of Deputy and Assistant Commissioners appointed on a voluntary basis, he is responsible to the Governor for the efficient operation of the corps.

Volunteer members receive comprehensive training as and where necessary in areas covering first-aid, squad drill, basic ambulance aid and practical ambulance manning, casualty evacuation, home nursing, clinical and hospital ward attachment, life-saving, leadership and management development. In November, an expert from Australia was commissioned to conduct training courses on disaster medicine for volunteer members who are medical and nursing professionals, to enhance their operational efficiency and effectiveness.

During emergencies, volunteer members would be deployed and supplied with the necessary medical resources to provide immediate first-aid treatment for the injured at the disaster scene, to convey casualties to hospitals, to render nursing care to patients at both acute and convalescent hospitals and to work in collaboration with other rescue forces.

If paramedical assistance is required, the AMS Emergency Response Task Force would be available at short notice. Medical officers, nurses and trained members of the force are equipped to provide nursing aid, minor surgery and other life-saving measures on the spot.

Apart from being in full readiness to perform emergency roles and functions, the AMS is committed to providing supplementary medical services to government departments and outside agencies for ambulance manning; lifeguard duties; clinical services in methadone clinics and refugee camps; and first-aid coverage at country parks, cycling tracks, school activities and major public functions.

During the year, the AMS continued to assist in the daily manning of 23 methadone clinics and to provide round-the-clock clinical manning at eight sick bays in five Vietnamese boat people centres. More than 681 966 man-hours were committed to operational tasks.

The AMS also provides first-aid training to frontline civil servants. A total of 4 050 government officers completed the basic first-aid certificate course and qualified as first-aiders in 1993 under this training scheme.

Environmental Hygiene

The Urban Council and Regional Council are responsible for environmental hygiene. Working under the two councils, respectively, the Urban Services Department and the Regional Services Department are responsible for street cleaning, collection and removal of refuse and nightsoil, the cleansing of gullies, management of public toilets and bathhouses, pest control and services for the dead.

A workforce of about 8 199 people is employed in cleansing duties, deploying a fleet of 583 specialised vehicles which include refuse collection vehicles, street-washers, mechanical sweepers, nightsoil collectors and gully emptiers.

Streets are swept, either manually or mechanically, from up to six times a day for busy thoroughfares to once every second day for village lanes. Streets and lanes are also hosed down when local conditions warrant. Hawker areas and refuse collection points are washed regularly.

There are 2 640 refuse collection points in the territory, with 1 466 bin sites in the New Territories. During the year, four permanent off-street refuse collection points were completed in the urban area. Two are in Mong Kok District, at Mong Kok Road and Bedford Road. The refuse collection point at Third Street, in Western District, was funded by the Land Development Corporation. The one at Hok Yuen Street, in Kowloon City District, is equipped with a water scrubber system, a much more effective de-odourising ventilation system than that used previously. The new system is now the standard for all other refuse collection points currently under construction or under planning. Refuse collection vehicles, equipped with compacting devices, call at refuse collection points up to three times daily to convey refuse to transfer stations and an incinerator for disposal.

About 5 204 tonnes of refuse and junk are collected daily, including 124 tonnes removed from outlying islands by a contractual barging service. Desludging services are provided free for public aqua privies and septic tanks. This service is provided for private facilities on a charge basis upon request. A daily nightsoil collection service is also provided free of charge to areas without a water-borne sewage system.

In a further effort to improve environmental hygiene, the Regional Services Department started night collection of market refuse in Tai Po and Sai Kung in May. This service will be extended in phases to other districts upon the commissioning of more refuse transfer stations.

Eleven public toilets were renovated under the Urban Council's public toilet refurbishment programme. The programme aims to provide well-lit, clean and well-managed public conveniences. A total of 37 toilets have been refurbished over the past three years and the programme will continue until all old-style toilets have been modernised.

The two departments continued to contract-out some of the cleansing services to private contractors, to reduce the direct involvement of departmental labour and enhance cost-effectiveness. In the urban area, the contracts covered 201 public toilets and bathhouses; and manual street-sweeping of Tai Kok Tsui, part of Wan Chai, and two squatter villages. The waste collection service in Tai Po township was contracted-out for a period of five years commencing in May. Meanwhile, the contracting-out of street cleansing was introduced in Kwai Tsing, and extended to Tsuen Wan, Yuen Long, Tai Po and Sha Tin in July. This was followed by the contracting-out of cleansing in remote areas in Sai Kung in September. The overall exercise brought significant savings and enabled the Regional Council to retrench some 530 staff. The performance of the contractors is closely monitored by supervisory staff.

The Regional Services Department commissioned two market research companies to conduct opinion surveys in areas where street cleansing was newly contracted-out, before and after the commencement of contracts. With the findings of the surveys as general guidelines, further proposals for the contracting-out of refuse collection and street cleansing will be explored.

During the year, the Keep Hong Kong Clean Campaign, organised by the Joint Urban Council/Regional Council Keep Hong Kong Clean Steering Committee, marked its 21st anniversary. In order to spread the 'keep clean' message throughout the year, the steering committee mounted a six-phase clean-up programme, covering the environment; water areas; roads; homes; squatter areas and villages; and the countryside and country parks. The campaign focussed on direct community involvement, education, and publicity through the media. The steering committee also introduced a Keep Hong Kong Clean Activities Funding Scheme. Under the scheme, voluntary agencies, local organisations and schools were encouraged to organise clean-up activities and apply to the two municipal councils for subsidies.

Law enforcement remained a major weapon against litter offenders. During the year, 36 766 litterbugs were fined a total of $11.9 million.

Controls

Staff of the two municipal services departments enforce the Public Health and Municipal Services Ordinance to ensure that standards of hygiene are maintained. The staff regularly inspect licensed and permitted premises, common parts of buildings, squatter areas, construction sites and undeveloped land. They respond to complaints about sanitary nuisances and vermin infestation.

For the prevention of vector-borne diseases, pest control staff carry out integrated programmes to control rodents, mosquitoes, flies and other public health pests. Measures taken included environmental improvement, eradication of breeding places, health education and law enforcement. Special surveillance is maintained to prevent outbreaks of malaria in Vietnamese migrant centres. Technical support is provided by the Pest Control Advisory Section of the Department of Health.

Environmental Health Education

The Health Education Unit of the Hygiene Division of the Department of Health promotes environmental health through education on a territory-wide basis. Under the auspices of the two municipal councils, the unit launched a number of educational campaigns in 1993. The most notable were the Environment and Health Drive held early in the year, and the Food Hygiene Campaign organised during the summer for members of the food trade and school teachers.

Publicity campaigns directed at the prevention of rodent infestation and nuisances caused by mosquitoes and dripping air-conditioners, as well as the promotion of good personal habits, were also staged during the year. Apart from talks and hotline services provided by the unit, health messages were disseminated through the mass media. Public health materials, including posters and leaflets, were also distributed to the general public at the unit's resource centre.

Food Hygiene

The health inspectorate of the Hygiene Division of the Department of Health, backed by a hygiene consultant, controls both imported and locally-produced food for sale. Supported by laboratory resources and assisted by a scientific advisory arm, the inspectorate ensures that consumers are able to buy good, wholesome food which is unadulterated, uncontaminated, properly described and of nutritious quality.

Food samples are taken regularly for chemical analyses, bacteriological examinations and toxicity tests to ascertain their fitness for human consumption. For the purpose of sampling for laboratory testing, food items are prioritised according to the nature of the food and the risks that they may pose to consumers. Complementary to regular laboratory analyses, field tests for pesticide residues are performed on imported vegetables at the points of entry into Hong Kong.

The growing number of food establishments, and the quantities and variety of food items available have increased the importance of law enforcement. Parallel to this is the increasing demand for services for health certification of foods for export and re-export.

The review of food legislation has been an on-going exercise with a view to ensuring that laws are consistent with international standards, guidelines and recommendations based on scientific evidence. This is important in order to provide a high standard of public health protection and to facilitate international trade in foods.

On the international scene, Hong Kong maintains close ties with the World Health Organisation, the Food and Agriculture Organisation of the United Nations and other international authoritative bodies on foods. As the bulk of the local food supply comes from China, the territory works closely with the Chinese authorities to promote food safety and better food hygiene. Regular meetings are held with officials from the Guangdong and Shenzhen Commodities Inspection Bureaux.

Food Premises

The Urban Services Department has categorised licensed food premises in the urban area into different grades according to their standards of hygiene. Its frequency of inspections is determined by the grades of the premises, to better utilise manpower and resources.

The department continued to adopt a demerit points system for suspension or cancellation of food business licences or permits in order to deter breaches of licensing and hygiene regulations. The system is regularly reviewed to ensure its effectiveness.

To assist applicants for restaurant licences and to better co-ordinate inter-departmental efforts, a central vetting panel was set up. It advises the applicants in the early stages whether the intended premises are suitable for licensed restaurants. The panel also gives initial advice on steps and actions to be taken to meet the licensing requirements.

The Regional Services Department continued to exercise strict control over food premises which failed to apply for a licence or which had not complied with the specified requirements. The weekly prosecution of repeated offenders has had the effect of dramatically reducing the number of unlicensed food businesses.

The two departments also work closely with the Department of Health in the investigation and control of food-poisoning outbreaks, substandard foods and infectious diseases.

Markets

The Urban Council operated 62 retail markets in the urban area in 1993. In these markets, 10 108 stalls offered commodities ranging from fresh food to household items.

Old and outdated markets have been gradually replaced by multi-purpose complexes managed by the council. The 16 existing complexes house new markets and cooked food centres on the lower floors, while the upper floors provide a variety of facilities for indoor sports activities, cultural and recreational pursuits. New markets with cooked food centres are built to meet not only hawker resiting commitments, but consumer demand.

The Electric Road Complex was opened to the public in March. The redevelopment of Tai Shing Street Market in Wong Tai Sin District was undertaken jointly with the Hong Kong Housing Society in late 1993, as part of the latter's redevelopment scheme for Kai Tak Estate. Also earmarked for redevelopment is Sai Ying Pun Market in Western District. To prepare for this, the renovation of Centre Street Market was completed to provide temporary accommodation for the stall lessees of Sai Ying Pun Market. Improvement works to the existing To Kwa Wan Market in Kowloon City District started. The works include the provision of air-conditioning for the cooked food centre. The cooked food centre at Sai Wan Ho Market was also under renovation for installation of air-conditioning. If the air-conditioning scheme proves successful and cost-effective, consideration will be given to extending it to other existing cooked food centres.

A scheme for contracting-out cleansing operations has been implemented in 28 markets in the urban area — 18 on Hong Kong Island and 10 in Kowloon. A pilot scheme was introduced for markets in the New Territories, at Sha Tin Market, Plover Cove Road Market and Tung Yick Market, in November. If successful, the scheme will be extended to other markets in future.

The Regional Council is responsible for the management of public markets in the New Territories. In 1993, a new market with 35 stalls was commissioned at Mui Wo. This brought the number of markets managed by the council to 47 — providing a total of 5 257 market stalls and 278 cooked food stalls. Another new air-conditioned market with 365 market stalls and 28 cooked food stalls is under construction at Shek Wu Hui and is scheduled for completion in mid–1994.

During the year, the council continued to improve its existing markets. Minor improvement works were carried out in nine markets nominated by the council's district committees. Sha Tin Market was identified as a pilot scheme for implementing long-term measures, including improvements to toilets, drainage, lighting and ventilation.

Other improvements are in the pipeline. The council's Working Group on Management of Markets has concluded a review on market policy and related management matters, and a report will be submitted to the council in early 1994.

Hawkers

The Urban Council is responsible for the licensing of street hawkers in the urban area while the Regional Council is responsible for their management in the New Territories. At the end of December 1993, there were 13 606 licensed hawkers in the territory — 780 less than in 1992. The decrease was due to a policy of not issuing or allowing succession of itinerant hawker licences, and to the resiting of on-street hawkers into new markets. The completion of the Java Road Market, Wong Nai Chung Market, Electric Road Market and Ap Lei Chau West Industrial Area Cooked Food Market in 1993 made it possible to resite 210 licensed hawkers formerly trading in the vicinity.

The Urban Council's policy of eventually eliminating itinerant hawker licences was announced in March. Itinerant hawker licences will cease to exist in April 1996. Until then, licence holders are offered the option of surrendering their licences in exchange for either an *ex gratia* payment at the revised rate of $30,000, a fixed-pitch hawker licence, or a market stall tenancy. By the end of 1993, 640 itinerant hawker licences had been surrendered under this policy.

Following the recommendations of the council's Working Party on Hawker and Related Policies, efforts have been made to relax the issue of hawker licences to a limited extent. About 263 fixed-pitch newspaper hawker licences have been issued. The issue of other licences will depend on the availability of suitable sites.

The report of a Regional Council working group tasked to examine the legislation, policies and operational strategies against illegal hawking and illegal shop extensions was presented in June. Some of the report's 36 recommendations have already been implemented.

Control over on-street trading is maintained by the municipal councils through the deployment of general duties teams, comprising 2 977 civilian staff trained in law enforcement. During the year, the teams secured 125 980 court convictions for hawking offences and helped to reduce the number of unlicensed hawkers to 7 641, a drop of 739 compared to the year before.

Abattoirs

There are two abattoirs in the urban areas and three slaughterhouses in the New Territories, including a new one on Cheung Chau which also serves the nearby islands. With the exception of Cheung Sha Wan Abattoir, which is run by the Urban Council, all the others are managed by licensed private operators. To meet long-term demand, a site has been reserved for a new slaughterhouse in Sheung Shui.

During the year, these abattoirs and slaughterhouses handled 3 437 915 pigs, 171 259 head of cattle and 18 514 goats, which accounted for virtually all of the local fresh meat supply. To ensure the wholesomeness of the meat, all slaughtered animals were inspected by qualified health inspectors of the municipal services departments.

The two departments also maintain vigilance against illegal slaughtering. In 1993, health inspectors carried out 40 raids on suspected illegal slaughterhouses, and two offenders were successfully prosecuted. Staff also carried out spot checks on meat stalls and 20 persons were prosecuted for possessing unstamped carcasses for sale.

Cemeteries and Crematoria

It is government policy to encourage cremation, rather than burial, of the dead. During the year, over 68 per cent of the territory's dead were cremated. Human remains buried in public cemeteries have to be exhumed after six years and are either cremated or re-interred in an urn cemetery.

The Urban Council operates one public funeral parlour in Kowloon which provides free funeral services for the needy. Two service halls at the parlour are also open for public use free-of-charge.

In the urban area, the council manages five public cemeteries and two public crematoria, and monitors 18 private cemeteries. Two war cemeteries are under the management of the Commonwealth War Graves Commission.

Additional cremators and columbaria are under construction at Cape Collinson Crematorium to cater for the increasing demand for cremation.

The Regional Council manages six public cemeteries and four public crematoria in the New Territories. It also oversees nine private cemeteries and six private crematoria.

Columbaria managed by the council are provided at Kwai Chung, Fu Shan, Cheung Chau, Wo Hop Shek, Lamma and Peng Chau for the deposit of cremated ashes.

12
SOCIAL WELFARE

HONG KONG, as a society, cares deeply about the welfare of its citizens. To achieve targets for the protection of the disadvantaged, spending on social welfare in 1993–94 was increased by 25 per cent to $7,963 million. This followed a government pledge to increase recurrent spending on social welfare by 26 per cent in real terms by 1997. To secure funding for major improvements during that period, a capital injection of $2.3 billion was made into the Lotteries Fund.

The Director of Social Welfare is responsible for carrying out government policies on social security and social welfare, based on the objectives set out in three White Papers — *Integrating the Disabled into the Community: A United Effort (1977), Primary Education and Pre-primary Services (1981), and Social Welfare into the 1990s and Beyond (1991).*

The government is advised on social welfare policy by two committees — the Social Welfare Advisory Committee, covering the whole area of social welfare, and the Rehabilitation Development Co-ordinating Committee, on matters of rehabilitation. Members of these committees are appointed by the Governor, with non-officials as chairmen.

In the provision of welfare services, the Social Welfare Department maintains a close working partnership with non-governmental organisations, most of which are affiliated to the Hong Kong Council of Social Service. A list of the council's member agencies is shown in Appendix 32.

During the year under review, five new nurseries, 15 small group homes, 240 foster care places, nine home help teams, 16 family aides and 60 places of integrated programme in child care centres were established. Two combined children and youth centres were also established through reprovisioning of existing centres. For the elderly, a further 1 061 meal and care-and-attention places, 11 social centres, three day care centres, two multi-service centres and a holiday centre were set up. For the disabled, three new sheltered workshops, five day activity centres, seven hostels, two care and attention homes for severely disabled persons and 17 places in supported housing were established. A total of two outreaching service teams for the elderly at risk and four outreaching social work teams were set up. Eight extra family life education workers and 18 school social workers were made available.

A thorough overhaul of the social security system was undertaken and a Comprehensive Social Security Assistance Scheme was introduced on July 1 to improve means-tested benefits. The package provides, as a consolidated sum, income support for the special needs of particular groups who formerly received assistance under two separate schemes, the Public Assistance Scheme and the Special Needs Allowance Scheme. The rates of benefits were increased between four per cent and 37 per cent for different groups of beneficiaries.

The Protection of Women and Juveniles (Amendment) Ordinance 1993 was enacted in April. Among other things, it aims at widening the circumstances in which a child may be considered to be in need of care or protection, and providing the Director of Social Welfare with more flexible powers of intervention and investigation. The amendment ordinance was implemented on November 1 under the name of the Protection of Children and Juveniles Ordinance (Cap. 213).

Co-ordinated efforts from multi-disciplinary professionals and various government departments are needed to tackle the problems of young people at risk, child abuse, teenage suicide, drug abuse, triad influence and premature sexual involvement, which have attracted considerable public concern. The Coordinating Committee for the Welfare of Children and Youth at Risk was appointed in April under the chairmanship of the Secretary for Health and Welfare to co-ordinate services and advise on policy directions. Under this committee, two working groups — the Working Group on Child Abuse and the Working Group on Services for Youth at Risk — were established under the chairmanship of the Director of Social Welfare in mid-1993 to examine the wide range of issues related to the problems and welfare of children and young people.

Taking into account the changed needs of young people, the Secretary for Health and Welfare appointed a working party in 1992 to review the services provided by children and youth centres. The working party produced a draft report in June 1993, proposing, *inter alia*, that an integrated model should be adopted in providing services for young people. Public views were invited and a final report was submitted for policy consideration in late 1993.

Community Chest

The Community Chest, which organises and co-ordinates fund-raising activities for its member agencies, raised $145 million in 1992–93, compared with $132 million in 1991–92. More details about the Community Chest are given at Appendix 32.

Social Security

Social security is a major social welfare programme aimed at meeting the needs of vulnerable groups in the community requiring financial or material assistance. The Comprehensive Social Security Assistance Scheme and Social Security Allowance Scheme are the key elements in the non-contributory social security system. They are supplemented by three other schemes: the Criminal and Law Enforcement Injuries Compensation Scheme, the Traffic Accident Victims Assistance Scheme and Emergency Relief.

Comprehensive social security assistance, which is means-tested, provides cash assistance to those in need. It is designed to raise the income of needy individuals and families to a level where essential requirements are met. Persons who have resided in Hong Kong for not less than one year may be eligible if their income and other resources are below the prescribed levels. But an able-bodied unemployed person aged between 15 and 59, who is available for work, is required to register with the Labour Department for job placement to qualify for assistance.

Under the pre-July scheme, public assistance payments used to comprise four components: basic allowance, rent allowance, supplements and special grants. Essential needs such as food, clothing, fuel and light were met by the basic allowance. Rates of the basic allowance were increased across-the-board by nine per cent, in April, to keep pace with inflation. The eligibility criteria under the two schemes remain the same.

The Comprehensive Social Security Assistance Scheme is built on three simple components: a range of standard rates for different categories of applicant, rent and special grants to meet individual needs. Depending on the needs of the applicant, the monthly standard rates range between $1,035 to $2,835 for a single adult; $1,260 to $3,055 for a single child; $895 to $2,570 for an adult family member; and $995 to $2,795 for a child in the family. To cover the cost of accommodation, a separate allowance is paid. Those who have received comprehensive social security assistance continuously for 12 months are given an annual long-term supplement to enable them to meet the cost of replacing household wares and durable goods: $1,145 for a single person; $2,290 for a family with two to four members; and $3,435 for a family with five or more members. In addition, special grants are given, where necessary, to meet other needs such as school fees, travel or special diets. To encourage self-help, an individual's monthly earnings of up to $775 may be disregarded in the calculation of assistance payable.

At the end of 1993, the number of comprehensive social security assistance cases was 92 000, compared with 79 700 public assistance cases in 1992. The majority of recipients were the elderly, the disabled and single parent families. Expenditure on comprehensive social security assistance during the year amounted to $2,073.8 million, representing an increase of 54.9 per cent from the previous year.

The Social Security Allowance Scheme, which replaced the Special Needs Allowance Scheme on July 1, provides flat-rate allowances for the severely disabled and the elderly. Any person who is certified to be severely disabled and who has resided continuously in Hong Kong for at least one year immediately before application, is eligible for a disability allowance. To be eligible for an old age allowance, a person must have resided in Hong Kong for at least five years since the age of 60.

Under the new scheme, persons receiving comprehensive social security assistance would be no longer eligible to apply for these payments. Their level of benefits will, however, be maintained under the new arrangements.

The allowances were revised upwards by nine per cent in April 1993 to reflect the rise in the cost of living.

A higher disability allowance, which is twice the normal rate, is payable to severely disabled persons who require constant attendance from others in their daily life but are not receiving such care in a government or subvented institution. The current monthly rate for the disability allowance is $900 and, for the higher disability allowance, $1,800. The allowance is non-means-tested.

Old age allowance is also non-means-tested for those aged 70 and above, and they are entitled to $510 per month. For those aged 65 to 69, the monthly allowance is set at $450, subject to a declaration that income and assets do not exceed the prescribed levels.

The number of people receiving disability and old age allowances at the end of the year was 468 600, compared with 501 200 at the end of 1992. Expenditure on social security allowances during the year was $3,051.9 million, representing an increase of 6.7 per cent over the previous year.

The Criminal and Law Enforcement Injuries Compensation Scheme provides cash assistance to people who are injured in crimes of violence or while helping to prevent crime in Hong Kong. It also extends compensation to those injured by law enforcement officers using weapons in the execution of their duties. Payments are made to their surviving dependent family members in the case of persons killed in any one of these circumstances.

This scheme, which is non-means-tested, is administered by the Criminal Injuries Compensation Board and the Law Enforcement Injuries Compensation Board. Both boards consist of the same chairman and members, who are appointed by the Governor, from outside the civil service. The secretariat to the board is provided by the Social Welfare Department, which is also responsible for the assessment and payment of compensation.

During the year, total payments amounted to $9.3 million, compared with $9.0 million in the preceding year.

The Traffic Accident Victims Assistance Scheme is a no-fault and non-means-tested scheme. It provides cash payments to victims of traffic accidents or their dependants. It is administered by the Director of Social Welfare in consultation with an advisory committee.

For a person to be eligible, the accident must be within the definition of the Traffic Accident Victims (Assistance Fund) Ordinance and must have been reported to the police. The application must be lodged within six months of the date of the accident. For an injury case, the victim must be medically certified to require at least three days' sick leave. Payments cover personal injury and death but not damage to property.

Under the scheme, an applicant retains his right to claim legal damages or compensation from other sources for the same accident. In case of a successful claim, he is required to refund either the payment received from the scheme or the amount of damages or compensation, whichever is the less.

During the year, 5 850 applications were received and 5 270 were approved for assistance, with payments totalling $89 million compared with $69 million in 1992.

Emergency relief is provided to victims of natural or other disasters in the form of material aid such as hot meals, eating utensils and other essential articles. Grants from the Emergency Relief Fund are also paid to disaster victims or their dependants to relieve hardship arising from personal injury or death.

During the year, emergency relief was given to 1 721 registered victims on 83 occasions. The Social Welfare Department also assisted in providing hot meals to refugees and boat people from Vietnam.

Aside from burial grants, the rates of grants payable under the Criminal and Law Enforcement Injuries Compensation Scheme, the Traffic Accident Victims Assistance Scheme and the Emergency Relief Fund were increased in September 1993 to cover the rise in living costs.

To prevent abuse of the various schemes, a special team investigates cases of suspected fraud or difficulties encountered in recovery of overpayment. During the year, the team completed investigations into 74 cases.

Social Security Appeal Board

The Social Security Appeal Board is an independent body comprising non-official members appointed by the Governor. It considers appeals from individuals against decisions by the Social Welfare Department concerning comprehensive social security assistance, social security allowance and traffic accident victims assistance payments. During the year, 145 appeals were heard by the board. Of these, 10 related to the comprehensive social security assistance, 131 to the social security allowance and four to the traffic accident victims assistance.

Services for Offenders

The Social Welfare Department has several statutory duties in the field of services for offenders. These duties are to put into effect the directions of the courts on the treatment of offenders through social work methods. The overall objective is to rehabilitate offenders through probation supervision, the Community Service Orders Scheme, residential training for young offenders and after-care services with the aim of reintegrating the offenders into the community.

A probation service is provided in 11 probation offices which serve 10 magistracies, the District Courts and the High Courts. Probation officers make inquiries into the background and home surroundings of offenders, as the court may direct, and of prisoners for consideration of sentence reduction. They also supervise offenders in complying with the requirements of probation orders. Probation applies to offenders of all age groups from seven years onwards. It allows offenders to remain in the community under supervision and subject to prescribed rules set by the courts. The probation officers work closely with the probationers' families with a family-oriented approach. To promote community involvement in the rehabilitation of offenders, volunteers are recruited to befriend probationers and residents of institutions, and to assist them in activities that do not require professional skills and knowledge.

The Community Service Orders Scheme is a community-based treatment with punitive and rehabilitative aims. It requires an offender over the age of 14, who is convicted of an offence punishable by imprisonment, to perform unpaid work of benefit to the community and to receive counselling and guidance from a probation officer. The scheme covers the 10 magistracies.

The Young Offender Assessment Panel, run jointly by the Social Welfare Department and the Correctional Services Department, provides magistrates with a co-ordinated view on the most appropriate programme of rehabilitation for convicted young offenders aged between 14 and 25.

The Social Welfare Department operates seven residential institutions with a total capacity of 636 places, each with a slightly different training programme to cater for the needs of the residents. Educational, pre-vocational and character training are provided to assist juvenile offenders to return to the community as law-abiding citizens. The Begonia Road Boys' Home and Ma Tau Wei Girls' Home each consist of a remand home and a probation institution for juvenile offenders and youths in need of statutory care and protection. The Pui Yin Juvenile Home is a remand home for boys. The Pui Chi Boys' Home provides residential training for juvenile probationers. The O Pui Shan Boys' Home and Castle Peak Boys' Home are reformatory schools for boys aged under 16 on admission. The Kwun Tong Hostel is a probation hostel for young men aged between 16 and 21. Greater emphasis has been placed on group counselling, work with parents, development of volunteerism and participation in community activities among the boys and girls undergoing residential training — all with very encouraging results. One of the projects planned and undertaken by the trainees was nominated to represent Hong Kong in the Commonwealth Youth Service Award 1993.

Plans are in hand to improve the residential and training facilities, including the conversion of a youth centre and hostel into a probation home for girls, building a new workshop block at the O Pui Shan Boys' Home, and the relocation of the Castle Peak Boys' Home and Begonia Road Boys' Home to Sha Tin and Ngau Chi Wan, respectively.

In addition to the work carried out by the Social Welfare Department, two subvented non-governmental organisations also provide hostel, employment, casework and volunteer services to help ex-offenders and young people with behavioural problems to be reintegrated within the community.

Family and Child Welfare

The Social Welfare Department and a number of non-governmental welfare organisations provide a variety of family and child care services with the overall objective of preserving and strengthening the family as a unit, through helping individuals and families to solve problems or to prevent them altogether.

Family life education aims to improve the quality of family life through the promotion of interpersonal relationships and social consciousness, which may help to prevent family breakdowns and social problems. A total of 67 family life education workers provide a wide range of family education programmes in the territory. The 1992–93 family life education publicity campaign adopted the main theme of *Happy Marriage and Responsible Parenthood*, and used a wide variety of publicity media, including television and radio programmes, and booklets on effective parenting. In support of the centralised publicity campaign, promotional and educational activities were organised by social workers at the district level.

The Family Life Education Resource Centre supports social workers in promotional and education work by providing resource materials and audio-visual equipment on loan.

The department operates a network of 30 family services centres, while the subvented welfare sector operates 23 such centres. The major services provided in family services centres include: family casework and counselling; care and protection of children and young people aged under 21; and referrals for schooling, housing, employment and financial assistance.

As a complement to the casework service, a family aide service is provided by 19 family services centres to develop clients' home management skills and child care techniques and to help families attain self-reliance.

The home help service, subvented by the government and operated by non-governmental organisations, provides meal services, personal care and household work services to those in need. At the end of the year, there were 73 home help teams.

Wai On Home, run by the department, and Harmony House, run by a non-governmental organisation, together provide short-term accommodation with 80 places for women and children who may be victims of domestic violence, and for young girls at risk.

The department continues its efforts to tackle the problem of street-sleeping. It has set up outreaching teams dedicated to helping street-sleepers. It also assists non-governmental welfare organisations to run temporary shelters, urban hostels and a day relief service for street-sleepers. The department is also identifying suitable premises to set up more hostels for the homeless in the urban area.

A wide range of child welfare services is provided. The Adoption Units are responsible for the local and overseas adoption of orphans, abandoned babies and children available for adoption. The Central Foster Care Unit promotes foster care services in Hong Kong, while the Child Custody Services Unit carries out statutory duties in respect of supervision or care arising from custody and guardianship matters handled in Family Courts or the High Court. The Child Protective Services Unit caters for abused children. The Working Group on Child Abuse advises the government on measures to tackle the problem of child abuse.

The Chuk Yuen Children's Reception Centre and the Sha Kok Children's Home provide temporary care to young children who may be abandoned or whose families are unable to provide care.

The department also runs the Wai Yee Hostel, which is a home for teenage girls with behaviour problems and who are in need of care and protection.

In addition to the department's work, subvented welfare organisations also provide residential child care services through children's homes, homes and hostels for boys and girls, foster care and small group homes. The 1991 Social Welfare White Paper stipulated that residential services are to be developed on the principle that a family setting is the best environment for the healthy development of a child and should be the preferred choice over an institutional setting, particularly for those under teen-age. While there will continue to be a diversity of options, so that children can be placed in the type of residential facility that best suits them, non-institutional care in the form of foster homes and small group homes will take precedence over institutional care in future developments. In 1993, there was expansion in both foster care places, from 240 to 480 places, and in small group homes, from 17 to 32 homes. Opportunities are also taken to convert existing large children's homes from institutional into non-institutional facilities when the need arises for the reprovisioning of these homes. Two large children's homes run by non-governmental organisations were in the process of being converted into small group homes during the year.

Child care centres are available for children under the age of six. Such centres must comply with the standards laid down in the Child Care Centres Ordinance and Regulations. They are subject to registration and inspection. At the end of the year, there were 35 778 places in day child care centres and 577 places in residential child care centres. New modes of child care services were being tried out as experimental projects to meet the changing needs of families. Seventy-five day nurseries provide an occasional child care service which is a flexible and temporary form of child care service on a half-day or full-day sessional basis for families who are unable to take care of children for brief periods. Families with a low income and a social need for their children to attend a child care centre, may make use of the Fee Assistance Scheme in meeting nursery fees. A total of 8 550 children were receiving fee assistance at the end of the year.

The Social Welfare Department operates a telephone hotline service, answering enquiries and providing professional advice to the public on social welfare matters.

Medical Social Service

The Social Welfare Department continues to provide medical social services in public hospitals and clinics to help patients and their families deal with the personal and family problems arising from illness and disability.

Care of the Elderly

The White Paper 'Social Welfare into the 1990s and Beyond' laid down care in the community and by the community as the guiding principle for the planning and development of services for the elderly. To help families look after their elderly members and to enable old people to live with dignity in the community for as long as possible, community support services are provided. These include home help, day care, social and recreational facilities, canteen services, community education and respite care. At the end of 1993, there were 73 home help teams, 140 social centres, 19 multi-service centres, 13 day care centres and 13 respite care places. Financial assistance includes social security assistance and allowance. Housing assistance comprising compassionate rehousing and priority allocation of public housing continues to be available for those eligible. Sheltered housing is provided in private housing flats as well as in public housing estates for 2 725 elderly people who are capable of living independently. To provide timely services to the elderly at risk, two outreaching projects are funded by government subventions.

Residential facilities are provided for those who, for health or other reasons, are unable to look after themselves and who have no relatives or friends to assist them. At the end of 1993, there were 1 273 hostel places, 6 137 home places and 4 716 care-and-attention places.

The Registration Office of Private Homes for the Elderly provides advice and assistance to private homes for the elderly to reach an acceptable service standard. Higher service standards are encouraged through the Voluntary Registration Scheme and through an offer to buy places from registered homes under the Bought Place Scheme.

To provide a regulatory framework and a set of uniform standards for all homes for old people, the Residential Care Home (Elderly Persons) Bill has been introduced in the Legislative Council.

Services for Young People

A wide range of services and activities are aimed at helping young people to become mature, responsible and contributing members of society. The services are designed for young people aged from six to 24 to foster the development of their personality, character, social aptitude, sense of civic responsibility and ability to use their leisure time constructively, and to enable those with adjustment problems to direct their energies towards positive goals in society.

At district level, apart from providing group work activities in community centres, the department promotes and co-ordinates youth programmes and volunteer groups through its youth offices. Since 1974, the department has been running the Opportunities for Youth Scheme. Every year young people are helped with funds to implement a variety of community service projects to meet specific social needs. Awards are given for outstanding projects to recognise the contributions of participants.

Children and youth centres, operated by subvented non-governmental organisations, serve as focal points for a variety of programmes and activities for the personal and social development of young people. The service is well developed and the provision meets 94 per cent of the demand. Hong Kong's youth population is projected to decline from 27.45 per cent of the general population in 1993–94 to 23.2 per cent in 1999–2000. To achieve cost-effectiveness, there is a need to redistribute resources by reprovisioning existing centres from areas where there is over-provision to newly-developed or redeveloped areas where there is a need for new centres. Two combined children and youth centres were opened in 1993 through reprovisioning, making a total of 216 children centres and 216 youth centres.

Outreaching social work attempts to cater for groups of young people at risk who do not normally participate in organised youth activities. To establish contact with these young people, social workers visit the places they are known to frequent. They provide counselling and guidance and other forms of services to help the young people overcome problems, develop their potential and become socially re-integrated. In 1993, four new outreaching social work teams were established. There were a total of 28 outreaching social work teams serving in priority areas with large youth populations, high population density and high juvenile crime rates.

All secondary schools are covered by the school social work service. Social workers based in schools identify and help students with personal, behavioural or family-related problems in adjusting to school life. Eighteen additional school social workers were provided in 1993, bringing the total to 168.

Uniformed organisations offer young people opportunities to join organised activities with progressive training programmes for the development of character and leadership to help them become responsible, self-reliant and caring members of the community. There are eight subvented welfare organisations with over 91 967 members operating a wide range of activities with different emphasis for different target groups of young people. The Duke of Edinburgh's Award Scheme offers a comprehensive programme focussing on development of the potential of young people, attracting a membership of 37 006 through its 20 operating authorities.

Rehabilitation of Disabled Persons

The objective of Hong Kong's rehabilitation services is to integrate disabled persons into the community. Services provided by government departments and non-governmental organisations assist disabled people to fully develop their physical, mental and social capabilities. These services are co-ordinated by the Commissioner for Rehabilitation, who also conducts regular reviews of the Rehabilitation Programme Plan, which projects the requirement for — and identifies the shortfall in — rehabilitation services for the following 10 years. The future development of rehabilitation services is being examined after the publication in 1992 of the Green Paper on rehabilitation entitled *Equal Opportunities and Full Participation: A Better Tomorrow for All.*

The Department of Health is responsible for providing immunisation programmes against various communicable diseases and for promoting health education to prevent disabilities. It also provides screening services for the early detection and identification of disabilities. The Hospital Authority is responsible for providing medical rehabilitation services. The Social Welfare Department is responsible for the planning and development of a wide range of social rehabilitation services, either through direct service provision or subvention to non-governmental organisations. The Education Department is responsible for the planning and development of education and related supportive services for disabled children of school age. The Labour Department is responsible for job placements for the hearing and visually impaired, the physically and mentally handicapped, and discharged mental patients. The Transport Department subvents a Rehabus Service for disabled persons who have difficulties in using public transport. The Vocational Training Council is responsible for providing and co-ordinating vocational training for the disabled.

At the end of the year, the Social Welfare Department and non-governmental organisations provided a total of 766 integrated programme places, 987 special child care places (including 54 residential places) and 905 early education and training centre places for pre-school disabled children. In addition, the service of a clinical psychologist was provided for autistic children in special child care centres. For disabled adults, there were 2 293 day activity centre places providing day care, daily living skills and work training for the mentally handicapped; 4 575 sheltered workshop places providing employment for disabled persons unable to compete in the open job market; and 2 548 hostel places and 17 supported housing places for those disabled persons who could neither live independently nor be adequately cared for by their families, or who lived in areas too remote from their places of training or employment. For aged blind persons unable to look after themselves adequately, or who were in need of care and attention, 339 places were provided in homes and care-and-attention homes for the aged blind. In addition, 200 long-stay care home places, 809 halfway house places and 110 day activity centre places were provided for discharged mental patients. Twenty-one social and recreational centres were provided for all categories of disabled persons.

The supported employment scheme introduced by the department continues to provide employment opportunities for disabled persons. Various supported employment service models are being developed.

To improve service quality, professional back-up from clinical psychologists, occupational therapists and physiotherapists is provided in all rehabilitation day centres and hostels. Other support services include the respite service, which provides short-term relief to families with mentally-handicapped persons, and five home-based training teams which help train mentally-handicapped persons while they await placement.

The Queen Elizabeth Foundation for the Mentally Handicapped, set up in August 1988, aims to further the welfare, education and training of mentally-handicapped persons and to promote their employment prospects. The management and use of the foundation's funds are determined by a council appointed by the Governor. During the year, the foundation allocated $9 million in the form of grants or sponsorships to 42 non-governmental organisations and three government departments, enabling them to undertake projects for the benefits of mentally-handicapped persons. The fund stood at $119 million on March 31, 1993.

Staff Development and Training

Training of professional social workers is provided by the universities, polytechnics and post-secondary colleges. The Social Welfare Department and non-governmental organisations assist in the provision of practical work placements for social work students from these institutions.

The department, through its Lady Trench Training Centre, provides various types of in-service training programmes such as orientation courses for newly-recruited staff, basic social work training for non-professional grade staff, induction training for staff transferred to a new service area and staff development programmes to provide knowledge and skills to help handle the increasingly complicated social problems. During the year, the training centre organised 266 programmes, seminars and workshops for 10 001 participants. It also operates a child care centre for 113 children aged between two and six years, which serves as a training facility for child care personnel.

To equip its staff with up-to-date, specialist skills in the various fields of professional practice, the department sponsors experienced members of staff to attend advanced local and overseas training courses and international conferences. During the year, 82 staff attended 38 such courses and conferences.

The Social Work Training Fund continues to provide financial assistance for individuals to pursue social work training in Hong Kong or overseas. In 1993, a total of 94 applicants were awarded either full or partial grants. It also provides funding support for other purposes, such as enlisting the services of overseas experts to provide training and consultation, and the printing of resource training materials for social workers.

The Advisory Committee on Social Work Training and Manpower Planning advises the government, through the Social Welfare Advisory Committee, on all matters relating to the education and training of social workers, including the planning of manpower to meet welfare service needs.

Research and Statistics

The department conducts surveys and maintains data systems for the monitoring and development of social welfare services. Eight surveys were carried out during the year. In conjunction with the Hong Kong Council of Social Service, the department runs the Social Welfare Manpower Planning System which collates information on individual social work personnel and on the demand for, and supply of, trained social workers for facilitating overall manpower planning in the welfare sector. The department also maintains 10 other data systems: the Integrated Law and Order Statistical System on offenders under the charge of the department; the Child Protection Registry; the Street Sleepers Registry; the Planned Welfare Projects Registry; the Director of Social Welfare Wards of High Court Registry; and five central referral systems for co-ordinating the referral of clients to various welfare institutions.

Subvention and Evaluation

Financial assistance is given to 164 non-governmental organisations for the provision of social welfare services in accordance with government policies. Financial assistance for capital and recurrent expenditure is also provided through the Lotteries Fund.

The Evaluation Unit of the department is responsible for monitoring and assessing services provided by the subvented non-governmental organisations. For this purpose, departmental staff make regular visits to the agencies which are in turn required to submit service statistics at specified intervals. Where appropriate, findings are submitted to the Subventions and Lotteries Fund Advisory Committee, which advises on the allocation of subventions and lotteries grants to agencies providing social welfare and rehabilitation services. During the year, the department conducted five in-depth evaluations of experimental projects and services operated by non-governmental organisations.

Community Building

A number of government departments and voluntary organisations contribute towards the community-building programme.

This programme, co-ordinated by the Community Building Policy Committee, serves to foster among the people of Hong Kong a sense of belonging, mutual care and civic responsibility as society undergoes rapid socio-economic changes.

Community-building efforts involve the provision of purpose-built facilities for group and community activities, the formation of citizens' organisations and the encouragement of community participation in the administration of public affairs, solving community problems, promoting social stability and improving the quality of life in general.

The City and New Territories Administration and the Social Welfare Department are the two departments principally responsible for implementing this programme.

The City and New Territories Administration, through its network of district offices, is primarily concerned with promoting mutual care and community spirit through local organisations, such as area committees, mutual aid committees, rural committees, kaifong welfare associations, women's organisations, and local arts and sports associations.

The Social Welfare Department is responsible for various aspects of group and community work aimed at promoting the development of individuals and groups and at fostering a sense of community responsibility.

Commission on Youth

The Commission on Youth was established in February 1990 with members appointed by the Governor. The main objectives were to advise the Governor on matters pertaining to youth, to initiate research, to promote co-operation and co-ordination in the provision of youth services and to serve as a focal liaison point with other international youth organisations for exchange programmes.

In April 1993, the commission completed the task of developing a Charter for Youth. The charter sets out important principles and ideals on youth development; it covers the protection and promotion of young people's interests and outlines the roles of all concerned in promoting youth affairs. To commemorate the formal launching of the charter, a promulgation conference was held on July 22.

The charter operates on a system of subscription, with organisations and individuals interested in promoting youth development becoming subscribers on a voluntary basis. By the end of the year, 332 organisations and 1 203 individuals had become subscribers to the charter.

The commission conducted two studies during the year. These were a study on youth participation in community activities; and on the education and career plans of young people. Working groups were also set up to examine the support system for the territory's youth, underage drinking and the moral values of Hong Kong's young people. To provide essential information for policy-makers and service providers, the commission also updated the publication *Youth in Hong Kong — A Statistical Profile*.

The commission has started to build a liaison network with youth and youth-related organisations to facilitate its work and to promote better co-ordination in furthering the welfare of youth.

Committee on the Promotion of Civic Education

The Committee on the Promotion of Civic Education was set up by government in May 1986 to promote civic awareness and responsibility throughout the community. Made up largely of non-government members, the committee advises government and community organisations on the objectives and scope of civic education. It encourages, through sponsorship, community efforts in organising civic education activities among different age groups.

The committee focussed on the concept of the rule of law and human rights in 1993–94. Its programmes included a four-day Civic Education Exhibition in July featuring human rights; the production of teaching kits for use in secondary schools; and seminars. A territory-wide civic education survey was also conducted to gauge public views on civic education subjects.

With the help of the Information Services Department, teleline messages on human rights were available free of charge to the public between July and September. A series of 13 radio programmes was produced in co-operation with Commercial Radio to promote key concepts of human rights and the rule of law.

The committee continued to offer sponsorship under the Community Participation Scheme to voluntary agencies and district civic education bodies to encourage them to organise civic education activities. A total of $1.2 million has been made available for 35 projects in 1993–94.

The committee continued to liaise with voluntary agencies and district civic education bodies, from whom its work has received strong support.

13 HOUSING

THE public housing programme is well on the way to achieving its objective of providing homes by the turn of the century for all those in need.

Of the 72 100 public sector flats produced in 1993, 36 700 were rental units and 35 400 were for sale.

About three million people — half the population — now live in subsidised public housing in some 874 000 flats in 286 estates throughout Hong Kong. Some 2.6 million live in 688 000 rental units while some 500 000 live in purchased flats.

The year saw public housing on a large scale enter its 40th year in Hong Kong, having begun after the Shek Kip Mei squatter fire in December 1953 left 53 000 people homeless. Significantly, 1993 also saw the award of ISO 9001 certification to the authority's Construction Branch.

The first phase of the 'sandwich' class housing loan scheme was implemented to help middle-income families buy homes. The scheme, offered to 1 000 families in 1993, was over-subscribed three-and-a-half times.

The government continued to provide land for the private sector to sustain a high level of supply of competitively-priced private flats.

The government estimates that, by 1997, nearly 55 per cent of families in Hong Kong will own their own homes.

The Housing Strategy

The government's Long Term Housing Strategy, on which the public housing programme is based, calls for the Hong Kong Housing Authority and the Hong Kong Housing Society to build a further 175 000 public rental flats and 187 000 public flats for sale between 1993 and the year 2001.

Of this, the Housing Society, a non-profit-making housing agency, is to produce 26 000 flats.

These public housing projections do not include the output of 281 000 flats in that period by the private sector, which is forecast to meet about 45 per cent of the overall needs of the community.

Public housing estates are developed as total living environments and include a wide range of community, commercial and transport facilities.

There is also a continuing programme to redevelop the older estates, to bring them up to the latest designs and standards.

A feature of the public housing effort is the increasing proportion of flats being offered for sale below market prices to those who are eligible, according to certain income criteria. This is in keeping with economic development and the rising aspirations of the people.

Housing Authority

The Housing Authority, which evolved from a number of bodies, was established on April 1, 1973, under the Housing Ordinance.

It was re-organised in April 1988 and given a separate financial identity and autonomy, together with sufficient flexibility to deal with the priorities set by the Long Term Housing Strategy.

It advises the Governor on all housing policy matters and through its executive arm, the Housing Department, plans and builds public sector housing, either for rent or ownership, and temporary housing areas.

The authority also manages public housing estates, home ownership courts, temporary housing areas, cottage areas, transit centres, flatted factories and ancillary commercial facilities throughout the territory, and administers the Private Sector Participation Scheme and the Home Purchase Loan Scheme. It acts as the government's agent to clear land, prevent and control squatting, and implement improvements to squatter areas.

The authority is made up of members appointed by the Governor for two-year terms. It is chaired by a non-official, and comprises 20 other non-official members and four official members. Its nine standing committees, on which sit 35 non-official committee members, deal with various aspects of housing policies such as development, building, commercial properties, establishment and finance, home ownership, management and operations, and the allocation and standards of vacant flats. Many of the members of the authority and the committees also serve the Hong Kong community as executive, legislative, urban or regional councillors, or as members of the Heung Yee Kuk, district boards, area committees, mutual aid committees and other government boards and committees. Some members are themselves residents of public housing estates.

An *ad hoc* committee was set up in November 1993 to conduct an overall review of the provision of housing for the elderly. Three other committees completed or were about to complete their work. The special committee on the clearance of the Kowloon Walled City, established in January 1987, is expected to end its work soon. Two other *ad hoc* committees completed examining the housing needs of the 'sandwich' class and the review on the policy on housing subsidy.

The authority will continue to provide homes at affordable rents and prices for the public. Under an arrangement which came into effect in April 1988, the government continues to ensure the availability of funds required for the housing programmes as set out in the Long Term Housing Strategy.

On March 31, 1993, the government's capital investment and contribution to housing stood at about $125.9 billion. This comprised permanent capital of $26.3 billion, contribution to domestic housing of $89.2 billion and non-domestic equity of $10.4 billion.

In the 1992–93 financial year, recurrent expenditure on the authority's domestic operations, covering mostly management and maintenance costs, totalled $5,383.7 million, while income from domestic operations was $5,861.6 million, generating a surplus of $477.9 million. However, after paying interest on the government's permanent capital, a deficit of $589.1 million was incurred.

The authority was able partly to offset this deficit from the net income derived from its non-domestic operations which, over the same period, generated a surplus of $609.5 million, after paying to the government interest on its permanent capital and the required dividends.

The authority itself financed capital programmes amounting to $7,851.4 million.

Rent Policy

Despite increasing operating and maintenance costs, rents for domestic premises in public housing estates have been maintained at low levels. This has been possible as a result of government subsidies in the form of free land and average low interest rates.

To meet the demand for more spacious allocation, the Ad Hoc Committee to Review Domestic Rent Policy and Allocation Standards recommended, in 1991, that tenants moving into public housing could in future choose to live at the minimum internal floor area allocation standard of seven square metres per person with the median rent-to-income ratio not exceeding 18.5 per cent, or at the existing minimum standard of 5.5 square metres per person with the rent-to-income ratio not exceeding 15 per cent.

With rents being charged at $47 per square metre for the newest urban estates and $26 for the newest New Territories estates, public housing tenants pay on average about eight per cent of their income on rent.

Rents are reviewed every two years and adjusted to take account of rates increases; maintenance and other costs; estate values in terms of location, facilities and services provided; and the tenants' ability to pay.

Housing Subsidy Policy

A modified housing subsidy policy was introduced in April. Under this policy, tenants who have lived in public housing for 10 years or more and whose incomes exceed twice the waiting list income limit, but are less than three times the waiting list income limit, are required to pay 1.5 times net rent plus rates. Only tenants whose incomes exceed three times the waiting list income limit are required to pay double net rent plus rates.

There are some 300 000 households with 10 years' residence in public housing, and 18 per cent of these are required to pay extra rent.

Rent Assistance

Domestic tenants facing financial hardship are granted temporary rent relief under the rent assistance scheme. In 1993, 300 families received assistance under the scheme.

Those tenants whose rent-to-income ratio exceeds 25 per cent, as a result of an increase in rent or a reduction in household income, may apply for a reduction of rent for a period of six months, renewable for a further six months.

The amount of reduction will be 25 per cent for tenants whose rent-to-income ratio exceeds 25 per cent, and 50 per cent for tenants whose ratio exceeds 33 per cent.

Tenants who still face financial difficulty after 12 months may seek a transfer to cheaper housing in the same district. They will be granted a domestic removal allowance and a rent-free period of one month on transfer.

A family which has already moved to cheaper housing because of hardship but whose rent-to-income ratio still exceeds 25 per cent will be entitled to further rent assistance, subject to review every six months.

Allocation

In 1993, 27 500 new flats and 12 600 vacated flats were let to the various categories of eligible applicants.

The largest allocation of some 14 500 flats (36 per cent) went to waiting list applicants. Applicants for public housing rentals through the waiting list are considered in the order of their registration and in accordance with their choice of districts. Accommodation is offered to those who, on investigation, are found eligible in respect of their family income and residence in Hong Kong. The income limits range from $7,600 for a family of two, to $20,000 for a family of 10 or more. The number of applications at the end of the year stood at 151 000. In addition, there were 19 000 applications on the single-person waiting list, established in January 1985. The income limit for single persons is $4,600.

The next largest group allocated flats were tenants affected by the comprehensive redevelopment programme (30 per cent), followed by families affected by development clearance (10 per cent).

The remainder of the flats went to junior civil servants, victims of fires and natural disasters, occupants of huts and other structures in dangerous locations, and compassionate cases recommended by the Social Welfare Department.

Computerisation of information on about 3.5 million applicants and tenants now enables housing allocation and duplication checks to be carried out effectively. It also produces useful statistical information.

Housing the Elderly

A priority scheme is provided under which elderly couples or single elderly persons applying in groups of two or more will be allocated public housing within two years. During the year, 1 700 people were rehoused under this scheme, bringing to 800 the number of flats allocated under this category.

Under a separate incentive scheme, families with elderly persons are allocated housing two years ahead of their normal waiting time. So far, 7 500 families have benefited from this scheme.

Since the introduction of the sheltered housing scheme in 1987, more than 2 000 housing units have been provided for able-bodied elderly persons aged 60 years or over who are self-reliant and independent. A warden service is also provided to deal with emergency situations.

Cases in which a higher level of health care is required are referred to the Social Welfare Department for transfer to more suitable housing.

Home Ownership Scheme

The Home Ownership Scheme (HOS) was established in 1978 to provide flats for sale at prices below market value to lower and middle-income families and public housing tenants.

Since then, 191 800 flats have been sold to eligible families. This figure includes 61 500 flats produced under the complementary Private Sector Participation Scheme (PSPS), which aims to make more use of the resources of the private sector to produce flats for sale at subsidised prices.

About 45 per cent of the families who bought under the schemes were public housing tenants who were required to surrender their rental flats in return.

Private sector applicants are not allowed to own domestic property and are subject to a household income limit of $20,000 per month. These restrictions, however, do not apply to public housing tenants, residents of temporary housing areas and cottage areas managed by the authority, households displaced by clearance of squatter areas for development, natural disaster victims and junior civil servants.

As an encouragement, public housing tenants are accorded higher priority than private sector applicants in selecting HOS flats. This incentive has been extended to prospective tenants, so that more rental flats will be available for applicants in greater need.

During the year, the allocation quota of flats for the private sector and public housing rental applicants was changed. Previously, private sector applicants were allocated one third of the flats in each development phase, but this figure was increased to 50 per cent.

Favourable mortgage terms are provided by 48 financial institutions for the purchase of HOS and PSPS flats, in return for the authority's indemnity against loss in cases of default. This enables purchasers to borrow between 90 and 95 per cent of the flat price, with repayment periods of up to 20 years.

During the year, the HOS and PSPS schemes were over-subscribed by 12 times. Some 13 300 flats were sold under the HOS scheme, and 5 600 flats under the PSPS scheme. A total of 1 200 flats were sold to eligible public housing rental applicants under the trial scheme allowing the option to rent or buy.

The prices of flats sold ranged from $441,900 for a flat with a saleable floor area of 37.3 square metres at Yan Shing Court, Fanling, to $1,587,200 for a flat of 59.9 square metres at Fu Keung Court, Wang Tau Hom. Prices were, on average, 43 per cent below market values.

The annual production of ownership flats will range from around 10 000 to 25 000 flats between 1994 and 1998. Of these, about 45 per cent will be upgraded flats in blocks originally intended for rental housing estates, thus providing a wider choice of flat sizes, standards, locations and prices.

Home Purchase Loan Scheme

Under the Home Purchase Loan Scheme, lower and middle-income families are given assistance to buy flats in the private sector. In 1993, 570 families benefited.

Eligible applicants are offered an interest-free loan of $200,000, repayable over the same period as the bank mortgage on the property, up to a maximum of 20 years.

A new option allows eligible applicants to opt for a monthly subsidy of $2,600 for 36 months, which is not repayable.

Since the start of the loan scheme in 1988, 8 090 loans and 250 subsidies have been granted. As a result, 4 550 public housing units have been recovered for allocation to other families.

Building Projects

Some 110 000 flats were at various stages of construction during the year, with most of the work being carried out on redevelopment of old housing estates in the urban areas.

Several phases of work had begun on rebuilding Sau Mau Ping Estate and Tsz Wan Shan Estate in Central Kowloon, while work on estates in Lam Tin and Ko Chiu Road in East Kowloon was well underway. The final phase of the redevelopment of Tsui Ping Estate in Kwun Tong had also started.

In Tseung Kwan O new town, not far from Kwun Tong, nearly 10 000 flats were under construction.

In the longer term, the area currently known as Tiu Keng Leng will be cleared to form part of the Tseung Kwan O new town. A total of 53 hectares will be produced to provide homes for 86 000 persons, half of them in public housing estates. The authority has agreed to undertake the site formation work for this area, including the necessary roads and infrastructure. Overall planning for the Tiu Keng Leng project has been completed and clearance will start next year, with completion of the first housing blocks expected in the year 2000.

Within the urban area, three sites will be developed for public housing on the West Kowloon Central Reclamation. The three separate sites, with a total area of seven hectares, will be developed comprehensively as a single project. The sites are constrained, however, by environmental factors and building height restrictions. Upon full development in 1999, they will house about 17 000 people in 5 250 flats, including 2 430 Home Ownership Scheme units.

The housing estate at Ma Hang Village, Stanley, in the southern part of Hong Kong, has been designed for development in three phases, with the aim of preserving and enhancing the characteristics of the original settlement and land form. The authority's proposals extend right to the shoreline, to the area around the Tin Hau temple, and will create an extension to the existing heart of Stanley. The focal point of this new development will be the rebuilt Murray House, which will be used as a commercial centre.

The housing projects in the new towns are generally on schedule.

The development plan for Tung Chung, the newest of the new towns, has been endorsed by the authority. Construction of public housing in Tung Chung will coincide with the work on Phase 1 of the North Lantau Development, which forms part of the new airport core projects. Up to 15 000 people will be accommodated in public housing and 5 000 people in private housing by late 1997.

Maintenance

Expenditure on maintenance and improvement works for the year amounted to $2.1 billion, representing an increase of 43 per cent over the previous year.

Several major improvement programmes were initiated during the year, including the refurbishment of 14 900 vacant flats and the upgrading of some commercial centres, at a total cost of $100 million. New and higher standards of refurbishment were introduced.

The improvement programme covering the reinforcement and re-wiring of the electrical supply to older blocks is also continuing and $85.6 million worth of electrical reinforcement work was completed within 102 buildings before the summer peak electrical demand.

Every opportunity is taken to improve the general environment of existing estates, and a programme has started on the extensive environmental upgrading of middle-aged estates. The first estate to receive this treatment, valued at $20 million, was Fuk Loi Estate in Tsuen Wan. At the same time, 30 estates were being redecorated.

The comprehensive repair programme for older estates is continuing, with structural repairs being completed on 56 blocks during the year.

To overcome the debonding problem of mosaic tiles used as an external finish for high-rise buildings, a consultancy was appointed to determine suitable survey techniques and to implement an action plan to supplement the extensive on-going remedial works programme.

The new comprehensive maintenance planning works system, referred to as CARE (Condition, Appraisal, Repair and Examination), was formally implemented. During the year, 18 estates came within the initial stages of the CARE programme, with extensive condition surveys being undertaken on each estate.

The Maintenance Assessment Scoring System was developed during the year to cover the authority's maintenance work. It aims to assess the performance of contractors and to form a basis for offering more tendering opportunities for those contractors who have done good work and can provide the required quality and service.

Redevelopment

Redevelopment of the older estates to bring them up to current standards is an integral part of public housing development.

Since the comprehensive redevelopment programme began in 1988, 225 old blocks have been redeveloped, improving living conditions for 65 000 families. The current five-year rolling redevelopment programme, covering 1993–94 to 1997–98, and involving 156 blocks and 58 000 families, began in May.

Affected tenants are formally notified 18 to 24 months before the clearance dates.

Construction

The first Harmony blocks completed in late 1992 in Tin Yiu Estate and Tin Shui Estate in Tin Shui Wai, Yuen Long, marked the start of a new era in public housing construction. Since then, there has been a continuing effort to enhance the design of the Harmony blocks.

Development studies were carried out to enhance the design through further improvement of the bathroom and kitchen layout, and to provide a better standard of finishes and fittings. Building services layout and pipe routes were also reviewed, and improved and built-in gondolas were introduced to facilitate maintenance to drainage and water supply pipes on external walls. The facades of domestic units in Harmony blocks contracted out after 1994 will have to be constructed of pre-cast units, a move which will further improve both efficiency of the building process and the quality of the finished product.

To deal effectively with building defects which have been reported and to provide feedback for further enhancement of designs, details and specifications, a defects-monitoring centre was established during the year.

Quality Assurance

Hong Kong's continuing efforts to improve the design, quality and general living environment of public housing gained further recognition during the year with the certification of the authority's Construction Branch to ISO 9001.

This certification confers international recognition on the branch as an organisation of assessed capability in respect of 'professional services for the planning; design; project management; and contract administration for the construction, maintenance and improvement of public housing developments'.

Through its leadership and encouragement, the authority also helped pave the way for more than 20 building contractors, including those on its own approved list of contractors, to be certified to ISO 9000, raising the overall standard of building construction in the territory.

The attainment of ISO 9000 certification by the construction industry, following audits carried out by the Hong Kong Quality Assurance Agency during the year, clearly demonstrates the progress that has been made in building construction. This is expected to further develop, giving assurance that all objectives pertaining to good professional services are achieved.

PASS System

Since the Performance Assessment Scoring System (PASS), which objectively monitors the performance of building contractors on the authority's projects, went into full operation in April 1991, the benchmark Target Quality Score (TQS) for contractors has been moving upwards to a high of 92 per cent. This indicates that the contractors are achieving better quality.

As an incentive towards better quality, contractors were selectively invited during the year to tender for new building contracts on the basis of their performance as measured by the scoring system.

Site Safety

Site safety has always been of major concern to the authority and stringent measures are enforced on all its sites in the interest of workers.

Site safety campaigns have been held in collaboration with the Labour Department and employer and workers' groups with much success, and will continue to be an yearly event.

Management

Visits to the estates are made regularly by the chairman and members of the authority to meet tenants and community representatives, and exchange views.

These visits are in addition to regular meetings with the community representatives, either at the authority's headquarters or at other venues. Open meetings of the authority are also held regularly, so that the public may attend and observe the proceedings.

Tight control is exercised over the cleansing services provided by contractors to ensure that a high standard of service is maintained.

Information Centres

For the benefit of residents of private buildings affected by redevelopment, the authority has established two Housing Information Centres in conjunction with the City and New Territories Administration. With the support of the Social Welfare Department, Labour Department, Education Department and Rating and Valuation Department, these centres provide enquiry and advisory services to the residents on matters relating to public housing, education, employment, social welfare, and their rights under existing tenancies.

The two information centres, at the Mongkok and Wan Chai District Offices, have proved popular and there are plans to provide a similar service in Tsuen Wan.

Welfare Services

At the end of the year, 950 welfare premises in the authority's estates and courts were let for welfare and community services at a concessionary rent of $25 per square metre a month. Non-domestic premises at less popular locations were also let at a fair market rate to community organisations.

The authority undertakes fitting-out works for some welfare projects and since 1984, 155 welfare projects have been fitted out.

The estate liaison officer scheme, providing outreaching services to elderly public housing tenants in various estates, has been extended. Under the scheme, housing management staff visit the elderly to offer assistance and encourage them to take part in various activities. Emergency alarm systems for elderly people are also being installed and, by the end of the year, 180 alarm sets had been provided in four estates.

Commercial Properties

The authority manages 1.28 million square metres of commercial space for shops, market stalls, banks, supermarkets, restaurants and flatted factory units. It also provides 65 000 carparks.

During the year, 14 more shopping centres with 44 000 square metres of lettable floor area, were built.

The authority's commercial space is let under some 30 300 separate tenancies and generated a rental income of $2.7 billion during the year, representing one-third of the total rental income of the authority.

The stock includes 17 660 flatted factory units in 17 flatted factories and 3 400 graded shops in former resettlement estates. These shops were initially let at very low rents which, despite moderate biennial increases since 1976, remain well below market levels.

In line with the policy not to subsidise commercial tenants, rents for commercial premises are fixed at market levels. During the year, 534 commercial premises were let by rental tendering, while another 113 premises with a total floor area of 21 200 square metres were let on negotiated terms. Negotiation provides a more flexible approach and assists in attracting anchor tenants, especially those who take up large spaces for the operation of superstores, Chinese restaurants and food courts.

Following the success of a trial scheme under which an entire market was let to a single operator in Yiu On Estate in Ma On Shan, three new markets were let to single operators. These are Fu Heng Market in Tai Po, Wah Kwai Market in Pok Fu Lam and Tin Shui Market in Tin Shui Wai.

Under a further trial scheme, an entire small shopping centre at Yiu Tung Estate in Shau Kei Wan was to be let to a single operator who would be responsible for comprehensive services from leasing to subsequent day-to-day management.

Improvements to shopping centres continue to play an important role in enhancing the trading potential of the shopping facilities. Such work was underway at 15 shopping centres. In particular, major upgrading schemes were being undertaken at two large district shopping centres at Lok Fu and Wong Tai Sin.

A co-ordinated strategy for the improvement of older shopping centres has been formulated and a five-year programme has been drawn up for the upgrading of 25 to 30 selected centres.

Parking

Since 1987, carparks and roads in 55 estates have been placed under the management of three private companies. In view of its success, the privatisation scheme will be extended to the authority's other rental estates.

Illegal parking in public housing estates remains a problem requiring constant attention. During the year, 18 800 offenders were prosecuted, resulting in fines totalling $5.3 million. Some 77 000 vehicles were impounded, costing the owners $15.5 million in charges.

As a further means to combat illegal parking, a recently approved fixed penalty ticket system will be introduced in 1994.

Squatter Control

As a result of rehousing through clearance and the waiting list, the squatter population has been reduced to 42 500 in the urban area and 223 000 in the New Territories.

The 1982 squatter structure survey provides a baseline for control of new squatting on government land and private agricultural land. Squatter control has been effectively maintained by carrying out daily patrols and regular hut-to-hut checks.

Meanwhile, the authority continues to undertake repairs and maintenance of services and facilities provided under the squatter area improvement programme. It is also responsible for settling electricity charges for public lights installed under this programme.

Squatter Clearance

During the year, 270 hectares of land were cleared, with 11 000 affected people given permanent rehousing and 6 500 given temporary rehousing. Some 300 industrial, commercial and agricultural undertakings affected by the clearances were awarded *ex gratia* allowances.

On the advice of the Geotechnical Engineering Office of the Civil Engineering Department, which carried out re-inspections of 70 villages in the New Territories, a non-development clearance programme was drawn up. Some 1 200 persons living in squatter huts on slopes vulnerable to landslips, in the event of heavy rain, were provided with either permanent or temporary housing.

A total of 2 000 people who lost their homes as a result of fires or natural disasters were given either permanent or temporary housing.

Temporary Housing

Temporary Housing Areas (THAs) consist of single or two-storey structures built to re-house people not yet eligible for permanent public housing upon clearance, fires or natural disasters.

There were 52 THAs in the territory, housing some 62 000 persons. In the next three years, 37 THAs will be cleared and 48 500 persons living in them will be rehoused.

The government aims to offer flats to all THA residents by 1997. By 1996, all THAs built before 1984 should be cleared.

Transit Centres

There were eight transit centres in the territory, with a capacity for 1 300 people. Transit centres provide short-term emergency accommodation for the homeless and victims of fires or natural disasters.

Cottage Areas

There were six cottage areas in the territory, housing 9 900 people. The largest one, at Tiu Keng Leng, is due for clearance.

Private Housing

In 1993, some 27 700 residential flats were built by the private sector. To increase the housing supply by the private sector, the government announced plans in October to provide additional staff for the Lands Department in 1994 to speed up the processing of lease modifications and land exchanges. In this way, an extra 2 000 flats, on top of the current 15 000 from this category, should reach the market each year.

To combat speculation activities in the property market, the administration introduced a series of measures, including stringent requirements on the presale of flats under construction and amendments to the Stamp Duty Ordinance to require the payment of stamp duty on all sale and purchase agreements for residential properties. Some local banks have tightened their mortgage lending policies. Residential property prices have steadied since August.

'Sandwich' Class Housing Scheme

A new middle-income housing scheme for the 'sandwich' class was introduced during the year, aiming to help families that are neither eligible for public housing nor able to afford to buy their own homes in the private sector.

The scheme, operated by the Housing Society, comprises a short-term and long-term programme.

Under the short-term scheme, a low-interest loan fund of $2 billion was set up to provide beneficiaries with a one-off loan as part of a down-payment for a flat.

In August, the first phase of the loan scheme was launched, offering to 1 000 beneficiaries low-interest loans of 20 per cent of the sale price of a flat, up to a limit of $500,000. Repayment at a low interest rate would only begin in the fourth year, when the beneficiary's financial position has improved.

The applicants had to have at least seven years' continuous residence in Hong Kong and the total monthly family income had to be within the range of $20,001–$40,000, among other requirements.

A total of 3 435 applications were received.

Under the long-term scheme, land is to be given to the Housing Society at a concessionary premium to build flats for sale to the 'sandwich' class at affordable prices.

Six sites were earmarked under the 1993–94 land disposal programme for this purpose. These sites are expected to produce about 5 000 flats for sale by 1996–97, with the first flats available in 1995.

Rent Control in the Private Sector

Statutory controls on rents and security of tenure in Hong Kong date back to 1921. The governing legislation is the Landlord and Tenant (Consolidation) Ordinance. Parts I and II of the ordinance apply controls over rent levels and give security of tenure in respect of certain domestic tenancies. For nearly all other domestic tenancies, Part IV of the ordinance gives security of tenure, but the tenant must pay the prevailing market rent.

The ordinance provides that, unless a tenant voluntarily vacates the premises, a landlord must apply on certain specified grounds and obtain an order from the Lands Tribunal before he can recover possession. Heavy penalties are prescribed for harassment of a protected tenant with intent to induce him to leave. However, provisions exist to facilitate an agreed surrender by the tenant of his protected tenancy in exchange for a consideration.

The Rating and Valuation Department publishes explanatory pamphlets to help people understand their position in relation to the legislation. It provides an advisory and mediatory service to deal with the many practical problems arising from rent controls. It also operates a scheme under which rent officers attend District Offices on certain days each week to deal with referred cases and answer enquiries on landlord and tenant matters.

The legislation is kept under review to improve its operation and to achieve the objective, recommended in 1981 by the Committee of Review, Landlord and Tenant (Consolidation) Ordinance and endorsed by the government, that as soon as circumstances permit, rent controls should be phased out. To this end, the ordinance was amended in July 1993, principally to allow controlled rents under Parts I and II to increase progressively up to market levels, so that rent controls can be removed by the end of 1996. However, security of tenure under Part IV will continue to apply.

Pre-war Premises

Legislation controlling rents and providing security of tenure for pre-war premises was introduced immediately after World War Two. In 1947, it was embodied in the Landlord and Tenant Ordinance and has since been re-enacted as Part I of the Landlord and Tenant (Consolidation) Ordinance.

Part I previously applied to both domestic and business premises, but from July 1, 1984, it has applied only to domestic premises. Substantially reconstructed buildings are, however, excluded from Part I controls.

Rent increases under Part I are controlled by reference to the standard rent of the premises (that is, the rent payable, on an unfurnished basis, on or most recently before December 25, 1941). The rent lawfully chargeable under the ordinance is the permitted rent, which cannot exceed the prevailing market rent of the premises.

In order to implement the policy of phasing out rent controls, the legislation was amended in July 1993 to allow permitted rents to be increased to 55 times the standard rent of the premises. The multiplier will be increased to 65 in July 1994, to 75 in July 1995 and to 85 in July 1996. In addition, the legislation provides that the new rent shall not be less than a specified percentage of the prevailing market rent. The minimum percentage has initially been set at 60 per cent but will be adjusted upwards to 70 per cent in July 1994, to 80 per cent in July 1995, and to 90 per cent in July 1996. The Commissioner of Rating and Valuation is empowered to certify the standard rent and the prevailing market rent.

The legislation provides for premises to be excluded from control if they are to be redeveloped, and generally, possession is subject to compensation being paid to the protected tenants. Jurisdiction under Part I is exercised by the Lands Tribunal, while technical functions are performed by the Commissioner of Rating and Valuation.

Post-war Premises

Apart from the period between 1966 and 1970, comprehensive legislation to control rent increases in post-war domestic premises has been in force in one form or another since

1963. This is now contained in Part II of the Landlord and Tenant (Consolidation) Ordinance.

Part II controls rent increases and provides security of tenure to tenancies and sub-tenancies in post-war domestic premises completed or substantially rebuilt after August 16, 1945 and before June 19, 1981. It does not, however, apply to new lettings created on or after June 10, 1983, or to tenancies of premises having a rateable value of or above $30,000 as at June 10, 1983.

Under Part II, landlords and tenants are free to agree on an increase in rent, but such agreements must be endorsed by the Commissioner of Rating and Valuation. Increases, except by agreement, are permitted only once every two years. Where an increase is not agreed, the landlord may apply to the Commissioner to certify the increase which may be made to the current rent. The permitted increase is arrived at by taking the lesser of (i) the difference between the prevailing market rent and the current rent, or (ii) 30 per cent of the current rent. However, if the increase so determined, when added to the current rent, results in a rent less than 75 per cent of the prevailing market rent, the permitted increase will be the amount necessary to bring the new rent up to that percentage of the prevailing market rent. The minimum percentage will be increased in stages to 80 per cent, 85 per cent and 90 per cent in the month of July in 1994, 1995 and 1996, respectively, to allow rent controls to be phased out by the end of 1996. Both the landlord and tenant may apply to the Commissioner for a review of his certificate and may also appeal to the Lands Tribunal against the Commissioner's review.

For nearly all domestic tenancies not subject to Part I or II controls, Part IV of the ordinance provides security of tenure for a sitting tenant who is prepared to pay the prevailing market rent on renewal of his tenancy. However, Part IV does not control rents. Under the legislation, a further tenancy must be granted to the existing tenant, unless the landlord can satisfy the Lands Tribunal that he requires the premises for his own occupation, or that he intends to rebuild the premises, or on one of the other grounds specified in the legislation. The parties are free to agree on the rent and terms for the new tenancy but, failing agreement, they can apply to the Lands Tribunal for a determination. Provisions also exist enabling tenancies to be transferred, under certain statutory conditions, from the ambit of Part II to Part IV.

Parts II and IV of the ordinance provide for the payment of statutory compensation to tenants dispossessed by the rebuilding of premises. Since July 1993, the basis of compensation has been revised to a multiple of 1.7 times the current rateable value of the concerned property.

14

LAND, PUBLIC WORKS AND UTILITIES

A CONSULTATION document on the future development pattern of Hong Kong, outlining options for the territory's growth up to the year 2011, was published in September.

The 'Territorial Development Strategy Review — Development Options' reviews the long-term land use, environmental and transport planning framework for the territory, taking into consideration Hong Kong's increasing integration with the Pearl River Delta and other parts of Southern China. The preferred development pattern will be finalised in 1994.

The year 1993 marked the 20th anniversary of new town development in Hong Kong. To date, over 8 800 hectares of land have been formed for the new towns, where as many as 2.5 million people live. Work has begun on a ninth new town at Tung Chung on Lantau.

Torrential rain brought by Typhoon Dot in September and Typhoon Ira in November caused serious flooding in parts of the territory, particularly in the northern New Territories.

Illegal land use, including the haphazard conversion of farmland into storage and dumping sites, has aggravated the flooding problem.

The government announced in October the setting up of a task force to clean up the New Territories over the next decade. It will take tougher enforcement action against unauthorised land use and undertake major improvement works.

The government, which has drawn up a comprehensive programme to reduce flood risks, is also looking at how to improve flood forecasting and warning capabilities.

The Organisational Framework

The primary objectives of the government's lands and works policies are to ensure an adequate supply of land to meet the short-term and long-term needs of the public and private sectors, to optimise the use of land within the framework of land use zoning and development strategies, and to ensure co-ordinated development in infrastructure and buildings.

Policy responsibility for land, private development and the implementation of the public works programme rests with the Planning, Environment and Lands Branch, and the Works Branch, each headed by a policy secretary. Both secretaries are members of the Land Development Policy Committee, which is chaired by the Chief Secretary and is responsible for overseeing all aspects of the physical development of the territory and for giving broad approval to all major proposals affecting the development or planned use of land.

The Secretary for Planning, Environment and Lands is chairman of the Development Progress Committee and the Port Progress Committee. These two committees are responsible for monitoring the general progress of the physical development of the territory, as well as considering and approving detailed planning briefs, layouts and development plans. He is also chairman of the Town Planning Board, and has policy responsibility for conservation.

In addition to his policy functions, the Secretary for Planning, Environment and Lands oversees the operation of the Buildings Department, Drainage Services Department, Environmental Protection Department, Lands Department and Planning Department, as well as the Land Registry, which is operated on a trading fund basis. He also oversees part of the work of the Agriculture and Fisheries Department, Civil Engineering Department, Electrical and Mechanical Services Department, Marine Department and Territory Development Department.

The Secretary for Works oversees, and has policy responsibility for, the operation and works agency activities of the Architectural Services Department, Civil Engineering Department, Drainage Services Department, Electrical and Mechanical Services Department, Highways Department, Territory Development Department and Water Supplies Department. The New Airport Projects Co-ordination Office (NAPCO) was set up in February 1991 under the Secretary for Works to co-ordinate the implementation of the Airport Core Programme (ACP).

Planning

Given the limited land resources in Hong Kong, it is a great challenge to plan for the competing demands of housing, commerce, industry, transportation and the utilities, as well as for recreation, education, medical and health care, and other community facilities.

Town planning is carried out by the Planning Department under policy directives from the Planning, Environment and Lands Branch. The department comprises two functional units: the Territorial and Sub-Regional Planning Branch and the District Planning Branch.

During the year, the department was involved with the drafting of a White Bill for the new Planning Ordinance; updating and reviewing the Territorial Development Strategy, the Northwest and Southwest New Territories Sub-Regional Development Strategies and the Hong Kong Planning Standards and Guidelines; and follow-up work on the Port and Airport Development Strategy, the Metroplan Selected Strategy, and the Rural Planning and Improvement Strategy.

It was also engaged in forward planning and development control for the districts, including co-ordination of various urban renewal efforts; and in undertaking enforcement action against unauthorised developments in designated rural areas.

Review of Town Planning Ordinance

The Town Planning Ordinance was first enacted in 1939. In 1987, the Executive Council ordered that an overall review of the ordinance should be undertaken, with a view to introducing new legislation to replace the existing one, to provide the necessary degree of guidance and control for planning and development to meet Hong Kong's changing circumstances.

Public consultation on the comprehensive review of the Town Planning Ordinance was carried out in 1992. As part of the comprehensive review, a special committee was set up to consider specifically the complex and contentious issue of compensation and betterment arising from planning actions. After careful consideration of the submissions and views from various sectors, the special committee completed its work and submitted a report to the Governor in the same year.

The administration completed analysis of the public comments received and the recommendations of the special committee. Proposals for the new Planning Ordinance have been drawn up. A White Bill is being drafted and will be published for further public consultation in 1994.

Hong Kong Planning Standards and Guidelines

The Hong Kong Planning Standards and Guidelines is a government manual of planning criteria and guidelines for determining the quantity, scale, location and site requirements of various land uses and facilities. The document is applied to planning studies, preparation or revision of town plans and development control. It is constantly under review to take account of changes in government policies, demographic characteristics as well as social and economic trends. Major work undertaken during the year included the formulation and revision of planning standards and guidelines for social welfare facilities, utility services, potentially hazardous installations as well as landscaping and conservation.

To promote public awareness of planning and to facilitate the use of the manual by non-government bodies, the document has been made available in various libraries. The document is also available for sale to the public, on a chapter by chapter basis.

Territorial Development Strategy

The Territorial Development Strategy (TDS) is the highest tier in the hierarchy of town plans in Hong Kong. It provides a broad, long-term framework on land use, transport and environmental matters for the planning and development of the territory. It aims to facilitate the continued growth of Hong Kong as a regional centre and international city.

A comprehensive review of the strategy was commenced in 1990, to assess the implications of the proposed port and airport developments and the current policies on environment and transport, taking into account the changing role of the territory in the context of recent economic and infrastructural developments in the Pearl River Delta region and the deeper hinterland in China.

The TDS review consists of three main streams of work. The first stream comprised appraisal and review studies, including identification and assessment of goals and objectives, key issues, development constraints and opportunities, evaluation criteria, and sectoral land use studies. The latter studies covered industry, housing, offices, recreation, rural land, landscaping, conservation and the environment. The second stream comprised formulation and evaluation of TDS development options on the basis of the results of the first stream. These two streams have been completed.

The result was the Territorial Development Strategy Review — Development Options, published in September for public consultation.

In the formulation of the TDS development options, which cover a time frame up to 2011, two development scenarios have been postulated to take account of the development in China. The first scenario assumes the Pearl River Delta area as Hong Kong's primary economic hinterland, while the second scenario includes both the Pearl River Delta area and some inner provinces of China as Hong Kong's economic hinterland.

The review has identified two major directions of growth in Hong Kong.

First, there is the east to west development axis, comprising the new port and airport facilities on North Lantau and the Western Harbour, plus the Metroplan proposals in the downtown area.

Second, with the rapid development along the east bank of the Pearl River and the Shenzhen Special Economic Zone, a southeast to northwest development axis from Hong Kong to Guangzhou is also gradually emerging.

Based on the broad development scenarios and directions of growth, six development options have been formulated on the basis of varying rates of economic growth, varying demand and supply of land for different uses, and varying roles of the public and private sectors as development agents.

The third stream of the TDS review will consist of the production of a recommended development strategy and a medium-term implementation plan. The TDS review is expected to be completed in 1994.

Sub-regional Development Strategies

The Sub-regional Development Strategies serve as a bridge between the TDS and district plans. They translate long-term, broad-brush territorial goals into district planning objectives for the five sub-regions of Hong Kong — the Metro area, Northeast New Territories (NENT), Southeast New Territories (SENT), Northwest New Territories (NWNT) and Southwest New Territories (SWNT).

The Metroplan Selected Strategy was approved by the Governor-in-Council in 1991 to provide a planning framework for public and private sector development. Rather than a programme by itself, it is a conceptual strategy for developing and upgrading the Metro sub-region, including Hong Kong Island, Kowloon and New Kowloon, Tsuen Wan and Kwai Tsing.

To follow up the Metroplan recommendations, work has started, with input from consultants, on a series of development statements for districts including West Kowloon, Southeast Kowloon (including the Hong Kong International Airport site), Tsuen Wan-Kwai Tsing, and Hong Kong Island West. A consultancy study has also been undertaken to establish the appropriate institutional framework and map out a coherent strategy to restructure and upgrade the obsolete industrial areas in the Metro sub-region. The first three studies were largely completed in 1993. The preparation of the Hong Kong Island West Development Statement, which commenced in late 1993, is expected to be completed in 1994.

Following the government's decision in 1989 on the Port and Airport Development Strategy (PADS), work on the review for the NWNT and SWNT sub-regions commenced in early 1990. Each of these reviews aims at producing for the sub-region an appropriate strategic development framework on land use, transport and the environment for the target year 2011.

An Interim Recommended Strategy on the NWNT Development Strategy is being formulated after examining the various development options. Strategic growth areas have also been identified. However, a recommended strategy cannot be finalised until the recommendations of the other territorial studies, such as the TDS, are ready. In the interim, existing Development Permission Area (DPA) Plans are required to be replaced by Outline Zoning Plans (OZPs) under the Town Planning (Amendment) Ordinance 1991. In order to provide a planning context for the preparation of these OZPs, the NWNT Development Statement Study has been commissioned. This study has produced Recommended Outline Development Plans, which will provide input in the preparation of OZPs in the rural NWNT.

An Interim Recommended Strategy has been formulated for the SWNT. It proposes that urban-type development be concentrated in North Lantau and the existing centres. Countryside areas will be conserved by the extension of country parks, and the designation of coastal and landscape protection areas. Suitable areas have been identified for recreation and tourism development in the sub-region. The strategy will be reviewed when the results of the TDS are available in 1994, before the SWNT Development Strategy is finalised.

Work on the NENT Development Strategy Review commenced in September 1993 to review current issues and formulate an up-to-date strategy for the sub-region. Results are expected to be available by early 1995. The SENT Development Strategy Review will commence in due course.

District Planning

Development projects are implemented in accordance with statutory or departmental district plans. These plans aim to regulate and provide guidance to development in terms of land use, building density and development characteristics, to ensure that they are in line with the planning objectives of the districts.

Statutory Planning

Statutory plans are prepared and published by the Town Planning Board (TPB) under the provisions of the Town Planning Ordinance. There are two types of statutory plans: Outline Zoning Plans (OZPs) and Development Permission Area Plans (DPA plans).

In 1993, one new OZP was published and 29 existing plans were amended by the TPB. In the same period, four new DPA plans were published and seven amended. At the end of the year, there were a total of 51 OZPs and 35 DPA plans.

The OZPs are prepared for existing and potential urban areas and show the proposed land uses, specific development restrictions within respective land use zones, and major road and other transport systems of individual planning scheme areas.

DPA plans have been prepared after the enactment of the Town Planning (Amendment) Ordinance 1991 for areas not previously covered by OZPs. So far, they have been prepared mainly for rural areas in the New Territories. DPA plans provide interim planning control and development guidance for selected areas, pending the preparation of OZPs within three years. While DPA plans may also indicate land use zones, the zonings are not comprehensive and there are many 'unspecified' areas where planning permission is required for developments other than those listed as always permitted. Development without the necessary planning permission will constitute an unauthorised development and will be subject to enforcement. The provisions for enforcement will continue to be applicable in the subject areas after the DPA plans are replaced by OZPs.

Under the provisions of the ordinance, any person affected by the statutory plans can make objections to the TPB. DPA plans are subject to the same publication and objection hearing procedures as OZPs.

During the year, a total of 96 objections to the statutory plans were lodged and 74 objections were considered by the TPB.

Attached to each statutory plan is a schedule of notes showing the uses which are always permitted in particular zones and other uses for which the TPB's permission must be sought. The provision for application for planning permission allows flexibility in land use planning and better control of development, to meet community needs and changing circumstances.

Under the provisions of the ordinance, an applicant who is aggrieved by a decision of the TPB may apply for a review of its decision. During the year, the board considered 735 applications for planning permission and reviewed 97 applications, compared to 608 and 96 applications, respectively, in 1992.

The Town Planning Appeal Board, which was set up in 1991, deals with appeals lodged by applicants who feel aggrieved by the decisions of the TPB upon review of their planning applications. During the year, 20 appeal cases were lodged. A total of 11 cases were heard by the appeal board, all of which were dismissed.

The TPB has promulgated 12 sets of guidelines for applications for various types of development. These are available to the public.

Departmental Plans

Apart from statutory plans, the Planning Department also prepares departmental Outline Development Plans (ODP) and Layout Plans (LP) for individual districts or parts of districts, to show the planned land uses, development restrictions and transport network in greater detail. These plans serve as a guide for land formation, implementation of public work projects as well as land sales and allocations. At the end of the year, there were a total of 32 ODPs and 246 LPs.

Enforcement

According to the Town Planning Ordinance, no person should undertake or continue development in a development permission area unless it is an existing use, or is permitted under the DPA plan, or has been approved by the TPB. Any development that does not satisfy any of these criteria is an unauthorised development. The Director of Planning can serve notices on the respective land owners and occupiers, requiring the unauthorised development to be discontinued by a specified date or demanding a reinstatement of the land. If the requirements of the notices are not complied with, the Director can initiate prosecution proceedings.

Frequent patrols were undertaken during the year within the DPAs by patrol teams established in the Planning Department. The teams also carried out detailed site inspections on suspected unauthorised developments. Most of the unauthorised uses were related to pond filling; site formation; open storage of vehicles, containers and construction materials as well as vehicle repair workshops. Overall, 540 warning letters for 91 cases, 503 enforcement notices for 73 cases, 15 stop notices for three cases and four reinstatement notices for one case were served in 1993. Prosecution was initiated with respect to 16 cases and 14 defendants in eight cases were found guilty.

Rural Planning and Improvement Strategy

The Rural Planning and Improvement Strategy (RPIS) aims to improve the quality of life in the rural areas of the New Territories. It is implemented at both strategic and district levels.

At the strategic level, land use policies are continuously reviewed to control incompatible developments and provide a more sustainable and cost-effective basis for public and private investments. In this regard, a number of reviews and studies have been, or are being, undertaken. They include the study on better utilisation of agricultural land and the review of the rural improvement concept.

At the district level, improvement projects are undertaken under the rural development programmes. These projects include village improvement and expansion works; provision of sewers and sewage treatment plants; improvement, reconstruction and expansion of village access roads; provision of local recreational facilities in village areas; works related to land drainage, river training and flood prevention schemes; and the provision and improvement of communal irrigation, field drainage and farm access in selected agricultural areas. These rural improvement projects are initiated, implemented and monitored by the various District Rural Development Working Groups, with a budget totalling about $4 billion over a span of 10 years.

The rural development programmes are overseen and monitored by the Rural Development Steering Committee, while the overall policy and development management aspects of the RPIS are monitored by the RPIS Monitoring Group.

New Towns and Rural Townships

The 20th anniversary of new town development in Hong Kong saw continued expansion in this area. This took the form of additional land formation, especially in the newer generation of new towns such as Tseung Kwan O and Tung Chung, and improvements to infrastructure and community facilities.

The extensive and rapid growth in the new towns has carried over to adjacent rural areas and even to the old urban areas. They are providing a new reference standard for future developments.

The over 8 800 hectares of land that have been formed for new town development is anticipated to increase by about 40 per cent when all the new towns are fully developed.

The quality of life for the 2.5 million new town residents has been improved. With careful planning and landscaping, the scenic assets and greenery in the new towns have generally been preserved or improved, along with some of the historic locations and civic heritage. A wealth of opportunities for recreation, leisure and culture is also available through the provision of town parks and open spaces, the generous reserve of green belts, active afforestation and planting, the provision of sports complexes, and recreation and cultural centres. Residents have a wide range of choices to suit their individual lifestyles.

The environmental impacts of the massive developments were carefully studied before the projects were launched. Air and noise pollution has been largely eliminated by landscaping works, buffer zones, attention to detail in building orientation and spacing. A careful mix of strategically positioned high-rise buildings with low-density developments blends easily with the natural landscape. These are often enhanced by local open spaces, creative use of river banks and water features, amenity areas and roadside planting. About five million trees have been planted, averaging two trees for every new town resident.

The new towns are served by a network of over 700 kilometres of roads which provide efficient traffic circulation and easy access to the old urban areas. Depending on the destinations, commuters also have alternative means of transport with the Mass Transit Railway, the Light Rail System, the Kowloon-Canton Railway, buses, ferries and taxis.

The sewage from the immense developments is conveyed by over 230 kilometres of trunk sewers to treatment plants installed in the respective new towns. Domestic and industrial discharge, topography and the ecology of the receiving waters have been taken into consideration.

The new towns are served by over 500 schools, 13 hospitals with over 8 400 beds, a large number of clinics and ambulance depots, and facilities for the aged, the young and the handicapped. There are 47 post offices catering for communications needs and over 100 markets supplying daily necessities. The provision of these community facilities and services, which grow with the towns, add to the social cohesion and civic pride of the new town communities.

With the continuing improvements to facilities, it is expected that more people will be attracted to make their homes in the new towns. The number of residents is expected to grow to the design capacity of 3.5 million people. The new towns symbolise the government's commitment to provide a sound basis for the further growth and prosperity of the territory. While each new town has an atmosphere and a character of its own, there is a common theme: a strong engineering, architectural, planning and landscaping framework is there to provide the basis and flexibility for sustained development and a closely-knit social fabric.

The experience gained in 20 years of new town development was shared with overseas delegates in September at the New Town Experience Conference, co-hosted by a local organising committee, supported by the government and local professional and development institutions, and the International Urban Development Association.

Tsuen Wan

Tsuen Wan new town embraces the areas of Tsuen Wan, Kwai Chung and Tsing Yi Island. Its population is expected to stabilise over the next 10 years at around 720 000. While new development and redevelopment continues, the gradual reduction in family sizes and increased provision of larger flats will result in a decrease in population in some areas, resulting in no overall increase.

In addition to the district's historic elements, the new town is characterised by the location of Hong Kong's container terminals in its midst in the Kwai Chung area. In September, the first berth of the new Container Terminal 8 (CT8) was commissioned. Completion of CT8 development is expected by March 1995. Container Terminal 9 (CT9) is planned for Southeast Tsing Yi. Detailed design for the duplicate Tsing Yi South Bridge has been finalised and the bridge's completion is tied to the opening of the first berth of CT9.

Major highway projects will further extend and reinforce the principal road network. In Kwai Chung, the completion of improvements to Kwai Chung Road South and Container Port Road has substantially benefited the traffic conditions along the Kwai Chung Road Corridor between Castle Peak Road and Mei Foo Bridge. Road improvement works to Hing Fong Road and Texaco Road (Phase II), and the realignment and dualling of Castle Peak Road in Tsuen Wan Area 2 are progressing satisfactorily.

School children in the new town will have more choices of conveniently located schools with the addition of the Shek Yam Estate primary school in Kwai Chung and the Cheung Hang Estate primary school in Tsing Yi. The indoor recreation centres in Wai Tsuen Road, Tsuen Wan and Lai Cho Road, Kwai Chung will be welcomed by a wide range of age groups. The completion of the sub-divisional fire station in Tsing Yi will cope with the future development there. Also under construction are the Tak Wah Park Phase II, the Tsing Yi Town Park Phase II and a divisional fire station at Lai King.

Sha Tin

Sha Tin new town is, to a large extent, complete and already home to over half a million people. Sha Tin, well known for its planning and integrated development, is situated at the head of Tolo Harbour.

The final reclamation contract at Ma On Shan, to be completed by early 1994, will add 23 hectares of land, boosting the total to over 1 850 hectares. Work on the last section of the primary road link to Ma On Shan Town Centre started in August and is scheduled for completion in 1996.

The programme to improve conditions in the many old villages in and around Sha Tin continued during the year. The village improvement schemes for Fo Tan and Tai Shui Hang were completed, and the combined scheme for the villages of Hin Tin, Sheung Keng Hau and Ha Keng Hau was in progress.

Community facilities were being reviewed for this mature new town, with additional schools added during the year.

The water quality in Shing Mun River and Tolo Harbour is expected to continue improving, with the completion in mid-1993 of the scheme to export the effluent from the Sha Tin sewage treatment works to the Kai Tak Nullah.

Tai Po

In the last 20 years, Tai Po has grown from a small market town of 25 000 into a new town with a population of 263 000, accommodated in 1 260 hectares of development area.

Most of the new town's engineering infrastructure is in place. Its infrastructure was further improved by the completion of several pedestrian bridges and subways. A further expansion of the Tai Po sewage treatment works was in progress to cater for the remaining development in the town area and the industrial estate.

Construction of the Nethersole Hospital started in April, while work on the Tai Po Convalescent/Infirmary Hospital started in September. On completion of these two hospitals, the needs of the region will be adequately met with a combined capacity of 1 662 beds in 1997.

Fanling and Sheung Shui

Fanling and Sheung Shui, just a few kilometres from China, have grown from a group of villages in 1973 to a town of 164 000 people. Their combined population is expected to increase to 215 000 by the turn of the century.

During the year, 26 hectares of land were formed for development, in addition to the nearly 500 hectares already produced for various uses. Flood control measures continued with the completion of the training of a section of the River Indus Minor and the rehabilitation of a moat at the village of Sheung Shui Tsuen.

The school building programme continued, while the Ta Kwu Ling Rural Centre was completed. Construction of the Regional Council's market complex at Shek Wu Hui was in progress. Design work on the North District Hospital started and construction will begin in 1994.

MOTOROLA

Previous page: *Tallest of the tall, Central Plaza dominates the skyline on Hong Kong Island.*

Above and right: *Art deco influences lend elegance to the interior of Central Plaza.*

Left: *Newly-completed, Entertainment Building rises on the prime Central site of its former namesake.*

Below: *Citybank Tower reflects the changing face of Central.*

Hong Kong's booming economy has spurred the development of numerous, multi-storied shopping complexes. Kowloon City Plaza **(above),** *is one of the latest.*

Times Square in Causeway Bay **(above and right),** *was another impressive landmark to open in 1993.*

Public housing has won many accolades for outstanding design. A recent award-winner was the commercial complex at the Housing Authority's Kwong Yuen Estate in Sha Tin **(above and left).**

Next page: *Nine Queen's Road Central makes a striking new addition to the downtown area.*

Tuen Mun

Tuen Mun, in the West New Territories, is developed mainly on land reclaimed from Castle Peak Bay and on platforms formed in the valley between Castle Peak and the Tai Lam Hills. Up to late 1993, about 1 000 hectares of land had been provided by the government and the private sector for development.

About 70 per cent of the town's population of some 430 000 live in public housing developments, which comprise 11 public rental estates and 14 home ownership and private sector participation schemes. Within the next five years, three more home ownership and private sector participation schemes will be developed to accommodate an additional 23 000 people. Together with some low-density private housing developments along the southeastern coast, the new town will provide homes for about 460 000 people by the mid-1990s.

A marina was substantially completed along the southeastern coast of the town during the year. This private development consists of 19 residential buildings, hotels, shops and recreational facilities, including berths for 300 boats.

Light manufacturing industries, including plastics, garments, metal, electronics and textiles, dominate in Tuen Mun. The existing industrial areas provide floor space for about 2 200 companies and jobs for about 40 000 people. Over 80 per cent of the workers employed in the factories live in the Tuen Mun and Yuen Long areas.

The backbone of the transport service serving the town, and linking it with Yuen Long, is the Light Rail Transit system. Provision has been made for its future extension within the Tuen Mun region.

A 125-hectare site in western Tuen Mun has been earmarked for special industries and a terminal for river trade with China to be developed by the private sector. Reclamation work for the special industry area is scheduled to commence in 1994. In late 1993, a planning and engineering feasibility study was completed for an even larger reclamation to the north of Tap Shek Kok in Tuen Mun West, for both deep waterfront industries and cargo-working terminal development. Construction work is about to begin on a new thermal power station, with a 5 000MW capacity, at Black Point.

Yuen Long, Tin Shui Wai and the Northwestern New Territories

Yuen Long town was first developed in the early 1970s. Its population, which stood at 120 000 at the end of the year, is expected to grow to 140 000 early in the next decade.

Development is spreading to the Tuen Mun-Yuen Long Corridor. The rural area is being rejuvenated, with new infrastructure providing for improved rural development.

To keep pace with the rapid development, five major infrastructure contracts in Tin Shui Wai were completed during the year, while another is in progress. Phased completion of these contracts provide access and service facilities to private and public housing developments.

Land formation for the first stage of the Light Rail Transit link to Tin Shui Wai was completed in late 1992 and train services commenced in early 1993. Both the Tin Shui Wai light rail routes to Yuen Long and Tuen Mun and the new town itself were officially opened by the Governor on March 26.

The two public housing estates, Tin Yiu Estate and Tin Shui Estate, are being completed in phases. The first residents moved into their new flats less than five years after major engineering works started in late 1987. They were followed shortly afterwards by the residents of the private development, Kingswood Villa. A third public housing development will commence in early 1994. Upon its completion in 1997, the new town population is expected to reach 140 000.

The provision of community facilities in Tin Shui Wai has been programmed to coincide with the population intake.

The first three parks to be developed in Tin Shui Wai opened to the public in March. The largest, forming a centrepiece for the town, was Phase One of the Tin Shui Wai District Park. The completion of large-scale roadside landscaping works contributed greatly to the greening of the town.

Long Tin Road and Long Ping Road, which connect the southeast of Tin Shui Wai to Yuen Long, were completed in early 1992. The Tuen Mun-Yuen Long Eastern Corridor was opened to traffic in July 1993. Construction of the Yuen Long Southern By-Pass and the Tin Shui Wai West Access was continuing. As these major roads move to completion, the traffic around this area will improve progressively.

For the disposal of sewage from existing and future developments, the Northwest New Territories Sewerage Scheme, comprising a sewage treatment plant, pumping station, nine-kilometre sewer tunnel and 3.1-kilometre submarine outfall, was commissioned early in the year. The $1.1 billion scheme represents the culmination of 10 years of planning and construction, and bears testimony to the government's effort to combat pollution, particularly to protect the ecology of the Deep Bay area.

The large tracts of low-lying land to the north and west of Yuen Long are particularly susceptible to flooding during heavy rains. A series of major flood prevention projects are planned to solve this problem and the year under review marked the commencement of another series of flood control works in the low-lying areas.

Tseung Kwan O and Sai Kung

The development of Tseung Kwan O new town, which started in 1982, is divided into three phases. The major part of the new development areas will be formed by reclaiming Tseung Kwan O Bay. About 66 million cubic metres of fill material will be required to complete the whole reclamation. The Phase I area has been substantially completed. Reclamation for the other phases has started, with the drawn-up programme extending beyond the year 2000. The population of the new town, which was 127 000 at the end of the year, will reach over 400 000 upon full development by 2010.

About 420 hectares of land have been formed at Tseung Kwan O new town. Engineering infrastructure has been provided to cater for private and public housing and the development of community facilities. Four public rental estates, six home ownership schemes and three private sector participation schemes have been occupied. More public housing and private sector development is on the way. Reclamation of the town centre area, currently in progress, is expected to be completed by the end of 1999.

Work continues for the provision of land and services for the Tseung Kwan O Industrial Estate. Upon completion in early 1996, 71 hectares of land will be available for industrial development. Reclamation is also in progress to develop the southern part of Siu Chik Sha for industrial use.

In preparation for further industrial development, a plan is being drawn up to develop a 100-hectare site to the south of Tseung Kwan O for deep waterfront industries and potentially hazardous installations.

Construction work is underway on the first major district open space in Tseung Kwan O, near the Po Lam housing estate. On completion in early 1994, the project will provide extensive sports facilities and sitting-out areas.

At Sai Kung, reclamation of Sai Kung Creek is in progress to provide land in 1994 for a rural public housing site.

Islands District

Hong Kong's ninth new town is beginning to rise at Tung Chung and Tai Ho on northern Lantau Island, to provide a supporting community for the new airport at nearby Chek Lap Kok.

A comprehensive development — incorporating residential, industrial and commercial facilities and all the necessary supporting infrastructure — is being designed to modern international standards.

The new town will comprise about 760 hectares of land. As well as playing a pivotal role at the gateway to Hong Kong, it will respond to the need for further development space. The contract for the first phase of the development at Tung Chung was in progress during the year.

The new town will comprise two discrete urban development areas at Tung Chung and Tai Ho, with proposed populations of 150 000 and 50 000, respectively, by the year 2011. Residential and commercial developments will be concentrated in the town centre and two district centres in Tung Chung and Tai Ho, each incorporating a Lantau Line railway station and public transport terminus. The town centre will provide the retail, commercial and cultural core of the new town. Other necessary retail and commercial facilities will be distributed in the district centres serving Tung Chung and Tai Ho, and local centres within housing areas. Land will be reserved at Siu Ho Wan for airport-related industrial uses. A number of major utilities, including a water treatment works centre, a sewage treatment works centre, a railway depot and a refuse transfer station, will also be located at Siu Ho Wan.

There will be four phases of development for the new town between now and 2011. The first phase, which is earmarked as one of the Airport Core Programme projects, will be completed by 1997 to coincide with the opening of the new airport and will accommodate about 20 000 residents at Tung Chung. Site formation work, involving substantial reclamation, is in progress.

Elsewhere, the design of the North Lantau sewage treatment works was nearing completion. Work is expected to commence on site in 1994, and is scheduled for completion in 1996.

Improvements to the living environment and facilities for residents and visitors to the Islands District continued during 1993.

In Cheung Chau, site clearance for the rural public housing estate and Home Ownership Scheme in Sin Yan Tseng had started, with site formation work to be completed in mid-1995. This rural public housing development, planned for completion in 1998, will provide about 400 housing units for some 1 550 residents.

Foundation work for the first rural public housing estate on Peng Chau was completed and building works began in mid-1993. Planning was also in hand for a fire station in Peng Chau, with construction to begin in 1994–95. Construction of a sewage treatment plant will start on the island in January 1994.

In Mui Wo, the construction of a fireboat berthing point and the upgrading of the existing sewerage system were in progress. An indoor recreation centre-cum-library was completed during the year.

Open space facilities and rehabilitation planting on North Lantau were under planning during the year.

Urban Development Areas

Work on the new urban development areas generally take account of the Metroplan. This document sets out a broad pattern of land use and guidelines for the planning and development of new areas, which integrate with the replanning and redevelopment of adjoining old areas in a co-ordinated manner.

Six development areas at Aldrich Bay, Siu Sai Wan, Hung Hom Bay, West Kowloon, Central and Wan Chai, and Belcher Bay — all involving reclamations in Victoria Harbour — are under planning or construction to meet forecast requirements in the 1990s and beyond.

On completion, they will provide more than 580 hectares of land for urban area expansion, as well as make up for land use deficiencies, such as lack of open space and other facilities, in adjacent old urban areas.

The Aldrich Bay development will produce about 28 hectares of land for private residential and public housing, open space and other uses. The newly-completed typhoon shelter has already been put into use, while reclamation of the old typhoon shelter started in August 1992, for completion in phases between 1995 to 1999.

The Siu Sai Wan development includes the formation of about 56 hectares of land for industrial, residential, government, institutional, community and other uses. Land formation has been completed and developments have already taken place.

Twenty hectares of land have so far been formed at Hung Hom Bay, with a further 16 hectares due for completion in 1994. The reclamation is destined for residential, commercial and community facilities, open space, transport interchange facilities and expansion of the existing Kowloon-Canton Railway freight yard. Two new ferry piers and a bus concourse, constructed near Whampoa Garden, were opened in 1991.

Steady progress was maintained in the West Kowloon Reclamation, which is being implemented in stages up until 1996. The reclaimed area of some 340 hectares, extending from Lai Chi Kok and Stonecutters Island in the north to Yau Ma Tei in the south, will provide land for private and public housing, commerce and industry, government, institutional and community facilities, open space and other uses. In accordance with the Metroplan, it will provide opportunities for thinning out the existing high-density developments in the West Kowloon hinterland, as well as providing strategic transport links to serve the new airport at Chek Lap Kok, namely the Airport Railway, the West Kowloon Expressway and Western Harbour Crossing.

More than half of the area has been reclaimed. The project commenced in August 1990 and is estimated to cost $12.5 billion. A new 70-hectare Yau Ma Tei replacement typhoon shelter, 14 hectares larger than the previous one, was completed and opened in October 1992, and reclamation of the original shelter commenced shortly afterwards with a target completion date of 1995. A new wholesale market, occupying 10 hectares of the new reclamation, was opened in September 1993. The opening was achieved only 21 months after the first section of reclamation appeared above sea level.

The Central and Wanchai Reclamation, extending along the Hong Kong Island waterfront from Sheung Wan to Causeway Bay, will cover an area of 108 hectares. Reclamation work started in late 1993 to create the 20 hectares needed in Phase I, adjoining Exchange Square. Upon completion in mid-1997, it will provide the site for the Central Terminus of the Airport Railway and allow for much needed expansion of the area's business district.

The Belcher Bay reclamation will create about 11 hectares of land, mainly for the construction of the Belcher Bay Link, a dual carriageway connecting the existing, upgraded, Connaught Road West with Smithfield in Kennedy Town. Both the reclamation and the construction of the link commenced in May for completion by 1996–97, to tie in with the opening of the Western Harbour Crossing.

Urban Renewal

In the course of preparing the Metroplan, the older urban districts were seen as offering redevelopment opportunities for comprehensive urban renewal, to create a better urban environment.

The government and private developers are both involved in the redevelopment of the older urban districts, where buildings are old and in dilapidated condition and where the provision of various community and infrastructure facilities is inadequate.

The Land Development Corporation (LDC) was established in 1988 to undertake, encourage, promote and facilitate urban renewal. Since its inception, about 30 projects have been initiated within the designated old urban districts. At the end of 1993, plans for five comprehensive redevelopment projects had been drawn up and gazetted under the Town Planning Ordinance.

Of the five redevelopment plans, the Jubilee Street, Wing Lok Street and Queen Street plans were approved by the Executive Council over the past two years. The Argyle Street/Shanghai Street plan was approved in July 1993. The Shamchun Street Scheme was abandoned by the LDC.

All private properties in the Wing Lok Street Scheme have been resumed and construction work has started. Resumption in the Jubilee Street Scheme had been largely completed by the year's end, with construction work about to commence. Upon completion, the two schemes will provide high-quality commercial buildings and much-needed open space and community facilities for the district. Acquisition of the properties in the Queen Street Scheme was in progress. The scheme will provide space for residential, commercial and office uses, supplemented by the provision of a multi-purpose social welfare complex, public open space, a cooked food centre and a day nursery to offset the shortfall of government, institutional and community facilities in the district.

In Kowloon, acquisition of the properties in the Argyle Street/Shanghai Street Scheme was underway. In addition to the provision of commercial space, there will be a public light bus terminus, a cooked food centre, a neighbourhood community centre and public open space facilities.

Apart from these schemes, the LDC has also undertaken several smaller commercial and residential redevelopment projects. On Hong Kong Island, the commercial development in Queen's Road Central and residential developments in Third Street and Tai Yuen Street were completed. Still under construction were residential development schemes in Li Chit Street and Wan Chai Road. In Kowloon, the construction of the residential development in Soy Street was in progress. Three other projects in Yim Po Fong Street, Dundas Street and Sai Yeung Choi Street, to provide commercial and residential space, were under active planning and construction work will start soon.

A survey on social attitudes towards urban renewal was completed early in the year. Its findings will provide useful information for the formulation of future urban renewal approaches and the implementation of the Metroplan.

The Hong Kong Housing Society has also contributed to the urban renewal process by undertaking a number of urban improvement schemes in the older areas. Four such projects were under construction — one in Yau Ma Tei, one in Sham Shui Po and two in Sheung Wan. They are expected to be completed in the next two years.

Planning Studies

During the year, the Planning Department provided planning input for a number of major reclamation and development projects, notably the Central and Wan Chai, the West Kowloon and the Green Island reclamations.

Studies were completed on the restructuring of obsolete industrial areas, and on a review of building density and height restrictions in Kowloon and New Kowloon. Studies on planning for vehicle repair workshops, density guidelines for private residential areas and the redevelopment of under-developed government sites were near completion.

In the New Territories, major forward planning studies covering North Lantau and the Lantau port peninsula were completed. Studies were being undertaken to identify back-up sites to meet the increasing demand for container and open storage sites, due to the rapid growth of the cross-border trade and associated transport and storage activities.

Other planning studies relating to the Territorial Development Strategy and the Sub-regional Development Strategies were also conducted during the year.

Building Development

The Private Sector

The administration of private buildings and building works control took a significant step forward on August 1, 1993, with the separation of the Buildings Ordinance Office from the former Buildings and Lands Department to become the new Buildings Department.

The reorganisation will lead to more effective management of building control activities, and help to ensure that statutory standards of safety and health are met in all buildings and building works in the private sector. With a clearer identity and greater autonomy in the control and use of its resources, the Buildings Department will respond more effectively to its expanding responsibilities, improve the delivery of services to the public and achieve greater cost-effectiveness.

Headed by the Director of Buildings, who is the Building Authority under the Buildings Ordinance, the department comprises the Control and Enforcement Division, Development Division, Specialist Division, Structural Engineering Division, and Litigation and Legislation Division.

During the year, the department continued to emphasise building safety in existing buildings. The on-going enhanced planned survey exercise, which commenced in 1989, continued to target its list of 16 700 identified buildings in need of detailed inspection. A total of 2 980 of these buildings were surveyed, resulting in the issue of 1 088 statutory orders requiring repair and, in a few instances, demolition.

Extensive operations to remove unauthorised and potentially dangerous projections from the external walls of buildings proved successful. Eighty-five buildings were targeted during the year, with over 11 000 projections from more than 6 000 flats being pinpointed for demolition. Due to the widespread publicity of earlier operations, flat-owners and owners' corporations were more aware of the serious problems inherent in unauthorised building works and, as a consequence, a large proportion of the projections were removed voluntarily. The impact of these clearance operations on the urban environment can be clearly seen. The department's success is underlined by the fact that it now receives requests from owners to initiate action on their buildings.

During the year, 416 occupation permits were issued for completed buildings, compared with 443 in 1992. The amount of usable floor area provided was three million square metres and the total cost of new building works was $28,164 million.

Following the relaxation of the airport height restrictions, the monotonous skyline of the Kowloon peninsula is being broken by building redevelopment.

A new concept in the design of industrial buildings is emerging. Curtain walling, neo-classic motifs and pinnacle roofs have been widely employed recently to enhance the appearance of these buildings. Another change is that factory units are becoming smaller in size and provided with air-conditioning.

A large luxury residential project, the Gold Coast Development, was completed at Castle Peak Bay. The suburban resort includes a 450-room hotel with international conference facilities, a Mediterranean-style shopping mall, a 300-berth marina and country club, plus high-rise residential towers and low-rise beach houses.

Site formation work commenced for a new power station at Black Point, Tuen Mun. Two 600MW blocks of additional generating capacity will be installed in the station in 1996 and 1997, respectively.

Environmental initiatives continue to be pursued. Following the completion of the consultation exercise on the draft handbook on Overall Thermal Transfer Value in buildings, the department is following up with amendments to the Buildings Ordinance. The aim is to achieve energy efficiency in buildings through mandatory control. To promote energy efficiency, the department participated in an annual award scheme for the design of energy-efficient buildings, organised by the Energy Efficiency Advisory Committee.

The Public Sector

The Architectural Services Department is a large multi-disciplinary organisation with responsibility for providing technical advice on building-related matters to all government departments, financial and project management of public building developments under the Public Works Programme and for subvented building projects financed by the government. It is also responsible for professional design services for government, Urban Council and Regional Council buildings; and provides maintenance and management services for buildings owned or occupied by the government, the municipal councils, and the British Forces in Hong Kong.

During 1992–93, the department had over 500 projects under study, design and construction, valued at $38 billion. In addition, the value of subvented projects monitored by the department amounted to $13 billion. Actual expenditure on building projects undertaken or monitored by the department came to $5.8 billion, while expenditure on routine maintenance and minor alteration works to properties amounted to $1 billion.

In the 12-month period to March 1993, tender prices for the projects undertaken dropped by about one per cent. Over the same period, labour and basic material costs rose by 10 per cent and 15 per cent, respectively.

The year saw considerable progress in implementing the government's policy of self-sufficiency in office buildings. The fitting-out of the third tower of the North Wanchai complex was completed and the tower is now occupied by the Inland Revenue and Environmental Protection Departments. Previous phases of the complex accommodated the Immigration Department, the Wanchai North Law Courts and other government departments.

A purpose-built office in Ho Man Tin now accommodates branches of the Highways Department under one roof. Also sharing the building is the Government Laboratory, and a fire services and ambulance depot.

In Tsuen Wan, a government office has been combined with a Regional Council library in a distinctive mid-town complex — the latter officially opened by the Governor in July.

Much of the planned infrastructure for the new airport has necessitated relocation of other facilities, such as the wholesale markets at Cheung Sha Wan and Kennedy Town. This work progressed well during the year, with Phase I of the relocated Cheung Sha Wan market being opened in October.

The government's continued commitment to improving facilities for handicapped persons was reflected in the completion of the third phase of a core programme to modify existing public buildings to facilitate access for the disabled. In total, 125 locations, ranging from hospitals and post offices to markets and playgrounds, have been provided with ramped access and, where feasible, special toilets.

Less evident to the public, but of significance, are the continuing series of buildings on hill-top sites across the territory. Most are for telecommunications or radar for the airport; others are related to communications links with China. There is an on-going programme to improve access to such sites by constructing helipads, where these are not already provided.

Major medical projects started during the year included the Extension Block at Princess Margaret Hospital, with a planned completion date of 1995; the redevelopment of the Jockey Club Institute of Radiology and Oncology at Queen Elizabeth Hospital, and the Phase I Redevelopment of the Castle Peak Hospital, both due to be completed in 1996. Also begun were the Princess Margaret Hospital refurbishment, and the Tai Po Infirmary and Convalescent Hospital, both planned for completion in 1997. Other projects under construction included the Queen Elizabeth Hospital refurbishment, due for completion in 1996; the Queen Mary Hospital extension and improvement, due for completion in 1995; the Cancer Centre at the Prince of Wales Hospital and the Shum Wan Laundry, both due for completion in 1994; the refurbishment of the existing Yau Ma Tei Jockey Club Polytechnic; the Wong Chuk Hang Complex for the Elderly; and a well-woman clinic. Projects completed during the year included the Siu Lam Hospital Extension, the Yau Ma Tei Jockey Club Polyclinic Extension, the Tin Shui Wai Clinic, the Tuen Mun Clinic and the new X-ray unit for accident and emergency services at the Tai Po Jockey Club Clinic.

Construction was completed on a number of Urban Council projects, including Quarry Bay Park, Wanchai Park, Shek Kip Mei Park Stage III, the greenhouse at the Hong Kong Zoological and Botanical Gardens, the Indoor Games Hall Lam Tin South, Sam Ka Tsuen Recreation Ground and Cape Collinson Columbarium. Work began on four market complexes and two leisure pools. Other projects under construction included the Squash Court Complex at Cornwall Street and the Un Chau Street Complex.

Regional Council projects completed included the Mui Wo Complex; the indoor recreation centre, swimming pool complex and sportsground at Tin Shui Wai; and two air-conditioned indoor recreation centres at Kwai Chung and Tsuen Wan. An air-conditioned market complex at Shek Wai Hui was nearing completion, and construction work commenced for a swimming pool complex and sportsground at Tsing Yi.

For the disciplined services, completed projects included a police post at Tap Mun, departmental quarters for Correctional Services staff at Lai Chi Kok and the final phase of Police Tactical Unit premises at Fanling. Projects underway included additional accommodation for the Sai Kung Police Station, a sub-divisional fire station at Tsing Yi, a divisional fire station at Lai King and police staff quarters at Tsing Yi. Other projects under construction were the new Police Headquarters Complex Phase II, the permanent container cargo-examination compound at the Kwai Chung Container Port Area, and quarters for the disciplined services at Fanling, Wong Tai Sin, Tseung Kwan O and Ngau Chi Wan.

In March, the reprovisioning of the HMS Tamar naval facilities was completed at Stonecutters Island, to enable relocation of the base from Central.

Five secondary schools were completed under the School Building Programme, and construction work on one primary school and five secondary schools was started during the year. Four special schools for handicapped children were completed during 1993 (including the Caritas Lok Yi School for severely mentally handicapped children at Lei King Wan), and work started on another three special schools.

The department's Subvented Projects Division has a vetting and advisory role to other departments and private organisations on buildings, repairs, and maintenance work funded by subvention. These include a wide range of schools and social welfare facilities, as well as the seven universities and polytechnics, the Hospital Authority and the Vocational Training Council.

The Property Services Branch provides routine maintenance and minor alteration works to over 7 000 buildings used by the government, Urban Council, Regional Council, Hospital Authority, subvented schools and agencies, and the British Forces. The number of major refurbishment and fitting-out projects again increased. These included noise-abatement measures at government and subvented schools, the refurbishment of the City Hall and the renovation of Caine House at Police Headquarters.

The department also gives advice on facilities to be provided to the government by private developers as a condition of land grants. Examples include office accommodation, transport interchanges and neighbourhood social welfare facilities.

Its Building Services Branch provides professional support in the design and supervision of the installation of all building services and electrical and mechanical systems for building projects undertaken by the department.

With the government committed to improving the environment, the branch is taking action to resolve the issue of chlorofluorocarbons (CFCs), and to improve indoor air quality and waste disposal systems.

As the commonly used refrigerants CFC and HCFC (hydrochlorofluorocarbons) are not ozone-friendly, and to follow the spirit of the revised Montreal Protocol, they are not specified as far as possible in all new air-conditioning designs for government-funded and subsidised projects with effect from June 1993. With the installation of Hong Kong's second non-CFC/HCFC refrigerating machine in Revenue Tower, Wanchai, two years ago, the department has been at the forefront in introducing good environmental practices to help protect the Earth's ozone layer. As a second step, the department, in collaboration with the Electrical and Mechanical Services Department, will retro-fit existing refrigerating machines with non-CFC refrigerants under a 10-year programme. The first project to be completed under this programme will be the Prince of Wales Hospital, where work commenced in July.

As today's multi-functional buildings accommodate not only offices but other facilities, such as computer centres and laboratories, the indoor environment is more vulnerable to air contamination. Air purifiers have been installed at Revenue Tower. Other important areas where the commitment to environmental awareness has been demonstrated include the installation of waste disposal and treatment systems in buildings where sewers are not available, as well as to boilers and incinerators.

It was altogether a significant year for the department. The design of the Kowloon Walled City Park received international recognition when the department was presented a Diploma of the Central Society of Horticulture of Germany at the fifth International Horticulture Exhibition (IGA Stuttgart Expo '93) in October. The achievement was the result of the concerted efforts of the project team, comprising architects from the new works group, landscape architecture group and antiquities group.

Land Administration

The Lands Administration Office of the new Lands Department, which was established on August 1 following the reorganisation of the Buildings and Lands Department, co-ordinates all aspects of land administration throughout the territory.

The office's main functions are to acquire land and make land available for the government's development programmes; to dispose of land in accordance with a programme approved by the Sino-British Land Commission; to manage all unallocated government land; and to ensure the use of private land complies with its lease conditions.

Land usage statistics are at Appendix 35.

Land Acquisition

When private property is needed in the public interest, which in most cases is for the implementation of public works projects, and cannot be acquired by negotiation, the use of compulsory powers becomes necessary. Property may then be acquired under the Crown Lands Resumption Ordinance, the Land Acquisition (Possessory Title) Ordinance, the Mass Transit Railway (Land Resumption and Related Provisions) Ordinance or the Roads (Works, Use and Compensation) Ordinance. These ordinances provide for payment of compensation, based on the value of the property, and for business loss, where appropriate, at the date of acquisition. If agreement cannot be reached on the amount payable, either party can refer the claim to the Lands Tribunal for adjudication.

Where land is acquired in the New Territories, a system of *ex gratia* payments applies, with enhanced rates paid for land situated within the new town development areas and progressively lower rates for land situated outside these areas. In the case of building land, an *ex gratia* payment is offered in addition to the statutory compensation available. A system of *ex gratia* payments also applies in the case of old scheduled lots acquired in the urban area. Additionally, an *ex gratia* Home Purchase Allowance is normally paid upon resumption of domestic units within the urban area.

During 1993, about 0.19 million square metres of private land was acquired in the New Territories to carry out various public works projects. The total land acquisition and clearance costs amounted to about $790 million. These projects included the Southeast New Territories Landfill at Tin Ha Wan in Tseung Kwan O, the thermal power station at Black Point in Tuen Mun, the Au Tau 'B' pumping station and the Western aqueduct in Yuen Long, the North Lantau Expressway (Phase II) on Lantau Island and a village sewerage disposal pipeline in the North District.

In the urban areas of Hong Kong Island and Kowloon, about $2.76 billion was paid in compensation for land and buildings acquired during the year for public works projects, either under compulsory powers or by agreement. These projects included the Ma Hang Redevelopment at Stanley, Rock Hill Street Extension in Sai Wan and open space development at Pak Tsz Lane in Sheung Wan.

Private streets continued to be resumed to facilitate their repair and maintenance by the government.

The Lands Administration Office was also much involved in acquisition and clearance work in connection with the implementation of urban renewal projects to be carried out by the Land Development Corporation and the Hong Kong Housing Society.

Land Disposal

All land in Hong Kong is held by the government, which sells or grants leasehold interests. Such grants and leases are made in accordance with the terms set out in Annex III to the Sino-British Joint Declaration on the Question of Hong Kong.

The new land to be granted is not to exceed 50 hectares a year, excluding land granted to the Hong Kong Housing Authority for public rental housing (the Land Commission may increase this limit and regularly does). The land disposal limit for 1993–94 is 127.8 hectares, with a five-hectare reserve. Premium income obtained from land transactions is shared equally, after deduction of the average cost of land production, between the Hong Kong Government and the future Hong Kong Special Administrative Region Government.

Land grants and leases are normally made for terms expiring not later than June 30, 2047. They are made at premium and nominal rental until June 30, 1997, after which an annual rent equivalent to three per cent of the property's rateable value will apply.

A land sales programme is issued at the beginning of each financial year and updated regularly, showing the details of public auctions and tenders normally held each month. Land in the New Territories is often sold by way of tender, restricted to holders of land exchange entitlements. These entitlements were used in the past for the acquisition of land in the New Territories, but since 1983 are no longer issued.

As a result of the buoyant property market, the premium received from the sale of sites in all sectors of the market showed significant increases.

Although most government land available for private sector development is sold by public auction or tender, land is also made available at nominal premium to the Housing Authority for its public rental estates and Home Ownership Scheme, and to non-profit-making charitable, medical and educational institutions which operate schools, hospitals, and social welfare and other community services.

During the year under review, a site in Fanling, with an area of 1.57 hectares, was sold under the Private Sector Participation Scheme. Eight sites were granted to the Housing Authority for the development of Home Ownership Scheme projects. These included three large sites comprising 3.46 hectares, 5.16 hectares and 3.11 hectares in Hong Kong East, Kowloon East and Ma On Shan, respectively.

Land for the construction of about 5 000 flats was granted in 1993–94 to the Hong Kong Housing Society, for an assisted housing scheme for Hong Kong's 'sandwich' class (those families not eligible for existing public housing assistance but unable to afford private sector flats).

Major land transactions and negotiations included the granting of a 46-hectare site in Tuen Mun for the Black Point Power Station; an 8.61-hectare site in Tuen Mun for the relocation of Lingnan College; five hectares of land for the first phase of the Third Industrial Estate at Tsueng Kwan O; and a nine-hectare site in Tuen Mun to relocate the Shiu Wing Steel Mill.

In the New Territories, six sites with a total area of 5.85 hectares were sold by tender restricted to holders of land exchange entitlements. These included a 2.08-hectare site in Fanling and two sites with a total area of 2.74 hectares at Tseung Kwan O. These sites were for commercial and residential use.

Land Registration

The Land Registration Ordinance provides for registration of all instruments affecting land in the Land Registry.

On August 1, 1993, the Land Registry became one of the first government departments to operate on a trading fund basis. A trading fund is a financial and accounting arrangement which requires a department, whose services are of a commercial nature, to operate on a commercial basis while remaining a government department. The basic objective is to improve the quality of service to customers.

Registration of land documents in Hong Kong is effected by means of a memorial form, containing the essential particulars of the instrument, which is then placed on a register showing the particular piece of land or individual premises affected. The registers provide a complete picture of the title to each property, from the grant of the government lease. They are available for search by the public on payment of a small fee. The memorials and a complete copy of each registered instrument are kept, and are also available for search by the public on payment of a fee.

The records of transactions affecting land on Hong Kong Island, Kowloon, New Kowloon and some of the urban areas of the New Territories are kept at the Urban Land Registry located at the Queensway Government Offices. Those relating to transactions affecting land in the remainder of the New Territories are kept at eight district land registries in the New Territories. Before any land transaction is completed, a land search to ascertain property ownership is made. During the year, 3 328 390 such public land searches were made and 631 849 instruments registered throughout the territory, compared with 3 207 280 and 685 136, respectively, in 1992. At the end of the year, there were 1 580 877 property owners, an increase of 75 874 over the previous year.

All instruments and memorials presented for registration in the Urban Land Registry are microfilmed, and the particulars of the land transactions are stored in computerised registers. To improve public search services in the urban areas, the registry is developing a computer network to provide on-line, direct search facilities at the offices of solicitors and other professional firms. This public network access for the land search service will be implemented around mid-1994. Instruments and memorials presented to the New Territories district land registries are still registered manually. They are made available to the public for search in their original form. Microfilming of the land documents registered in the New Territories has started. Conversion of the information kept in these registries into computerised data will start in mid-1994. The microfilming and computerisation of New Territories land records will provide a more efficient service.

The Land Registration Ordinance also provides that all instruments registered under it shall have priority according to their respective dates of registration, unless they are registered within one month of execution, in which case priority relates back to the date of the instrument. For charging orders made by the court and pending court actions, priority runs from the day following the date of registration. The ordinance further provides that unregistered instruments, other than *bona fide* leases at a rack rent for a term not exceeding three years, shall be null and void as against any subsequent *bona fide* purchaser or mortgagee for valuable consideration.

Registration is essential to the protection of title, but does not guarantee it. Approval in principle has been given by the government to change the present system of land registration to one of title registration. Legislation to implement the titles registration system is being drafted.

Land registration statistics are at Appendix 34.

Government Conveyancing

Following the reorganisation of the Buildings and Lands Department, its Legal Advisory and Conveyancing Office has become part of the new Lands Department. The office provides professional legal services to the government for all government land transactions and associated matters. It is responsible for the issue, renewal, variation and termination of government leases as well as the drafting and completion of conditions of sale, grants and exchanges of government land, the apportionment of government rents and premia, and the recovery of outstanding rents. It provides conveyancing services for the Housing Authority in connection with the sale of flats built under the Home Ownership Scheme, and for the Financial Secretary Incorporated in connection with the extension of non-renewable government leases, the purchase and sale of government accommodation in private developments, mortgages to secure interest-free loans to private schools, the purchase of properties for government staff quarters and group housing schemes for the elderly. It is also responsible for the processing of the Consent Applications which are governed by the rules of the Land Authority's Consent Scheme. During the year, 14 applications involving 3 820 units in the urban areas were approved and in the New Territories, 46 applications involving 26 665 units were approved.

Survey and Mapping

The Survey and Mapping Office of the Lands Department is responsible for defining and recording land boundaries of all existing and new land developments, providing and maintaining the territory-wide survey control system, mapping the territory at various scales for land administration, engineering and other government purposes, and managing a computerised land information system.

Geodetic control systems, which are horizontal and vertical control networks covering the whole territory, have been established and are maintained to a high degree of accuracy. These systems provide the necessary origin and control points for cadastral (property boundary), topographical mapping, engineering and other surveys.

Cadastral surveying is one of the more important functions of the office, defining land boundaries for disposal and redevelopment, among other administrative purposes. The office maintains a comprehensive record of all leasehold and government land boundaries in the territory, with most urban area records stored in digital form and the New Territories records kept in graphical form.

The office's mapping coverage of Hong Kong is extensive. The most definitive series of maps and the foundation of all other mapping is the large-scale (1:1 000) basic topographic series (3 000 sheets). Smaller-scaled maps include the monochrome map series at 1:5 000 (157 sheets) and the coloured map series at 1:20 000 (16 sheets). Two monochrome street map series at 1:10 000 and 1:15 000 of the urban areas in Hong Kong, Kowloon and parts of the New Territories are produced for special uses and as a base for the popular guide-book *Hong Kong Guide—Streets and Places*. Demand for leisure maps, in the form of the Countryside Series and the Tourist Guide, is strong.

The Survey and Mapping Office provides cartographic services for many government departments. These include full-colour mapping for geological purposes, base maps for weather forecasting, aeronautical charts, electoral boundary maps and pollution control plans.

Its Reprographic Unit also provides services in photo-reproduction and plan copying, and serves as an essential back-up for in-house map reduction and other cartographic activities.

A computerised land information system is being installed in District Survey Offices in phases, as digital map data and land records become available. The system processes and analyses land information, and is a useful tool for handling enquiries on land status. The system also automates the production of large-scale maps and cadastral plans. Up-to-date mapping and boundary information can be made readily available to users. Besides producing standard 1:1 000 survey sheets containing full topographical features, the system can also produce plans according to the user's specifications. Mapping information in digital form may be supplied to the public on payment of a fee. Direct on-line access to the central mapping data is also possible. Data conversion for the districts is being speeded up by contracting-out the work and is scheduled for completion in 1994.

The office's Photogrammetric Survey Section provides aerial photographs and photogrammetric mapping, as well as data for engineering design work, environmental studies and town planning work, and volumetric calculations for quarry and controlled tipping operations. The Air Survey Unit is also on call for quick response photography in emergency operations such as storms, flooding and landslips.

Drainage Services

The Drainage Services Department is committed to a programme of works to upgrade Hong Kong's drainage systems to significantly reduce water pollution and flooding as far as possible, at an estimated cost of some $20 billion over the next 10 years.

It is responsible for planning, designing, constructing, operating and maintaining the sewerage, sewage treatment and stormwater drainage infrastructures.

To serve the community, the department has pledged to attend expeditiously to complaints on drainage matters, such as blocked drains, and to promptly process applications for drainage connections for private developments.

Treatment and Disposal of Foul Water

The treatment and disposal of foul water, including domestic sewage and trade and industrial effluent, is based on standards, strategies and programmes drawn up by the Environmental Protection Department.

The projects on foul water disposal are broadly divided into three categories: sewerage or sewage treatment projects which were in the public works programme before the new strategy to combat water pollution evolved; 'sewerage masterplan schemes' which are territory-wide sewerage rehabilitation and improvement projects; and the 'strategic sewage disposal scheme' under the new strategy. The latter is a massive project to collect all the sewage from Hong Kong Island, Kowloon, Tsuen Wan, Kwai Chung and Tseung Kwan O into a deep tunnel, intercepting sewer system that will discharge the sewage, after treatment on Stonecutters Island and Mount Davis, through a long sea outfall into the Dangan Channel, south of Lamma Island.

Under the existing projects category, the largest project in hand was the Tolo Harbour Effluent Export Scheme. This will export the sewage effluent from the Sha Tin and Tai Po sewage treatment works, away from the enclosed Tolo Harbour, into Victoria Harbour, where it can be more satisfactorily diluted through tidal flows. The works comprise sewage pumping stations, rising mains, submarine pipelines and a sewer tunnel, of 3.2-metre in diameter and 7.5 kilometres in length, under Tsz Wan Shan. Stage I of the works between Sha Tin and Victoria Harbour will be completed in 1994 and includes the construction of the sewer tunnel. Stage II of the works between Tai Po and Sha Tin started in late 1992, for completion in mid-1995, and includes the construction of a one-metre diameter, six-kilometre long, steel rising main buried under the seabed of Tolo Harbour.

Other projects underway in this category included the construction of a sewage screening plant to serve a population of 1.2 million in the Tsuen Wan and Kwai Chung area, a sewage pumping station and intercepting sewer at Ap Lei Chau, and a sewerage system at Hung Hom. The Northwest New Territories Sewerage Scheme was commissioned in March.

Under the sewerage masterplan schemes, planning and design work was in hand to improve the sewage collection, treatment and disposal facilities in Tsuen Wan; Kwai Chung and Tsing Yi; North, South and Northwest Kowloon; Central; Western and Wanchai West.

Construction work was underway in the Southern district of Hong Kong Island. In Stanley, a sewage treatment works was being constructed underground, in a cavern, and is due for commissioning in mid-1994, along with the completion of other sewerage rehabilitation and improvement works in the Stanley and Tai Tam areas. The works in Repulse Bay and Shek O are expected to be completed towards the end of 1995. In East Kowloon, a system of new trunk sewers and pumping stations is expected to be completed in early 1994.

Engineering feasibility studies for the implementation of the strategic sewage disposal scheme were completed during the year. Detailed design work for the Principal Collection and Treatment System started and construction is planned to commence in mid-1994.

Stormwater Drainage and Flood Control

The North and Northwest New Territories are particularly vulnerable to flooding.

Damage caused by flooding was widespread when typhoons Dot and Ira struck the territory in September and November, respectively. During the November typhoon, some 400 000 Tuen Mun residents were left without running water for four days due to the flooding of the Fu Tei fresh water pumping station.

The Drainage Services Department completed a study reviewing rainfall, stream flows and flooding predictions in 1993, with the aim of drawing up basin management plans for the main rivers in the North and Northwest New Territories and examining in more detail potential local flood mitigation measures. This was a follow-up to a territory-wide study in 1990.

In addition, pamphlets giving advice on what to do and what not to do in a flooding situation were distributed through the District Offices to people living in flood-prone areas.

The government commenced work during the year on the first stage of its largest scheme to alleviate the flooding problem in Northwest New Territories. Valued at $1.1 billion, this involves the construction of 14 kilometres of flood-ways and concrete-lined nullahs for the improvement of the Kam Tin River and Shan Pui River in Yuen Long. Design work for the remaining stages of this scheme and for the construction of main drainage channels in Ngau Tam Mei and San Tin, also in Northwest New Territories, is now in progress.

As an associated measure, about a dozen flood water pumping systems have also been constructed and are in operation to mitigate the impact of flooding in low-lying villages in the New Territories. Six more are planned.

The government is also working closely with the Shenzhen Municipality to resolve the flooding problem associated with the Shenzhen River, which divides Hong Kong and Shenzhen. The solution proposed involves the straightening, widening and deepening of some 17 kilometres of the river, to enhance its flow to reduce the flood risk in the catchments on both sides of the river. Preparatory work has been agreed upon by the two sides and is in progress.

The Land Drainage Bill, introduced in the Legislative Council in the middle of the year, is an essential component of the strategy to alleviate flooding in the New Territories. When passed into law, it will authorise government staff to access, inspect, clear and maintain important watercourses running through or bordering on private land, as a further attempt to reduce the risk of flooding.

Operation and Maintenance of the Drainage System

With the commissioning of each additional item of infrastructure, there is a consequential increased commitment in operations and maintenance. The volume of sewage treated territory-wide has increased from 385 million cubic metres in 1989 to 635 million cubic metres in 1993, of which 146 million cubic metres receive full biological treatment.

Since the establishment of the department, the approach to operation and maintenance of the public drainage system has progressively shifted from crisis management to preventive maintenance. The efficient maintenance of the drainage infrastructure is essential to ensure the proper and effective disposal of foul and storm water, and to prevent blockages and leaks which also cause foul odours, flooding or other nuisances to the public. The department now maintains 2 900 kilometres of watercourses, drains and sewers. These are increasing at the rate of 130 kilometres per year. Some 45 000 clearance exercises are carried out yearly to remove over 250 000 cubic metres of silt from drains and watercourses, to keep them free-flowing and their pollution level low.

The department also operates an Emergency Storm Damage Organisation. The organisation is run by staff working on a rotational basis and is supported by the department's own labour force and contractors. Its operation ensures that emergency situations are dealt with efficiently.

Geotechnical Control

The Geotechnical Engineering Office (GEO) of the Civil Engineering Department was established after the landslip disasters of the 1970s, and the control of geotechnical aspects of construction works, in the interest of public safety, continues to be one of its foremost duties. Checks were made on 7 000 design proposals during the year.

Work to upgrade unsatisfactory old slopes to modern safety standards is continuing. Private sector resources are now being employed to accelerate the Landslip Preventive Measures Programme. During 1993, landslip preventive works were completed on 90 slopes and retaining walls, at a cost of $70 million, within the programme. Preliminary studies were carried out on 1 200 slopes and retaining walls, and detailed geotechnical investigations were finished on 100 slopes and retaining walls. Work was completed on the extension to the Mid-Levels boulder fence above Conduit Road, together with the *in situ* stabilisation of large boulders in the boulder field behind the fence, at a cost of $5.6 million. Upgrading work on the slopes of an old landfill borrow area at Fung Shing Street, Ngau Chi Wan, was also completed at a cost of $7 million.

The GEO operates the Landslip Warning System and a 24-hour emergency service to provide advice to protect public safety when landslips occur. Exceptionally heavy rainfall on June 16 resulted in about 100 landslip incidents, one of which involved a fatality. GEO staff attending these incidents gave advice on immediate measures to reduce danger, as well as on permanent remedial measures.

The GEO's public education campaign continued, to increase awareness of the importance of slope maintenance and the responsibility of land owners to maintain their slopes.

A revised edition of *Geoguide 1: Guide to Retaining Wall Design* was produced. Publication of the document will provide upgraded technical standards in this area. The GEO also published a document on granular and geotextile filters with the same objective.

The Hong Kong Geological Survey prepared 1:20 000 scale geological maps for the Tung Chung, Tai O and Cheung Chau districts. Compilation of memoirs relating to the Northeast New Territories and Lantau Island neared completion during the year, with publication scheduled for 1994. Work also started on the compilation of a comprehensive publication on the geology of Hong Kong.

A programme of systematic land inspections continued to identify old fill slopes and retaining walls, using aerial photography. Following publication of engineering geology maps and reports on the North Lantau development area, work commenced on a study of potential hazards related to slopes in the Tung Chung Valley. New geophysical techniques were introduced to assist with developing the stratigraphic model for offshore sediments. Other geophysical surveys were completed in Tolo Harbour, North Lantau and North Lamma. These will help to identify geological structures and buried marble in development areas.

The computerised borehole database for Lantau was completed, and work commenced on the database for the urban areas of Hong Kong and Kowloon. Standards were also being established for the computerisation of ground investigation records by contractors and consultants. Satellite photographs covering the territory were obtained to generate special purpose images, partly for monitoring suspended sediment offshore; while digital terrain models were under development for use in on-going landslide studies.

The Geotechnical Information Unit (GIU) houses the largest collection of geotechnical data in Hong Kong. It served more than 3 100 users during the year.

The Marine Geotechnology Section carried out research and development work for Port and Airport Development Strategy (PADS) projects, notably on foundations for marine structures and reclamations, and the sea-bed pits for the containment of contaminated mud dredged from development areas.

During the year, there were further improvements to ground investigation, geophysical surveys and soil and rock testing services provided for public works projects. An in-house quality assurance system was in the process of being implemented in the Ground Investigation Section of the Materials Division. A requirement has been introduced for ground investigation data to be submitted in a digital format, with the ultimate aim of setting up a territory-wide database.

A number of major ground investigations were undertaken for the Lantau Port and Tseung Kwan O Development Studies, the Strategic Sewage Disposal Scheme, various reclamation projects, new highway tunnels and for environmental studies at landfill sites. Major marine ground investigation and geophysical surveys were also carried out for the Fill Management Studies. Geophysical and hydrographical surveys were executed to study the environmental effects of dredging activities and marine dumping in Hong Kong waters. An increasing number of chemical analyses, including heavy metal testing, were undertaken for studies on contaminated marine mud.

The GEO manages the Public Works Central Laboratory at Kowloon Bay and seven public works regional laboratories in various parts of the territory. Over 300 000 tests on various construction materials were carried out during 1993. The laboratories are accredited under the Hong Kong Laboratory Accreditation Scheme to carry out tests on construction materials, in addition to providing laboratory calibration services. They are currently preparing for accreditation of soils testing.

Fill Management

The territory's fill resources are managed by the Fill Management Committee, whose secretariat is a unit of the Geotechnical Engineering Office (GEO) of the Civil Engineering Department. The committee was set up in 1989 to make decisions on the reservation, allocation and efficient utilisation of fill resources for government and major private projects.

Up to the end of 1993, some 270 million cubic metres of marine fill had been allocated or reserved and of this amount, approximately 120 million cubic metres had been extracted from the seabed for the construction of reclamations. A further 250 million cubic metres of fill from marine sources and a similar quantity from land sources are needed for reclamations over the next 15 years.

A second role of the committee is to plan the marine disposal of dredged mud, including contaminated mud, and to allocate disposal capacity at the gazetted marine spoil grounds.

During the year under review, 100 million cubic metres of uncontaminated mud and five million cubic metres of contaminated mud were disposed of under licences issued by the Environmental Protection Department. The uncontaminated mud was dumped in spoil grounds and in worked-out borrow areas, and the contaminated mud was placed in disposal pits specially designed to ensure containment.

Water Supplies

Water from China

China is the major single source of water supply for Hong Kong, and all future increases in demand will be met from this source. This arrangement dates back to 1960, when a scheme was first formulated for receiving a piped supply of 22.7 million cubic metres a year. The annual supply from China stipulated under the agreements has increased to 630 million cubic metres for the period from March 1993 to February 1994, and this will continue to increase in stages to 840 million cubic metres by the year 2000. Apart from the fixed quantities of supply stipulated in the agreements, there are provisions for the purchase of additional supplies from China in years of low rainfall in Hong Kong.

Following the agreement reached with the Chinese authorities in December 1989 to increase the China water supply up to a maximum of 1 100 million cubic metres per year to cope with anticipated demands beyond 1994 and into the early 2000s, a conceptual plan was developed for the necessary works to receive and distribute the additional supply. The works are being implemented in stages, with Stage I works to be substantially completed by the end of 1994. These works include some 22 kilometres of large-diameter delivery pipes; new pumping stations at Muk Wu, Tai Po Tau, Au Tau and Sai O; and major improvements to an existing pumping station at Tai Mei Tuk. Work on the first contract commenced in December 1991, and work on all the pumping stations and pipelines is now in progress.

Water Storage and Consumption

Full supply was maintained throughout the year. At the end of 1993, there were 386 million cubic metres of water in storage, compared with 315 million cubic metres at the end of 1992, with 331 million cubic metres being stored in Hong Kong's two largest reservoirs, High Island and Plover Cove. Rainfall for the year was 2 344 millimetres, compared with the average of 2 214 millimetres. Water piped from China during the year totalled 627 million cubic metres.

A peak consumption of 2.78 million cubic metres per day was recorded, compared with the 1992 peak of 2.82 million cubic metres. The average daily consumption throughout the year was 2.51 million cubic metres, an increase of 3.3 per cent compared with the 1992 average of 2.43 million cubic metres. The consumption of potable water totalled 915 million cubic metres, compared with 889 million cubic metres in 1992. In addition, 129 million cubic metres of sea water for flushing was supplied, compared with 127 million cubic metres in 1992.

Water Works

The water distribution system continued to be extended and enlarged to meet urban and rural demands in the territory. This included expansion of the distribution network to supply remote villages in the New Territories.

Construction for the Au Tau Treatment Works Stage II, a new intake tower in Tai Lam Chung Reservoir, Sham Tseng Treatment Works Stage I, and extension of the Sheung Shui Treatment Works and Yau Kom Tau Treatment Works were in progress.

The detailed design for the Ma On Shan Treatment Works was completed in December. Tenders were invited from pre-qualified contractors, with a view to starting construction in April 1994.

Planning was in hand for the major new treatment works at Ngau Tam Mei. Further planning for the improvement of system capacity was also in progress to meet the demand arising from new developments in central and western Hong Kong Island—including the new reclamation areas in Central and Wan Chai—Sham Tseng, Kwun Tong, Yuen Long, Tin Shui Wai and the northwestern New Territories.

Design work for additional service reservoirs, pumping stations and water supply networks in Ap Lei Chau and Repulse Bay was completed, while that for Tuen Mun, Yau Kom Tau, Tsuen Wan, Tsing Yi, Tseung Kwan O, and the western Mid-Levels was in progress. The design for the flushing water supply system for Ma On Shan and Tai Po was substantially completed.

Design work was also in hand for the improvement of water supply to the metropolitan southeastern area of Kowloon, the enhancement of Tai Tam Tuk Pumping Station and the major renovation of the sea water supply system for central Kowloon.

Consultants were commissioned to carry out a feasibility study on the treatment and disposal of sludge generated by the existing treatment works. The consultancy agreement commenced in August and will be completed in early 1994.

Work on the permanent water supply system for the new airport at Chek Lap Kok and other developments in North Lantau associated with the Port and Airport Development Strategy was being implemented in stages. The Stage I works, to be commissioned by mid-1996, include submarine and land mains, a water treatment works, pumping stations, a service reservoir and an aqueduct between Siu Ho Wan and Silvermine Bay.

Tai Wan Salt Water Pumping Station, which provides flushing water to a large area of East Kowloon, was upgraded by replacing the diesel-driven pumps with electrically-driven units capable of a greater output.

Improvements to chlorine storage facilities in the Tsuen Wan Treatment Works, Yau Kom Tau Treatment Works, Tai Po Tau Treatment Works, Tuen Mun Treatment Works and Tai Lam Chung Prechlorination House were completed at the end of the year. The improvements formed part of the mitigation measures recommended by consultants to improve the safety of chlorine storage. Major design work commenced for the extension of Tai Lam Chung Prechlorination House.

Water Accounts and Customer Relations

The number of the Water Supplies Department's consumer accounts continued to rise at a rate of about three per cent and the consumer account base expanded to approximately 2.01 million accounts at the end of 1993. Computer systems were widely employed to provide efficient enquiry services; to handle applications for water supply and change of consumer particulars; and to issue demand notes for water charges, connection fees and water deposits. In July, a new Electronic Meter Reading System, employing hand-held computers, was introduced to further improve the efficiency of the meter reading and billing processes. An Interactive Voice Response System will be introduced in early 1994 to provide a round-the-clock enquiry service on water supply matters. Efforts to promote the autopay service continued, and the number of consumer accounts using autopay for payment of water charges reached 251 000, or about 12 per cent of all consumers.

A number of computer systems were being developed for the handling of water quality complaints, automating the process of closing water accounts, and preparing cost estimates of capital works projects.

The department issued its performance pledges in March. Standards of service were publicised. In July, a customer liaison group, comprising members randomly selected from the department's computerised database of consumers, was set up to provide a channel of communication on customers' needs and expectations of service standards.

Electricity

Electricity is provided by two commercial companies — the Hongkong Electric Company Limited (HEC), which supplies Hong Kong Island and the neighbouring islands of Ap Lei Chau and Lamma; and China Light and Power Company Limited (CLP), which supplies the whole of Kowloon and the New Territories, including Lantau and a number of outlying islands. The supply to consumers is at 50 Hz alternating current, while the voltage is being upgraded to 220 volts single phase and 380 volts three phase from 200 and 346 volts, respectively.

The two supply companies are investor-owned and do not operate on a franchise basis. The government monitors their financial arrangements through mutually agreed scheme of control agreements. New agreements with CLP and HEC came into effect on October 1, 1993 and January 1, 1994, respectively. Both will last for 15 years. The agreements require each company to seek the approval of the government for certain aspects of their financing plans, including projected tariff levels.

In 1985, the Hong Kong Nuclear Investment Company (a wholly-owned subsidiary of CLP) and the Guangdong Nuclear Investment Company (wholly owned by the Chinese Ministry of Nuclear Industry) signed the joint venture contract for the formation of the Guangdong Nuclear Power Joint Venture Company, to construct and operate a nuclear power station at Daya Bay in Guangdong.

When completed, the Guangdong Nuclear Power Station will comprise two 985MW pressurised water reactors. The first unit will be put to commercial operation in February 1994, while the commissioning of the second unit is scheduled for mid-1994. About 70 per cent of the power from the station will be purchased by CLP to meet part of the longer-term demand for electricity in its area of supply.

The operations of the three generating companies affiliated to CLP — Peninsula Electric Power Company Limited (PEPCO), Kowloon Electricity Supply Company Limited (KESCO) and Castle Peak Power Company Limited (CAPCO) — were consolidated under CAPCO in April 1992. CAPCO's present generating facilities include the Tsing Yi 'A' (796MW), Tsing Yi 'B' (876MW), Castle Peak 'A' (1 752MW), Castle Peak 'B' (2 708MW) and Penny's Bay (300MW) power stations. The total installed capacity is 6 432MW. The government has also approved the installation by CLP of four 600MW blocks of additional generating capacity, the first two of which will be installed in a new power station at Black Point, Tuen Mun, in 1996 and 1997, respectively. The other two blocks will be commissioned within the periods 1998 to 2000 and 1999 to 2001. All will be fuelled by natural gas piped from the Yacheng 13-1 gas field off Hainan Island in China.

CAPCO is 60 per cent owned by Exxon Energy Limited and 40 per cent by CLP, while the associated transmission and distribution systems are wholly owned by CLP. CLP's transmission system operates at 400kV, 132kV and 66kV, and distribution is effected mainly at 33 kV, 11kV and 380 volts.

CLP has more than 173 primary and over 7 916 secondary sub-stations in its transmission and distribution network. An extra high voltage transmission system at 400kV was completed in 1986 to transmit power from the Castle Peak Stations to the various load centres. Currently it comprises a double-circuit overhead line system encircling the New Territories, underground cables and eight extra high voltage sub-stations. Construction and planning work for the addition of new extra high voltage sub-stations and for reinforcement of the existing system is in progress.

In HEC's supply areas, electricity is supplied entirely from the Lamma Power Station. At the end of 1993, the total installed capacity at the Lamma Power Station was 2 605MW. There are plans to add a further 350MW unit to Lamma in late 1995.

HEC's transmission system operates at 275kV, 132kV and 66kV, and distribution is effected mainly at 11kV and 380 volts. With the exception of a small proportion of 132kV overhead transmission lines, all supplies are transmitted and distributed by underground or submarine cables.

The transmission systems of CLP and HEC are interconnected by a cross-harbour link. This provides emergency back-up and achieves cost savings to consumers through economic energy transfers between the two systems and a reduction in the amount of generating capacity that needs to be kept as spinning reserve against the tripping of other units. The interconnection, commissioned in 1981, currently has a capacity of 720MVA.

CLP's system is also interconnected with that of the Guangdong General Power Company of China and electricity is exported to Guangdong province. Such sales, which are made from existing reserve generating capacity, are governed by an agreement with the government, signed in March 1992, under which CLP's consumers receive priority of supply and 80 per cent of the profit from the sales.

Also, in July 1985, CLP signed a contract with the China Merchants Steam Navigation Company Limited for the supply of electricity, for a 10-year period starting from late 1986, to the industrial zone of Shekou and the adjacent Chi Wan area, both in Guangdong. The arrangements, which afford Shekou a reliable electricity supply without subsidy from Hong Kong consumers, is illustrative of the close co-operation on energy matters which has developed on both sides of the border.

CLP, through its affiliated company, the Hong Kong Pumped Storage Development Company Limited, has purchased the right to use 50 per cent of the capacity of the Guangzhou Pumped Storage Power Station, located at Conghua. The total installed capacity of the current phase is 1 200MW. The first two 300MW units were commissioned in 1993, with the other two scheduled for commissioning in 1994. Off-peak electricity from the Castle Peak Stations and Guangdong Nuclear Power Station is used to pump water from a lower reservoir to an upper one. The water is allowed to flow downhill during the day to generate electricity to meet Hong Kong's peak demand.

The Electricity Ordinance, enacted in 1990, provides, among other things, for the registration of electrical workers and contractors. To ensure that electrical work is carried out by qualified personnel, only registered electrical workers and contractors are allowed to practise, with effect from June 1, 1992. To be eligible for registration, they must possess the necessary experience and qualifications. The registration of electrical workers and contractors started in November 1990 and November 1991, respectively. At the end of December 1993, over 53 000 and 7 200 qualified electrical workers and contractors, respectively, had been registered.

To further enhance public safety, the government is planning to introduce statutory controls over electrical products and the power supply industry. Initially, legislation will provide control over plugs and adaptors. Comprehensive legislation on electrical product safety will be enacted in 1995 to provide control over all domestic electrical products. The introduction of the new Electricity Supply Regulations is scheduled for 1996.

In May 1990, the government decided that the electricity supply voltage in Hong Kong should be upgraded from 200 volts single phase or 346 volts three phase to 220 volts single phase or 380 volts three phase. A Supply Voltage Advisory Committee was appointed in February 1991 to advise on the implementation of voltage upgrading in the territory. The voltage upgrading is being carried out in two phases and will be completed in about six years. Phase I conversion, covering existing installations inside government buildings, started in August 1990 and was completed in November 1992. Phase II conversion, covering existing installations in Housing Authority and private sector buildings, commenced in January 1993 and will take about four years to complete.

Electricity statistics and sales figures are at Appendix 36.

Gas

Gas is widely used throughout the territory for domestic, commercial and industrial purposes. Two main types of fuel gas are available: Towngas, distributed by the Hong Kong and China Gas Company Limited (HKCG); and liquefied petroleum gas (LPG), supplied by major oil companies based in Hong Kong, namely Shell, Mobil, Esso, Caltex, Concord Oil and China Resources. Towngas is mainly supplied as a manufactured gas, but for some customers, substitute natural gas (SNG) is supplied under the Towngas trademark. The constituents of LPG are butane and propane, mixed in approximate proportions of 75 per cent and 25 per cent, respectively.

The total number of gas customers is about 1.865 million. In 1993, Towngas accounted for 65 per cent of the total fuel gas sold in energy terms and LPG for 35 per cent.

HKCG manufactures Towngas at two plants, at Ma Tau Kok and the Tai Po Industrial Estate. Both use naphtha as a feedstock. They currently have output capacities of 2.2 million and 8.4 million cubic metres per day, respectively.

Towngas is distributed through an integrated distribution system to about 985 000 customers for cooking and heating purposes. The mains network extends to the urban areas of Hong Kong Island, including Aberdeen, Repulse Bay, Stanley and Ap Lei Chau; Kowloon; and many new towns in the New Territories, including Sha Tin and Tai Po, Yuen Long and Tsing Yi Island. HKCG is currently constructing a 90-kilometre network transmission pipeline in the New Territories. The new transmission line is designed to operate at elevated pressure and will provide an additional 0.8 million cubic metres of line pack storage capacity.

SNG is distributed by HKCG under the Towngas trademark from a temporary plant located in Tuen Mun, specifically designed and operated to provide the gas requirements of the new town. The plant will remain *in situ* until the new transmission pipeline connecting Tai Po to Tuen Mun has been completed.

LPG is imported to Hong Kong by sea. About 59 per cent of total sales is distributed to customers, via dealer networks, in portable cylinders. The remaining 41 per cent is distributed through piped gas systems from bulk LPG storage and vaporiser installations, which are located in, or adjacent to, the developments being supplied.

There are about 444 LPG distributors operating within the territory. Additionally, 23 LPG site operators manage 510 bulk storage installations under government-monitored arrangements. Altogether, there are 880 000 LPG customers.

In 1982, the government introduced a piped gas policy to discourage the use of gas cylinders in domestic dwellings. At the same time, it also began a programme of encouraging the upgrading of sub-standard gas water heaters. The percentage of domestic dwellings using cylinders fell to less than 30 per cent in 1993, and the number of upgraded gas water heaters amounted to some 67 815. Apart from suicide cases, there were three fatalities arising from fuel gas incidents during the past year.

As a further means of safeguarding the general public and gas consumers, the Gas Safety Ordinance was introduced in 1991. The ordinance and its subsidiary regulations constitute a comprehensive package of gas safety legislation, covering all aspects of fuel gas importation, manufacture, storage, transport, supply and use of gas. The Director of Electrical and Mechanical Services was appointed the Gas Authority, and the Gas Safety Advisory Committee was established for the purpose of advising the authority on all relevant matters. Since April 1992, it has been necessary for all gas supply companies, gas installers and contractors to be registered with the Gas Authority in order to carry out their operations. In 1993, seven gas supply companies, 2 759 gas installers and 371 gas contractors were registered under the scheme. In addition, the administrative arrangements for controlling safety in the transportation of LPG in tankers and cylinder wagons were transferred from the Director of Fire Services to the Gas Authority.

The government and the fuel gas supply industry have adopted risk assessment techniques for the detailed examination of all appropriate potentially hazardous gas installations. The risk assessments facilitate the taking of remedial measures where necessary, with the aim of ensuring that residents in the vicinity of these installations are not exposed to unacceptable risk levels.

Professional Registration

The Architects Registration Ordinance and the Engineers Registration Ordinance were enacted in 1990. Registration boards were set up and, by the end of 1993, there were 960 registered architects and 930 registered professional engineers. The Surveyors Registration Ordinance and the Planners Registration Ordinance were enacted in 1991, leading to the registration of about 240 professional surveyors and 100 professional planners. Registration for all four professions requires, in addition to approved professional qualifications, ordinary residence and at least one year's professional experience in Hong Kong.

15
TRANSPORT

A NEW franchised bus service on Hong Kong Island, the start of work on the third harbour road crossing, increased expenditure on transport infrastructure and the release of a report on future strategic rail development topped the transport agenda during the year.

To promote healthy competition in the provision of public transport services, Citybus Limited successfully took over, from the China Motor Bus Company (CMB), the operation of 24 Hong Kong Island routes and two cross-harbour tunnel routes in September. Despite initial teething problems, the new service was soon having a positive impact on the overall quality of bus services on the island. The remaining island routes continue to be operated by CMB under a new franchise.

Work began in October on the Western Harbour Crossing, linking new reclamations on both sides of the harbour, following the award of a 'build, operate and transfer' franchise to a private consortium. On completion in 1997, the crossing will provide a fast road link from Hong Kong Island, via the West Kowloon Expressway and North Lantau Expressway, to developments on Lantau Island and the new airport.

Work also began on the construction of additional climbing lanes on the Tuen Mun Highway, to improve traffic flow between the Northwest New Territories and urban Kowloon.

At the year's end, a prequalification exercise was underway to select a contractor to build the Ting Kau Bridge, which will be funded by the government. The bridge, together with the Tai Lam Tunnel and the Yuen Long Approach Road, will form the country park section of Route 3, which will provide a fast link between the border and the container port in Kwai Chung. Construction of the latter two sections of Route 3 will be privatised under a 'build, operate and transfer' franchise, tenders for which were invited on December 3.

Proposals for future railway development were mapped out in the Railway Development Study, published in April for public consultation. The study recommends that priority should be given to a Mass Transit Railway extension to Tseung Kwan O and to the construction of a railway line in the Western New Territories. This proposed railway line could accommodate a freight service between the border and the container port, long-distance passenger services to China, and commuter services to the Northwest New Territories. Public opinion collected in the consultation exercise is being assessed, before the government decides on the railway development strategy.

During the year, construction work continued on the major transport links from the new airport at Chek Lap Kok to the urban area.

Emphasis continued to be placed on improving the efficiency with which transport and related services are delivered to the public.

Another significant event was the introduction of fare concessions by the franchised bus and ferry companies for elderly passengers.

This chapter also looks at Hong Kong's port and aviation services.

The Administrative Framework

The Transport Branch of the Government Secretariat, headed by the Secretary for Transport, is responsible for overall policy formulation, direction and co-ordination of internal transport matters. The Secretary for Transport is assisted by the Transport Advisory Committee, which advises the Governor in Council on major transport policies and issues. The committee has 11 appointed members, including the chairman and six government officials, and is supported by a Transport Complaints Unit, which received 12 793 complaint cases on traffic and transport matters in 1993. The Secretary for Transport also chairs the Transport Policy Co-ordinating Committee, which oversees the formulation and implementation of major internal transport policies. On local transport matters, the government is advised by the district boards, and their traffic and transport committees.

The Commissioner for Transport, the head of the Transport Department, is the authority for administering the Road Traffic Ordinance and legislation regulating public transport operations other than railways. His responsibilities cover strategic transport planning, road traffic management, government road tunnels, car parks and metered parking spaces, and the regulation of internal roads and waterborne public transport. He is also the authority for the licensing of drivers and the registration, licensing and inspection of vehicles.

While the police force is the principal agency for enforcing traffic legislation and prosecuting offenders, the prosecutions unit of the Transport Department handles prosecutions involving safety defects found on buses, disqualifications under the Driving Offence Points System, and breaches of vehicle safety regulations and government tunnel regulations. In 1993, the unit handled 23 prosecutions in respect of buses, 5 158 cases for which disqualification was sought under the Driving Offence Points System, and 433 prosecutions in respect of breaches of tunnel and other regulations.

A Transport Tribunal, set up under the Road Traffic Ordinance and chaired by a non-government official, provides the public with a channel of appeal against decisions made by the Commissioner for Transport in respect of the registration and licensing of vehicles, the issue of hire car permits and passenger service licences, and designation of car-testing centres.

The Transport Department also operates an Emergency Transport Co-ordination Centre, which co-ordinates special traffic and transport arrangements during serious traffic and transport disruptions, rainstorms and typhoons. The centre undertook 13 operations in 1993.

To tackle the area-wide traffic congestion at the Kwai Chung container port, the police operate, when necessary, the Emergency Container Port Traffic Control Centre jointly with representatives of the Transport Department, Kwai Tsing District Office, the three terminal operators, the Container Tractor Owners Association and the Container Transportation Employee's General Union. The control centre is located within the container port and is equipped with a Closed Circuit Television system and efficient communication links. During the year, it operated three times.

The Director of Highways heads the Highways Department, which is responsible for designing and building all highways, their repair and maintenance, and also for studying new railway proposals.

Planning

The updating of the Second Comprehensive Transport Study was completed during the year. This facilitates the planning of territorial transport networks and the managing of the demand for road use up to the year 2011.

A freight transport strategy, to meet the projected freight demand and improve the efficiency of goods movements up to 2011, is being developed through the Freight Transport Study.

Meanwhile, the railway development strategy is being formulated, taking account of views expressed following public consultation on the Railway Development Study.

The Travel Characteristics Survey, which provides up-to-date information on house-hold trips and socio-economic data, was completed in early 1993. The results are being used for transport planning purposes, including updating the existing transport planning models.

A Parking Demand Study has commenced, to update the parking inventory and to forecast future demand, so as to identify the shortfalls in parking provisions for the territory.

Cross-Border Traffic

There are three road crossing points between Hong Kong and China — at Sha Tau Kok, Man Kam To and Lok Ma Chau. The total capacity of the three crossings is about 40 000 vehicles per day. The crossings open at 7 am each day and while the Sha Tau Kok crossing closes at 6 pm, the other two close at 10 pm.

Cross-border vehicular traffic increased by about 12 per cent during the year, compared with 1992. The increase was registered mainly at Lok Ma Chau. The average daily traffic figures at the three crossing points in 1993 were about 1 700, 9 400, and 9 000 at Sha Tau Kok, Man Kam To and Lok Ma Chau, respectively. Goods vehicles accounted for 96 per cent of the traffic, reflecting the rapid growth in trade and industrial links with China. At the end of the year, 25 companies operated tourist coach services across the border.

The Kowloon-Canton Railway continued to play an important role in carrying freight and passenger traffic between Hong Kong and China. Some 2.28 million revenue tonnes of freight were brought into Hong Kong by rail, compared to 2.81 million tonnes in 1992. Exports to China by rail accounted for 1.21 million revenue tonnes, an increase of 2.5 per cent from the 1.18 million tonnes carried in 1992. There are five goods yards at Hung Hom, Ho Man Tin, Mong Kok, Sha Tin and Fo Tan, and a marshalling yard at Lo Wu. Freight trains are hauled by a fleet of 12 diesel locomotives. A Hung Hom-Daleng railway container shuttle service was commissioned on December 7, 1992. Some 41 million rail passengers crossed the border in 1993, compared to 38 million the previous year. A further extension of the terminal building at Lo Wu is being constructed to cope with growth in rail traffic. The project is scheduled for completion in early 1995.

Ferry services between Hong Kong and China carried 6.5 million passengers, compared with 5.1 million in 1992. At the end of the year, there were 29 ferry routes between Hong Kong and China, operated by eight companies.

The opening of the Shenzhen Airport in October 1991 provided a further impetus to the growth of cross-border traffic, and coach and ferry services now operate between the airport and Hong Kong.

Construction of Phase I of the Guangzhou-Shenzhen-Zhuhai Superhighway linking Guangzhou and Huanggang started in January 1992. When completed, it will further increase cross-border traffic, particularly through Lok Ma Chau.

The Road Network

Hong Kong's roads have one of the highest vehicle densities in the world. At the end of 1993, there were 439 719 licensed vehicles and about 1 625 kilometres of roads — 418 on Hong Kong Island, 394 in Kowloon and 813 in the New Territories, representing 271 vehicles per kilometre of road. This high vehicle density, combined with the difficult terrain and dense building development, poses a constant challenge to transport planning, road construction and maintenance. There are eight major road tunnels, over 818 flyovers and bridges, 446 footbridges and 278 subways to assist the mobility of vehicles and people.

To cope with increasing transport demands, the Highways Department has continued an extensive construction programme, with about 60 road projects currently under construction and 30 being actively planned.

The department's budget for the financial year ending March 1994 totals $7,681 million, of which $7,043 million is for major highway construction, and $638 million for road and public lighting maintenance.

Strategic Road Network

The spine of the strategic road network is Route 1, which runs from Aberdeen on the southern shore of Hong Kong Island, and cuts through Kowloon peninsula and the New Territories, to the Lok Ma Chau border crossing point.

On Hong Kong Island, Route 8 runs along the northern shore from the Cross Harbour Tunnel, via the Island Eastern Corridor, to Shau Kei Wan and Chai Wan in the east. Route 7 stretches westwards from the Cross Harbour Tunnel along the northern shore, via Gloucester Road, Harcourt Road and Connaught Road, to Hill Road at Kennedy Town.

On the mainland, Route 2 runs from the Kowloon Bay Reclamation, through the Airport Tunnel, via the East and West Kowloon Corridors, Tsuen Wan Road, Tuen Mun Road and Yuen Long Northern Bypass to the junction of Castle Peak Road and Lok Ma Chau Border Link Road. Route 4 runs along the base of the foothills separating Kowloon from the New Territories, and connects Lai Chi Kok with Kwun Tong and with Tseung Kwan O through the Tseung Kwan O Tunnel. Route 5, another strategic road, is a seven-kilometre, two-way trunk road connecting Sha Tin with Tsuen Wan, via the Shing Mun Tunnels. It forms part of the New Territories Circular Road System.

Route 6 covers the Eastern Harbour Crossing, Kwun Tong Bypass, Tate's Cairn Tunnel and the approach road linking Tate's Cairn Tunnel to the Tolo Highway.

Improvements to Major Road Networks

In the northern New Territories, the remaining section of the New Territories Circular Road from Pak Shek Au to Au Tau was completed during the year under review.

The Yuen Long to Tuen Mun Eastern Corridor was completed in July to provide an eastern continuation of Route 2. This corridor is a dual, two-lane trunk road along the eastern side of Castle Peak Road, connecting with the Yuen Long Southern Bypass, construction of which started in early 1992 and is scheduled for completion in late 1994.

To improve cross-border traffic and access to the northwest New Territories, the country park section of Route 3 is under planning, for completion by late 1998. It will be a dual, three-lane carriageway, connecting Ting Kau with Yuen Long. The private sector will be invited to build the section from Au Tau to Ting Kau under a franchise arrangement.

New Airport Access

The relocation of the airport to Chek Lap Kok requires additional road links to serve the new airport and its supporting community. Work is underway on the major highway projects which will cater for airport traffic, including the Western Harbour Crossing, the West Kowloon Expressway, the Kwai Chung and Tsing Yi sections of Route 3, the Lantau Fixed Crossing and the North Lantau Expressway.

The Airport Core Programme also includes a rail link, which will provide both a fast and efficient train service to the new airport and a domestic service to bring relief to the Nathan Road Corridor of the Mass Transit Railway. The rail link will, in addition, serve new developments on the West Kowloon Reclamation and in Tung Chung new town, and provide a third cross harbour rail link.

For more details, see Chapter 16.

Environmental Impact of Road Construction

The environmental impact of new road projects is carefully appraised at the planning stage by the Highways Department. Where practical, measures such as landscaping works, artificial contouring of surrounding hillsides and installation of noise barriers are considered. Measures taken include the application of pre-cast decorative concrete panels to the retaining wall of the Gascoigne Road Flyover project, and the installation of an enclosed-type noise barrier in a section of the Tate's Cairn Tunnel approach road near Richland Gardens in Kowloon Bay. Where necessary, consideration is also given to providing air-conditioning units and double-glazing in domestic premises where noise levels cannot be brought within the required standard by other means.

Road Opening Works

The highways provide space to install various utility services, such as water and gas mains, sewers, and electricity and telephone cables, besides serving as carriageways for vehicles and pedestrians. To cope with the demand resulting from the rapid development of Hong Kong, utility companies often have to excavate the carriageways and footpaths to maintain services by renewal, repair and enlargement of pipes, cables and ducts. On average, 170 new road openings are started every working day. These are co-ordinated and controlled by the Highways Department through a permit system, under which utility companies are required to carry out works to a required standard and in a limited period of time. In order to co-ordinate these works and to minimise traffic disruption, the department holds monthly Road Opening Co-ordinating Committee meetings with the utility companies, police and the Transport Department. Consideration is being given to improving the management of road openings, to reduce their duration and frequency.

Tunnels

In January, the management of the Lion Rock Tunnel, Airport Tunnel, Shing Mun Tunnels and Tseung Kwan O Tunnel was contracted out, following competitive tendering, to reduce the need for staff resources and to improve efficiency. The contractors are responsible for operating and managing the tunnels on behalf of the government. Toll charges remain under government control.

Lion Rock Tunnel, which links Kowloon and Sha Tin, began single tube operation in 1967, with a second tube added in 1978. It is the most heavily-used government tunnel and was used by 78 000 vehicles a day in 1993.

The toll-free Airport Tunnel provides direct road access from Hung Hom to Hong Kong International Airport. It also passes underneath the airport runway to Kowloon Bay. Opened in 1982, it was used by an average of 55 000 vehicles per day in 1993.

The Shing Mun Tunnels, opened to traffic in 1990, link Sha Tin to Tsuen Wan. The average daily traffic, which has increased steadily since opening, was 47 000 vehicles during the year under review.

Tseung Kwan O Tunnel was opened in 1990. Linking Kowloon to Tseung Kwan O new town, it was used by 23 000 vehicles daily.

The Aberdeen Tunnel was opened in 1982. It links the north and south sides of Hong Kong Island, with a daily traffic volume of 56 000 vehicles in 1993.

The Cross Harbour Tunnel, the Eastern Harbour Crossing and the Tate's Cairn Tunnel were all built by the private sector under 'build, operate and transfer' franchises.

The Cross Harbour Tunnel, opened in 1972, connects Causeway Bay on Hong Kong Island and Hung Hom in Kowloon. Used by an average of 122 000 vehicles each day in 1993, it is one of the world's busiest four-lane road tunnels. The tolls ranged from $4 to $30, including a government passage tax.

The Eastern Harbour Crossing is Hong Kong's second cross-harbour road tunnel. Opened in 1989, it links Quarry Bay on Hong Kong Island and Cha Kwo Ling in Kowloon. It is connected by an elevated section of Route 6 to the Kowloon portal of the Tate's Cairn Tunnel. At the end of the year, traffic in this tunnel averaged 80 000 vehicles per day. The tolls ranged from $5 to $30.

Tate's Cairn Tunnel was opened to traffic in 1991, to provide an additional direct road link between the northeastern New Territories and Kowloon. Measuring four kilometres from portal to portal, it is the longest road tunnel in the territory. The daily traffic flow at the Tate's Cairn Tunnel increased to 78 000 vehicles a day at the end of 1993. The tolls ranged from $4 to $8.

In August, automatic tunnel toll collection (autotoll) was introduced in the Cross Harbour Tunnel and the Aberdeen Tunnel, to enable motorists to drive through toll booths without stopping and to reduce tunnel operating costs.

The automatic toll collection, based on microwave technology, was initially for one toll lane in each direction, following amendments to the Road Tunnels (Government) Ordinance and Cross Harbour Tunnel Bylaws. Drivers need not stop to pay tolls as the toll is automatically deducted from the vehicle user's account. At the end of the year, there were about 23 800 registered autotoll users, making daily averages of 18 600 and 14 400 trips through the Cross Harbour and the Aberdeen Tunnels, respectively.

Traffic Management and Control

To facilitate a smoother traffic flow, an extensive programme of traffic management and control measures is being implemented.

At the end of the year, there were 1 130 signalised junctions in the territory, comprising 440 in Kowloon, 300 on Hong Kong Island and 390 in the New Territories.

In Kowloon, 360 signalised junctions were under the control of the existing Kowloon Area Traffic Control (ATC) System, which has been in operation for more than 16 years. The system is now being replaced to increase its capacity and update the technology. One notable feature of the new system, to be commissioned in 1995, will be 'traffic responsive control', under which signal timings can be automatically adjusted in response to changes in traffic flows. This should minimise delays for road users. In addition, planning work has started on the enhancement of the Closed Circuit Television (CCTV) system in Kowloon to provide a wider area coverage for traffic surveillance.

On Hong Kong Island, the majority of the signalised junctions on the northern shore, from Kennedy Town to Shau Kei Wan, are under the control of the Hong Kong Area Traffic Control system. The system is being expanded to Chai Wan and the Southern District. At the end of 1993, 240 junctions on Hong Kong Island were under ATC control and 35 CCTV cameras were in use.

A new ATC System is now being installed in Tsuen Wan. At the end of the year, about 70 signalised junctions in Tsuen Wan, Kwai Chung and Tsing Yi were under computer control. The final system, to be completed in 1995, will include traffic responsive control and a CCTV system.

Following the installation at Tsuen Wan new town, the ATC system will be extended to Sha Tin new town, and planning work has already started for implementation in early 1995.

Parking

The management and operation of on-street, metered parking spaces are scheduled to be contracted out in early 1994 to improve efficiency.

On-street parking, usually metered, is provided only at locations where traffic conditions permit. At the end of the year, there were 13 000 metered spaces throughout the territory, most of which operate between 8 am and midnight from Mondays to Saturdays. In Causeway Bay, Happy Valley and Tsim Sha Tsui, where parking demand is high, their operation has been extended to include Sundays and public holidays to facilitate a better turnover of parking spaces. In June 1993, tenders were called to invite a contractor to take over the management of parking meters from the Transport Department from March 1994.

The government also owns 14 multi-storey carparks, which provide 8 200 parking spaces. They are operated and managed by two private companies under two separate management contracts. Off-street public parking is also provided by the Civil Aviation Department at Hong Kong International Airport, and by the Kowloon-Canton Railway Corporation at its terminus. The private sector also operates multi-storey and open-air public carparks in commercial buildings, public and private housing estates and open-air lots — providing over 100 000 parking spaces.

Licensing

The total number of licensed vehicles in all classes was 439 719 at the end of the year — an increase of 7.8 per cent over 1992.

The number of new private cars registered fell from 41 878 in 1992 to 41 480 in 1993, a decrease of 0.95 per cent. Despite the use of financial restraint measures — which included increasing the first registration tax of new private cars from a range of 80–100 per cent to 90–120 per cent of the cars' Cost Insurance Freightage values in March 1991 — the total number of licensed cars in December was 259 874, a growth of 9.64 per cent over the past year.

Registered goods vehicles increased to 143 805 in December, up by 2.36 per cent compared with the 140 491 goods vehicles of a year earlier. Included in these were 106 068 light goods vehicles, which increased by 0.44 per cent from 1992. In line with the policy to restrain the ownership and use of this class of vehicles, the first registration tax and annual licensing fees of van-type light goods vehicles were increased in 1991 by 50 per cent and 90 per cent, or $4,140 and $2,115, respectively. This has had the effect of reducing the number of light goods vehicles, but slightly increasing the number of medium goods vehicles. At the year's end, the number of licensed light goods vehicles stood at 86 709, a decrease of 1.95 per cent from the same period in 1992. Meanwhile, the number of medium goods vehicles increased by 7.93 per cent to 32 386 by end-1993.

There were 1 008 270 licensed drivers at the year's end, an increase of 4.89 per cent from 1992. The average number of new learner-drivers increased from 6 164 per month in 1992 to 6 541 per month in 1993.

Since the introduction of the Driving Offence Points System in August 1984, 22 076 drivers have been disqualified. A total of 242 718 warning notices have been served and 380 757 drivers have incurred penalty points for committing offences scheduled under the Road Traffic (Driving Offence Points) Ordinance. The figures for 1993 were 5 158, 41 767 and 25 737, respectively.

A performance pledge scheme for the services provided by the Transport Department in the issue of learner and full driving licences, and registration and licensing of vehicles was introduced in December 1992. Plans are in hand to extend the scheme to other licensing and vehicle examination services. Two customer liaison groups, covering the licensing services on Hong Kong Island, and in Kowloon and the New Territories, were formed in September to gauge customers' opinions on services provided and improvements desired. A Best Licensing Service Award Scheme was launched in June and 10 licensing staff were given awards.

Vehicle Examination

Vehicle examination activities continued to expand, through the efforts of examination centres operated by the government or its contractors, and the private sector.

Two lanes of computer-controlled equipment were put into full operation in September at the Kowloon Bay Vehicle Examination Centre for urban taxi inspections. A taximeter test machine was also installed in August at the Sheung Kwai Chung Vehicle Examination Centre for New Territories taxis.

With effect from June, it became necessary for all light goods vehicles to pass a roadworthiness inspection every year, before they can be relicensed. Medium and heavy goods vehicles manufactured before 1989 also require annual inspection. It is planned that all goods vehicles should be inspected annually by the end of 1994.

Private cars over six years old are also required to pass an inspection before relicensing. The private car inspection scheme was operated at 24 designated car testing centres. From

13506
GEMINI SEAS
13506

HIT
EVER GLOBE

Previous page: *A traditional Chinese junk under full sail is now a rare sight in Victoria Harbour, where power craft rule the waves.*

Left: *Tugs assist a giant vessel at the world's busiest container port at Kwai Chung.*

THE PRINCE OF WALES BUILDING
PHILIPS
PHILIPS
YASHICA
SAMSUNG
Carlsberg
THE SWANK SHOP
MOTOR

Left: *The graceful oceanliner Queen Elizabeth II is an annual visitor to Hong Kong's Ocean Terminal.*

Below: *Despite the advent of harbour tunnels, the familiar green and white Star Ferry vessels still busily shuttle passengers between Hong Kong Island and Kowloon.*

NEC

Opposite page: *An extensive assortment of working craft ply the local waters.*

Hong Kong's port services provide rapid turnaround times for the world's shipping **(above).**

Left: *Like neat rows of slippers, fishing boats at Shau Kei Wan await nightfall.*

Private motor yachts form an exclusive colony in a section of the Causeway Bay Typhoon Shelter **(above)**.

Left: *A range of sailing and motor yachts lie at their moorings at the Royal Hong Kong Yacht Club, which celebrates its centenary in 1994.*

June, these testing centres also inspected all light goods vehicles over one year old and with a gross vehicle weight under 1.9 tonnes.

All public transport vehicles continued to be inspected annually, while the random daily spot checks of in-service franchised buses were increased.

Road Safety

Traffic accidents involving injury increased by one per cent in 1993. There were 15 420 accidents, of which 3 395 were serious and 333 fatal. This compares with 15 322 accidents in 1992, of which 3 438 were serious and 318 fatal. In-depth investigations were carried out at 149 traffic accident blackspots in order to identify accident causes. Remedial accident prevention measures were recommended at 130 of these locations. Similar measures, when implemented, have been shown to reduce accidents by 30 per cent on average.

Accident records are updated daily with the microcomputer-based traffic accident data system, installed in 1991. Accident statistics and map plots are retrieved, compiled and analysed for traffic accident blackspot analysis and road safety strategy formulation. (Accident statistics are at Appendix 39.)

As an aid to police enforcement, a red light camera pilot scheme was commenced in January to deter red light running at signal-controlled junctions. The experiment showed the equipment was effective and a plan is being drawn up to expand the system.

Road safety campaigns continued to play an important role in reducing traffic accidents. The major themes of the year's campaigns were pedestrian safety, targeted at young people and the elderly; and safety for drivers, targeted in particular at light goods vehicle, private car and motorcycle drivers. Posters, television announcements and leaflets were produced and widely distributed. A series of radio and television road safety programmes were broadcast. In anticipation of new legislation on the fitting and wearing of rear seatbelts in private cars, efforts have been made to educate the public on the subject. Two new short films, on seatbelt wearing and drink-driving, were produced and broadcast on television during the year.

At the year's end, the Road Safety Association of Hong Kong operated 224 school road safety patrols, while school staff patrols operated at 562 schools, with the objective of ensuring the safety of school children on their way to and from school. The Road Safety Council, an advisory body, continued to co-ordinate all road safety matters in the territory.

Public Transport

The Hong Kong public transport system is notable for its variety of modes and operators, its intensity of usage, and the absence of government subsidies. A network of rail, ferry, bus and other transport services extends to almost every part of the territory.

Railways

There are five rail systems, comprising a heavily-utilised mass transit system, a busy suburban railway, a modern light railway, a traditional street tramway and The Peak funicular railway. The first three rail systems are operated by public corporations, wholly owned by the government. The others are owned by private operators.

Mass Transit Railway

The Mass Transit Railway Corporation (MTRC) operates a three-line metro system, comprising 43 route-kilometres with 38 stations, served by a fleet of 671 cars operating in eight-car trains. The system was opened in stages between October 1979 and August 1989.

Patronage increased slightly during the year, and by the year's end, the railway was carrying 2.13 million passengers a day. It is one of the busiest underground railways in the world. Adult fares ranged from $3.50 to $9 per trip, according to distances travelled.

Plans for the construction and financing of the Airport Railway are in hand. The new railway, when built, will consist of two separate rail services: a dedicated express service linking the new airport at Chek Lap Kok to Central, with stations at the airport, Tsing Yi, West Kowloon and Central; and a domestic service between Tung Chung and Central, with stations at Tung Chung, Tsing Yi, Lai King, Tai Kok Tsui, West Kowloon and Central. The domestic service will interchange with the Tsuen Wan line of the existing MTR system at Lai King and with the Island Line at Central, bringing relief to the MTR Nathan Road corridor.

Kowloon-Canton Railway

The Kowloon-Canton Railway was opened in 1910 and was double-tracked and electrified in the early 1980s. Operation of the system, formerly run by a government department, was vested in the Kowloon-Canton Railway Corporation (KCRC) in 1982.

The 34-kilometre railway provides a suburban service to the new towns in the northeastern New Territories, a freight service to and from China, and passenger services to and from Guangzhou and Foshan. The suburban service has grown substantially since the introduction of electric trains, and in 1993, the railway handled 569 500 passenger journeys daily. Passenger traffic is carried in a fleet of 351 cars, operated in train formations of 12 cars. There are 13 stations along the railway. A major programme to replace old escalators and install additional ones began in 1991 and continued throughout the year. In the 10 years beginning late 1993, the KCRC plans to spend about $600 million to further reduce noise levels at major residential developments along the entire line, by constructing covered or semi-covered noise barriers at 18 locations.

Light Rail Transit

The KCRC also owns and operates the 31-kilometre Light Rail Transit (LRT) system, in the northwestern New Territories, which began operating in 1988. An extension was opened in January 1993, between Tin Shui Estate and Castle Peak Road at Tong Fong/Hung Shui Kiu. The extension increased to 55 the stops served by the system. Nine services are provided on the network by a fleet of 100 cars, which operate either singly or in pairs. At the end of the year, 291 942 boardings a day were handled on the LRT and its feeder bus services within the transit service area between Tuen Mun and Yuen Long. The LRT operates zonal fares and provides free transfers from one route to another within the zone and to and from feeder buses. Ordinary adult fares ranged from $3 to $4.30.

In June, the boarding and alighting restrictions on buses operated by the Kowloon Motor Bus Company (1933) Limited in the transit service area were lifted, to provide a greater choice to passengers travelling within the area.

A further extension of the LRT in Tin Shui Wai new town, from Tin Shui Estate to the Tin Shui Wai town centre, is expected to be completed in 1994. The system route length will then be increased to 31.8 kilometres, and the number of stops to 57.

Trams

Electric trams have been operating on Hong Kong Island since 1904. Hongkong Tramways Limited has six overlapping services, using 13 kilometres of double track along the north shore of Hong Kong Island, between Kennedy Town and Shau Kei Wan, and nearly three kilometres of single track around Happy Valley. The 163 trams, including two open-balcony trams for tourists and private hire, make up the only fully double-decker tram fleet in the world. All of the original trams had been rebuilt by 1991. Tramway patronage rose marginally during 1993, with an average of 340 000 boardings daily. Fares remained at $1 for adults and $0.50 for children.

Funicular Rail

Hong Kong's other 'tramway' is a cable-hauled funicular railway, operated by the Peak Tramways Company Limited from Central to The Peak. The 1.4-kilometre line began operation in 1888 and climbs 373 metres on gradients as steep as one-in-two. The line was modernised in 1989. The service caters largely for sightseers but also serves Peak district commuters. The line serves an average of 9 000 passengers a day. One-way fares for adults and children were $10 and $4, respectively.

Road Passenger Transport

Road passenger transport accounted for two-thirds of all public transport journeys. Over half of the journeys made by road were on franchised buses, with the remainder handled by green minibuses, public light buses, taxis and non-franchised buses.

Franchised Buses

The standard and capacity of franchised bus services continued to improve through planning and co-ordination. There are four franchised bus companies, which together carried 3.4 million passengers daily on a network of 469 regular routes.

The largest operator is the Kowloon Motor Bus Company (1933) Limited (KMB), which ran 299 bus routes in Kowloon and the New Territories; 38 cross-harbour routes jointly with the China Motor Bus Company; two cross harbour routes with Citybus Limited and three cross harbour routes of its own. As a continuing effort to improve service quality, KMB has introduced 11 air-conditioned bus routes. KMB also operates 'Airbus' services to and from the airport, comprising three routes to Hong Kong Island and two within Kowloon.

The KMB fleet at the end of the year comprised 3 197 registered vehicles, with 2 579 double-decker conventional buses, and 312 and 306 air-conditioned double and single-decker buses, respectively. Each can seat between 24 and 164 passengers. In 1993, KMB made 966 million passenger trips and operated 243 million kilometres, compared with 970 million passenger trips and 234 million kilometres in 1992. KMB's current franchise extends until August 31, 1997. Fares ranged from $1.00 to $23.00 for non air-conditioned services, and from $2.20 to $25.50 for air-conditioned services.

To attract commuters who might otherwise have used and overloaded the section of the Mass Transit Railway (MTR) along Nathan Road, a total of 29 air-conditioned 'Nathan' bus routes were operated during the year, from the New Territories and North Kowloon to Hong Kong Island and South Kowloon. These services helped keep the MTR passenger flows along Nathan Road at acceptable and safe levels.

From April, elderly passengers aged 65 and over became entitled to concessionary fares on every KMB route, except the Airbus services.

Bus services on Hong Kong Island are provided by two operators. The China Motor Bus Company (CMB) operates 91 routes on the island and, jointly with KMB, 38 cross-harbour routes. At the end of 1993, CMB's fleet comprised 991 double-deckers and 23 single-deckers. Eighty-one double-deckers and all the single-deckers were air-conditioned. They made 236 million passenger trips and travelled 48 million kilometres during the year, compared with 263 million and 52 million, respectively, the previous year. CMB purchased 20 air-conditioned double-deckers in 1993 to improve services. Fares ranged from $1.80 to $25.50. With effect from June 6, elderly passengers aged 65 and over became entitled to concessionary fares on most CMB routes. The company's franchise has been extended to August 31, 1995.

Citybus Limited (Citybus) is the other franchised operator on Hong Kong Island. The company had been running non-franchised bus services since 1979. In August 1991, it was awarded a franchise to operate a route between Central and MacDonnell Road.

To promote healthy competition among transport operators, 24 Hong Kong Island routes and two cross-harbour tunnel routes, withdrawn from CMB, were awarded to Citybus under a three-year franchise which took effect on September 1, 1993. The cross-harbour routes are operated jointly with KMB. At the end of the year, Citybus had a fleet of 200 franchised double-decker buses, of which half were air-conditioned. Fares ranged from $1.80 to $4.50 for non-air-conditioned trips, and from $2.50 to $12.00 for air-conditioned services. Elderly passengers aged 60 and over became entitled to concessionary fares from September on Hong Kong Island routes. Overall, Citybus's franchised bus services made 22 million passenger trips and travelled 3.6 million kilometres during the year.

The New Lantao Bus Company (1973) Limited (NLB) operates six regular, and one recreational, franchised routes on Lantau Island, with a fleet of 51 single-decker and five double-decker buses. Most NLB services connect with the ferries at Mui Wo. Operational efficiency was improved in September 1991 by the opening of a new bus depot in Mui Wo. The average weekday patronage rate for NLB in 1993 was 8 920 passengers. Boosted by recreational traffic, the average patronage on Sundays and public holidays was 21 847 passengers. Fares ranged from $1.20 to $21.00. With effect from September, elderly passengers aged 65 and above can pay half-fare on all NLB services on Mondays to Saturdays, except public holidays. To meet peak recreational demand, NLB introduced (in June 1991) a special service between Mui Wo and Po Lin Monastery, using air-conditioned coaches ferried to Lantau at weekends. During the year, the average patronage on this special service was 3 605 passengers per day. In July, NLB was awarded a new two-year franchise until March 31, 1997.

Minibuses

Hong Kong's minibuses are licensed to carry a maximum of 16 seated passengers. There were 6 904 minibuses in 1993. Of these, 4 350 were public light buses (PLB), and 2 554 private light buses. The PLBs are authorised to carry passengers at separate fares. The private light buses are authorised only to carry group passengers and the collection of separate fares is not permitted.

The operation of PLBs is regulated by a passenger service licence. There are two types of PLBs. Green PLBs provide services according to fixed schedules. There were 1 620 of these, operating on 230 approved routes, each with fixed fares and timetables. They carried 728 000 passengers a day. Red PLBs operate without a schedule. They do not have fixed routes, timetables and fares. In 1993, there were about 2 709 red PLBs, which carried about 1 007 000 passengers daily.

In line with government policy to convert more red PLBs to operate on scheduled routes, more new scheduled routes will be identified. During the year, one green minibus selection exercise, with 16 routes requiring 80 minibuses, was conducted, for competitive bidding by minibus operators.

Taxis

At the end of 1993, there were 14 950 urban taxis, 2 738 New Territories taxis and 40 Lantau taxis, carrying, respectively, an average of 1 085 000, 192 000 and 1 070 passengers daily.

A Transport Advisory Committee (TAC) working group continued its review of the government's policies on taxis. An exercise launched by the TAC in 1992 to seek public views on various measures, identified by the working group, for improvement of taxi services was completed during the year. The working group is formulating recommendations for the consideration of the TAC.

Non-Franchised Bus Operators

Residents' coach services were introduced in 1982 to give commuters an extra choice. These services operate primarily during peak hours, supplementing services provided by the franchised bus operators. They are flexible, to respond to local market demands. This helps keep down the number of franchised buses that would otherwise be left idle during off-peak hours. Residents' organisations may invite a non-franchised bus operator to operate such a service under a passenger service licence issued by the Transport Department. Residents' services operate in accordance with approved schedules, which specify the routing, timetable, and stopping places.

At the end of the year, there were 91 residents' services running 85 000 passenger trips a day. Vehicles used on these services ranged from small coaches to double-decker buses. Thirteen residents' services were introduced during the year, providing bus services from various residential areas, mainly in the New Territories, the Mid-Levels and the southern part of Hong Kong Island.

Non-franchised bus operators also serve the needs of factory employees, tourists and students on a group hire basis.

At the end of 1993, the licensed fleet of non-franchised buses totalled 4 098 vehicles, of which 219 were double-deckers. An increasing proportion of these vehicles were air-conditioned.

Ferries

Ferries are essential for travelling to Hong Kong's outlying islands and provide an important link to the new towns in the northwest New Territories. In the inner harbour, they are a supplementary mode of transport to cross-harbour buses and the Mass Transit Railway. Existing services are provided largely by two franchised operators — the 'Star' Ferry Company Limited and the Hongkong & Yaumati Ferry Company Limited (HYF).

The Star Ferry operated 12 vessels across the harbour and, during the year, carried 35 720 673 passengers on its three routes. Fares ranged from $1.50 to $1.80. Passengers aged 65 and above can enjoy free travel on all Star Ferry services.

HYF owned 83 licensed vessels and operated 16 ferry routes, including passenger and vehicular services across the harbour, hoverferry services to the northwest New Territories, services to the outlying islands and charter services. In 1993, the company carried 99 807 passengers and 6 565 vehicles daily. Elderly passengers aged 65 or above can enjoy half-fare concessions during off-peak hours in ordinary class services from Mondays to Fridays, except on public holidays.

A further 18 other ferry services were operated by eight licensed operators, including the service to Discovery Bay, Lantau. These were supplemented by *kaitos*, or local village ferry services, which were licensed to serve remote coastal settlements. At the end of the year, 89 *kaitos* were in operation.

The Port

Hong Kong has the busiest container port in the world, handling more than nine million TEUs (20-foot equivalent units) in 1993. It is also one of the busiest in terms of vessel arrivals, and cargo and passenger throughput. Some 165 000 ocean-going and river trade vessels arrive in Hong Kong annually, handling over 100 million tonnes of cargo, and over 20 million international passengers, most of whom are carried on the world's largest fleet of high-speed ferries.

Details of international movements of vessels, passengers and cargo are given at Appendix 37.

The port has always been, and continues to be, crucial to Hong Kong's economy and prosperity. It handles about 90 per cent of the territory's trade. Port and related industries generate about 15 per cent of Hong Kong's Gross Domestic Product, provide some 350 000 jobs and keep 20 per cent of all companies in business.

To maintain its strategic significance as a conduit for Hong Kong's trade, as an *entrepôt* for China and as a hub port for world trade, the port must continue to grow. Planning for growth flows from the Port and Airport Development Strategy to a Port Development Plan, covering container terminals and other less obvious but equally vital facilities such as cargo-working areas, typhoon shelters, anchorages, container back-up land, shipyard sites and berths for deep waterfront industries. The pace of development is geared to meet the forecast demand up to the year 2011. It is reviewed regularly to ensure that facilities are available when they are needed, taking into account the latest forecasts of demand.

The government has always taken the view that generally it should not undertake commercial activities which can be provided more efficiently by the private sector. Hong Kong leads the world in this respect and the port is an excellent example. Most port facilities, such as the container terminals and dockyards, are privately built, owned and operated. Services such as stevedoring, tugs and pilotage are also provided directly by the private sector. The Port Development Plan envisages a continuing high level of private sector involvement in providing port facilities and services.

The valuable advice given by users and operators of port facilities is an important factor in the port's success. A wide range of interests from the private sector are represented in advisory and consultative bodies, including the Port Development Board, which advises the government on port planning and development; the Port Operations Committee, which advises the Director of Marine on the operational needs of the port; and the Provisional Local Vessel Advisory Committee, which advises on local craft matters.

The Container Port

Of the 9.2 million containers loaded and discharged in 1993, about 63 per cent (or 5.8 million TEUs) were handled at the Kwai Chung Container Port, and another 30 per cent (or 2.8 million TEUs) were handled by ships at mid-stream mooring buoys and anchorages. All eight container terminals at Kwai Chung are privately owned and operated, and will have a total of 16 berths for ocean-going vessels by early 1995. The first of four berths of the latest terminal, Container Terminal 8, became operational in July 1993. The other three berths are under construction and will be completed at about six-month intervals. While Container Terminal 8 is being built, planning for the construction of Container Terminal 9, at southeast Tsing Yi Island, is at an advanced stage and preliminary design work is underway for Container Terminals 10 and 11.

International Ferry Services

The number of international passengers using the ferry terminals managed by the Marine Department is increasing. In 1993, 6.7 million passengers used the China Ferry Terminal in Tsim Sha Tsui and 13 million used the Macau Ferry Terminal in Central. The total was a three per cent increase from 1992. Most of these passengers travelled on the world's largest fleet of modern, high-speed passenger craft, comprising jetfoils, hydrofoils, sidewall hovercraft and catamarans operating from Hong Kong to Macau and various ports in China.

The department has introduced statutory requirements to enhance safety, by predicting and minimising the effects of shipboard system failures and improving crew training.

Port Services

The port is administered by the Marine Department. The department's mission is to enhance Hong Kong's role as one of the world's great ports by ensuring that ships can enter port, work their cargoes and depart as quickly and safely as possible. In line with the government's public sector reform programme, the department has published a performance pledge, outlining the standards of service its customers can expect. In a further step to improve and meet the ever-growing demand for its services, the department is commercialising its operations. It aims to become a trading fund department and a self-financing commercial entity within the government in two years.

Hong Kong waters are covered by a Vessel Traffic Service (VTS), to ensure a safe and expeditious marine traffic flow in the densely-populated port. The system is run by the department and participation is compulsory for ocean-going vessels of 300 gross registered tonnes (GRT) and above. The system comprises a computer-assisted radar network, a computer database and VHF radio telephone communications. Coupled with a comprehensive system of navigational aids, fairways, traffic separation schemes and harbour patrols, it helps Hong Kong maintain a low level of marine accidents by world standards.

Ships over 5 000 GRT and certain other vessels are required to engage pilots when moving within the port and its approaches. The Director of Marine regulates and controls the pilotage service, although the pilots themselves operate as a private company.

The number of vessels using the port and requiring pilotage is increasing rapidly. A Pilotage Review Consultancy Study was commissioned by the department in March, to review the present pilotage system and to make recommendations for any changes necessary to meet the needs of the port in the most efficient and cost-effective manner for the period 1994 to 2011.

The main recommendations of the consultants include shifting the present pilot boarding station located at Green Island to the outer entrance of East Lamma Channel; extending compulsory pilotage to all ships exceeding 3 000 GRT; creating a corporate body responsible for pilotage services and all related matters; and establishing a close operational relationship between the VTS and pilots for improved efficiency and safety in the port. These recommendations are currently under examination and consideration by the department prior to implementation.

The department's launches patrol the main harbour area and its approaches, maintain order and respond to emergencies. They are in continuous radio contact with the VTS through the department's Vessel Traffic Centre (VTC). Well-equipped fleets of fire boats, tugs, oil-pollution control vessels and marine police launches are also available to respond to emergencies.

Immigration and quarantine services, including advance clearance, may be applied for by radio through the VTC. The Western Quarantine Anchorage provides these services round-the-clock while services are available between 6 am and 6 pm daily at the Eastern Quarantine Anchorage.

The department provides and maintains 76 mooring buoys within the port for ships to work cargo in the stream. The buoys can be booked through the VTC. There are two classes of buoys, suitable for vessels up to 137 and 183 metres in length. Most are typhoon moorings to which vessels may remain secured during tropical storms.

A large number of harbour craft are essential to the efficient running of the port. During the year, over 1 700 lighters and 400 motorised cargo boats transported cargo to and from ocean-going ships in the anchorages and at buoys in the harbour, and private or public cargo-working areas ashore. These are part of Hong Kong's 16 000 local vessels which include ferries, barges, workboats, fishing boats and pleasure vessels.

Bunkering facilities within the port are readily available at commercial wharves and oil terminals, or from a large fleet of private bunkering barges. Fresh water can also be provided alongside berths, or from a private fleet of water boats.

The port has extensive facilities for repairing, dry-docking and slipping all types of vessels of up to 150 000 deadweight tonnes, including oil rigs. Smaller shipyards are able to build and maintain workboats and pleasure vessels.

In the latter part of the year, the department initiated a prototype Dangerous Goods Control System in an attempt to establish more accurately the quantities and types of dangerous goods being moved into and out of Hong Kong. When the results of the prototype control system are established, the department will introduce a stricter control regime utilising the International Maritime Dangerous Goods (IMDG) Code as a cornerstone.

The increase in the number and size of ships visiting the port and the increasing pace of reclamation have increased the need for accurate and up-to-date hydrographic surveys and charts. The department is establishing its own hydrographic office to meet this demand.

The department also provides refuse collection and scavenging craft, which collect and scavenge some 5 100 tonnes of refuse annually from ocean-going ships and Hong Kong waters.

The Chemical Waste Treatment Centre commissioned on Tsing Yi Island during the year provides, among other things, reception facilities for treating oily and chemical wastes from ships as required under the International Convention for the Prevention of Pollution from Ships (MARPOL).

Port State Control

A total of 50 ocean-going ships visiting Hong Kong were inspected in 1993, to check compliance with international safety and environmental protection conventions. This represented about 0.9 per cent of ships visiting Hong Kong. Of the ships inspected, about 75 per cent required deficiencies to be made good before they could sail. Hong Kong supports international co-operation in maritime safety and in December 1993, signed an Asia-Pacific region Memorandum of Understanding on Port State Control to enhance the effectiveness of these inspections at sea.

Local Vessel Survey and Related Services

A plan-approval and safety survey service is provided for local vessels operating within the waters of Hong Kong. The requirements for the certification, safety and control of local craft are being rationalised to enhance safety, by clearly delineating the duties and responsibilities of owners, operators and the government.

A free inspection and advice service is provided to promote safe working practices in ship repairing, ship-breaking and cargo-handling afloat.

Government Fleet

The Government fleet of about 330 powered vessels provided by the Marine Department is highly visible in the port. In addition to harbour patrol launches, fire boats and police vessels, the government has launches used for immigration, port health and customs clearance, and surveys of international shipping. The fleet also includes lighters, airport rescue craft, pollution control craft, floating clinics and launches for transporting government staff.

All government vessels are specially designed to meet their users' needs. The department designs and procures new vessels, maintains the whole fleet, and mans and operates about 70 general purpose craft. In 1991, the government awarded a $300-million contract to an Australian shipbuilder for the construction of six police patrol and command launches. The six launches were delivered in 1992 and 1993.

Maritime Search and Rescue

By international agreement, the Marine Department is the Maritime Search and Rescue Co-ordinator for the area of the South China Sea north of latitude 10°N and west of longitude 120°E, excluding the immediate coastal waters of neighbouring states.

The Maritime Search and Rescue Co-ordination Centre (MRCC) is manned continuously and monitors all emergency communications channels. Radio communications equipment for the Global Maritime Distress and Safety System (GMDSS) is also available and used in the centre. Search and rescue missions can be activated and run by professionally-trained staff. Fully-equipped search and rescue vessels and aircraft are available, and additional assistance can be obtained from other rescue co-ordination centres in the region.

In 1993, the MRCC responded to over 200 distress calls, of which at least 75 involved major operations. These cases varied from simple casualty evacuations of injured fishermen from vessels, to the rescue of an entire crew from a sinking vessel in a typhoon. In between, there were groundings, fires, collisions, sinkings and man overboard cases.

During the year, three major incidents highlighted the work of the MRCC. The first involved the rescue of crew members from a sinking vessel during Typhoon Koryn on June 27. Five helicopters and a fixed wing aircraft were involved in the rescue some 71 miles east-southeast of Hong Kong, under appalling weather conditions, and 24 persons were saved.

The second case, on August 21, involved co-ordination with the rescue centre at Stavanger, Norway, which was first advised by satellite of a sinking vessel in heavy weather 332 miles southeast of Hong Kong. The MRCC subsequently tasked a Super King Air of the Government Flying Service (GFS) to the scene, and assisted in locating the sinking vessel and guiding other ships in the vicinity to the distress position. The MRCC instigated urgent marine information broadcasts over the NAVTEX service and 15 vessels responded. Three vessels arrived at the scene and effected the rescue of all 21 persons on board, before the vessel eventually sank.

The third case, on October 29, involved the rescue of a Korean seaman who fell overboard before midnight from his ship 270 miles southeast of Hong Kong and was not discovered missing until the following morning. The MRCC, having considered the sea surface currents in that area, tasked a Super King Air from the GFS to do a track line search. Eventually, the man was rescued and returned to his ship just before dusk, after being in the water for 18 hours.

Seafarers

The falling levels of recruitment of local seafarers is a major concern to the government and Hong Kong shipowners. Together with the Merchant Navy Training Board, training institutions and seafarers' unions, they are trying to increase the recruitment of trainee officers by promoting seafaring careers. As part of this effort, the Hong Kong Shipowners' Association is sponsoring 40 cadets and trainees.

In addition, the government, the Merchant Navy Training Board and the training institutions have given considerable attention to improving training for Hong Kong seafarers. The Vocational Training Council, a quasi-government body, has built and operates a modern and well-equipped Seamen's Training Centre. The centre provides training courses for new entrants and in-service training for seamen, to comply with the requirements of the International Convention on Standards of Training, Certification and Watchkeeping for Seafarers, as well as other marine courses for local seafaring needs.

The Marine Department monitors training leading to the acquisition of maritime qualifications. It then examines candidates for certificates of competency for service on vessels of all sizes and types, operating both internationally and locally.

The department's Seamen's Recruiting Office and the Mercantile Marine Office register and supervise the employment of about 3 000 seafarers.

Participation in the International Maritime Organisation

Hong Kong is independently represented as an associate member of the International Maritime Organisation, and in accordance with the Sino-British Joint Declaration on the Question of Hong Kong, this status will continue after 1997. The territory has made a considerable contribution to the International Maritime Organisation's work in the development of the Protocol to the 1977 International Convention for the Safety of Fishing Vessels, international eyesight standards, and the Code of Safety for High Speed Craft.

Hong Kong's Shipping Register

The Hong Kong Shipping Register is administered by the Marine Department. It recognises the commercial realities of the shipping industry but, more importantly, reflects the government's commitment to the highest international standards of maritime safety and environmental protection. Its supporting legislation embodies international standards for vessel construction, equipment and manning, and is consistent with Hong Kong's obligations under International Maritime Organisation and International Labour Organisation conventions, including those on safety of life at sea, training and certification of crew, and protection of the marine environment. Statutory surveys of Hong Kong-registered vessels are undertaken worldwide by the department's surveyors or authorised classification societies, to ensure that these standards are met.

The register had a total fleet of 597 vessels, amounting to 7.75 million gross registered tonnes (GRT) at the end of 1993. This represents an increase of 14 ships (2.4%) and 0.43 million GRT (5.87%) over 1992.

Shipping

Hong Kong is a prominent centre for ship-owning, ship-financing and ship-management. Most local shipowners and connected businesses are represented by the Hong Kong Shipowners Association, whose members control a significant percentage of the world's tonnage.

The association promotes and protects Hong Kong shipowners and ship-managers, plus the growing number of companies which support them.

At the end of 1993, its members' fleet stood at 1 294 ocean-going vessels totalling 60.5 million deadweight tonnes and 33.9 million GRT. The association is either a member of, or works closely with, all significant international maritime bodies to contribute to major developments in merchant shipping worldwide.

At the end of 1993, membership of the association comprised 85 ship-owning and ship-managing companies, 124 associate members and one honorary member (the Director of Marine). The associate members include the major banks, classification societies, maritime lawyers, average adjusters, ship agencies, ship brokers, shipbuilders, ship repairers, surveyors and insurers. This broad-based membership makes a particularly effective forum for liaison with the government and international bodies.

The combined fleet of the association's members was registered in 32 different countries in early 1993, chiefly Liberia and Panama followed by Hong Kong; total tonnages on those three registers were 20.8 million, 17.3 million and 8.5 million deadweight tonnes, respectively.

Civil Aviation

It was another year of strong growth, both in passenger and cargo throughput, at Hong Kong International Airport, at Kai Tak.

A total of 24.5 million passengers passed through the terminal, an increase of 10.9 per cent over the 22.1 million in the previous year.

Some 1.14 million tonnes of cargo, valued at $390,096 million, were handled, compared with 956 906 tonnes, valued at $332,655 million, in 1992. Air transport continued to play an important role in Hong Kong's external trade. Of Hong Kong's total trade in imports, exports and re-exports, air transport carried about 19 per cent, 30 per cent and 14 per cent in value terms, respectively. The United States remained the major market for exports and re-exports by air, accounting for 38 per cent and 27 per cent, respectively.

An increase of 11.7 per cent in aircraft movements was recorded in 1993, bringing the annual total to 135 100, of which 78 per cent were wide-bodied aircraft.

On November 4, a Boeing 747 aircraft from Taipei overran the runway at Kai Tak on landing and ended up in Victoria Harbour. At the time, Hong Kong was affected by weather associated with Severe Tropical Storm Ira, which was some 300 nautical miles to the south-southwest. All 296 passengers and crew of the China Airlines jet were rescued. Twenty-three passengers were sent to hospital for observation or treatment and two were admitted in fair condition. None of the crew was injured. An investigation team is looking into the cause of the accident.

Following three incidents involving a loss of standard separation between aircraft in the first six months of the year, the Director of Civil Aviation commissioned the United Kingdom's Civil Aviation Authority (UKCAA) Air Traffic Control Inspectorate to carry out an independent audit of air traffic control procedures at the airport. Among other findings, the UKCAA Inspectorate pointed out that the 'opposite runway' mode of operating at Kai Tak posed a hazard to flight safety and recommended that it be withdrawn as soon as possible. Based upon this advice, the Director of Civil Aviation suspended this mode of operation with effect from October 29.

Improvements to Hong Kong International Airport

The programme of improvements to the airport at Kai Tak, which started in 1988, is expected to continue until 1994. It is aimed at enabling the airport to meet continuing high growth in passenger and cargo throughput until the commissioning of the new airport at Chek Lap Kok in 1997.

In February, work started on the construction of additional accommodation for airline commercially important persons, to replace an existing facility. Upon its completion in the first quarter of 1994, the area occupied by the existing facility will be converted into a waiting area.

Other improvements being implemented within the passenger terminal building include the widening of the departure pier in the departure lounge, the construction of an additional bus dock to serve passengers transferring to aircraft positioned on outer parking bays, and the installation of escalators for disembarking passengers.

A new Check-in Information Display System was commissioned and brought into use in the middle of the year. To further optimise check-in counter utilisation, a computerised Check-in Counter Allocation System is being planned for implementation in early 1995.

To improve ground access to the airport, a number of road works are being carried out. They include the provision of a roundabout connecting Concorde Road and Prince Edward Road East, a bridge crossing the Kai Tak Nullah, an upramp from Concorde Road, and further improvements to the transport terminus to increase taxi queuing space. The second floor of the airport's multi-storey carpark is being converted to a passenger set-down area to supplement the existing departures kerbside. This work is due to be completed in early 1994. The new passenger set-down area will be connected to the existing terminal building via an additional link bridge and two lifts, which are expected to be completed towards the end of 1994.

The runway resurfacing and regrooving works were completed in February 1993, two months ahead of schedule.

During the year, 10 additional parking bays for B747-sized aircraft and two new taxiway bridges, which provided a taxiway system linking the new South Apron with the runway, were brought into operation. Construction of one more B747 parking bay on the South Apron also commenced, with completion expected in June 1994.

A computerised aircraft parking bay allocation system was commissioned in August. The system automates the assignment of parking bays, optimising the utilisation of the aircraft parking areas.

As part of a continuing process to upgrade security at the airport, work commenced in November to replace the airport perimeter fence. This is expected to be completed in late 1994. Tenders for an Integrated Access Control and Permit Production System were called in June. This system, when fully operational in May 1994, will facilitate the issue of airport permits and enhance access security.

The Airport Fire Contingent took delivery of a specially-designed low draught fire rescue vessel that can pass underneath the newly-completed Taxiway Bridge No. 3, linking the South Apron with the runway. This ensures that adequate fire and rescue cover is provided in waters surrounding the runway promontory. To further enhance the fire-fighting and rescue capability at Kai Tak, a contract for an additional fire appliance equipped with a jackless hydraulic rescue platform was concluded in November. Delivery is expected in late 1994.

Air Services

Hong Kong is home to three international airlines. During the year, Cathay Pacific Airways (CPA), the largest of the three, commenced scheduled passenger services to Cairns and Colombo in October, and to Mauritius in November; and scheduled cargo services to Vancouver in October. To cope with the increasing scale of its operations, CPA acquired three B747-400s and one L1011. At the end of 1993, its fleet comprised 19 L1011s, seven B747-200s, six B747-300s, 17 B747-400s and four B747-200 freighters — a total of 53 aircraft.

Hong Kong Dragon Airlines (Dragonair) continued to operate scheduled services to seven cities in China and four other destinations in Asia, together with non-scheduled passenger services to a number of other cities, mostly in China and Japan. The airline commenced scheduled services to Phnom Penh, Kota Kinabalu and Sendai in August, October and December, respectively, and regular passenger charters to Ningbo in June; but suspended its scheduled service to Kathmandu in January. With the completion of its B737 replacement programme, Dragonair now operates six A320 and two L1011 aircraft.

Air Hong Kong (AHK) continued to operate scheduled all-cargo services to Manchester, Brussels, Nagoya, Ho Chi Minh City and Singapore, and non-scheduled cargo services to a number of destinations in Asia, using three B747F and one B707F aircraft. In September, the airline commenced scheduled all-cargo services to Kuala Lumpur.

The year saw the introduction of scheduled air services to Hong Kong by Varig Brazilian Airlines in January, Biman Bangladesh Airlines and British Asia Airways in March, Southern Air Transport in May and Cambodia International Airlines in August. As a result, the number of scheduled airlines serving Hong Kong increased to 55. During the year, these airlines operated about 1 200 direct round-trip services weekly between Hong Kong and some 94 other cities. In addition to the scheduled services, an average of 240 non-scheduled flights were operated by both scheduled and non-scheduled airlines each week.

In accordance with the relevant provisions of the Sino-British Joint Declaration, the process of separating Hong Kong's air services agreements from those of the United Kingdom continued. Two more agreements, with Sri Lanka and Australia respectively, were signed during the year, bringing the total to 10.

In 1993, the Air Transport Licensing Authority granted nine licences to Hong Kong airlines: one to CPA, four to Dragonair and four to AHK. At the end of the year, CPA held licences to operate scheduled services to 63 cities, Dragonair to 60 cities and AHK to 37 cities.

16
THE AIRPORT CORE PROGRAMME

CONSTRUCTION work on the Airport Core Programme (ACP) saw good progress in 1993. By the end of the year, 39 contracts worth a total of over $46 billion had been placed, within budget estimates, by the government, the Provisional Airport Authority (PAA) and the franchisee for the Western Harbour Crossing (WHC).

Over one-third of the 1 248-hectare site for the new international airport, at Chek Lap Kok off North Lantau, had been formed by December.

Major developments during the year included the start of physical work on the West Kowloon Expressway in August, and on the WHC — Hong Kong's third cross-harbour tunnel — and Phase I of the Central reclamation in September.

Hong Kong's externally-oriented economy depends greatly on modern, efficient and expanding air transport for its continued growth. Efficient road and rail transport facilities are also essential, along with land for development.

The ACP is designed to provide these facilities in 10 interlinked projects, which will build a base for economic expansion well into the next century. Hong Kong's key role as a centre for international and regional aviation will be enhanced by the new modern airport located away from centres of urban population and capable of operating round-the-clock. Associated infrastructure developments will relieve traffic congestion, and open up new land for urban development and the further expansion of port facilities. The new land will also provide space for recreational activities and have substantial overall environmental benefits.

The 10 projects in the ACP comprise the new airport, which will replace the existing one at Kai Tak; six road and rail projects, including extensive tunnels and bridges, stretching from Central District under the harbour, along the west shore of Kowloon peninsula, across the islands of Tsing Yi and Ma Wan, and along the North Lantau coast; two major land reclamations in West Kowloon and Central District (in addition to the land reclaimed for the airport); and a new town at Tung Chung on North Lantau.

Overall, the programme is based on sound financial principles, with good returns for government investments and extensive involvement of the private sector. Cost-effective concepts and designs have been drawn up for individual projects. Contracts are placed on the basis of open and fair tender evaluations, and there are strong and comprehensive financial and project management controls. Comprehensive consultative arrangements and community and public relations programmes have been developed.

The Need to Replace Kai Tak

A new airport is urgently needed because the international airport at Kai Tak, which has only one runway, is approaching its full capacity of around 28 million passengers a year and cannot viably be enlarged. In terms of international traffic, it is already the world's fourth busiest airport for passengers and third busiest for freight. It handles about 67 per cent of Hong Kong's nine million visitors a year and 30 per cent of its domestic exports. It also plays an important role in the development of southern China, as well as Hong Kong.

In 1993, the throughput of passengers was growing at about 12 per cent. This level of growth means that Kai Tak will be unable to accommodate forecast passenger demand before the new airport's planned opening date in 1997. Hong Kong's economy will, therefore, begin to suffer: for example, the economic disbenefits to Hong Kong of not going ahead with the airport have been estimated to be at least $420 billion, in money of the day (MOD), over the period 1997–2010. This represents only quantifiable losses; it does not include indirect losses caused by the declining effectiveness of Hong Kong as an international trading and financial centre providing comprehensive business services, which could double the estimate.

The ACP was conceived in 1991 out of the Port and Airport Development Strategy (PADS), which had been unveiled in 1989 after years of study. PADS had been designed to provide, in the most cost-effective way, for the growth of both the port and the airport. It covers major extensions to Hong Kong's container port and other developments, which are proceeding separately; while the 10 ACP projects are all associated with the opening of the airport at Chek Lap Kok (with the first of two planned runways).

Memorandum of Understanding

In September 1991, the Prime Ministers of Britain and China signed the Memorandum of Understanding Concerning the Construction of the New Airport in Hong Kong and Related Questions (MOU). The memorandum recognises the 'urgent need for a new airport in Hong Kong in order to ensure and develop its prosperity and stability', and the 'need for the airport project to be cost-effective'. It requires the Hong Kong Government to complete the ACP projects 'to the maximum extent possible' by June 30, 1997, and states that the Chinese Government will 'support the construction of the new airport and related projects'.

During 1993, the Airport Committee, which was set up in accordance with the MOU under the auspices of the Sino-British Joint Liaison Group (JLG), held four meetings. Agreement was reached on the award of the Western Harbour Crossing franchise, and the start of the Central Reclamation Phase I works. Discussions continued on overall financing arrangements for the airport and airport railway projects.

The Consultative Committee on the New Airport and Related Projects (ACC) and its four sub-committees (on the airport and its related land development projects; planning, environment and people's livelihood; traffic and transport; and financial matters) held a total of 14 meetings during the year. A wide range of subjects related to the ACP were discussed. The second term of the ACC began in November.

The MOU provides that an Airport Authority will be established and that the ordinance setting up the body will be modelled, as far as possible, on the Mass Transit Railway Corporation Ordinance. A draft Bill has been passed to the Chinese side of the Airport Committee for comment. Public views will also be sought on the draft Bill in early 1994.

Implementing and Financing the ACP

The ACP is being implemented by the government, two statutory corporations wholly owned by the government, and a franchisee appointed for the WHC. The government is carrying out direct capital works projects to reclaim land and to build highways and a new town near the airport. The PAA is responsible for planning and developing the airport until a permanent statutory body is established. The Mass Transit Railway Corporation (MTRC) is responsible for building and operating the airport railway. The WHC is being designed, built and operated by the Western Harbour Tunnel Company Limited under a 30-year franchise.

The cost of the 10 ACP projects was estimated in 1992 to be $163.7 billion in MOD. (Sometimes known as out-turn prices, MOD takes into account the impact of inflation on the value of the dollar while projects are designed and built, providing a realistic projection of out-turn prices. This is particularly relevant to the ACP because most contracts are let on a fixed-price lump sum basis, which means that contract prices have been adjusted to cover inflation over the contract period.)

Within the $163.7 billion, the government's capital expenditure is estimated at approximately $60 billion. This is expected to amount, between 1992–93 and 1996–97, to 25 per cent of the government's total capital expenditure. The remaining 75 per cent of its capital expenditure will be spent on social services projects and other essential construction activities.

The ACP cost estimate is being reviewed and is expected to be reduced to $158.2 billion in MOD.

The programme provides extensive opportunities for private sector participation. Besides the franchise for the WHC, these include a range of important commercial franchises at the airport, plus commercial lending and real estate development associated with the airport and the airport railway.

Benefits for the Community

The main benefits for the community, in addition to the airport itself, will come from improved road and rail facilities, which will ease congestion in West Kowloon and open up North Lantau. The closure of Kai Tak will also provide substantial environmental benefits for the 350 000 residents living under its flight paths, who will escape the noise of aircraft. The overall benefits to Hong Kong's economy will also be substantial.

The government's proposed financial investment in the projects will yield substantial benefits for taxpayers. It is estimated that by the year 2020, the new airport, the Lantau Fixed Crossing, and the airport railway will generate over $300 billion in additional revenue for the government.

Formation of Land

The ACP involves the creation of 1 669 hectares of new land, comprising a 1 248-hectare platform for the new airport (composed of 920 hectares of reclaimed land, and the islands of Chek Lap Kok and Lam Chau off northern Lantau, which will be levelled); 67 hectares of reclamation along the northern shore of Lantau for Phase I of Tung Chung new town; a 334-hectare reclamation at West Kowloon; and a 20-hectare section of a larger reclamation adjacent to Central and Western districts on Hong Kong Island.

The West Kowloon reclamation will provide housing for 91 000 people and some five hectares of commercial space, as well as vital road and rail arteries linking Kowloon with the new airport and northwestern New Territories. By the end of 1993, the reclamation was about 65 per cent complete, with about 220 hectares of land formed.

Construction of Phase I of the Cheung Sha Wan wholesale market complex on the West Kowloon reclamation was completed on time and within budget, and opened for use in October. It is designed to operate round-the-clock, every day of the year, and to handle more than 1 000 tonnes of fresh produce every day.

Phase I of the Central reclamation will provide opportunities for the development of Hong Kong's central business district, plus a site for the Central terminus of the airport railway. Reclamation work, which began in September, necessitated the relocation of the Discovery Bay Ferry Pier to the Star Ferry East Pier, and the Tsim Sha Tsui East hoverferry service to Queen's Pier.

Tung Chung new town will ultimately occupy two valleys at Tung Chung and Tai Ho on northern Lantau and a coastal strip of reclamation in between. It is planned to house 20 000 people by 1997 and up to 200 000 people by 2011. In addition to providing support services for the new airport, it will accommodate commercial and industrial developments and will serve as an impressive gateway to Hong Kong for visitors. There will be a mixture of private, public rental, and home ownership scheme housing, several shopping centres, an office and hotel complex in the town centre, and a 52-hectare industrial park. Extensive landscaping will shield the town from the airport to the northwest and provide generous recreational areas, supplemented by the backdrop of the Lantau Country Park to the south. Strong emphasis has been placed on community facilities and both local and long-distance rail and bus transport. At the year's end, about 50 hectares of land had been formed.

The Airport at Chek Lap Kok

Detailed planning of the airport facilities, and construction of the airport platform at Chek Lap Kok, progressed rapidly in 1993. The PAA, a statutory corporation set up in April 1990 with the Hong Kong Government as its sole shareholder, is planning and developing an airport which will be operationally safe and efficient, environmentally friendly, and commercially viable. Operationally, the new airport will expand on the quality and range of aviation services available at the existing airport. At the same time, it will set new directions in terms of commercial operations and expand the role of Hong Kong's airport as the regional transportation hub.

The new airport has been scheduled to open the first of its two runways in 1997. It will be able to handle 35 million passengers and 1.5 million tonnes of air cargo a year. Airport facilities are being designed by the PAA so that they can be expanded in stages and cater for forecast growth, in both passenger and cargo throughput, to 87 million passengers and nine million tonnes of cargo by the year 2040. Because of its location off North Lantau, the airport will be able to operate round-the-clock without causing noise problems for Hong Kong's urban areas.

Out of a total of 100 works contracts planned by the PAA for the new airport, four major construction contracts and various smaller contracts — with a total value of $9.7 billion — have been awarded. The $9 billion airport site preparation contract, which is the largest contract in the ACP, covers a period of 41 months. Work started in December 1992 and involves moving an average of 400 000 cubic metres of fill a day. More than 450 hectares of land had been formed by the end of 1993. Three smaller works contracts let by the PAA for advance works at Chek Lap Kok, and for trans-shipment facilities at Lok On Pai, have been completed.

The detailed design of the passenger terminal building is continuing and is expected to be substantially completed by the second quarter of 1994. The airport's passenger terminal complex will provide a dynamic gateway to Hong Kong. It is to be a large, low building with a roof line inspired by the concept of flight. With a length of 1.2 kilometres and a floor area of over 490 000 square metres, it will be the focal point of the airport.

A ground transportation centre located adjacent to the passenger terminal will make the airport easily accessible. The centre will contain arrivals and departures platforms for the Airport Express railway, a designated coach staging area, tour group check-in facilities, a limousine pick-up area, a 24-taxi simultaneous pick-up system, and facilities for short and long-term parking. There will also be a ferry terminal nearby. More than 35 000 square metres of space will be provided in the arrivals and departures halls and the concourse area for 150 commercial outlets.

By the end of 1993, 18 design consultancies had been awarded. They covered the designs of the permanent utilities, stormwater drainage, sewerage and irrigation, temporary utilities, airfield tunnels, airfield pavements, airfield ground lighting, apron lighting, marine geology of Chek Lap Kok, waste management, airport expressway, rail link and roads, modularisation and workforce accommodation, integrated transportation centre and approach roads, airport railway, on-airport aviation fuel services system, communications systems, security systems, perimeter fence and ancillaries as well as urban design guidelines and standards.

The PAA is preparing to award more than 80 works contracts. Tenders were invited in mid-July for the development of an automated people-mover system and an automated baggage-handling system within the terminal.

The commercial opportunities at Chek Lap Kok will be as diverse as Hong Kong's own economic profile. As a business, the airport will encourage competition, quality services and private sector participation. It will offer a world-class service to all of its users — passengers, airlines, air-cargo shippers, the travel and tourism industry, and the commercial licensees and concessionaires who will establish their businesses at the airport.

There will be more than one licence for most airside developments including air-cargo handling, aircraft maintenance and aircraft catering. The first drafts of the business plan specification brief on cargo-handling and aircraft maintenance were issued to potential franchisees for comments in March and May, respectively. The first draft of the brief for the aviation fuel supply system was issued in August. The market assessment for the licensed provision of aircraft catering services has been completed. Expressions of interest for the design of the on-airport fuel distribution service system were called for in July and processing work for the licence continues.

By the end of the year, the Finance Committee of the Legislative Council had approved a total advance of $14,591 million to enable the PAA to fund the site preparation contract and the key consultancies mentioned above, and to proceed with the airport development in general. Such funding enabled the PAA to take important steps forward on the airport, while the government continues to seek agreement with China on the overall airport financing plan.

The Finance Committee had further approved a sum of $289 million for key consultancies relating to the provision of government facilities at the new airport. These covered civil aviation and meteorological equipment, and advance site investigations. Consultancies for a mechanisation system for the Air Mail Centre and for terminal doppler weather radar and operational windshear warning systems have been awarded.

New Transport Facilities

The ACP includes five major highway projects designed to cater for the new airport's traffic and to relieve congestion on existing roads. They comprise the WHC, West Kowloon Expressway, the Kwai Chung and Tsing Yi sections of Route 3, the Lantau Fixed Crossing, and the North Lantau Expressway. Contracts to construct all five projects are now underway.

Together with the airport railway, these highways will also provide a rapid transit system between Tung Chung new town and the Central District, stimulating developments on North Lantau in the same way that the Kowloon-Canton Railway triggered development in the eastern New Territories when it was first double-tracked and electrified over a decade ago.

Congestion will also be relieved in West Kowloon, Kwai Chung and Tsing Yi. For example, when the West Kowloon Expressway opens, the peak hour traffic volume on the existing West Kowloon Corridor is projected to drop by as much as 40 per cent.

New Highways

The WHC will be a dual, three-lane, immersed tube road tunnel linking the West Kowloon Expressway on the West Kowloon reclamation with a new section of elevated road in the Western district on Hong Kong Island, connecting with Connaught Road Central. It will comprise a two-kilometre tunnel, associated approach roads, a major road interchange on Hong Kong Island and a toll plaza on Kowloon side. Aside from providing a key part of the airport highway route, it will relieve congestion at the two existing cross-harbour tunnels. On June 18, the JLG's Airport Committee endorsed the WHC project, and the Western Harbour Crossing Bill was subsequently passed by the Legislative Council in July. The formal project agreement was signed on September 2, with the Western Harbour Tunnel Company Limited, to finance, construct and operate the tunnel under a 30-year franchise. Physical work, which started in September, is aimed at completion by mid-1997.

The West Kowloon Expressway will link the northern portal of the Western Harbour Crossing to Lai Chi Kok, forming an important part of Route 3, with a dual, three-lane carriageway. It will serve developments on the West Kowloon reclamation and help relieve pressure on existing local and distributor roads in central and western Kowloon. Physical work on the expressway started in August. A further section of Route 3 will connect Kwai Chung with the Lantau Fixed Crossing through Tsing Yi, with a dual, four-lane viaduct in Kwai Chung. Three major contracts on Route 3, covering the construction of the Cheung Ching Tunnel, Kwai Chung Viaduct and Rambler Channel Bridge, were awarded in 1993 for completion in early 1997.

The two-deck Lantau Fixed Crossing, carrying a railway as well as roads, will comprise the Tsing Ma suspension bridge linking Tsing Yi to Ma Wan; viaducts crossing Ma Wan; and the Kap Shui Mun Bridge, with a cable-stayed design, linking Ma Wan to Lantau. The Tsing Ma Bridge will become internationally-known as a major Hong Kong landmark. Its main span of about 1.4 kilometres will be the world's longest carrying both road and railway, and its concrete towers will be 206 metres tall, as high as some of the tallest office buildings in Central District. Construction of the Tsing Ma Bridge was about 37 per cent complete at the end of the year. Design of the Kap Shui Mun Bridge was underway, with preliminary site clearance and physical works starting concurrently in March 1993.

The North Lantau Expressway will be a 12.5-kilometre dual, three-lane carriageway along the northern coast of Lantau, linking the Lantau Fixed Crossing to Tung Chung new town and the airport at Chek Lap Kok. Construction of the expressway is being carried out in three sections. Work on the Tai Ho and Yam O sections started in 1992 and were about 51 per cent and 25 per cent complete, respectively, at the year's end. The contract to construct the Tung Chung section was awarded in September 1993.

Airport Railway

The 34-kilometre airport railway has been planned to provide two separate rail services, operating mainly on the same tracks but with separate platforms. These will be: a fast passenger link to the airport at Chek Lap Kok, called the Airport Express, and a domestic service called the Lantau Line. Both will have maximum operating speeds of 135 kilometres per hour, compared to 80 kilometres per hour on existing Mass Transit Railway (MTR) lines.

The Airport Express is designed as an all-seated, business class-type express service providing a 23-minute link between the Central District on Hong Kong Island and the airport, with only two stops at Kowloon and Tsing Yi. It is envisaged that six-car trains will be used initially at eight-minute frequencies, increasing, as required, to a maximum of 10-car trains, operating at 4.5-minute frequencies.

Serving northern Lantau, western Kowloon, and Central, the Lantau Line is designed as a conventional mass transit commuter service. It will bring much needed relief to the MTR's Tsuen Wan Line, particularly along the Nathan Road Corridor where the railway is presently carrying its capacity of 77 500 passengers during the morning peak hours. Stations are planned at Central, West Kowloon, Tai Kok Tsui, Lai King, Tsing Yi and Tung Chung new town, with provision for additional stations later.

Five sites, totalling approximately 62 hectares, have been identified along the railway route for residential and commercial property development. They are at Central, West Kowloon, Tai Kok Tsui, Tsing Yi and Tung Chung.

During 1993, the MTRC carried out detailed design and planning work for the railway. Tender documentation was well advanced and the corporation began calling tenders for civil, electrical and mechanical works.

To avoid interface problems that may arise between the government works on the Central reclamation and the MTRC's railway station works, the government has entrusted management of the Phase I Central reclamation work to the corporation. Work on this $1.7 billion (MOD) contract commenced on September 1. The contract will provide the site for the railway's Hong Kong Central station, which will be the terminus for both the Lantau Line and the Airport Express Line.

Government Contracts and Tenders

A total of 34 government construction contracts, worth about $31.3 billion, had been awarded by the end of 1993. Sixteen of these contracts, worth more than $12 billion, were awarded in the course of the year. All were awarded within budget estimates and were proceeding smoothly. They represented 78 per cent of the total value of the government's ACP contracts, and over 90 per cent of the total highways.

The contracts awarded during the year included the Tung Chung section of the North Lantau Expressway at a cost of $920 million; three sections (for the Cheung Ching Tunnel, Kwai Chung Viaduct and Rambler Channel Bridge) of Route 3 for a total of $3.4 billion; the north and south sections of the West Kowloon Expressway for a total of $2.1 billion; the Lantau Fixed Crossing toll plaza advance works and traffic control system for a total cost of $456 million; a variety of land formation and sewerage and drainage works on the West Kowloon reclamation for a total of $3.1 billion; engineering works for the Phase I Central reclamation awarded at a cost of $1.6 billion; and water supply works to North Lantau at a total cost of $942 million.

The government welcomes international participation in the contracts and is strictly applying its traditional 'level playing field' approach on tendering procedures and the award of contracts.

A significant number of international companies, from a wide range of countries, have won construction and site investigation contracts, often in joint ventures. By the end of 1993, Japan had won the largest share by value with 27 per cent of the total, followed by Hong Kong (17 per cent), United Kingdom (14 per cent), the Netherlands (11 per cent), the People's Republic of China (eight per cent), France (seven per cent), Belgium (six per cent), Australia (four per cent), the United States of America (two per cent), New Zealand (two per cent), Germany (one per cent), Italy (0.6 per cent), and South Africa (0.4 per cent). Firms winning consultancies have come from the United Kingdom, United States of America, the Netherlands, Germany, Australia, Canada, Denmark, Sweden, Switzerland, New Zealand, France, Japan and Hong Kong.

The selection of contractors, whether local or multi-national, is strictly based on their ability to meet the government's requirements in terms of completion time, standards and specifications, and the lowest acceptable price.

Management and Cost Controls

Following the establishment of an overall strategy on the scope of the ACP, its critical programme objectives, and its budget, regular reviews were conducted in 1993. The strategy is the basis for the overall programme and its project management system. Fixed-price, lump sum contracts are being used for most projects to minimise risks to the government, especially from inflation and changes in the estimation of quantities.

A cost control system has been introduced for the ACP, laying down procedures for monitoring, scrutinising and controlling costs during the design and construction of the government-funded projects. Early warnings of possible cost increases are reported to the New Airport Projects Co-ordination Office (NAPCO) and relevant department heads. Proposed design changes leading to higher costs have to be fully justified and approved before detailed design can start. This system enables upward trends, which could lead to cost increases, to be identified early. If cost increases are accepted, off-setting savings are sought in the same or other ACP projects.

Government works departments, and other participants such as the PAA, MTRC, and the Western Harbour Crossing franchisee, have full responsibility for their own project-level planning, execution, control and management. They are required to complete projects on time and within budget, and to report progress and co-ordinate their work through NAPCO.

NAPCO's job is to ensure compliance with ACP plans, programmes and budgets, and to act as a focal point for the management of project interfaces and resolution of problems. It is made up of staff from the government and the ACP project management consultant.

In addition to the cost control systems, its highly competitive tendering system has also enabled the government to obtain value for money on the ACP contracts.

Protecting the Environment

Environmental impact assessment (EIA) studies have been undertaken for each of the ACP projects, sometimes at both the feasibility and detailed design stages, as an integral part of project planning and design. These studies have generally shown that, with suitable mitigation measures in place, the projects will be environmentally acceptable when they are built and operating.

The island being formed at Chek Lap Kok for the airport platform has been designed to allow tidal water to flow between the airport and the North Lantau coastline, thereby flushing partially enclosed areas of water to the east. Most of the natural coastline to the west of Tung Chung will be retained. Several mitigation measures have been initiated for the loss of wildlife habitats along North Lantau and at Chek Lap Kok. These include ecological studies of local wetlands, seagrass beds and mangrove communities; relocation of a colony of Romer's Tree Frogs from Chek Lap Kok; and replanting of mangrove communities and woodlands.

Extensive environmental monitoring and audit programmes are being put in place by the respective project offices to ensure acceptable environmental performance of individual projects. To supplement the efforts of the project offices, an environmental project office for the West Kowloon project area was established by the Environmental Protection Department (EPD) in 1992. A similar office was set up for the Kwai Chung and Tsing Yi area in 1993. Both offices consist of EPD staff and specialist environmental consultancy teams. Their task is to monitor and audit the cumulative environmental effects of the construction works and to ensure that environmental issues are quickly identified and acted upon by the works agents. The offices also assist the government in dealing with local community concerns on environmental issues arising from the construction works.

Safety at Work

The government continues to promote safety at work and is making headway in the implementation of safety measures on the ACP construction sites.

The Airport Core Programme Construction Safety Manual was published in 1992, setting out the government's policy and objectives, and safety measures.

During 1993, a package of safety measures was implemented on the construction sites. Contractors were required to prepare safety plans, employ full-time safety personnel on site, provide training to their workers and management, and establish site safety committees. These measures, which were incorporated in each contract, were intended to ensure there was an effective safety management system on each site from the moment work commenced.

Safety standards on sites were closely monitored. A site safety management committee was established in each site to monitor each contractor's compliance with safety requirements. A safety management unit was established by the government to visit the ACP sites to audit their construction safety standards. In addition, a database was compiled to assist with the monitoring of accident rates, analysis of the causes of accidents, and formulation of prevention measures.

Other measures taken to complement these safety efforts included accident prevention and safety management training courses conducted for site staff. Safety promotion campaigns and awards were organised to increase awareness, especially among construction workers. Up to the end of 1993, the industrial accident rate for ACP contracts was 98 per thousand workers per year, compared with the corresponding rate for the construction industry as a whole of 302 in 1992. The government has committed itself to further improvements in the safety records of ACP and non-ACP works sites.

Community and Public Relations

A comprehensive programme of community and public relations activities was implemented during 1993. For schools, a primary teaching kit was produced and two exhibitions were organised. Publications included six ACP newsletters and three regional pamphlets on ACP projects for West Kowloon, Kwai Tsing, and Central and Western districts. Boat tours of ACP sites were also organised for various groups, including members of the Legislative Council, the ACC, the Urban Council, the Regional Council and district boards, consular representatives and the media. Four overseas exhibitions were mounted in Osaka, Seattle, New York and Singapore, and two local exhibitions were held in Sham Shui Po and Kwai Tsing districts. Briefings were given to a wide range of audiences, including about 800 visitors to Hong Kong.

17
PORT DEVELOPMENT

HONG KONG's port throughput continued to record a strong growth rate. In 1993, the number of containers handled increased by 15 per cent to total 9.2 million TEUs (20-foot equivalent units). This followed increases of 29 per cent in 1992 and 21 per cent in 1991. The massive increases ensured that Hong Kong retained its position as the world's busiest container port.

The port handles more containers a year than does the whole of Britain. Only the United States and Japan have a bigger container throughput than Hong Kong.

To meet rising demand, Hong Kong must, between now and the year 2011, increase its handling capacity by one million TEUs each year. That is the equivalent of building, every year, a port the size of Oakland, California, or Felixstowe, Britain's busiest container port.

The territory will build a completely new port on the northeast of Lantau Island to handle this huge rise in throughput. This will involve one of the world's biggest civil engineering projects.

A total of 17 new container berths are planned for Lantau, but it is envisaged that as many as 24 berths could be in operation by 2011. Hong Kong's present container port at Kwai Chung has 15 berths, with another seven to be built by 1995.

Aside from container berths, the new port at Lantau will need back-up and cargo working areas, ship-repair facilities, a river trade terminal to handle vessels from China and an extensive road network, including an expressway. New channels must be dredged to provide marine access and breakwaters constructed to shelter working container vessels from wave action. Eventually a link, by tunnel or bridge, will connect Lantau directly with Hong Kong Island.

Planning is also underway for a dedicated rail link that will connect the new port and the present facilities at Kwai Chung with China's upgraded rail network. This will enable containers to be sent by rail from most of mainland China.

For, like Kwai Chung, the new port will not just serve Hong Kong. The territory owes its very existence to its position as an *entrepôt* for China. With the modernisation of China's economy and its opening up to world markets, that *entrepôt* trade has assumed a renewed importance.

The port at Lantau will begin to operate in 1997, when the Lantau Fixed Crossing — which includes one of the world's longest suspension bridges — comes into operation. The bridge will provide transport access to both the new port, and the new airport at Chek Lap Kok.

While Hong Kong awaits the new facilities on Lantau, the port must handle ever-increasing amounts of cargo. To cope with this demand, two new container terminals have been planned close to the present container port — at Stonecutters Island (Terminal 8) and Southeast Tsing Yi Island (Terminal 9).

The first berth at Terminal 8 started operations in July 1993 and three more berths will come into operation by early 1995.

The Terminal 8 project involves the reclamation of 111 hectares of land to the north of Stonecutters Island. Of this, 58 hectares will house the four-berth terminal, while 53 hectares will be used for back-up facilities.

As with Hong Kong's other seven terminals, private companies are designing, building and operating Terminal 8. The government awarded the development rights to a consortium formed by Modern Terminals Limited, Hong Kong International Terminals Limited (the two major terminal operators at Kwai Chung), and China Ocean Shipping Company.

In November 1992, the government announced the offer of development and operating rights for Terminal 9 to a consortium comprising Modern Terminals Limited, Hongkong International Terminals Limited and the Tsing Yi Container Terminal Consortium. The terminal will comprise 60 hectares containing four berths, with a total capacity of 1.6 million TEUs a year — the same start-up capacity as Terminal 8. A further 26 hectares will be available for back-up purposes and 39 hectares for industrial and community use.

It was originally planned that the first berth at Terminal 9 would be operating by mid-1995, when Terminal 8 is expected to be at full capacity. Although there has been some difficulty in meeting the August 1993 date for starting construction work, plans to minimise the delay and to mitigate its effects are being developed. (For further details on the port, see Chapter 15.)

Port Development Board

As the majority of port facilities and services are provided by private companies, Hong Kong has never created a port authority. However, with a development as massive and extensive as the new Lantau port, there is a need for a co-ordinating body to keep development plans up to date and to act as a link between the private and government bodies involved. The Port Development Board (PDB) fills that role.

Set up in April 1990, the board has a non-official chairman and advises the Governor, through the Secretary for Economic Services, on all aspects of port planning and development.

Specifically, the PDB's brief is to assess development needs in the light of changing demand, port capacity, productivity and performance. It considers the competitiveness of Hong Kong compared with other major regional ports.

The board recommends strategies for creating new port facilities and co-ordinates government and private sector involvement in developing them. It acts as a focal point for ideas and opinions expressed by port operators or anyone affected by port expansion.

Originally, the PDB had three committees to help it plan for special needs in the port: the Ship Repair Facilities Committee, the River Trade Cargo Activities Committee and the Mid-Stream Operations Committee. In 1991, board members endorsed the setting up of the Port Land and Transport Committee, and the Container Handling Committee.

The Port Land and Transport Committee advises the government on land required to support port cargo handling facilities. This includes land for ancillary port operations and transport systems required to ensure smooth movement of cargo to and from the port. The shortage of land for mid-stream operations was one of its main concerns during the year under review.

The Container Handling Committee provides data, analyses and advice to the government on container handling facilities. It examines worldwide containerisation trends, Hong Kong's position in the Asia-Pacific Region and the increased potential for containerisation in China.

A working group was also established in 1992 to examine institutional arrangements for future port development.

Future Growth

The PDB's Port Cargo Forecasts Study of 1993 found that total port traffic would continue to grow by 6.7 per cent a year between 1992 and 2011, when total throughput would reach 349.4 million tonnes. This would comprise 207.6 million tonnes of inward cargo and 141.8 million tonnes of outward cargo. More than 75 per cent of the cargo would be carried by ocean-going vessels and the rest by river vessels.

Trans-shipment traffic would account for seven per cent of the ocean traffic in 2011, a substantial decrease from the 20 per cent in 1992.

Analysed by commodity, inward cargo carried by ocean-going vessels in 2011 would consist mainly of petroleum products (31 per cent), coal (12 per cent), and chemical and related products (10 per cent). About 47 per cent of the cargo is expected to be containerised, 31 per cent liquid bulk, 18 per cent dry bulk, and four per cent break-bulk.

Outward cargo would comprise mainly manufactured articles (40 per cent), machinery and transport equipment (19 per cent), and petroleum products (14 per cent). Analysed by cargo type, 83 per cent of the cargo would be containerised, 14 per cent liquid bulk and three per cent break-bulk.

From these figures, a preliminary estimate is that by 2011, the new port will need at least 17 additional container berths, each with a quay length of 320 metres; about 9 600 metres of cargo-working seafrontage; some 300 hectares of land for back-up areas; and about 4 000 hectares of buoy and anchorage area to support port operations.

The board has also concluded that the new port infrastructure must include ship repair facilities to service the growing fleet of ocean-going vessels calling at Hong Kong. Besides servicing these vessels, such repair facilities will ensure that the port can recover quickly from a major maritime accident or from storm damage.

Ship repairing is among the oldest industries in Hong Kong, and the PDB has recommended planning a dockyard industry supporting a minimum of eight floating or dry docks (supported by alongside berths or finger piers) by the mid-1990s, with flexibility to increase the number of docks to at least 10 by 2006.

Port Layout at Lantau

In October 1989, the government announced that both the new airport and new port would be built on Lantau Island. Although its Port and Airport Development Study (PADS) determined the general site of the port, stretching southeast from Penny's Bay on Lantau towards Hong Kong Island, the study did not decide its exact pattern.

Since August 1991, consultants have been carrying out the Lantau Port and Western Harbour Development Studies, on behalf of the government, to decide the best layout for the new port. They delivered their final report to the government in May 1993.

The consultants examined five options including a peninsula, a series of connected islands with berth entrances to the east and to the west, and east and west-facing basins. They evaluated different configurations from port and harbour aspects, marine risk and navigation, environmental impact, transport and traffic links, and onshore land planning.

The evaluation showed a strong preference for the west-facing island layout. Among the main advantages, its long-term development potential is much higher than for other configurations.

The preferred western approach channel allows for better marine traffic arrangements and manoeuvring into and out of the port basins. Ship-to-ship and ship-to-ferry encounter risk would be low, typhoon evacuation fast, and traffic control needs small.

Water quality impacts are similar for all concepts. But west-facing islands will mean better air quality because the expressway serving the port will be located further from residential areas in Discovery Bay and on Peng Chau. From an on-shore and general planning viewpoint, the layout is also compatible with developments in Discovery Bay and on Peng Chau.

While there are no great differences for traffic and transport arrangements, the west-facing island layout will give better direct port access.

It will also mean the lowest cost for Phase One development of the port. Comprising the first four berths of Terminal 10, this will be the most expensive phase. It will include flyovers, road junctions, interchanges and other infrastructure that must be in place before later phases begin.

Since planning and construction of new terminal facilities need a five-year lead time, close attention is paid to throughput figures to determine when to trigger the next phase of development. During the year, Terminal 11, the second to be built on Lantau, was triggered. Terminal 10 was triggered in 1992.

Mid-Stream and River Traffic

While 63 per cent of Hong Kong's container throughput in terms of TEUs was handled by the container terminals in 1993, 30 per cent was handled by mid-stream operations and seven per cent by river trade vessels. The 1993 Port Cargo Forecasts Study has estimated that container traffic carried by ocean-going vessels will continue to grow by 6.9 per cent per annum between 1992 and 2011, when total throughput to be handled at the container terminals and mid-stream will reach 26.7 million TEUs. River trade container throughput is expected to increase at 14 per cent per annum during the period, amounting to 5.1 million TEUs in 2011.

From its early days, Hong Kong has been a buoyage port, with most cargoes handled over the sides of ships into or out of lighters moored alongside vessels. Some ships are also worked at anchor. Even with the growth of containerisation, the port still handles much of its cargo in these ways. Lighters carry containers to and from ships moored or anchored mid-stream.

Mid-stream container throughput grew at an average annual growth rate of 27 per cent over the past five years. The year under review saw a 14 per cent increase in mid-stream container handling, to a total of 2.8 million TEUs.

While there has been a huge increase in the number of containers handled mid-stream, it has not been possible to increase to the same extent the amount of land available for mid-stream operators. This is largely due to the demand for land by Hong Kong's other development projects. This problem is being addressed by the Port Development Board, which has initiated an extensive search for both short-term and permanent sites.

An increasing volume of goods trans-shipped to and from China through Hong Kong now moves by river boats down the Pearl River, for generations the gateway to trade with China. In 1993, 21 million tonnes of goods were handled by 76 000 river trade vessels in this manner. To cater specifically for this growth, private companies will build and operate a River Trade Terminal at Tuen Mun on the mainland north of Lantau. Expressions of interest in this connection were being evaluated within the government. The terminal is planned to be available in 1997.

Development Studies

The port development plan and its associated programme will be reviewed regularly to ensure that it remains relevant to Hong Kong's needs and that it can be achieved within the required time.

As part of this process, the PDB's Secretariat conducted a survey of Chinese ports, from the Vietnam border extending to the northeast along the coast of China. Although some ports showed potential for development, none emerged as a serious rival to Hong Kong as the main port to serve the rapidly developing South China region. While other ports in the region will be developed or expanded, these will be complementary to, rather than in competition with, Hong Kong.

Through the refinement of periodic strategy reviews and the regular monitoring of the progress and updating of the port development plan and programme, the competitive advantage of Hong Kong can be assured well into the 21st century.

18
PUBLIC ORDER

HONG KONG is one of the safest cities in the world. The crime rate in 1993 was the lowest in the past 10 years.

There remain areas of concern, however, and the fight against crime continues without remission. There is an increased police presence on the streets and better cross-border co-operation against crime.

The Royal Hong Kong Police was up to its full establishment for the first time in a decade. The police recruited 1 367 junior police officers, while in the same period 1 010 left the force. The wastage rate was about two per cent lower than that of the previous year.

There was increased alarm, however, about corruption, with a 44 per cent rise in complaints recorded by the Independent Commission Against Corruption. In October, the government announced additional resources for the commission in 1994.

The Fire Services Department celebrated its 125th anniversary during the year. The department, which started out modestly as a fire brigade of 66 officers and 100 volunteers in 1868, is now completely localised with more than 8 000 staff, operating more than 90 fire stations and ambulance depots.

New Year's Day began with a tragic event. Twenty-one people were trampled to death in crowd revelry in Lan Kwai Fong, Central, where thousands gathered to welcome in 1993. The Governor ordered an immediate inquiry to look at how to prevent similar tragedies.

The Organisational Structure

The government gives high priority to the fight against crime and the maintenance of public order. The Fight Crime Committee, chaired by the Chief Secretary, provides valuable advice and puts forward recommendations on areas of public concern and on measures to improve the maintenance of law and order.

The Royal Hong Kong Police has operational responsibility for crime prevention and detection, the maintenance of public order and, since April 1992, has fully resumed responsibility for the detection of illegal immigrants on the border.

The Immigration Department, through its control of the entry and exit points, and activities directed at discovering illegal immigrants, contributes significantly to the maintenance of law and order.

In anti-narcotics operations, the police maintain close liaison with the Customs and Excise Department. The latter also maintains links with overseas customs authorities and plays a major part in combating smuggling and enforcing the Copyright Ordinance.

The Independent Commission Against Corruption enforces the Prevention of Bribery Ordinance and promotes greater community awareness of the evils of corruption.

The Correctional Services Department administers the penal system and runs correctional and rehabilitative programmes. The department also manages five detention centres for Vietnamese migrants.

The Fire Services Department gives advice on fire protection and provides fire-fighting and rescue services. It also operates the main ambulance service.

Fight Crime Committee

In 1993, the Fight Crime Committee continued to provide advice on measures to combat crime. Specific subjects considered included measures to counter organised and serious crimes, the regulation of the security and guarding services industry, witness protection, the post-release supervision scheme for ex-offenders, student triad activities, and crime involving juvenile and young offenders.

An *ad hoc* group of the Legislative Council continued a detailed study of the Organised and Serious Crimes Bill. The Bill was introduced into the council in July 1992. Its objective is to effectively tackle organised crime, including triad-related crime, and other serious crimes through, among other things, enhanced investigative powers and provisions to enable heavier sentences to be imposed.

The Security and Guarding Services Bill was introduced into the Legislative Council on November 10, 1993. The Bill aims at regulating the security and guarding services industry through a licensing system to be run on two levels, namely, the licensing of persons who undertake security work (including watchmen) and the licensing of security companies.

The Fight Crime Committee set up an *ad hoc* committee to review existing witness protection arrangements in late 1992. It endorsed the *ad hoc* committee's final report and recommendations in April 1993. Major recommendations on witness protection endorsed by the Fight Crime Committee include the establishment of a witness protection programme and provision of sufficient funding for the programme; the review of witness accommodation in court and in custody; improvements to the existing witness assurance and assistance arrangements; and the launching of an education programme to inform the public of the witness protection programme, and the assurance and assistance arrangements.

The committee examined, in July 1991, how the post-release supervision scheme could operate. The scheme aims to rehabilitate ex-offenders, reduce the threat posed by some to public safety, reduce the chances of recidivism and turn them into useful members of society. The Post-Release Supervision Bill, which sets out the framework of the scheme, is under preparation. It is expected that the Bill will be introduced into the Legislative Council in early 1994.

The committee has devoted much of its attention to the problem of juvenile crime, in particular, triad activities in schools. An inter-departmental working group was set up in August 1992 to consider ways to provide support to schools to tackle student triad activities. The committee examined, in November 1993, the final report of the working group and endorsed its recommendations, which include integration of community resources to tackle the problems; provision of guidelines and training for discipline teachers to handle student behavioural problems; stepping up police presence near schools; and strengthening liaison among the police, discipline personnel and social workers.

A sub-committee of the Fight Crime Committee commissioned, in September 1992, the research team of the Social Science Research Centre of the University of Hong Kong to conduct a study on the social causes of juvenile crime. The research team completed all major field work during the year and it is expected that the research study will be completed in early 1994.

The Young Offenders Assessment Panel continued to provide advice to the courts on the rehabilitation programmes most likely to reform juveniles and young people. A special Outward Bound Course has also been arranged for inmates of Correctional Services Department facilities.

District Fight Crime Committees continued to play an important role. They monitored the crime situation in their districts, and helped foster both community awareness of the need to prevent crime and community participation in combating crime.

Police Force

The overall crime rate remained steady in 1993, with a slight reduction in violent cases. While armed gangs continued to be a cause for concern, better intelligence and improved co-operation with China led to the arrest of several ringleaders and the break-up of gangs responsible for some of the most violent crimes over the past two years.

In addition to the return of criminals from China, cross-border liaison helped to eliminate a number of syndicates involved in the theft and smuggling of luxury cars to China. The anti-smuggling task force set up in 1991 successfully curtailed the activities of speedboats, while intelligence passed to Chinese security forces enabled them to capture smugglers at their home bases. Several batches of stolen luxury cars recovered in China were returned to Hong Kong during the year.

Further afield, Hong Kong police collaborated in the detection of a major credit card forgery syndicate and played a major role in the worldwide crackdown on drug trafficking.

To maintain Hong Kong's record of being one of the safest cities in the world, the Police Force places high priority on deploying sufficient manpower to counter, prevent and reduce crime. Recent recruitment has brought the Force up to its full establishment of 27 263 disciplined officers. The year under review saw the former New Territories Region split into two and the opening of several new police stations.

Equipment and support services are also keeping pace with the latest technology. New revolvers, with more effective ammunition, were issued to officers for better protection against criminals who carry powerful weapons. The officers can now practise their marksmanship at a state-of-the-art firing range, at the Police Tactical Unit base at Fanling, which is believed to be unrivalled in the world. The marine police also completed a major reprovisioning exercise during the year when it commissioned five new command launches and six inshore patrol boats, bringing its fleet up to 166 boats — the biggest fleet of its kind. In the air, the Force gained the use of two Black Hawk helicopters operated by the newly-formed Government Flying Service. They will enable rapid deployment of personnel, as well as support, for other operations.

The Force has also promulgated performance pledges to improve its service to the public. In addition, a public opinion survey, on views and perceptions of the police by the public, was being conducted. The results will provide valuable input for projecting a positive image of the Force to the public. Also under study was a consultant report on possible ways to improve the senior command structure of the Force.

Crime

The total number of crimes reported to the police in 1993 was 82 564, a decrease of 1.8 per cent compared with 84 056 in 1992. The crime rate stood at 1 395 cases per 100 000 of the population. This represented a drop of 3.6 per cent, compared with 1992.

Violent crime, which includes murder, wounding, serious assault, rape, indecent assault, kidnapping, blackmail, criminal intimidation, robbery and arson, registered a decline in the year, with a total of 17 454 cases recorded, compared to 18 567 in 1992. Robbery, wounding and serious assault accounted for some 21 per cent of the total number of violent crimes in 1993.

The situation regarding vehicle theft improved considerably. Overall, 4 630 motor vehicles were reported missing in 1993, a sharp decrease of 33.1 per cent compared with 1992.

The number of robberies involving the use of firearms — both genuine and pistol-like objects — was 291, a drop of 127 compared with 1992.

A total of 40 227 crimes, or 48.7 per cent, were detected in 1993, and some 45 042 persons were arrested for various criminal offences. Of the persons arrested, 6 644 were juvenile offenders (aged under 16 years) and 8 733 were young persons (aged between 16 and 20 years).

Organised Crime and Triads

In 1993, there was a marked decrease in armed robberies. The decrease was attributed to a series of successful police operations against armed criminal syndicates and improved co-operation with the Chinese authorities. This co-operation led to more criminals seeking refuge in China being arrested and sent back to Hong Kong.

The overall decline in the number of missing vehicles could be attributed to the vigorous enforcement by the Hong Kong and Chinese authorities. Action taken included the neutralisation of a number of major cross-border smuggling syndicates and increasing the maximum sentence for taking a conveyance without authority from three to seven years. Improved car security by manufacturers and owners, as a result of mounting pressure from insurance companies, was also a factor.

A new trend emerged in 1993, featuring an upsurge in the theft and smuggling of left-hand-drive vehicles. It was assessed that the majority of stolen luxury cars were smuggled into China.

Action against triads remained a priority, and resulted in successful prosecutions against both office-bearers and members.

The Organised and Serious Crimes Bill, under study by an *ad hoc* group of the Legislative Council, will enable the police to tackle organised and serious crimes more effectively. The Bill was designed to give the police more power to obtain information from witnesses; allow the courts to confiscate the proceeds of crime; and enable the prosecution, in respect of certain offences, to provide the courts with more information upon conviction, to assist the courts in awarding more deterrent sentences.

Commercial Crime

The Commercial Crime Bureau's Fraud Division continued investigation into fraud in the trading and financial sectors. The activities of unscrupulous foreign exchange companies caused much public concern, and in one case alone, some 300 investors suffered losses of over $100 million. New legislation on fringe foreign exchange trading, in the form of the Leverage Foreign Exchange Trading Bill, was put before the Legislative Council. Upon enactment of the Bill, the Commercial Crime Bureau will be able to resolve this longstanding and difficult problem.

In April, the Computer Crimes Ordinance was enacted and a special section was established in the bureau to investigate the new offences created by the ordinance. For the first time, hacking and damaging computers or their software became offences. This brought Hong Kong into line with other jurisdictions.

During the year, the Counterfeit and Forgery Division was successful in combating both the manufacture and use of forged credit cards, and the production of counterfeit currency. In one case, a major international forged credit card syndicate was neutralised in an operation involving Hong Kong, European and North American law enforcement agencies. In another case, a raid on a printing workshop yielded counterfeit US$100 notes with a face value of over US$7 million.

Narcotics

The territory continued to suffer from its relative proximity to the production area in the Golden Triangle, which accounted for almost 70 per cent of the world's total output of opiates.

The year saw an abundant supply of (almost exclusively) No. 4 heroin in the local market, the price and purity of which continued to show a downward trend. By the year's end, the purity was 41.36 per cent, compared to a high in the early 1990s of more than 70 per cent. The retail price was approximately $332 per gram.

Some 269.15 kilogrammes of opiate drugs, comprising opium and No. 4 heroin, were seized, compared with 611.99 kilogrammes in 1992. There were 12 600 arrests for narcotics offences, compared with 9 600 in the previous year.

Heroin remained the major drug abused by more than 90 per cent of the total addict population. Although also popular with young persons, increases were noted in cough mixture abuse (up 25 per cent) and cannabis abuse (up 23 per cent). Continuing the trend of the last few years, there were also increases in the number of young persons arrested for drug offences. They comprised almost 19 per cent of the total drug arrests during the year.

Narcotics enforcement recorded a productive year, with noticeable successes against local distribution syndicates, particularly heroin-cutting centres. Successes in 1993 included the neutralisation of 30 such facilities, as well as seizures of 72.91 kilogrammes of heroin.

In August 1992, Section 25 of the Drug Trafficking (Recovery of Proceeds) Ordinance, which contains the offence of 'assisting another to retain the benefit of trafficking', was overruled by a High Court Judge. The section was considered inconsistent with Article 11 of the Bill of Rights Ordinance. In May 1993, the Privy Council of the House of Lords reversed that decision. The total amount of assets seized by police since the enactment of the ordinance was HK$145,460,359.

Crime Prevention

The Crime Prevention Bureau continued to promote the principles of crime prevention through public awareness programmes and the provision of professional advice to the community. The security of high-risk premises, particularly banks, was accorded high priority, followed by domestic security and vehicle-related crime.

Anti-crime education for juveniles continued through the medium of the 'Robotcop', which was used in more than 200 displays in schools, youth organisations and public exhibitions throughout the year. Shop theft by juveniles was further targeted by the introduction of the life-size 'cardboard policeman', which attracted a positive response from retail outlets.

A new unit dedicated to the security of computers was set up, to undertake specialist training of crime prevention officers and the formulation of advisory publications for public dissemination.

Crime Information

The Criminal Records Bureau is the sole repository for criminal records in Hong Kong. It houses complete records on all persons convicted of crime in the territory.

The records and indices held by the bureau comprise details of wanted persons, suspected offenders, missing persons, stolen property, outstanding warrants and missing vehicles. At the end of the year, the indices held particulars of some 548 447 criminal records, 11 180 wanted persons, 1 201 missing persons, 6 227 outstanding warrants and 5 404 missing vehicles. During 1993, the Enhanced Police Operational Nominal Index Computer System (EPONICS) dealt with a total of 2 701 186 enquiries.

Ballistics and Firearms Identification

The Ballistics and Firearms Identification Bureau handled 318 cases involving the use or possession of a firearm during the year. This was a slight decrease over the previous year's figure of 338 cases. Weapons recovered were mainly self-loading pistols, although two fully-automatic Chinese type 56 assault rifles were also seized in one armed incident. As in previous years, the pistols recovered were mainly of the very powerful and penetrating 7.62 × 25 mm calibre, with countries of manufacture as diverse as China, Poland, Russia, Czechoslovakia and Hungary.

In addition to the forensic examination of firearms and ammunition, the bureau also dealt with the scientific aspects of gunshot residue examinations. These tests, which can prove beyond reasonable doubt whether a person has or has not recently fired a weapon, have proved invaluable in the investigation of armed crime incidents.

Identification

The Identification Bureau provides support to all formations in the Force in respect of fingerprint technology and forensic photography.

In terms of fingerprint identifications, improved levels of efficiency and service were achieved by the bureau in 1993, following the partial computerisation of the Force's fingerprint records. The Computer Assisted Fingerprint Identification System (CAFIS) reduced considerably the time taken to process fingerprints found at scenes of crime. The computer, coupled with the more traditional methods of searching fingerprints, led to 1 201 persons being identified as being linked with 1 279 criminal cases during the year. Computerisation of the remainder of the bureau's fingerprint records continued.

During the year, officers from the Scenes of Crime Section attended 25 220 crimes scenes. Various measures were introduced to shorten the time taken to reach the scene of crime.

The Main Fingerprint Collection Section, which is principally responsible for confirming people's previous criminal convictions, processed the fingerprints of 205 928 persons, leading to the discovery of 83 796 persons who had criminal records.

Interpol
The Hong Kong National Central Bureau of the International Criminal Police Organisation, more commonly known as Interpol, is one of its most active members in the Southeast Asian region.

The bureau aims to ensure and promote the widest possible mutual assistance among all police authorities, within the limits of the laws existing in different member countries and in the spirit of the Declaration of Human Rights.

It acts as a co-ordination centre in dealing with criminal information and associated inquiries between Hong Kong and the rest of the world, and disseminates information on behalf of the Force to participating countries. It also maintains close liaison with most local consulate officials.

Two officers are seconded to the Interpol General Secretariat in Lyons, France, to maintain close liaison with the secretariat there.

As part of the improved liaison and co-operation with China, two Chinese liaison officers were stationed in Hong Kong during the year.

Public Order
There were no incidents of major public disorder in Hong Kong in 1993.

During the year, the Police Tactical Unit (PTU) Companies were deployed in a wide variety of roles, including a number of large-scale anti-illegal immigrant operations. They also assisted the Correctional Services Department in duties related to Vietnamese migrants.

PTU tactical training continued to expand, with an emphasis on weapons tactics and Internal Security (IS) training. Several improvements in equipment were made. It is expected that the PTU Companies will soon have the capability to operate using Black Hawk helicopters. By the end of the year, a total of 2 210 officers were trained in the PTU Companies. In addition, officers of District IS Companies, CID officers and women police also underwent training under scheduled programmes of the PTU.

Illegal Immigration
It was another busy year for the police dealing with increased numbers of illegal immigrants. A total of 35 193 illegals from China were arrested in the territory by the police, representing a 4.4 per cent increase over 1992.

Among those arrested, 62 per cent claimed to have entered the territory by boat and the remainder over land. An increasing number of those coming by land resorted to hiding in trains or cargo vehicles, rather than risking climbing the border fence.

The police continued their responsibility for the border and, on average, deployed over 500 officers each day to counter the influx.

About 60 per cent of arrested illegals had entered the territory on previous occasions. There were also indications that the majority came in to look for job opportunities. Many returned to the mainland voluntarily after working for several months and remitting money back home. This resulted in the police targeting anti-illegal immigrant operations at work premises. Prosecutions were directed against employers breaking the law.

Vietnamese Migrants
Vietnamese migrants (VMs) are held in detention centres throughout Hong Kong, with the majority detained at the Whitehead Detention Centre. The screening of VMs was near

completion at the year's end, with over 90 per cent of the group having been processed. The majority of these people were screened out, pending repatriation to Vietnam either through the Voluntary Repatriation Scheme or the Orderly Repatriation Scheme. Those screened in either have been resettled or are awaiting resettlement in other countries.

It was agreed with the Vietnamese authorities in 1991 that those who were screened in would be resettled, while those screened out would be repatriated to Vietnam. This policy had an immediate deterrent effect, and in 1992 and 1993, the number of arrivals dropped remarkably. There were only 101 arrivals in 1993, compared to 12 in 1992. Every effort was also made to encourage those VMs who had been screened out to return voluntarily to Vietnam. Flights were arranged every month and resettlement programmes were in operation in Vietnam.

There were no major incidents in the VM detention camps. However, searches of camps for homemade weapons, illegal items and alcohol-brewing equipment, and the transportation of VMs between centres and from the centres to the airport under the Orderly Repatriation Programme continued to place heavy demands on police resources.

From June to August, over 2 400 ex-China Vietnamese (ECVIIs) arrived in Hong Kong. All of them were from Beihai in Guangxi Province. The influx apparently stemmed from a re-zoning of the ECVIIs, who were living in illegal squatter areas there. Discussions were held with the mainland authorities and it was agreed that all the ECVIIs would be repatriated to China.

On December 31, the total number of Vietnamese migrants in Hong Kong stood at 32 052, of whom 1 846 were accorded refugee status, 27 564 were classified as non-refugees, 1 687 were awaiting screening and 955 were ECVIIs. Resettlement accounted for 2 571, and 318 births were recorded. A total of 450 were repatriated to Vietnam under the Orderly Repatriation Programme. The figure for voluntary repatriation was 12 301, while 1 518 ECVIIs were returned to China.

Traffic

Traffic congestion was another main area of concern in 1993. Vehicle registrations approached the half million mark at the end of the year. With the steady increase in trade between Hong Kong and other countries, long queues at border crossing points and container terminals led to instances of chronic congestion. Urgent action was being taken by the government to control the length of these queues. A number of well-publicised serious accidents on expressways, which caused severe delays to traffic, highlighted the additional problems associated with high traffic densities and shortage of road space. The increase in vehicular traffic was also keenly felt with regard to parking. About 1.91 million tickets for parking offences were issued, an increase of 41.4 per cent. It became apparent that the deterrent effect of a parking ticket at its existing fine level had been eroded by inflation and prosperity, putting increased pressure on scarce police resources. Legislative amendments were in hand to deal with the situation.

Although traffic accident and casualty rates remained at the same level as that of two years ago, the fatality and serious injury rates were three times greater than those arising from criminal activity. The most common causes of accidents were, again, speed-related. Police action continued to focus on offences which were most likely to result in accidents, through a Selective Traffic Enforcement Policy (STEP), which directs priorities for enforcement action according to accident causation factors.

Marine Region

It was a year of change for many in the sea divisions of the marine police, as the Marine Region of the Royal Hong Kong Police brought into service 21 new launches, of three different types, as part of a fleet modernisation programme.

The upsurge in illegal immigration placed considerable demands on the Marine Region. The problem of smuggling also persisted during 1993, but suitable resources were deployed to combat such illegal activities. A dramatic decrease was recorded in the large-scale smuggling of electrical goods and stolen vehicles. Factors behind this included changes to the law in China to restrict the import of vehicle parts and a ban on the registration of right-hand-drive vehicles. Fluctuations in the value of the Chinese currency also made the smuggling of electrical goods less profitable. Smugglers continued to vary their methods of operation, and enforcement agencies maintained a flexible approach to tackle the problem. This sustained high-priority effort on all fronts saw record seizures of goods and vessels during the year.

Policing of the remote communities in Mirs Bay received a boost with the opening of a new police post on the small island of Tap Mun, and the installation of improved communications equipment in the post on Peng Chau Island. The construction of a police post on Kat O Island commenced in December.

Bomb Disposal

The Explosive Ordnance Disposal (EOD) Unit expanded to an establishment of six full-time operators, with the recruitment of the first local Assistant Force Bomb Disposal Officer. The operators rendered safe over 5 025 explosive devices, ranging from improvised bombs made by criminals to unexploded shells, aircraft bombs and pyrotechnics.

Fortunately, the year saw a reduction in the use of hand grenades by criminals in Hong Kong, and much of the work of the EOD Unit involved the safe defusing and recovery of large pieces of ordnance from the many dredgers operating in the territory's waters.

The unit continued to upgrade its equipment and response capabilities in line with worldwide improvements in EOD technology. Together with the increased use of helicopter deployment, this resulted in a faster response time, with a corresponding reduction in disruption to the public.

Community Relations

The long-standing objective of enlisting public support in the fight against crime continued through 1993, with emphasis on preventive measures to protect personal property. A wide range of publicity materials was issued to spread the messages that individual crime victims suffered losses, that the community as a whole bore the costs and that these effects could be minimised by individual watchfulness.

The Good Citizen Award Scheme and the Good Citizen of the Year Award Scheme, introduced in 1972 and 1984, respectively, continued to serve as effective means of promoting public involvement in the fight against crime. Jointly administered by the police and the Hong Kong General Chamber of Commerce, the two schemes have so far seen 2 342 and 26 persons, respectively, presented with the awards.

In its 13th year of operation, the police hotline, 527 7177, was still the most popular channel for the public to report crime information. A total of 6 974 calls were received, resulting in 822 arrests for various crimes.

Crime information forms, an alternative means of reporting crime information, were also widely used, with 2 570 completed forms received, leading to 428 arrests.

The Junior Police Call (JPC) remained popular, with some 178 030 active members at the year's end. Apart from involvement in fight crime activities and crime prevention campaigns, members were provided with a wide range of sports, recreational and academic programmes, organised with a view to fostering a positive attitude towards a healthy life. Members also participated in a wide range of community services such as flag-selling and fund-raising for charity, tree-planting and environmental protection programmes. The JPC helps to guide its members towards becoming responsible and law-abiding citizens.

The Force jointly produced the television programmes *Crime Watch*, *Police Call* and *Police Report* with Radio Television Hong Kong. These programmes are broadcast on a regular basis on both the English and Chinese channels of the two local television stations. In addition to the reconstruction of undetected crime cases and delivering appeals to witnesses for related information, special features were made of current crime trends and problems, as well as the various facets of police work. The programmes enjoyed a consistently high audience rating.

During the year, there were altogether 97 visits to the Force by 1 126 local and 397 overseas personalities.

Planning and Development

On April 1, the New Territories Region was split into two regions, North and South, with their regional headquarters at Tai Po and Ma On Shan, respectively.

Force planning concentrated on developments taking place on North Lantau, and on building up resources for newly-developed areas in the New Territories. An interim police station at Tung Chung on North Lantau was completed in November. It provides a base for enhanced police coverage until the permanent police stations at the new airport at Chek Lap Kok and Tung Chung new town become operational.

The West Kowloon Reclamation project was closely monitored, as was the Southeast Kowloon Development Study, in anticipation of additional police services required in Southeast Kowloon after the redevelopment of Kai Tak Airport.

A $111 million firing range complex was completed at the Police Tactical Unit base at Fanling during the year. This houses a 100-metre range, nine indoor ranges and a Close Quarter Battle House.

In Kowloon East Region, work commenced on an indoor firing range, comprising eight mini-ranges and an indoor conventional 25-metre range. When this project is completed in 1995, the Force will have five indoor firing ranges equipped with the most sophisticated weapons training facilities.

Elsewhere, the Ma Liu Shui Marine North Division Base and Tap Mun Island Police Post were completed, while work commenced on the construction of a new post on Kat O Island and a new Marine Police Training School at the former Sai Wan Ho Pier.

Refurbishment or expansion programmes at seven police stations were also completed, and work to improve the Police Training School ranges continued.

Construction of married quarters for junior police officers at Tsing Yi was completed, providing 288 units for occupancy in December. Another 408 units are due for completion at Fanling in July 1994. During 1993, funds were approved for the construction of another two blocks at Wong Tai Sin, comprising 429 married quarters. Piling work for both of these blocks started in July and completion is expected by mid-1996. Funds were also sought for the refurbishment of 152 quarters at Queen's Hill Camp near Fanling. Planning was well advanced for a new Marine Regional Headquarters complex at Sai Wan Ho, to replace the existing one in Tsim Sha Tsui.

The construction of a 32-storey tower block at Police Headquarters in Arsenal Street commenced in mid-1992. On completion in late 1995, this building will accommodate most of the Police Headquarters crime and security formations.

Communications

The programme to replace outdated and inefficient telephone exchanges in police facilities was concluded during the year, and the network of facsimile machines expanded to reduce the time of routine transmission of documents throughout the Force. Facsimile machines were also installed in the Regional Command and Control Centres in Kowloon, Hong Kong Island and the New Territories to enable members of the public who have a hearing impairment to access the '999' emergency system.

A computer-based Force Directory Enquiries System was commissioned in June to enable quick tracing of key officers in the Force, with a view to answering urgent enquiries from both within and outside the Force.

A Casualty Enquiry System, with sufficient lines to handle public enquiries in the event of a major disaster, was installed. To back up internal security and anti-crime activities in the territory, new portable radios, mobile radios and associated repeater equipment, designed specially for these needs, were provided to Regional Crime Units and the Police Tactical Unit.

Sophisticated navigation and communications equipment was installed in each of the six new divisional command launches put into service, to make police operations at sea possible even under the most severe weather. The Marine Radio Workshop also enhanced its capability to take up first line support of the advanced technologies employed in these systems.

Planning for the communications needs of police facilities at the new airport and all associated rail links continued during the year, alongside the design of a new and better radio system for traffic police.

Information Technology

In January, the government accepted the financial implications, estimated at some $526 million, for the implementation of the Force's Information Technology Strategy. Throughout the year, the Information Technology Branch was heavily committed to planning for the five major groups of computer systems which are integral to the strategy.

These systems are the Communal Information System, Force Criminal Investigation System, Force Operations Support System, Force Administrative Support System and Free-standing Systems.

The Communal Information System will facilitate day-to-day operations and the collation of management information at district, regional and headquarters levels. A pilot project, which has been running in Wanchai district for two years, has been successful, establishing the conceptual basis for future force-wide application. The Force Criminal Investigation System will provide enhanced computer facilities for the investigation and detection of crime. The Force Operations Support System will maintain a comprehensive database for the support of operations throughout the Force. The Force Administrative Support System will support the general administration of the Force by centrally maintaining personnel, training, leave, allowances, accounting and financial records, as well as a database from which related management and statistical information can be obtained. The Free-standing Systems will cater for specific local needs which are largely self-contained within specific formations, such as the Police Training School, police stores, marine police and Special Branch.

Planning also commenced for the Police Data Communications Network, which will link the various systems within the strategy with one another and with existing systems.

At the end of September, implementation of the first stage of Phase II of the Enhanced Command and Control Computer System was completed, with the incorporation and/or enhancement of three sub-systems to assist in managing resources and incidents; the provision of terminals to all police stations and district, regional and Force headquarters; and the provision of separate operational environments for internal security and training duties. Work also continued throughout the year on the three final sub-systems to provide management information, location identification and intruder alarm identification. Its completion is expected by mid-1994.

System development work for the extension of the Criminal Intelligence Computer System to the Narcotics Bureau and Commercial Crime Bureau was completed, and the fully-expanded system went into operation in August. This has enhanced the Force's intelligence gathering and analysis capabilities in these complex areas of law enforcement.

Transport

The police vehicle fleet continued to expand and modernise to keep pace with developments. At the end of the year, it stood at 2 314. Significant progress was also made to obtain improved performance from the fleet by the evaluation of several major vehicle types prior to purchase. The introduction of a charging system by the Electrical and Mechanical Services Department placed fleet maintenance on a commercial footing, and resulted in the Force exercising tighter control over servicing standards and vehicle availability.

During the year, increased emphasis was placed on the standard of police drivers. An operational driving course was introduced in early 1993 to enhance the ability of the Force to respond to emergencies and other difficult situations. Several instructors attended overseas driving courses as part of a continuing programme to upgrade driving skills and, in pursuit of Force policy, to become fully self-sufficient in driver training.

Planning also continued to upgrade the Force Transport Management Information System and to acquire an automated Fuel Dispensing System.

Research

The Research Branch completed a comprehensive study into the posts held and the tasks undertaken by women police officers within the Force during the year. Also studied and reported on were projects concerning the future use of bilingual forms within the Force, the value and necessity of the 'morning conference' system of management, the need for and level of protection required to combat firearm threats to police vehicles and their occupants, and a study into the effectiveness of the transfer of responsibility to regions of the Enhanced Command and Control Computer Systems.

Other projects under review included a proposed development of the management functions of the driver cadre to regions, and a proposed study of the beat patrol system.

Inspection Services Wing

Regular Force inspections to ensure effective and efficient operations and administration, which resumed in April 1992, were suspended in June 1993, to concentrate resources on a major management, manning and command structure study of the Force as a whole. A total of 20 inspections were conducted during this fourth cycle inspection period.

Police Licensing Office

The Commissioner of Police, through the Police Licensing Office, is the Licensing Authority for various licences and permits. As the Societies Officer, he also accepts notification of the establishment of local societies.

In 1993, 709 societies notified the Societies Officer of their establishment and 381 societies were dissolved. At the year's end, a total of 6 127 societies had provided notification of their establishment.

An average of 2 153 people applied for registration as watchmen each month. In 1993, 21 158 watchmen were registered, of whom 1 173 were licensed to carry firearms. At the end of 1993, a total of 134 810 watchmen were registered.

A total of 1 669 persons were licensed to possess arms for competition or target shooting, while 178 persons applied for arms licences.

At the end of the year, 1 026 notifications of public meetings were processed. A further 290 licences for public processions, 1 297 permits for the use of loudspeakers and 768 lion dance permits were issued.

A total of 27 applications for massage establishment licences, 40 applications for auctioneer licences, nine applications for marine store dealer licences, four applications for pawnbroker licences and 53 applications for temporary liquor licences were processed during the year.

Police Dog Unit

The Police Dog Unit located at Ping Shan in Yuen Long recorded an establishment of 104 dogs, including labradors and springer spaniels, trained to patrol, track and detect dangerous drugs and explosives. The unit ran a variety of training courses, and the successful handlers and dogs were deployed throughout Hong Kong. Numerous demonstrations were also performed for social and charity activities.

Complaints Against Police

The Complaints Against Police Office investigates all complaints from the public concerning the conduct and behaviour of members of the Police Force, including civilian staff and auxiliary police officers. The investigation of the complaints is monitored by the independent Police Complaints Committee.

In 1993, 3 374 complaints were received, an increase of 145 cases or 4.5 per cent over 1992. Over 97.7 per cent of complaints were made by persons either involved with or subjected to constabulary action. Complaints of assault, neglect of duty and conduct/manner made up the majority of cases, comprising 79.7 per cent of total complaints. Investigations into 3 520 cases were completed, with 100 cases or 2.8 per cent substantiated and 34 cases or one per cent classified as false. Altogether, 2 338 cases or 66.4 per cent of all complaints were either withdrawn or not pursuable. A total of 576 cases, representing 16.4 per cent of all complaints, were dealt with by way of the new Informal Resolution Scheme. Overall, 17 police officers were disciplined and two charged with offences resulting from the complaints. In addition, 204 officers were the subject of corrective action.

The Complaints Against Police Office is also responsible for advising Force members on how complaints can be prevented. Throughout the year, lectures and seminars on complaint prevention were organised for junior police officers, with the aim of improving public relations and reducing situations of conflict. A Complaints Prevention Committee, made up of various ranks in the Force, was set up in 1992 to identify and eradicate areas which may lead to complaints.

Recruitment

As at December 31, 1993, the Force establishment stood at 27 263 and 6 026 for disciplined and civilian staff, respectively. The strength of the Force had improved and was 27 251 and 5 782, respectively.

During the year, 8 879 applications for the post of constable were received, with 1 367 recruits subsequently taken on strength.

With regard to the recruitment of inspectors, 37 local direct-entry officers were appointed, while 41 junior police officers were promoted. In addition, 20 overseas officers were taken on strength.

The year saw a healthy recruitment situation and a significant reduction in wastage levels.

Training

Training is a vital part of a police officer's career, starting with initial training on recruitment, followed by in-service training (which takes place both locally and, in some cases, overseas) and training after promotion.

Newly-recruited inspectors and constables are sent to the Police Training School at Wong Chuk Hang, a modern 18-hectare campus, for their initial training. The 36-week inspectors' and the 24-week constables' courses cover similar subjects, including criminal law, social studies, police and court procedures, drill, firearms, first aid, physical fitness, swimming, life-saving and self-defence. Inspectors also study management theory and practical leadership. As part of recruit training, expatriate inspectors study colloquial Cantonese, while functional English is taught to local inspectors.

An officer is kept up-to-date with new legislation and procedures by in-service training at regular intervals throughout his service. In addition, there are tailor-made courses for officers in more specialised branches involved, among other things, in marine, traffic, financial investigation and instructional work. Language courses on English, Mandarin and Vietnamese are also run in conjunction with the Civil Service Training Centre. During the year, about 50 officers were sent to the United Kingdom, Canada, the United States, New Zealand, Australia and Malaysia for management, specialist and technical training.

The Higher Training Division provides progressive levels of management training and self-development courses for inspectors, chief inspectors and newly-promoted superintendents. The courses are designed to be mind-broadening and to provide a wider perspective of social and political developments in Hong Kong, as well as an opportunity to practise research techniques, and operational and strategic planning. This is achieved through lectures and discussions with senior police officers, academics and members of the Legislative Council. Visits to commercial and industrial organisations are arranged. The emphasis is on researching and solving contemporary management problems affecting diverse areas of the police force.

Promotion training for junior police officers takes place as soon as possible, after an officer's promotion, at the Police Training School. The instruction is designed to equip officers with the management and decision-making skills necessary for their new ranks.

At the Detective Training School, courses at standard and advanced levels are conducted to improve the standard of criminal investigation throughout the Force. A number of specialised courses are also run there, including an 11-day training course for officers who may be required to deal with victims of sexual assault and child abuse.

Throughout the year, emphasis continued to be placed on weapons training. All male officers were trained to use the new type of revolver, ammunition and associated equipment before these items were introduced for normal duty study. Further training was provided to front-line officers to induce greater awareness of shooting tactics on the street.

Following the trampling disaster in Lan Kwai Fong on January 1, plans are in place to upgrade the level of First Aid Refresher Training given and to make supervisory officers more aware of crowd psychology.

Promotions

Promotion prospects in the Force remained good at most levels. During the year, a total of 40 officers were promoted to the rank of senior superintendent of police and above, 31 chief inspectors advanced to superintendent, 60 senior inspectors to chief inspector, 104 sergeants to station sergeant and 367 constables to sergeant. In addition, 10 exceptionally experienced station sergeants advanced to the rank of inspector.

Overall, 267 officers retired from the Force, 31 officers were invalided, 530 resigned, six were compulsorily retired and 33 were either dismissed or had their services terminated in 1993.

Awards

A total of 882 officers were awarded the Colonial Police Long Service Medal after 18 years of continuous police service; 366 officers were awarded the 1st Clasp to the Medal after 25 years' service and another 292 officers were awarded the 2nd Clasp after 30 years' service. In addition, four officers were awarded the Queen's Police Medal for Distinguished Service and 27 officers the Colonial Police Medal for Meritorious Service. Three officers received the Queen's Gallantry Medal and four officers were awarded His Excellency the Governor's Commendation.

Welfare

The Welfare Branch provides a wide range of services, including personal welfare, psychological consultation, assistance on retirement, catering, and sports and recreation for all members of the force and their families.

During the year, social work staff conducted 3 605 casework interviews in the five regional welfare offices and the two sub-offices, and made 6 352 casework visits to sick officers and family members of officers in hospital, places of work or their home.

Family life education continued to play an important part in the welfare programme, with emphasis on good parental guidance and personal finance management.

A total of 1 877 children of regular and auxiliary police officers were awarded bursaries from the two police education trust funds. The Police Children's Education Trust distributed $4,152,000 and the Police Education and Welfare Trust distributed $1,075,325, to assist them to pursue various levels of education.

Force Housing

The Force manages a total of 11 586 quarters, of which 10 403 are for junior police officers. These include 288 new quarters at the Tsing Yi Police Married Quarters and 152 ex-military quarters at Queen's Hill Camp. The construction of 408 quarters in Fanling and 429 quarters in Wong Tai Sin are underway and scheduled for completion by 1994 and 1996, respectively. In 1993, the Force was again allocated 400 units under the Disciplined Services Quota of the Government Public Housing Scheme. Other alternative sources of accommodation which remain open to eligible junior police officers include the Home Purchase Scheme, Housing Loan Scheme and Home Ownership Scheme.

The programme to refurbish 4 500 married quarters for junior police officers over a nine-year period was progressing well. Since the introduction of the scheme in 1987, 1 621 quarters have been refurbished, resulting in a marked improvement in the structural condition and standard of these old blocks of quarters.

The policy to provide housing for all eligible married police officers, including those in the inspectorate and superintendent cadres, continued to be implemented progressively. Efforts were made to acquire more quarters of higher grading to replace the current sub-standard ones, rather than opting for sheer numbers.

Royal Hong Kong Auxiliary Police Force

Manned entirely by part-time volunteers from all walks of life, the Royal Hong Kong Auxiliary Police Force has a proud history dating back to 1914.

The traditional role of the Force was to provide the regular police with additional manpower for emergencies. Subsequent to the Fight Violent Crime Campaign in 1973, the auxiliary police have provided increasing support and are presently fully integrated with their regular counterparts in a wide variety of daily constabulary duties in the field of crime prevention, neighbourhood policing, traffic control, special duties and community relations. The auxiliary police also provide support in communications duties in police command and control centres.

The strength of the Force at the end of the year was 5 629, out of a total establishment of 5 746 officers of all ranks. Approximately 10.8 per cent of the Force was composed of women officers.

Between January to March, the average daily turnout for normal constabulary duty was 850 officers. From April to the end of 1993, this turnout was reduced to 750 officers in the light of improvements in the operational strength of the regular force.

Customs and Excise

The Customs and Excise Department is organised into five major branches — the Headquarters Branch, Operations Branch, Investigation Branch, Trade Controls Branch and the Civil Secretariat. It is primarily responsible for the collection and protection of revenue payable under the Dutiable Commodities Ordinance, the suppression of illicit trafficking in narcotics, the prevention and detection of smuggling, and the enforcement of intellectual property rights protection.

The department has an establishment of 3 914 posts.

Revenue Protection

The department is responsible for collecting and protecting duty revenue on four groups of dutiable commodities in Hong Kong — liquor, tobacco, hydrocarbon oil and methyl alcohol.

The smuggling of dutiable cigarettes into Hong Kong from China continued to be a problem during the year, primarily due to the substantial difference in cigarette prices across the border. Illegal sales of dutiable cigarettes have proliferated in Hong Kong as a result. To combat these activities, enforcement action was stepped up, leading to the detection of 3 272 cases and the seizure of 50 million cigarettes with a duty potential of $29 million.

The illegal use of industrial diesel oil by motor vehicles remained prevalent. Some 244 persons were arrested and 69 659 litres of industrial diesel oil were seized.

In addition to enforcement action, the Dutiable Commodities (Amendment) (No. 2) Ordinance 1993 was enacted on July 23 to streamline the procedures for the forfeiture and disposal of seized articles.

Anti-Narcotics Operations

The department plays an important role in the prevention and suppression of illicit trafficking in narcotics and other dangerous drugs.

The strategy in attacking drug offenders is directed at all levels, including import, export, manufacturing, distribution and peddling.

Apart from suppressing drug trafficking activities locally, the department also exchanges intelligence and co-operates closely with the Royal Hong Kong Police, overseas customs authorities and other law enforcement agencies in the fight against drug traffickers at the international level. In 1993, the department successfully extradited six persons to the United States for trial in connection with drug offences.

During the year, the department prosecuted 1 010 persons for drug offences and seized 75 kilogrammes of heroin, 38 kilogrammes of opium and 137 kilogrammes of cannabis.

Recovery of Drug Trafficking Proceeds

The department and the police have joint responsibility for enforcing the Drug Trafficking (Recovery of Proceeds) Ordinance, which is an effective tool in confiscating assets derived from drug trafficking.

During the year, the department successfully obtained four court orders restraining realisable properties suspected to be the proceeds of drug trafficking, with a total value of $0.7 million. Five cases were concluded, with the confiscation of drug proceeds totalling $3.1 million.

The department also completed its first successful case under the bilateral agreement between Hong Kong and the United States for the confiscation of drug proceeds. Assets worth some $2 million, belonging to a convicted drug trafficker in the United States, were ordered by a court to be confiscated in Hong Kong.

Anti-smuggling and Import and Export Controls

During the year, the department detected 568 smuggling cases under the Import and Export Ordinance, arrested 752 persons and seized $171 million worth of goods.

Smuggling between Hong Kong and China remained prevalent. At sea, stolen luxury saloon cars were being smuggled by high-powered speed-boats, while electrical appliances were shipped out by Chinese territorial trading or fishing vessels. The situation was, however, contained towards the end of the year, due to the assiduous efforts of the Joint Police/Customs Anti-smuggling Task Force and various enforcement units of the department. On land, smugglers made use of the busy cross-border traffic to smuggle vehicles, computer parts, telecommunications equipment and electrical appliances out of the territory. These goods were often smuggled by concealing them inside false compartments in containers, or by disguising or mixing them with other cargoes under false declarations.

A legislative amendment, the Import and Export (Amendment) Ordinance 1993, was introduced on August 6 to simplify and speed up the forfeiture of seized articles, vessels and vehicles. Under the new legislation, the maximum penalty for importing and exporting strategic commodities has also been increased to seven years' imprisonment and an unlimited fine.

Strategic Commodities

The department is responsible for the enforcement of import and export control of strategic commodities. The objectives of these controls are to inspire international confidence in Hong Kong's ability to contain the spread of these commodities to countries of arms proliferation concern and to ensure continued access for Hong Kong to high technology equipment. Enforcement of these controls also prevents Hong Kong from being used as a centre from which weapons of mass destruction or their component parts can be distributed on a large scale. During the year, the department carried out physical examinations at entry and exit points, and consignment checks at traders' premises to ensure that imports and exports of controlled goods were properly licensed. Detailed investigations were also made into suspected illegal diversions with a view to prosecution.

Customs Co-operation Council

Hong Kong is a member of the Customs Co-operation Council (CCC), established to improve and rationalise international customs operations and facilitate international trade.

The department takes part regularly in the CCC's annual plenary meetings, and other seminars and meetings on enforcement, customs techniques, computer technology and intellectual property rights protection. The department also contributes to CCC regional projects by organising and assisting in the running of training courses on narcotics investigation and ship rummaging techniques, for other CCC members within the Economic and Social Commission for Asia and the Pacific Region.

Enforcement of Intellectual Property Rights Protection

The department is the sole agency responsible for investigating complaints relating to infringements of copyright and trade marks, as well as false trade descriptions under the Copyright Ordinance and the Trade Descriptions Ordinance. Apart from enforcement action, close liaison is maintained with copyright and trade mark owners, the legal profession, intellectual property rights organisations and foreign enforcement agencies to advance intellectual property rights protection.

During the year, the department seized $29 million worth of goods under the Copyright Ordinance. Its continued enforcement efforts greatly reduced piracy involving television and computer games. Meanwhile, a new type of music piracy emerged, involving the infringement of compact discs. Large quantities of illegally-produced compact discs were seized from hawkers, distribution centres and border control points.

The department also seized $176 million worth of counterfeit and falsely-labelled goods in 1993. Due to vigorous enforcement action, most of the syndicates were forced to set up their manufacturing bases outside Hong Kong. Efforts were also made to eradicate fake watches, leather goods and clothing from retail outlets.

Performance Pledges

In response to the 'Serving the Community' scheme launched by the government, the department announced its performance pledges in September. These cover services including cargo and vehicular traffic clearance at control points, the processing of applications for licences and permits, customs attendance and counter services. The establishment of users' committees is being investigated, to reinforce the pledges by involving representatives of major trades and members of the public in monitoring the standard of services supplied.

Police Complaints Committee

The main function of the Police Complaints Committee is to monitor and review investigations, by the Complaints Against Police Office (CAPO) of the Royal Hong Kong Police, of complaints made against the police by members of the public. Set up in 1986 to replace the former UMELCO Police Group, the committee is an independent body appointed by the Governor. The chairman is normally drawn from the Executive Council, while the two vice-chairmen are drawn from the Legislative Council. Committee members include eight Justices of the Peace, the Attorney General or his representative and the Commissioner for Administrative Complaints.

During the year, the committee endorsed 3 520 complaint cases, after being satisfied that each case had been thoroughly and impartially investigated by CAPO. Arising from the reviewing of these complaint cases, the committee proposed a number of changes to police practices, procedures and instructions, with a view to improving the overall effectiveness of the complaint system and assisting the Commissioner of Police in minimising public complaints against the police.

Independent Commission Against Corruption

The Independent Commission Against Corruption (ICAC) is independent of the civil service; its Commissioner is directly responsible to the Governor. It fights corruption on three fronts: investigation, prevention and education. This work is carried out through three functional departments — Operations, Corruption Prevention and Community Relations.

The ICAC received a total of 3 284 reports of corruption allegations in 1993. Of these 1 798 reports concerned the private sector, which was an increase of 54 per cent compared with 1992. Another 1 365 reports were made against civil servants, an increase of 32 per cent. There were 113 reports against employees of public bodies, compared with 58 in 1992.

Some members of the public regard the ICAC as a conduit for general grievances against various government departments. During the year under review, the ICAC received 2 443 non-corruption complaints, 1 243 of which were subsequently referred to the government departments concerned.

Operations

The Operations Department receives and investigates reports of suspected corruption offences under the Prevention of Bribery Ordinance and the ICAC Ordinance, and deals with election malpractices under the Corrupt and Illegal Practices Ordinance.

In 1993, the department received 3 284 reports, of which 2 244 contained sufficient information for investigations to commence. The department's caseload was at an all time high of 1 375 at the year's end. Altogether, 643 persons were prosecuted, and 61 cautioned for lesser breaches of the law.

To strengthen the department's ability to investigate corruption, the government will provide additional resources for the ICAC to set up another investigation group, with nearly 40 officers, in 1994.

The department continues to closely monitor the effects of the Bill of Rights Ordinance on ICAC-related legislation, to ensure that the ICAC can effectively maintain its capability to investigate corruption and that its legislation remains compatible with that ordinance.

Video-recording of interviews with suspects continued to play an important role in the department's investigations and is now a standard practice, providing evidence of a high quality.

Computerisation has also significantly aided investigations, particularly in highly complex cases.

Corruption Prevention

The Corruption Prevention Department identifies and eliminates opportunities for corruption in government, public bodies and organisations receiving government subvention. It also provides free and confidential corruption prevention advice to private sector organisations upon request.

The work of the department consists of studies of new subject areas, the review or 'monitoring' of previous studies and giving corruption prevention advice through consultation and participation in a wide variety of committees and working groups. In 1993, the department conducted 102 studies of specific activities covering policy, law, procedures and management controls.

During the year, the department assisted the Urban Services Department in tightening the procedures for hawker control, and also gave assistance to the Provisional Airport Authority in setting up a purchasing system. The customs cargo-processing procedures at the border were strengthened to assist detection and prevent corrupt collusion with cross-border smugglers.

To ensure that equitable compensation packages are offered to owners and tenants affected by urban renewal projects, the department reviewed the compensation policy and procedures of the Land Development Corporation. The department also took part in a review of the public housing decoration contractors system, with a view to allowing rental estate tenants a larger choice in their selection of decorators and give the Housing Department greater control over unscrupulous decorators.

Obtaining a restaurant licence can take six months to a year and many restaurants commence business before being licensed. The department worked closely with the Urban Services Department and Regional Services Department to speed up and improve the process. Measures included closer co-ordination of the government departments involved and making the process clearer to applicants.

The department's Advisory Services Group provided tailor-made advice to 176 organisations during the year, covering purchasing, merchandising and the legality of offering or accepting rebates. The group also assisted companies to draw up policies on business ethics. With the issue, in mid-1993, of the Secretary for Home Affairs' code of practice on procurement of supplies and services by owners' corporations of buildings, requests for advice on that subject increased considerably.

Community Relations

The Community Relations Department educates the public against the evils of corruption and enlists community support to fight the problem; it also aims to promote higher ethical standards in social and business matters. It works through the mass media, as well as personal approaches to different target audiences.

The department's eight regional offices act as a focal point for carrying out anti-corruption liaison work and providing preventive education services to the local community.

The department continued to place emphasis on the commercial and manufacturing sectors. Corruption prevention packages were produced for various trades to help chief executives identify corruption-prone areas in their companies and to take preventive measures. During the year, the department established personal contacts with 3 476 companies to introduce these packages to them. The department also used direct mail to put across anti-corruption messages to 5 748 small companies in the plastics and restaurant industries.

With the rapidly increasing volume of trade across the border with China, there was growing concern about some business practices infringing the anti-bribery laws of Hong Kong. In response, the department produced a set of comprehensive guidelines on the legality of such practices and suggested various measures for corruption prevention. Over 10 000 copies were printed for distribution to Hong Kong-China trade operators. For the longer term, the department will deploy additional manpower for in-depth study of the problem and development of co-operation with China's anti-corruption agencies.

A total of 37 organisations from both the private and public sectors took part in the department's Community Participation Programme, under which they organised their own anti-corruption activities, receiving a small ICAC subsidy towards the cost of these activities.

The department also conducted talks and seminars for some 19 680 existing staff members and new recruits of government departments and public bodies during the year.

On the media front, it continued to make use of television and radio advertisements, as well as advertising on buses to motivate the public to support the ICAC's work and to report corruption offences.

For primary and secondary schools, the department initiated a school-based curriculum development programme, through which 6 235 students in seven schools teamed up with ICAC officers to develop a moral education curriculum targeted specifically at the needs of students. The programme is still in the pilot stage. After evaluation, the department will consider extending it to a larger number of schools.

International Co-operation

International inter-agency co-operation is essential to combat corruption, which can cross all borders and boundaries.

In May, the Commissioner gave a speech at the 10th Commonwealth Law Conference in Cyprus; and in October, he led an ICAC delegation to China to visit the Guangdong Provincial People's Procuratorate in Guangzhou and the Supreme People's Procuratorate in Beijing for a general exchange of views and experience. In November, the Commissioner and other ICAC officials participated in the Sixth International Anti-Corruption Conference held in Cancun, Mexico. While in the region, the Commissioner also attended the First Latin American Conference on the Struggle Against Administrative Corruption in Bogota, Colombia.

During the year, the ICAC received 70 visitors from law enforcement agencies and other organisations in various countries. On the investigation side, the Operations Department sent its officers overseas on more than 119 occasions for enquiries into various cases.

Checks and Balances

To minimise the possibility of any abuse of power, the ICAC is subject to a stringent system of checks and balances. At the policy level, the ICAC is guided by the Advisory Committee on Corruption, which reviews and advises the Commissioner on all aspects of anti-corruption policy, strategy and legislation. It comprises seven prominent citizens and one government official.

An investigation can only be completed by a decision to prosecute made independently by the Attorney General, or on the authorisation of the Operations Review Committee, which has to be satisfied that the enquiry has been exhaustively pursued and merits no further investigative action. The Operations Review Committee comprises the Attorney General, the Commissioner of Police, and six civic leaders appointed by the Governor, and is chaired by the Commissioner Against Corruption.

Two other committees, the Citizens Advisory Committee on Community Relations and the Corruption Prevention Advisory Committee, review and advise on the work of the Community Relations Department and Corruption Prevention Department, respectively.

Members of the public can lodge formal complaints against ICAC officers to the ICAC Complaints Committee. Its membership comprises four members of the Executive and Legislative Councils, two prominent citizens, the Attorney General and the Commissioner for Administrative Complaints.

In addition, the Operations Department has an internal investigation group, which monitors and investigates complaints or allegations of corruption against ICAC officers.

The Way Ahead

The ICAC will mark its 20th year of operation in February 1994. It is committed to combating corruption vigorously through effective law enforcement, education and prevention, so as to contribute to the upholding of the rule of law, as well as the stability and prosperity, in Hong Kong.

Government Laboratory

The Forensic Science Division of the Government Laboratory provides expert scientific evidence in courts of law in Hong Kong. It also provides specialist skills to all government departments concerned with law and order, and, increasingly, to a private sector seeking assistance, on a fee-paying basis, in civil litigation and criminal defence cases.

During the year, the division examined 198 572 exhibits and samples, of which 900 exhibits (involving 81 cases) came from the private sector.

The nine specialist sections of the division are organised into two groups. The Physical and Biochemical Evidence Group concentrates on the analysis of trace evidence associated with crimes of violence and fraud such as homicide, rape, arson, hit-and-run, and questioned documents, which involves expert opinion. The Drugs and Toxicology Group is involved with drug analysis and the evidence given is of scientific fact.

Within the Physical and Biochemical Evidence Group, the greatest expansion in work has been in DNA profiling, which has proved to be a useful tool in confirming serial rape cases. Although the workload of the group was similar to that of the previous year, there was a substantial increase in the number of both homicide and sexual assault cases, by 23 per cent and six per cent, respectively. In terms of technology improvement, a new Scanning Electron Microscope, with an energy-dispersive analyser, was installed. This allows the fully-automated analysis of gunshot residue samples.

The Drugs and Toxicology Group dealt with a record number of cases for the analysis of drug seizures. During the year, over 102 000 drug items (an increase of 30 per cent over 1992) were examined. As in previous years, the great majority of the cases involved opiate drugs (over 78 000 items), but the presence of cannabis continued to be a growing problem. With increased seizures of cocaine, amphetamines, benzodiazepines, and for the first time in Hong Kong, the amphetamine-related designer drugs of the 'Ecstasy' type, drug abuse in Hong Kong appeared to be following international trends more closely. More stringent legislative controls over cough syrups were enacted at the start of the year, with an immediate positive effect. Requests for drug urinalysis continued to grow, with 56 681 sample tests conducted during the year, an increase of 13 per cent over 1992. The results of those tests indicated the rising trend of non-opiate drug abuse.

In line with government policy, the Forensic Science Division is presently engaged in formulating performance parameters and targets, to ensure greater efficiency in the future.

Immigration Department

By controlling entry to Hong Kong, the Immigration Department plays an important role in maintaining law and order.

Through examination at control points and the vetting of visa applications, undesirable persons, including international criminals and terrorists, are detected and refused entry. In 1993, 19 075 such travellers and persons not in possession of proper documentation were refused permission to land and 2 702 persons were refused visas.

Detection of Forged Travel Documents

A total of 2 347 forged travel documents were detected during the year, representing a decrease of 17.4 per cent on the 2 840 detected in 1992.

Strict measures were taken to guard against the use of forged travel documents by travellers, as well as illegal immigrants. Intelligence on forgery activities was collected and quickly disseminated. Frequent contacts with local and overseas law enforcement agencies and consulates were maintained. Special operations were mounted against forgery syndicates.

Interception of Wanted Persons
During the year, 113 992 persons were intercepted at immigration control points, and immigration and registration of persons offices. Of these, 749 were wanted in connection with murder cases, 2 795 were suspected robbers, 55 089 were suspected of involvement in the trafficking of dangerous drugs and 45 334 were wanted in connection with other criminal offences. In addition, 186 known or suspected terrorists were identified at points of entry.

Illegal Immigration
The availability of employment opportunities in Hong Kong continued to attract large numbers of illegal immigrants to the territory. The lower wages accepted by these immigrants encouraged unscrupulous employers to offer them employment. Frequent checks were, therefore, conducted at targeted locations, including construction sites, factories, restaurants and other places of employment.

Illegal immigrants arrested at these places were prosecuted and sentenced to imprisonment, before being repatriated to their places of origin. Employers of illegal immigrants, including principal contractors in the construction industry, were also prosecuted and fined and, in serious cases, custodial sentences were imposed. In 1993, 77 employers of illegal immigrants were prosecuted. In addition, publicity continued to emphasise that there will be no amnesties.

In 1993, a total of 44 146 illegal immigrants were apprehended and repatriated. This figure, which includes arrests by the police and the number of illegal immigrants caught working, represented an increase of 2.4 per cent on the 43 096 apprehended in 1992.

Investigation and Prosecution of Immigration Offences
A total of 11 905 charges were laid against persons who had committed various immigrations offences. These included remaining in Hong Kong illegally, breaching conditions of stay, making false statements or representations, and using or possessing forged documents.

Deportation and Removal
The department is responsible for the application, issue and execution of deportation and removal orders. During the year, 7 441 persons who had been convicted of possessing or trafficking in dangerous drugs, deception, theft and other criminal offences were considered for deportation. Subsequently, 295 were deported. In addition, 1 894 persons were removed from Hong Kong under removal orders. These included 1 317 illegal immigrants, mostly of Chinese origin, and 577 persons who had breached their conditions of stay.

Fire Services
The Fire Services Department is responsible for fire-fighting and rescue on land, sea and at the airport within Hong Kong's territorial boundary. It also provides the major ambulance service and gives advice on fire protection measures to the public.

The year marked an important chapter in the department's history: the service commemorated its 125th anniversary; it started recruiting female station officers, in a bid to help relieve recruitment difficulties; and it introduced a pilot scheme for a paramedic ambulance service. In addition, the department seconded a local fire officer to a British fire services college as its first overseas instructor.

The department's 125th anniversary was celebrated with a series of commemorative events. The highlights included a review by the Governor of fire services personnel and appliances at the Sha Tin Fire Station Complex on October 27. Many senior fire and ambulance officials from China and overseas attended.

Fire Suppression

During 1993, the department responded to a total of 28 804 fire calls, 54 of which were classified as major fires of No. 3 alarm and above. Careless handling or disposal of smoking materials remained a major cause of fires, totalling 4 779 cases in all.

The fires claimed 32 lives and injured 618 people. Among the injured were 37 firemen. A total of 25 788 people were rescued by Fire Services personnel.

Notable fire incidents during the year included a No. 3 alarm at a home for the elderly in Boundary Street in June, which killed two women and injured 30 others; a No. 4 alarm in a factory building in Lee Chung Street in August, injuring 15 people; and the gutting of the casino ship *New Orient Princess* in August, in which firemen battled the blaze for several days.

Shenzhen Fire

A fire broke out at a dangerous goods storage depot in Shenzhen on the afternoon of August 5, leading to a series of explosions in which 15 people died and more than 100 others were injured.

In response to the Xinhua News Agency's approach for assistance from the Hong Kong Government, the Director of Fire Services and two senior fire officers flew to the fire scene by helicopter that same night to assess the situation and determine how the Hong Kong Fire Services might help. A fleet of fire engines and fire officers were placed on standby at the Sheung Shui Fire Station, in case of call-out.

Preparations were made for several helicopters and a team of fire services personnel to take off from Hong Kong for the fire scene again the next morning to water-bomb the scene of the incident. In the event, the pre-dawn mission was called off at the last minute, when the Hong Kong Government was informed that the fire had been brought under control by the Shenzhen authorities.

This was the first time the Hong Kong Fire Services had been asked for help by its Chinese counterparts.

Special Services

Apart from fire-fighting, the department also provides wide-ranging rescue services to people in incidents such as traffic accidents, trapped lifts, lock-in cases, gas leakages, industrial accidents, attempts to jump from a height, house collapses and landslides.

In 1993, the department received 18 500 calls for special services. The most significant alerts were the Lan Kwai Fong tragedy in the early hours of New Year's Day, when 21 people died and more than 80 others were injured; the collapse of a passenger hoist in Java

Road in June, in which 12 workers were killed; and an incident involving a China Airlines jumbo jet in November, in which 296 passengers and crew were rescued from the wrecked plane at sea without major injuries.

Ambulance Services

It was a busy year for the Ambulance Service, which handled a total of 442 304 emergency and non-emergency calls — an average of 1 212 calls per day — providing assistance to 560 358 patients and casualties.

The launching of a pilot scheme for a paramedic ambulance service in June marked a new era for the service, enhancing its standard of pre-hospital care for the community. Three paramedic ambulances were put on a trial run for a year, with the aim of eventually operating 33 paramedic ambulances round-the-clock. During the year, two paramedic courses were conducted locally for selected ambulance personnel by visiting instructors from the Paramedic Academy from British Columbia, Canada, in collaboration with Hospital Authority physicians. A total of six ambulance officers and 35 ambulance supervisors successfully completed the courses and became qualified.

Meanwhile, plans to hive-off the non-emergency ambulance service to the Hospital Authority in phases will be implemented from mid-March next year. The arrangement will allow ambulance personnel to undertake the more urgent and serious cases, and will provide a more cost-effective ambulance service.

Communications

The computerised mobilising and communications system in the Fire Services Communication Centre enables all movements of fire appliances, ambulances, fire boats and officers to be kept up-to-date, so that appropriate appliances, equipment and manpower can be despatched to cope with different emergencies quickly and efficiently.

The system helps the department to achieve a better prescribed graded response time (GRT) to all fire and emergency calls. During the year, 88.9 per cent of all structural fire calls and 92.5 per cent of emergency ambulance calls were attended within the GRT and the target travel time, respectively.

Fire Prevention

The department is responsible for formulating and enforcing fire safety regulations and policies, as well as assisting and advising the public on fire protection measures and the abatement of fire hazards.

The Fire Protection Bureau places great emphasis on public education on fire prevention. With the help of the Information Services Department, a major publicity campaign on electricity safety was launched during the year. In addition, fire officers gave 428 talks to 17 167 people from different sectors of the community. These were supplemented by exhibitions and demonstrations.

During the year, the number of fire hazard complaints totalled 5 004, indicating a growing public concern over fire safety and an increasing awareness of the services provided by the department.

Fire Services personnel made 72 562 inspections of all types of premises, and issued 3 329 abatement notices for the removal of fire hazards during the year. There were 206 prosecutions in cases of non-compliance, with fines amounting to about $0.8 million. In addition, prosecutions for obstructing the means of escape in buildings resulted in 150 convictions, with total fines of $0.6 million.

The department also imposes fire service requirements for new buildings, to ensure compliance with fire safety standards. Some 7 502 submissions of building plans, including the new airport-related projects, were processed during the year.

Appliances and Workshops

The department operates some 700 modern appliances and vehicles, fitted with up-to-date fire-fighting and rescue equipment. During the year, 49 new or replacement appliances and vehicles of various kinds were put into service. These included a new pumping appliance with excellent road-holding characteristics and manoeuvrability. A smaller rescue launch, which can carry out fire-fighting and rescue operations in shallow waters, was provided to the Airport Fire Contingent by the Civil Aviation Department.

The Workshops Section of the department is constantly evaluating new products from different parts of the world, to see if they can be used locally.

The safety of service members in fire-fighting and rescue operations is a prime concern of the department. A total of 6 500 fire-resistant gloves of better quality were procured by the Stores and Supplies Section during the year, for the use of operational personnel. In addition, 22 sets of the Rapid Intervention System, a multi-functional handy tool, were provided for service members, to facilitate rescue work.

Staff Training

The department has two major training schools. The Fire Services Training School at Pat Heung, New Territories, provides initial training for all ranks. The Ambulance Command Training School at Ma On Shan provides initial, refresher and advanced training to all ambulance personnel. The various training courses range from three to 26 weeks in duration.

Altogether, 345 recruits — comprising 50 station officers, eight senior firemen (control), five senior firewomen (control) and 282 firemen — successfully completed their initial training in 1993.

The Fire Services Training School also provided training to 745 staff of other government departments and private organisations on basic fire-fighting and the use of breathing apparatus. In response to requests from fire services of other countries, the school provided training for their officers. The Ambulance Command Training School provided training to 46 staff of other government departments on basic ambulance aid and to 13 officers from other countries.

To meet operational needs and for career development purposes, 29 officers were sent to China, Singapore, Germany, the United Kingdom, the United States of America and Japan for management and professional training. In-service training was provided to 128 fire and 2 635 ambulance personnel.

The Driving Training School conducted appliance driving and operation courses for 743 officers and other ranks.

Establishment and Recruitment

At the end of 1993, the department had an establishment of 7 281 and 733 for uniformed and civilian staff, respectively. The department continued its recruitment exercise with the appointment of 43 station officers, seven ambulance officers, 15 senior firemen and firewomen (control), and 285 firemen.

For the first time in its history, the department opened its recruitment of station officers to female applicants in April. The two qualified new recruits undertook their initial training at the Pat Heung Training School in October with their male counterparts.

Overseas Secondment

The professionalism of Hong Kong Fire Services personnel was again recognised internationally following the secondment, in September, of a local fire officer to the Fire Services College at Moreton-in-Marsh, United Kingdom, as an instructor in high-rise building fire methodology and ship fire-fighting techniques.

This was the first time a local fire officer had been seconded overseas as an instructor, as well as a first for the college in engaging a non-UK instructor. The secondment is for two years.

Buildings and Quarters

In line with government policy to provide an emergency response to all areas within target response times according to the category of risk, the department continued to plan and build fire stations and ambulance depots at strategic locations, to cope with local developments.

At the end of the year, there were 64 fire stations, 29 ambulance depots and stations, and five fire boat stations in the territory. Planning is in hand for the provision of 829 additional married quarters for firemen and ambulancemen.

Correctional Services

The Correctional Services Department administers a wide range of services for both adult and young offenders, drug addicts and the criminally insane, broadly under two programme areas — prison management and re-integration. The department also manages detention centres for Vietnamese migrants and Ex-China Vietnamese Illegal Immigrants.

At the end of 1993, the department was managing 20 correctional institutions, three halfway houses, a staff training institute, an emergency support group, two custodial wards (one each at the Queen Mary Hospital and Queen Elizabeth Hospital), and five detention centres for Vietnamese migrants. A total of 7 060 staff were looking after 10 869 inmates, 21 639 Vietnamese migrants, 930 Ex-China Vietnamese Illegal Immigrants, and 3 346 persons under supervision after discharge from custody.

During the year, the number of Vietnamese migrants continued to decrease as a consequence of the implementation of the Orderly Return Programme. The workload of the department in managing Vietnamese migrants, however, remained heavy. This was due to its taking over the management of two Voluntary Repatriation Departure Centres from the police, and the influx of the Ex-China Vietnamese Illegal Immigrants from late June to early August.

On April 1, the former Escort Unit was re-organised into the Emergency Support Group, and took over from the police escort duties in connection with remand cases in the magistracies. In addition to providing an escort service, the group is also responsible for providing back-up emergency support services to all institutions.

Male Offenders
Prisoners are assigned to institutions according to their security rating, which takes into account, among other things, the risk they pose to the community and whether or not they are first offenders.

There are 12 prisons for adult male prisoners. The four prisons of maximum security are Stanley Prison, Shek Pik Prison, the Siu Lam Psychiatric Centre and Lai Chi Kok Reception Centre. There are four prisons of medium security, namely, Ma Po Ping Prison, Tung Tau Correctional Institution, Victoria Prison and Hei Ling Chau Correctional Institution. The remaining four prisons of minimum security are Tai Lam Correctional Institution, Pik Uk Prison, Tong Fuk Centre and Ma Hang Prison.

Stanley Prison and Shek Pik Prison house prisoners serving long sentences or life imprisonment. The Siu Lam Psychiatric Centre accommodates the criminally insane and those requiring psychiatric treatment. Adult males awaiting trial, or remanded in custody during court hearings, are detained at the Lai Chi Kok Reception Centre, which also has a separate section for male civil debtors. Victoria Prison houses illegal immigrants pending their repatriation to China, while a special section at Ma Hang Prison has been set aside for elderly prisoners. Adult prisoners released under the Pre-release Employment Scheme are provided with accommodation at Phoenix House, a halfway house for adult and young offenders.

Young Male Offenders
The department administers four correctional programmes for young male offenders under the Prisons, Training Centres, Drug Addiction Treatment Centres and Detention Centres Ordinances.

The maximum security Pik Uk Correctional Institution is run as a reception centre and training centre, as well as a prison, for young offenders under 25 years of age, including those who are remanded for pre-sentencing reports on their suitability for admission to the detention centre, training centre and drug addiction treatment centre programmes.

Cape Collinson Correctional Institution houses those between the ages of 14 and 17 years; and Lai King Training Centre, those between 18 and 20 years who have been sentenced to participate in the training centre programme.

The Lai Sun Correctional Institution on Hei Ling Chau accommodates young prisoners aged between 14 and 20 years. To cope with the increased penal population, part of the Sha Tsui Detention Centre has been set aside since April 1989 to hold young prisoners between 14 and 20 years of age.

An effective detention centre programme is carried out at the Sha Tsui Detention Centre. There are two sections, one for young offenders aged between 14 and 20 years, and the other for young adults aged between 21 and 24. The detention centre programme emphasises strict discipline, strenuous training, hard work and a vigorous routine.

Young offenders identified as having special needs on discharge from a training centre or detention centre are housed at Phoenix House for up to three months, before they are permitted to live at home or in other places while continuing to be under after-care supervision. Young male offenders released from prisons under the Pre-release Employment Scheme are also accommodated at Phoenix House. Residents of this halfway house must go out to work, or attend full-time school, during the day and return in the evening.

Female Offenders

Adult females serve their sentences at the Tai Lam Centre for Women, which also has sections for remand prisoners and those undergoing drug addiction treatment. Most of the women are employed in an industrial laundry, which provides services to government departments and public hospitals.

Female offenders under 21 years-of-age are held at the Tai Tam Gap Correctional Institution, where separate sections are provided for training centre inmates, drug addiction treatment centre inmates, young prisoners and those on remand.

Bauhinia House serves as a halfway house for women and girls released under supervision from the training centre or under the Pre-release Employment Scheme. Residents of this halfway house also go out to work, or attend full-time school, during the day and return in the evening.

Drug Addiction Treatment

Drug addicts found guilty of an offence punishable by imprisonment may be sentenced to a drug addiction treatment centre under the Drug Addiction Treatment Centres Ordinance. They can be detained from two to 12 months, depending on their progress. In-centre treatment is followed by 12 months of statutory after-care supervision.

Male drug addicts are treated at the Hei Ling Chau Addiction Treatment Centre, while female adult addicts receive treatment at the Tai Lam Centre for Women and the young are detained at the Tai Tam Gap Correctional Institution.

The drug addiction treatment programme aims to detoxify, restore physical health and, through the application of therapeutic and rehabilitative treatment, wean addicts from their dependence on drugs.

Assistance is also given to addiction treatment centre inmates with post-release employment and accommodation. Temporary accommodation is available at New Life House, a halfway house for those in need of such support immediately after release.

Young Offender Assessment Panel

The Young Offender Assessment Panel, comprising staff from the Correctional Services and Social Welfare Departments, was established in April 1987 to provide magistrates with recommendations on the most appropriate programmes of rehabilitation for young offenders between 14 and 25 years-of-age. The service provided by the panel is available to juvenile courts and certain magistracies.

Education and Vocational Training

Offenders under the age of 21 attend educational and vocational training classes, conducted by qualified teachers and instructors.

For educational classes, textbooks compiled by the department are used to provide inmates with suitable and practical learning material matching their maturity in personality growth and development.

Adult offenders attend evening classes, on a voluntary basis, run by part-time teachers recruited by the department. Self-study packages and external correspondence courses are also available for those who are interested.

Both young and adult offenders are encouraged to take part in public examinations, organised by the City and Guilds of London Institute, Pitman Examinations Institute,

London Chamber of Commerce and Industry, and the Hong Kong Examinations Authority. Young inmates are permitted to sit for the Hong Kong Certificate of Education Examination as school candidates, and formal classes up to certificate level are provided for them, while adult inmates can sit for the examination as private candidates. Some offenders, mostly adults, have also participated in degree courses offered by the local Open Learning Institute and other academic institutes.

A wide spectrum of vocational training programmes is provided to help young inmates acquire employable skills, develop good working habits and obtain qualifications for further training. Upon their discharge, they may be referred to other vocational training organisations, such as the Vocational Training Council, the Construction Industry Training Authority and the Clothing Industry Training Authority, to further their training.

Medical Services

All institutions have their own medical units providing basic treatment and health and dental care, including radiodiagnostic and pathological examinations and prophylactic inoculations. Inmates requiring specialist treatment are either referred to a visiting consultant or to specialist clinics in public hospitals. Those requiring hospitalisation are usually kept in custodial wards at Queen Mary and Queen Elizabeth Hospitals, under the charge of correctional services officers. Although HIV infection and AIDS are not a problem among the penal population, the department is committed to a programme of education and prevention.

The Siu Lam Psychiatric Centre treats prisoners with mental health problems and offers psychiatric consultations and assessments for inmates referred by other institutions and the courts.

Ante-natal and post-natal care is provided within institutions for female inmates, but babies are normally delivered in public hospitals.

Psychological Services

Clinical psychologists and specially-trained officers provide a wide range of counselling services for inmates with emotional difficulties, and behavioural and personality problems. Professional consultation is offered to courts, various review boards and institutional managements to facilitate their decision-making with regard to the disposal, treatment and management of offenders. Research projects are also regularly undertaken to improve treatment programmes and reduce recidivism.

Visiting Justices

Justices of the Peace, appointed by the Governor, visit penal institutions and the centres for Vietnamese migrants, either fortnightly or monthly depending on the type of institution. They investigate complaints, inspect diets and report on living and working conditions. They may also advise the Commissioner of Correctional Services on the employment of prisoners and job opportunities after release.

Inspectorate and Management Services

The Inspectorate and Management Services Division studies the efficacy and efficiency of departmental policies and the management of prison establishments, to optimise the level and quality of services provided. The division comprises three units, tasked with the responsibility to streamline procedures to meet the changing needs of the community by reviewing standing instructions, department manuals, rules and regulations; to inspect, and to furnish specialist advice on how to improve, physical and procedural security measures in penal institutions; to maintain an intelligence pool on prisoners' subversive activities; and to redress grievances and investigate complaints lodged by prisoners and the public, as well as correctional services staff.

After-care Services

After-care services are provided to inmates discharged from training, detention and drug addiction treatment centres; and to prisoners who participate in the Release Under Supervision and Pre-release Employment Schemes. The primary objective of after-care is to assist offenders in their rehabilitation and re-integration into the community. It also plays an essential role in enhancing their determination to lead an industrious and law-abiding life upon discharge.

After-care commences immediately after the admission of an inmate into an institution, or when a prisoner has been approved to participate in the Release Under Supervision and Pre-release Employment Schemes. Each inmate is assigned an after-care officer, who will provide him with appropriate support and guidance, enabling him to adapt to the institutional programme and to prepare him for subsequent discharge. A sound relationship between the inmate, his family and the after-care officer is developed, to help the inmate overcome obstacles to rehabilitation.

Inmates are assisted, through individual and group counselling, to gain a better insight into problems arising from their personal and social inadequacies. They are helped to become better prepared to cope with difficulties upon release.

Under the provisions of the Prisoners (Release under Supervision) Ordinance, prisoners, other than those serving life sentences or subject to deportation upon discharge, who have served not less than half or 20 months (whichever period is the longer) of a sentence of three years or more may apply to join the Release Under Supervision Scheme for the remaining portion of their sentences; and those who are serving sentences of two years or more and are within six months of completing their sentences, after taking into consideration remission, may apply to join the Pre-release Employment Scheme. Following approval by the Release Under Supervision Board, successful applicants are discharged or permitted to go out to work and reside in a designated hostel, under the supervision of after-care officers, for the balance of their sentences. The aim of the scheme is to enable suitable, eligible and motivated prisoners to serve their sentences in an open environment under close supervision. Prisoners who breach supervision conditions may be recalled to serve the remainder of their sentences or charged in court with a breach of the supervision order.

The success of the after-care programmes is measured by the percentage of supervisees who complete supervision without re-conviction and, where applicable, remain drug-free. At the end of 1993, the annual success rates were 94 per cent for detention centre inmates, 69 per cent for male training centre inmates, 94 per cent for female training centre inmates, 78 per cent for young male prisoners, 100 per cent for young female prisoners, 63 per cent for male drug addiction treatment centre inmates, 74 per cent for female drug addiction treatment centre inmates, 100 per cent for the Release Under Supervision Scheme and 100 per cent for the Pre-release Employment Scheme.

Correctional Services Industries
Correctional services industries aim to keep prisoners and inmates gainfully employed, reducing the risk of unrest through boredom and lack of constructive activities. The industries also help to reduce government expenditure by providing products and services to government departments and public organisations.

All convicted prisoners who are medically fit are required by law to work six days per week. Prisoners are paid for their work, and they can use their earnings to purchase food extras and other canteen items approved by the management. More importantly, they acquire the habit of doing useful work through participation in industrial production, eventually helping them to find a job after release.

The Correctional Services Industries section runs various trades, the largest being laundry and garment-making. Other trades include silk-screening, printing, envelope-making, book-binding, shoe-making, knitting, fibreglass work, metal work, leather work and carpentry. The commercial value of goods and services provided for the year was estimated at $364 million.

Detention Centres
The award of automatic refugee status to Vietnamese people reaching Hong Kong was discontinued following a change in policy on June 16, 1988. In May 1990, the department ceased to be responsible for managing closed centres for refugees, a task first undertaken in July 1982.

Under the existing policy, Vietnamese people arriving in Hong Kong will be screened by immigration officers, while being held in detention centres, to determine their status. Those screened-in as refugees are transferred to open centres, while those screened-out will remain in the detention centres until arrangements can be made for their repatriation. Any person who has been screened-out may appeal to a Refugee Status Review Board, which has the power to overturn that decision.

The department manages five centres for Vietnamese migrants held pending their screening or repatriation. These are the detention centres at Chi Ma Wan, Nei Kwu Chau, Whitehead and High Island; and the reception centre at Green Island.

Voluntary agencies, co-ordinated by the United Nations High Commissioner for Refugees (UNHCR), continue to provide valuable services in the detention centres, complementing those provided by the department.

Staff Training
The department's Staff Training Institute is responsible for the planning and implementation of training programmes for both new and serving officers.

All recruit officers and assistant officers (grade II) must undergo a recruit training course for a period of 26 weeks and 23 weeks, respectively. The training syllabus covers the relevant laws of Hong Kong, rules and regulations, counselling, social work, prison management, basic psychology, penology, criminology, first aid, foot-drill, self-defence, emergency response tactics, physical training, weapons training, field placement and adventure training.

Development training and job-orientated courses are provided throughout the year for serving officers to update their professional knowledge, to prepare them for promotion and to equip selected officers for duties in specialised fields such as counselling, after-care, nursing, psychological services, dog-handling, emergency services and physical education. Weekly in-service training is carried out within institutions to cater for their individual needs.

Attachment training to other government departments and overseas penal settings is also organised, from time to time, for officers of middle management level and above.

Non-government Organisations

A number of organisations assist the department in providing services to help inmates re-integrate into the community. These include the Society for the Rehabilitation of Offenders, Hong Kong Caritas Lop Heep Club, Hong Kong Christian Kun Sun Association, Wu Oi Christian Centre and the Prisoners' Friends' Association. They provide services such as case work, counselling, hostel accommodation, employment assistance, recreational activities and care for those with a history of mental illness.

Civil Aid Services

The Civil Aid Services (CAS) is an auxiliary emergency relief organisation. Its main role is to support government departments in tackling emergency situations. The CAS is financed by the government and has an establishment of 3 634 uniformed and disciplined adult volunteers, 3 232 cadets and 126 permanent staff.

Role and Responsibilities

The work of the CAS has a heavy emphasis on coping with natural disasters. Its volunteers are trained to perform duties during tropical cyclones, landslips and flooding; to search for and rescue persons trapped in collapsed buildings; to fight forest fires and patrol country parks; to manage refugee camps; to combat oil pollution at sea; to assist the police in crowd control and incident management; and to perform first aid, casualty-handling and evacuations. They also carry out difficult mountain rescue operations. On any weekend or public holiday, it is normal for over 500 volunteers to be on duty.

Civic Duties

The CAS is also heavily committed to performing civic duties. During the year, adult volunteers help to organise and provide crowd control, communications and marshalling services in charity fund-raising activities, government campaigns and at other public functions.

Vietnamese Migrant Duties

The permanent staff and volunteers of the CAS manage two Vietnamese refugee and migrant centres — the New Horizons Vietnamese Refugee Departure Centre (for Vietnamese refugees who have been accepted for resettlement overseas) and the Kai Tak Vietnamese Migrant Transit Centre (for Vietnamese migrants awaiting voluntary repatriation to Vietnam, and Vietnamese women at an advanced stage of pregnancy and their accompanying relatives from other detention centres. Vietnamese migrants seeking medical advice and treatment are also lodged temporarily at the Kai Tak Centre).

The work in these centres is both physically and psychologically demanding. Duties are performed under difficult conditions, and a good deal of dedication and patience is required of those involved. CAS volunteers, who have met all demands made on them, have been involved in refugee management since 1975 and continuously since 1988. This work will continue for the foreseeable future.

Service Training
Service training is divided into centralised courses and unit training, both designed to promote and maintain the operational efficiency of the CAS. The centralised courses in 1993–94 embrace a wide variety of subjects. In addition to normal counter-disaster courses, first aid, fire-fighting and conventional rescue instruction have been included.

Regular overseas training programmes are organised for both permanent training staff and volunteer officers. In 1993, one officer joined a Royal Air Force expedition to Nepal, and two officers attended disaster management courses at the Australian Emergency Management Institute in Melbourne. A CAS delegation visited Royal Air Force Mountain Rescue Service establishments in the United Kingdom, to explore advanced mountain rescue techniques and training facilities. A contingent of senior CAS officers was invited to visit the civil defence organisation in Guangzhou, China, in November to study its disaster management and exchange experiences and views on related subjects.

Cadet Corps
The Cadet Corps comprises 24 all-boy units, three all-girl units and five mixed units throughout the territory. Cadets join up when they are aged between 12 to 15 years, and undertake a series of training courses. Their tuition includes training in basic mechanical and electrical engineering, carpentry and fibre-glass moulding, printing and book-binding, as well as in photography and interior design. The cadets are also trained in countryside preservation, first aid, crowd control psychology, road safety, rock-climbing, orienteering, expeditions and trekking. They are encouraged to participate in the Duke of Edinburgh Award Scheme. In 1993, six cadets qualified for the gold award, 18 for the silver and 80 for the bronze awards. At 18, the cadets leave the corps and may join the adult voluntary services.

Government Flying Service
The Government Flying Service (GFS) superseded the Royal Hong Kong Auxiliary Air Force on April 1, carrying forward an establishment of 254 permanent staff comprising aircrew, groundcrew and administrators. The GFS is a full-time disciplined service, operating in accordance with civil aviation rules. Apart from providing flying services to support the work of various government departments and agencies, the GFS also provides a 24-hour emergency air ambulance and search and rescue service.

The GFS operates a fleet of 16 aircraft: two twin-engined Beech Super King Airs, four Slingsby Firefly trainers, eight Sikorsky S-76 helicopters and two Sikorsky S-70 helicopters (Black Hawks). In 1993, over 6 000 hours were flown. A total of 984 requests for emergency medical evacuation and rescue were received. Some of these came from the local fishing fleet of about 5 000 boats, many of which now have high-frequency radios and portable telephones, enabling them to call for assistance when necessary. Altogether, 114 search and rescue operations were carried out, involving both helicopters and aeroplanes.

The rescue operation during Typhoon Koryn, on June 27, stood out as an outstanding example of its type. During the operation, GFS aircrews had to work under winds of more than 80 knots but — in concert with RAF helicopter crews — succeeded in saving 24 lives from the wrecked freighter *Lian Gang*. GFS and RAF crews were again involved in search and rescue missions during Severe Tropical Storm Becky on September 17. With winds in excess of 70 knots, many survivors were plucked from the rough seas and pitching decks of floundering vessels.

The Police Force and the Correctional Services Department made frequent use of helicopters for operational and training purposes. Helicopters also routinely took engineering staff to hilltops, to carry out maintenance and repair work on communication repeater stations. The Super King Airs supported both the Police and Customs in anti-smuggling operations, and were heavily employed by the Lands Department for aerial surveys, photography and map-making. The Fireflys provided pilot training for cadet pilots.

During the year, about 13 249 government officers were flown to various areas in the course of their duties. Flying services were also provided to give official overseas visitors an overview of the territory.

During the dry season, the helicopters assisted in over 60 fire-fighting operations, dropping over 835 tonnes of water on bush and forest fires in areas inaccessible to conventional fire-fighting appliances.

Under the pilot localisation programme, three more cadets completed their training and were promoted to the rank of Pilot II, making a total of 10 Pilot IIs. Six cadets were still under training, while three more will start training in 1994.

An extensive engineering upgrade programme was undertaken throughout the year. This enabled the Civil Aviation Department to award the GFS the first Hong Kong Aircraft Maintenance Organisation Approval in accordance with the new legal standard known as Hong Kong Requirement 145, which permits the unit to service and maintain its entire fleet of aircraft. It expects to achieve ISO 9000 certification in early 1994.

19
TRAVEL AND TOURISM

TOURISM, one of Hong Kong's largest service industries, continued to set records during the year under review. In addition, regulation of the outbound travel industry was strengthened.

Tourism

Tourism is the territory's second largest earner of foreign exchange.

A record 7.2 million international visitors (excluding travellers from China) came to Hong Kong in 1993, an increase of five per cent from the previous year. The Hong Kong Tourist Association (HKTA) started to include visitors from China in visitor arrival statistics in April. Visitor arrivals from China (foreign residents and China nationals) grew by 50.8 per cent in 1993 to 1.7 million. Total visitor arrivals were, therefore, 8.9 million — an increase of 11.6 per cent.

Tourism earnings (excluding spending by visitors from China) registered an increase of 10 per cent, setting another record at $53.2 billion.

Hong Kong remained Asia's most popular travel destination. Aside from China, the biggest influx of visitors in recent years has been from neighbouring areas in the Asian region, notably Taiwan, which accounted for 19.9 per cent of total arrivals in 1993. Other major markets were West Europe (11.7 per cent), North America (10.6 per cent), and Australia and New Zealand (3.5 per cent).

To cater for the accommodation needs of the continuing increase in visitors to Hong Kong, four new hotels opened in 1993, bringing the total number of rooms available in the territory to 34 000.

Hong Kong Tourist Association

The HKTA was established by the Hong Kong Government in 1957 to develop the territory's tourism industry. The association works to increase the number of visitors to Hong Kong; promotes the improvement of visitor facilities; secures overseas publicity for the territory's attractions; co-ordinates the activities of the tourism industry; and advises the government on industry-related matters.

The chairman and members of the board of management of the HKTA are appointed by the Governor. The association receives an annual subvention from the government. It also derives funds from membership dues; the sale of publications and souvenirs; and from its own commercial tours.

At the end of 1993, the association had 1 699 members, comprising airlines, hotels, travel agents, tour operators and retail, restaurant and other visitor service establishments.

The HKTA maintains two information and gift centres: in the basement of Jardine House in Central and at the Kowloon Star Ferry concourse. In addition, it operates two information counters at the Hong Kong International Airport at Kai Tak. Together, these centres assisted 2.4 million visitors in 1993.

The association runs a general information telephone service in 13 languages for visitors in Hong Kong and a special shopping information service. Together, these lines handled enquiries from 58 165 visitors in 1993. In addition, the association's Infofax service provided information to 5 738 members of the local and overseas travel trade and consumers. This covered such topics as sightseeing, shopping, dining, special interest activities and a calendar of events.

The association provided visitors with some 11.2 million pieces of literature in 12 languages, while continuing to update its publications for the travel trade and overseas consumers. Special emphasis was placed on the production of support material which focusses on the requirements of particular market segments, such as families, senior citizens, honeymooners and sports enthusiasts. The association also continued to advertise, both as a single entity and in co-operation with airlines, tour operators and travel agents, to promote the territory worldwide, in print and on television.

The HKTA has a network of 17 overseas offices whose primary function is to market Hong Kong as a travel destination. It also has an agreement with Cathay Pacific Airways Limited for the airline to act as the association's information agent in an additional 42 cities around the world.

The year 1993 was an active one for the HKTA. It headed Hong Kong delegations to 16 major travel trade events overseas, including the World Travel Market in London and the International Tourism Bourse in Berlin.

In conjunction with travel industry partners such as the Hong Kong Hotels Association and airlines, the HKTA carried out various promotions overseas. These included a Southeast Asia Roadshow to Bangkok, Singapore, Kuala Lumpur, Jakarta and Manila; Hong Kong/Macau update seminars in five Japanese cities; and a Hong Kong travel mission to Taiwan.

In co-operation with Cathay Pacific Airways Limited, the HKTA continued the Friends of Hong Kong Super City programme, which aims to develop a corps of Hong Kong and Cathay Pacific supporters, within Southeast Asia travel agencies which have a track record of promoting Hong Kong. The programme enables travel agency staff to provide more informed advice about Hong Kong when discussing holiday plans with their clients.

Familiarisation visits to Hong Kong were arranged for 3 248 travel agents. A further 501 visiting travel trade personnel were briefed to encourage them to include Hong Kong in their clients' travel itineraries or to persuade tour wholesalers to extend the Hong Kong portion of their current Far East tour packages. A Hong Kong Salutes Europe promotion brought some 70 chief executives and decision-makers from top European travel agencies and tour operators to Hong Kong in September to experience first-hand the latest developments in the territory.

During the year, the association also worked with the some 150 Hong Kong-based foreign correspondents or news organisations, and assisted 1 800 visiting overseas media representatives with their coverage of Hong Kong. For example, in February, a special

Sumo in Hong Kong tournament involved 40 sumo wrestlers and resulted in extensive international coverage, particularly in Japan. Some 60 food writers and members of television crews were brought in to cover the 1993 Hong Kong Food Festival, resulting in extensive overseas publicity for Hong Kong's culinary attractions.

In its marketing of Hong Kong as a tourist destination, the HKTA organised a series of events to promote the territory as a year-round travel destination—highlighting its special blend of East and West, and extensive range of top-quality attractions. The Hong Kong Dragon Boat Festival—International Races, organised for the 18th consecutive year in early July, were a major attraction and received widespread international publicity. A total of 30 overseas and 129 local crews competed in the race programme and a series of charity races raised $1.02 million for the Community Chest.

The HKTA also carried out overseas promotions for other special events, such as the Hong Kong Arts Festival, the musical *Barnum*, the Image Hong Kong photographic event, the Cathay Pacific/Hongkong Bank Invitation Seven-A-Side Rugby Tournament and the Cathay Pacific/Wharf Holdings International Cricket Sixes, highlighting Hong Kong's role as a major venue for arts and sports.

In addition, the association operated a number of special interest tours for visitors, including The Land Between Tour, the Come Horseracing tour, the Family Insight Tour, the Sports and Recreation Tour and the Heritage Tour.

The association's marketing theme, 'Hong Kong—Stay an Extra Day', remained instrumental in encouraging visitors to stay longer. The HKTA continued to use the 'Hong Kong *à la carte*' promotion, which rewards visitors booking a longer-than-average Hong Kong holiday with a booklet of special offers from retail, dining, sightseeing and entertainment establishments. More than 228 400 booklets have been distributed overseas since the start of the scheme in 1991.

The association continued to actively promote Hong Kong as a venue for conventions and incentive travel business. Efforts in this area were rewarded by a 10 per cent increase in 1993 in the number of delegates attending conventions and exhibitions in Hong Kong. Highlights included the 35th World Congress of Surgery International Surgical Week in August and the 1993 Junior Chamber International Hong Kong Congress in November, bringing in 2 500 and 12 000 delegates, respectively.

Locally, to highlight the tourism industry's contribution to Hong Kong and to enhance the community's support for the industry, the HKTA organised the second Hong Kong Tourism Day in December. The programme's activities included a charity walk and a tree-planting ceremony. Throughout the year, a public announcement with the theme 'Tourism Works for Hong Kong' continued to be televised on all four local channels to highlight the contribution of the industry to the territory's economic well-being.

The association recognises the importance of training in the industry to maintain Hong Kong's high reputation for service. Its Industry Training Department runs various programmes for staff in the retail trade, as well as courses designed specifically for tour co-ordinators and restaurant personnel. To attract school-leavers to the industry, the association organises annually the Tourism Employees Preparatory Programme, while the complementary Job Bazaar enables prospective employers to meet participants in this programme. There is also a free Tourism Employees Recruitment Service.

The HKTA continued to encourage higher levels of courtesy through the ongoing Hong Kong Cares courtesy campaign. During the year, the association organised a Hong Kong

Cares Courtesy Awards Programme for members of the service industry, which received more than 1 500 nominations from visitors from 46 countries. For the first time, the association joined forces with Radio Television Hong Kong's Radio 2 service to promote this programme of activities. The campaign closed with the Courteous Hong Kong, Beautiful City carnival in May. The bi-annual Hong Kong Tour Co-ordinator of the Year Award programme was also held in 1993, drawing more than 10 000 nominations from visitors.

For the 26th year, the HKTA organised the Student Ambassador Programme, under which 100 students heading overseas for their tertiary education took part in a month-long programme of briefings to increase their awareness of various aspects of Hong Kong, which would enable them to talk more knowledgeably about their home. The Tourism Ambassador Badge scheme for Hong Kong's Scouts also continued to be popular. A total of 200 Scouts have now earned their badge by attending a special workshop on the tourism industry in Hong Kong and by helping visitors at the HKTA's information and gift centres.

The association publishes regular reports on the performance of the tourism industry and conducts surveys which monitor changes in the basic demographics of all visitors, their activities, spending patterns and attitudes towards Hong Kong's tourism facilities.

Outbound Travel

Hong Kong's outbound travel business is operated by some 1 100 travel agents who are licensed by the Registrar of Travel Agents under the Travel Agents Ordinance. The ordinance provides the statutory framework for regulation of the outbound travel industry. To be licensed, a travel agent must be a member of the Travel Industry Council of Hong Kong.

The council is an approved organisation of travel agents in Hong Kong. It comprises eight association members: Hong Kong Association of Travel Agents Limited; Federation of Hong Kong Travellers Limited; International Chinese Tourist Association Limited; Society of International Air Transport Association Passenger Agents Limited; Hong Kong Taiwan Tourist Operators Association Limited; Hong Kong Association of China Travel Organisers Limited; Hong Kong Outbound Tour Operators' Association Limited; and Hongkong Japanese Tour Operators Association Limited. The council regulates member travel agents through codes of practice and directives. Members who breach the rules of self-regulation risk losing their council membership and their licence to operate.

The self-regulatory scheme for the industry was strengthened with the implementation of the Travel Agents (Amendment) Ordinance 1993 on October 15, 1993. The reforms include the enhancement of the regulatory regime for the outbound travel industry; the offer of increased protection to consumers; the provision of a secure source of finance for the council to carry out its self-regulatory efforts; the establishment of a Travel Industry Compensation Fund for the payment of *ex gratia* compensation to aggrieved outbound travellers; and an independent management board appointed by the Governor to administer the fund. The fund took over the assets and liabilities of two former compensation funds—the Travel Agents' Reserve Fund under the Travel Agents Ordinance; and the Travel Industry Council Reserve Fund, which was introduced in 1988. If a licensed travel agency collapses, aggrieved outbound travellers may claim *ex gratia* compensation of 80 per cent of their paid outbound tour fares from the new fund.

The amending ordinance also clarifies the scope of leviable outbound travel services and provides for the splitting of the former levy on outbound package tour fares into two discrete sums: a fund levy and a council levy, both payable by licensed travel agents on the outbound fares paid by travellers. The two levies are specified by the Financial Secretary from time to time and are currently imposed on outbound travel fares at the specified rates of 0.35 per cent for the fund levy and at 0.15 per cent for the council levy. The fund levy goes to the Travel Industry Compensation Fund for the protection of outbound travellers, whereas the council levy goes to the Travel Industry Council of Hong Kong to help finance its self-regulatory efforts. A licensed travel agent who fails to pay either one of the two levies, risks losing his licence.

In 1993, no travel agencies collapsed. The new fund had a balance of $138 million at the end of the year.

20
THE ARMED SERVICES

THE announcement of plans for the deployment of British forces in Hong Kong up to 1997 and the transfer of naval operations to a new base on Stonecutters Island highlighted 1993 for the territory's multinational Armed Services.

The Hong Kong garrison comprises Gurkhas from Nepal, who make up nearly half the garrison strength; locally-recruited Hong Kong Chinese; and service personnel from the United Kingdom. In addition, the territory has its own locally-raised regiment of part-time soldiers — the Royal Hong Kong Regiment (The Volunteers).

The garrison includes elements of the Royal Navy, Army and Royal Air Force, all of which are supported by a civilian work force, predominantly composed of locally-recruited Hong Kong Chinese.

Garrison's Role

The garrison's principal role is to provide a tangible demonstration of the United Kingdom's sovereignty and commitment to Hong Kong until 1997, in this way contributing to security, stability and prosperity in the territory.

In order to meet this role, the garrison must retain a balanced and flexible capability to assist the Hong Kong Government, if and when necessary, in a number of tasks. These include assistance in the maintenance of stability, security and confidence within the territory; maintenance of the territorial integrity of Hong Kong's boundaries; support to Royal Hong Kong Police operations; disaster and emergency relief; and contributing to regional security.

Commander British Forces

The Commander British Forces, with the rank of major-general, is in overall command of the Royal Navy, Army and Royal Air Force elements based in Hong Kong.

The Garrison

The garrison numbers about 9 500 men and women, comprising 7 200 military and some 2 300 civilian support staff.

The Royal Navy headquarters at HMS Tamar was closed in May and naval operations were transferred to a new base on Stonecutters Island. The HMS Tamar title was also transferred along with the move of the three Peacock-class patrol craft and operational and support facilities. Headquarters British Forces continue to operate from the Prince of Wales Building on the old west Tamar site, now renamed the Prince of Wales Barracks.

During 1993, the Royal Navy remained active in operations at sea to counter smuggling and illegal immigration in support of the Royal Hong Kong Police. It was also called upon in its search and rescue role when maritime disasters struck civilian shipping.

The Army comprises the largest element of the garrison, although its numbers will continue to decline as functions are transferred to civil agencies. At present, the Army element consists of one United Kingdom infantry battalion (1st Battalion The Black Watch) and two Gurkha battalions supported by Gurkha engineer, signals and transport regiments. Army units in Hong Kong are completed by an Army Air Corps squadron equipped with Scout helicopters, and a maritime troop (part of the transport regiment) which operates three landing craft. Many of these units will be reduced and, in some cases, disbanded during 1994.

The Royal Air Force is based at Sek Kong in the New Territories, where it operates a squadron of Wessex helicopters.

The Future Size and Shape of the Garrison

Outline plans for the deployment of British forces in Hong Kong up to 1997 were announced by the Ministry of Defence in July. Units of all three services — the Army, Royal Navy and Royal Air Force — will remain in Hong Kong until June 1997. However, the garrison will continue to be reduced in stages over the intervening period as local forces assume responsibility for its former operational tasks.

In the latter part of 1994, the 1st Battalion The Black Watch will return to the UK and the two Gurkha battalions will merge to form the 1st Battalion The Royal Gurkha Rifles. An infantry battalion will be based in Hong Kong until June 1997. The strength of logistic and other supporting units will be reduced in line with that of front-line units.

The three Royal Navy patrol craft presently in Hong Kong will remain until June 1997. Royal Air Force helicopters will also remain until 1997, although their numbers may be reduced.

Thus, for the final two years of British sovereignty, the garrison will be about 3 000 strong, comprising a headquarters, an infantry battalion group, logistic support, naval patrol craft and Royal Air Force helicopters.

Training and Operations

As the garrison is unique in its makeup, so it is also in its ability to use its blend of troops and skills in a wide range of training and operations. This involves a busy programme throughout the year with combined exercises involving the three services and the Royal Hong Kong Regiment, as well as Five Power Defence Agreement exercises with the armed forces of Singapore, Malaysia, Australia and New Zealand.

Exercises are held in Hong Kong in locations like Lantau Island and the New Territories, but Hong Kong lacks suitable areas for realistic training with some of the weaponry with which British forces are normally equipped. As a result, some exercises are held overseas in order to maintain a high standard of military skills.

In June 1993, three Wessex helicopters from the RAF's No. 28 Squadron joined aircraft from the Government Flying Service in rescuing 24 crew members of a cargo vessel which sank near Hong Kong at the height of Typhoon Koryn. In August, troops from the Queen's Gurkha Engineers based in Hong Kong travelled to Nepal to assist with disaster relief operations following extensive flooding in that country. Individuals from the garrison were also called upon to assist with United Nations operations, including those in Cambodia.

Vietnamese Migrants

In 1993, despite the small number of Vietnamese migrants arriving in Hong Kong, the garrison continued to provide logistical and technical support in dealing with the problem.

The temporary camp for Vietnamese migrants at the western end of RAF Sek Kong was closed in January this year. The Lo Wu training camp, previously used as a departure centre for migrants awaiting voluntary return to Vietnam, was also closed in May 1993.

During the year, the Army's maritime troop moved some 8 500 migrants between locations and the Royal Navy assisted in the transfer of hundreds of returnees under the Orderly Repatriation Programme.

The Garrison and the Community

The garrison contributes to the well-being of the wider community in many ways. Apart from the high-profile events which highlight the garrison's presence, there is much behind-the-scenes activity which largely goes unreported.

When a typhoon threatens, the garrison automatically moves to a higher state of alert. Emergency communications are set up and troops placed on standby for any tasks they might be given. The troops are backed up by a wide range of equipment and supplies held in disaster relief stores.

The Royal Navy operates the only decompression chamber in the region to treat divers who may have re-surfaced too quickly. There is also a clearance diving team ready to assist civilian authorities in underwater tasks.

Local people bring a wide variety of skills to the garrison, either in uniform as members of the Hong Kong Military Service Corps or the Chinese Division of the Royal Navy, or as civilians in a wide range of jobs. Apart from supplying essential translation skills, they are to be found working as drivers, medical orderlies, teachers, secretaries, book-keepers, military police, guards, dog-handlers, signallers or mechanics.

Just as the community plays an important part in the life of the garrison, the garrison itself takes an active role in the lives of local communities. In addition to participation in displays, band performances and open days enjoyed by thousands of people, smaller groups of servicemen and women support a wide variety of charities and involve themselves in projects concerning the young, the elderly and the disabled.

Every year the Queen's Gurkha Signals provide logistic support for Trailwalker, when hundreds of enthusiasts walk the length of the MacLehose Trail to raise funds for charity. The popularity of this event increases year by year, both in terms of the number of teams taking part and in terms of money raised, presently amounting to over $7.5 million *per annum*.

Open days held by all the elements of the garrison continued to attract large attendances and raised tens of thousands of dollars for charity.

Garrison teams and individuals also played a leading role in the territory's sporting programme. Gurkha military engineers provided the design expertise and manpower for the construction of various youth projects, and several hundred youngsters attended camps run by the garrison to experience a variety of activities, including physical training and assault courses, shooting, map-reading, first aid, hill-walking, canoeing and sailing.

Royal Hong Kong Regiment (The Volunteers)

The Royal Hong Kong Regiment (The Volunteers) was formed in May 1854, when the Crimean War led to a reduction in the British military presence in Hong Kong.

The regiment, then known as the Hong Kong Volunteer Defence Corps, was heavily involved in the battle for Hong Kong in December 1941, during which over 2 200 soldiers and officers were mobilised. The corps lost over 200 personnel, killed or missing, during the battle and was awarded 19 decorations and 18 mentions in despatches for gallantry and service during the war.

Today, it is a light reconnaissance regiment of part-time volunteers. Its role includes reconnaissance, anti-illegal immigration operations and assistance to other government departments in the event of natural disasters. It is administered and financed by the Hong Kong Government but if called out, it is commanded by the Commander British Forces and forms part of 48 Gurkha Infantry Brigade. The regiment will be disbanded in September 1995. By then, it will have existed in various forms for 141 years.

The regiment has an establishment of 946 volunteers and 54 permanent staff, including nine regular officers and soldiers on loan from the British Army, one of whom is the Commanding Officer. The volunteers come from all walks of life and are of various nationalities, although over 97 per cent are Chinese. In June, a total of 175 recruits, of whom 34 were female, successfully completed their six-month basic training. They are the regiment's final cadre of recruits.

The Regiment consists of four sabre squadrons, a home guard squadron and a headquarters squadron which includes a women's troop, with a strength of 88, who provide support in various operational duties as searchers, interpreters and radio operators. The regiment also runs a junior leaders' corps of around 300 boys, aged from 14 to 17, which provides training in youth activities and leadership skills.

Each year, selected volunteers are sent for overseas training and on attachments to British Army regiments in the United Kingdom. Officer cadets receive military training at the Royal Military Academy, Sandhurst, before they receive their commissions.

The training commitment for each volunteer is two evenings and one weekend each month. There are also centrally-organised regimental training programmes such as military courses, regimental camps and exercises. The camps, which are the highlight of the year's training, take place over eight days in May and November. In addition, the Volunteers are deployed on the border for anti-illegal immigration operations. Working alongside the police, the Volunteers captured a total of 97 illegal immigrants during their border operation in May.

21
COMMUNICATIONS AND THE MEDIA

THE sophisticated telecommunications industry saw major developments in 1993, including the establishment in July of the Office of the Telecommunications Authority (OFTA) to steer Hong Kong towards an increasingly competitive market.

Existing and prospective telecommunications operators in the territory are planning infrastructural investments of some $45 billion over the next 10 years.

During 1993, Hong Kong became the first major city in the world to have a completely digital telecommunications network.

The territory also reported the second highest rate of mobile phone use in the world, the greatest number of paging subscribers per head of population, the highest rate of international telecoms use and the second largest number of fax machines per head of population.

The scheme of control of Hong Kong Telephone Company Limited was replaced by a price-capping arrangement, International Direct Dialling charges were reduced and the intention to license additional local fixed telecommunications networks was announced.

Subscription television sprang to life on October 31, bringing with it the world's first 24-hour news service in Chinese.

A further 19 new newspapers and 139 new periodicals joined the ranks of Hong Kong's flourishing free press in 1993.

The News Media

The news media in Hong Kong includes nearly 77 daily newspapers (including one in Braille), around 619 periodicals, two private television companies, a subscription television service, a regional satellite television service, one government radio-television station, two commercial radio stations and a radio station for the British Forces.

The availability in Hong Kong of the latest in telecommunications technology, together with growing interest in Hong Kong affairs, has attracted a large number of international news agencies, newspapers with international readership and overseas broadcasting corporations to establish regional offices in the territory. In addition, many international news media representatives have their regional base here. Regional publications are also produced here very successfully, underlining the territory's strong position as a financial, industrial, trading and communications centre.

The news media play a significant role in the territory's precautionary measures against sudden climatic threats — alerting, informing and advising the public in the event of typhoons or rainstorms.

The Press

The Hong Kong press consists of 77 newspapers and 619 periodicals, which have a high readership. They include 41 Chinese-language dailies and seven English-language dailies. Of the Chinese-language dailies, 33 cover mainly general news, both local and overseas; three focus on finance; and the rest cover entertainment news, especially television and cinema news. The larger papers include overseas Chinese communities in their distribution networks, and some have editions printed outside Hong Kong, in particular in the United States, Canada, the United Kingdom and Australia. One of the English dailies publishes a daily Braille edition, in conjunction with the Hong Kong Society for the Blind. A total of four news agency bulletins, issued in Chinese, English and Japanese, are also registered as newspapers.

Hong Kong is the Southeast Asian base for many newspapers, magazines, news agencies and electronic media. Among the international news agencies with offices in Hong Kong are Associated Press, Reuters, United Press International, Agence France-Presse, Kyodo News Service of Japan, Agencia EFE of Spain, and LUSA of Portugal. *Newsweek* and *Time* magazines have editions printed in Hong Kong, which is also the base for the regional magazines *Asiaweek* and *Far Eastern Economic Review*. The *Asian Wall Street Journal* and the *International Herald Tribune* are also printed here.

Several organisations represent and cater for people working in the news media in Hong Kong. The Newspaper Society of Hong Kong represents Chinese and English newspaper proprietors. It is empowered to act in matters affecting the interests of its members. The Hong Kong Journalists Association, which celebrated its 25th anniversary in 1993, is the only territory-wide trade union for journalists. It seeks to recommend better training, pay and conditions in journalism, and advises its members in the event of disputes with employers. The association is also active in issues related to freedom of the media and serves as a watchdog of professional ethical standards. The Foreign Correspondents' Club offers its members social facilities and a range of professional activities, including news conferences, briefings and films. The Hong Kong Press Club provides an opportunity for journalists to meet socially.

A sum of $300,000 was allocated by the Vocational Training Council to its Journalism Training Board and Advertising, Public Relations and Publishing Training Board to conduct about a dozen upgrading courses for journalists working for the mass media. The most popular ones covered Putonghua for journalists (held by the City Polytechnic of Hong Kong), interviewing techniques (by the British Council), oral communication skills for journalists (by the Hong Kong Polytechnic) and advertising management (by the 4A's). The Journalism Training Board also provided a subsidy of $20,000 to the Hong Kong Journalists' Association for the conduct of a number of short seminars and talks for reporters.

Information Policy

The government's information machinery was reorganised with effect from October 15, 1993, when the Home Affairs Branch assumed overall responsibility for policy formulation on information and related matters.

Under the reorganisation, the Information Co-ordinator in the Chief Secretary's Office took responsibility for the government's public relations strategy, with the Information Services Department as the executive agency for policy implementation.

The main aims are to ensure an open exchange of information in the community and to keep the media fully informed of the government's plans and policies, so that members of the public are kept aware of the government activities which affect their lives.

The Information Co-ordinator advises the government on the presentation of its policies, and on public relations matters generally, both within Hong Kong and overseas.

Information Services Department

The Information Services Department, also known as Government Information Services (GIS), provides the link between the administration and the media and, through the latter, enhances public understanding of Government policies, decisions and activities.

The department is organised into five divisions — the News and Media Research, Publicity, Overseas Public Relations, Visits and Administration divisions. It has a staff of about 550. Of these, 359 are Information Grade officers, with 229 deployed in government departments, policy branches in the Government Secretariat and Hong Kong Government offices overseas.

News and Media Research Division

The News and Media Research Division maintains direct contact with the media on a 24-hour basis. It is responsible for disseminating government information through a teleprinter network to over 80 newspapers, news agencies, television and radio stations, and other individual organisations. It also has a facsimile transmission system serving 29 outlets, which is particularly important for communicating in the Chinese language.

The division produces a Daily Information Bulletin in both English and Chinese, which contains about 20 of the more important press releases on an average day.

It runs a Press Enquiry Service which operates round the clock. It has a comprehensive press library, holding press cuttings and copies of all government press releases, and a smaller reference library for use by journalists, researchers and students.

The division keeps the government informed of public opinion as expressed in the media by producing a media summary every morning, and special reports on matters of topical and special interest.

Publicity Division

The Publicity Division is responsible for government publications, promotional campaigns, advertisements, creative and design work and government photography.

Its Publishing Sub-division handles more than 8 000 separate titles. It produces a wide variety of government publications, including the Hong Kong Annual Report. Every year, it distributes some six million copies of publications such as books, fact sheets, brochures, pamphlets, posters and government forms. Associated with this output, the sub-division sells some four million copies of books and miscellaneous printed materials annually.

The sub-division arranges and places all government advertising in the media, both locally and overseas. These come to around 4 500 notices, with over 14 000 placements annually.

The Promotions Sub-division organises about 10 major government campaigns and more than 40 general publicity programmes yearly, to educate the public on major issues of concern and create public awareness of civic responsibilities. Publicity messages are disseminated through films, publications, radio announcements, press advertisements, exhibitions and other promotional activities such as launch ceremonies, float parades, concerts and variety shows. Increased efforts have been made to get the message across to a wide sector of the community through joint programme production and coverage with the electronic media, as well as district activities in support of campaign themes.

In 1993, 10 major government campaigns were organised. Issues of general concern, such as environmental protection, road safety, AIDS prevention, crime prevention and the fight against drug abuse, continued to be matters of priority. Other topics promoted during the year included registering for British National (Overseas) passports, energy conservation and civic education.

The Creative Sub-Division is responsible for all government design and display services, and film and photographic work.

Overseas Public Relations Division

The Overseas Public Relations Division devises the government's overseas public relations strategy, co-ordinates all international publicity efforts, monitors Hong Kong's image overseas and handles VIP visits.

Its Overseas Public Relations Sub-Division co-ordinates the government's publicity efforts overseas. It produces and distributes material worldwide, including feature articles, books, pamphlets and television newsclips. The sub-division also runs a sponsored visitors programme, under which influential journalists are invited to visit Hong Kong to gain a better understanding of the territory. It provides assistance for other visiting journalists requiring information and interviews with government officials, business and community leaders, and maintains close liaison with news agencies and foreign correspondents based in Hong Kong.

The sub-division is in constant touch with the information and public relations units of the government's overseas offices, providing them with the necessary information to present an accurate and up-to-date picture of Hong Kong.

The Overseas Projects Sub-Division mounts promotional activities for projecting Hong Kong's image overseas. Very often, these projects are organised in conjunction with the private sector. It also assists overseas bodies in organising activities in Hong Kong which foster bilateral links.

In carrying out these tasks, the sub-division maintains close liaison with the government's overseas offices; consuls-general and commissioners of foreign countries in Hong Kong; various organisations involved in promoting the territory, such as the Hong Kong Trade Development Council and the Hong Kong Tourist Association; chambers of commerce and major corporations in Hong Kong.

Visits Division

The Visits Division sponsors and invites VIP visitors, including influential politicians, parliamentarians and businessmen from countries with close relations with Hong Kong, to visit the territory. It plans, organises and co-ordinates their visit programmes and briefings with the aim of improving their understanding of Hong Kong.

The division runs a speakers programme as well, under which arrangements are made for senior government officials and prominent local personalities to address targeted audiences overseas. These programmes are complemented by participation in international seminars, cultural activities and other events.

Administration Division
The Administration Division provides administrative, personnel and financial support services for the department.

Hong Kong's Image Overseas
One of the main objectives of the government's information policy is to project an accurate image of Hong Kong to overseas communities.

As international interest in the major issues confronting Hong Kong has increased, so the government, in co-operation with leading organisations in the private sector, has expanded the programme of joint promotional activities mounted overseas.

Overseas Offices
The Hong Kong Government's overseas public relations efforts are concentrated on its major business partners in North America, Europe and the Asia-Pacific region. Its overseas offices in these regions play a leading role in promoting Hong Kong.

London
The News and Public Relations Unit of the Hong Kong Government Office in London works closely with GIS to provide a press service on Hong Kong matters for the British media, and for Hong Kong journalists based in the United Kingdom. The unit maintains close contact with journalists, from both national and regional media, briefs and helps plan programmes for media visiting Hong Kong, and assists visiting journalists from Hong Kong. It provides enquiry and information services for the public about events and developments in Hong Kong, backed by a very comprehensive library. The unit also organises a panel of speakers of about 100 former government officers and businessmen, who have retired or now work in Britain.

The unit monitors British parliamentary proceedings and both national and regional media coverage of Hong Kong affairs, responding where necessary to inaccurate reports. It also publishes a newsletter, *Dateline Hong Kong*, which is distributed among organisations and individuals with a close interest in the territory.

North America
In North America, media relations are conducted through the government's Economic and Trade Offices in Washington, New York, San Francisco and Toronto. These offices provide a general news and information service for the media and work with GIS to produce news releases, features and articles tailored to the specific requirements of American and Canadian publications. Close contact is maintained with journalists in all major centres of both countries. The units also provide them with assistance and information for preparing articles on Hong Kong and help journalists visiting Hong Kong with briefings, research material and interviews. Each year, the information units of these offices organise, in conjuction with GIS, a series of sponsored visits to Hong Kong by American and Canadian journalists.

The units also handle numerous public and business enquiries on all types of issues. To supplement this service, a monthly digest of events and happenings in Hong Kong is produced and mailed to contacts throughout North America. The units participate in a variety of exhibitions and seminars to establish further contact with the electronic and print media, and to publicise Hong Kong. The units also monitor coverage of relevant issues in the American and Canadian news media.

To further strengthen Hong Kong-United States ties, the Governor, the Right Honourable Christopher Patten, made his first official visit to the United States in May. During his visit to Washington, the Governor met the United States President Mr Bill Clinton, the Senate Majority Leader Mr George Mitchell, various cabinet members and congressional leaders. He then travelled to New York to meet leading members of the business and financial community.

In the United States, a public relations firm is also used to implement a public relations plan and strategy for Hong Kong. It also assists with organising speaking platforms and tours for visiting speakers from Hong Kong and senior officers of the Economic and Trade Offices in North America.

Europe

Among its responsibilities, the Hong Kong Economic and Trade Office in Brussels is charged with overseeing the government's public relations and publicity efforts in the European Community and its member states (except the United Kingdom, which is the responsibility of the London Office), and in Switzerland and Austria. The public relations and press team in the office works closely with Hong Kong and the 'Hong Kong family' in Europe to give information about the territory to contacts in both the public and private sectors and in the media in Europe, to develop and sustain their interest in Hong Kong affairs. The Brussels team also monitors and collects information appearing in the European media which is of relevance or importance to Hong Kong.

Under the sponsored visitors programme, the Brussels Office invites opinion leaders and decision-makers from the European Commission, the governments of member states and major European businesses to visit Hong Kong, to enable them to have a better understanding of the territory's needs and importance. Members of the European Parliament and European media are also included in this programme. In addition, the Brussels Office arranges speaking engagements in many EC countries for senior Hong Kong Government officials and leading members of the Hong Kong community, to explain recent developments.

The biggest promotion Hong Kong has ever staged in continental Europe, Hong Kong '93, was held towards the end of the year. The promotion was centred on Hong Kong's major trading partners in the region — Germany, France and the Netherlands.

The highlights included a film festival in Paris, jointly organised with the famous La Cinematheque Française, and featuring 20 top Hong Kong films from the early 1980s to the present; an exhibition on Hong Kong architecture, arranged in association with the prestigious German Museum of Architecture in Frankfurt, displaying models and design plans of some of Hong Kong's dazzling skyscrapers, such as the Bank of China building and the HongkongBank building; and special functions in The Hague, featuring the Academy for Performing Arts, and in Paris, where Hong Kong's designers took centre stage with some of their latest fashion creations. A series of business conferences with the theme 'Hong Kong Means Business' was also held in Frankfurt, Paris and Amsterdam.

Japan
The Hong Kong Economic and Trade Office in Tokyo is responsible for the government's public relations efforts in Japan. It liaises with Japanese ministries and other organisations, and arranges programmes for Japanese officials and other VIPs to visit Hong Kong. It also organises speaking engagements for senior government officers in Japan.

Its information unit provides enquiry and information services concerning events and developments in Hong Kong; maintains close contacts with the local media; briefs and helps plan programmes for media representatives visiting Hong Kong; and monitors the local media coverage of Hong Kong affairs, responding where necessary to reports of relevance to Hong Kong. The office also maintains contacts with other Hong Kong-based organisations and companies in Japan with a view to optimising the territory's overall promotional efforts.

Australia and New Zealand
There are at present no Hong Kong Government offices in Australia and New Zealand, but a public relations firm has been appointed to provide public relations coverage in this region.

Printing and Publishing
A reputation for good printing quality, quick and reliable delivery, and competitive prices continues to boost the international status of Hong Kong's printing industry. The territory is a leading centre for printing and publishing, with 4 820 printing establishments employing 40 918 people, and more than 200 publishing houses, including many from overseas which have set up offices or regional headquarters in Hong Kong. Hong Kong printers are investing substantially in advanced machinery and equipment, and are taking positive steps to develop the United States market.

The industry constitutes 12 per cent of all manufacturing establishments and eight per cent of employment in the manufacturing sector. A majority of the printing factories (76 per cent) are engaged in general jobbing work, and most of the remainder deal with related work, such as typesetting and book-binding. There are also 21 newspaper printers.

Use of the latest technology, especially computerised equipment, has enabled the industry to become highly specialised. The local electronics industry contributes to the plant and equipment of both the more sophisticated printing companies and of publishers, who are becoming increasingly involved in the use of data and word-processing systems for editorial production and stock control. The output data can be converted or interfaced with typesetting equipment at a realistic cost, to provide publishers with the additional benefits of fast and cost-efficient printing. An increasing number of Chinese language word-processors are being installed to meet demand.

Domestic exports of printed matter increased in value terms by one per cent over the previous year. Material printed locally with a total value of $4,447 million was exported, with the United States, China, the United Kingdom, Taiwan and Australia being the main customers. Books, pamphlets, newspapers, journals and periodicals accounted for 68 per cent of exports of printed products. The biggest customers for this reading material were the United States, the United Kingdom and Australia.

Overall, the printing and publishing industries contributed five per cent of the gross output of the manufacturing sector.

Telecommunications Services

Hong Kong continues to enjoy a wide range of efficient telecommunications services at fair and reasonable prices.

The territory has one of the highest telephone densities in Southeast Asia. At the year's end, there were an estimated 3.8 million telephones served by three million exchange lines, representing a density of 65 telephones for every 100 people.

Basic public telecommunications services are provided under franchise. Under the Telephone Ordinance, the Hong Kong Telephone Company Limited has the exclusive right until June 30, 1995 to provide a public voice telephone service by wire within Hong Kong. Hong Kong Telecom International Limited has been granted an exclusive licence until September 30, 2006, to provide a range of public international telecommunications services, including telephone, telex and telegram services and leased circuits for data and facsimile traffic.

Following a decision to further liberalise the telecommunications industry, the government announced in November 1993 its intention to license three new fixed telecommunications networks to provide competition to the Hong Kong Telephone Company Limited — in data and facsimile services initially, and in voice telephony beyond June 1995.

A new price-capping scheme for the Hong Kong Telephone Company Limited was implemented in August 1993. By limiting overall price increases to four per cent below the prevailing rate of inflation, the new scheme ensures that local telephone charges will decrease significantly in real terms, while providing a reasonable degree of incentive for continued investment and improved efficiency.

The local public switched telephone network became fully digitalised during the year and Hong Kong now has one of the most advanced networks in the world. Through the fully digital network, customers in the territory enjoy a wider range of high quality telecommunications services.

The popularity of facsimile communications continued to grow at the expense of telex traffic, which dropped by 8.9 per cent to 39 million minutes in 1993. In contrast, the number of facsimile lines reached 228 000 by the end of the year, with Hong Kong having more fax machines per head of population than anywhere else apart from Japan. A wide range of advanced data communication facilities is also provided by a public packet-switched data network called Datapak, which is operated by the Hong Kong Telephone Company Limited.

Hong Kong is connected to the rest of the world by overland and submarine cables, satellites and terrestrial radio links. The more important cables include the Hong Kong-Guangdong optical fibre cable, the Hong Kong-Shenzhen optical fibre cable, the Singapore-Hong Kong-Taiwan submarine cable, the Hong Kong-Luzon submarine cable, the Hong Kong-Japan-Korea optical fibre submarine cable, the Hong Kong-Taiwan 2 optical fibre submarine cable and the Asia Pacific Cable (APC). Hong Kong Telecom International Limited operates a satellite earth station at Stanley with six Standard-A, two Standard-B and one Standard-G antennas communicating with international satellites over the Indian Ocean and the Pacific Ocean. Two Inmarsat satellite antennas are being constructed and will be ready for service in 1994.

The only remaining external terrestrial radio links are with China, Macau and Laos.

In 1993, international telephone traffic grew by 24 per cent to 2 522 million minutes. More than 220 overseas countries and territories, and more than 1 080 cities in China can be called, using the International Direct Dialling (IDD) service. Following the agreement reached between the government and Hong Kong Telecom International Limited, an overall eight per cent reduction in IDD charges came into effect on August 1, 1993. Further price reductions, at an annual rate of two per cent, will continue to be made in the next two years. Furthermore, as part of Hong Kong's move to liberalise the telecommunications industry, companies and organisations may also be licensed to provide their own external telecommunications links.

A wide variety of competitive public telecommunications services are, in addition, provided by other companies under Public Non-Exclusive Telecommunications Services (PNETS) and Public Radiocommunications Service (PRS) licences granted by the Telecommunications Authority. Such services include public mobile radio telephone, public mobile data communications, one-way data message, public community repeater, electronic mail (text mail and voicc mail), electronic data interchange (EDI), value-added facsimile transmission (for example, text-facsimile conversion), second generation cordless telephone (Telepoint), digital public mobile radio telephone and videotext services. In December, 54 PNETS licences and 13 PRS licences were in force.

Special arrangements have been agreed upon between Hong Kong and the United Kingdom, the United States, Japan and Australia to facilitate the use of international private leased circuits (IPLCs) for data communications and enhanced facsimile services. Under these arrangements, operators of international value-added network services (IVANS) may use IPLCs to carry third party traffic at normal flat-rate tariffs. In June 1993, the provision of IVANS was further liberalised to allow operators to extend their services to any territory using IPLCs, as long as the services are within the permitted scope and the arrangement is permissible under the national law of the distant territory. The scope of IVANS permitted in Hong Kong was also expanded to include value-added voice services and managed data network services.

Public mobile radio telephone services (PMRS) continued to expand at a fast pace. During the year, the number of customers increased from 233 500 to 289 500. Hong Kong has the highest per capita rate of mobile phone penetration in the world outside Scandinavia. To cater for future growth in demand and to promote competition in this market, in 1992 the Telecommunications Authority licensed a new operator to provide digital PMRS using the GSM standard. This new digital service was launched in January 1993. In addition, the three existing PMRS operators were in the process of digitalising their analogue systems. One launched its digital system in October 1992 and another started service in July 1993.

Hong Kong also has the highest penetrations in the world, on a per capita basis, for radio paging services. In December, 1 254 000 pagers had been licensed (approximately one in 4.7 people). In addition to the established numeric and alphanumeric paging, there are services conveying messages in Chinese characters. An international radio paging service using the 931 MHz frequency was also introduced in April.

Following the introduction of second generation cordless telephone (CT2) services in 1992 by two licensed operators, a third operator launched its service in March 1993. In December, there were 130 500 CT2 customers.

A Hong Kong-registered company, Asia Satellite Telecommunications Company Limited, operates the regional telecommunications satellite, AsiaSat-1. Following its successful launch in April 1990, AsiaSat-1 offers telecommunications services to the region, from the Middle East to Japan. The company has further plans to launch a second satellite, AsiaSat-2, in early 1995. Another company established in Hong Kong in 1992, APT Satellite Company Limited, plans to launch two regional telecommunications satellites, APSTAR-1 and APSTAR-2, in 1994 and 1995, respectively.

The new telecommunications regulatory body, the Office of the Telecommunications Authority (OFTA), was established on July 1. This marked a significant milestone in the development of telecommunications regulation in Hong Kong. OFTA has not only taken over all the tasks previously performed by the Telecommunications Branch of the Post Office, but is also charged with major responsibilities to steer Hong Kong through the transition to an increasingly competitive and complex telecommunications market.

OFTA is headed by the Director-General of Telecommunications, who has been concurrently appointed by the Governor as the Telecommunications Authority under the Telecommunication Ordinance. The Director-General of Telecommunications administers the Telecommunication Ordinance and the Telephone Ordinance, which govern the establishment and operation of all telecommunications services. He also acts as an adviser to the government on matters concerning the development of public telecommunications services, and is a member of the Broadcasting Authority.

Another major function carried out by OFTA is the management of the radio spectrum. This comprises the planning and allocation of the spectrum to radio users, investigating and eliminating radio interference, co-ordinating the use of radio frequencies with neighbouring administrations, and inspecting radio equipment to ensure its suitability for use in Hong Kong. To cope with the increasing volume and complexity of the frequency co-ordination work, OFTA upgraded its spectrum management computer system during the year.

Under the Telecommunication Ordinance, OFTA issues licences for all forms of radio communications in Hong Kong. It conducts examinations of radio-operating personnel and issues certificates to suitably qualified persons in compliance with the Radio Regulations of the International Telecommunication Union. It also inspects ship radio and radar installations.

OFTA also provides advisory and planning services for the communications requirements of government departments and subvented institutions, co-ordinates and regulates the use of radio communications sites, monitors the technical performance of broadcast services and investigates complaints concerning reception quality.

Broadcasting Authority

The regulation of commercial television and sound broadcasting is the responsibility of the Broadcasting Authority, a statutory body established in September 1987. The authority has 12 members, nine of whom are appointed non-official members representing a cross-section of the community, and three government officers. Its major function is to secure the programme, advertising and technical standards of broadcasting licensees, through provisions in the Television Ordinance, the Telecommunication Ordinance and the Broadcasting Authority Ordinance. In April, the authority's jurisdiction was extended to cover subscription television, which was introduced in October. Other licensees include the two commercial radio, one satellite television and two wireless television stations.

During the year, the authority advised the government on the terms and conditions under which the licence for the subscription television service was issued. The authority also assisted the government in conducting a policy review on radio broadcasting, and made a number of changes to the codes of practice on programme and advertising standards for radio. In addition, the authority embarked on a television broadcasting survey which is expected to yield useful data for the mid-term review of the wireless television licences to be carried out in 1994.

Complaints Committee

All complaints relating to television and radio broadcasting are considered by the Complaints Committee of the Broadcasting Authority unless they are of a trivial or frivolous nature. Complaints may be lodged in writing or through a 24-hour hotline provided by the authority. During the year, the authority dealt with 637 complaints concerning quality and standards of television and radio programmes and advertisements. Acting on the recommendations of the Complaints Committee, the authority issued five warnings and nine serious warnings to the two wireless television stations. Three financial penalties were imposed on the two wireless television stations. It also issued two warnings and two serious warnings to the two commercial radio stations, and imposed a financial penalty on one of the commercial radio stations.

Working Group on Review of Codes of Practice

The authority's Working Group on Review of Codes of Practice met regularly during the year to review the codes of practice on programme, advertising and technical standards for television and radio services. As a result, revisions were made to provisions governing financial advertising, local property advertising, the portrayal of superstition in programmes, programme sponsorship, definition of an advertisement, and supplementary standards on medical preparations and treatments.

The working group drew up a new code to regulate the scheduling of programmes on wireless television. In the context of the radio broadcasting review conducted during the year, the working group recommended the relaxation of restrictions on sponsorship of news programmes on radio and streamlining of provisions governing the protection of children and young listeners.

The working group also drew up new codes of practice on programme and home shopping standards to regulate the newly-introduced subscription television service.

Television Viewing Advisory Panels

The Television Viewing Advisory Panels, whose members represent different sections of the community, provide the authority with opinions and suggestions on television broadcasts. The scheme has been in operation for over 10 years. Nineteen district television viewing groups, with a total membership of about 600, have been formed in the Hong Kong, Kowloon and New Territories regions. There are also three regional panels with membership drawn from the 19 district television viewing groups, a television advisory panel on English language services and a special advisory panel on children's and youth programmes. All these panels are chaired by the authority's members.

Television Broadcasting

Wireless Television

Television viewing remained Hong Kong's most popular leisure activity in 1993, with more than 98 per cent of households owning one or more television sets. Sixty-nine per cent also owned a video cassette recorder. Each of the television licensees, Television Broadcasts Limited (TVB) and Asia Television Limited (ATV), provides one Chinese and one English language channel and together, on average, they transmitted over 580 hours of programming per week — an increase of about three per cent compared with 1992.

Competition between the two wireless television stations remained keen. Both tried to strengthen their audience share, and efforts were made to diversify programme contents and to enrich programme scheduling. A variety of programmes such as musicals, magazine shows and 'infotainment' programmes were screened during prime time in addition to serialised dramas. More feature films were also shown by both stations.

On the Chinese channels, locally produced serialised dramas remained the main attraction, with plots revolving around romance, human conflicts, kung fu fantasies, and police and gangster confrontations. Feature films and made-for-television films continued to enjoy a steady share of popularity, while beauty pageants, game contests, charity fund-raising events and musical specials constituted standard fare. Foreign serials dubbed into Cantonese were also broadcast at prime time.

On the English channels, films, imported dramas and musical specials remained major attractions. Documentaries, arts and cultural programmes were featured regularly in the programme line-up. Feature films and cartoons in foreign languages formed part of the off-peak programming.

News and information programmes remained an important part of the programming on all channels, and Putonghua news programmes and financial reports were also introduced. The two English channels continued to carry live satellite telecasts of news programmes from the United States.

Coverage of international sports events was given priority in programme scheduling during the year. Satellite feeds were often used to provide live coverage of sports events, including soccer and tennis.

There was an increase in the use of multi-channel sound television broadcasts with the Near Instantaneously Companded Audio Multiplex (NICAM) system. Feature films, documentaries and sports programmes were broadcast in bilingual format, enabling English services to attract more Chinese-speaking viewers.

The two wireless television stations also embarked on the testing of teletext transmission.

For the transmission of television signals, there were altogether 24 transposer stations. Of these, 23 had adopted the combined broad-band antenna system, to offer a more standardised control of the quality of transmission signals.

Satellite Television

STAR TV provides the satellite television and sound service from Hong Kong to the Asian region. Five channels providing news, sports, music, entertainment and Chinese programmes are receivable in countries as far apart as Japan and Turkey, Indonesia and Mongolia. The service is predominantly in the English language but also includes Putonghua programming. An additional channel in various Indian languages was launched in October 1992, but is not receivable in Hong Kong. The STAR TV service also carries the BBC World Service programmes.

At the end of 1993, over 325 000 homes in Hong Kong were able to receive STAR TV's service and other satellite television programme services through Satellite Master Antenna Television (SMATV) systems.

Subscription Television

The year marked the introduction of subscription television in Hong Kong.

Following a comprehensive review of the television broadcasting environment in Hong Kong, the government drew up a regulatory framework to encourage the introduction of a subscription television service. Tenders were invited to establish the service and the licence was awarded to Wharf Cable Limited in June 1993. The licence covers a 12-year period. Wharf Cable Limited launched its service, delivered by microwave initially, on October 31. Eight channels are available, providing the world's first round-the-clock news service in Chinese, films, sports, children's and other entertainment programmes. The microwave system used for delivery will eventually be replaced by an optical fibre cable network, when the capacity of the system will be increased to a maximum of 39 channels.

Radio Television Hong Kong (Television)

Radio Television Hong Kong (RTHK) produced 10 hours of public affairs television programmes each week during the year. Of these, five hours of programmes were broadcast during prime time throughout the week on the Chinese channels of the two commercial stations (TVB and ATV). Programmes, usually averaging half an hour in length, were also shown on the English channels.

RTHK programmes fall basically into six categories: current affairs, drama, information and community services, variety and quiz shows, children's and youth programmes, and general educational programmes. According to a report on the media, the average viewer size of RTHK programmes during prime time on TVB and ATV was 1 273 000 and 330 000, respectively. An annual independent survey on qualitative rating showed continued public support for RTHK programmes.

Most of RTHK's programmes focus on promoting civic responsibility and social awareness. Current affairs programmes remained in great demand. Through the weekly *Common Sense*, *Headliner*, *City Forum*, *The Hong Kong Connection*, *Today in Legco* and *Media Watch*, current issues were explored and analysed to provide better public understanding of social events. For the younger generation, this was done through a new programme series *Children News Magazine*.

For drama, the focus was on the lives of particular social groups. *Drama Featuring Disabled People* highlighted the successful integration of this group into the community; *Youth Drama* gave an in-depth description of young people's behaviour; and the *Housing Anniversary Series* featured the lives of people in public housing. In the variety area, a series of programmes promoted rehabilitation. *Project Sunshine* successfully served as a fund-raiser for Caritas Hong Kong; *Rehabilitation Special*, jointly organised with the Health and Welfare Branch, sought to promote the integration of the disabled into society; and the *4th Talent Quest for the Disabled* helped to arouse their interest, and develop their talents, in the performing arts.

Programmes designed for youth and children were another focus of production. *Value of Life* aimed at imparting to youth a positive attitude towards life. *CYC Drama* depicted youngsters' participation in the Community Youth Club activities, and their school and family lives. *New Working Generation* featured young people in various career fields.

In educational programmes, language continued to be strongly featured. *One Minute's English* continued to teach English in an easy-to-understand manner. The *Putonghua* series continued to facilitate learning the language in an entertaining and lively style.

There were also programmes associated with different aspects of daily life and social issues. *Human Relations* and *Serve the Needy* helped to arouse concern for other people. *Crucial Moments* focussed especially on patients with serious illnesses. The *Environment Programme* pressed home the importance of environmental protection. *Law Programme* highlighted aspects of the rule of law and human rights in a drama format. The new series of *Doctor and You* continued to encourage public interest in health and medical knowledge, and the *Sex Education* series promoted family life education.

RTHK's Educational Television Division and the Education Department continued to produce curriculum-based and special educational programmes for schools. These programmes, transmitted on the commercial television channels for eight hours every weekday during the academic year, were watched by about 604 000 school children from Primary 3 to Secondary 3.

Sound Broadcasting

Fifteen radio channels are broadcasting in Hong Kong — seven operated by RTHK, three by Hong Kong Commercial Broadcasting Company Limited (CRHK), three by Metro Broadcast Corporation Limited (MB) and two by the British Forces Broadcasting Service (BFBS).

Radio Television Hong Kong (Radio)

RTHK, a publicly-funded station, is charged with providing balanced and objective broadcasting services which inform, educate and entertain the people of Hong Kong. Its news and public affairs programmes aim to provide timely, accurate and in-depth news reports. The Director of Broadcasting is the station's editor-in-chief.

RTHK broadcasts 1 148 hours a week. Its main Chinese and English services, Radio 1 and Radio 3, respectively, operate 24 hours a day. Each of the station's seven channels has established an individual identity.

Radio 1 is the main news and information channel of the Chinese Programme Service. It provides fast, accurate and in-depth news, and financial, traffic and weather reports. Major political and social events are covered extensively and the public mood of the moment is gauged through the channel's phone-in programmes *Talkabout* and *Headliner*. The three-hour public affairs magazine programme *Newsrama* is a major feature of the channel bringing to listeners up-to-the-minute happenings around the territory.

Two major new programmes were introduced on Radio 1. The *Putonghua Roundabout* is targeted at Putonghua-speaking residents and visitors, and carries news, reviews, phone-ins and reports on activities in Putonghua-speaking countries and communities through reports and link-ups with overseas Chinese radio stations. The new *District Board* programme stimulates interest in local affairs through the coverage of activities in the territory's 19 district boards.

Radio 2 provides programmes in Chinese ranging from civic education to entertainment. Following a spate of student suicides, Radio 2 launched a new programme, *Youth Hotline* which proved an instant success. The programme opens up a venue for young people to air, and share, their problems with others of their own age, and for professional counselling to be provided, without the disclosure of the callers' identity. *Solar Project*, which encourages the younger generation to play a positive role in community affairs, continued to be well supported. In 1993, the programme launched a fund-raising concert in Shanghai with the Shanghai East Radio, and publicity visits were also made to various parts of China. Another major event was the annual *Top Ten Chinese Gold Songs Award Presentation Concert*, which promoted local musical talent and raised funds for charitable organisations.

Radio 3 is very much a part of the multi-national English-speaking community of Hong Kong. It is committed to maintaining a high quality English-language service and has boosted its speech content to offset cutbacks in English-language programming by commercial stations. The channel's flagship is its morning current affairs programme *Hong Kong Today*, which provides a comprehensive review of daily news and current affairs in the territory. *Drive Time* showcases a magazine programme, with studio guests giving their views on controversial issues of the day, international phone links and a review of the day's financial and stock markets by experts. Weekends feature documentaries, specialist music and programmes for Indian and Filipino communities.

Radio 4, the bilingual channel for fine music and the arts, broadcasts a wide range of fine music programmes and regular relays of concerts held at major cultural venues in the territory. In order to extend and broaden its audience profile, the channel has adopted a less formal presentation style. The channel promotes local musical talent and creative music through live studio recitals, commissions, and various projects such as *Young Music Makers*, *Musicrama '93* and participation in the International Rostrum of Composers. The weekly magazines *Signals* and *Kaleidoscope* help promote the arts.

Radio 5 broadcasts educational, cultural and minority interest programmes like Cantonese opera, provincial music and features in Putonghua. The *Care for the Elderly* programme has now become an annual project and involves visits to various hostels for the elderly by popular personalities.

Radio 6 relays the BBC World Service round-the-clock. It broadcasts a wide range of programmes from news and current affairs, sport and documentaries to dramas, fine music and programmes for young people.

Radio 7 broadcasts news summaries, financial data and traffic information at 15-minute intervals on weekdays and 30-minute intervals on weekends. During typhoons, heavy rainstorms and other emergencies, special announcements are carried frequently. The channel plays middle-of-the-road music.

RTHK maintains regular links with broadcasting associations and overseas radio stations. The station co-produced programmes with radio stations in China and other ethnic Chinese stations. Through these exchanges, overseas Chinese communities and local audiences were able to keep in touch on a regular basis.

On the technical side, RTHK made a fundamental change to its radio presentation in 1993. A fully integrated music and audio storage system replaced the traditional on-air facilities. The new system is touch-screen operated, with superb sound quality comparable to that of a compact disk. It allows automation of, and simultaneous access to, CD tracks in juke-boxes and audio items located in mass storage. Its database management offers programming flexibility for on-air events.

Commercial Radio

Commercial Radio operates two Chinese services (CR1 and CR2) on FM frequencies and one English service (Quote AM 864) on an AM frequency on a 24-hour basis.

News and current affairs programmes such as the *Breakfast Show*, *Morning This Minute* and *Hong Kong This Minute* are the main features on CR1.

CR2 continues to appeal to students and young people by promoting local pop music. The channel demonstrated its commitment to community service by launching the Man-Yan-Bong Volunteer Service campaign to serve different groups in need and to encourage youth participation in volunteer services.

Quote AM 864 broadcasts in a unique total-music format, uninterrupted by DJ comment.

Joining forces with other organisations and the print media, Commercial Radio also devoted considerable efforts to raising funds for the needy in 1993, partly through the launching of the Action Jackson Charity Drive.

Metro Broadcast

Metro Broadcast went on the air in July 1991, ending a 32-year monopoly on commercial radio broadcasting in Hong Kong. Metro operates three channels of formatted radio — two on FM and one on the AM band.

The two FM channels are both music services — FM Select and Hit Radio. FM Select offers bilingual broadcasts in Cantonese and English to a more mature audience aged 25 and above, largely featuring evergreen songs from the Thirties onwards. Hit Radio is a contemporary hit radio station, playing the current Chinese and Western pop hits.

Metro Broadcast used to provide a 24-hour English news service (Metro News) on its AM frequency, but the format was revised in May and the channel was renamed Metro Plus. The channel now offers a bilingual service, blending five hours of English news programmes with Chinese and English songs. Ethnic programmes in Tagalog are also presented during weekend evenings.

The station has emerged as a major concert producer. During the year, it demonstrated its commitment to community affairs by staging the second 'Fathers Without Wives' charity concert at the Hong Kong Convention and Exhibition Centre, and a Mother's Day concert. The station was also the official radio sponsor for a rapidly accelerating schedule of appearances by top international artists. In 1993, these included Chicago, Public Enemy, Bryan Adams, Foreigner, the Brecker Brothers, Elton John, Bobby Brown, the Bolshoi Ballet, Bon Jovi and Kenny G.

In China, Metro has become a major producer of programming for Chinese radio, having a national programme daily on China Radio International's countrywide network, and a daily programme for the Pearl River Delta over Radio Foshan. The programmes are known as JOY FM and HIT FM, respectively, and enjoy wide popularity.

British Forces Broadcasting Service

The British Forces Broadcasting Service (BFBS) is part of the Services Sound and Vision Corporation, a worldwide organisation providing entertainment, information and training films, video, and broadcast television and radio services for the British Forces, under contract to the Ministry of Defence.

BFBS provides two radio services in Hong Kong, designed for the particular needs of the English and Gurkha service audiences.

Nepali programmes, broadcast for 90 hours each week from Sek Kong in the New Territories, cater for the Brigade of Gurkhas, providing music and features reflecting daily life with the brigade in Hong Kong, as well as providing news from Nepal and other Gurkha units throughout the British Army.

The English-language channel broadcasts 24 hours-a-day from both Sek Kong, and the Prince of Wales Barracks in Central. This service includes music, hourly news, reviews, sports coverage, quizzes and phone-in competitions. Extensive use is made of a satellite circuit from London to relay the news and BBC programmes such as *The World This Weekend* and *Sport on Radio 5*.

BFBS London has a brief to keep its overseas listeners in touch with home, and provides live overnight and weekend programmes to Hong Kong, and a number of specialist music programmes presented by some of Britain's leading broadcasting personalities.

BFBS is essentially a welfare service, and stations around the world join together each year to raise money for the Wireless for the Blind appeal and other charities.

Film Industry

Despite the popularity of video clubs and the widespread ownership of video cassette recorders, cinema-going remained a popular leisure activity. Attendances in 1993 totalled 45 million, compared with 47 million in 1992. The number of cinemas increased from 175 in 1992 to 190 in 1993. Mini-cinemas in many cases replaced large cinemas and proved popular.

While imported films continued to be popular, good quality local films were still the favourites. During the year, locally-produced films totalled 126 (including 19 co-productions) compared with 376 (including 11 co-productions) in 1992. Action films and comedies continued to dominate the market. The biggest box-office hits for the year included *Jurassic Park* which grossed $61.9 million, *Flirting Scholar* ($40.17 million), *King of Beggars* ($38.62 million) and *All's Well End's Well Too* ($35.48 million). The film *Cageman* won the Best Movie, Best Director, Best Supporting Actor and Best Screenplay awards at the 12th Hong Kong Film Awards.

Films are classified into three categories: those approved for exhibition to persons of any age (Category I); those advertised as 'not suitable for children' (Category II); and those to be exhibited only to people aged 18 years or above (Category III). Classification standards are based on the results of regular surveys of community views. A statutory panel of advisers, comprising about 300 members drawn from a wide cross-section of the community, assists in the classification process.

During the year, 1 399 films intended for public exhibition were submitted for classification, compared with 1 190 in 1992. Of these, 249 were classified Category I, 501 Category II (62 with excisions) and 649 Category III (379 with excisions). A total of 7 294 items, including video tapes, slides and laser discs, were exempted from classification.

The Film Censorship (Amendment) Ordinance 1993 was enacted in July and will come into operation in January 1994. This regulates the release of cinema films in the form of videotape and laser disc.

Postal Services

In 1993, the Hong Kong Post Office surpassed the one billion mark in mail traffic handled. A total of 1 035 million letters and parcels (a daily average of 2.8 million) were handled, representing an increase of 5.5 per cent over 1992. Approximately 10 380 tonnes of letter mail and 5 414 tonnes of parcels were despatched abroad by air — a slight decrease of

1.4 per cent from 1992. With the growth in population and the increase in business activities in the territory, the range and level of services provided by the Post Office have also multiplied.

The Speedpost service, which provides a door-to-door collection and delivery service for customers sending time-sensitive documents, samples or merchandise, continued to grow. One of the pioneers of this service, the Post Office handled 4.3 million items in 1993, an increase of 7.5 per cent over 1992. This makes the Hong Kong Post Office the third largest exporter of Speedpost in the world, after the United States Postal Service and Japan. In the case of incoming traffic, Hong Kong ranked second in the world, after the United States Postal Service. The service is now available to 61 countries, including all of the territory's major trading partners.

A high-quality postal service has been an important factor in Hong Kong's development as a leading business, financial and industrial centre. The Post Office provides two mail deliveries each weekday to commercial and industrial areas and one delivery to residential areas.

In April, the Post Office announced its performance pledges. Performance standards and targets were set for counter, delivery and Speedpost services. Most local letters are delivered within one working day after collection from a posting box or over post office counters. Bulk postings and second class mail take slightly longer. Air mail to overseas destinations is usually despatched within 24 hours of posting. Air mail arriving from overseas is normally delivered by the next working day.

During the year, Mong Kok Post Office and Sai Wan Ho Post Office moved to larger premises to provide improved facilities to cope with the rising postal demands in those districts. The counter section of Tai Po Post Office was also relocated, to release more space for the expansion of the postal delivery team serving Tai Po District. To make way for developments, Kwai Fong Post Office, The Peak Post Office and Pok Fu Lam Post Office were also relocated. For the same reason, Ma Tau Wai Post Office and Tsuen Wing Street Post Office were replaced by To Kwa Wan Post Office and Texaco Road Post Office, respectively. In addition, one new post office at Lee On Estate in Ma On Shan was opened — bringing the total number of post offices in the territory to 123.

To lower operating costs and enhance efficiency, the Post Office maintained its efforts to automate its mail-handling process. The Mechanised Letter Sorting System, introduced in mid-1990, was extended, with an order placed during the year for two additional letter sorting machines, for the Sha Tin Central Post Office and the Tuen Mun Central Post Office.

The introduction of the new electronic stamp vending machines at 10 major post offices in 1992 has proved to be a success. Another 13 post offices were provided with the new machines in 1993. In addition, six electronic stamp vending machines were installed at self-service suites located at Kowloon-Canton Railway stations and other focal points, providing greater convenience to the public. More will be ordered for installation at other post offices in the coming years.

Overall, 100 electronic scales, which can automatically calculate the postage of the mail item according to its weight and destination, were provided at the 15 busiest post offices during the year, replacing the mechanical letter scales. They are useful in reducing counter transaction time and improving accuracy. Additional scales will be purchased over the next few years, with a view to replacing all mechanical letter scales.

Studies are in hand to computerise the Speedpost acceptance and accounting procedures, as well as to improve tracking of outward mail. The feasibility of introducing a self-service automatic mailing system is also being considered.

The Post Office issued five sets of special stamps in 1993. These featured the Year of the Cock, Chinese string musical instruments, the 40th anniversary of the coronation of Her Majesty Queen Elizabeth II, science and technology in the territory and Hong Kong goldfish.

Several philatelic products were also issued during the year, including new FRAMA (electronic postage) labels for the Year of the Cock. The second Hong Kong Classics Series of definitive stamp sheets was released in July. This $10 definitive stamp sheet bore reproductions of the four special stamps issued in 1935 to commemorate the Silver Jubilee of the reign of King George V. Another definitive stamp sheet was released in August to publicise the HONG KONG '94 Stamp Exhibition to be held in February 1994. This event, which is being jointly organised by the Hong Kong Post Office, will be the first regional stamp exhibition in the territory. An attractively-designed definitive stamp sheet was issued in October to mark the participation by the Post Office in the international stamp exhibition BANGKOK '93.

22
RELIGION AND CUSTOM

IN Hong Kong, every major faith is practised in complete freedom.

Buddhist monasteries and Taoist temples co-exist with Christian churches, mosques, and Hindu and Sikh temples. All major religious bodies have established schools which offer a general education apart from religious instruction. Ancestral worship is also widely practised in Hong Kong since the local people are still greatly influenced by Confucianism which, though not a religion, teaches a moral code based on human relations.

Traditional Festivals

Many customs of the Hong Kong people are observed in their celebration of traditional Chinese festivals, which offer occasions for family union and feasting.

There are five major Chinese festivals, all of which are statutory public holidays. Foremost of these is the Lunar New Year which is celebrated, in the first few days of the first moon, with visits and gifts being exchanged between friends and relatives and children receiving 'lucky' money. The Ching Ming Festival in the spring is the traditional occasion for visiting ancestral graves. The Dragon Boat Festival is celebrated on the fifth day of the fifth moon in early summer. This festival, which was originally held in memory of an ancient Chinese poet who committed suicide by jumping into a river, has developed into a joyous event characterised by dragon boat races and the eating of rice dumplings cooked in lotus leaves.

The Mid-Autumn Festival falls on the 15th day of the eighth moon and gifts of mooncakes, fruit and wine are exchanged. Adults and children carry colourful lanterns to the parks and countryside at night to have a picnic supper and appreciate the full moon. The Chung Yeung Festival, on the ninth day of the ninth moon, is another occasion for visiting ancestral graves. Many people celebrate the festival by climbing hills in remembrance of an ancient Chinese family which fled to the top of a high mountain to escape plague and death.

Buddhism and Taoism

Buddhists from around the world celebrated a milestone event in the territory at the end of the year. On December 29, thousands gathered at the Po Lin Monastery on Lantau Island to inaugurate the Tian Tan Buddha — the largest outdoor bronze statue of Buddha in the world.

Buddhism and Taoism, the leading Chinese religions, maintain a strong hold on the population, especially among older folk.

There are about 360 Chinese temples in Hong Kong. Some temples are centuries old, built by fishermen or early settlers. Because of the short supply of land, some temples are established in multi-storey buildings to cater for the spiritual needs of smaller circles of city-dwellers.

All Chinese temples are required to be registered under the Chinese Temples Ordinance. The Chinese Temples Committee manages some 40 public temples and the income, from donations by worshippers, is used for preservation and restoration not only of public temples but also privately-owned ones of historical value. Any surplus is put towards a charity fund.

Each temple is dedicated to one or two deities whose images are enshrined in the main hall, with side halls housing images of subsidiary deities. Since Buddhism and Taoism are both accepted as traditional Chinese religions, Buddhist and Taoist deities are often honoured together within one temple. Leading deities include Buddha, Kwun Yum (the Buddhist Goddess of Mercy), and Lui Cho (a Taoist god).

There is also a diversity of deified mortals traditionally worshipped as a result of their performance of actual or mythical feats. Foremost of these is Tin Hau, the Queen of Heaven and Protectress of Seafarers, worshipped originally by the fishing population but now by others in the community as well — reflecting Hong Kong's dependence on fishing and trade by sea. There are at least 24 Tin Hau temples in Hong Kong, the most famous being the one in Joss House Bay, which is visited by tens of thousands of worshippers each year during the Tin Hau Festival on the 23rd day of the third moon.

Other deified mortals include Kwan Tai, the God of War and Righteousness; Pak Tai, lord of the North and Patron of Cheung Chau Island; Hung Shing, God of the South Seas and weather prophet; and Wong Tai Sin, a Taoist deity, in whose honour a 72-year-old temple, built in traditional Chinese architectural style in northeastern Kowloon, enjoys great popularity. Dedicated to the gods of literary attainment and martial valour, Man Mo Temple in Hollywood Road on Hong Kong Island is also very popular. It is run by the Tung Wah Group of Hospitals, a charitable organisation. The Che Kung Temple at Sha Tin in the New Territories is dedicated to a general in the Sung Dynasty.

Protestant Community

The presence of the Protestant community dates back to 1841. In the 150 years since the first Protestant church came into being, the community has grown to 258 000 in over 900 congregations which comprise 52 denominations and independent churches. The Baptists form the largest denomination followed by the Lutherans. Other major denominations are the Adventist, Anglican, Christian and Missionary Alliance, Church of Christ in China (representing the Presbyterian and Congregational traditions), Methodist and Pentecostal. With their emphasis on youth work, many congregations have a high proportion of young people. Since the 1970s, the number of independent churches has increased significantly due to the strong evangelical zeal of lay Christians.

The Protestant churches are also deeply involved in education, health care and social welfare. Protestant organisations operate three post-secondary colleges — Chung Chi College at the Chinese University of Hong Kong, Hong Kong Baptist College and Lingnan College. They run 122 secondary schools, 141 primary schools and 146 kindergartens. In addition, they operate 13 theological seminaries and Bible institutes, 16 Christian publishing houses and 57 Christian book shops.

They also run seven hospitals with 2 126 beds, 24 clinics and 61 social service organisations that provide a wide range of social services, including 108 community and youth centres, 35 day care-centres, eight children's homes, 27 homes for the elderly, 78 centres for the elderly, three schools for the deaf, 10 training centres for the mentally handicapped and 20 camp sites. Five international hotel-type guest houses are managed by the YMCA and YWCA.

Ninety-six para-church agencies and various Christian action groups have been established to minister to the needs of the Protestant community and to respond to current issues and concerns in Hong Kong society at large. The church is involved in overseas aid by supporting emergency relief and development projects in third world countries. The 'Five Loaves and Two Fish' campaign, sponsored by the Hong Kong Christian Council, was the first overseas aid project initiated in Hong Kong. Two weekly newspapers, *The Christian Weekly* and *The Christian Times*, bring news and comments from a Christian perspective to the Christian community.

Two ecumenical bodies facilitate co-operative work among the Protestant churches in Hong Kong. The older of the two, dating back to 1915, is the Hong Kong Chinese Christian Churches Union with a membership of 259 congregations. The second co-operative body is the Hong Kong Christian Council, formed in 1954. Major mainline denominations and ecumenical services constitute the membership core of the council, which is committed to building closer relationships among all churches in Hong Kong as well as with churches overseas, and with encouraging local Christians to play an active part in the development of Hong Kong society. It seeks to serve the wider community through its auxiliary agencies such as the Hong Kong Christian Service, Christian Industrial Committee, United Christian Hospital, Pamela Youde Nethersole Eastern Hospital and the Christian Family Service Centre. The council runs weekly 'Alternative Tours', which give visitors and residents an opportunity to see how the church is serving the community.

In the area of social concern, the Protestant community has played an active role in arousing public interest in Hong Kong's democratic development and has supported such issues as labour welfare and the guarantee of human rights in Hong Kong in the future.

Roman Catholic Community

The Roman Catholic Church has been present in Hong Kong since the territory's early days. The church was established as a mission prefecture in 1841 and as an apostolic vicariate in 1874. It became a diocese in 1946.

In 1969, Francis Chen-peng Hsu was installed as the first Chinese bishop of the Hong Kong diocese, and he was succeeded in 1973 by Peter Wang-kei Lei. The present bishop, John Baptist Cheng-chung Wu, was consecrated in 1975, and was made Cardinal in 1988.

About 249 180 people, or five per cent of the population, are Catholics. They are served by 253 priests, 64 brothers, and 632 sisters. There are 63 parishes and 34 centres for Mass. The majority of the services and other religious activities are conducted in Chinese, with a few churches providing services in English.

The diocese has established its own administrative structure while maintaining traditional links with the Pope and with other Catholic communities around the world. It uses the same scriptures and has similar ecclesial communions as in the universal Church throughout the world, with which it maintains close fellowship. The assistant secretary-general of the Federation of Asian Bishops' Conference has his office in Hong Kong.

Christmas lights make a spectacular appearance in early December, signalling the start of a dazzling nightly display that continues, with progressive updates in the designs and message content, through to the Lunar New Year.

Fireworks in Victoria Harbour are an established tradition at the Lunar New Year, along with buying a peach tree in blossom **(below),** *to bring good fortune.*

St.Valentine's Day is gaining rapidly in popularity each year, with this happy couple **(above)** *selecting the festival as an auspicious time to embark upon marriage.*

Left: *Mid-Autumn Festival is an outright favourite with youngsters, for its lanterns, night-time picnics, moon cakes, and entitlement to stay-up late.*

As a spin-off from the traditional Dragon Boat Festival, the Hong Kong Dragon Boat Festival—International Races were staged in early July, for the 18th consecutive year, attracting 30 overseas and 129 local crews.

HONG
KONG

San Miguel

Above and right: *Hong Kong's close links with the sea guarantee the Tin Hau Festival is always one of the year's most colourful and noisy events, for this is the birthday of the Queen of Heaven and Protectress of Seafarers.*

Opposite page: *Captivated by the atmosphere and pageantry of the Tin Hau Festival, people of many nationalities join the crowds.*

(一) 進人廟內
寶燭一律不得帶入廟
燭請在廟前露

Every 10 years, villagers of Yuen Long **(above)** *celebrate Ta Chiu Festival, to thank the deities and request continued protection.*

Right: *Halloween antics in Central.*

Along with its apostolic work, one of the prime concerns of the diocese has been for the well-being of all the people of Hong Kong. In education, there are 270 Catholic schools and kindergartens, which have about 315 353 pupils. The Catholic Board of Education assists in this area. The medical and social services include six hospitals, 13 clinics, 17 social centres, seven hostels, 29 homes for the aged, one home for the handicapped and many self-help clubs and associations. Caritas is the official social welfare arm of the church in Hong Kong.

These services are open to all people — indeed, 95 per cent of those who have benefited from the wide range of services provided by the diocese are not Catholics.

To reach people through the media, the diocese publishes two weekly newspapers, *Kung Kao Po* and *The Sunday Examiner*. In addition, the Diocesan Audio-Visual Centre produces tapes and films for use in schools and parishes and the Hong Kong Catholic Social Communications Office acts as an overall information and public relations channel for the diocese.

Muslim Community

There are about 50 000 Muslims in Hong Kong. More than half of them are Chinese with the rest being either locally-born non-Chinese or believers from Pakistan, India, Malaysia, Indonesia and Middle Eastern and African countries. Four principal mosques are used daily for prayers. The oldest is the Jamia Mosque in Shelley Street on Hong Kong Island, which was built before the turn of the century and rebuilt in 1915. It can accommodate a congregation of 400.

Also on Hong Kong Island is the Masjid Ammar and Osman Ramju Sadick Islamic Centre. Opened in 1981, this eight-storey centre in Wan Chai houses a mosque on two floors, a community hall, a library, a medical clinic, classrooms and offices. The mosque, which is managed by the Islamic Union of Hong Kong, can accommodate 700 people but up to 1 500, if necessary, by using other available space in the centre.

Situated on what is sometimes called the 'Golden Mile' in Nathan Road is the Kowloon Mosque and Islamic Centre, which was opened in May 1984 and which replaced an old mosque built in 1896. This imposing building, with white marble finishing, is a distinctive landmark in Tsim Sha Tsui. The mosque can accommodate a congregation of about 2 000 and has, in addition to the three prayer halls, a community hall, a medical clinic and a library.

There are two Muslim cemeteries, both on Hong Kong Island — one at Happy Valley and the other at Cape Collinson, Chai Wan. The Cape Collinson cemetery also has a mosque.

The co-ordinating body for all Islamic religious affairs is the Incorporated Trustees of the Islamic Community Fund of Hong Kong. A board of trustees nominated by the Islamic Union of Hong Kong, the Pakistan Association, the Indian Muslim Association and the Dawoodi Bohra Association, is responsible for the management and maintenance of mosques and cemeteries. The trustees are also responsible for organising the celebration of Muslim festivals and other religious events. Charitable work among the Muslim community, including financial aid for the needy, medical facilities and assisted education, is conducted through various local Muslim organisations.

Hindu Community

The religious and social activities of Hong Kong's 12 000-strong Hindu community are centred on the Hindu Temple in Happy Valley. The Hindu Association of Hong Kong is responsible for the upkeep of the temple, which is also used for meditation periods, yoga classes and other community activities. Naming, engagement and marriage ceremonies are performed at the temple according to Hindu rites. Devotional music sessions and religious discourses are held every Sunday morning and Monday evening. The Sunday sessions are followed by a free community meal.

The Hindu Temple is an approved place of worship for the performance of marriages and the issue of marriage certificates under the Marriage Ordinance.

The temple is frequently visited by swamis and learned men from overseas who deliver spiritual lectures. All major Hindu festivals are observed, the more important ones being *Holi*, the *Birth of Lord Krishna*, *Shivaratri*, *Dussehra* and *Diwali*.

Other important services are the administration of last rites and arranging for cremation and related ceremonies. The temple is also responsible for the upkeep of the Hindu crematorium at Cape Collinson.

Sikh Community

The Sikhs — distinguished by their stylised turbans and unshorn hair — first came to Hong Kong from the Punjab, in North India, as part of the British Armed Forces in the 19th century. Because of their generally strong physique, they also comprised a large segment of the Royal Hong Kong Police Force before World War II.

Today, members of the community are engaged in a variety of occupations. The centre of their religious and cultural activities is the Sikh Temple at 371 Queen's Road East, Wan Chai, Hong Kong. A special feature of the temple, which was established in 1901, is the provision of free meals and short-term accommodation for overseas visitors of any faith. Religious services, which include hymn-singing, readings from the *Guru Granth* (the Sikh Holy Book) and sermons by the priest, are held every Sunday morning. The temple also houses a library containing a good selection of books on the Sikh religion and culture, and runs a 'starters' school for Indian children aged between four and six to prepare them for English primary schools in Hong Kong.

The main holy days and festivals observed are the birthdays of Guru Nanak (founder of the faith), Guru Gobind Singh (the 10th Guru) and *Baisakhi* (birthday of all Sikhs).

Jewish Community

Hong Kong's Jewish community — comprising families from various parts of the world — worships on Friday evenings, Saturday mornings and Jewish holidays at the Synagogue *Ohel Leah* in Robinson Road, Hong Kong Island. The synagogue was built in 1901 on land given by Sir Jacob Sassoon and his family. The original site included a Rabbi's residence and school, as well as a recreation club for the 1 000 people in the congregation. There is also a Jewish Cemetery, which is located at Happy Valley.

The site adjoining the synagogue, which once housed the school and club, is currently under reconstruction and the club has been temporarily relocated in Melbourne Plaza, Central. It has two restaurants serving Kosher meals prepared under rabbinical supervision, from 8 am to 11 pm daily, and a specialist library with information on the history of Judaism in Hong Kong and China.

Other Faiths

As well as the major religions practised in Hong Kong, faiths such as that of the Baha'is and Zoroastrianism have also found their place here.

23
RECREATION, SPORTS AND THE ARTS

IMPROVING recreational, sporting and cultural facilities has helped to enhance the quality of life in Hong Kong.

The territory's residents have access to a wide range of leisure activities. Many of these are provided by the Urban and Regional Councils, which are autonomous bodies empowered to formulate policies for the provision and management of cultural and recreational facilities in their respective areas. They build and operate games halls and pitches, swimming pools and parks, museums, libraries and other recreational facilities, as well as organising and supporting a host of cultural, sporting and recreational activities.

The government's policies on recreation, sport, culture and heritage matters are co-ordinated by the Recreation and Culture Branch headed by the Secretary for Recreation and Culture. He is assisted by several expert bodies, including the Council for the Performing Arts, Antiquities Advisory Board, Sports Development Board and Hong Kong Sports Institute. Many other individuals and associations play an essential role in creating and improving opportunities for fulfilling sports and leisure activities in Hong Kong.

Highlights of the year included the setting up of the Hong Kong Film Archive, which is scheduled to be completed by 1997, and the opening in July of the Regional Council's computerised central library in Tsuen Wan, the largest public library in Hong Kong. Work on the redevelopment of the Hong Kong Stadium continued to make good progress. The stadium, which will give Hong Kong world class facilities for staging large-scale sporting and other spectator events, will be ready for use in early 1994. A horse-riding school was completed in Tuen Mun at the end of the year and will also be opened to the public in early 1994. Other innovations during the year were the Urban Council's first Green Hong Kong campaign and the Regional Council's Greening Scheme.

There were other multifaceted events which have become traditional and which, over the years, have gone from strength to strength, always developing and improving. These included the 17th Hong Kong International Film Festival and the 12th International Arts Carnival.

Promoting Hong Kong's heritage, the Regional Council, with the assistance of the Heung Yee Kuk, launched a highly successful New Territories Relics Collection Campaign in March. The 5 000-plus items collected during the campaign period will be exhibited in the Heritage Museum planned for Sha Tin.

There were also important developments in the organisational structures for both sports and the arts. Proposals were brought forward for the integration of the Sports

Development Board and Hong Kong Sports Institute to ensure that local resources in the sports field are deployed in the most cost-effective manner for the further development of sports and the training of Hong Kong athletes for international events.

In March, the Recreation and Culture Branch published a review of the arts policy which evoked a lively response from the community. It was concluded that Hong Kong has now reached a new stage of development in culture and the arts, the needs of which can best be served by a statutory arts council. Such a council would replace the Council for the Performing Arts, not only providing more effective and strategic support to the performing arts but also allowing for the needs of other art fora, such as the visual and literary arts, to be addressed. A working group was appointed by the Governor in October to prepare for the establishment of the Provisional Arts Development Council in early 1994.

The Arts

In world terms, Hong Kong's arts community is still in its youth, with all the characteristics of dynamism, new ideas and rapid growth which that implies. While talent and creativity have always been present, it is only in recent years that, with financial support from both the public and private sectors, the arts community has been able to capitalise on its creativity and increase the number and range of its activities. As a result, there are now two professional orchestras, three full-time dance companies, three professional drama groups and hundreds of amateur groups, including orchestras, bands, choirs, dance groups and drama clubs. The Urban and Regional Councils run arts venues throughout Hong Kong, so that access to cultural presentations is no longer confined to people living in the main urban areas. The two councils have also become patrons of the arts in their own right, either by funding performing groups directly, or assisting them with presentations.

The government's arts policy review consultation document, in March, provided a survey of the state of arts development over the past decade, highlighting achievements and problems and making recommendations on the way forward. Almost 600 responses were received from the arts community during the three-month consultation period (ending on June 30) and these were both substantial and well considered. This consultation exercise proved most useful in providing an open, widespread and healthy debate on the future of the arts. While diverse opinions on many aspects were expressed, there was broad consensus on the key recommendations that the government's responsibilities for arts development should be expanded to include the visual and literary arts and that a statutory arts council should be established.

In response to the feedback collected during the consultation exercise, the government decided to move forward quickly towards the establishment of a new statutory and independent body named the Hong Kong Arts Development Council for the further development of the arts in general, and to provide a capital grant of $100 million, in addition to the existing resources spent on the arts, to the council. To this end, a working group was appointed by the Governor in October. Its target is to enable the new council to commence functioning as a non-statutory advisory body on April 1, 1994, with a view to its future transformation into a statutory body with executive powers with effect from April 1, 1995.

Council for the Performing Arts

The government's support for the performing arts is co-ordinated by the Secretary for Recreation and Culture, on the advice of the Council for the Performing Arts. The council, which comprises 15 appointed and two official members, is responsible for advising the government on the development of the performing arts and the disbursement of funds on performing arts activities. It has expert committees on specific aspects of the arts, including music, drama, dance, arts services and Chinese opera, and also advises on general issues such as business sponsorship, promotion of performing arts in schools and audience-building.

The council continued its efforts to promote business sponsorship through the matching grant scheme, under which arts groups receive a dollar for each dollar of business sponsorship they secure, up to a maximum of $100,000 for each project. With the objective of promoting local talent, a competition for original script-writing was held for the third consecutive year. A reception was held by the council in June at which business sponsors were honoured with commemorative certificates and awards were presented to the winners of the script-writing competition. The occasion was also used to announce the findings of a survey commissioned by the council on the population's attitude to the arts. The survey provided empirical data for planning and resource allocation for performing arts development. A summary of the survey findings was sent to major performing arts groups in Hong Kong for reference. Conscious of the need for audience-building, the council sponsored a conference organised by the Arts Resource and Information Centre on developing future arts audiences in October. The conference was well attended by representatives of performing arts companies and school principals.

On the advice of the council, five performing arts organisations — the Chung Ying Theatre Company, the Hong Kong Ballet, the City Contemporary Dance Company, the Exploration Theatre and the Hong Kong Arts Festival — received general support grants totalling about $31.1 million in 1993–94. In addition, $1.5 million was awarded to the Hong Kong Sinfonietta as a seeding grant and about $4.1 million to other local performing arts groups as grants for individual projects.

The rapid emergence of numerous small performing arts companies in recent years has led to increased demands for financial support from government. To meet these demands and to further enhance the development of the arts, in May, the government established an Arts Development Fund under the Sir David Trench Fund for Recreation with the injection of a capital grant of $30 million. The money is disbursed by the Secretary for Recreation and Culture on the council's advice.

Performing Groups

Hong Kong Philharmonic Orchestra

The Hong Kong Philharmonic Orchestra, funded by the Urban Council with contributions from major business corporations, began its 18th professional season under the leadership of its Music Director, David Atherton. The orchestra's Principal Guest Conductor is Kenneth Jean and the Resident Conductor is Yip Wing-sie.

In addition to its regular season and school concerts in the Hong Kong Cultural Centre, the City Hall and the New Territories, the orchestra made its first — and highly successful — visit to Taiwan in May.

The second half of the 1992–93 season featured an unusual *Double Delight* series of four concerts, each with two soloists either in collaboration with another artist or performing a solo concerto. Well-known artists who appeared included British pianists Peter Donohoe and Martin Roscoe.

The *Atherton and Friends* series brought the season to a splendid close with three renowned string instrumentalists playing solo, double or triple concertos during four weekends, giving Hong Kong audiences the opportunity to enjoy some of the most popular, and several rarely-heard, string masterpieces.

Highlights of the first half of the 1992–93 season were the appearances of internationally-acclaimed artists such as French horn player Barry Tuckwell, tenor Robert Tear, pianist John Lill and organist Peter Hurford.

The year also saw the release of an educational music video featuring Saint-Saens' *Carnival of the Animals*, a melange of animated puppets and theatre. The video was the first such family video shown in Hong Kong.

Hong Kong Repertory Theatre

The Hong Kong Repertory Theatre staged nine productions in 121 performances in 1993, attracting 55 820 people.

Two of the productions, Shakespeare's *King Lear* and Jerry Sterner's *Other People's Money*, were staged in Cantonese and Putonghua and directed by the company's Artistic Director, Daniel Yang. A revival production and a new production, both on Hong Kong themes and written by the company's Playwright-in-Residence, Raymond To, were also featured. The others were mostly translated plays.

Apart from staging its regular productions, the company also toured schools and community centres regularly, giving free performances, lecture-demonstrations and workshops. In 1993, the company gave 62 such performances to a total audience of 15 000.

Hong Kong Chinese Orchestra

The Hong Kong Chinese Orchestra is Hong Kong's only professional Chinese music orchestra.

In 1993, the 85-member orchestra celebrated its 16th professional season and gave 106 performances under the baton of its new Music Director, Henry Shek, and various local and overseas guest conductors, attracting 90 196 people.

Apart from regular concerts, the orchestra presented ensemble concerts, participated in district arts festivals, and organised free outreach performances at community arts centres and schools. In November, the orchestra gave two performances in Guangzhou, China.

Recognised as one of the world's leading Chinese orchestras, it explores new frontiers in Chinese music by experimenting with new techniques and styles. The orchestra has continued to expand its repertoire by commissioning new works by both local and overseas composers.

Hong Kong Dance Company

The Hong Kong Dance Company is the only professional Chinese dance company in the territory to present Chinese traditional and folk dances and full-length dance dramas choreographed on Chinese and Hong Kong themes.

In 1993, the company presented five productions — a new dance drama choreographed by the company's Rehearsal Master Leung Kwok-shing, two revivals, a dancers' choreography showcase and a dance showcase of the minority nationalities of China. A total of 21 performances were staged, attracting 12 945 people. In addition, the company also gave free performances and lecture-demonstrations, in schools and community arts centres, to 39 800 people.

The Chung Ying Theatre Company

The Chung Ying Theatre Company continued to serve local audiences of all ages with the ongoing support of the Council for the Performing Arts. In 1993, the company once again presented locally-commissioned works, continuing to encourage local playwrights and directors. The first local work was *The Legend of a Storyteller*, by Cheung Tat-ming, in collaboration with guest director Fredric Mao, for the 1993 Hong Kong Arts Festival. The second was *Taxi Driver* by James Cheung, directed by Suen Wai-fong as part of Chung Ying's Studio Shorts '93 at the Hong Kong Arts Centre's Shouson Theatre. Finally, the company introduced young playwright Annie Chan to local audiences in June, with her first work *Ah Mew's Move*, directed by Wong Yuen-ling at the City Hall Theatre.

The company also devised original works as part of an internal programme to extend and develop the performing skills of its members. Drawing upon techniques explored during a period of study leave last year, veteran Chung Ying Director and actor Lee Chun-chow worked with other company members to create the unique production *Oops! Back Again* in September at the Shouson Theatre. Guest Director Gerry Flanagan, who had previously worked with Chung Ying to devise the popular clowning production *Fools, Fools, Fools*, returned to the company in November to direct a newly-devised mask production *Don't Let Go!*

A further highlight of 1993 for Chung Ying was an invitation to participate in the Vancouver Children's Festival, an international showcase of work for young audiences. The company presented *Monkey See Monkey Do*, directed by Artistic Director Chris Johnson, in Vancouver and at related festivals in Calgary and Saskatoon — a total of 21 performances. The production returned in August to play at the Hong Kong Cultural Centre's Fun Week.

Another theatre work in the 1993 programme for young audiences was *Whale* by David Holman, directed by Chris Johnson at the Sai Wan Ho Civic Centre for July's International Carnival. The unique feature of this production was the appearance on stage of 30 local children with Chung Ying's players.

The company continued its school touring programme with Canadian playwright Dennis Foon's *Skin*, which toured secondary schools before being presented on stage as part of Studio Shorts '93. The popular story-telling and story-building programme introduced by the company continued to be a success throughout 1993, with presentations at venues as varied as Ocean Park, schools and regional centres.

City Contemporary Dance Company

The City Contemporary Dance Company, Hong Kong's first professional modern dance company, participated in the Hong Kong Arts Festival 1993 with the dance production *Quadrille*. This featured original music compositions and dance works by eight local professional choreographers and composers. A multi-media concert *Box Side 10 — Lock Head Jig* performed jointly with The Box, an experimental pop music group, was presented in March. *Journey to the West*, a family dance drama, choreographed by Artistic Director Willy Tsao, was re-staged at the Hong Kong Academy for the Performing Arts' Lyric Theatre in the summer. A new version of *Journey to the West — The Red Baby King* was also commissioned by the Regional Council for the Christmas and New Year holiday seasons.

The company collaborated with overseas dance artists from Columbia, the United States and Australia in its productions of *Solid Longing*, *Chronicle of a Floating City* and *Tales of a Middle Kingdom* to promote cultural links with overseas dance communities.

The company also continued to hold evening dance classes and to tour primary and secondary schools to develop audiences. Other audience-building projects included the staging of the jazz ballet programme *City Romance* at various civic centres, and the organisation of *Modern Dance Performance Workshops*, sponsored by the Regional Council, to promote dance education and appreciation.

Hong Kong Ballet

The year was an exciting one for the Hong Kong Ballet under the artistic direction of Bruce Steivel, who has focussed on the development of the company both at home and abroad. In 1993, the Hong Kong Ballet toured the east coast of the United States for the first time. The company also performed in Macau in October. These events provided useful feedback for the company as its performances were measured against the international standards of dance today.

At home, the Hong Kong Ballet premiered a new full-length ballet *Cinderella* for the Hong Kong Arts Festival in February, commissioned by the Regional Council, and also two one-act ballets *The Strangers* and *Danses Concertantes*. *The Strangers* employed local talents throughout, from choreography to music composition. The Regional Council also commissioned the company's staging of *La Sylphide and Napoli Divertissements* for its International Children's Arts Festival. The company experimented with the concept of a ballet season in September, staging *Cinderella* and a triple bill *Contemporanza*, jointly presented with the Urban Council. The company was also invited to give two public performances at Government House. Audiences enjoyed an exciting and entertaining year, which concluded with the staging of the world's most popular ballet *The Nutcracker*.

The outreach activities of the company's education unit, which included participatory courses, workshops and special theatre performances, continued to cater for the growing audiences of ballet throughout the territory.

The Exploration Theatre

Established in 1982, the Exploration Theatre was the first theatrical company supported by the Council for the Performing Arts under the seeding grant scheme in 1989. The artistic merit and the professional standard attained by the company in the intervening years won the recognition of the council when it elevated the company to general support grant status in 1993 for the first time.

The company continued to promote local original works. Its Easter production *Ah Dum's Family*, written by local playwright Cheung Tat-ming, was a successful satirical black comedy. *What About Marrying Me*?, written by Mok Hei, was a light comedy which depicted with subtlety and humour the theme of love today. Two shorter original works, written by new playwright Fung Kin-sun and Cheung Tat-ming, were also brought to audiences in the New Territories in the winter season.

In summer, the company successfully brought together dramatists James Mark, Mok Yan-lan and Hardy Tsoi, to act in its August production *Driving Miss Daisy*, directed by Chung King-fai.

On the educational front, the company took its original works *Green Life* and *Dear Papa & Mama* to 76 schools and colleges, and organised over 22 acting workshops for young people and schools.

Hong Kong Sinfonietta
The Hong Kong Sinfonietta, which comprises young local musicians, was established in 1990. The Sinfonietta has been supported by the Council for the Performing Arts under the seeding grant scheme since 1991. Apart from providing performance opportunities for local musicians, it also offers orchestral support to local performing groups. Its repertoire includes traditional orchestral pieces and works by local composers.

The Sinfonietta has accompanied many performing groups, such as the Hong Kong Oratorio Society, the Bolshoi Ballet, the Hong Kong Ballet and the Pacific Chorale.

Its 1993 concerts included the *Outstanding Young Local Talent Concerts* and *Angelic Melody*. The Sinfonietta also presented student concerts and foyer performances. In August, the Sinfonietta accompanied the Hong Kong Oratorio Society in two successful concerts in Xiamen in China, becoming the first two Hong Kong performing groups to have toured China together.

Hong Kong Academy for Performing Arts
As Hong Kong's major tertiary institution for vocational training in the performing arts, the Hong Kong Academy for Performing Arts aims to foster and provide training, education and research in the performing and technical arts, and houses some of the territory's premier arts venues, a library and a television complex. Emphasis is placed on both Western and Chinese traditions in the performing arts. The academy has been accredited by the Hong Kong Council for Academic Accreditation and it brings together under one roof schools of dance, drama, music, and theatre and television arts.

The School of Dance trains dancers in ballet, Chinese dance, modern dance, and musical theatre dance. The School of Drama prepares actors, directors and playwrights for the theatre and television. The School of Music provides professional training in Chinese and Western music for players, singers and composers. The School of Technical Arts prepares students for careers in theatre and television including management; directing; costume, set, sound and lighting design; property-making and set construction.

The central core of the academy's teaching programme are the full-time degree, advanced diploma, diploma and certificate courses. Bachelor of Fine Arts degree courses have recently been introduced, and the academy is planning to introduce Masters degree programmes in the near future.

In the 1993–94 academic year, 584 students were enrolled in full-time courses and 812 students in junior courses in dance and music for talented young people of school age. Continuing education in dance for evening part-time students was also offered by the School of Dance on a seasonal basis.

The School of Dance enjoyed a busy academic year. The main event was the Graduation Concert held in the Lyric Theatre in May, followed by a performance in Guangzhou. Other productions included creative projects in February and March, a faculty concert in March, a repertory concert in May and, with the School of Music, a Rodgers and Hammerstein evening in June. The School of Dance also participated in the Japan Asia Dance Event '93 in Tokyo during the summer. The major dance event of autumn was *Animal Fantasies*, designed to appeal particularly to young audiences.

In March, the School of Drama mounted one of the academy's major productions of the year — the Broadway musical *West Side Story*. The school also presented three Directing and Design Majors productions including Max Fisch's *The Chinese Wall* in January, Marc Camoletti's *Happy Birthday* in March and William Gibson's *The Miracle Worker* in May. An adaptation of four of the Wakefield mystery plays, *Looking For Rainbow*, was also staged in May. The production was then taken to San Francisco and Los Angeles as part of a summer study tour. Special Guest Director Travis Preston was invited from the United States to direct Jean Genet's *The Balcony* in November. The school received many honours at the 2nd Hong Kong Drama Awards. A total of 12 prizes out of 27 were awarded to academy staff and graduates.

During the year, the academy gave a highly successful series of concerts at Government House at the invitation of the Governor, who regularly joined the packed audiences of over 300, drawn from all over the territory. In March and April, the School of Music presented a highly-acclaimed performance of Handel's opera *Semele*. The next operatic venture comprised scenes from Mozart's *The Magic Flute* and Massenet's *Werther*, marking the opening of the two-week long Summer Music Festival of concerts and recitals given by students of the academy. Monday lunch-time concerts and Friday piano departmental concerts continued as established features of academy musical life, while another series of Young Professional Musicians Platform concerts offered varied programmes of Chinese and European music. The opera performance at the end of the year was one of Mozart's happiest and most tuneful works *Marriage of Figaro*. Academy composition students also distinguished themselves, receiving all five awards in the Hong Kong Composers' Guild New Generation '93 Competition.

The School of Technical Arts (Theatre) was involved in all the dance, drama and opera productions, with design and management students contributing significantly to the success of many events. A Technical Arts Graduation Exhibition '93 was organised by students before their graduation in June. The *Sunset Pop Concert*, produced by sound and lighting students, was held in the Drama Theatre in June before a full house. The school also participated in a study tour of Italy and Greece during the summer.

The Division of Technical Arts (TV/Film) expanded its activities significantly. Students and staff participated in several significant interactions with the academy's other schools through exercises involving videotaping various academy productions.

Business for Art

Business for Art is a non-profit organisation established in 1990 by a group of prominent business people in Hong Kong to encourage, assist and promote local arts in all forms to enrich the cultural life in the territory. It supports projects and programmes that draw public attention to cultural activities and bring the visual, creative and performing arts not only to those with cultivated tastes but also to those who might otherwise not be exposed to the arts. Business for Art also helps young artists to establish themselves and promotes opportunities for displaying their work.

The organisation published the *Arts Patron* quarterly bilingual magazine to promote business sponsorship and arts projects. *Arts Patron* was distributed to business, arts and media organisations and individuals in Hong Kong as well as overseas.

Sponsored by Business for Art, two scholarships were set up to support interested persons or professionals in the field of art administration and museum study, to do an attachment at the Museum of Contemporary Art in Ghent for three months in early 1994.

Hong Kong Arts Centre

Hong Kong Arts Centre is an independent, non-profit organisation founded in 1977 to promote arts and culture. Its funding is derived from rental income, box office receipts, corporate sponsorship and donations from individuals. It incorporates the 439-seat Shouson Theatre, the 193-seat Lim Por Yen Film Theatre, the 80-seat McAulay Studio, the Pao Sui Loong and Pao Yue Kong Galleries, the Atrium Gallery, rehearsal rooms, art and craft studios, music practice rooms and classrooms.

As a multi-discipline arts organisation, Hong Kong Arts Centre offers a platform for contemporary work in the performing, visual and cinematic arts as well as featuring new, *avant garde* and multi-media art forms. It encourages the work of non-established artists of all disciplines and the development of indigenous art forms. Resources are also dedicated to outreach work in arts education offered by established artists, art historians and theorists, to promote the appreciation of all art forms and activities.

In 1993, the centre was visited by over 993 000 people, many of whom attended the 925 stage and screen performances, 81 exhibitions and 525 arts-related classes and courses held within its venues. Highlights of the year included the exhibitions *China's New Art — Post 1989; the Art of Jörge Immendorff; Art in Belgium: Cyclic Identity; Cries and Whispers; British Paintings of the 1980s; Guan Wai Lung: the King of Calendar Painting*; the film programmes *The Great Japanese Animator: Osamu Tezuka; A Tribute to Jean-Pierre Melville & Pedro Almodovar Retrospective*; and the education programmes *Summer Art Camp 93; School of Visual Arts; New York Co-presentation: A Study of Digital Culture.*

British Council

One of the aims of the British Council in Hong Kong is to foster cultural understanding between Britain and Hong Kong through a balanced programme of music, drama, dance, exhibitions, film shows and related masterclasses and workshops catering to the interests of local residents. The council works in conjunction with local organisations and supports collaborative projects between British artists and local performing companies.

In 1993, the council jointly organised a number of arts events, including the Royal Shakespeare Company's performance of *The Comedy of Errors*; the debut of Adventures in Motion Pictures, an exciting British modern dance company; the opera *Der Rosenkavalier*, produced by Stephen Lawless for the Hong Kong Arts Festival; and several acts in the Hong Kong Festival Fringe. It also arranged a visit by Peter Blake to coincide with a pop art exhibition of his works; a visit by Gerry Flanagan to direct *Don't Let Go!* for the Chung Ying Theatre Company; a Film Week featuring the best of current British productions; and a jazz cabaret by the Westbrook Trio.

Cultural Events

Hong Kong Arts Festival

Founded in 1973, the annual Hong Kong Arts Festival brings a rich artistic experience to the people of Hong Kong. More than 1 000 artists and off-stage staff participated in the 1993 festival, which lasted 23 days and presented a total of 38 programmes. Over 100 000 people attended the 145 performances held at 16 venues throughout Hong Kong.

Among the many distinguished international stars and companies appearing in the festival were the Spanish tenor Jose Carreras, Irish flautist James Galway, the Borodin String Quartet, the Paris Opera Ballet and the Royal Shakespeare Company.

Other highlights of the festival included traditional music and dance from Tibet, water puppets from Vietnam, Butoh dance founder Kazuo Ohno, a silent film *Napoleon*, lasting five-and-a-half hours, and an exhibition of *New Art in China Post '89*. The renowned Camerata Salzburg and Oslo Philharmonic Orchestra made their Hong Kong debuts, while New York's Ensemble for Early Music made a welcomed return to present Monteverdi's masterpieces.

The *Fantasy in the Arts* series examined the important role which fantasy plays in artistic creation. Programmes included the special opera production of Richard Strauss' *Der Rosenkavalier*, the ballet classics *Cinderella* and *Don Quixote*, the dance *Deadly Serious*, the Shakespearean play *The Comedy of Errors*, as well as performances by mime magician Jeff McBride, the Polivka Theatre Company and Velo Theatre.

Hong Kong's most distinguished musicians were presented in a series of four concerts, and The Group of Experimental Cantonese Opera Hong Kong offered a unique reinterpretation of a popular Kunju opera.

Hong Kong Festival Fringe

Since its founding 11 years ago, the Festival Fringe has developed from an annual open arts festival into a successful year-round operation that gives the emerging artists of Hong Kong the opportunity to hone their skills and create new works.

The 1993 Festival Fringe, staged over three weeks in January and February, was attended by some 300 000 people. Over 200 groups and individual artists from Hong Kong and overseas took part.

Operating from the Fringe Club, the Festival Fringe staff also organised and mounted new shows, exhibitions, workshops and an active outreach programme. The Fringe Club houses two studio theatres, exhibition galleries, a pottery studio with showroom, rehearsal studios, a restaurant, a bar and offices.

Urban Council Presentations

To offer cultural programmes for people of all ages, the Urban Council presented a wide variety of performances by local and overseas artists in 1993. A total of 308 performances were organised, attracting 253 900 people.

Music-lovers enjoyed the classical repertoire of the Royal Concertgebouw Orchestra; light symphonies by the Budapest Strauss Symphony Orchestra; popular favourites by the Hong Kong Philharmonic Orchestra in the outdoor free concert *Symphony Under the Stars '93*; evenings of jazz with the Aparis and the Westbrook Trios; the singing of Barbara Hendricks, Dmitri Hvorostovsky and the Chanticleer; and ensemble works by the Guildhall String Ensemble and the I Solisti Veneti. There was added enjoyment from the music of a host of instrumental virtuosi, including pianists Emanuel Ax, Kong Xiangdong and Yefim Bronfman; violinists Jane Peters, Gidon Kremer and Isaac Stern; organists Graham Barber and Peter Hurford; guitarist Julian Bream and cellist Janos Starker.

For dance enthusiasts, there was *Romeo and Juliet* by the Birmingham Royal Ballet; *1980* by the Pina Bausch Wuppertal Dance Theatre; the World Professional Ballroom and

Latin American Dance; and the colourful Lezginka, the State Dance Company of Daghestan.

Theatrical and operatic offerings included drama performances by the local Actors Family, Carlsberg Wanchai Theatre, Kwun Tong Theatre, Spotlight Productions, Horizonte Drama Society and British Red Shift Theatre; mime performances by the Japanese Mugon-geki Company; Chinese opera by the Hing Fung Ming Opera Troupe and a local production of Verdi's opera *Rigoletto*.

Hong Kong International Film Festival

The Hong Kong International Film Festival presented by the council is one of the world's major annual, non-competitive, film festivals.

The 17th festival in 1993 presented 185 films from 30 countries. The films were divided into 13 sections: world cinema, declarations of American independents, a tribute to John Cassavetes, Asian cinema, focus on Abbas Kiarostami, Hong Kong Panorama 92–3, Truth or Dare: Documentaries East and West, a tribute to Shinsuke Ogawa, archival treasures, The Zone, animation, Hong Kong Cinema Retrospective: Mandarin Films and Popular Songs 40s–60s, and Hong Kong Independent Short Film Competition.

Apart from the screening of films, several fringe activities were held during the festival. Over 400 posters and stills of the participating films were displayed at an exhibition at the City Hall Exhibition Hall, which attracted over 13 000 visitors. Seminars focussing on the two topics 'Mandarin Films and Popular Songs: An Actress's Perspective' and 'Hong Kong Independent Short Film Competition: A Discussion on Movie and Techniques' also attracted high attendances.

Over 89 000 tickets were sold during the festival.

Hong Kong Independent Short Film Competition

The Hong Kong Independent Short Film Competition aims to promote the production of quality non-commercial short films and to encourage creative independent film production in the territory.

The prize presentation ceremony of the competition was held during the opening reception of the 17th Hong Kong International Film Festival and all the winning entries were screened during the film festival.

Chinese Music Festival

The Chinese Music Festival is a new Urban Council venture. It ran for 22 days in October and November with 10 prominent music groups from China, Taiwan and Hong Kong performing traditional, ethnic Chinese music and contemporary music works. Outstanding overseas Chinese instrumentalists were also invited to perform with prominent local musicians.

Other special features of the festival included an exhibition of Chinese musical instruments, two Chinese music days and a series of lecture-demonstrations.

Highlights of the festival included performances by the Central Philharmonic Orchestra, the Inner Mongolian Chorus, various pipa and huqin players and the council's Hong Kong Chinese Orchestra.

International Arts Carnival

The annual International Arts Carnival entered its 12th year in 1993. It aims to stimulate the interest of children and young people in the performing arts and to provide them with cultural programmes during their summer vacation.

The carnival took place in July and August, and featured 30 performances of magic, mime, puppetry, ballet, Cantonese opera, children's musical works and drama. The shows were staged by four overseas and seven local groups. In addition, a free fun fair comprising a marching band, variety show, puppet show, cartoon video wall, games, and arts and crafts stalls was held at the Hong Kong Cultural Centre piazza.

The programmes offered half-price tickets for students and senior citizens and attracted 81 863 patrons.

Entertainment Programmes

During the year, the Urban Council staged 253 entertainment programmes in parks, playgrounds, community halls, housing estates and community arts centres in the urban areas. Most of these programmes, which were attended by over 101 900 people, were free.

Annual territory-wide events organised by the council included the Spring Lantern Festival, Summer Fun Festival, the Mid-Autumn Lantern Carnival, Christmas Carnival and the District Cantonese Opera Parade. About 551 700 people attended these events.

The council also played a part in the co-ordination of the 1993 Lunar New Year fireworks display and was a co-organiser of the Hong Kong Dragon Boat Festival International Races and the Concert in the Stadium. On New Year's Eve, it supported the territory-wide pilot project 'Countdown '94'.

Regional Council Presentations

The Regional Council presented a diverse programme of music, opera, drama, dance, film shows and other performing arts to cater to the tastes of local residents and develop new audiences. The number of events totalled 478 and reached an audience of some 284 000 in 1993.

By presenting established artists of high standing and popular appeal, and novel programmes, the council aims to broaden the horizons of concert-goers. During the year, overseas artists and companies appearing under the council's auspices included Fou Ts'ong, the Moscow Philharmonic Orchestra, Le Jeune Ballet de France, the Mantovani Orchestra, Lin Hwai-min's Cloud Gate Dance Theatre from Taiwan, and violinist Ruggiero Ricci.

Chinese opera presentations were also high on the list of performances: the Wu Zhou Cantonese Opera Troupe from Guangxi, Yu Kuizhi with the Peking Opera Academy of China, and the Hebei Clapper Opera Troupe all performed for local audiences at the council's venues.

The council's collaboration with the Hong Kong Arts Festival Society broke new ground in 1993. Besides jointly presenting the Oslo Philharmonic Orchestra and the magician Jeff Mcbride, for the first time the council commissioned a local programme as a contribution to the festival. The nine performances of the commissioned programme — the Hong Kong Ballet's *Cinderella* — were played to full houses at the council's three town halls.

Support for local performing companies became a regular feature of the council's cultural promotion efforts, with performances by the Hong Kong Ballet, City Contemporary Dance Company, High Noon Production Company, Sha Tin Theatre Company and the Hong Kong Philharmonic Orchestra. Through co-operation with the Urban Council, the Hong Kong Dance Company and the Hong Kong Repertory Theatre brought their repertoires to the venues of the council and presented *The Story of Zhou Xuan* and *I Have a Date with Spring*, respectively.

Dance and Drama Animateur Scheme
The successful 1992 Dance Animateur Scheme, in which a dance animateur set up outreach classes and developed interest groups among schools and voluntary organisations, continued in 1993. A similar scheme was organised in five districts in co-operation with the Prospects Theatre Company to stimulate interest and develop skills in drama among students. A total of 25 schools, with some 650 participants, have joined the two schemes.

International Children's Arts Festival
The International Children's Arts Festival, into its fourth year in 1993, is an annual event organised by the council to bring cultural activities to young people and their families during the summer. Highlights of the 1993 festival included performances by the Beijing Youth Jing Kun Arts Troupe from China, the Little Angel Marionette Theatre from the United Kingdom, magician Peter Samuelson and the comedy group Waldo-Woodhead from the USA. Contributions by local artists included special programmes by the Hong Kong Symphony Orchestra and Anonymity Dramatic Club; and the Hong Kong Ballet's *La Sylphide and Napoli Divertissements*, another new production commissioned by the council. In view of the popularity of participatory programmes, Chung Ying Theatre Company was invited again to organise two drama workshops — *Story-Building Time* and *Story-Telling Time*. The festival drew a total attendance of 56 200 at three 'fun' days and open days, 12 drama workshops, 36 stage performances and a children's painting exhibition.

Silk Road Arts Festival
A showcase of the cultural heritage and folkloric life of the Silk Road, the festival featured a diversity of programmes, including *The Ancient Music of Dunhuang* by the Dunhuang Art Ensemble of Gansu, Chinese instrumental concerts by the Song and Dance Theatre of Shaanxi, *Waist Drums* and *Seeding Songs* from Shaanxi, and *Tai Ping Drums* from Gansu. Top-billing was also given to ethnic performances from Xinjiang by the Ethnic Song and Dance Troupe of Xinjiang, *Mukam* — music and dance of Southern Xinjiang, and a dance drama *The Lilting Flute of the Silk Sea* by the Fujian Provincial Song and Dance Theatre.

In order to promote the festival and add variety, outdoor programmes were held in areas without convenient access to the civic centres. Three fairs featured performances and demonstrations of folk arts and crafts. Pre-performance talks and demonstrations were also held to promote understanding and appreciation of the performances. About 72 000 people participated in the festival programmes.

Besides the cultural programmes, an exhibition of precious artifacts of the Tang Dynasty was mounted at Sha Tin Town Hall with the assistance of the Shaanxi Archaeology Institute of China. The exhibition attracted 30 000 people.

Visual Arts
The Regional Council's Best of Visual Arts scheme provides opportunities for local visual artists to exhibit their works in major civic centres. Under this scheme, local artists and art organisations are presented in one-person or joint exhibitions of painting, calligraphy, sculpture, ceramics and print-making.

In 1993, a total of 18 exhibitions were held, attracting 14 400 visitors.

Entertainment Programmes
The council regularly presents free cultural and entertainment programmes in community halls, playgrounds and open spaces to provide community leisure activities for residents in the vicinity. In 1993, 362 programmes were organised, attracting 215 700 people.

These free programmes, including Chinese instrumental music, Western music, Chinese folk dance, modern dance, Cantonese opera, puppet shows, pop shows and variety shows, brought professional performances to the general public and provided opportunities for budding artists to improve their performing skills. The performances also helped preserve Chinese cultural heritage such as puppetry and acrobatic art.

Venues
Most performance venues in Hong Kong are built and operated by the Urban and Regional Councils. They range from major facilities, such as the Hong Kong Cultural Centre, to smaller multi-purpose centres used for district-based cultural activities.

Urban Council Venues
Hong Kong Cultural Centre
Hong Kong Cultural Centre, an international landmark on the Tsim Sha Tsui waterfront, is a leading performing arts venue in the territory.

Its oval-shaped, 2 085-seat Concert Hall has played host to numerous local artists and many of the world's finest orchestras and soloists. Internationally-renowned artists appearing there in 1993 included Jose Carreras, Barbara Hendricks, Isaac Stern, James Galway, Emanuel Ax, Janos Starker, the Royal Concertgebouw Orchestra, the Philadelphia Orchestra and the Oslo Philharmonic Orchestra.

The Grand Theatre, with its advanced stage facilities, has accommodated a diversity of functions ranging from highly complicated theatrical productions to film shows. In 1993, audiences saw performances there by the Bolshoi Ballet, the Pina Bausch Wuppertal Dance Theatre, the Birmingham Royal Ballet, the Paris Opera Ballet and the Byelorussian Ballet.

The Studio Theatre with its variable stage configurations has proven to be a valuable venue for small-scale functions and drama productions requiring an intimate atmosphere.

To promote the centre and nurture the arts in the territory, a total of 234 free foyer, outdoor and educational programmes were presented, attracting a total of 81 680 participants.

In 1993, 3.5 million patrons visited the centre.

City Hall
Since its opening in 1962, the City Hall has become synonymous with the development of the arts and culture in Hong Kong. It continues to be one of the council's major cultural venues while retaining its popularity as a centre in the urban area for the performing and

visual arts. The 1 488-seat Concert Hall and 465-seat Theatre are ideal venues for local music and theatre groups.

Significant events presented in the City Hall during the year included the 1993 Hong Kong Arts Festival, the 17th Hong Kong International Film Festival, concerts by the Hong Kong Philharmonic Orchestra and recitals by Julian Bream and Kong Xiangdong.

During the year, 193 000 people attended 414 performances in the Concert Hall, Theatre and Recital Hall. In addition, 67 exhibitions were held in the Exhibition Hall and Exhibition Gallery.

Beginning in July, the City Hall underwent a major renovation. All the performing venues and exhibition halls were closed for varying periods.

Community Arts Centres

The Urban Council operates four community arts centres to promote district-based cultural activities.

Ngau Chi Wan Civic Centre has a 443-seat theatre, a 350-square-metre exhibition hall, a 90-seat lecture room, two music practice rooms and a dance practice area. During the year, the theatre was used for 212 events, including drama, Cantonese opera, variety shows and ceremonies for a total audience of 51 868.

Sheung Wan Civic Centre comprises a 511-seat theatre, a 150-seat lecture hall, an exhibition hall, a rehearsal hall, a dance practice room, four music practice rooms and two art studios. The council's performing companies — the Hong Kong Chinese Orchestra, the Hong Kong Repertory Theatre and the Hong Kong Dance Company — are housed in the centre. During the year, 74 044 people attended 470 performances in the centre's theatre and lecture hall.

Sai Wan Ho Civic Centre features a 471-seat theatre, a multi-purpose cultural activities hall, three art studios and two music practice rooms. In 1993, 84 971 people attended 298 performances in the theatre. The cultural activities hall was extensively used for a variety of functions, including performances and exhibitions. The centre also ran a ceramics workshop which offered 51 pottery classes for children, young people and adults.

The Ko Shan Theatre is the only semi-open air theatre in Hong Kong. It has 3 000 seats of which 2 000 are in the open. The theatre is suitable for a broad range of cultural and entertainment events. Cantonese operas and other operatic recitals are frequently staged there, with rock concerts the second most popular events. In 1993, 120 000 people attended 190 performances. The theatre will undergo major improvement works in 1994.

Indoor Stadia

The Hong Kong Coliseum and Queen Elizabeth Stadium, which the council manages, are two of Asia's best equipped, multi-purpose, indoor stadia.

The 12 500-seat coliseum is a popular venue not only for pop concerts by local and international performers, but also for world-class entertainment spectaculars. In 1993, performances staged at the coliseum included Sumo wrestling, Elton John's *The One* tour, Walt Disney's *World On Ice*, the World Volleyball Grand Prix and 1993 JCI Hong Kong Congress.

The giant video screen which hangs above the centre of the arena is a special feature of the facility.

The year 1993 marked the 10th anniversary of the coliseum. Over 12 000 people from various social service groups, including children, young people, senior citizens and the disabled, were invited to celebrate the milestone at two ice shows in April. The celebration activities also featured a youth band performance and a demonstration of gymnastics and wushu techniques at the piazza level.

The compact 3 500-seat Queen Elizabeth Stadium plays host to various medium-sized productions, ranging from sports events to pop concerts, and from cultural programmes to conventions. Highlights in 1993 included a silent film classic programme *Napoleon*, with live orchestral accompaniment conducted by the internationally-renowned composer and conductor Carl Davis, and a concert by James Galway and Cleo Laine — both of which were presented by the 1993 Hong Kong Arts Festival. Other events included the Asian Badminton Championship, the World Volleyball League and Shizuka Kudo in Concert.

In addition to the arena, the stadium provides facilities for recreational activities, such as badminton, squash, volleyball, basketball, table tennis and gymnastics, and committee rooms for lectures and meetings.

Redevelopment of Hong Kong Stadium

The redevelopment of the Hong Kong Stadium, costing $850 million, is funded and handled by the Royal Hong Kong Jockey Club. On completion in March 1994, its seating capacity will be increased to 40 000. The new stadium will be managed by the Urban Council, and will provide a first-class venue for world class sports events, pop and rock concerts, and other spectator events.

The partially-completed stadium was opened for the Hong Kong Rugby Sevens and major soccer matches in March and April. More than 60 000 spectators attended.

Computerised Ticketing

The Urban Council operates URBTIX (Urban Ticketing System), a computerised system providing a full range of ticketing services primarily in support of cultural and entertainment events. URBTIX not only sells tickets for the council's own presentations, but acts as a ticketing agent for events presented by the Regional Council, Hong Kong Arts Centre, the Academy for the Performing Arts and other organisations.

URBTIX services include counter bookings and prior reservations by telephone. Postal bookings are normally available for major events. The system also handles credit card phone orders from its registered patrons.

URBTIX operates a network of 18 outlets throughout the territory, all equipped with on-line sales terminals. During the year, 4.1 million tickets were sold through the system.

Regional Council Venues

The Regional Council manages six civic centres — three major ones in Sha Tin, Tsuen Wan and Tuen Mun, and three others in Yuen Long, Tai Po and Sheung Shui.

Centrally-located in the town centres, each major civic centre houses a 1 400-seat multi-purpose auditorium designed for staging performances ranging from symphony concerts to ballets. Other facilities include a cultural activities hall, an exhibition gallery, lecture rooms, rehearsal areas, and music and dance studios. All facilities are offered for public hiring at reasonable charges. The civic centres are well served by public transport and there are restaurants, shopping centres and carparks in their vicinity. A renovation programme for the Tsuen Wan Town Hall was completed during the year.

For the smaller civic centres, an 800-seat auditorium and ancillary function rooms are provided.

Music Office

The Music Office, a part of the Recreation and Culture Branch, plays an active role in providing instrumental music instruction and promoting interest in music among young people.

The Instrumental Music Training Scheme is open to young people between six and 23 years of age. Over 600 training classes in both Western and Chinese instruments were conducted for about 3 000 trainees in five music centres. To help young people take up musical training, the Music Office hires out musical instruments to its trainees at a modest charge. Trainees are provided with aural and theory instruction as well as orchestral and band training. Masterclasses and seminars are conducted by local and overseas visiting musicians. For talented young musicians, special training is provided.

The Music Office presently manages one symphony orchestra, four string orchestras, five Chinese orchestras, five symphonic bands and two choirs.

To promote interest in music, the office also organises an annual music gala and various music festivals. A major activity is the *Music for the Millions* concerts. Over 160 such concerts were presented in schools, community and welfare facilities throughout Hong Kong for a total audience of 73 000. The office also encourages the handicapped to enjoy music by holding concerts and training sessions at special schools.

The office organises international music exchanges to foster mutual understanding among young musicians and to broaden their horizons. In August, the Hong Kong Youth Symphonic Band made a concert tour of Brisbane, Armidale and Sydney in Australia. The office also hosted visits by various youth music groups from Canada and Australia.

Hong Kong Jockey Club Music Fund

The Hong Kong Jockey Club Music Fund was set up in December 1979 with a donation of $10 million from the Royal Hong Kong Jockey Club for the promotion and development of music, dance and other related activities. It is a non-statutory trust fund, administered by a board of trustees. In 1993, the fund awarded 132 grants and nine scholarships totalling $2,685,000 enabling young people to study music and dance abroad, and assisting local schools and organisations to acquire or repair musical instruments and dance equipment.

Museums

Hong Kong Museum of Art

The Hong Kong Museum of Art has received popular support since its opening in 1991 in new premises in Tsim Sha Tsui. In 1993, the museum entertained 361 296 visitors and 889 school parties with 32 858 students.

The museum's permanent galleries on contemporary Hong Kong art, historical pictures, Chinese antiquities and Chinese fine art continued to display selected items from the museum collection on a rotation basis. The special exhibition gallery was devoted to the staging of local and overseas exhibitions on both Chinese and Western art.

The Art of Cheung Yee, The Urban Council Fine Art Award Winners and *The Hong Kong Artists* exhibitions were organised to promote local art and artists. The *Kagoshima Art* exhibition, jointly presented with the Kagoshima Prefectural Government, introduced paintings and prints by artists from the southern Japanese prefecture. Several joint presentations offered the best of Asian art to the public. *Treasures of Asian Art: Selections from the Mr and Mrs John D. Rockefeller 3rd Collection, the Asia Society, New York*, was a joint presentation with the Asia Society — Hong Kong Centre; *Transcending Turmoil: Painting at the Close of China's Empire 1796–1911* was jointly presented with the Phoenix Art Museum, U.S.A.; and *Treasures of Chang'an: Capital of the Silk Road* was a joint presentation with the Archaeological Overseas Exhibitions Company of Shaanxi Province and the Hong Kong Culture and Art Foundation. *Berlin Art Scene — A Double Mentality*, a joint presentation with the Goethe Institute, Hong Kong, and the *Rodin Sculpture* exhibition, a joint presentation with the AFAA, Ministry of Foreign Affairs, France, and the Rodin Museum, provided special features on Western arts. Special tours were arranged for blind and handicapped visitors to the *Rodin Sculpture* exhibition in May.

The Xubaizhai Gallery, displaying the world-renowned Xubaizhai collection of ancient Chinese paintings and calligraphy donated by Mr Low Chuck-tiew, was officially opened in September 1992. Its inaugural exhibition, *A Gift of Heritage*, was followed by *The Enduring Spirit: Chinese Painting and Calligraphy from the Xubaizhai Collection*, dedicated to the memory of Mr Low.

The Flagstaff House Museum of Tea Ware organised exhibitions on Chinese tea drinking, including *The Art of the Yixing Potter* and *Tea Wares by Hong Kong Potters*. Display items for the latter exhibition were selected from a local tea ware competition. A new wing comprising an exhibition gallery and an educational activities hall is being planned.

The Hong Kong Visual Arts Centre was built to provide studio facilities for practising artists. The centre provides workshop facilities for ceramics, sculpture and print-making for hire to artists at subsidised rates. In addition to the hiring of the exhibition gallery, artist studios, seminar rooms and lecture hall, the centre also organised exhibitions, art courses, workshops, lectures and art video programmes. *Selected Treasures: A Treasury of Canadian Craft*, a joint presentation with the Canadian Government, reflected the spirit and culture of Canada through its arts and crafts.

To develop the role of the museum as a visual arts education centre, various educational activities were organised. These included small-scale exhibitions, art lectures, demonstrations, workshops, guided tours, gallery talks, art video programmes and travelling exhibitions. They attracted a total of 44 432 participants.

Hong Kong Space Museum

The Hong Kong Space Museum provided an educational and entertaining experience for visitors through its 55 groups of interactive exhibits housed in the Hall of Astronomy and the Hall of Space Science. In 1993, 252 816 people visited the exhibition halls. In addition to permanent exhibitions on astronomy and space science, a temporary exhibition entitled *Hawaii* was also held.

Major attractions offered by the museum's Space Theatre included four Omnimax film shows (entitled *Antarctica*, *Hawaii*, *Seasons* and *Tropical Rainforest*) and three sky shows (*From Fiction to Science, The Voyager Encounters* and *Eyes in the Sky*). Two educational programmes (*The New Solar System* and *The Friendly Sky*) were also arranged for students. The shows attracted 500 000 people.

The museum published a 1994 astro-calendar and a Space Museum guidebook. Other activities included 25 lectures, four lecture series and 24 film shows on astronomy, space science and related topics.

Hong Kong Science Museum

The Hong Kong Science Museum was a popular venue for visitors to explore the world of science and technology. During 1993, a total of 473 200 visitors from all walks of life visited the museum.

The exhibits covered basic scientific principles, mathematics, earth science, life science, the daily application of technology, energy, communication, transportation and high-tech items such as computers and robotics. The most prominent exhibit was a 20-metre high energy machine. Many exhibits were hands-on displays which were not only entertaining but also educational. During 1993, a 12-seat Venturer Simulator was installed in the Hall of Transportation to provide visitors with a life-like experience of different adventures.

To supplement the exhibition programmes, the museum organised special thematic exhibitions. The *Dinosaurs Alive!* exhibition, from November 1993 to March 1994, features eight robotic dinosaurs and a variety of hands-on exhibits, multi-media programmes and extension activities. By the year's end, a total of 70 000 visitors had seen the 'dinosaurs'.

To promote public interest in science, the museum organised a wide range of activities including science lectures, workshops, seminars, film shows and 'fun' science experiments for different target groups. The museum worked in collaboration with the British Council and the Education Department to present the *Science Alive* lecture series to over 3 000 teachers and students. To promote health knowledge, a series of science seminars on AIDS was arranged in association with the Education Department and the Department of Health, attended by a total of 800 teachers and principals. Another lecture series on the eye also proved to be highly popular and was repeated three times. The 'fun' science experiments, a programme specially-designed for children, enabled over 1 000 youngsters to enjoy learning science through performing interesting and stimulating experiments.

A new computer classroom with group teaching facilities was set up in the museum. Specially-designed computer courses with input from computer professionals were also organised for the public.

Hong Kong Film Archive

The Urban Council decided to set up the Hong Kong Film Archive at an estimated cost of $50 million in December 1992. The archive building is scheduled to be completed in 1997.

As Hong Kong is the third largest film production centre in the world, churning out over 100 films each year, the archive will preserve the territory's rich film heritage.

The archive, when completed, will not only fulfil its archival functions of acquiring, preserving, cataloguing, studying and documenting Hong Kong films and related materials, but also encourage public access to its collection through film programmes and exhibitions.

With a net area of about 2 500 square metres, the film archive will include environment-controlled film stores, conservation laboratories, a small cinema for film shows and seminars, an exhibition hall, and a research and study centre.

The archive office has already started acquiring films and related material, mainly through donations and voluntary deposits by owners.

Heritage

Growing awareness of the importance to the community of Hong Kong's cultural and historical heritage is reflected in the activities of the museums run by the Urban and Regional Councils, and the work of the Antiquities Advisory Board as well as the Antiquities and Monuments Office. The Secretary for Recreation and Culture is the antiquities authority and implements the provisions of the Antiquities and Monuments Ordinance. Through exhibitions, guided tours, publications, local studies and community involvement projects, the museums and Antiquities and Monuments Office seek to achieve their twin objectives of preserving Hong Kong's heritage and increasing public awareness of its importance.

Heritage preservation was given a further boost with the establishment of the Lord Wilson Heritage Trust at the beginning of the year. With the help of the trust and the Antiquities Advisory Board, the first heritage trail in Hong Kong was opened at Ping Shan in Yuen Long, providing the public with easy access to restored historical buildings and monuments along the trail. In addition, funding support was given to community organisations and schools for a variety of heritage-related activities. Other projects being planned by the trust included the production of a learning package on local history for use by students in junior secondary forms and other publicity programmes targeted at arousing the younger generation's awareness and interest in heritage preservation.

Hong Kong Museum of History

The year saw a diversified and lively programme of exhibitions and educational activities at the Hong Kong Museum of History. These started with a very popular exhibition, *Dress in Hong Kong — A Century of Change and Customs*, which displayed the museum's valuable collection of costumes. The exhibition closed in April after attracting 66 900 visitors. An exhibition entitled *Education in Hong Kong: Past and Present* was mounted from June to September with the aim of illustrating the development of local education since the early days of Hong Kong.

A large-scale archaeological exhibition on the discoveries of the ancient Yue tribe in South China came next, jointly presented with the Anthropology Museum of Zhongshan University in Guangzhou and the Shenzhen Museum. On display were over 200 items of unearthed artifacts from Fengkai, Xiqiaoshan, Shenzhen and Hong Kong, reflecting the lifestyle of the ancient Yue people from the prehistoric period to the Han dynasty. The exhibition was attended by 17 259 visitors in the first month of its opening. A two-day seminar was held to complement the exhibition.

The permanent exhibition, *The Story of Hong Kong*, which illustrates the development of Hong Kong from a small fishing village to a metropolis, remained open throughout the year and attracted 172 986 people.

The museum's educational activities drew a high attendance. Weekend programmes included lectures, demonstrations and video shows. The traditional handicraft courses and field visits to historic sites in the New Territories were all over-subscribed, as were the student workshops on *Experiencing Archaeology* and *Rubbing Chinese Folk Woodblock Prints*. The seminar on the history of Hong Kong, jointly organised with the Education Department for history teachers, was fully attended. Other extension services, such as travelling exhibitions and the loan of slide packs and videos, were much in demand.

The second inter-school competition of study projects on the traditional trade and crafts in Hong Kong was launched and received an encouraging response.

In 1993, the museum embarked upon various research projects. These included a special research project into the historical background of the Lei Yue Mun fortifications and their role in Hong Kong's coastal defence, and a project on Chinese antique maps of the Hong Kong region.

The Lei Cheng Uk Branch Museum presented a new display on the costumes of the Han dynasty and attracted 45 295 visitors. At the Law Uk Folk Museum, a thematic exhibition on Chinese and Japanese folk art was presented alongside its permanent display of rural furniture and farming implements. The exhibition was attended by 49 711 visitors.

Sheung Yiu Folk Museum

Situated at a scenic spot in Sai Kung, this museum is housed in a fortified Hakka village built in the late 19th century. The 500-square-metre village comprises eight domestic units, pig pens, an open courtyard and an entrance gate tower, and is situated on a raised platform about two metres above ground level. The village, together with a nearby lime kiln, was gazetted as a monument in 1981. Period furniture and local farming implements are displayed. The museum building was renovated, and planning for reorganising the structure and the exhibits for visitors was put in hand in 1993. Despite its remoteness, the museum attracted 56 000 visitors.

The Hong Kong Railway Museum

This open-air museum, occupying an area of 6 500 square metres, is located in the town centre of Tai Po Market. It comprises the old Tai Po Market railway station building, six passenger coaches dating from 1911 to 1974, and an educational audio-visual room housed in a mock-up of an electric train. The station building, in Chinese decorative style, was built in 1913. The museum attracted 210 000 visitors in 1993.

Sam Tung Uk Museum

The museum, located close to the Mass Transit Railway terminus in Tsuen Wan, was originally an old Hakka walled village built in 1786. The layout of the 2 000-square-metre village resembles a chequer-board with an entrance hall, an assembly hall and an ancestral hall along the central axis. The village was declared a monument in 1981 because of its historical significance. After restoration, it was furnished with traditional Hakka furniture and farming implements. The largest museum of its kind in Hong Kong, it attracted 370 000 visitors in 1993.

Two exhibitions were staged at the museum during the year. *The Heritage of Cantonese Opera* marked the completion of efforts by the museum to record, collect and acquire 3 835 opera-related artifacts in the past five years. The second exhibition, *On Track: the Story of Hong Kong Rail Transport*, presented a colourful collection of memorabilia, models and preserved documents illustrating the history and future development of the five modes of railway transport in Hong Kong.

Antiquities Advisory Board

The Antiquities Advisory Board has 14 appointed members drawn from a variety of backgrounds. They include archaeologists, historians, architects, anthropologists, planners and curators. The board advises the government on the sites and structures which merit protection through declaration as monuments.

In 1993, the enclosing walls and corner-towers of Kun Lung Wai in Lung Yeuk Tau, Fanling, and the exterior of the main building of the Helena May, were declared monuments. The *wai* has a history of some 250 years, witnessing the lengthy settlement of the Tang clan in the area. The Helena May building, opened in 1916 to provide accommodation for single working women, is a fine example of architecture in the late Victorian/Edwardian classical revival style. The Antiquities Advisory Board also examined a number of historical buildings, including Chinese temples, and graded them in accordance with their historical significance, architectural merit and other factors.

The full restoration of Ching Shu Hin, an elegant Qing dynasty residence of the Tang clan at Ping Shan in Yuen Long, and the walls of Kun Lung Wai in Fanling, was completed during the year with funding support from the Royal Hong Kong Jockey Club and the government, respectively. Other major restoration and repair projects launched during the year included the Yi Tai Study Hall in Kam Tin and the Yu Kiu Ancestral Hall in Ping Shan.

University students were employed during the summer to conduct a survey of Chinese temples in Kowloon, which provided preliminary historical and architectural information on the buildings as a basis for further study.

The Antiquities and Monuments Office continued to maintain close links with government departments and private developers to ensure that all archaeological sites which would be affected by development were brought to its attention during the planning stage. As a result, it proved possible to preserve intact some of the sites, such as the Late Neolithic site at Pa Tau Kwu in North Lantau and the Yuan dynasty kiln complex at Ha Law Wan, Chek Lap Kok.

Intensive archaeological surveys were conducted of areas to be developed. Such investigations included the archaeological survey of Tung Chung and Kau Shat Wan, the headland at Sha Lo Wan West in Lantau and the historical and archaeological survey of Ma Wan. These surveys were undertaken by local as well as overseas experts and professional institutions. The surveys succeeded in retrieving important archaeological information on the areas investigated, enabling appropriate rescue operations to be organised prior to the commencement of development works.

Many of these surveys and subsequent rescue operations were made possible by substantial donations from the developers concerned and from the Royal Hong Kong Jockey Club.

The Antiquities and Monuments Office encouraged public interest in local heritage issues through a full programme with an emphasis on education and links with school curricula. Field studies, seminars and lectures were organised for youth groups, students and teachers. Exhibitions on various local heritage themes were produced and staged at the exhibition hall in the Tsim Sha Tsui office and other suitable venues. A booklet introducing the history, relics and traditions of the Islands District was published by the Islands District Board with the assistance of the office. Another similar publication, covering the Eastern District, was underway. Various community involvement projects such as grass-cutting and cleaning-up at historic sites were arranged. These were aimed at cultivating among the younger generation an interest in Hong Kong's past and a sense of civic responsibility.

The Ping Shan heritage trail, the first heritage trail in the territory, was opened during the year. Located at Ping Shan in Yuen Long, it is about one kilometre in length. The trail links a number of historical Chinese buildings and monuments within easy walking distance, and provides the public with an opportunity to experience the social and cultural development of the New Territories over the past centuries in a convenient half-day excursion.

Public Libraries

Urban Council Libraries

The Urban Council Public Libraries continued to increase in number, and in size, during 1993. In May, the third mobile library was put on the road, and the Electric Road Public Library was opened in August. In addition, the first phase of renovation works to expand the City Hall Public Library was finished. When this renovation is completed, in April 1994, the City Hall Public Library will occupy more than eight floors of the High Block.

The Urban Council operates 31 public libraries, including a specialised library on the arts at the Hong Kong Cultural Centre. Under the current expansion programme, the number of libraries will be increased to 42 in the next few years.

The Hong Kong Central Library, being planned in the Causeway Bay area, will have a net usable area of about 18 000 square metres and will provide a central reference library for storing all major reference materials of the library system under one roof. Two other libraries, both joint venture projects with the private sector, were also under construction in 1993. They were a district library at Shung Ling Street in Wong Tai Sin and a small library in Tsim Sha Tsui East.

Facilities provided by the libraries included lending services for adults and children, newspapers and periodicals services, audio-visual services, students' study rooms, a wide range of extension activities as well as block loan services to non-profit-making organisations and penal institutions. Reading machines for the blind were also available in the City Hall Public Library and Kowloon Central Library.

A start was made in June on the full-scale implementation of the Library Computerisation Project. The system will have English and Chinese capabilities to provide a more efficient service to the public. The first computerised library is expected to come into operation in April 1994. It is planned that the computerisation project will be fully implemented by mid-1995.

The year saw a major enhancement in reference services. The libraries have subscribed to about 100 bibliographical and information databases on Compact Disc — Read Only Memory (CD-ROM). A computer network was installed in 1993 to centralise most of the CD-ROM databases in the City Hall Reference Library and to make information readily available to the Kowloon Central Reference Library, Arts Library and district libraries through dial access. In addition, planning was in hand to introduce on-line search facilities to local and overseas databases to locate up-to-date information for readers in early 1994.

The installation of book detection systems in the council's libraries continued during the year, bringing to 25 the total number of libraries with this equipment. Readers using these libraries are permitted to keep their bags and belongings with them.

In 1993, the library collection increased to 2.8 million items, including 2.7 million books and 161 122 audio-visual items. The council libraries will continue to acquire suitable materials to increase the library stock to 3.4 million items, to reach the target of one item per head of the urban population. The libraries also subscribed to 1 282 titles of local and overseas newspapers and periodicals.

A total of nine million books and 270 600 audio-cassette tapes were loaned during the year, while 18.5 million books were read in the libraries. The year also saw the registration of 86 000 new members, bringing the total membership to 1 914 000.

The three reference libraries at the City Hall, Kowloon Central Library and Arts Library were heavily used, with a total of 77 900 reference enquiries handled by the staff and 837 000 reference books consulted.

Urban Council libraries also housed a number of unique collections for public use. These included the British Standards, the Hok Hoi collection of classical Chinese thread-sewn rare books, the Kotewall collection of old Chinese and English books, the Royal Asiatic Society collection on Hong Kong and China studies, the Oriental Ceramic Society collection, the Royal Institution of Naval Architects and the Institute of Marine Engineers collection, the Hong Kong Stock Exchange collection and the course materials of the Open Learning Institute of Hong Kong. The City Hall Library is the depository library for Hong Kong, United Nations, World Bank, Asian Development Bank, General Agreement on Tariffs and Trade and World Food Programme publications.

A competition on creative writing in Chinese was organised to cultivate interest in this area. The winning entries were published for sale to encourage wider participation and provide healthy reading materials. Since the inception of the awards in 1979, 54 titles have been published.

The second Hong Kong Biennial Awards for Chinese Literature were organised in recognition of the achievements of local writers.

To publicise the high standard of books printed and published locally, a competition on the best produced books in Hong Kong was organised jointly with the Hong Kong Trade Development Council. The 20 winning entries were exhibited at the Hong Kong Book Fair in July.

A reading programme for young people was held to arouse interest in reading. Since its launch in 1984, over 90 000 young people have enrolled as members in the programme and have read a total of 1.4 million books.

A wide range of other extension activities and outreach programmes were organised by the libraries. These included book exhibitions, interest clubs, subject talks, children's hours, computer literacy projects and library visits. These attracted 2.9 million people.

Regional Council Libraries

The Regional Council operates 22 public libraries and three mobile libraries serving 36 regular stops. These libraries, with a registered membership of 920 000, had a total stock of 1.8 million books and 101 000 items of audio-visual material.

Public library services were particularly well received in the developing new towns. In 1993, 5.81 million books and audio cassettes were lent for home use. Sha Tin Central Library, the council's first central library and the most heavily patronised library in Hong Kong, registered a record issue of 8 350 items of library materials in a single day on July 16, 1993.

To further strengthen the council's library services, its third central library, in Tsuen Wan, opened in July. The Mui Wo Public Library was also relocated in the new Regional Council Mui Wo complex to better serve local users.

The project to computerise the council's library services proceeded ahead of schedule. The first computerised library, at South Kwai Chung, came into operation in February, and computerisation of all other council libraries was advanced to November 1993. The smooth implementation of the project enabled the public to enjoy a better library service four months ahead of the original completion date.

The mainframe computer in the Regional Council Building was installed in October 1992. Installation of the network of communication equipment and terminals in the 25 branch libraries began in December 1992 and took only 11 months to complete. Some 300 terminals at the council's libraries are now connected to the system.

Conversion of the 360 000 library catalogue cards to the computer bibliographic database was made in January 1993. In the following months, the council's staff labelled two million library items with bar codes, and linked them to their respective records in the computer bibliographic database.

The exercise to re-register readers for the issue of new computerised borrower's cards commenced in September 1992 and, at the end of 1993, over 365 000 readers carried the new cards.

The introduction of the computerised system greatly improved the efficiency and quality of library services. Other benefits, such as enhanced management information, were also passed on the public through better library planning and a more cost-effective service.

To promote greater use of the library services, extension activities such as book exhibitions, subject talks, and interest groups were organised regularly for different age groups. These activities formed an integral part of the public library services and during the year, some 2.29 million people participated.

A highly popular and ongoing computer literacy project was organised at the central libraries at Sha Tin and Tuen Mun and at the North Kwai Chung Public Library. In all, 2 669 people attended the computer lectures and interest clubs.

Since 1991, the council has organised an annual Shih or T'zu poetry-writing competition to promote interest in the basic use of Chinese tones. The 1993 poetry writing competition featuring Shih composition attracted wide public interest and received more than 900 entries.

Educational kits in the form of discovery boxes were provided in the council's central and district libraries. They were enjoyed by children in the story hours and interest clubs and became a regular form of library extension activity.

In collaboration with the Education Department, study rooms were provided in Tsuen Wan, Sha Tin and Tuen Mun central libraries and in district libraries at South Kwai Chung, North Kwai Chung, Yuen Long, Sai Kung, Cheung Chau and Tai Po, providing a total of 1 218 seats. To cater to the needs of students, these study rooms are open from 7:30 am to 9:30 pm every day from mid-March to the end of June each year. Study rooms will also be provided in central and district libraries under planning.

Books Registration Office

Hong Kong is one of the four largest printing centres in the world and is renowned for the quality of its products and low prices. The Books Registration Office enforces the Books Registration Ordinance and supervises the collection of publications from publishers and printers. Under the ordinance, all books first published, produced or printed locally are preserved permanently in depository libraries after registration with the office. During the year, a total of 7 290 books and 9 800 periodicals were registered with the office. A bibliography of registered books is gazetted at quarterly intervals.

The office is the local agent for the International Standard Book Numbering System (ISBN), and helps to promote its use among publishers and book-selling trades. In all, 1 355 publishers' identifiers conforming to ISBN were issued.

Sports and Recreation

Sports and recreational activities and facilities are many and varied in Hong Kong. The Urban and Regional Councils develop and manage facilities which include sports grounds, playgrounds, indoor games halls, holiday camps, swimming pools and beaches. The two municipal councils also organise training courses and sporting competitions for people of all ages and abilities, and encourage passive recreation by providing parks and landscaping services within their respective areas.

The Sir David Trench Fund for Recreation disburses grants for the construction and improvement of recreational and sporting facilities as well as for the purchase of equipment.

Sports Development Board

The Hong Kong Sports Development Board is a statutory body responsible for promoting the development of sports and physical recreation in Hong Kong. In the 1992–93 financial year, $55 million was allocated to the board. Of this, over $31 million was used for sports development purposes which included funding support to the Amateur Sports Federation and Olympic Committee of Hong Kong for expenses relating to the 1992 Olympic Games, and to national sports associations for their staff salaries, office expenses and sports development programmes. It was also used for special projects undertaken by the board, including international exchange programmes, community sports programmes, and the organisation in conjunction with the University of Canberra and Hong Kong Sports Institute of degree courses in sports administration and coaching in the territory.

The concept of identifying target sports and providing them with increased resources for development is one of the fundamentals of Hong Kong's sports policy. Seven target sports have been identified: badminton, football, rowing, squash, swimming, table tennis and windsurfing. Others will be added to the list on a performance-related basis.

Progress has been made in the coach education field since the inception in 1991 of the Hong Kong Coaching Committee. The committee was jointly formed by the Sports Development Board, the Amateur Sports Federation and Olympic Committee of Hong Kong and the Hong Kong Sports Institute. The major component of the programme is the Hong Kong Coach Accreditation Programme. The support given to this initiative by national sports associations bodes well for future development. In 1992–93, about $3 million was allocated to these programmes.

The Sports Aid Foundation Fund and the Sports Aid for the Disabled Fund, administered by the board, increased substantially its level of support to leading athletes. A total of 108 athletes who satisfied the criteria were grant-aided in 1992–93. The total allocation exceeded $2 million.

The board has been active in securing additional funds from the commercial sector in support of development programmes organised by national sports associations. The Sports

Sponsorship Advisory Service, officially launched in June 1992, generated $9 million in sponsorship funding in 1992–93, with a number of agreements running for several years.

Sporting Achievements

Athletes from Hong Kong participated in many international competitions and enjoyed some significant successes.

In windsurfing, Lee Lai-shan won a gold medal in the ladies' lightweight international race board class while Wong Tak-sum won a bronze medal in the men's lightweight international race board class at the Asian Boardsailing Championships 1993. At the UK Eurolymp Championships 1993, Lee Lai-shan won a gold medal in the ladies' Olympic class and Wong Tak-sum a silver medal in the men's lightweight Olympic class. Lee Lai-shan also won the championships in the ladies' Olympic class at the German Windsurfing championships 1993 and the IMCO European Windsurfing Championships 1993.

In table tennis, Chan Suk-yuen, Chan Tan-lui, Chai Po-wa and Wong Wing-san won a silver medal in the women's team event at the First Asian Team Cup Table Tennis Tournament. Chan Tan-lui and Chai Po-wa won bronze medals in the women's doubles at the 42nd World Table Tennis Championships.

At the 6th Asian Junior Squash Championships, Jackie Lee won a gold medal in the men's individual event, while Rebecca Chiu won a bronze medal in the women's individual. Rebecca Chiu, Sally Hawkes, Eva Yam and Angel Choi then went on to win a bronze medal in the women's team event.

At the 1993 Special Olympics World Winter Games, Leung Sai-ho and Tsang Lai-king each won a gold medal in the men's Grade 2 figure skating and women's Grade 2 figure skating, respectively. In speed-skating, Chong Sin-hon won a gold medal in the women's 800 metres event and a bronze medal in the 300 metres event. Lau Kwok-yee won a silver medal in the women's 300 metres event. Law Cheuk-kei won a bronze medal in the men's 100 metres event and a bronze medal in the men's 1 000 metres event.

At the Asian Karatedo Invitation Championships 1993, Chat Him-ching won a gold medal in the men's under 60 kilogramme Kumite event and Ng Suet-lai a silver medal in the women's Kata event. Lau Wai-kwong and Shaz Shahid won bronze medals in the men's 65–70 kilogramme Kumite event, and together with Leung Chi-lap, Tam Tak-ming, Tang Chung-kay and Lam Lap-sun, they won a bronze medal in the men's team Kumite event. Tse Sun-yue and Wong Pui-wah won bronze medals in the men's Kata and women's Kata event, respectively.

At the First East Asian Games 1993, Ho Kim-fai won a gold medal in the women's lightweight single scull event. Lui Kam-chi and Chiang Wing-hung won bronze medals in the men's lightweight doubles scull event in rowing. In wushu, Leung Yat-ho won a silver medal in the men's nanquan and Ng Siu-ching won a silver medal in the women's three events combined. Ng Siu-ching and Li Fai also won bronze medals in the women's nanquan and women's three events combined, respectively. In badminton, Chan Siu-kwong, Ng Pak-kum, Wong Wai-lap, Chow Kin-man, Chan Kin-ngai and Ng Liang-hua won a bronze medal in the men's team event, while Wong Chun-fun, Chung Hoi-yuk, Chan Oi-ni, Cheng Yin-sat, Tung Chau-man and Ngan Fai won a bronze medal in the women's team event. Chan Siu-kwong and Chung Hoi-yuk also won bronze medals in the mixed doubles event. In swimming, Michael Wright won a bronze medal in the men's 50-metre freestyle event.

Hong Kong Sports Institute

The aim of the Hong Kong Sports Institute is to provide an environment in which athletic talent can be identified, nurtured and developed. This aim implies the pursuit of excellence by athletes and coaches.

The mandate of the institute is sixfold: athlete development; coach education and development; sports science, sports medicine and research; resource information; international exchanges and co-operation with other bodies.

In 1992–93, the institute offered a sports scholarship scheme in 18 sports for over 230 elite local athletes. Scholarship holders received different levels of support services in coaching, facilities, accommodation, dietary advice, sports science, sports medicine, fitness training, overseas training and support for education and employment. The 18 sports covered were archery, cycling, diving, badminton, sports for the disabled, fencing, gymnastics, rowing, soccer, squash, swimming, table tennis, tennis, ten-pin bowling, track and field, triathlon, windsurfing and wushu.

During the year, the government made a one-off grant of $100 million to the institute, which has been placed under the Hong Kong Sports Development Board Trust Fund. This is to be used for the development of sports science and sports medicine, and for the training of elite athletes preparing for major events over the next four years. This contribution will enable the institute to capitalise on the momentum so far gained in the area of top level training and development.

The institute also encouraged the general public to participate in sports by running various sports clubs, including clubs for tennis, squash, swimming and badminton, and by organising sports courses at different levels.

Amateur Sports Federation and Olympic Committee of Hong Kong

The Amateur Sports Federation and Olympic Committee of Hong Kong, recognised by the International Olympic Committee in 1951 as the national Olympic committee of the territory, controls Hong Kong's participation in the Olympic, Commonwealth, Asian, East Asian and World Games. It plays a major role in promoting sports in Hong Kong by encouraging participation in international competitions by its 60 affiliated sports associations. It is the acknowledged voice of sport in Hong Kong and throughout the sports world.

One of the objectives of the federation is the promotion of sports education. For more than two decades it has sponsored sports leaders, administrators, coaches, technical officials and athletes to attend courses and conferences held locally and overseas.

It organises monthly courses on sports leadership, sports administration, sports medicine, sports science, plus courses on sport management and sport coaching in conjunction with the United States Sports Academy. It sends Hong Kong representatives to the annual International Olympic Academy and sponsors three Olympic Solidarity courses each year.

Special sports activities during the year included seminars organised by the Hong Kong Olympic Academy on the prevention and management of foot and ankle injuries, and educational opportunities and career prospects in sport and physical education in the

1990s. Five weekend seminars on sports management were also organised in conjunction with the University of Oregon.

The federation, along with governing sports bodies and the municipal councils, organises the Hong Kong Festival of Sport annually. This large-scale community-building event, held since 1958, attracts wide participation and continues for more than two months.

Urban Council

The Urban Council manages a wide range of sports and recreational facilities, and runs numerous low-cost introductory courses to attract participation by people of all ages. The council also encourages and promotes sporting activities by subsidising competitions organised by various governing bodies.

On Hong Kong Island, three major projects were completed in 1993, namely the Quarry Bay Park, the Peak Road Garden and the Harcourt Garden. The former offers a wide range of recreational facilities including eight tennis courts, a cycling path, a seven-a-side soccer pitch, a jogging track, two basketball courts, two children's play areas and several landscaped areas. The other two venues each provide a landscaped plaza, a children's play area and a landscaped garden.

In Kowloon, two major projects were also completed during the year. The Sam Ka Tsuen Recreation Ground comprises two basketball-cum-volleyball courts, a seven-a-side soccer pitch, a five-a-side soccer pitch, two children's play areas and several landscaped areas. The Shek Kip Mei Park Stage III provides a natural grass soccer-cum-rugby pitch, a seven-a-side soccer pitch, two basketball courts, a jogging track with fitness stations and two landscaped areas. These two new venues offer both active and passive recreational facilities for people of all ages.

Apart from providing new facilities, the council continues to upgrade its existing facilities. During the year, the Smithfield Road Children's Playground, Fat Hing Street Playground, Wun Sha Street Playground, Albany Road Children's Playground, Tong Mei Road Children's Playground and Lei Cheng Uk Playground were improved. New and innovative children's play equipment was added to these playgrounds. The Victoria Park bowling green was resurfaced with artificial turf. To meet the need of schools, additional spectator stands at Aberdeen Sports Ground were provided and a new sports ground at Siu Sai Wan, with a seating capacity of 12 000, is being planned.

The council also embarked on its first adventure playground project. The adventure playground at Fung Tak Road in Wong Tai Sin will feature selected episodes from the well-known Chinese fable *The Adventures of the Monkey King*. Taking advantage of the natural topography of the site, the legendary Water Curtain Cave, the birthplace of the Monkey King, will be featured as well as the Mountain of Five Fingers, the Crystal Palace and the Flamed Mountain.

Regional Council

Under the auspices of the Regional Council, over 400 000 people took part in 5 570 training courses, competitions and recreation programmes, including water sports, ball games, racquet games, athletics, archery, fencing, cycling, gymnastics, multigym-fitness and dancing. Region-wide activities were well received with more than 8 000 participants.

A very popular programme provided opportunities for participants and school children to watch demonstrations by Hong Kong's world-class table tennis players. About 2 000 participants were attracted.

With a view to promoting sports among students in the territory, the council, in conjunction with the New Territories School Sports Association, Hong Kong Amateur Athletic Association, Hong Kong Table Tennis Association and the Education Department, launched a youth sports training programme. This pilot programme comprised two phases — teacher training and youth training. Over 100 teachers and 1 000 students from 50 schools in the New Territories took part in the programme.

With regard to the special needs of the disabled in sports, the council provided a total subsidy of $279,000 in 1993 to voluntary agencies to organise 105 sporting events for the physically and mentally handicapped.

A sports subsidy scheme has been in operation since 1986 to encourage sports associations to organise competitions, training courses and spectator events. During 1993, subsidies amounting to $3.75 million were allocated for 190 projects, benefiting 155 000 people. Training courses were organised for some 350 instructors in various sports.

As a catalyst to the promotion of sports and recreational events at the district level, a variety of programmes, including basic training courses, camping, excursions, competitions and fun days, were mounted in each of the nine districts in the council's area. In 1993, $12 million was allocated for the organisation of 5 380 district programmes which drew 245 000 participants.

Major Events and Festivals

Among the larger recreation events organised by the Regional Council in 1993 were the Corporate Games, Masters Games, Carnival for the Elderly, Kite-Flying Festival and Sand Sculpture Competition, which together attracted 15 000 participants.

The council also took an active part in promoting International Challenge Day 1993 and the Agricultural Carnival 1993 — two special events which were warmly received by the public. International Challenge Day, held on May 26, was a worldwide competition aimed at encouraging citizens of participating cities to take up regular fitness activities. Over 76 per cent of Hong Kong residents took part in some 500 events organised by the two municipal councils, or completed 15 minutes of physical exercise on the day. The overwhelming response helped Hong Kong beat Vancouver, its paired rival in the competition.

The Agricultural Carnival was held to revive the agricultural show last organised by the Agriculture and Fisheries Department in 1972 at Sek Kong. The carnival was staged at Kwai Chung Sports Ground in December 1993 and January 1994 and was jointly presented with the Agriculture and Fisheries Department, the Vegetable Marketing Organisation and the Joint Federation of the Hong Kong Agricultural and Fisheries Production and Marketing Societies. Carnival attractions included competitions and exhibitions of prize livestock, horticultural products, fish and pets; displays and demonstrations of modern and high-tech farming practices; associated commercial activities; and entertainment programmes. A total of 300 000 people visited the carnival.

A ticket to ride bought a trip to enchantment for this little girl **(above),** *during a family fun fair at the Cultural Centre, Tsim Sha Tsui.* **Right:** *Other fair-goers preferred more hair-raising thrills during Lunar New Year celebrations at Victoria Park.*

Pure entertainment can come in many shapes, even in the form of this giant pumpkin **(right),** *which amused the crowds at an agricultural carnival at the Kwai Chung Sports Ground.*

Below: *Enjoying the sunshine and a break from routine, these restless young artists found it hard to be serious on a class excursion to Hong Kong Park.*

Dinosaurs were a hot topic with youngsters everywhere in 1993, and Hong Kong was no exception. Among the many attractions with a prehistoric theme, was the Dinosaurs Alive exhibition at the Hong Kong Science Museum **(above)**.

Left: *In keeping with the spirit of their growing community, residents of Discovery Bay, Lantau Island, held their own colourful festival in November.*

Ice-skating artistry holds an audience spellbound at the Hong Kong Coliseum **(above and right).**

Opposite page: *A furry aristocrat earns a hug from an adoring fan at the Hong Kong Kennel Club's 64th All Breeds Championship Dog Show in March.*

Year after year, the Hong Kong International Rugby Sevens scores top points with both players and crowds for its superb standard of rugger, good-natured patriotism and electric atmosphere **(left and below)**.

There was something for everyone at this holiday fun fair in Morse Park, Kowloon; daredevils could choose to take their frights seated **(above)**, *or* **(left)** *standing up.*

It was a vintage year for public entertainment, with no shortage of talent — as these aspiring young stars were keen to prove, on the opening day of Kid's World, at Ocean Park in July **(above and right).**

Sports and Recreation Venues

In 1993, eight new sports and recreation venues were completed in the Regional Council area. In the spirit of 'sports for all', the council's efforts to popularise horse-riding and golf were realised when its first riding school, with a stable of 60 horses, was completed in Tuen Mun at the end of 1993. It will be opened for public use in early 1994. A golf driving range alongside the school is targeted for completion in 1994–95. The recreation complex, built on a 25-hectare site, is fully funded by the Royal Hong Kong Jockey Club.

The council now manages 29 indoor recreation centres, 13 swimming pool complexes, 97 tennis courts, 105 squash courts and 12 sportsgrounds.

An electronic display board was installed at the Tai Po Sportsground, the first venue to be fitted with this device in the council's area. Furthermore, two fully air-conditioned indoor recreation centres at Tsuen Wan and Kwai Tsing were completed and indoor tennis facilities were included at the Kwai Chung and Tai Po Indoor Recreation Centres.

The council has three water sports centres (Tai Mei Tuk, Chong Hing and Wong Shek) and three holiday camps (Lady MacLehose Holiday Village, Sai Kung Outdoor Recreation Centre, and Tso Kung Tam Outdoor Recreation Centre.) During the year, 69 000 people made use of the water sports centres and 301 200 of the holiday camps. Wall-climbing was introduced at the holiday camps, where more than 600 youngsters aged between eight and 11 took part in a memorable summer camp.

District Festivals Subsidy Scheme

Under the District Festivals Subsidy Scheme, the Regional Council assists local bodies to organise recreational, sports and cultural activities most suited to their districts. These include arts and sports festivals, dragon boat races, Mid-Autumn Festival celebrations, and Lunar New Year carnivals.

During the year, $10.7 million was allocated to the nine New Territories districts under the jurisdiction of the council, in support of 61 festival celebrations. Over 800 000 residents participated.

Beaches and Swimming Pools

Swimming is one of Hong Kong's most popular forms of summer recreation. During 1993, some 12.4 million people visited the beaches and another 6.1 million enjoyed using the numerous public swimming pools managed by the two municipal councils. Due to reports of shark attacks at Silver Strand Beach and Seung Sze Wan in Sai Kung, and shark sightings elsewhere, swimmers were warned off beaches managed by the Regional Council for a brief period during the summer. Following initial concern by the Department of Health over the quality of water at the public swimming pools, water samples were taken for testing and were afterwards confirmed to meet world health standards.

There are at present 42 gazetted bathing beaches: 12 on Hong Kong Island managed by the Urban Council and 30 in the New Territories managed by the Regional Council. Facilities provided at these beaches range from changing rooms, toilets, showers, first-aid posts, lookout towers and light refreshment kiosks to picnic areas and other ancillary facilities. The water quality of these beaches is regularly monitored, with the findings made public.

The two councils manage 27 public swimming pool complexes: 14 in the Urban Council area and 13 in the Regional Council area. The competition pools in these complexes are built to international standards. The Regional Council also provides leisure pool facilities, such as water slides and splash pools, at Hin Tin, Sheung Shui, Tai Po, Tsuen Wan and Tuen Mun pools.

The councils regularly organise learn-to-swim classes to promote water safety. During the year, over 1 870 swimming classes and training programmes were held for more than 39 240 people.

The councils also encourage the formation of lifeguard clubs at their swimming venues. These clubs help maintain a steady supply of voluntary lifeguards to augment regular lifeguard services. At the end of the year, the number of lifeguard clubs operating in the Urban and Regional Council areas were 13 and eight, respectively.

Three public swimming pool projects are under planning in the urban areas. Construction of two leisure pool projects at Hammer Hill Road and Jordan Valley started in late 1993. The first leisure pools to be built by the Urban Council, they will provide varied play equipment in the form of pirate ships, water slides and jets, lily pads and log walks.

To bring the message of safe swimming to a wide spectrum of the public, the Urban Council launched another water safety campaign in 1993. Major functions of the campaign included a launching ceremony, in conjunction with the Hong Kong Life Guard Club, of the Governor's Shield Lifeguard Grand Parade 1993 at Repulse Bay Beach; the water safety slogan competition, which attracted 3 636 entries; the water safety poster design competition in which 450 students took part; and a series of promotional activities performed by the *Water Safety Ambassador* dressed in a dolphin outfit at the council's aquatic venues during the peak swimming season.

The Regional Council also implemented a package of safety measures to strengthen safety at beaches against any threat of shark attack. These included distributing information leaflets and setting up additional lookout posts to provide a better view of the beach areas and adjacent waters. The council also secured the assistance of the Government Flying Service in deploying its light aircraft for shark-patrol exercises during weekends and public holidays during the swimming season. The council also worked on a shark prevention net trial scheme with a view to installing nets at three selected beaches by the beginning of the swimming season in 1994.

Summer Youth Programme

The territory-wide Summer Youth Programme is organised each year for children and young people aged between six and 25. Social and recreational programmes and community service activities help the participants to develop their skills, appreciate human relationships, understand the community in which they live and enhance their sense of responsibility to the community.

In 1993, the Summer Youth Programme was officially launched on July 10, bearing the central theme *Share the Fun, Serve the Community*. A Silver Jubilee Day was also held on August 8 to celebrate the 25th anniversary of the Summer Youth Programme. Between July and September, about 14 100 activities were organised involving 1.36 million young people. The total expenditure of the programme was around $39 million. The Royal Hong Kong Jockey Club donated $14 million and the balance was met by the government, district boards, the Urban Council, Regional Council, private donations and participants' fees. A total of 24 outstanding volunteers were awarded Summer Youth Programme scholarships and attended training courses organised by the Outward Bound School and other institutions.

Ocean Park

Located on the southern side of Hong Kong Island, Ocean Park is Southeast Asia's largest oceanarium and Hong Kong's premier theme park. Built on a site of 87 hectares, Ocean Park also includes Water World and Middle Kingdom, a Chinese cultural village.

More than three million people visited Ocean Park in 1993, while total attendance since the park opened in 1977 passed the 37-million mark.

Built on hilly land, the headland and lowland areas of Ocean Park are linked by a cable car system, and from the Tai Shue Wan entrance at Middle Kingdom by a 225-metre covered outdoor escalator.

In the summer of 1993, Ocean Park opened its newest attraction, Kids' World. Featuring family rides, games, shows, two creative play areas and a Dolphin University, the facility is built for the enjoyment of the whole family, especially children.

The $30 million Ocean Park Tower — built as part of the park's $600 million five-year expansion plan that runs through to 1997 — is the tallest observation tower in Asia. The tower was opened in 1992 to mark the park's 15th anniversary. Seventy-two metres tall and 200 metres above sea level, it offers a 360-degree bird's eye view of Hong Kong and the nearby harbours and islands.

In the headland area, there are six exciting rides. Marineland includes a 3 500-seat ocean theatre staging regular shows featuring the killer whale, dolphins and sealions; the newly-renovated wave cove has sealions, seals and penguins; and a $40-million shark aquarium is home to more than 80 sharks of 20 species. In addition, a new-look atoll reef — exhibiting more than 5 000 fish — will re-open after its $50 million renovation.

In the lowland gardens are the goldfish pagoda with over 100 species of goldfish; a butterfly house with 1 500 butterflies; a greenhouse complex and the new Kids' World.

Water World is the first and largest water playpark in Asia. It has two main pools, three 'fun' slides and a Lazy River. Water World has attracted more than three million swimmers since it opened in 1984.

Middle Kingdom recreates 5 000 years of Chinese history in 13 dynasties with temples, shrines, pavilions, pagodas and palaces. It features theatrical cultural performances, street demonstrations in Chinese arts and crafts, acrobatic and kung fu shows and lion dances.

In addition, the aviaries house more than 2 000 birds of 150 species. There is also a bird theatre, a parrot garden and a flamingo pond.

Outward Bound School

The Outward Bound Trust of Hong Kong Limited is a private registered charity and part of a worldwide network of 31 schools, providing training programmes for personal and professional development in an outdoor adventure environment on land and sea.

The purpose of the courses is to enhance in the individual self-confidence, resourcefulness, leadership, communication skills and personal effectiveness. In addition to open courses for the general public, special programmes are run for the handicapped, socially-deprived and juvenile delinquents, as well as employees of major corporations, smaller businesses, senior government officers, and teachers.

More than 25 per cent of the enrolment is supported by an active bursary scheme enabling Outward Bound to reach the deserving and financially-disadvantaged members of the community. Seventy per cent of the courses are for the general public, youth organisations and special populations, while the rest are contract courses for corporate groups and education institutions.

The courses are residential with an average course length of 10 days. The programmes operate from three centres: a sail training ship, the brigantine *Ji Fung*; a 74-bed base at Tai Mong Tsai, Sai Kung; and the Sir Murray MacLehose Training Base on the island of Double Haven in Mirs Bay.

There has been a significant increase in demand for Outward Bound training from corporations and businesses which recognise that the courses are an effective team-building and training strategy for older adults, resulting in a continuous increase in the demand for 'team building', 'adult challenge', and special 'contract' courses.

In 1993, the school operated over 150 courses for over 3 600 trainees. New initiatives included an international course, in collaboration with the Kenya Outward Bound School, and two training voyages to Japan on the *Ji Fung*, in collaboration with the Japan Outward Bound Trust.

A study group has been formed to explore the feasibility of operating courses for organisations in the People's Republic of China.

Financing is provided through tuition income and charitable donations which enable the participation of young people who are unable to afford the full course fee.

The operations base at Tai Mong Tsai underwent major renovations funded by a grant from the Royal Hong Kong Jockey Club, and plans are being developed to create an additional 36-bed, self-sustaining facility in Ah Kung Wan.

In 1994, Hong Kong will host the Fifth International Outward Bound Conference.

Adventure Ship

The Adventure Ship Project has been operating in Hong Kong for 16 years. It is a registered charity which maintains a 27.5-metre Chinese sailing junk, *Huan*, providing nautical training trips for underprivileged and handicapped children. The project is mainly funded by the Community Chest and the Hong Kong Jockey Club (Charities) Limited.

Each year, over 6 000 young people from children and youth centres, institutions for the handicapped, outreach teams and schools have benefited from these programmes.

The training programme consists of day trips or overnight trips (up to three days and two nights). The vessel is equipped to accommodate 60 youngsters on day trips and 50 on overnight voyages. 'Disciplined Entertainment' is the main theme of the training programme. Once on board, participants are regarded as members of the crew and take part in the operational routines. Under the guidance of experienced instructors, they are trained to face new challenges and participate in team-spirit building activities. The programmes have been devised to cope with various weather conditions and special requirements for children of different aptitudes and backgrounds.

The Adventure Ship Project has created new horizons for many thousands of young people, enabling them to enrich their experience while discovering the beautiful scenery of Hong Kong.

Youth Hostels

The Hong Kong Youth Hostels Association is a registered charity providing outdoor leisure opportunities for young people, particularly the 18 to 26 age group, although members may be of any age. The association has seven operational hostels, mostly away from the urban areas and in scenic spots. The association has over 32 000 members, who may make use of the 5 000 hostels throughout the world, enabling them to stay in economical accommodation of a good standard while travelling abroad.

The programme of upgrading accommodation continued throughout 1993. A number of small rooms were created at the existing hostels and these were furnished to higher standards and air-conditioned. The main event of the year was the opening, by the Governor of Hong Kong, of the new Bradbury Lodge Youth Hostel at Plover Cove. The hostel immediately enjoyed high occupation rates, largely due to the good transportation links and the many recreational facilities in the area.

Urban Council Parks

The Urban Council has an extensive building programme for large modern parks.

The first of these, Kowloon Park, features many special attractions including a sports complex with an ultra-modern Olympic pool, indoor and outdoor leisure pools and an air-conditioned indoor games hall. The park also contains a history museum, an aviary, a popular bird lake, a sculpture walk, a creative playground and a garden piazza for the staging of a wide range of cultural and entertainment activities.

A second major park located on Hong Kong Island, Hong Kong Park, was opened to the public in May 1991. It was constructed as a joint venture between the council and the Royal Hong Kong Jockey Club, which donated $170 million of the total cost of $398 million. Among the park's facilities are the 3 000-square-metre walk-in Edward Youde Aviary, the Forsgate Conservatory and spectacular water features. The Flagstaff House Museum of Tea Ware and Hong Kong Squash Centre are also part of the park. Educational activities are organised for school children in the park, with emphasis on conserving the natural environment and wild life resources.

The third major park development, Lei Yue Mun Park, occupies the historic site of the old Lyemun Barracks. The site was first developed by the council in 1987 as a holiday camp and activity centre. In view of its popularity, the council is providing more attractions in the park for visitors. One of the newly-added attractions is a horse-riding school funded and built by the Royal Hong Kong Jockey Club. Other attractions under planning include a museum, an indoor leisure centre and a free-form pool.

Kowloon Walled City Park

The Kowloon Walled City site will be developed into a Chinese-style landscaped garden with the restored *yamen* building as a focal point. Other attractions will include a chess garden, a pine mound, a rock garden, a piazza, a lily pond, a stone tablet garden and a children's playground. Relics of the Walled City, including two cannons, five stone inscriptions and three old wells, will be preserved at various locations inside the park. This park, to be managed by the Urban Council, will be integrated with the existing Carpenter Road Park to form a regional facility for local residents and tourists.

The project is being funded by the government at a cost of $59 million. Work on the park will start in early 1994 and is scheduled for completion by mid-1995.

Zoological and Botanical Gardens

The Hong Kong Zoological and Botanical Gardens are the oldest and among the most popular public gardens in the territory. Situated on a 5.35-hectare site overlooking Government House, the gardens contain a wide variety of plants and animals, and are notable for their pleasant environment and imaginative use of space.

The gardens were constructed between 1861 and 1871, divided by Albany Road. The old garden, on the east side of the road, houses an extensive bird collection while the new garden, opened in 1871, houses various mammals. The botanical section is mainly located in the old garden.

The Urban Council, which manages the facility, puts considerable emphasis on the breeding and conservation of endangered species. The gardens house 12 endangered species of mammals, birds and reptiles and, despite the urban environment, provide a most successful breeding centre. This has been borne out by the increased breeding loans arranged through the relevant international breeding programmes for endangered species.

The bird collection is one of the most comprehensive in Asia, with over 1 000 birds of 300 species. Though less comprehensive, the mammal collection is varied and interesting. The mammals include the echidna, an egg-laying mammal; and the jaguar, the world's third largest cat. To further enrich the zoological collection, a reptile enclosure is being developed on the site of the old greenhouse and will be stocked in early 1994.

As the sale and transfer of stock among countries is becoming increasingly difficult, in-house breeding is now essential and has resulted in the development of local expertise in husbandry, aided by improved veterinary support for monitoring health and diagnostic laboratory work.

The gardens feature more than 500 species of trees and shrubs. The fountain terrace contains a large central fountain, and the landscaped surrounds include more than 250 species of ornamental shrubs and flowering plants.

The medicinal plant collection, established in 1987, has generated much interest. To update the display facilities, the shade house built some 40 years ago was demolished and a new greenhouse was built on the same site. It now houses some 200 species of orchids, ferns, cacti, succulents and other indoor plants.

In recent years, the educational role of the gardens has been further developed. Numerous school and club visits have been arranged.

Regional Council Parks

Over 510 parks and gardens of various sizes, including four town parks, are managed by the Regional Council.

Tuen Mun Town Park is the largest park in the New Territories. Occupying an area of 12.5 hectares, the park has an ornamental lake for rowing and a 160-metre water cascade, the largest of its kind in Hong Kong. Other features include an open-air performance arena, a children's playground and a skating rink. North District Central Park covers 9.6 hectares and is provided with a sports hall, amphitheatre, artificial lake and children's playground. The 8.5-hectare Sha Tin Central Park, with its Chinese garden and adventure playground, is the council's most popular park. Special features of the 7.5-hectare Yuen Long Town Park include a seven-level pagoda with a built-in aviary which houses more than 210 birds of 50 species. The park also has the first gateball pitch in the Regional Council area.

Country Parks

Despite Hong Kong's largely urban environment, opportunities for outdoor recreation are not lacking. No place is far from green countryside and there are 21 country parks covering some 40 per cent of the territory's total land area. Over 10 million visits were made to these parks during 1993. They are most popular during the cool, dry months from October to April.

The Director of Agriculture and Fisheries is the Country Parks Authority. With the advice of the Country Parks Board and its various committees, he is responsible for the management of land and provision of facilities within the country parks. These facilities include picnic and barbecue areas, walking trails, rain shelters, toilets, information posts and visitor centres.

Horticulture and Landscape Services

Urban Council

The Urban Council is heavily committed to improving the urban environment with landscaping. Its staff provide a full range of landscaping services including design and planning, plant production, planting, maintenance and conservation. All new projects undertaken by the council are expected to have a landscape element where possible. The council also plays a key role in preserving trees in the urban areas and in extending planting areas along the highways.

In 1993, the Urban Council planted about 9 000 trees and 800 000 flowering shrubs. About 90 per cent of the plants were produced in its own plant nurseries with the balance from commercial stocks.

To foster a greener Hong Kong, the council initiated the Green Hong Kong Campaign and designated 1993 as the Greening Year. The large-scale campaign was the first-ever greening campaign organised in Hong Kong. The Urban Council committed over $10 million in the year for this project which included tree planting in streets and on slopes. In addition, a series of community involvement activities such as talks and seminars, tree planting by the community, mini-flower shows, open days and guided visits to plant nurseries and major parks, and territory-wide potted plants competitions were organised to arouse public awareness of the need for greening Hong Kong. The 10 urban district boards, related government departments and voluntary greening organisations pledged their support for this meaningful campaign.

Apart from planting more trees, the council is also concerned with tree preservation. Its horticultural staff have been actively involved in preserving existing trees on development sites, and planting compensatory vegetation if the removal of the trees is unavoidable.

The council has put on display over 100 species of plants introduced from various countries such as Australia, South Africa, Taiwan, the USA and Southeast Asia at the Hong Kong Park's Forsgate Conservatory. Plants of special interests include *Victoria amazonica*, the largest water lilies; *Dendrocalamus sinicus*, the largest bamboo; and *Raphia raffia*, whose leaves are the biggest in the plant world.

Regional Council

The Regional Council maintains 693 hectares of greenery in parks, gardens, sportsgrounds, soccer pitches, games areas and children's playgrounds in the New Territories. It also manages amenity plots and soft landscape along highways and roads. In 1993, over

470 827 trees, shrubs, palms, creepers, ground covers and seasonal flowers were planted in parks, playgrounds and roadside amenities.

The council manages four nurseries in Tsuen Wan, Tuen Mun, Sha Tin and Tai Po. Tung Tze Nursery in Tai Po, which covers four hectares, is the biggest. In 1993, the nurseries together produced 3 741 trees, 179 823 shrubs, 87 329 ground covers, 1 120 creepers and 191 976 seasonal flowers.

Among the council's amenities features are its theme gardens. At Hing Fong Road Playground in Kwai Tsing, there is a scented garden, while Fanling Recreation Ground in North District has a hibiscus garden. Residents of Sai Kung can rest in the shade of palms at Sha Tsui Playground Garden. Sheung Chuen Park in Yuen Long is graced with conifers. Roses carpet the garden at Tuen Mun Town Park, while Yuen Long Town Park boasts an azalea garden and Sha Tin Central Park an assorted seasonal flower garden.

In 1993, to promote interest in gardening and educate the public on the importance of keeping Hong Kong green, the Regional Council organised 21 horticultural classes, and conducted 25 guided tours and lectures for visitors at open days at the nurseries as part of a greening scheme. Stickers and bookmarks were produced and distributed to visitors and school children to encourage their awareness of the plants and greenery around them. The message was also broadcast at the Regional Council stall at the Third China National Flower Show held in Beijing in April 1993.

Hong Kong Flower Show

Since 1987, the Urban Council and the Regional Council have jointly organised the annual Hong Kong Flower Show. The show has become a major public event popular with professional horticulturists as well as amateur plant-lovers.

The 1993 show, held at the Sha Tin Town Hall and Sha Tin Central Park in March, attracted more than 80 horticultural organisations from 12 countries, and was visited by 300 000 people.

24
THE ENVIRONMENT

BEHIND the changing face of Hong Kong lie environmental problems which are common to most developed countries. The territory's rapid growth of population, industry and commerce remain at the root of pollution by human activities.

The government has substantially increased spending to clean up the environment in recent years. In 1993–94, this category of expenditure made up 2.6 per cent of public spending, totalling $4,045 million, compared to 0.8 per cent in 1988–89.

The year 1993 ended with the publication of an environmental review, entitled 'A Green Challenge for the Community', in which future courses of government action were outlined and a challenge was issued to the Hong Kong people to accept a share of the responsibility for improving the environment.

Much progress was made during the year towards controlling and eliminating pollution.

Additional measures were introduced to control air, water, waste and noise pollution. These included controls on the handling and disposal of chemical waste; and the extension of the Water Pollution Control Ordinance to two new control zones that cover the industrial areas at Tsing Yi and Eastern Hong Kong. A review of the livestock waste control programme led to more effective controls on this form of organic pollutants.

Details of a programme of sewage improvement schemes, costing $12 billion (in 1993 prices), were announced in September, for completion by 1997. The programme aims to clean up Victoria Harbour, where as much as 50 per cent of the territory's sewage goes untreated, and to improve sewage services in other areas. It includes proposals for the introduction in 1994 of a sewage services charging scheme, under which users will contribute towards the costs of better services under a 'polluter pays' principle.

Sewerage master plan studies were completed for North and South Kowloon, Chai Wan and Shau Kei Wan, and Tuen Mun. The Drainage Services Department has begun to implement these plans in phases.

The award of contracts for two new strategic landfills and one additional refuse transfer station was an important step forward in the government's waste disposal strategy.

Legislative amendments to the Air Pollution Control Ordinance extended its scope to cover more air-polluting industries and environmental asbestos, and increased penalties and fines. Further controls under the Ozone Layer Protection Ordinance accelerated the phasing out of ozone-depleting substances as part of a global programme.

In October, the government announced plans to set up a task force, bringing together a number of its departments, to clean up pollution in the New Territories over the next decade. The new measures will involve tougher enforcement action against unauthorised land use.

Plans for a $50 million Environment and Conservation Fund for Hong Kong were also announced, to help pay for environmental education and research.

The establishment of marine parks and marine reserves was approved to protect and manage unspoilt areas for conservation, education and recreation. In the first phase, Hoi Ha Wan and Yan Chau Tong in Sai Kung were recommended for designation as marine parks while Cape D'Aguilar on southern Hong Kong Island was proposed for designation as a marine reserve. The relevant legislation is expected to be ready in 1994.

The Environmental Protection Department set up three more local control offices during the year, bringing to five the total number of such offices. These offices deal with local issues, promptly responding to complaints from local residents and keeping potential pollution blackspots under closer supervision than was possible with centralised control.

The government is reviewing the implications, for its environmental and related policies, of recommendations which arose from the United Nations Conference on the Environment and Development, held in Rio de Janeiro in 1992.

This chapter also looks at Hong Kong's climate, topography, hydrography, and fauna and flora.

The State of the Environment

A 1989 White Paper entitled 'Pollution in Hong Kong — A Time to Act' acknowledged that the reason the environment was in an unsatisfactory state was largely a result of the earlier lack of emphasis placed on this area by the government.

A series of measures has been introduced over the years to ensure that greater emphasis is given to environmental matters in planning decisions.

In December, the government issued 'A Green Challenge for the Community', which was its second review of the 1989 White Paper.

Aside from stressing the need for public awareness and participation to improve the environment, the document examined the progress of the government's environmental protection programme, set down the basis for future action and explained new initiatives for improving the performance of the government and the community.

For the first time, 10 foundation stones were set down to assist the development of collective responsibility, including sustaining the environment for future generations, private sector participation and the adoption of the 'polluter pays' principle.

The government also proposed eight sets of regulations for 1994 — to ban open burning, control construction dust, control percussive piling and other construction noise, control the management of asbestos, control vehicle emissions, introduce sewage charges, introduce charges for some categories of solid waste disposals at landfills, and introduce charges for the disposal of chemical waste.

Urban Environmental Quality

The government has committed a great deal of money and effort to meeting the challenges of Hong Kong's older urban areas. These offer a dense mix of housing, community facilities, and commerce and industry — with an infrastructure that falls short of modern standards. Poor urban landscaping, incompatible neighbouring uses, air and water pollution, noise, and waste disposal problems are common.

Hong Kong's objectives for air quality are comparable to internationally-recognised air quality standards for the protection of public health. The actual air quality does not always meet the objectives. Total suspended particulates, respirable suspended particulates and nitrogen dioxide are often high. In 1993, the highest annual averages recorded were 320 micrograms per cubic metre of total suspended particulates and 180 micrograms per cubic metre of respirable suspended particulates, both at levels above the objectives. Nitrogen dioxide was near its objective of 80 micrograms per cubic metre. Emissions from motor vehicles are the main source of these pollutants, and preparatory work for the introduction of cleaner automobile fuel and tighter standards for heavy duty diesel vehicles was undertaken. A scheme to largely replace the use of light duty diesel with unleaded petrol is being formulated.

The ever-increasing demand for transport has led to serious noise problems in areas close to major roads and rail transport corridors. The continued re-paving of roads with quieter surfaces and noise-insulating of schools brought further relief to more Hong Kong residents. The Kowloon-Canton Railway Corporation embarked on a massive 10-year programme to abate the noise along its entire railway line through the use of noise barriers and enclosures. The Mass Transit Railway Corporation also started to implement a noise mitigation programme for its rolling stock, railway tracks and maintenance depots.

Urban sewerage grew alongside the city without an overall controlling strategy. The Environmental Protection Department has estimated that, due to the many expedient connections between foul sewerage and storm drains, only half the city's sewage — a million tonnes a day — gets any treatment before it flows into the sea. The resulting load of water pollution has a severe impact on confined areas such as typhoon shelters. In the worst of these, such as the Kowloon Bay typhoon shelter beside Kai Tak airport, foul-smelling and toxic gases stem from the polluted water. A major $500 million re-sewerage project is under construction under Stage I of the East Kowloon sewerage master plan to bring substantial relief to the area by late 1994.

In the harbour, water quality does not reach desired standards. The median concentration of dissolved oxygen, a good indicator of water quality, is close to 50 per cent saturation — the minimum level the water quality objectives allow. Phase I of the strategic sewage disposal scheme, for which detailed investigations and design are in progress, will reduce harbour pollution significantly. The declaration of two more water control zones (the Western Buffer and Eastern Buffer Water Control Zones) in 1993 will also reduce pollution in the harbour through the enforcement of the Water Pollution Control Ordinance.

With the community's growing expectations for a better environment, the need for a cost-effective, secure and environmentally acceptable waste management programme has been recognised.

Consideration is also being given to the control of special categories of waste, such as clinical waste, decomposing carcasses and various types of sludge.

The comprehensive control of the handling and disposal of chemical waste commenced in May with the opening of the chemical waste treatment centre and full implementation of the Waste Disposal (Chemical Waste) (General) Regulation. Hong Kong is now able to stop the widespread malpractice of dumping untreated chemical waste into the territory's sewers and surface waters, in this way improving the water quality in the receiving waters, particularly the inner harbour.

The Environment of New Towns

The development of new towns in what were formerly rural areas, on the nuclei of small fishing or market towns, has helped sustain economic growth in Hong Kong.

To some extent, the territory's new towns face the same environmental problems as the old urban areas. However, they have been better planned. They tend to be more spacious, and are better provided with sewers and facilities for waste disposal. On the negative side, water pollution in the rivers, streams and sea has become a problem.

With the declaration of the Northwestern Water Control Zone in 1992, the protection of the Water Pollution Control Ordinance was extended to all new towns.

The decline in water quality in Tolo Harbour — where a major part of the pollution comes from effluent from industrial and commercial areas reaching storm water drains, and sewage discharge from village areas — appears to have been halted. Through the enforcement of the ordinance, a large number of the unauthorised or expedient connections have been rectified. Implementation of the Sewerage Master Plan for the Tolo Harbour area will eliminate direct sewage discharge from the villages into surface water. The nutrient-rich effluent from the Sha Tin sewage treatment works has contributed to the poor water quality in Tolo Harbour. As a major element of the Tolo Harbour Action Plan, a tunnel diverting the treated effluent from the treatment works to an environmentally less sensitive area is scheduled for completion in 1994. Flows from the Tai Po sewage treatment works will be connected into the scheme in 1995.

Another pollution problem is the high concentration of heavy metals in industrial discharges. These have upset the performance of the government's sewage treatment works. However, statutory controls have been successful in reducing the pollution loading in the various water control zones.

Rural Areas and the Sea

While some rural areas are badly polluted, others offer tremendous opportunities for conservation and recreation.

In the developed parts of the New Territories, water pollution in many rivers and streams remains severe. Some streams have recorded a degree of pollution equivalent to 10 times the strength of raw domestic sewage, and a thick, foul crust can be observed on the streams. This pollution poses a serious health risk when it passes through towns such as Yuen Long and Tuen Mun. With effective legislative controls, significant improvements in water quality have been achieved in some rivers such as the Mui Wo River and Tai Po Kau Stream.

The cause of much of this pollution is the territory's livestock industry. Before 1987, the total amount of waste produced annually by about 700 000 pigs and 12 million poultry in Hong Kong was 840 000 tonnes. This was equivalent to the pollution load of the raw sewage from a population of two million people. Most of it ended up in Hong Kong's small streams and rivers and eventually, the sea. By the end of 1993, this load had been reduced to 330 000 tonnes.

In the sea, away from the urban areas and confined bays, water quality objectives are met most of the time. However, dredging and dumping as part of the process of land formation and construction continued to affect the marine environment. Extensive areas of muddy water were visible at times, and some fishermen complained of reduced catches. Illegal dumping and short dumping of spoil (outside the designated areas) damage marine life.

Bathing beaches are an important recreational resource. Due to the great effort expended on pollution control in critical areas, the water quality of most of Hong Kong's beaches has improved. However, due to the recent rapid development in Tuen Mun and Tsuen Wan districts, beaches in these two districts are still sporadically polluted by domestic sewage discharged from the beach hinterlands where sewerage facilities will need to be improved.

To safeguard the public against swimming in polluted waters, the Environmental Protection Department has adopted strict *E. coli* (a bacterium) standards for water quality control in bathing beaches. This standard relates to the degree of faecal pollution and was devised by the department after a very thorough study of the health risks that local bathers face. The following table shows how beaches were classified in 1992 and 1993.

Annual beach rank	Bathing season geometric mean of *E. coli* count per 100 mL of beach water	Health risk cases per 1 000 swimmers	Number of beaches	
			1992	1993
Good	Up to 24	Undetectable	22	22
Fair	25 to 180	Under 10	22	19
Poor	181 to 610	10 to 15	9	12
Very Poor	More than 610	Over 15	3	3

Unfortunately, complaints occur even at beaches that are free from sewage pollution, usually because of floating refuse and occasionally because of slime caused by algae.

Protecting the Environment

The Administrative Framework

The Environmental Protection Department is the government's main store of expertise in pollution control and environmental management. Its tasks include: providing advice on policy; implementing programmes to meet policy goals for all aspects of pollution; undertaking environmental planning and assessment; devising, enforcing and reviewing the effectiveness of all environmental legislation, and recommending new or amended legislation; and planning and developing facilities for liquid and solid waste disposal.

Other departments also play a major role in protecting Hong Kong's environment. The Planning Department takes care of the environment in government urban and rural planning at strategic and local level. The Drainage Services Department designs, builds, operates and maintains sewerage and sewage treatment and disposal facilities throughout the territory. The Territory Development Department carries out sewerage and sewage disposal works in new towns. The Urban Services Department and Regional Services Department provide refuse collection services and maintain environmental hygiene. The Civil Engineering Department oversees and operates landfills for the disposal of waste. The Agriculture and Fisheries Department is responsible for wildlife and countryside conservation; manages agricultural weirs; and operates and maintains departmental farm waste treatment facilities. The Electrical and Mechanical Services Department operates refuse incinerators and promotes energy efficiency. The Marine Department clears floating refuse and oil from harbour waters, and enforces the law on oil spills.

Planning Against Pollution

Environmental planning aims to achieve land uses that are environmentally acceptable and compatible among neighbours. A pro-active approach is adopted to anticipate and avoid environmental problems which may arise from developments, and to promote environmental improvements. It is carried out through input at various levels of planning, often assisted by environmental impact assessment (EIA) studies. A legislative proposal is being formulated to require both the conduct of EIA studies before developments are carried out, and the full implementation of any recommended environmental measures. This legislation is expected to go before the Legislative Council in 1994.

The Governor's policy speech in October 1992 set out important initiatives to strengthen environmental planning. All submissions on policy matters going before the Executive Council must now report on environmental implications. Government departments have also been asked to take more responsibility for their own environmental performance. Apart from the Governor's initiatives, all submissions on public sector projects to the Public Works Sub-committee of the Finance Committee must also include information on environmental implications before funding approval can be given.

At the strategic level, a review of the Territorial Development Strategy, the overall blueprint for developing Hong Kong, is being undertaken to recommend improvements to the territory's land use, environmental and transport framework. The study aims to improve not only the efficiency of the territory but, more importantly, the quality of life. As part of the review, a territorial environmental profile was completed and published. A series of development options are being examined and evaluated, with a view to ensuring that development aspirations can be accommodated within the limits of local and regional environmental targets. The results so far indicate the difficulty of sustaining a clean and healthy environment without placing a limit on development.

Environmentally-desirable land-use changes are being more precisely defined through sub-regional development strategy reviews and district development statements. Environmental planning studies are being undertaken as part of the Metroplan-derived district development statements. In 1993, both the Tsuen Wan and Kwai Tsing development statement, and the Southeast Kowloon study were nearing completion, while work on the development statements for Hong Kong West and for Central and East Kowloon were progressing. These statements also deal with industrial and residential interfaces.

Building on a previous report endorsed by the Hong Kong-Guangdong Environmental Protection Liaison Group, work on defining the cumulative environmental effects of developments in and around Deep Bay continued in 1993. An EIA is being commissioned for the proposed Shenzhen River regulation project. It aims to examine the environmental acceptability of the project, with a view to preserving and protecting the important and unique environments at Mai Po and Inner Deep Bay, the Fu Tien Nature Reserve on the Shenzhen side and other important conservation assets in the region.

At the district level, hazardous and polluting facilities are gradually being resited away from densely populated areas as long-term solutions. Examples of such removals are the cement plants at Kennedy Town and Tsing Yi; the Kennedy Town Abattoir; Hok Un Power Station; Ma Tau Kok Gas Works; and some of the oil depots on Tsing Yi Island.

The EIA process has now been applied to all major new development and redevelopment sites under the Hong Kong Housing Authority, Hong Kong Housing Society and Land Development Corporation. Traffic noise and sewerage constraints are two common issues. Carrying out these EIAs has resulted in more effective and less costly solutions, as well as a better environment for the future residents than would have been the case.

Environmental issues associated with proposals to develop golf courses in rural areas or areas of conservation value emerged as an important concern that aroused considerable public reaction. The key environmental questions were the compatibility of the golf course development with nature conservation, the effects of the use of chemicals associated with the maintenance and operation of golf courses, and the disposal of sewage from the residential and recreational developments that often go with the golf courses. It has now become standard for an EIA study to address the key environmental issues before any golf course proposal is considered by the government.

Port and Airport Development

During 1993, the environmental focus for the Port and Airport Development Strategy (PADS) was the implementation of the recommendations of EIA studies on the project. PADS has been designed to provide, in the most cost-effective way, for the growth of both the port and the airport.

The contract for site formation work for the new airport at Chek Lap Kok was awarded in November 1992. Environmental protection measures have been incorporated into the contract to control the effects of dredging and site formation on water quality, noise on existing dwellings on the nearby North Lantau and Peng Chau coastlines, and dust pollution, particularly from rock-blasting. An environmental monitoring and audit programme is in place to closely monitor the actual effects of the construction work and to ensure effective implementation of the required protection measures.

Dredging and reclamation work for the Tung Chung new town and North Lantau Expressway, and construction of the Lantau Fixed Crossing continued in 1993. For the Tung Chung project, a number of dwellings affected by construction noise will be insulated and air-conditioned. An EIA study on the expressway project has shown that the effects of construction would be acceptable. Mitigation measures will be required for noise nuisance from round-the-clock work on the Lantau Fixed Crossing and from future airport railway operations. Comprehensive monitoring and auditing is being carried out to contain the actual impacts, within acceptable bounds.

A number of major port development studies were completed to provide a framework for future developments. The major difficulty has been finding ways to accommodate these gigantic port developments without significant accompanying environmental decline as a result of increased land-based, port-related activities. The results of EIA studies for Lantau Port and the West Harbour Development called for measures to minimise the impacts of construction and operations. These include the adoption of an island design to minimise the impact on water quality, and the use of quiet port equipment and barriers to mitigate the impact of operational noise.

Noise from the operation of the planned Container Terminal 9, the control of both on-site dredging of contaminated mud and off-site dumping activities, and the dredging of marine sand in the East Lamma Channel, are three major environmental issues. Detailed environmental protection clauses were, or will be, incorporated in the land grant documents for these projects to forestall adverse consequences.

Since 1992, the West Kowloon Environmental Project Office has performed an important role in initiating practicable preventive or remedial measures to deal with dust, noise and water quality aspects of several construction contracts in West Kowloon. In 1993, a second environmental project office was set up to deal with the cumulative effects arising from the construction works taking place in Kwai Chung and Tsing Yi. The two areas are affected by projects such as Route 3, the airport railway and other non-airport core projects such as Container Terminal 9 and the South Tsing Yi Bridge. As with the West Kowloon office, this project office will take a pro-active approach in identifying cumulative environmental problems, proposing effective mitigation measures and keeping the public informed on the environmental performance of the projects.

Measures to deal with noise from the future operation of these projects were also devised. To minimise the noise from traffic, the need for 7.5 kilometres of roadside noise barriers was identified for Route 3 and the West Kowloon and North Lantau Expressways. A 205-metre road enclosure will need to be built over a busy distributor road serving the South Tsing Yi Bridge.

Implementation plans were drawn up for the provision of noise insulation for about 3 000 homes which will be affected by traffic using the Western Harbour Crossing and the operation of the Duplicate South Tsing Yi Bridge.

For the airport railway, detailed work was undertaken on land-use compatibility, the design of residential tower blocks to be located on or near railway stations, and the provision of noise mitigation measures, including noise barriers. By drawing early attention to noise considerations at the planning stage, it should be possible to avoid the need for difficult retro-fitting in the future.

Noise from future aircraft operations at the new airport at Chek Lap Kok has been carefully predicted, and the generated Noise Exposure Forecast (NEF) contours are being used to guide land-use planning in the airport's vicinity.

Power Generation

To meet the rising demand for electricity in the coming decades, the two local power companies have submitted separate proposals to the government for increasing generation capacities. Approval has been granted for the initial phase of the expansion plans.

Hong Kong Electric Company Limited proposes to build two additional 350 megawatt, coal-fired, generating units at its Lamma Island site. An EIA study for the expansion plan was completed in 1993. To reduce air pollution from the additional coal-fired generating units, flue gas desulphurisation systems will be installed. The company will also limit the sulphur content in the coal it uses. The chosen flue gas desulphurisation system will produce a large amount of solid gypsum that will require disposal. An arrangement has been made by the company to export the solid gypsum to other countries for industrial re-use in an environmentally acceptable manner. As for pulverised fuel ash, industrial use is the preferred option. Its use in reclamation works under certain conditions has also been accepted as a long-term option.

China Light and Power Company Limited proposes the construction of an additional 6 000 megawatt facility at Black Point in Tuen Mun. The environmental factor was an important consideration in the choice of the site. The company plans, as Phase 1 of the new power station development, to build four 600 megawatt combined cycle generating units fired on natural gas, with light industrial diesel oil as the backup fuel. A full-scale EIA study on the proposed gas-fired units concluded that the environmental impact can be controlled within acceptable limits. The use of natural gas will greatly reduce air pollution and help to minimise the emission of greenhouse gases thought to contribute to global warming.

At the same time, the government has implemented energy efficiency programmes to reduce the use of energy. Such efforts will help conserve non-renewable energy resources and mitigate human impact on climate change.

Marine Borrow and Dumping Areas

The construction of the new airport requires 170 million cubic metres of marine fill and 134 million cubic metres of land-based fill. A total of 4.9 million and 139 million cubic metres of contaminated and uncontaminated mud, respectively, will require disposal. These huge quantities pose an immense challenge.

An EIA study on the South Mirs Bay borrow area showed that an unacceptable environmental impact and significant economic loss would be incurred by the fishing and mariculture industries from dredging in that area. As a result, the proposed dredging in South Mirs Bay and Ching Chau were cancelled by the government's Fill Management Committee.

The EIA study on the East Lamma Channel, completed in 1993, also indicated dredging would result in significant adverse effects on gazetted beaches, mariculture zones, capture fisheries and corals. The results led the government to significantly reduce the area of dredging to about half the original size, and to impose stringent controls and monitoring requirements on the proponent and contractors using the borrow area.

There was considerable professional and public concern about dredged mud. The disposal of contaminated mud at East Sha Chau was a case in point. To prevent adverse effects, the mud disposal would need to be controlled by using environmentally acceptable mud disposal methods and sealing the pit with suitable materials after it reaches the designed capacity. Active and full-time pit management, and intensive environmental monitoring would also be required.

Rural Developments

Under the Rural Planning and Improvement Strategy, the government is committed to improving the quality of life in rural areas. The strategy has moved forward, with efforts to terminate thousands of polluting short-term land uses. Village sewage improvement schemes have also been carried out in the rural areas of the New Territories.

As a result of the revision of the livestock waste control scheme, anyone wishing to keep livestock has to apply for a licence. This provides a powerful planning tool to ensure environmental compatibility with other planned or prevailing land uses.

Hazardous Installations

The government's risk management policy on potentially hazardous installations (PHIs) is to minimise risks to the public by requiring the PHIs to be constructed and operated to the highest standards and by controlling the land use within their vicinity. In 1988, the government introduced a set of Interim Risk Guidelines to determine the acceptability of risk associated with a PHI. The guidelines were formally adopted in 1993, and will be incorporated into the Hong Kong Planning Standards and Guidelines in 1994. An 'as low as reasonably practicable' principle was introduced into the guidelines to ensure implementation of all risk reduction measures which are practicable and cost-effective. The Hong Kong Risk Guidelines now limit public risks from PHIs to levels which are comparable with the most stringent international standards.

Chlorine has long been used in Hong Kong for water disinfection at water treatment works and swimming pools. Chlorine is toxic and potential risks to nearby residents from chlorine storage and use have been evaluated for all water treatment works, which are classified as PHIs. The risk assessments confirmed compliance with the Risk Guidelines following the introduction of several mitigation measures, including improvement in chlorine handling procedures, the replacement of bulk storage tanks with one tonne or 50-kilogramme containers, and the installation of chlorine absorption systems. These risk mitigation measures were fully implemented by the end of 1993. The Urban Services Department and Regional Services Department have agreed to phase out the use of conventional chlorine gas dosing systems for swimming pools in the future. The departments are converting to smaller cylinders for chlorine in the interim and are gradually adopting other safer sterilisation systems.

Legislation and Pollution Control

Hong Kong has six main pieces of legislation to control pollution. They are: the Waste Disposal Ordinance; the Water Pollution Control Ordinance; the Air Pollution Control Ordinance; the Noise Control Ordinance; the Ozone Layer Protection Ordinance and the Dumping At Sea Act (Overseas Territories) Order. Most of these include subsidiary regulations and other statutory provisions, such as technical memoranda, that give specific effect to the intentions of the principal laws.

The government has adopted a system of environmental quality objectives as a general principle in its pollution control laws. The objectives are set at levels that will protect conservation goals, such as the protection of public health or the preservation of a natural ecosystem. This system usually gives the required environmental benefit at the least cost. The limits it imposes on pollutant emissions are no more stringent or costly than is necessary to achieve the conservation goal. It also makes the maximum safe use of the environment's capacity to neutralise pollution.

Industrial and Commercial Emissions

Industrial and commercial success in Hong Kong has been achieved at the expense of severe degradation of the environment. The penalty is being paid in the form of adverse ecological changes, a heavy but usually hidden financial burden on the community, and great risks to community health.

The government's pollution control strategy aims not to harm industry and commerce, but to work in partnership with firms, so that all may benefit from a better environment. There are often direct economic benefits to be gained from activities that benefit the environment, such as recycling and the adoption of clean technology in manufacturing. These methods are better than pollution control techniques that have to be applied after a waste material has become a potential pollutant.

The government would prefer industry and commerce to recognise the benefits of waste minimisation and pollution prevention, but it is inevitable that this is not an entirely voluntary process and legislative control is required. Nowhere is this more apparent than in the case of the Water Pollution Control Ordinance, which first came into operation in 1987, and has been gradually extended to a series of water control zones. These zones were in 1993 extended to some of the most heavily industrialised areas, though the major industrial areas surrounding Victoria Harbour have yet to be covered.

The Eastern Buffer and Western Buffer Water Control Zones were declared on June 1. The Eastern Buffer Water Control Zone covers Chai Wan and Shau Kei Wan, while the Western Buffer Water Control Zone covers Tsing Yi Island, part of Tsuen Wan (to the west of Tai Chung Road), Sham Tseng, Aberdeen, Ap Lei Chau and Pok Fu Lam. This includes six gazetted beaches along Castle Peak Road.

The Southern and Tolo Harbour Supplementary Water Control Zones, which cover the catchments of Tai Tam, Shek Pik, Plover Cove and Shing Mun Reservoirs, were also declared on June 1. All water-gathering grounds in the New Territories are now covered by the water control zones.

The Victoria Harbour Water Control Zone, which will be the last water control zone to be declared, will shortly be covered, in phases.

The Western Buffer Water Control Zone has, among all the existing water control zones, the highest concentration of electroplaters, printed circuit board manufacturers, and bleaching and dyeing factories. Together, they generate over 20 000 cubic metres of industrial effluent daily, mostly untreated. Control efforts are now focussed on these industries to reduce the pollutants, in particular the toxic metals and alkaline waste, which greatly affect the water quality of the Rambler Channel.

All trade effluents discharged into a water control zone must be covered by a licence, which will specify the maximum amount of pollutants that may be discharged. The standards vary from place to place in accordance with the conservation goals and water quality objectives for the receiving water body. Licence standards usually follow a set of published guidelines.

Considerable efforts are made to ensure that effluents meet the standards set in licences. In 1993, Environmental Protection Department inspectors took more than 4 000 effluent samples and conducted over 13 000 laboratory tests.

These control measures have had great success. For example, in Tolo Harbour, the first water control zone, more than 100 'expedient' connections were rectified. The organic pollution load on the harbour has been reduced by 75 per cent. Concentrations of heavy metals in the processed sludge of the Sha Tin sewage treatment works have been reduced to such an extent that the sludge now meets the stringent standards that apply to marine disposal. In the Southern Water Control Zone, over 90 per cent of private sewage treatment plants now operate satisfactorily and the water quality of many popular bathing beaches has improved as a result.

In Yuen Long and Tuen Mun, a total of 16 000 cubic metres per day of industrial and commercial effluents have been diverted from storm drains to the foul sewerage system. This is equivalent to the organic pollution load from a population of over 80 000 people. In the established zones of Port Shelter and Junk Bay, the reduction is as much as 70 and 50 per cent, respectively, of the organic pollution load.

In all control zones, the department estimates that so far, it has achieved an average of about 50 per cent reduction in the target pollution load by enforcing the Water Pollution Control Ordinance. Even more positive results are expected when the controls have been fully implemented.

Pollution in the once notorious Ho Chung River — the black river of Sai Kung — has improved dramatically due to effective control of the major industrial polluters. An interceptor scheme, diverting further pollution away from the river for treatment, is expected to be in operation by early 1994.

The Waste Disposal Ordinance is complementary to the Water Pollution Control Ordinance in controlling industrial pollution. It provides the statutory framework for the management of all solid and semi-solid waste in Hong Kong.

The Waste Disposal (Chemical Waste) (General) Regulation was enforced in stages and full control was achieved over all chemical waste from industry and commerce in May, from the point of production to point of disposal. Chemical waste producers must register with the Environmental Protection Department. They must pack, label, and temporarily store their chemical waste in a safe and proper manner before delivery to licensed facilities for treatment and disposal. Only facilities capable of treating, recycling or disposing of chemical waste in an environmentally acceptable manner can obtain a licence. Licensing control also applies to the collection and transportation of chemical waste. The licence conditions require a sound operation employing fully-trained and skilful staff, and proper equipment and vehicles.

A system of consignment notes, called trip tickets, are used in the 'cradle to grave' control of chemical waste. A tailor-made computer information management system tracks waste movements through the trip ticket records. All responsible parties, including the waste producer, the waste collector and the reception manager of the waste disposal site, must supply accurate details of each consignment of waste.

Coinciding with the full enforcement of the Waste Disposal (Chemical Waste) (General) Regulation was the commissioning of the Chemical Waste Treatment Centre, which is run by a government contractor. The treatment centre is the main licensed disposal facility and collector for chemical waste generated in Hong Kong. Its operator provides a fleet of vehicles for the collection of waste from the waste producers.

To assist chemical waste producers to comply with the new regulations, guidebooks, leaflets and codes of practices were published, seminars organised, and a telephone hotline set up to explain the legislation.

In addition to liquid and solid wastes, many factories and commercial enterprises produce emissions to the air. The Environmental Protection Department operates air pollution controls under the Air Pollution Control Ordinance. Subsidiary regulations under the ordinance provide specific controls on furnaces and chimneys, dark smoke emissions, fuel composition and specified processes. Regulations have been proposed to ban open burning of waste materials and to reduce dust emissions from construction work.

The installation and alteration of furnaces, ovens and chimneys need prior approval from the department. This commonly affects industrial furnaces, restaurant stoves and chimneys serving emergency generators. The requirement for prior approval is to prevent emissions from new installations causing air pollution problems when they come into operation, and to ensure that district air quality objectives will not be violated. During 1993, the department processed 656 applications.

Nuisance and environmental problems caused by dark smoke emissions, which commonly result from poor maintenance or incorrect operation of fuel burners, arouse great public concern, especially when factories are near homes. The Air Pollution Control (Smoke) Regulations provide controls on dark smoke emission, limiting the darkness of smoke to Ringelmann shade number 1 which corresponds to 20 per cent opacity.

In July 1990, the Air Pollution Control (Fuel Restriction) Regulations banned fuel oils with a sulphur content over 0.5 per cent by weight or a viscosity over six centistokes at 40°C. The sulphur content of solid fuels is limited to one per cent by weight. Due to the unfavourable topography of the Sha Tin area, which restricts atmospheric dispersion, only gaseous fuels may be used there.

The enforcement of the fuel restriction regulations has successfully reduced emissions of sulphur dioxide by 80 per cent. These regulations have also reduced nitrogen oxides and particulates.

Certain industrial facilities and processes, including power utilities, incinerators, gas production plants, metallurgical factories and cement plants, which are liable to cause significant air pollution, are targeted for control under the licensing system provided by the Air Pollution Control Ordinance and the specified processes regulations.

However, most of these facilities are presently exempted from licensing control. At the end of 1993, there were 83 exempted premises while only 60 licences were in force. As the exempted premises are not obliged to adopt the best practicable means to control air pollution, they continue to cause problems.

To tackle this situation, the Air Pollution Control (Amendment) Ordinance enacted in February 1993, will allow the phased removal of these exemptions by 1997. In addition, the number of specified processes covered by the amended ordinance increased from 23 to 31. The eight new processes are pathological waste incinerators, organic chemical works, petroleum works, zinc galvanising works, rendering works, non-ferrous metallurgical works, glass works and paint works. Together with the proposal to adopt a technical memorandum approach in issuing air pollution abatement notices, these new measures will further reduce air pollution in Hong Kong.

Enforcement of the air pollution law involves complaint investigations, providing technical advice, issuing warning notices to require polluters to abate their emissions, and prosecution. During 1993, 1 939 complaint cases were investigated; there were 7 919 inspections of plant; 1 813 cases were given technical advice; 60 warning notices were issued; and there were 227 successful prosecutions. Fines on offenders ranged from $300 to $30,000.

Noise from industrial or commercial premises is controlled under the Noise Control Ordinance. The department responds to complaints and may serve noise abatement notices that require a reduction of excessive noise by a given date. Failure to comply with the notices is an offence, liable to prosecution. During 1993, 2 300 complaints were investigated; 250 noise abatement notices were served; and 150 offenders were prosecuted. Fines on noise offenders ranged from $1,000 to $80,000.

Transport

Transport by road and rail can cause air pollution and noise nuisance, while shipping is more likely to cause water pollution through inappropriate waste disposal.

Large diesel vehicles are major contributors to vehicle emissions. The government is developing control strategies that include up-to-date emission standards for large vehicles and tightened inspection and maintenance requirements for certain classes of vehicles to reduce emissions.

Since April 1991, all petrol stations must sell unleaded petrol, to ensure its availability for cars with catalytic converters. The market share of unleaded petrol, which is cheaper, averaged about 64 per cent in 1993.

The Air Pollution Control (Vehicle Design Standards) (Emission) Regulations became effective in January 1992. These regulations require that all new vehicles of 2.5 tonnes or less must meet stringent emission standards. To comply, petrol-fuelled cars must be fitted with catalytic converter emission control devices and engine management systems. The regulations also require that all petrol-fuelled cars registered after January 1992 must use unleaded petrol. Plans are in hand to lower the sulphur content of vehicle diesel fuel oil by 1995.

The existing scheme for reporting smoky vehicles was revised in October 1991. Smoky vehicles that are observed are now directed to take remedial action and to attend a designated testing centre to confirm that the smoke problem has been rectified. There are 20 centres in operation, and they conducted approximately 42 000 smoke tests in 1993.

The government is also considering a scheme which will see the eventual replacement of diesel-powered taxis, public light buses and light goods vehicles by cleaner, unleaded petrol-fuelled counterparts. Using a system of duty rebates to equalise the operating costs of both types of vehicles during the five-year period when both are on the road, the scheme will eliminate most smoky vehicles and contribute to much-needed reductions in health-threatening levels of air pollutants.

Traffic noise is a problem in some areas. A practical way to minimise sleep disturbance is to divert traffic, particularly heavy vehicles, from noise-sensitive receivers. A recent amendment to the Road Traffic Ordinance enables the regulation of traffic on environmental grounds, and this will be used to route heavy traffic away from residences in Ma Hang.

Under the Quiet Road Surface Programme, which aims to reduce the traffic noise impact on residents living close to high-speed trunk roads, 6.1 kilometres of roads were resurfaced with a quieter porous bitumen material. This brought relief to the residents of some 8 400 dwellings. A further 2.1 kilometres of roads are scheduled to be resurfaced in 1994.

The Noise Insulation Programme for Schools provides noise insulation for windows and air-conditioning for school classrooms affected by excessive levels of aircraft and traffic noise. To date, some 3 000 classrooms have been acoustically treated, benefiting 140 000 students. A further 4 500 classrooms will receive similar treatment in the coming two years.

Noise from the operation of rail transport is controlled under the Noise Control Ordinance. In 1993, the Mass Transit Railway Corporation started to implement a noise mitigation programme for its rolling stock, railway tracks and maintenance depots. The Kowloon-Canton Railway Corporation also launched a 10-year noise reduction programme to alleviate the railway noise at 18 populated locations along its line.

Controls on the discharge of oily wastes, noxious liquids and other harmful materials from ships have been introduced under the Merchant Shipping (Prevention and Control of Pollution) Ordinance. Among other things, the law sets minimum requirements aboard ocean-going and local vessels to prevent polluting discharges.

Construction and Demolition

The noise and vibration of the percussive pile-driver, once so characteristic of Hong Kong's massive construction programme, is now minimised by restrictions on its operations. The construction industry is no less active, however, and still generates noise, smoke and dust. It also produces vast quantities of solid waste that need safe disposal.

The Noise Control Ordinance, its regulations and two technical memoranda, are the major instruments for the control of construction noise. The Environmental Protection Department controls the operation of powered mechanical equipment in general construction work during weekdays from 7 pm to 7 am and on Sundays and public holidays by means of a construction noise permit system. The department assesses permit applications in accordance with noise criteria and procedures contained in the technical memoranda. The permits generally specify the number and type of equipment that may be used within a certain period of time. The ordinance also bans percussive piling from 7 pm to 7 am on weekdays and at all times on Sundays and public holidays. Percussive piling at other times is controlled by the permit system, which confines operations to specific hours. This system employs a time restriction mechanism so that those piling operations which most affect noise sensitive receivers will work fewer hours. This encourages contractors to use quieter piling methods. During 1993, there were 520 permit applications; 504 permits issued; and five prosecutions.

The department has also started to control specific types of particularly noisy construction equipment. Hand-held percussive breakers and air-compressors, which affect tens of thousands of people when used in building demolition and road works, were the first batch to be controlled. The import, manufacture, supply or use of such equipment for construction purposes must comply with relevant stringent noise emission standards. The equipment must also be fitted with 'green' noise emission labels when being operated. During 1993, there were 2 650 label applications, 2 631 labels issued and 27 prosecutions.

Whenever practicable, the department requires the use of silenced equipment and the adoption of noise reduction measures. The department and the police respond to complaints relating to night-time construction work, and carry out inspections. During 1993, there were 1 790 permit applications; 1 482 permits issued; and 34 prosecutions.

A bill to amend the Noise Control Ordinance to further limit the noise effects of construction work carried out at night and on general holidays was introduced into the Legislative Council. The amendment seeks to essentially ban such activities in populated and other particularly sensitive areas.

Construction under the airport core programme continued and, in 1993, the department issued 170 permits for such work in the restricted hours, with stringent noise mitigation measures. A monitoring programme ensured that construction noise levels were within acceptable limits.

A significant air pollution concern in construction and demolition is the control of asbestos. The Air Pollution Control (Amendment) Ordinance 1993 introduced a full range of measures for the control of materials containing asbestos in buildings and ships; the registration of asbestos consultants, contractors, supervisors and laboratories; and a ban on the import and sale of asbestos (amosite and crocidolite). To pave the way for effective enforcement of the new regulations, the department had installed a transmission electron microscope in 1991. This provides analytical support for the definitive identification of asbestos fibres.

During 1993, the department made 780 inspections, mainly on building demolition and renovation sites, temporary housing areas, housing estates and private buildings, to ensure any asbestos materials involved were handled and disposed of properly in accordance with the requirements of the Waste Disposal (Chemical Waste) Regulation. Its asbestos laboratory, which is covered by the Hong Kong Laboratory Accreditation Scheme, analysed 347 bulk samples and 155 air samples.

Construction and demolition waste, including dredged material, that meet a tight quality specification, may be dumped at sea, subject to licensing controls under the Dumping at

Sea Act 1974 (Overseas Territories) Order 1975. Anyone who intends to dump dredged marine spoil or excavated material that is unsuitable for reclamation purposes must first obtain a licence from the Director of Environmental Protection.

Spoil grounds have been designated for the disposal of dredged marine spoil or excavated material unsuitable for reclamation. All marine dumping activities must be carried out at these designated areas in an appropriate manner in accordance with marine dumping licences.

The large number of port and airport-related projects has generated a vast quantity of materials requiring marine disposal. This increase in dumping activities has been accompanied by a corresponding increase in illegal dumping. In view of the serious impact of illegal spoil dumping on marine life, the department has revised its marine dumping action plan. Since January 2, 1993, a vessel must be equipped with an automatic self-monitoring device before it can be listed in a marine dumping licence. The device will track all dumping operations by keeping a continuous record of the position and draft of the vessel, so that the authorities can trace any illegal dumping in a more cost-effective manner.

The department maintains strict enforcement through frequent marine patrols, which have been supplemented by the introduction of helicopters patrols. Offenders who are caught are prosecuted, and repeat offenders face having their licences revoked or applications for new licences refused. Serious cases are taken to the district courts where higher fines can be imposed.

Livestock

Indiscriminate disposal of waste from the livestock industry is one of the main causes of pollution in streams in the New Territories, and constitutes a health hazard. A Bill to amend the Waste Disposal Ordinance to prevent pollution by livestock waste was submitted to the Legislative Council in late 1993 to increase the maximum penalties and make the law easier to enforce. Livestock-keeping will be banned in all urban and environmentally sensitive areas of Hong Kong. Where they are allowed, livestock farms will be controlled by licensing to ensure that the farms are equipped with proper waste treatment systems.

Complementing these controls is an administrative scheme to help affected operators. If an operator wishes to continue in business, he is eligible for a grant and a loan to help him pay for pollution control facilities. Since the start of the scheme, about $1.6 million has been paid out in capital grants and loans. If an operator chooses instead to cease business, he is eligible for an allowance to help tide him over until he finds other employment. About $590 million has been paid out in allowances to date, of which about $100 million was handed out in 1993.

During the year under review, the livestock waste control scheme stopped pollution equivalent to the raw sewage from 200 000 people being discharged into the environment. This brought to about 60 per cent the total reduction in livestock waste pollution since the 1987 inception of the control scheme.

Ozone — A Global Responsibility

To control ozone-depleting substances and fulfil Hong Kong's obligations as a party to the Montreal Protocol on Substances that Deplete the Ozone Layer, the Ozone Layer Protection Ordinance was enacted in 1989. This ordinance prohibits local manufacturing of chlorofluorocarbons (CFCs) and bromofluorocarbons (halons), and imposes restrictions on the import and export of these substances through licensing and quota controls. The ordinance was amended in 1992 and the control of ozone-depleting substances extended to cover 1, 1, 1-trichloroethane, carbon tetrachloride and 10 other fully halogenated CFCs with effect from January 1, 1993.

In 1993, there was one prosecution under the ordinance, with a $10,000 fine imposed.

In a meeting of the parties to the Montreal Protocol in Copenhagen in November 1992, it was further agreed that the schedule to phase out ozone-depleting substances should be substantially accelerated. The use of halons will have to be completely phased out by 1994 and CFCs, carbon tetrachloride and 1, 1, 1-trichloroethane by 1996. In the interim, local consumption of CFCs will have to be reduced by 75 per cent in 1994. These controls are being implemented through the existing quota system.

The Montreal Protocol also requires all parties to prohibit the import of a list of products containing CFCs or halons from non-party countries, with effect from May 1993. The Ozone Layer Protection (Products Containing Scheduled Substances) (Import Banning) Regulations were enacted in 1993 to effect such control.

The Ozone Layer Protection (Controlled Refrigerants) Regulations were also approved by the Legislative Council in 1993, to be effective on a date to be appointed. The regulations prohibit the intentional venting of CFC-based refrigerants from large air-conditioning units and from motor vehicle air-conditioners. While this regulation aims at minimising the emission of CFCs into the atmosphere and reducing the demand for virgin materials, it will also encourage the recovery and recycling of CFCs by industries, which will help meet the tight phasing-out schedule. Subsidiary legislation banning the venting of CFCs into the atmosphere during the decommissioning or servicing of air-conditioning or refrigeration units is being prepared.

Neighbourhood Noise

Noise from domestic premises and public places is classified as neighbourhood noise. The police handle complaints about such noise. During 1993, the police dealt with 400 complaints and prosecuted 20 offenders.

Provision of Facilities and Services

Every day, Hong Kong produces two million tonnes of sewage and 7 900 tonnes of municipal solid waste. The government has adopted detailed strategies to deal with these challenges.

The sewage strategy requires improved sewage collection facilities under sewerage master plans, and a system of deep tunnels and treatment works to treat and dispose of the sewage from the Victoria Harbour area.

Continued work on developing and implementing the sewerage master plans made good progress during the year. Site investigation and engineering studies continued, and detailed design started, for the strategic sewage disposal scheme.

Domestic, commercial and industrial waste, collectively referred to as municipal solid waste, is forecast to increase by 3.2 per cent annually over the next 14 years. By the year 2006, some 12 300 tonnes of municipal solid waste will require collection and disposal each day. The waste disposal plan, setting out the framework for management of all waste types, was published in late 1989. The plan specifies the waste disposal strategy for the territory, and sets out a programme for phasing out old facilities and for the provision of new facilities and services.

Sewerage Master Plans

The existing provision of sewerage in Hong Kong is inadequate. There is a complete absence of sewerage in many developed areas and villages in the rural areas. In areas with some sewerage, there is widespread under-capacity, heavy siltation and numerous 'expedient' connections of sewage discharges to the storm drains, particularly in the older industrial areas.

To overcome the problem, the government is preparing a total of 16 comprehensive sewerage master plans, covering all sewage catchments in Hong Kong. These plans form the basis for providing adequate sewer networks to collect and convey sewage to the treatment facilities. By the end of the year, 11 sewerage master plan studies had been completed, while four were partly complete and one had yet to start.

Sewage Treatment and Disposal

The construction of improvements proposed in Stage 1 of the East Kowloon sewerage master plan continued and is scheduled for completion in mid-1994. The improvement work includes the provision of a relief sewer, dry weather flow interceptors, two pumping stations and associated sewage pumping mains.

A new sewerage system for Hong Kong Island South, proposed in the sewerage master plan study for that area, is being built. The system includes underground sewage treatment works for Stanley, a screening plant and sewerage at Shek O, and a number of pumping stations, one of which will pump sewage from the Repulse Bay area to an existing treatment facility at Aberdeen.

Stage 1 of the Tolo Harbour effluent export scheme, which transfers the treated effluent from the Sha Tin sewage treatment works and which is an important element of the Tolo Harbour Action Plan, was scheduled for completion in 1994. It aims to reduce the amount of pollution entering Tolo Harbour. Completion of Stage 2 between Tai Po and Sha Tin is expected in 1995, when treated effluent from both the Tai Po and Sha Tin sewage treatment works will be removed entirely from the Tolo Harbour catchment, and discharged to less sensitive waters.

The Northwest New Territories sewerage scheme was completed in March 1993. Sewage generated from the Yuen Long peripheral area, covering North Tuen Mun, Yuen Long, the Tuen Mun Corridor, Tin Shui Wai, and Au Tau and Long Ping, is collected by this sewerage system for treatment before discharge to Urmston Road via an outfall.

Charging Scheme for Sewage Services

A $12 billion programme of sewage improvement schemes, to be completed by 1997, was announced in September.

It included proposals for the introduction in 1994 of a sewage services charging scheme, under which users will contribute towards the costs of rapidly improving sewage services.

The programme comprises an $8.1 billion high-priority programme, which will clean up 70 per cent of the pollution in Victoria Harbour, plus $4 billion of public works expenditure on other ongoing sewage improvement schemes.

Under the application of the 'polluter pays' principle, those who cause the pollution will contribute financially to part of the programme.

Charges will be modest for households. Industry and commerce will pay more through a trade effluent surcharge because they create more pollution. The government hopes that the charging scheme will encourage them to take remedial measures such as more careful use of water and effluent treatment.

Legislation to give effect to the charging arrangements will be introduced into the Legislative Council in 1994.

The high-priority programme comprises a deep tunnel sewerage system running from Hong Kong Island East to Tseung Kwan O and Tsuen Wan, with treatment works on Stonecutters Island, as well as improvements to associated local sewerage networks.

The ongoing sewage improvement schemes comprise more than 30 projects funded under the public works programme.

Landfills

Most municipal solid waste is currently disposed of at three landfills, located at Tseung Kwan O, Shuen Wan and Pillar Point Valley. Much of the rest is incinerated. The current territorial waste disposal strategy is to develop three other large landfills in remote areas of the New Territories, to provide the necessary capacity for disposal of waste for the next 20 years.

These landfills will be served by a network of refuse transfer stations located in the urban area. The landfills and transfer stations will be designed, constructed and operated to high environmental standards by experienced waste management contractors.

Contracts for the design, construction and operation of the West New Territories Landfill and the Southeast New Territories Landfill were awarded in 1993. The contract for the Northeast New Territories Landfill is expected to be awarded in 1994. The West New Territories Landfill was commissioned in November and the expected dates of commissioning for the Southeast New Territories Landfill and Northeast New Territories Landfill are mid-1994 and early 1995, respectively.

Due to rapid development in the territory, the amount of construction waste arriving at the landfills has increased dramatically in the past few years. Some 11 000 tonnes of such waste was created every day during 1993. The disposal of such large quantities of this waste at existing landfills has led to a short-term critical shortage of waste disposal capacity. To overcome this problem, the capacity of the existing landfills is being increased. Arrangements have also been made to advance some reclamation activities, so that suitable construction wastes can be used to create land, instead of using up valuable landfill space.

The decomposition of refuse produces large quantities of a highly polluting liquid called leachate, and gases which may be explosive. As a precaution, studies are being conducted on the collection, treatment and disposal of landfill gas and leachate produced at existing and fully used-up landfill sites. These studies will identify solutions to mitigate the landfill gas and leachate problems, and finalise the requirements for fitting pollution control systems and landfill restoration works. Future land-use of the restored landfills will also be considered. A gas control system was installed at Sai Tso Wan Landfill in 1991 and the system is operating satisfactorily, with no sign of gas migration off the site.

The phased restoration works programme developed under a study for the fully used-up urban landfills at Jordan Valley, Ma Yau Tong Centre, Ma Yau Tong West, Gin Drinkers'

Bay and Ngau Chi Wan started in 1993. Studies on the restoration of Tseung Kwan O Landfill, the Northwest New Territories Landfill and Shuen Wan Landfill were commissioned in 1993 and the restoration programme will commence after completion of the studies in 1994.

Refuse Transfer Stations

As part of its waste disposal strategy, the government is developing a network of refuse transfer stations. These will centralise the collection of refuse and ensure that its transport to remote landfill sites is effective and economical.

The development of transfer stations, built to high environmental standards, will enable the government to close the poorly-located incinerators currently operating in Hong Kong. This will eliminate a significant source of air pollution in the urban area.

The transfer stations will receive waste collected by small refuse collection vehicles and enable its delivery, in bulk, to the landfills in sealed containers, by road or sea transport.

The first transfer station, at Kowloon Bay, has been in service since April 1991. It processes an average of 1 600 tonnes of municipal refuse per day.

The second transfer station, Island East Transfer Station, was commissioned in November 1992 and is processing an average of 1 300 tonnes of refuse per day. Collected refuse is compacted into sealed containers and then delivered to landfill sites by purpose-built vessels. With the commissioning of this transfer station, the incinerator at Kennedy Town was shut down in March 1993 to improve the air quality in the vicinity.

The contract for the third refuse transfer station, at Sha Tin, was awarded in July 1993. The station is expected to be operational in late 1994.

A study on the feasibility of building an underground transfer station on a rock cavern site on western Hong Kong Island was commissioned in 1992. Detailed planning of this underground transfer station is in progress and tenders will be invited in 1994. Consultancy studies for refuse transfer stations for the outlying islands, Northwest New Territories and West Kowloon commenced in 1992, with a target commissioning date of 1996. Studies for a refuse transfer station in North Lantau Island also started in early 1993.

Chemical and Special Wastes

There were, until recently, no central treatment facilities for chemical waste in Hong Kong and there were practical, technological and financial obstacles to local industries having their own. This led the government, in December 1990, to appoint a specialist contractor to design, build and operate a chemical waste treatment centre on Tsing Yi Island.

The centre, commissioned in April 1993, is the first integrated facility for chemical waste in the region. It collects, transports, treats and disposes of chemical waste, helping the waste producers to comply with the law. It serves also as the regional reception point for oily and noxious liquid wastes from ships. This meets Hong Kong's obligations under the International Convention for the Prevention of Pollution from Ships and its Protocol (the Marpol Convention).

With the coming into force of chemical waste regulations, all chemical waste producers must properly store and dispose of their chemical waste. A trip ticket system involving the waste producers, licensed collectors and licensed disposal points, tracks the movement of chemical waste. Most of the chemical waste goes to the treatment centre but some, such as asbestos, is sent to landfills for disposal.

The asbestos waste action plan, introduced in 1990, has been replaced by statutory control under the Waste Disposal (Chemical Waste) Regulation, ensuring that waste producers and disposal contractors follow safety guidelines in the code of practice on asbestos waste.

Under a five-year trial programme, treated sludge from the waterworks and sewage treatment processes at Sha Tin are disposed of at sea some 15 kilometres east of Waglan Island. Approximately 40 000 cubic metres of sludge is dispersed every month at the spoil ground, which was selected after detailed study. Monitoring of the water, marine sediment quality and biotic community at the spoil ground is continuing, to provide an early indication of any adverse effects on the environment.

A study of the long-term arrangements for the disposal of waterworks and sewage sludge looked into both new and well-established technologies, including energy recovery. It recommended that sludge be dehydrated, dried, and buried in landfills.

In view of the unsatisfactory disposal arrangements for clinical waste, animal carcasses and some security waste, a central incinerator is planned to dispose of such waste. A consultancy study is underway and the tender for constructing the facility is expected to be called in late 1994.

The government has appointed a contractor to collect livestock waste that would otherwise be indiscriminately dumped into streams and rivers in the New Territories. In 1993, some 2 000 tonnes of solid livestock waste were collected and sent to the government-operated composting plant at Sha Ling for recycling.

Monitoring and Investigations

The assessment of progress towards policy goals is one of the key activities of the Environmental Protection Department. Its routine monitoring and special investigations form the basis for the strategic planning, provision of facilities and statutory controls that aim to improve the environment.

The department has a new marine pollution investigation vessel, the *Dr Catherine Lam*, which is used to monitor water quality in all 10 existing and proposed water control zones. It has a network of nearly 100 monitoring points in inland waters, and keeps 42 publicly-managed bathing beaches under surveillance. The results of this monitoring, which goes back to 1972, form a comprehensive record of the chemical, physical and microbiological quality of Hong Kong's waters.

All the data are published regularly, and can be made available to scientists and engineers on computer disks or tapes to contribute to their work. Members of the public are usually most interested in the summary reports of bathing water quality, which are issued to the media every two weeks during summer.

Standards and objectives for water quality draw heavily on the results of water quality monitoring and a number of special investigations that the department carries out. During 1993, work continued to analyse the results of a third phase of a long-term investigation to quantify the link between the pollution of bathing waters and health risks. This study was conducted in co-operation with the Chinese University of Hong Kong.

Mathematical models are used in much of the department's water quality assessment work. The department also provides a service to other government departments whose activities might have a major impact on the flow and quality of sea water around Hong Kong.

Another field of investigation is the impact of toxic chemicals in the environment. This leads to an assessment of the safety of specific materials for use in the local environment and to the refinement of effluent standards.

The department operates an air quality monitoring network consisting of 11 stations. The stations are equipped with continuous ambient monitoring instruments for measuring sulphur dioxide, nitrogen oxides, respirable and total suspended particulates (dusts), photochemical oxidants, carbon monoxide and lead.

The results of measurements at the Kwai Chung, Central and Western, and Mong Kok monitoring stations are reported and published each month. These stations broadly represent air quality in districts close to industrial areas, in combined commercial-residential districts, and near road traffic in built-up urban areas.

The department also operates a mobile air quality laboratory. In 1993, it was deployed to measure air quality in various semi-confined transport interchanges. Preliminary findings showed that the air quality at some of these locations was quite unacceptable.

In view of concerns about high nitrogen dioxide levels adjacent to roads, a territory-wide survey of nitrogen oxide concentrations was carried out to supplement measurements made at the fixed air quality monitoring stations. About 60 passive diffusion tube samplers were used to record nitrogen oxide levels. The results confirmed the previous findings that nitrogen oxide levels are generally high throughout Hong Kong's busy road network.

The department conducts surveys on municipal solid waste twice a year to collect up-to-date information for planning future waste disposal facilities. Compared to 1992 findings, total municipal solid waste quantities disposed of at the landfills and incinerators increased by 15 per cent to 9 100 tonnes per day. The increase was due to a nine per cent increase in the amount of domestic waste, and a 28 per cent and 30 per cent increase in the amount of industrial and commercial waste, respectively, delivered to the landfills and incinerators. Construction waste delivered to the landfills, however, decreased by nine per cent.

Local waste recovery activities continued to play an important role in waste management, resulting in the export of substantial quantities of recovered waste materials for recycling overseas. A total of 1.3 million tonnes of waste materials, including waste paper, metals and plastic, were exported in 1993, generating export earnings of $2.2 billion. About 500 000 tonnes of waste paper, used lubricating oil, metals, plastic scrap and glass were reprocessed locally.

The government encourages waste avoidance, which embraces waste minimisation, recovery and recycling, recognising that it is a useful means to bring about a reduction in quantities of waste requiring disposal. A Waste Reduction Study is being carried out to develop a strategic plan for waste avoidance in the territory. The plan would include various practical measures to facilitate waste prevention, minimisation, re-use, recovery through sorting, separation and recycling in the territory. The application of advanced technologies to reduce the bulk of municipal waste requiring disposal will also be examined.

A study conducted by the department in March found that a large proportion of construction waste could be used to create land after sorting and removal of undesirable materials, comprising mainly non-inert materials such as wood, paper, plastic, bamboo and general refuse. The survey ascertained that the sorting of construction waste at source is practical and achievable.

The department also carries out noise monitoring and surveys. It is concerned about traffic in densely-populated and congested metropolitan areas. Resurfacing noisy roads with quiet surfacing material will continue to provide relief for adversely affected people.

Government Laboratory

The Government Laboratory provides a wide range of chemical testing services to government departments, principally the Environmental Protection Department, in relation to environmental protection. These services include the testing of air particulates, deposition samples, river and marine water samples, sediment samples and waste water samples for a variety of pollution level indicators. About 220 000 tests were conducted in 1993.

Apart from analysing routine environmental samples for monitoring purposes, the Government Chemist also functions as a referee analyst under a number of regulations and ordinances. Fuel oil samples and industrial waste water samples are tested for compliance with the Air Pollution Control (Fuel Restriction) Regulations and the Water Pollution Control Ordinance, respectively. With the recent enactment of the Waste Disposal (Chemical Waste) (General) Regulation, testing of chemical waste from local industry is also undertaken.

About 800 samples were tested for enforcement and prosecution purposes in 1993.

Climate

Hong Kong's climate is sub-tropical, tending towards the temperate for nearly half the year. During November and December, there are pleasant breezes, plenty of sunshine and comfortable temperatures. Many people regard these as the best months of the year. January and February are more cloudy, with occasional cold fronts followed by dry northerly winds. It is not uncommon for temperatures to drop below 10°C in urban areas. The lowest temperature ever recorded at the Royal Observatory was 0°C, although sub-zero temperatures and frost occur at times on high ground and in the New Territories.

March and April can also be very pleasant although there are occasional spells of high humidity. Fog and drizzle can be particularly troublesome on high ground which is exposed to the southeast, and air traffic and ferry services are occasionally disrupted because of reduced visibility.

May to August are hot and humid with occasional showers and thunderstorms, particularly during the mornings. Afternoon temperatures often exceed 31°C whereas at night, temperatures generally remain around 26°C with high humidity. There is usually a fine dry spell in July, which may last for one to two weeks, or even longer in some years.

September is the month during which Hong Kong is most likely to be affected by typhoons, although tropical cyclones of varying strength are not unusual at any time between May and November. On average, about 31 tropical cyclones form over the western North Pacific and China seas every year, and about half of them reach typhoon strength (with maximum winds of 118 kilometres per hour or more).

When a tropical cyclone is about 700 to 1 000 kilometres southeast of Hong Kong, the weather is usually fine and exceptionally hot, but isolated thunderstorms sometimes occur in the evenings. If the cyclone's centre comes closer to the territory, winds will increase and rain can become heavy and widespread. The heavy rain may last for a few days, and subsequent landslips and flooding sometimes cause considerably more damage than the winds.

The mean annual rainfall ranges from around 1 300 millimetres at Waglan Island to more than 3 000 millimetres in the vicinity of Tai Mo Shan. About 80 per cent of the rain falls between May and September. The wettest month is August — when rain occurs about four days out of seven — for which the monthly average at the Royal Observatory is 391.4 millimetres. The driest month is January, when the monthly average is only 23.4 millimetres and rain falls only about six days in the month.

Severe weather phenomena that can affect Hong Kong include tropical cyclones, strong winter and summer monsoon winds, monsoon troughs and thunderstorms with associated squalls that are most frequent from April to September. Waterspouts and hailstorms occur infrequently, while snow and tornadoes are rare.

Climatological data are given in Appendix 45.

The Year's Weather

The year 1993 was eventful. Extremes in seasonal temperature variations were marked by a prolonged cold spell in January and an unusually hot and dry summer in July and August. In a year of frequent tropical cyclone activity, the No. 8 Gale or Storm signals were hoisted four times, just once short of the record set in 1964. The rather long typhoon season spanned from late June to early November. Apart from seasonal monsoon rain in June, severe rainstorms also occurred with the passage of tropical cyclones, most notably during Dot in September and Ira in November. The total rainfall during the year amounted to 2 343.9 millimetres, six per cent above the annual mean of 2 214.3 millimetres.

One of the most persistent cold spells ever experienced in Hong Kong occurred in January. Daily minimum temperatures were below 12°C for 16 consecutive days from January 15, and daily mean temperatures were below 12°C for 11 consecutive days, the longest duration since 1887. Freezing conditions were experienced on high ground on the morning of January 16 and temperatures at Tai Mo Shan went down to –2°C. The monthly rainfall of 33.5 millimetres was 43 per cent above the January normal.

Without significant surges of cold air from the north, February was unseasonably mild. The monthly mean temperature of 18°C and the monthly mean minimum temperature of 16.3°C were, in their respective categories, the fourth highest on record for the month of February. The monthly rainfall of one millimetre was only about two per cent of the February normal of 48 millimetres, making it the seventh driest February on record.

March was warmer, cloudier, and more humid than normal. The first thunderstorm of the year occurred on March 16.

April was relatively cool and cloudy, with the northeast monsoon active late in the season. Although rainfall was recorded at the Royal Observatory for 23 days in the month, the monthly total of 136.3 millimetres was still 16 per cent below the April normal of 161.5 millimetres.

The weather in May was typical of the season in both temperature and precipitation. Most of the rain was associated with monsoon troughs which affected the South China coastal areas from time to time.

With moist southwest monsoons and the presence of active troughs near the South China coast, June was cloudier than normal and unusually humid. The mean dew point of 25.2°C was the second highest ever recorded in June. Torrential downpours on June 11 and 16 caused widespread flooding in the urban area, necessitating the issuance of Rainstorm Red Warnings on both occasions and a Rainstorm Black Warning in the latter case. The year's first tropical cyclone to affect Hong Kong was Typhoon Koryn, which necessitated the hoisting of the No. 8 Gale or Storm Signal on June 27. With only one rain-free day in the month, the monthly total rainfall of 485.2 millimetres was 29 per cent above the June normal of 376.0 millimetres.

July was unusually hot. The mean minimum temperature of 27.6°C and the mean air temperature of 29.4°C ranked, respectively, the highest and second highest on record for July. Overall, it was a relatively dry month although more than 100 millimetres of rain fell during the passage of Severe Tropical Storm Lewis. The monthly rainfall of 213.7 millimetres was 34 per cent below the July normal of 323.5 millimetres.

The very hot and dry conditions continued into August. The monthly mean minimum temperature of 26.8°C was the fifth highest on record for August. The monthly rainfall amounted to 182.8 millimetres only, less than half of the August normal of 391.4 millimetres. This was despite the stormy weather brought by Typhoon Tasha on August 20, when the No. 8 Gale or Storm signal was hoisted for the second time in the year.

Then came three typhoons in quick succession within a fortnight in September. Becky and Dot necessitated the hoisting of the No. 8 Gale or Storm signals on September 17 and 26, respectively. The 223.9 millimetres of rain brought by Dot on September 26 was the third highest daily amount on record for September. By early next morning, the northern part of the New Territories was inundated with flood water as deep as seven metres in some areas. With a monthly rainfall of 655.9 millimetres, more than twice the September normal of 299.7 millimetres, September 1993 became the fifth wettest September on record.

October was much drier and slightly cooler than normal. This was due to the dominance of continental anti-cyclones which led to the third highest October monthly mean pressure of 1 016.2 hectopascals. The monthly rainfall of 87.8 millimetres was 39 per cent below the October normal of 144.8 millimetres.

November was unusually cloudy and humid. The monthly rainfall of 144.6 millimetres, more than four times the November normal of 35.1 millimetres, and the 131.2 hours of bright sunshine in the month were, respectively, the fifth highest and sixth lowest on record for November. The most significant weather event was the late-season passage of Typhoon Ira. Rain associated with Ira was quite exceptional as intense convection embedded within one of its trailing rainbands brought concentrated heavy rain of more than 700 millimetres to the western part of the territory on November 4 and 5. There were extensive landslides on Lantau Island and widespread flooding in Tuen Mun and Yuen Long. An inundated water treatment plant in Tuen Mun and burst water mains on Cheung Chau Island resulted in a cut-off of fresh water supply to these areas for a period of four days.

December was slightly cooler and cloudier than normal. Apart from a humid spell early in the month, it was rather dry. The monthly rainfall of 15.7 millimetres was 42 per cent below the December normal of 27.3 millimetres. The winter monsoon was active before Christmas, giving rise to some cold mornings and days of low humidity. The weather turned noticeably milder during the period leading up to the New Year.

Topography and Geology

The topography of Hong Kong is characterised by steep granitic and volcanic mountains. Much of the terrain at the foot of the mountains is blanketed by slope deposits transported by erosion and mass movement from the hillsides. Some 40 per cent of the exposed land is volcanic in origin and about 20 per cent is granitic, while slope deposits cover 15 per cent. A further 20 per cent is alluvial in nature, while about five per cent of the land is currently formed by reclamation and fill.

The highest peak is Tai Mo Shan (957 metres), located in the central New Territories. Four other peaks exceed 750 metres, all on Lantau Island. Victoria Peak, the highest on Hong Kong Island and best known as a major tourist attraction, is ranked 18th in the territory with an elevation of 554 metres.

The territory lies on the edge of the ancient Sinian land mass formed more than 600 million years ago, and which now extends from Shandong in northern China to the Gulf of Hainan. The oldest geological strata forming Hong Kong's land mass were deposited beneath the sea but were subsequently folded and faulted in mountain-building earth movements. A second period of mountain-building, beginning about 160 million years ago, was accompanied by explosive volcanic activity which deposited thick layers of ash and lava. Large granitic intrusions accompanied this volcanism, which lasted up to about 136 million years ago. These mountains were subsequently eroded, and the material washed from the slopes into the valleys, plains and shallow seas formed flat-lying sedimentary rocks and soft sediment deposits.

During the Quaternary period of the last 1.6 million years, world sea levels fell and rose several times. There were four major glaciations when water was taken up to form great ice sheets. In Southeast Asia, the sea level fell to between 120–150 metres below its present level, which would have exposed an area of continental shelf about 130 kilometres wide to the south of Hong Kong. During these low sea-level periods, the Pearl River deposited alluvial sand and silt over this wide plain. As the ice began to melt at the end of the last glaciation, sea levels rose, reaching their present level about 6 000 years ago. The returning sea deposited fine clays and silts (marine mud) over the earlier alluvial deposits. Sea level fluctuations during the Quaternary have therefore resulted in a sequence of mud, sand and gravel up to 100 metres thick in the present offshore area.

The erosion of the hills accelerated following destruction of the natural vegetation during the widespread colonisation of the area in the Sung Dynasty (960–1279). Hong Kong's rocks are generally deeply weathered, and much of the terrain is prone to landslips. More than 20 per cent of the terrain in the territory shows evidence of instability.

Generally, the weathered granitic and volcanic rocks can be excavated quite easily for use as reclamation material. However, sand dredged from offshore areas provides the most valuable fill resource. Hong Kong has few mineral resources, although iron and tungsten were once extracted in significant amounts, and deposits of lead, silver, zinc, quartz, kaolin, beryl and graphite have been mined in small quantities. Granites in Hong Kong were once extensively quarried for masonry, but are now mainly used as aggregates.

The natural landscape in the urban areas has been extensively modified as a result of site formation associated with development. Many of the natural granitic hills have been removed, and the material used as fill for the various reclamations. Almost 4 000 hectares of the developed land is reclamation.

Much of the undeveloped terrain in Hong Kong consists of steeply-sloping ground where soils are thin and nutrient-deficient. These soils support only grassland or shrubland, except in protected valleys where small areas of broad leaf woodland survive, or in water catchments and country parks where re-afforestation has succeeded in establishing pines and deciduous trees.

An important agricultural area is the alluvial plain around Yuen Long in the northwestern New Territories. These alluvial lowlands were probably formed within the last 33 000 years, and some areas are still prone to flooding. There are more than 5 000 hectares of floodplain in the territory and much of it is located in Yuen Long district. The natural deposition of sediment is continuing around the Deep Bay area, where brackish fish ponds have been established successfully in areas that once were mudflats, mangrove swamps or salt-water rice paddies.

As Hong Kong lacks large rivers, lakes or underground water supplies, reservoirs have been constructed in large valleys such as Shek Pik and Tai Lam Chung, and in coastal areas such as Plover Cove and High Island, where embayments and channels have been enclosed by large dams. In most instances, the catchment areas of the reservoirs have been designated as country parks.

A description of the onshore and offshore geology can be found in a series of new geological maps and memoirs produced and published at a scale of 1:20 000 by the Hong Kong Geological Survey, located within the Geotechnical Engineering Office. Detailed geological reports and maps at 1:5 000 scale have been published for Yuen Long, and are being prepared for Ma On Shan, North Lantau and Tsing Yi. Information about the terrain is also contained in the 55 maps and 12 reports of the Geotechnical Area Studies Programme. Published documents are available at the Government Publications Sales Centre.

Hydrography and Oceanography

Approximately two-thirds of the territory of Hong Kong, or almost 1 830 square kilometres, is covered by the sea. Historically, the sea has been very important, as a highway for international shipping and in the form of a large and sheltered anchorage. Hong Kong is one of the busiest ports in the world. Offshore areas have assumed greater importance in recent years with the increasing number of engineering projects offshore, including reclamations, the construction of tunnels and pipelines and cable-laying. They are also an important source of fill.

Maximum water depths reach a little over 30 metres in the southeastern corner of territorial waters to the south of Mirs Bay. More commonly, water depths range between 10–15 metres, with a generally flat and featureless muddy seabed that slopes gently southwards. Several deeper channels occur in constricted tidal pathways, for example in Urmston Road, the East Lamma Channel, Lei Yue Mun, Sheung Sz Mun and Lo Chau Mun.

Terrestrial Fauna

The physical and climatic environment of Hong Kong provides woody and grassy habitats for a wide variety of native animal and plant life. Under the pressures of urbanisation, larger animal species are rarely seen, but reptiles, amphibians, birds and many kinds of insects are common.

Most of Hong Kong's countryside is protected by the Forests and Countryside Ordinance, the Wild Animals Protection Ordinance, the Country Parks Ordinance, and the Animals and Plants (Protection of Endangered Species) Ordinance.

One of the most important sites in Hong Kong for wildlife is the Mai Po Marshes. A restricted area under the Wild Animals Protection Ordinance, and managed jointly by the

Agriculture and Fisheries Department and the World Wide Fund for Nature (Hong Kong), it is an internationally significant site for migratory and resident birdlife. Its 380 hectares of mudflats, shrimp ponds and dwarf mangroves provide a rich habitat, particularly for ducks and waders. More than 250 species of birds have been observed in this area, and at least 110 of them are rarely seen elsewhere in the territory. Yim Tso Ha, also a restricted area, is the largest egretry in Hong Kong. Five species — the Chinese Pond Heron, Night Heron, Cattle Egret, Little Egret and Great Egret — nest there regularly, and occasionally the rare Swinhoe's egret can be seen. Hundreds of egrets can be found there during the nesting season between April and September. Egretries are also found at Mai Po Village, A Chau, Jim Uk, Tsim Bei Tsui, Lok Ma Chau, Ho Pui Tsuen and Tai Po Market.

Although traditional fung shui woods near old villages and temples are increasingly affected by development, they continue to provide an important habitat for many birds. Sightings in wooded areas include an assortment of warblers, flycatchers and robins.

Areas around the Kowloon reservoirs are inhabited by monkeys descended from animals which had been released or had escaped from captivity. There are breeding groups of both long-tailed macaques, rhesus monkeys and their hybrids. Smaller mammals are common, with the woodland shrew, house shrew and bats prevalent in some rural areas. The Chinese porcupine, with its strikingly-coloured black and white quills, is still present in parts of the New Territories and Hong Kong Island.

Occasional reports are still received of sightings of less common species such as the leopard cat, civet cat, ferret badger, pangolin and barking deer. However, the increasing obtrusion of human activity into the countryside means an uncertain future for these species. Wild boar in some remote areas occasionally cause damage to farm crops.

Snakes, lizards and frogs are plentiful in Hong Kong. There are also various species of terrapins and turtles. Most of the local snakes are not poisonous, and death from snakebite is rare. The poisonous land snakes are: the banded krait, with black and yellow bands; the many-banded krait, with black and white bands; Macclelland's coral snake, which is coral red with narrow, black transverse bars; the Chinese cobra and the hamadryad or king cobra, both of which are hooded; the rare mountain pit viper; the red-necked keelback with a red patch on the neck; and the white-lipped pit viper or bamboo snake. The bamboo snake is bright green and less venomous than others, but it is not easily seen and strikes readily if approached. The king cobra, kraits and corals prey almost exclusively on other snakes.

Several species of sea snakes, all of which are venomous, are to be found in Hong Kong waters. However, they have never been known to attack bathers.

Two amphibians of special interest are the Hong Kong newt and Romer's tree frog, which have not been recorded elsewhere.

There are more than 200 recorded species and forms of colourful butterflies, some of which, as caterpillars, cause considerable damage to farm crops. These include the two commonly-found species of cabbage whites, the swallowtails, and the beautiful but less common small blue. Among the many local moths are the giant silkworm moths, including the cynthia, fawn, atlas and moon. The atlas has an average wing span of 23 centimetres and the moon, 18 centimetres.

Two local plant bugs are especially noted for their colour and shape. They are the rare, spotted tea bug, which has been recorded only on hilltops; and the lantern fly, which has delicately coloured wings and a remarkably long forehead. Dragonflies and damselflies are common, as are wasps and metallic-coloured beetles. Of particular interest is the giant red-spotted longhorn beetle which feeds on mountain tallow and wood-oil trees. Many other species of longhorn beetles infest living or weakened trees.

Since its introduction into Hong Kong in 1938, the African giant snail has become a major pest to vegetable crops and gardens. Farmers are also troubled by several types of slugs. One of these, veronicella, is large and black and sufficiently different from the other slugs to be placed in a separate family.

Aquatic Fauna

Hong Kong lies some 320 kilometres south of the Tropic of Cancer on the southern coast of China. Located at the junction of the vast temperate Palaearctic Japonic zoogeographical regions and the huge Indo-Pacific Province, Hong Kong possesses very diverse varieties of aquatic animals and plants. There are over 150 commercially important species of fish, crustaceans and molluscs.

The waters of Hong Kong can be divided into three sectors. Under the influence of the Pearl River, the biggest river in southern China, the western sector is predominantly brackish. The area to the east is more oceanic while the central sector is transitional between brackish and oceanic. In some localities, notably the Tolo Harbour region, pollution associated with recent rapid urban development has decimated the abundance and diversity of aquatic life. Pollution-sensitive organisms such as coral are now found only in a few clean yet remote oceanic areas in the northeast. Nevertheless, various locations still serve as spawning and nursery grounds for many aquatic species, and these in turn attract transient predators such as Spanish mackerel, little tuna, dolphinfish, sailfish and sharks.

Shark sightings have been recorded in Hong Kong waters. Most are small to medium in size and pose little danger to humans. However, two fatal attacks, believed to have been caused by tiger sharks, were recorded in June in Sai Kung waters.

Four species of whales and eight species of dolphins have been recorded in Hong Kong waters and strandings occur quite frequently. The black finless porpoise and the Chinese white dolphin are the most common in terms of occurrence. In 1993, 12 strandings were reported.

Flora

Situated near the northern limit of the distribution of tropical Asian flora, Hong Kong has an abundant variety of plant life. It is estimated that there are about 2 700 species of vascular plants, both native and introduced.

With the introduction of various conservation measures, hillsides and slopes which were formerly bare ground have now been planted with trees of both local and exotic species. In addition to greening and beautifying the countryside, woodlands are also important as habitats for wildlife, in the management of water catchments and in providing recreational opportunities for the public.

Remnants of the original forest cover, either scrub forest or well-developed woodlands, are still found in steep ravines. They have survived the destructive influences of man through their location in precipitous topography and the moist winter micro-climate.

Countryside Conservation and Management

The Agriculture and Fisheries Department is the principal government agency responsible for the conservation and management of Hong Kong's countryside. The Forests and Countryside Ordinance provides for the general protection of vegetation, and special protection is given to certain plants, including native camellias, magnolias, orchids, azaleas and the Chinese new year flower.

The Wild Animals Protection Ordinance prohibits the hunting of wild animals or the possession, sale or export of protected wild animals. It also restricts the entry of unauthorised members of the public to important wildlife habitats, the Mai Po Marshes and the Yim Tso Ha Egretry.

The Country Parks Ordinance provides for the designation, control and management of the most important areas of countryside as country parks and special areas, and enables them to be developed for recreational, conservation and educational purposes. It gives particular protection to vegetation and wildlife. There are now 21 country parks and 14 special areas, covering about 40 per cent of the land area in the territory. There were over 10 million visitors to country parks in 1993.

Overall enforcement of the ordinances is carried out by nature wardens and park wardens. These officers also provide information at seven visitor centres and escort groups on guided visits.

In addition to general conservation of the countryside, Hong Kong has adopted the concept of identifying and conserving sites of special scientific interest, such as a site where a rare tree or a rare species of butterfly can be found. Fifty sites have so far been identified.

The department is also responsible for the co-ordination and implementation of off-site ecological mitigation measures, recommended by consultants, to alleviate adverse effects of the new airport and related projects.

Meteorological Services

Royal Observatory

The Royal Observatory was established in 1883, mainly to provide scientific information for the safe navigation of ships. In the ensuing century, the observatory has evolved in line with the changing needs of the community. The scope of its studies and services now covers the fields of hydrometeorology, climatology, physical oceanography, applied meteorology and radiation monitoring and assessment. The observatory also operates the official time service for Hong Kong, provides basic astronomical information and maintains a seismological monitoring network.

Its most visible services are weather forecasting and warnings of hazardous weather — responsibilities borne by the Central Forecasting Office at the observatory's headquarters. Regular weather programmes for the public are presented on television by professional meteorologists from Mondays to Saturdays. Live interviews and briefings are also given by forecasters over the radio and television when the situation warrants. Two special bulletins, with accompanying weather charts as illustrations, are prepared for the press each day. Bulletins and advice are also issued to meet the diverse requirements of specialist users such as the shipping, aviation, fishing, recreation and oil-prospecting industries.

Whenever Hong Kong is threatened by tropical cyclones, frequent warnings with advice on necessary precautions are widely disseminated. The heavy rain on May 8, 1992 led to the introduction of a colour-coded rainstorm alert and warning system. A rainstorm warning is now issued whenever Hong Kong is affected by heavy rain which may cause serious road flooding and traffic congestion. The observatory also issues warnings on thunderstorms, flooding, landslips, storm surges, fire danger, strong monsoon winds and frost.

For people requiring instant access to weather forecasts or tropical cyclone information, the observatory operates a dial-a-weather service. The demand for this service continues to grow. There are now 27 lines for public weather forecasts and four lines for South China coastal waters bulletins. Close to 12 million calls were handled in 1993. On average, more than 30 000 calls were handled daily.

Information is also provided to the INFOTEX and INFOFAX services, which make available by telex and telefax a large variety of routine weather information, including pictorial data such as the daily weather map. Weather information is also made available for access by terminals connected to a commercial communications and paging network.

In response to the difficulties experienced by fishermen in receiving the South China coastal waters bulletins through regular radio broadcasts, a special arrangement has been made with Hongkong Telecom International to broadcast the forecasts three times a day, and up to four times when tropical cyclone warning signals are hoisted.

In planning the meteorological facilities required to support the new airport under construction at Chek Lap Kok, the observatory has taken steps to engage consultants to design and acquire state-of-the-art systems for meteorological data processing, information distribution, and wind shear detection and warning.

Weather Forecasting, Monitoring and Prediction

To provide the wide range of meteorological services described in the previous section, the observatory maintains a weather watch round-the-clock. Weather observers at the Royal Observatory Headquarters and Hong Kong International Airport make regular observations on local weather conditions. Additional observations are made by volunteers and collaborating agencies at other remote locations.

Apart from manual observation, a network of automatic weather stations telemeters real-time weather data to the Central Forecasting Office from Cheung Chau, King's Park, Ta Kwu Ling, Lau Fau Shan, Tsing Yi, Sha Tin, Tuen Mun, Wong Chuk Hang, Tai Po Kau, Sai Kung, Tseung Kwan O, Sha Lo Wan and Waglan Island. These stations provide a comprehensive coverage of regional weather variations. For aviation safety, wind conditions at the airport and its vicinity are monitored continuously by a network of anemometers. In collaboration with the Guangdong Meteorological Bureau, the observatory also operates an automatic weather station at Huangmao Zhou, an island 40 kilometres south of Lantau Island and strategically located for monitoring tropical cyclones approaching from the south.

Rainfall information is important for water resources management and also because of the susceptibility of slopes to landslips in heavy rain. A dense network of 143 raingauge stations provides information on the spatial distribution and intensity of rainfall in various parts of Hong Kong. Sixty-nine of these stations are equipped to provide up-to-the-minute information every five minutes. Rain cloud development, movement and intensity within 512 kilometres of Hong Kong are monitored by a digital radar system which also produces objective short-term rainfall estimates at selected locations. A lightning detection system locates cloud-to-ground lightning within a range of about 130 kilometres and a spherics recorder is used to register thunderstorm activity within a range of about 100 kilometres. Assimilation of all information is essential for assessing the likelihood of flooding and landslips.

For the real-time monitoring of floods in northwestern New Territories, water-level and rainfall information at Kam Tin is telemetered directly to the observatory's headquarters. Tide data are collected from eight gauges in the territory for operational warnings of coastal flooding. Numerical models are used to predict the likelihood of storm surges in tropical cyclone situations. Storm surge warnings are issued when a significant rise in the sea-level is forecast.

Besides surface observations, upper air conditions are measured by radiosondes carried by balloons launched at the King's Park Meteorological Station. For an overview of weather systems, hourly high-resolution cloud pictures are received from the Japanese Geostationary Meteorological Satellite. The satellite imageries, which cover East Asia and the western Pacific, greatly facilitate the monitoring of weather systems outside the range of the radar system.

Weather prediction requires constant meteorological data exchange with other countries. This is achieved through telecommunication circuits dedicated to the transmission of meteorological data. The observatory exchanges meteorological data with overseas centres via three international circuits: the Hong Kong-Beijing circuit, the Hong Kong-Tokyo circuit and the Hong Kong-Bangkok circuit.

In recent years, the vagaries and evolution of weather have become better understood through experience gained in analysing and interpreting the outputs of numerical weather prediction models run at the Royal Observatory and other major meteorological centres abroad. With the continuing advances in the accuracy and reliability of numerical model outputs, weather forecasts can now be issued several days ahead with confidence.

Radiation Measurement and Assessment

In line with its responsibilities for emergency response services relating to inclement weather and other natural disasters, the observatory would co-ordinate and formulate technical emergency advice should an unlikely accidental release of radioactivity occur at the Guangdong Nuclear Power Station at Daya Bay, which will begin commercial operations in February 1994. To fulfil this responsibility, the observatory has established an Environmental Radiation Monitoring Programme to monitor radiation levels in Hong Kong. The programme, which began in 1987, entails the collection and measurement of samples of air, water, soil and food regularly at a number of locations in the territory. Measurements from 1987 to 1991 have been analysed to determine the background radiation level in Hong Kong and the results were published in early 1993. A Radiation Monitoring Network has also been established to continuously monitor the ambient gamma dose rate in the territory and to provide an alert in case of any deviation of dose rate from the background level. Since 1993, the collected data has been published monthly. In the event of an emergency, the observatory will monitor and assess the radiological and meteorological information collected to estimate the transport, dispersion and deposition of any radioactivity over the territory, and provide technical advice to the government on any necessary counter-measures.

Climate, Oceanographic and Geophysical Services

The Royal Observatory carries out climate, oceanographic and geophysical studies. Its professional advice is often sought by consultants working on government or private projects. When an engineering project demands substantial data collection and analyses over a prolonged period, special studies are conducted.

A climatological information service is provided to meet the needs of the general public and to cater for the specialised interests of shipping, aviation, agriculture, fisheries, engineering, industry, judicial proceedings, and recreational planning. In particular, analyses on the probabilities of high winds, heavy rain, waves and surges are undertaken, using mathematical models as well as statistics of extremes. The observatory carries out extensive data analyses and research, the results of which are published in various forms. These publications are not only useful in support of the observatory's own operations, but are also very much in demand by engineers working on hydrological forecasting, water resources planning, drainage design, water quality control, reservoir design and operation, irrigation and infrastructure projects.

Climate change is another subject of interest and concern. The observatory participates actively in international climate programmes and, through the World Meteorological Organisation, keeps abreast of the findings and recommendations made by the Intergovernmental Panel on Climate Change.

To monitor earthquakes and seismicity, three short-period seismometers are operated at Cheung Chau, High Island and Tsim Bei Tsui. Long-period seismographs at the observatory's headquarters record tremors occurring throughout the world. Strong-motion accelerographs are operated at the observatory's headquarters and Tate's Cairn. About 130 earth tremors with epicentres within 320 kilometres of Hong Kong are detected annually. Reports of significant tremors are routinely made known to the general public via the media. Seismic data are used by structural engineers in the design of buildings. Such data are also made available to local and overseas scientific institutions for their studies.

The Hong Kong Time Standard is provided by a caesium beam atomic clock at the observatory headquarters. Accuracy within fractions of a microsecond a day is maintained. The time service is operated by relaying a six-pip time signal to Radio Television Hong Kong for broadcast.

25
POPULATION AND IMMIGRATION

THE population of Hong Kong passed the six million figure for the first time in 1993. There were 6 019 900 people in the territory at the end of the year, comprising 3 058 300 males and 2 961 600 females.

This represented an increase of 117 800 persons, or two per cent, from the population estimate for the end of 1992.

The rise was due to 41 300 more births than deaths and a net inflow of 76 500 arrivals.

It is estimated that some 60 per cent of the territory's population was born in Hong Kong and some 34 per cent in China, according to the last population census carried out in 1991.

Illegal immigrants from China continued to pose a problem, with 37 517 arrested. This was a five per cent increase compared to 1992. The year saw the first case of an employer hiring illegal immigrants being sentenced to imprisonment by the courts. A total of 77 such employers were prosecuted in 1993.

A sudden influx of 2 389 ex-China Vietnamese illegal immigrants arrived in the middle of the year. By the year's end, 1 514 had been repatriated to China — by air and land transport. The use of chartered and commercial flights to return 1 342 in the group represented the first airborne repatriation from Hong Kong to China.

The Vietnamese migrant population in the territory continued to drop. A detailed report on Vietnamese migrants is included later in this chapter.

The 10-Year Trend

The population at the end of the year represented an increase of 11.9 per cent on the 1983 population estimate of 5 377 400.

The annual growth rate of the population averaged 1.1 per cent over the 10-year period. The average annual growth of the population was 1.1 per cent during 1984–88, and 1.2 per cent during 1989–93. Despite a decrease in the number of births in the second half of the decade, the population still grew at about the same rate as in the first half, due to a larger net inflow of persons into the territory.

The rate of natural increase in the population dropped steadily over the 10-year period from 11 to 6.8 per 1 000. This was the result of the declining birth rate — down from 16 per 1 000 in 1983 to 12 per 1 000 in 1993 — and a stable death rate, at about five per 1 000.

With its land area of only 1 078 square kilometres, Hong Kong is one of the most densely-populated places in the world. The overall population density per square kilometre was 5 700 in 1993. The figure conceals wide variations among different areas in the territory. The density on Hong Kong Island, and in Kowloon and New Kowloon was 26 180 people per square kilometre, while that of the New Territories was 2 790 per square kilometre. As a result of the continuing development of the new towns, there has been a substantial redistribution of the population from Kowloon and New Kowloon to the New Territories during the past decade. There was no significant change in the population on Hong Kong Island. The proportion of the resident population on Hong Kong Island was 21.7 per cent; in Kowloon and New Kowloon it was 33.5 per cent; and in the New Territories it was 44.5 per cent.

The age distribution of the population has changed considerably over the past 10 years. In 1983, 24.1 per cent of the population was aged under 15 years; in 1993, the figure was 20 per cent. On the other hand, the proportion of people aged 65 and above has risen from seven per cent to 9.2 per cent over the same period. Along with these changes, the population aged between 15 and 64 years increased from 68.9 per cent in 1983 to 70.8 per cent in 1993. The dependency ratio — the ratio of the young and the aged to people in the 15 to 64 age group — has, however, dropped from 451 per 1 000 in 1983 to 412 per 1 000 in 1993.

Compared with 10 years ago, the ratio of males to females in the population has declined. In 1993, there were 1 033 males per 1 000 females; in 1983, the figure was 1 074.

More statistics are given in Appendix 28.

Immigration Department

The work of the Immigration Department falls into two main streams — controlling people moving into and out of Hong Kong, and providing travel documents and registration facilities for local residents. The work embraces such diverse fields as the issue of travel documents; visas and identity cards; naturalisation; and the registration of births, deaths and marriages. Considerable effort also goes into detecting and prosecuting those who breach the immigration laws, and removing those who have entered Hong Kong illegally.

Immigration policies are framed to limit permanent population growth brought about by immigration into Hong Kong, and to control the entry of foreign workers. Every effort is made to streamline immigration procedures for Hong Kong residents, tourists and businessmen. At the same time, the department aims to prevent both the entry of undesirable persons and the departure of persons wanted for criminal offences.

To take full advantage of advanced information technology and to improve the efficiency, quality and cost-effectiveness of services provided to the public, the department is implementing a long-term information systems strategy. The new system, which is expected to improve the department's productivity by 10 to 15 per cent, is likely to take three years to come on line.

Much of the department's work requires international co-operation, to facilitate legitimate travel as well as stop illegal immigration. Immigration officers make regular visits overseas to maintain and enhance liaison with colleagues in other immigration control enforcement agencies.

Immigration Control

Passenger traffic continued to increase in 1993. A total of 82.2 million passengers travelled in and out of Hong Kong, up 6.8 per cent from the 77 million in 1992. Movements to and from China also increased by 9.4 per cent, from 48 million in 1992 to 52.5 million.

The number of visitors travelling to Hong Kong increased from eight million in 1992 to 8.9 million in 1993, up 11.3 per cent. These included 1.8 million from Taiwan and 1.6 million from China.

To facilitate residents of China visiting Hong Kong, holders of Chinese two-way permits could, with effect from January, enter Hong Kong by sea. Previously, they could only enter by land via Lo Wu.

From August, the requirement for residents of China to obtain a visa for transitting Hong Kong was waived. These travellers can now stay in Hong Kong for seven days without a visa on their way to and from a third country.

Legal Immigration

During the year, 32 900 residents of China came to Hong Kong for settlement. Of these, 13 250 were wives, 14 504 were children and 1 370 were husbands of local residents. Entering Hong Kong for the purpose of family reunion, they made up 89 per cent of all new arrivals.

In November, an agreement was reached with the Chinese Government to increase the size of the one-way permit quota from 75 to 105 a day — making a total of around 38 000 a year.

Illegal Immigration

With its booming economy and proximity to China, Hong Kong is vulnerable to influxes of illegal immigrants from China. During the year, the number of illegal immigrants arrested continued to increase. The daily average arrest figure for 1993 was 103, compared with 97 in 1992 and 70 in 1991. Most illegal immigrants came to Hong Kong for jobs, attracted by higher wages. Frequent checks were therefore conducted on construction sites, factories and other places of employment. Illegal immigrants found at places of work were prosecuted. Their employers were also prosecuted. Most were fined but, in serious cases, prison sentences were imposed.

Emigration

Emigration has been a constant feature of life in Hong Kong. The number of persons leaving Hong Kong increased from an average of 20 000 a year in the early 1980s to 30 000 in 1987, and reached 66 000 in 1992. The increase has been attributed to a combination of factors, including concern about Hong Kong's future after the change of sovereignty in 1997 and immigration opportunities in the more popular destination countries. As a result of the recent economic downturn and reduced intake of some destination countries, however, in 1993, the number of emigrants was estimated at about 54 000.

Of those who emigrated in 1993, about one-third were in professional, technical, administrative and managerial occupations. To counter the outflow of talent, the government has adopted a threefold strategy — it is more flexible over proposals for importing skills from neighbouring countries, it has increased the number of graduates from Hong Kong's tertiary institutions and it is facilitating the return of former migrants. There were signs that an increasing number of people who had emigrated are returning to Hong Kong. It was estimated that at least 12 per cent of persons who emigrated in the 10 years before 1992 have returned to Hong Kong.

The government, with the assistance of other governments, also sought to retain people in Hong Kong through various schemes, such as the British Nationality Selection Scheme and the United States' deferred immigrant visas scheme. The British Nationality Selection Scheme, which began in December 1990, enables up to 50 000 persons and their dependants to acquire British citizenship without having to leave Hong Kong. The first phase of the scheme will end on January 1, 1994. By the end of 1993, a total of 96 811 persons, comprising 36 139 principal applicants and 60 672 dependants, were registered as British citizens under the scheme. The remaining places will be distributed in the second phase, which will begin on January 3, 1994. The special provision in the United States Immigration Act of 1990, which allows the deferred take-up of immigrant visas up to the end of 2001, would enable beneficiaries to have the confidence to continue to stay and work in Hong Kong.

Personal Documentation

During the year, 457 000 passports were issued, up 90 per cent from 1992. This total included 412 744 British National (Overseas) passports, compared to 150 123 in 1992. The sharp increase was partly attributable to the introduction of a worldwide phased programme for registration of the British National (Overseas) passport in July 1993. Eligible persons are called forward by age groups to apply for British National (Overseas) passports before specific cut-off dates. The aim of the programme is to ensure that all Hong Kong British Dependent Territories citizens who wish to obtain British National (Overseas) status are issued with such passports before 1997. At the end of 1993, 843 840 persons had been registered as British Nationals (Overseas). From July 1993, Hong Kong British Dependent Territories citizens are allowed to hold both valid British Dependent Territories Citizen and British National (Overseas) passports.

The demand for Certificates of Identity increased slightly by 2.4 per cent to 130 500. There was a decrease in the demand for re-entry permits, which accounted for 25 per cent of the 786 000 travel documents issued.

Following the completion of the Second Identity Card Re-issue Exercise in December 1991, all identity cards issued before July 1987 were declared invalid. There are now two types of new identity cards — the Hong Kong Permanent Identity Card, which states that the holder has the right of abode in Hong Kong, and the Hong Kong Identity Card, which does not state that right. These identity cards will remain valid beyond July 1, 1997, until they are replaced by the future Hong Kong Special Administrative Region government.

In 1993, 610 000 new identity cards were issued: 294 200 to new arrivals and persons who reached the age of 11 or 18, and 238 300 to persons who had lost or damaged their identity cards or whose identity cards required amendments.

Naturalisation

There was a continued surge in the number of applications for naturalisation. A total of 23 474 applications were received, a major increase from the 5 381 applications of 1992. The surge was partly attributed to the nationality requirement stipulated for the second tranche of the British Nationality Scheme.

Marriages

Marriages in Hong Kong are governed by the Marriage Ordinance and the Marriage Reform Ordinance.

Under the Marriage Ordinance, at least 15 days' notice of an intended marriage must be given to the Registrar of Marriages. The registrar has discretionary powers to reduce the period of notice or to grant a special licence dispensing with notice altogether — but this is done only in exceptional circumstances.

Marriages may take place at any of the 222 places of public worship licensed for the celebration of marriages, or at any of the 10 full-time marriage registries and three part-time sub-registries. During the year, 39 537 marriages were performed in the registries and 2 144 at the licensed places of worship. All records are maintained permanently in the General Register Office.

The Marriage Reform Ordinance provides that all marriages entered into in Hong Kong on or after October 7, 1971, shall imply the voluntary union, for life, of one man and one woman to the exclusion of all others. They may be contracted only in accordance with the Marriage Ordinance. Certain customary marriages and unions known as 'modern marriages' remain valid, provided they were entered into before October 7, 1971. Such marriages may be post-registered or dissolved. During the year, 25 customary and 42 'modern marriages' were post-registered.

Special arrangements have been made to enable Vietnamese illegal immigrants in detention centres to register their marriages in Hong Kong. In 1993, 992 marriages were contracted under these arrangements.

The Registrar of Marriages is also responsible for issuing Certificates of Absence of Marriage Records to local residents. During the year, 30 329 such certificates were issued, down 8.86 per cent from the 33 276 issued in 1992.

Births and Deaths

The registration of births and deaths is compulsory. The General Register Office keeps all such records.

During the year, 71 799 live births and 30 225 deaths were registered, compared with 72 206 and 30 528, respectively, in 1992. The figures, when adjusted for under-registration, gave a natural increase in population for 1993 of about 41 300 (0.7 per cent) — the lowest percentage-wise over the past 10 years.

A birth which has not been registered within one year may be post-registered with the consent of the Registrar of Births and Deaths, on payment of a fee of $200. During the year, 337 births were post-registered.

Birth registration services in the urban area are provided by two main registries, on Hong Kong Island and in Kowloon. There are five birth registries in the rural areas. In the outlying areas and islands, births are normally registered at rural committee offices by visiting district registrars. Visiting services are also provided to register the births of babies born in detention centres to Vietnamese illegal immigrants (1 214 in 1993).

There are two death registries, on Hong Kong Island and in Kowloon. Deaths in the rural areas are registered at local police stations.

Establishment and Training

At the end of the year, the department had an establishment of 3 502 disciplined staff — four (0.1 per cent) more than in 1992. Its civilian staff numbered 2 109, compared to 2 072 in 1992. A total of 189 immigration assistants were recruited in 1993.

The department provides training for both new and serving officers. Recruits undergo a 12-week induction course which covers law, immigration policies and procedures, foot-drill, physical training, swimming, first-aid and practical attachments. As part of the career development programme, in-service and specialised training are also provided within the department and in outside organisations.

During the year, 168 recruits completed their induction training. A further 3 273 serving officers received various types of job-related, management, development and other continuation training. Of these, 12 officers were selected for overseas attachment and training.

Vietnamese Migrants

The Vietnamese migrant population in Hong Kong camps continued to decline. In 1993, only 101 Vietnamese migrants arrived in Hong Kong, while over 15 322 were either settled overseas or repatriated to Vietnam. The corresponding figures for 1992 were 12 and 16 051, respectively.

The government's policy towards Vietnamese migrants is based on the Comprehensive Plan of Action (CPA), which was endorsed by the international community in Geneva in June 1989. The CPA provides that while those Vietnamese migrants who are classified as refugees under the terms of the 1951 United Nations Convention and 1967 Protocol are eligible for resettlement, those who are found not to be refugees should return to Vietnam. In October 1991, agreement was reached with the Vietnamese Government on the orderly repatriation of all Vietnamese migrants found to be non-refugees. A total of 817 persons have since been returned to Vietnam under this programme. The momentum of the voluntary repatriation programme organised by the United Nations High Commissioner for Refugees (UNHCR) was also maintained during 1993. Over 12 301 persons returned to Vietnam voluntarily — an average of 1 025 per month.

It is important that migrants returning to Vietnam should be assured that they may do so safely and without fear of persecution. The Hong Kong Government will not send back to Vietnam anyone whom they, or the UNHCR, believe is a genuine refugee. The Vietnamese Government has given firm guarantees that no returnees will be persecuted. All returnees are closely monitored on their return by the UNHCR to ensure that the guarantees are fully respected. Since March 1989, over 38 613 Vietnamese migrants have returned to Vietnam from Hong Kong and there has not been a single substantiated case of persecution to date.

At the same time, the Hong Kong Government and the international community recognise that while the economy in Vietnam has been improving gradually, returnees may have difficulties in re-establishing themselves on their return. The UNHCR therefore provides financial assistance to returnees to help them to resume their normal lives in Vietnam. The reintegration assistance programme run by the European Community in Vietnam offers returnees job-creation schemes, training courses and start-up loans for businesses. It also helps finance local infrastructure and health projects. To complement these international efforts, the Hong Kong Government contributed a further $15 million in May 1993 to finance small-scale infrastructure projects in the poorer migrant-producing areas in Vietnam, to raise living standards and increase employment opportunities for returnees.

At the end of 1993, there were 29 251 Vietnamese migrants and 1 846 refugees in Hong Kong. Of the Vietnamese migrants, over 27 564 had been screened out and 1 687 were awaiting screening. Those screened out have the right to have their cases reviewed by an independent Refugee Status Review Board (RSRB). UNHCR officials are involved in monitoring the screening process and in preparing cases for review by the board. To speed up the pace of refugee status determination, additional resources were injected into the screening process during the year. Over 100 immigration officers, 65 temporary Vietnamese interpreters and six RSRB panels are now engaged in screening work.

Since the introduction of screening in June 1988, 6 212 people have been screened in as refugees and 50 858 have been screened out. At the review stage, in 18 532 cases involving 38 555 persons, the first instance decision has been upheld, and in 932 cases involving 2 417 people, it has been reversed. The UNHCR has determined 1 134 people to be refugees under its own mandate.

The resettlement of refugees continued satisfactorily in 1993. During the year, 2 571 refugees were resettled overseas, with Canada, Australia, and the United States remaining the three major resettlement countries. The figure includes the 937 refugees who left Hong Kong for the Regional Refugee Transit Centre in Bataan.

The cost of looking after the Vietnamese migrants and refugees in Hong Kong amounted to $1,209 million in 1993. The Hong Kong Government met $1,014 million of this cost. The United Kingdom Government contributed $76 million specifically for the UNHCR's programme in Hong Kong. The UNHCR agreed to meet $195 million of the 1993 cost, but at the end of the year, it had yet to repay the Hong Kong Government an outstanding debt of $870 million accumulated since 1989.

In view of the gradual reduction in the size of the camp population, the Shek Kong Detention Centre was closed in January. The Lo Wu Camp, which was previously used as a departure centre for migrants awaiting voluntary return to Vietnam, was closed in May. The Hei Ling Chau Detention Centre was also closed in October.

While there was a gradual reduction in the Vietnamese population in Hong Kong camps, Hong Kong faced the sudden influx of 2 389 ex-China Vietnamese illegal immigrants (ECVIIs) in the middle of the year. The ECVIIs are those Vietnamese migrants who were previously resettled in China before their arrival in Hong Kong. Once they have sought and obtained asylum in China, they have no further claim to refugee status or resettlement. The ECVIIs are therefore regarded as illegal immigrants and are repatriated upon confirmation of their previous residency in China. Following discussion with the Chinese Government, agreement was reached with China in August to repatriate all the ECVIIs stranded in Hong Kong camps. The repatriation process was carried out by air for the first time and by land. At the end of the year, 1 514 ECVIIs — aside from those whose identities had yet to be verified by the Chinese authorities — had returned to China.

Hong Kong is still faced with a major humanitarian problem in trying to care for over 31 097 people in Vietnamese detention and refugee centres. However, an end to the problem is now in sight. Given the existing arrival and departure trends, which are expected to continue, the aim is to close all the camps by 1996.

26
HISTORY

HONG KONG moved into its remaining four years of British sovereignty at midnight on June 30.

Accordingly, preparations for the territory's transfer to China have advanced in many areas in the nine years since the signing of the Sino-British Joint Declaration on the Question of Hong Kong on December 19, 1984.

Under the agreement, British administration and jurisdiction over Hong Kong will continue to June 30, 1997, and Hong Kong will, from July 1, 1997, become a Special Administrative Region (SAR) of the People's Republic of China.

The Joint Declaration, signed between the then British Prime Minister, Mrs Margaret Thatcher and the then Chinese Prime Minister, Mr Zhao Ziyang, provides that for 50 years after 1997, Hong Kong's lifestyle will remain unchanged. The territory will enjoy a high degree of autonomy, except in foreign and defence affairs, and China's socialist system and policies will not be practised in the SAR. (For further details on the Joint Declaration, see Chapter 4.)

In recent years, Hong Kong's relationship with China has strengthened in breath and depth — not only in terms of business ties but government contacts and the flow of people in both directions.

This close relationship is the product of culture, location and history.

Hong Kong's history has been one of material and social improvement: the expansion of cities and towns by cutting into hillsides; reclaiming the land from the sea; and the building of homes, schools, hospitals and other public facilities to meet the demands of the growing population. It is also a tribute to the dynamic drive of its people and their determination to meet all challenges.

Archaeological Background

Archaeological studies in Hong Kong, which began in the 1920s, have uncovered ancient artifacts and other evidence of human activity at numerous sites along the winding shoreline, testifying to events which span more than 6 000 years. The interpretation of these events is still a matter of academic discussion. Archaeologically, Hong Kong is but a tiny part of the far greater cultural sphere of South China, itself as yet imperfectly known.

Despite suggestions that local prehistoric cultures had developed out of incursions from North China or from Southeast Asia, a growing number of scholars believe that the prehistoric cultures within the South China region evolved locally, independent of any major outside influences. There is little dispute, on the other hand, that these earliest periods, from the close of the 4th millennium BC, must be seen within the framework of a changing environment, which saw sea levels rising from depths as low as 100 metres below the present — inexorably submerging vast tracts of coastal plain and establishing a basically modern shoreline and ecology to which human groups in the area had to adapt or perish.

The stone tools, pottery and other artifacts relied on for an insight into the lives of Hong Kong's ancient inhabitants are, for the most part, preserved in coastal deposits. This pattern of coastal settlement points to a strong maritime orientation and an economy geared to the exploitation of marine resources. However, it would be unwise to over-emphasise this point, since the discovery of archaeological remains is influenced by many factors governing their survival. For example, the erosion of the hilly terrain has been severe, and evidence of inland settlement, though scanty, is not totally absent.

Recent excavations have revealed two main neolithic cultures lying in stratified sequence. At the lower, older level, there is coarse, cord-marked pottery, together with a fine, soft fragile pottery decorated with incised lines, perforations and occasionally painted. Chipped and polished stone tools are also present. Current indications suggest a 4th millennium BC date for this initial phase.

Cord-marked pottery and chipped stone tools continue as long-lived traditions into the higher, later levels in which appears a new ceramic form decorated with a wide range of impressed geometric patterns. In this phase, beginning in the mid-3rd millennium BC, polished stone tools show better workmanship and a proliferation of forms, some with steps and shoulders — features probably connected with improvements in hafting techniques. Ornaments such as rings, some slotted, in a range of sizes were also made, sometimes with exquisite craftsmanship, from quartz and other suitable stones.

The final phase of Hong Kong's prehistory is marked by the appearance of bronze at about the middle of the 2nd millennium BC. Bronze artifacts do not seem to have been in common use, but fine specimens of weapons, swords, arrowheads and halberds, and tools such as socketed axes and fish hooks have been excavated from Hong Kong sites. There is evidence, too, from Kwo Lo Wan on Chek Lap Kok Island, and Tung Wan and Sha Lo Wan on Lantau Island, in the form of stone moulds, that the metal was actually worked locally.

The pottery of the Bronze Age comprises a continuation of the earlier cord-impressed and geometric traditions and a new ware, fired at a much higher temperature leading to vitrification. This so-called hard geometric ware is decorated with designs, many of which are reminiscent of the geometric patterns of the late neolithic period, but with their own distinctive style, including the well-known 'Kui-dragon' or 'double F' pattern, so characteristic of this period.

Archaeology is silent on questions such as the ethnic and linguistic affinities of the ancient peoples. However, the start of recorded history has ancient Chinese literary records speaking of maritime peoples occupying China's southeastern seaboard and known as 'Yue'. It is probable, therefore, that at least some of Hong Kong's prehistoric inhabitants belonged to the 'Hundred Yue', as this diverse group of peoples was often called.

Interesting archaeological features almost certainly made by these people include the rock carvings, most of which are geometric in style, on Kau Sai, Po Toi, Cheung Chau and Tung Lung islands; at Shek Pik on Lantau Island; and at Big Wave Bay and Wong Chuk Hang on Hong Kong Island.

The military conquest of South China, by the north, during the Qin (221–207 BC) and Han (206 BC–220 AD) dynasties must have brought increasing numbers of Han settlers into the region and exerted a variety of influences on the indigenous populations. These events are testified to by the discovery, in excavations, of coins of the Qin and Han periods. But the outstanding monument to this turbulent period must undoubtedly be the fine brick-built tomb uncovered at Lei Cheng Uk in 1955 with its fine array of typical Han tomb furniture, dateable from the early to middle Eastern Han period.

Archaeological remains from later historic periods are at present still poorly known. Recent work has thrown a welcome light on one aspect of life in the Hong Kong of the Tang Dynasty (618–907 AD), through a study of the dome-shaped lime kilns which are an almost ubiquitous feature of the territory's beaches. Lime, a valuable commodity useful for caulking and protecting wooden boats against marine organisms, waterproofing containers, dressing the acid soils of agricultural fields and building, among other purposes, clearly played an important role in the economy of the period.

Strong traditions link Hong Kong with the events surrounding the Mongol incursions and the concluding chapters of the Song Dynasty in the 13th century AD. The Sung Wong Toi inscription, now relocated near the entrance to the Hong Kong International Airport; the Song Inscription on the grounds of the Tin Hau temple at Joss House Bay; caches of Song coins from Shek Pik, Mai Po, and recently, Kellett Island; and celadons of Song type from various sites, especially Nim Shue Wan and Shek Pik on Lantau Island, date from this period.

Recent archaeological studies are beginning to throw fresh light on events in Hong Kong during the Ming (1368–1644) and Qing (1644–1911) dynasties. These include an analysis of considerable quantities of Ming blue and white porcelain collected in recent years from a site at Penny's Bay, Lantau. The results suggest that this porcelain is very fine quality export ware of the kind which found its way to the courts of Southeast Asia and the West, and dates from the first few decades of the 16th century AD. The excavation of the Qing period fort on Tung Lung Island has already revealed fascinating details of the internal arrangements of the fortification and the everyday utensils of a remote garrison during the final stages of Imperial China.

A Place from Which to Trade

In its early days, the territory was regarded as an uninviting prospect for settlement. A population of about 3 650 was scattered over 20 villages and hamlets, and 2 000 fishermen lived on board their boats in the harbour. Its mountainous terrain deficient in fertile land and water, Hong Kong possessed only one natural asset, a fine and sheltered anchorage. Largely the reason for the British presence which began in the 1840s, Victoria Harbour was strategically located on the trade routes of the Far East, and was soon to become the hub of a burgeoning *entrepôt* trade with China.

Hong Kong's development into a commercial centre began with its founding as a settlement under the British flag in 1841. At the end of the 18th century, the British dominated the foreign trade at Canton (Guangzhou) but found conditions unsatisfactory, mainly because of the conflicting viewpoints of two quite dissimilar civilisations.

The Chinese regarded themselves as the only civilised people and foreigners trading at Canton were subject to residential and other restrictions. Confined to the factory area, they were allowed to remain only for the trading season, during which they had to leave their families at Macau. They were forbidden to enter the city and to learn the Chinese language. Shipping dues were arbitrarily varied and generally, much bickering resulted between the British and Chinese traders. Yet, there was mutual trust and the spoken word alone was sufficient for even the largest transactions.

Trade had been in China's favour and silver flowed in until the growth of the opium trade — from 1800 onwards — reversed this trend. The outflow of silver became more marked from 1834, after the East India Company lost its monopoly of the China trade, and the foreign free traders, hoping to get rich quickly, joined the lucrative opium trade which the Chinese had made illegal in 1799. This led to the appointment of Lin Zexu (Lin Tse-hsu) in March 1839 as special Commissioner in Canton with orders to stamp out the opium trade. A week later, he surrounded the foreign factories with troops, stopped food supplies and refused to allow anyone to leave until all stocks of opium had been surrendered, and dealers and ships' masters had signed a bond not to import opium on pain of execution. Captain Charles Elliot, RN, the British Government's representative as Superintendent of Trade, was shut up with the rest and authorised the surrender of 20 283 chests of opium after a siege of six weeks.

Elliot would not allow normal trade to resume until he had reported fully to the British Government and received instructions. The British community retired to Macau and, when warned by the Portuguese Governor that he could not be responsible for their safety, took refuge on board ships in Hong Kong harbour in the summer of 1839.

Lord Palmerston, then the Foreign Secretary, decided that the time had come for a settlement of Sino-British commercial relations. Arguing that, in surrendering the opium, the British in Canton had been forced to ransom their lives — though, in fact, their lives had never been in danger — he demanded either a commercial treaty that would put trade relations on a satisfactory footing, or the cession of a small island where the British could live free from threats under their own flag.

An expeditionary force arrived in June 1840 to back these demands, and thus began the so-called First Opium War (1840–42). Hostilities alternated with negotiations until agreement was reached between Elliot and Qishan (Keshen), the Manchu Commissioner. (Lin had been replaced by Qishan after his exile in disgrace over the preliminaries of a treaty.)

Under the Convention of Chuenpi (Chuanbi) signed on January 20, 1841, Hong Kong Island was ceded to Britain. A naval landing party hoisted the British flag at Possession Point on January 26, 1841, and the island was formally occupied. In June, Elliot began to sell plots of land and settlement began.

Neither side accepted the Chuenpi terms. The cession of a part of China aroused shame and anger among the Chinese, and the unfortunate Qishan was ordered to Peking (Beijing) in chains. Palmerston was equally dissatisfied with Hong Kong, which he contemptuously described as "a barren island with hardly a house upon it", and refused to accept it as the island station that had been demanded as an alternative to a commercial treaty.

"You have treated my instructions as if they were waste paper," Palmerston told Elliot in a magisterial rebuke, and replaced him. Elliot's successor, Sir Henry Pottinger, arrived in August 1841 and conducted hostilities with determination. A year later, after pushing up the Yangtze River (Chang Jiang) and threatening to assault Nanking (Nanjing), he brought the hostilities to an end by the Treaty of Nanking, signed on August 29, 1842.

In the meantime, the Whig Government in England had fallen and, in 1841, the new Tory Foreign Secretary, Lord Aberdeen, issued revised instructions to Pottinger, dropping the demand for an island.

Pottinger, who had returned to Hong Kong during the winter lull in the campaign, was pleased with the progress of the new settlement and, in the Treaty of Nanking, deviated from his instructions by demanding both a treaty and an island, thus securing Hong Kong. In addition, five Chinese ports, including Canton, were opened for trade. The commercial treaty was embodied in the supplementary Treaty of the Bogue (Humen) in October 1843, by which the Chinese were allowed free access to Hong Kong Island for trading purposes.

Lease of the New Territories

The Second Anglo-Chinese War (1856–58) arose out of disputes over the interpretation of the earlier treaties and over the boarding of a British lorcha, the *Arrow*, by Chinese in search of suspected pirates. The Treaty of Tientsin (Tianjin) in 1858, which ended the war, gave the British the privilege of diplomatic representation in China. The first British envoy, Sir Frederick Bruce, who had been the first Colonial Secretary in Hong Kong, was fired on at Taku (Dagu) Bar on his way to Peking to present his credentials, and hostilities were renewed from 1859–60.

The troops serving on this second expedition camped on Kowloon peninsula, as the territory's earliest photographs show. Finding it healthy, they wished to retain it as a military cantonment, with the result that Sir Harry Parkes, Consul at Canton, secured from the Viceroy the perpetual lease of the peninsula as far as Boundary Street, including Stonecutters Island. The Convention of Peking in 1860, which ended the hostilities, provided for its outright cession.

Other European countries and Japan subsequently demanded concessions from China, particularly after Germany, France and Russia rescued China from the worst consequences of its defeat by Japan in 1895. In the ensuing tension, Britain felt that efficient defence of Hong Kong harbour demanded control of the land around it.

By a convention signed in Peking on June 9, 1898, respecting an extension of Hong Kong territory, the New Territories — comprising the area north of Kowloon up to the Shum Chun (Shenzhen) River, and 235 islands — was leased for 99 years. The move was directed against France and Russia, not against China whose warships were allowed to use the wharf at Kowloon City. There, Chinese authority was permitted to continue 'except insofar as may be inconsistent with the military requirements for the defence of Hong Kong'. However, an Order-in-Council of December 27, 1899, revoked this clause and the British unilaterally took over Kowloon City. There was some desultory opposition when the British took over the New Territories in April 1899, but this soon disappeared. The area was declared to be part of the overall territory of Hong Kong but was administered separately from the urban area.

Initial Growth

The new settlement did not go well at first. It attracted unruly elements, while fever and typhoons threatened life and property. Crime was rife. The population rose from 32 983 (31 463 Chinese) in 1851 to 878 947 (859 425 Chinese) in 1931. The Chinese influx was unexpected because it was not anticipated they would choose to live under a foreign flag.

The Chinese asked only to be left alone and thrived under a liberal British rule. Hong Kong became a centre of Chinese emigration and trade with Chinese communities abroad. Ocean-going shipping using the port increased from 2 889 ships in 1860 to 23 881 in 1939. The dominance of the China trade forced Hong Kong to conform to Chinese usage and to adopt the silver dollar as the currency unit in 1862. In 1935, when China went off silver, Hong Kong had to follow suit with an equivalent 'managed' dollar.

Hong Kong's administration followed the normal pattern for a British territory overseas, with a governor nominated by Whitehall and nominated Executive and Legislative Councils with official majorities. The first non-government members of the Legislative Council were nominated in 1850, and the first Chinese in 1880; the first non-government members of the Executive Council appeared in 1896, and the first Chinese in 1926. In 1972, the long-standing arrangement that two electoral bodies — the Hong Kong General Chamber of Commerce and the Unofficial Justices of the Peace — were each allowed to nominate a member to the Legislative Council, was discontinued.

The British residents pressed strongly for self-government on a number of occasions, but the home government consistently refused to allow the Chinese majority to be subject to the control of a small European minority.

A Sanitary Board was set up in 1883, became partly elected in 1887, and developed into the Urban Council in 1936.

The intention, at first, was to govern the Chinese through Chinese magistrates seconded from the mainland. But this system of two parallel administrations was only half-heartedly applied and broke down mainly because of the weight of crime. It was completely abandoned in 1865 in favour of the principle of equality of all races before the law. In that year, the Governor's instructions were significantly amended to forbid him to assent to any ordinance 'whereby persons of African or Asiatic birth may be subjected to any disabilities or restrictions to which persons of European birth or descent are not also subjected'. Government policy was *laissez-faire*, treating Hong Kong as a market place where all were free to come and go, and where the government held the scales impartially.

Public and utility services developed — the Hong Kong and China Gas Company in 1861, the Peak Tram in 1885, the Hongkong Electric Company in 1889, China Light and Power in 1903, the electric tramways in 1904 and the then government-owned Kowloon-Canton Railway, completed in 1910. There were successive reclamations dating from 1851 — notably one completed in 1904 in Central District, which produced Chater Road, Connaught Road and Des Voeux Road, and another in Wan Chai between 1921 and 1929.

A system of public education began in 1847 with grants to the Chinese vernacular schools. Later, in 1873, the voluntary schools — mainly run by missionaries — were included in a grant scheme. The College of Medicine for the Chinese, founded in 1887, developed into the University of Hong Kong in 1911 and offered arts, engineering and medical faculties.

After the Chinese revolution of 1911, which overthrew the Manchu Dynasty, there was a long period of unrest in China and large numbers of people found shelter in Hong Kong. The agitation continued after Chinese participation in World War I brought in its wake strong nationalist and anti-foreign sentiment — inspired both by disappointment over failure at the Versailles peace conference to regain the German concessions in Shantung (Shandong), and by the post-war radicalism of the Kuomintang. The Chinese sought to abolish all foreign treaty privileges in China. Foreign goods were boycotted and the unrest spread to Hong Kong, where a seamen's strike in 1922 was followed by a serious general strike in 1925–26 under pressure from Canton. This petered out, though not before causing considerable disruption in Hong Kong. Britain, with the largest foreign stake in China, was at that time a main target of anti-foreign sentiment, but in this odious role, it was soon to be replaced by Japan.

The 1930s and World War II

During World War I, Japan presented its '21 demands' to China. Then, in 1931, Japan occupied Manchuria and the attempt to detach China's northern provinces led to open war in 1937. Canton (Guangzhou) fell to the Japanese in 1938, resulting in a mass flight of refugees to Hong Kong. It was estimated that some 100 000 refugees entered in 1937, 500 000 in 1938 and 150 000 in 1939 — bringing Hong Kong's population at the outbreak of World War II to an estimated 1.6 million. It was thought that at the height of the influx, about 500 000 people were sleeping in the streets.

Japan entered World War II when, on December 7, 1941, its aircraft bombed United States warships at Pearl Harbour. At approximately the same time, Japanese armed forces attacked Hong Kong (December 8, 1941, local time). The Japanese invaded Hong Kong from across the mainland border and, subsequently, the British were forced to withdraw from the New Territories and Kowloon on to Hong Kong Island. After a week of stubborn resistance on the island, the defenders — including the then Hong Kong Volunteer Defence Corps — were overwhelmed and Hong Kong surrendered on Christmas Day. The Japanese occupation lasted for three years and eight months.

Trade virtually disappeared, currency lost its value, the supply of food was disrupted, and government services and public utilities were seriously impaired. Many residents moved to Macau — the Portuguese province hospitably opening its doors to them. Towards the latter part of the occupation, the Japanese sought to ease the food problems by organising mass deportations. In the face of increasing oppression, the bulk of the community remained loyal to the allied cause. Chinese guerillas operated in the New Territories and escaping allied personnel were assisted by the rural population.

Soon after news of the Japanese surrender was received on August 14, 1945, a provisional government was set up by the Colonial Secretary, Mr (later Sir) Frank Gimson. On August 30, Rear Admiral Sir Cecil Harcourt arrived with units of the British Pacific Fleet, to establish a temporary military government. Civil government was formally restored on May 1, 1946, when Sir Mark Young resumed his interrupted governorship.

The Post-War Years

Following the Japanese surrender, Chinese civilians — many of whom had moved into China during the war — returned at the rate of almost 100 000 a month. The population, which by August 1945 had been reduced to about 600 000, rose by the end of 1947 to an estimated 1.8 million. Then, in the period 1948–49, as the forces of the Chinese Nationalist Government began to face defeat in civil war at the hands of the communists, Hong Kong received an influx unparalleled in its history. Hundreds of thousands of people — mainly from Kwangtung (Guangdong) Province, Shanghai and other commercial centres — entered the territory during 1949 and the spring of 1950. By mid-1950, the population had swelled to an estimated 2.2 million. Since then, it has continued to rise and now totals six million.

After a period of economic stagnation caused by the United Nations' embargo on trade with China, Hong Kong began to industrialise. No longer could the territory rely solely on its port to provide prosperity for its greatly increased population. From the start, the industrial revolution was based on cotton textiles, gradually adding woollens and, in the late 1960s, man-made fibres and made-up garments. Although the share of total exports held by textiles and clothing has declined over the past 10 years, these still make up around 40 per cent of domestic exports by value. While textiles remain the mainstay of Hong Kong's economy, major contributions are made by electronic products, watches and clocks, plastic goods and other light industries.

Associated with events in China, 1966 saw mounting tension in Hong Kong. During 1967, this developed into a series of civil disturbances, affecting all aspects of life and temporarily paralysing the economy. But, by the year's-end, the disturbances were contained and the community continued its tradition of peaceful progress.

In the post-war years, Hong Kong continued to expand its role as an *entrepôt* with its neighbours and trade with China was no exception. Coupled with tourism, this led to vast improvements in communications, with an increasing number of people entering China from or through Hong Kong, a natural gateway, each year. One of the territory's carriers, Hong Kong Dragon Airlines, and three Chinese airlines — China Southern Airlines, Air China and China Eastern Airlines — operate both scheduled and non-scheduled services between Hong Kong and cities in China. Additionally, three other Chinese airlines — China Southwest Airlines, China Northern Airlines and China Northwest Airlines — operate non-scheduled services between Hong Kong and destinations in China. The Kowloon-Canton Railway Corporation runs, jointly with the Guangzhou Railway (Group) Corporation, four daily 'through' trains in each direction between Kowloon and Guangzhou, and one daily 'through' train in each direction between Kowloon and Foshan. A number of direct bus services operate different routes into Guangdong and other parts of southern China. There are also daily ferry services to Guangzhou and other ports in South China.

To keep pace with the development, strong emphasis is placed by the government on infrastructural improvements. As a result, the territory has been transformed into a modern city with efficient road and rail links, tunnels and flyovers, as well as multi-lane highways which have opened up previously remote areas.

The development of Hong Kong's economic base has enabled the government to increase spending on housing, education, social welfare and health over the years — from $16,261 million in 1983–84 to an estimated $70,060 million in 1993–94.

Starting with emergency measures to house some 53 000 people made homeless in the Shek Kip Mei squatter fire in 1953, Hong Kong's public housing programme now provides rental and self-owned flats of an increasingly higher standard for about three million people, or half the population.

Given impetus by the Long Term Housing Strategy, which aims to provide affordable housing for all those in need by the turn of the century, the programme is being implemented by the Housing Authority.

Expenditure on education facilities and improvements for Hong Kong's young and vibrant population has always been one of the major considerations in budget preparations. There are now free and compulsory primary and junior secondary school places for every student up to the age of 15 years. In 1993, the government was able to provide subsidised Secondary 4 places for about 84.9 per cent of the 15-year-olds in a continuing programme.

In the field of social welfare, major advances have been made by both the government and non-government organisations in the past decade, with expenditure increasing from $1,842 million in 1983–84 to $7,963 million during 1993–94.

Medical and health services are also undergoing vigorous development programmes which will provide two more major public hospitals and some 15 additional clinics and polyclinics over the next decade.

A comprehensive system of labour legislation has been developed to provide for employees' benefits and protection, work injury compensation, industrial safety and occupational health. Due to the restructuring of the Hong Kong economy, the service industry replaced manufacturing as the largest employer in 1982.

APPENDICES

APPENDIX 1

Units of Measurement

The Legislative Council enacted a new Weights and Measures Ordinance on July 8, 1987, to replace the legislation made in 1885.

The new ordinance, which came into operation in January 1989, provides comprehensively for a modern system of units of measurement and defines the weights and measures that are lawful for use for trade in Hong Kong.

The government's long-term policy aim is that ultimately only metric units will be used in Hong Kong. However, given Hong Kong's long usage of traditional Chinese and British Imperial units, it is accepted that it will take many years before this policy aim is achieved. Furthermore, Hong Kong's heavy reliance on international trade requires that its industrialists and manufacturers must supply goods to their customers' specifications. Some of Hong Kong's major overseas markets have yet to fully adopt the metric system.

The definitions of units of measurement, and the units of measurement and permitted symbols or abbreviations of units of measurement lawful for use for trade in Hong Kong are contained in the first and second schedules to the Weights and Measures Ordinance. The Weights and Measures Conversion Table which sets out equivalent units of measurement in the Chinese, Imperial, metric and United States systems of measurement is contained in the Weights and Measures Order 1990 made under Section 7 of the Weights and Measures Ordinance. These are reproduced below.

FIRST SCHEDULE

DEFINITIONS OF UNITS OF MEASUREMENT

PART I

Measurement of Length

(*a*) *Metric Units*

1 kilometre	= 1 000 metres
1 metre	= the length of the path travelled by light in vacuum during a time interval of $\frac{1}{299\,792\,458}$ of a second
1 decimetre	= 0.1 metre
1 centimetre	= 0.01 metre
1 millimetre	= 0.001 metre

(*b*) *Imperial Units*

1 mile	= 1 760 yards
1 furlong	= 220 yards
1 chain	= 22 yards
1 yard	= 0.914 4 metre exactly
1 foot	= $\frac{1}{3}$ yard
1 inch	= $\frac{1}{36}$ yard

(*c*) *Chinese Units*

1 chek	= 0.371 475 metre
1 tsun	= 0.1 chek
1 fan	= 0.1 tsun

PART II

Measurement of Area

(*a*) *Metric Units*

1 hectare	= 100 ares
1 are	= 100 square metres
1 square metre	= an area equal to that of a square each side of which measures one metre
1 square decimetre	= 0.01 square metre
1 square centimetre	= 0.01 square decimetre
1 square millimetre	= 0.01 square centimetre

(*b*) *Imperial Units*

1 square mile	= 640 acres
1 acre	= 4 840 square yards
1 rood	= 1 210 square yards
1 square yard	= an area equal to that of a square each side of which measures one yard
1 square foot	= $\frac{1}{9}$ square yard
1 square inch	= $\frac{1}{144}$ square foot

PART III

Measurement of Volume

(a) *Metric Units*

1 cubic metre	= a volume equal to that of a cube each edge of which measures one metre
1 cubic decimetre	= 0.001 cubic metre
1 cubic centimetre	= 0.001 cubic decimetre
1 litre	= a volume equal to that of a cubic decimetre
1 decilitre	= 0.1 litre
1 centilitre	= 0.01 litre
1 millilitre	= 0.001 litre

(b) *Imperial Units*

1 cubic yard	= a volume equal to that of a cube each edge of which measures one yard
1 cubic foot	= $\frac{1}{27}$ cubic yard
1 cubic inch	= $\frac{1}{1\,728}$ cubic foot

PART IV

Measurement of Capacity

(a) *Metric Units*

1 hectolitre	= 100 litres
1 litre	= a volume equal to that of a cubic decimetre
1 decilitre	= 0.1 litre
1 centilitre	= 0.01 litre
1 millilitre	= 0.001 litre

(b) *Imperial Units*

1 gallon	= 4.546 09 cubic decimetres
1 quart	= $\frac{1}{4}$ gallon
1 pint	= $\frac{1}{2}$ quart
1 gill	= $\frac{1}{4}$ pint
1 fluid ounce	= $\frac{1}{20}$ pint

PART V

Measurement of Mass or Weight

(a) *Metric Units*

1 tonne	= 1 000 kilograms
1 kilogram	= a unit of mass equal to the international prototype of the kilogram kept by the International Bureau of Weights and Measures
1 gram	= 0.001 kilogram
1 metric carat	= $\frac{1}{5}$ gram
1 milligram	= 0.001 gram

(b) *Imperial Units*

1 ton	= 2 240 pounds
1 hundredweight	= 112 pounds
1 quarter	= 28 pounds
1 stone	= 14 pounds
1 pound	= 0.453 592 37 kilogram exactly
1 ounce	= $\frac{1}{16}$ pound
1 dram	= $\frac{1}{256}$ pound
1 grain	= $\frac{1}{7\,000}$ pound
1 ounce troy	= $\frac{12}{175}$ pound

(c) *Chinese Units*

1 picul (tam)	= 100 catties
1 catty (kan)	= 0.604 789 82 kilogram
1 tael (leung)	= $\frac{1}{16}$ catty
1 mace (tsin)	= $\frac{1}{160}$ catty
1 candareen (fan)	= $\frac{1}{1\,600}$ catty
1 tael troy	= 37.429 grams
1 mace troy	= $\frac{1}{10}$ tael troy
1 candareen troy	= $\frac{1}{10}$ mace troy

SECOND SCHEDULE

UNITS OF MEASUREMENT AND PERMITTED SYMBOLS OR ABBREVIATIONS OF UNITS OF MEASUREMENT LAWFUL FOR USE FOR TRADE

PART I

Measurement of Length

Metric Units		*Imperial Units*		*Chinese Units*
kilometre	km	mile		chek
metre	m	chain		tsun
centimetre	cm	yard	yd	fan
millimetre	mm	foot	ft	
		inch	in	

PART II

Measurement of Area

Metric Units		*Imperial Units*	
hectare	ha	square mile	
are	a	acre	
square metre	m^2	square yard	yd^2
square decimetre	dm^2	square foot	ft^2
square centimetre	cm^2	square inch	in^2
square millimetre	mm^2		

PART III

Measurement of Volume

Metric Units		*Imperial Units*	
cubic metre	m^3	cubic yard	yd^3
cubic decimetre	dm^3	cubic foot	ft^3
cubic centimetre	cm^3	cubic inch	in^3
litre	L		

PART IV

Measurement of Capacity

Metric Units		*Imperial Units*	
cubic metre	m^3	gallon	gal
hectolitre	hL	quart	qt
litre	L	pint	pt
millilitre	mL	gill	
		fluid ounce	fl. oz

PART V

Measurement of Mass or Weight

Metric Units		*Imperial Units*		*Chinese Units*
tonne	t	ton		picul
kilogram	kg	hundredweight	cwt	catty
gram	g	quarter	qr	tael
carat (metric)	CM	stone		mace
milligram	mg	pound	lb	candareen
		ounce	oz	tael troy
		dram	dr	mace troy
		grain	gr	candareen troy
		ounce, troy	oz tr	

WEIGHTS AND MEASURES ORDER 1990

WEIGHTS AND MEASURES CONVERSION TABLE

1. Measurement of Length (see note 2)

(*a*)

	Metric Units and Symbols	*Imperial Units*	*Chinese Units*
1 kilometre	km = 1 000 metres	= 0.621 371 mile	= 2 691.97 cheks
1 metre	m	= 3.280 84 feet	= 2.691 97 cheks
1 centimetre	cm = 0.01 metre	= 0.393 701 inch	= 2.691 97 fans
1 millimetre	mm = 0.001 metre	= 0.039 370 1 inch	= 0.269 197 fan

(*b*)

	Imperial Units and Symbols	*Metric Units*	*Chinese Units*
1 mile	= 1 760 yards	= 1.609 344 kilometres exactly	= 4 332.31 cheks
1 chain	= 22 yards	= 20.116 8 metres exactly	= 54.153 8 cheks
1 yard	yd = 1/22 chain	= 0.914 4 metre exactly	= 2.461 54 cheks
1 foot	ft = 1/3 yard	= 30.48 centimetres exactly	= 8.205 13 tsuns
1 inch	in = 1/36 yard	= 25.4 millimetres exactly	= 6.837 61 fans

(*c*)

	Chinese Units	*Metric Units*	*Imperial Units*
1 chek		= 0.371 475 metre	= 1.218 75 feet
1 tsun	= 0.1 chek	= 3.714 75 centimetres	= 1.462 50 inches
1 fan	= 0.1 tsun	= 3.714 75 millimetres	= 0.146 250 inch

2. Measurement of Area (see note 3)

(*a*)

	Metric Units and Symbols	*Imperial Units*
1 hectare	ha = 100 ares	= 2.471 05 acres
1 are	a = 100 square metres	= 119.599 square yards
1 square metre	m^2	= 10.763 9 square feet
1 square decimetre	dm^2 = 0.01 square metre	= 15.500 0 square inches
1 square centimetre	cm^2 = 0.01 square decimetre	= 0.155 000 square inch
1 square millimetre	mm^2 = 0.01 square centimetre	= 0.001 550 00 square inch

(*b*)

	Imperial Units and Symbols	*Metric Units*
1 square mile	= 640 acres	= 258.999 hectares
1 acre	= 4 840 square yards	= 40.468 6 ares
1 square yard	yd^2	= 0.836 127 square metre
1 square foot	ft^2 = 1/9 square yard	= 0.092 903 0 square metre
1 square inch	in^2 = 1/144 square foot	= 6.451 6 square centimetres exactly

3. Measurement of Volume (see note 4)

(*a*)

	Metric Units and Symbols	*Imperial Units*
1 cubic metre	m^3	= 1.307 95 cubic yards
1 cubic decimetre	dm^3 = 0.001 cubic metre	= 0.035 314 7 cubic foot
1 cubic centimetre	cm^3 = 0.001 cubic decimetre	= 0.061 023 7 cubic inch
1 litre	L = 1 cubic decimetre	= 61.023 7 cubic inches

(*b*)

	Imperial Units and Symbols	*Metric Units*
1 cubic yard	yd^3	= 0.764 555 cubic metre
1 cubic foot	ft^3 = 1/27 cubic yard	= 28.316 8 cubic decimetres or litres
1 cubic inch	in^3 = 1/172 8 cubic foot	= 16.387 1 cubic centimetres

4. Measurement of Capacity

(*a*)

	Metric Units and Symbols	*Imperial Units*	*US Units*
1 cubic metre	m^3 = 1 000 litres	= 219.969 gallons	= 264.172 gallons
1 hectolitre	hL = 100 litres	= 21.996 9 gallons	= 26.417 2 gallons
1 litre	L	= 35.195 1 fluid ounces = 1.759 75 pints	= 33.814 0 fluid ounces = 2.113 38 liquid pints = 1.816 17 dry pints
1 millilitre	mL = 0.001 litre	= 0.035 195 1 fluid ounce	= 0.033 814 0 fluid ounce

(b)	Imperial Units and Symbols		Metric Units	US Units
	1 gallon	gal = 160 fluid ounces	= 4.546 09 litres	= 1.200 95 gallons
	1 quart	qt = 1/4 gallon	= 1.136 52 litres	= 1.200 95 liquid quarts = 1.032 06 dry quarts
	1 pint	pt = 1/2 quart	= 0.568 261 litre	= 1.200 95 liquid pints = 1.032 06 dry pints
	1 gill	= 1/4 pint	= 142.065 millilitres	= 1.200 95 gills
	1 fluid ounce	fl oz = 1/20 pint	= 28.413 1 millilitres	= 0.960 760 fluid ounce

(c)	US Units		Metric Units	Imperial Units
	1 gallon	= 128 fluid ounces	= 3.785 41 litres	= 0.832 674 gallon
	1 liquid quart	= 1/4 gallon	= 0.946 353 litre	= 0.832 674 quart
	1 liquid pint	= 1/2 liquid quart	= 0.473 176 litre	= 0.832 674 pint
	1 gill	= 1/4 liquid pint	= 0.118 294 litre	= 0.832 674 gill
	1 fluid ounce	= 1/16 liquid pint	= 29.573 5 millilitres	= 1.040 84 fluid ounces
	1 dry quart		= 1.101 22 litres	= 0.968 939 quart
	1 dry pint	= 1/2 dry quart	= 0.550 610 litre	= 0.968 939 pint

5. Measurement of Mass or Weight (see note 5)

(a)	Metric Units and Symbols		Imperial Units	Chinese Units	US Units
	1 tonne	t = 1 000 kilograms	= 0.984 207 ton	= 16.534 7 piculs	= 1.102 31 short tons
	1 kilogram	kg	= 2.204 62 pounds	= 1.653 47 catties	= 2.204 62 pounds
	1 gram	g = 0.001 kilogram	= 0.035 274 0 ounce	= 0.026 455 5 tael	= 0.035 274 0 ounce
	1 metric carat	CM = 0.2 gram	= 3.086 47 grains	= 0.052 911 0 mace	= 3.086 47 grains
	1 gram	g	= 0.032 150 7 ounce troy	= 2.671 73 candareen troy	= 0.032 150 7 ounce troy

(b)	Imperial Units and Symbols		Metric Units	Chinese Units	US Units
	1 ton	= 2 240 pounds	= 1.016 05 tonnes	= 16.800 0 piculs	= 1.12 short tons exactly
	1 hundredweight	cwt = 112 pounds	= 50.802 3 kilograms	= 84.000 0 catties	= 1.12 short hundredweights exactly
	1 quarter	qr = 28 pounds	= 12.700 6 kilograms	= 21.000 0 catties	= 1 quarter
	1 stone	= 14 pounds	= 6.350 29 kilograms	= 10.500 0 catties	= 1 stone
	1 pound	lb = 16 ounces = 256 drams = 7 000 grains	= 0.453 592 37 kilogram exactly	= 0.750 000 catty	= 1 pound
	1 ounce	oz = 1/16 pound	= 28.349 5 grams	= 0.750 000 tael	= 1 ounce
	1 dram	dr = 1/256 pound	= 1.771 85 grams	= 0.468 750 mace	= 1 dram
	1 grain	gr = 1/7 000 pound	= 0.064 798 9 gram	= 0.171 429 candareen	= 1 grain
	1 ounce troy	oz tr = 12/175 pound	= 31.103 5 grams	= 0.831 000 tael troy	= 1 ounce troy

(c)	Chinese Units		Metric Units	Imperial Units	US Units
	1 picul	= 100 catties	= 60.479 0 kilograms	= 133.333 pounds	= 133.333 pounds
	1 catty		= 0.604 789 82 kilogram	= 21.333 3 ounces	= 21.333 3 ounces
	1 tael	= 1/16 catty	= 37.799 4 grams	= 1.333 33 ounces	= 1.333 33 ounces
	1 mace	= 1/160 catty	= 3.779 94 grams	= 2.133 33 drams	= 2.133 33 drams
	1 candareen	= 1/1 600 catty	= 377.994 milligrams	= 5.833 33 grains	= 5.833 33 grains
	1 tael troy		= 37.429 grams	= 1.203 37 ounces troy	= 1.203 37 ounces troy
	1 mace troy	= 1/10 tael troy	= 3 742.9 milligrams	= 0.120 337 ounce troy	= 0.120 337 ounce troy
	1 candareen troy	= 1/10 mace troy	= 374.29 milligrams	= 0.012 033 7 ounce troy	= 0.012 033 7 ounce troy

(d)	US Units		Metric Units	Imperial Units
	1 short ton	= 2 000 pounds	= 0.907 185 tonne	= 0.892 857 ton
	1 short hundredweight	= 0.05 short ton	= 45.359 2 kilograms	= 0.892 857 hundredweight

Notes

1. 'US' means United States.
2. In item 1, US units of length are the same as those in the Imperial system.
3. In item 2, US units of area are the same as those in the Imperial system.
4. In item 3, US units of volume are the same as those in the Imperial system.
5. In item 5, except short ton and short hundredweight, US units of mass or weight are the same as those in the Imperial system.

APPENDIX 2
(Chapter 2: Constitution and Administration)

The Executive Council

Type of appointment	*Names of Members on January 2, 1994*
	Presided over by His Excellency the Governor The Right Honourable Christopher Francis PATTEN
	Members:
Ex-officio	The Chief Secretary The Honourable Mrs Anson CHAN, CBE, JP
Ex-officio	The Financial Secretary The Honourable Sir Hamish MACLEOD, KBE, JP
Ex-officio	The Attorney General The Honourable J. F. MATHEWS, CMG, JP
Appointed	The Right Honourable The Baroness DUNN, DBE, JP
Appointed	The Honourable Rosanna WONG Yick-ming, OBE, JP
Appointed	The Honourable Denis CHANG Khen-lee, QC, JP
Appointed	Professor the Honourable Edward CHEN Kwan-yiu, JP
Appointed	Dr the Honourable Raymond CH'IEN Kuo-fung, JP
Appointed	The Honourable Andrew LI Kwok-nang, CBE, QC, JP
Appointed	Professor the Honourable Felice LIEH MAK, OBE, JP
Appointed	The Honourable Michael SZE Cho-cheung, ISO, JP (Secretary for Constitutional Affairs)
Appointed	The Honourable TUNG Chee-hwa
Appointed	The Honourable John Malcolm GRAY, JP

APPENDIX 3

(Chapter 2: Constitution and Administration)

The Legislative Council

Type of appointment	*Names of Members on January 2, 1994*
	President:
Appointed	The Honourable J. J. SWAINE, CBE, LLD, QC, JP
	Members:
Ex-officio	The Chief Secretary The Honourable Mrs Anson CHAN, CBE, JP
Ex-officio	The Financial Secretary The Honourable Sir Hamish MACLEOD, KBE, JP
Ex-officio	The Attorney General The Honourable J. F. MATHEWS, CMG, JP
Appointed	The Honourable Allen LEE Peng-fei, CBE, JP
Appointed	The Honourable Mrs Selina CHOW LIANG Shuk-yee, OBE, JP
Elected	The Honourable HUI Yin-fat, OBE, JP (Social Services Functional Constituency)
Elected	The Honourable Martin LEE Chu-ming, QC, JP (Hong Kong Island East Constituency)
Elected	Dr the Honourable David LI Kwok-po, OBE, LLD, JP (Finance and Financial Services Functional Constituency)
Elected	The Honourable NGAI Shiu-kit, OBE, JP (Industrial Functional Constituency)
Elected	The Honourable PANG Chun-hoi, MBE (Labour Functional Constituency)
Elected	The Honourable SZETO Wah (Kowloon East Constituency)
Elected	The Honourable TAM Yiu-chung (Labour Functional Constituency)
Elected	The Honourable Andrew WONG Wang-fat, OBE, JP (New Territories East Constituency)
Elected	The Honourable LAU Wong-fat, OBE, JP (Rural Functional Constituency)
Elected	The Honourable Edward HO Sing-tin, OBE, JP (Engineering, Architectural, Surveying and Planning Functional Constituency)
Elected	The Honourable Ronald Joseph ARCULLI, OBE, JP (Real Estate and Construction Functional Constituency)

Type of appointment	*Names of Members on January 2, 1994*
Appointed	The Honourable Martin Gilbert BARROW, OBE, JP
Appointed	The Honourable Mrs Peggy LAM, OBE, JP
Appointed	The Honourable Mrs Miriam LAU Kin-yee, OBE, JP
Appointed	The Honourable LAU Wah-sum, OBE, JP
Elected	Dr the Honourable LEONG Che-hung, OBE, JP (Medical and Health Care Functional Constituency)
Elected	The Honourable James David MCGREGOR, OBE, ISO, JP (Commercial Functional Constituency)
Elected	The Honourable Mrs Elsie TU, CBE (Urban Council Functional Constituency)
Elected	The Honourable Peter WONG Hong-yuen, OBE, JP (Accountancy Functional Constituency)
Elected	The Honourable Albert CHAN Wai-yip (New Territories South Constituency)
Appointed	The Honourable Vincent CHENG Hoi-chuen, OBE, JP
Appointed	The Honourable Moses CHENG Mo-chi
Appointed	The Honourable Marvin CHEUNG Kin-tung, OBE, JP
Elected	The Honourable CHEUNG Man-kwong (Teaching Functional Constituency)
Elected	The Honourable CHIM Pui-chung (Finance and Financial Services Functional Constituency)
Elected	Rev the Honourable FUNG Chi-wood (New Territories North Constituency)
Elected	The Honourable Frederick FUNG Kin-kee (Kowloon West Constituency)
Appointed	The Honourable Timothy HA Wing-ho, MBE, JP
Elected	The Honourable Michael HO Mun-ka (Medical and Health Care Functional Constituency)
Elected	Dr the Honourable HUANG Chen-ya (Hong Kong Island West Constituency)
Elected	The Honourable Simon IP Sik-on, OBE, JP (Legal Functional Constituency)
Appointed	Dr the Honourable LAM Kui-chun
Elected	Dr the Honourable Conrad LAM Kui-shing, JP (Kowloon Central Constituency)

Type of appointment	*Names of Members on January 2, 1994*
Elected	The Honourable LAU Chin-shek (Kowloon Central Constituency)
Elected	The Honourable Emily LAU Wai-hing (New Territories East Constituency)
Elected	The Honourable LEE Wing-tat (New Territories South Constituency)
Appointed	The Honourable Eric LI Ka-cheung, JP
Elected	The Honourable Fred LI Wah-ming (Kowloon East Constituency)
Elected	The Honourable MAN Sai-cheong (Hong Kong Island East Constituency)
Appointed	The Honourable Steven POON Kwok-lim
Appointed	The Honourable Henry TANG Ying-yen, JP
Elected	The Honourable TIK Chi-yuen (New Territories North Constituency)
Elected	The Honourable James TO Kun-sun (Kowloon West Constituency)
Elected	Dr the Honourable Samuel WONG Ping-wai, MBE, JP (Engineering, Architectural, Surveying and Planning Functional Constituency)
Elected	Dr the Honourable Philip WONG Yu-hong (Commercial Functional Constituency)
Elected	Dr the Honourable YEUNG Sum (Hong Kong Island West Constituency)
Elected	The Honourable Howard YOUNG, JP (Tourism Functional Constituency)
Elected	The Honourable Zachary WONG Wai-yin (New Territories West Constituency)
Elected	Dr the Honourable TANG Siu-tong, JP (New Territories West Constituency)
Appointed	The Honourable Christine LOH Kung-wai
Appointed	The Honourable Roger LUK Koon-hoo
Appointed	The Honourable Anna WU Hung-yuk
Elected	The Honourable James TIEN Pei-chun, OBE, JP (Industrial Functional Constituency)
Elected	The Honourable Alfred TSO Shiu-wai (Regional Council Functional Constituency)

APPENDIX 4

(Chapter 2: Constitution and Administration)

Urban Council

Names of Members on January 2, 1994

Chairman:

Elected by Urban Council — Dr Ronald LEUNG Ding-bong, OBE, JP (A)

Vice-Chairman:

Elected by Urban Council — Mr Lo King-man, MBE, JP (A)

Members:

Mr B. A. BERNACCHI, OBE, QC, JP (E)
The Honourable Mrs Elsie TU, CBE (E)
Miss Cecilia YEUNG Lai-yin (E)
Mr Stephen LAU Man-lung, OBE, JP (A)
Mr Joseph CHAN Yuek-sut (E)
Mr PAO Ping-wing, JP (E)
The Honourable Frederick FUNG Kin-kee (E)
Dr the Honourable Samuel WONG Ping-wai, MBE, JP (A)
The Honourable Marvin CHEUNG Kin-tung, OBE, JP (A)
The Honourable MAN Sai-cheong (E)
Mr CHAN Kwok-ming (E)
Mr Ronnie WONG Man-chiu, JP (A)
Mrs Eleanor LING Ching-man, JP (A)
Mr Paul YOUNG Tze-kong, JP (A)
Dr Stan CHEUNG Tsang-kay, JP (A)
Mr Jason YUEN King-yuk (A)
Mr MA Lee-wo (E)
Mr MOK Ying-fan (E)
Mr Daniel WONG Kwok-tung (E)
Mr CHAN Tak-chor (R)
Miss Christina TING Yuk-chee, JP (R)
Mr Ambrose CHEUNG Wing-sum, JP (R)
Mr Albert POON Shun-kwok (R)
Mr FUNG Kwong-chung (R)
Mr Vincent CHOW Wing-shing (A)
Ms Carlye TSUI Wai-ling, JP (A)
Mr Ronald POON Cho-yiu (A)
Professor LEUNG Ping-chung (A)
Mr WONG Shui-lai (E)
Mr San Stephen WONG Hon-ching (E)
Mr CHIANG Sai-cheong (E)
The Honourable Fred LI Wah-ming (E)
Mr WONG Siu-yee (R)
Ms YEUNG Kam-chun (R)
Mr YIM Kwok-on (R)
Ms Anna TANG King-yung (R)
Mr IP Kwok-chung (R)
Mr Justein WONG Chun, JP (A)

Note: (E) = Elected. (A) = Appointed. (R) = District Board Representative.

APPENDIX 5

(Chapter 2: Constitution and Administration)

Regional Council

Names of Members on January 2, 1994

Chairman:
Mr CHEUNG Yan-lung, CBE, JP (A)

Vice-Chairman:
Dr PANG Hok-tuen, JP (A)

Members:
The Honourable Albert CHAN Wai-yip (E)
Mr CHAU Chun-wing (A)
Mr CHAU How-chen, MBE, JP (A)
Mr CHEUNG Hon-chung (E)
Mr CHEUNG Hon-kau, MBE (A)
Mr CHEUNG Kan-kwai (A)
Mr CHEUNG Kuen, MBE (R)
Dr Fanny CHEUNG Mui-ching, JP (A)
Mr CHOW Yick-hay (E)
Mr CHOW Yuk-tong (R)
Mr FONG Loi (A)
Rev the Honourable FUNG Chi-wood (E)
Mr FUNG Pak-tai (E)
Dr HO Man-wui, JP (A)
Mr HO Sun-kuen, JP (A)
Mr LAI Kwok-iu (R)
Mr Daniel LAM Wai-keung, JP (Ex)
Mr LAM Wing-yin (E)
Mr LAU Kong-wah (E)
The Honourable LAU Wong-fat, OBE, JP (Ex)
Mr LIU Ching-leung, JP (Ex)
Mr NGAN Kam-chuen (E)
Mr POON Chin-hung (A)
Mr SIN Chung-kai (R)
Mr SO Shiu-shing (R)
Mr TANG Pui-tat (R)
Mr TING Yin-wah (E)
The Honourable Alfred TSO Shiu-wai (E)
Mr WAN Yuet-kau (R)
Mr Johnston WONG Hong-chung (E)
Mr WONG Luen-kin (R)
Mr WONG Po-ming, JP (A)
Mr David YEUNG Fuk-kwong (R)
Mr YIM Tin-sang (E)

Note: (A) = Appointed. (E) = Elected. (R) = Representative (District Board). (Ex) = Ex-officio (Heung Yee Kuk).

APPENDIX 6

I. Overseas Representation in Hong Kong

(A) Commonwealth Countries

Countries	*Represented by*
Antigua and Barbuda	Honorary Consul
Australia	Consul-General
Bangladesh	Commissioner
Barbados	Honorary Consul
Belize	Honorary Consul
Botswana	Consul-in-Charge
Canada	Commissioner
Commonwealth of Dominica	Consul-General
Cyprus	Honorary Consul
Gambia	Honorary Consul
Grenada	Honorary Consul
India	Commissioner
Jamaica	Honorary Consul
Malaysia	Commissioner
Maldives	Honorary Consul
Malta	Honorary Consul
Mauritius	Honorary Consul
New Zealand	Commissioner
Nigeria	Commissioner
Pakistan	Consul-General
Papua New Guinea	Honorary Consul
St Lucia	Honorary Consul
Seychelles	Honorary Consul
Singapore	Commissioner
Sri Lanka	Honorary Consul
Tonga	Honorary Consul
Trinidad and Tobago	Honorary Consul
Western Samoa	Honorary Consul

(There also is a Senior British Trade Commissioner)

(B) Foreign Countries

Countries	*Represented by*
Argentina	Consul-General
Austria	Consul-General
Belgium	Consul-General
Benin	Honorary Consul
Bhutan	Honorary Consul
Brazil	Consul-General
Cape Verde	Consul-in-Charge
Central African Republic	Honorary Consul
Chile	Consul-General
Colombia	Consul-General
Costa Rica	Consul-General
Cote D'Ivoire	Honorary Consul
Cuba	Honorary Consul
Denmark	Consul-General
Djibouti	Honorary Consul
Dominican Republic	Consul-General
Egypt	Consul-General
Fiji	Honorary Consul
Finland	Consul-General
France	Consul-General
Gabon	Honorary Consul
Germany	Consul-General
Greece	Consul-General
Guinea	Honorary Consul
Honduras	Honorary Consul
Iceland	Honorary Consul
Indonesia	Consul-General
Israel	Consul-General
Italy	Consul-General
Japan	Consul-General
Jordan	Honorary Consul
Korea	Consul-General
Liberia	Honorary Consul
Luxembourg	Honorary Consul
Marshall Islands	Consul-General
Mexico	Consul-General
Monaco	Honorary Consul
Mongolia	Honorary Consul
Morocco	Honorary Consul
Mozambique	Honorary Consul
Myanmar	Consul-General
Netherlands	Consul-General
Nicaragua	Honorary Consul
Norway	Consul-General
Oman	Honorary Consul
Panama	Consul-General
Paraguay	Honorary Consul
Peru	Consul-General
Philippines	Consul-General
Poland	Consul-in-Charge
Portugal	Consul-General
South Africa	Consul-General
Spain	Consul-General
Sweden	Consul-General
Switzerland	Consul-General
Thailand	Consul-General
Togo	Honorary Consul
Tunisia	Honorary Consul
Turkey	Consul-General
United States of America	Consul-General
Uruguay	Consul-General
Venezuela	Consul-General

II. Hong Kong Representation Overseas

GOVERNMENT OFFICES

EUROPE

Brussels
Hong Kong Economic and Trade Office,
Avenue de Tervuren 188A,
1150 Brussels,
Belgium.
Tel.: (322) 775 0088
Fax: (322) 770 0980

Geneva
Hong Kong Economic and Trade Office,
37–39 rue de Vermont, 1211 Geneva 20, Switzerland.
Tel.: (022) 734-90-40 Telex: 414196 HKGV CH
Fax: (022) 733-99-04
(022) 740-15-01

London
Hong Kong Government Office,
6 Grafton Street, London W1X 3LB, England.
Tel.: (071) 499-9821 Cable: HONGAID LONDON
Fax: (071) 495-5033
(071) 493-1964

NORTH AMERICA

New York
Hong Kong Economic and Trade Office,
British Consulate General, 680 Fifth Avenue,
22nd Floor, New York, NY 10019, USA.
Tel.: (212) 265-8888 Fax: (212) 974-3209

San Francisco
Hong Kong Economic and Trade Office,
British Consulate General, 222 Kearny Street,
Suite 402, San Francisco, CA 94108, USA.
Tel.: (415) 397-2215 Fax: (415) 421-0646

Washington
Hong Kong Economic and Trade Office,
British Embassy, 1150, 18th Street,
NW Suite 475, Washington DC 20036, USA.
Tel.: (202) 331-8947
Cable: PRODROME WASHINGTON
Fax: (202) 331-8958

Toronto
Hong Kong Economic and Trade Office,
174 St. George Street, Toronto, Ontario,
M5R 2M7, Canada.
Tel.: (416) 924-5544
Fax: (416) 924-3599

ASIA

Tokyo
Hong Kong Economic and Trade Office,
7th Floor, Nishi-Azabu Mitsui Building,
4-17-30, Nishi-Azabu,
Minato-ku, Tokyo 106, Japan.
Tel.: 81-3-3498-8808 Fax: 81-3-3498-8815

Industrial Promotion Units

EUROPE

Brussels
Hong Kong Economic and Trade Office,
Avenue de Tervuren 188A,
1150 Brussels,
Belgium.
Tel.: (322) 775 0088
Fax: (322) 770 0980

London
Industrial Promotion Unit,
Hong Kong Government Office,
6 Grafton Street, London W1X 3LB, England.
Fax: (071) 495-5033

NORTH AMERICA

New York
Industrial Promotion Unit,
Hong Kong Economic and Trade Office,
680 Fifth Avenue, 22nd Floor, New York.
NY 10019, USA.
Tel.: (212) 265-7232 Fax: 212 974-3209

San Francisco
Industrial Promotion Unit,
Hong Kong Economic and Trade Office,
222 Kearny Street,
Suite 402, San Francisco, CA 94108, USA.
Tel.: (415) 956-4560 Fax: (415) 421-0646

ASIA

Tokyo
Industrial Promotion Unit,
Hong Kong Economic and Trade Office,
7th Floor, Nishi-Azabu Mitsui Building,
4-17-30, Nishi-Azabu, Minato-ku,
Tokyo 106, Japan.
Tel.: 81-3-3498-8808 Fax: 81-3-3498-8815

OTHER ORGANISATIONS

Hong Kong Trade Development Council

EUROPE

Amsterdam
Prinsengracht 771, Ground Floor,
1017 JZ Amsterdam, The Netherlands.
Tel.: 31-(020)-627-7101
Cable: CONOTRAD AMSTERDAM
Fax: 31-(020)-622-8529

Athens
52, Aegialias Street, Paradissos,
GR 15125 Amaroussion, Athens, Greece.
Tel.: 30-(1)-689-4189 Fax: 30-(1)-685-0832
(Trade enquiries only)

Barcelona
Balmes, 184 Atico 3,
08006 Barcelona, Spain.
Tel.: 34-(3)-415-8382
34-(3)-415-6628
34-(3)-415-9458
Fax: 34-(3)-416-0148

Budapest
Dorottya utca 8, H-1051 Budapest, Hungary.
Tel.: 36-(1)-266-1988
Fax: 36-(1)-266-1944

Frankfurt
Kreuzerhohl 5–7, 60439 Frankfurt,
Germany.
Tel.: 49-(069)-586011
Cable: CONOTRAD FRANKFURT
Fax: 49-(069)-5890752
Postal Address: P.O. Box 500551
60394 Frankfurt, Germany.

Istanbul
Piyalepasa Bulvari, Kastel Is Merkezi,
D. Blok Kat: 5, 80370 Piyalepasa,
Istanbul, Turkey.
Tel.: 90-(1)-237-02-25 Fax: 90-(1)-254-98-67

London
Swire House, Ground Floor, 59 Buckingham Gate,
London SW1E 6AJ, England.
Tel.: (44)-071-828-1661
Cable: CONOTRAD LONDON SW1
Fax: 44-(071)-828-9976
For trade enquiries in the UK
call 0800-282-980

Milan
2 Piazzetta Pattari, 20122 Milan, Italy.
Tel.: 39-(02)-865405, 865715
Cable: KONGTRAD MILAN
Fax: 39-(02)-860304

Paris
18, rue d'Aguesseau,
75008 Paris, France.
Tel.: 33-(01)-47-42-41-50 Telex: 283098 HKTDC F
Fax: 33-(01)-47-42-77-44

Stockholm
Kungsgatan 6, S-111 43 Stockholm, Sweden.
Tel.: 46-(08)-4115690
Cable: CONOTRAD STOCKHOLM
Telex: 11993 TDC S Fax: 46-(08)-7231630
Postal Address: P.O. Box 7505
S-103 92 Stockholm, Sweden.

Vienna
Rotenturmstrasse 1-3/8/24, A-1010 Vienna, Austria.
Tel.: 43-(01)-533-98-18
Cable: CONOTRADREP WIEN
Fax: 43-(01)-535-31-56

Warsaw
Ul Flory 9 PL-00586, Warsaw, Poland.
Tel.: 48-(22)-496-068
Fax: 48-(22)-493-584

Zurich
Seestrasse 135, P.O. Box CH-8027 Zurich,
Switzerland.
Tel.: 41-(01)-281-31-55 Fax: 41-(01)-281-31-91

NORTH AMERICA

For trade enquiries in the US
call 1-800-TDC-HKTE

Chicago
333 N. Michigan Ave., Suite 2028,
Chicago, IL 60601, USA.
Tel.: 1-(312)-726-4515
Cable: CONOTRAD CHICAGO
Fax: 1-(312)-726-2441

Dallas
Suite 120, World Trade Centre,
2050 Stemmons Freeway, Dallas, TX 75207, USA.
Tel.: 1-(214)-748-8162
Cable: HONGTRADS DALLAS
Fax: 1-(214)-742-6701
Postal Address: P.O. Box 58329
Dallas, TX 75258, USA.

Los Angeles
Los Angeles World Trade Centre,
350 S. Figueroa Street, Suite #282,
Los Angeles, CA 90071–1386, USA.
Tel.: 1-(213)-622-3194
Cable: CONOTRAD LOS ANGELES
Fax: 1-(213)-613-1490

Miami
Courvoisier Centre II, Suite 509,
601 Brickell Key Drive,
Miami, FL 33131, USA.
Tel.: 1-(305)-577-0414 Fax: 1-(305)-372-9142

New York
219 East 46th Street,
New York, NY10017, USA.
Tel.: 1-(212)-838-8688 Fax: 1-(212)-838-8941

San Francisco
c/o Hong Kong Economic and Trade Office,
222 Kearny Street, 4th Floor, Suite 402
San Francisco, CA 94108, USA.
Tel.: (1)-415-677-9038
Fax: (1)-415-421-0646
(Trade enquiries only)

Toronto
Suite 1100, National Building, 347 Bay Street,
Toronto, Ont. M5H 2R7, Canada.
Tel.: 1-(416)-366-3594
Cable: CONOTRAD TORONTO
Fax: 1-(416)-366-1569

Vancouver
1500 Georgia Street West,
11th Floor, Vancouver, B.C.
Canada. V6G 3B6
Tel.: 1-(604)-685-0883, 669-4444
Fax: 1-(604)-681-0093

LATIN AMERICA

Buenos Aires
Reconquista 513, Piso 3, (1003) Buenos Aires,
Argentina, Republic of Argentina.
Tel.: 54-(1)-314-2636 Fax: 54-(1)-314-8304

Mexico City
Manuel E. Izaguirre # 13, 3er piso Ciudad Satelite,
Mexico City 53310, Mexico.
Tel.: 52-(5)-572-41-13, 572-41-31
Fax: 52-(5)-393-59-40

Panama City
Condominio Plaza Internacional
Primer Alto, Oficina No. 27
Edificio del Banco Nacional de Panama
Via Espana y Calle 55
Panama City, Republica de Panama.
Tel.: (507) 69-5894, 69-5611, 69-5109
Fax: (507) 69-6183
Postal Address: Apdo. Post. 6-4510
El Dorado, Panama City, Panama

ASIA

Bangkok
20th Floor, TST Tower, 21 Vibhavadi Rangsit Road,
Bangkok 10900, Thailand.
Tel.: 66-(2)-273-8800 Fax: 66-(2)-273-8880

Beijing
Room 901, 9th Floor, CITIC Building,
19 Jianguomenwai Dajie, Beijing, 100004, PRC.
Tel.: 86-(01)-512-8661 Fax: 86-(01)-500-3285

Guangzhou
Unit A, 26th Floor,
Guangdong International Building, Annex A,
339 Huanshi Dong Lu, Guangzhou 510060, PRC.
Tel.: 86-(20)-3312889, 3311068
Fax: 86-(20)-3311081

Ho Chi Minh City
93 Nguyen Dinh Chieu Street, District 3,
Ho Chi Minh City, Vietnam.
Tel.: 84-(8)-242-058 Fax: 84-(8)-230-115

Nagoya
Sakae-Machi Building, 4th Floor, 3-23-31 Nishiki,
Naka-ku, Nagoya 460, Japan.
Tel.: 81-(052)-971-3626 Fax: 81-(052)-962-0613

Osaka
Osaka Ekimae Dai-San Building, 6th Floor,
1-1-3 Umeda, Kita-ku, Osaka 530, Japan.
Tel.: 81-(06)-344-5211
Cable: CONNOTRADD OSAKA
Fax: 81-(06)-347-0791

Seoul
720–721, KFSB Building, 16–2, Yoidodong,
Youngdeungpoku, Seoul, Korea.
Tel.: 82-(02)-782-6115/7 Fax: 82-(02)-782-6118

Shanghai
Room 1004, 10th Floor, Shanghai Union Building,
100 Yanan Dong Lu, Shanghai 200002, PRC.
Tel.: 86-(21)-326-4196, 326-5935
Telex: 30175 TDCSH CN Fax: 86-(21)-328-7478

Shenzhen
Unit 08, 14th Floor,
Shenzhen Development Centre Building,
Renminnan Road, Shenzhen, PRC.
Tel.: 86-(755)-228-0112/3 Fax: 86-(755)-228-0114

Singapore
20 Kallang Avenue, 3rd Floor, Pico Creative Centre,
Singapore 1233.
Tel.: 65-293-7977 Fax: 65-299-5218

Taipei
7th Floor, 315 Sung Chiang Road,
Taipei, Taiwan.
Tel.: 886-(2)-516-6085 Fax: 886-(2)-502-2115

Tokyo
Toho Twin Tower Building,
4th Floor, 1-5-2 Yurakucho,
Chiyoda-ku, Tokyo 100, Japan.
Tel.: 81-(03)-3502-3251/5 Fax: 81-(03)-3591-6484

AUSTRALIA

Sydney
71 York Street, Sydney, NSW 2000, Australia.
Tel.: 61-(02)-299-8343 Fax: 61-(02)-290-1889
Postal Address: G.P.O. Box 3877
Sydney, NSW 2001, Australia

MIDDLE EAST

Dubai
New Juma Al-Majid Building,
Dubai Sharjah Road, Dubai, U.A.E.
Tel.: 971-(4)-625255 Cable: MARKETS DUBAI
Telex: 46361 MARKET EM Fax: 971-(4)-663764
Postal Address: P.O. Box 7434 Dubai, U.A.E.

Hong Kong Tourist Association

EUROPE

Barcelona
c/o Sergat Espana S.L., Pau Casals,
08021 Barcelona, Spain.
Tel.: (3) 414-1794 Fax: (3) 201-8657

Frankfurt
Wiesenau 1, D 60323 Frankfurt am Main,
Federal Republic of Germany.
Tel.: (069) 722-841 Fax: (069) 721-244

London
4th/5th Floors, 125 Pall Mall,
London SW1Y 5EA, UK.
Tel.: (071) 930-4775 Fax: (071) 930-4777

Paris
Escalier C, 8eme etage, 53 rue Francois ler,
75008 Paris, France.
Tel.: (01) 4720-3954 Fax: (01) 4723-0965

Rome
c/o Sergat Italia, s.r.l., Piazza Dei Cenci 7/A,
00186 Roma, Italy.
Tel.: (06) 688-013-36 Fax: (06) 687-3644

NORTH AMERICA

Chicago
333 North Michigan Avenue,
Suite 2400, Chicago, IL 60601-3966, USA.
Tel.: (312) 782-3872 Fax: (312) 782-0864

Los Angeles
Suite 1220, 10940 Wilshire Boulevard,
Los Angeles, CA 90024-3915, USA.
Tel.: (310) 208-4582 Fax: (310) 208-1869

New York
5th Floor, 590 Fifth Avenue, New York,
NY 10036-4706 USA.
Tel.: (212) 869-5008/9 Fax: (212) 730-2605

Toronto
347 Bay Street, Suite 909,
Toronto, Ontario, M5H 2R7, Canada.
Tel.: (416) 366-2389 Fax: (416) 366-1098

ASIA

Tokyo
4th Floor, Toho Twin Tower Building,
1-5-2 Yurakucho, Chiyoda-ku, Tokyo 100, Japan.
Tel.: (03) 3503-0731 Fax: (03) 3503-0736
Telex: 072 2225678 LUYUTO J

Osaka
8th Floor, Osaka Saitama Building,
3-5-13 Awaji-machi, Chuo-ku, Osaka 541, Japan.
Tel.: (06) 229-9240 Fax: (06) 229-9648

Singapore
13-08 Ocean Building, 10 Collyer Quay,
Singapore 0104, Republic of Singapore.
Tel.: (65) 532-3668 Fax: (65) 534-3592
Telex: 087 28515 LUYUSN RS

Taipei
7th Floor, 18 Chang An East Road,
Sec. 1, Taipei, Taiwan.
Tel.: (02) 581-2967 Fax: (02) 581-6062

Seoul
Suite 1204, Sungji Building,
538 Dowha-Dong, Mapo-Gu, Seoul, Korea.
Tel.: (02) 706-5811 Fax: (02) 706-5813

SOUTH AFRICA

Johannesburg
c/o Development Promotions (Pty.) Ltd.,
7th Floor, Everite House,
20 De Korte Street, Braamfontein 2001.
Tel.: (011) 339-4865 Fax: (011) 339-2474
Telex: 421741/421740

AUSTRALIA

Sydney
Level 5, 55 Harrington Street,
The Rocks, Sydney, NSW 2000, Australia.
Tel.: (02) 251-2855 Fax: (02) 247-8812

NEW ZEALAND

Auckland
P.O. Box 2120, Auckland, New Zealand.
Tel.: (09) 520-3316 Fax: (09) 520-3327

APPENDIX 7

(Chapter 5: The Economy)

Gross Domestic Product by Expenditure Components at Current Market Prices

			$ Million
Expenditure Components of GDP	*1991*	*1992**	*1993†*
Private consumption expenditure	390,913	449,342	510,889
Government consumption expenditure	51,530	64,175	72,161
Gross domestic fixed capital formation	177,332	205,738	225,976
Change in stocks	4,098	12,732	6,828
Total exports of goods (f.o.b.)	765,886	924,952	1,046,248
Less imports of goods (c.i.f.)	782,042	958,462	1,075,712
Exports of services	121,570	143,397	164,464
Less imports of services	86,357	96,467	103,041
Total expenditure on gross domestic product at current market prices	**642,930**	**745,407**	**847,813**
Per capita GDP at current market prices ($)	**111,721**	**128,264**	**143,236**

Gross Domestic Product by Expenditure Components at Constant (1980) Market Prices

Expenditure Components of GDP			
Private consumption expenditure	178,876	192,574	206,517
Government consumption expenditure	17,553	19,906	20,352
Gross domestic fixed capital formation	75,995	83,304	87,848
Change in stocks	2,023	6,338	3,755
Total exports of goods (f.o.b.)	438,139	522,104	590,170
Less imports of goods (c.i.f.)	446,952	546,820	616,851
Exports of services	57,055	63,346	68,459
Less imports of services	49,255	52,699	56,405
Total expenditure on gross domestic product at constant (1980) market prices	**273,434**	**288,053**	**303,845**
Per capita GDP at constant (1980) market prices ($)	**47,514**	**49,566**	**51,334**

Note: * The estimates are subject to revisions later on as more data become available.
† Preliminary estimates.

Gross Domestic Product at Current Prices by Economic Activity

	1990		*1991*		*1992**	
	$ Million	*%*	*$ Million*	*%*	*$ Million*	*%*
1. Agriculture and fishing	1,432	0.3	1,441	0.2	1,468	0.2
2. Mining and quarrying	210	@	222	@	236	@
3. Manufacturing	92,241	17.2	92,693	15.2	93,041	13.2
4. Electricity, gas and water	12,612	2.3	13,521	2.2	15,639	2.2
5. Construction	29,836	5.6	34,486	5.6	36,467	5.2
6. Wholesale, retail and import/export trades, restaurants and hotels	130,542	24.3	155,616	25.5	187,241	26.6
7. Transport, storage and communication	50,526	9.4	57,746	9.5	67,599	9.6
8. Financing, insurance, real estate and business services	111,825	20.8	138,892	22.7	168,289	23.9
9. Community, social and personal services	80,334	15.0	94,563	15.5	110,729	15.8
10. Ownership of premises	58,141	10.8	66,548	10.9	77,559	11.0
less imputed bank service charge	30,829	5.7	44,737	7.3	54,572	7.7
Gross domestic product at factor cost (production-based estimate)	536,870	100.0	610,991	100.0	703,696	100.0
Indirect taxes less subsidies	29,614		36,323		48,777	
Gross domestic product at market prices (production-based estimate)	566,484		647,314		752,473	
Gross domestic product at market prices (expenditure-based estimate)	558,859		642,930		745,407	
Statistical discrepancy	1.4%		0.7%		0.9%	

Note: * The estimates are subject to revisions later on as more data become available.
@Less than 0.05.

APPENDIX 8
(Chapter 5: The Economy)
Public Expenditure by Function

$ Million

Item	Actual 1991–92			Actual 1992–93			Revised Estimate 1993–94		
	Recurrent	*Capital*	*Total*	*Recurrent*	*Capital*	*Total*	*Recurrent*	*Capital*	*Total*
Economic	**4,797**	**1,072**	**5,869**	**5,360**	**2,161**	**7,521**	**6,023**	**6,537**	**12,560**
Security									
Internal security	10,995	1,289	12,284	12,451	1,037	13,488	13,696	621	14,317
Immigration	1,051	82	1,133	1,165	42	1,207	1,322	40	1,362
Other	1,140	20	1,160	1,556	34	1,590	1,742	20	1,762
Sub-total	**13,186**	**1,391**	**14,577**	**15,172**	**1,113**	**16,285**	**16,760**	**681**	**17,441**
Social Services									
Social welfare	6,606	307	6,913	7,561	275	7,836	9,534	480	10,014
Health	9,785	1,379	11,164	12,340	1,297	13,637	14,586	3,982	18,568
Sub-total	**16,391**	**1,686**	**18,077**	**19,901**	**1,572**	**21,473**	**24,120**	**4,462**	**28,582**
Education	**16,235**	**2,660**	**18,895**	**18,895**	**2,744**	**21,639**	**22,189**	**2,914**	**25,103**
Environment	**752**	**1,925**	**2,677**	**789**	**2,340**	**3,129**	**1,317**	**1,914**	**3,231**
Community and external affairs									
Recreation, culture and amenities	4,352	1,389	5,741	4,858	1,071	5,929	5,695	2,075	7,770
District and community relations	696	16	712	717	16	733	817	17	834
Other	289	20	309	314	20	334	354	19	373
Sub-total	**5,337**	**1,425**	**6,762**	**5,889**	**1,107**	**6,996**	**6,866**	**2,111**	**8,977**
Infrastructure									
Transport	1,262	2,486	3,748	1,413	4,514	5,927	1,585	7,575	9,160
Land and buildings	1,918	5,169	7,087	2,106	5,827	7,933	2,473	7,854	10,327
Water supply	2,761	649	3,410	2,511	1,113	3,624	2,843	1,281	4,124
Sub-total	**5,941**	**8,304**	**14,245**	**6,030**	**11,454**	**17,484**	**6,901**	**16,710**	**23,611**
Support	**13,129**	**1,614**	**14,743**	**14,140**	**1,894**	**16,034**	**15,930**	**6,302**	**22,232**
Housing	**5,123**	**7,454**	**12,577**	**5,082**	**7,850**	**12,932**	**6,566**	**10,196**	**16,762**
Total	**80,891**	**27,531**	**108,422**	**91,258**	**32,235**	**123,493**	**106,672**	**51,827**	**158,499**

APPENDIX 8A

Public Expenditure by Function

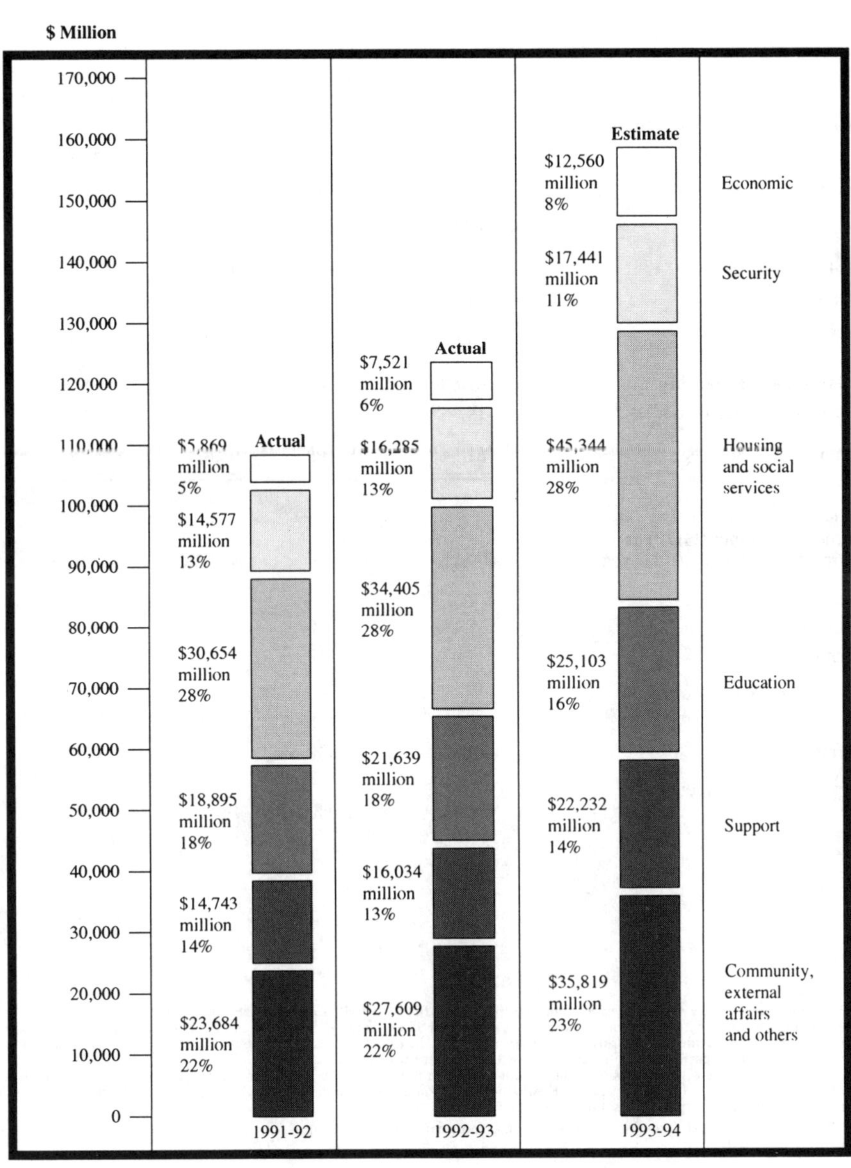

APPENDIX 9

(Chapter 5: The Economy)

Government Expenditure and the Economy

					$ Million
	Actual 1989–90	*Actual 1990–91*	*Actual 1991–92*	*Actual 1992–93*	*Revised Estimate 1993–94*
Government Expenditure (see Appendix 10)					
Operating Expenditure	50,106	61,469	71,677	85,024	97,820
Less: Grant to Regional Council	(273)	(274)	—	(2,300)	—
	49,833	61,195	71,677	82,724	97,820
Capital Expenditure	18,973	17,873	18,720	22,247	39,212
Less: Debt repayment	(1,000)	—	—	—	(1,200)
	17,973	17,873	18,720	22,247	38,012
Total Government Expenditure	**67,806**	**79,068**	**90,397**	**104,971**	**135,832**
Add: Other public sector bodies	14,139	16,130	18,025	18,522	22,667
Total Public Expenditure§	**81,945**	**95,198**	**108,422**	**123,493**	**158,499**
Gross Domestic Product (GDP) at current market prices (calendar year)	499,157	558,859	642,930	745,407*	847,813†
Growth in GDP:					
Nominal terms	15.1%	12.0%	15.0%	15.9*	13.7†
Real terms	2.8%	3.2%	4.1%	5.3*	5.5†
Growth in Public Expenditure:					
Nominal terms	26.5%	16.2%	13.9%	13.9%	28.4%
Real terms	10.8%	2.3%	3.3%	3.7%	17.7%
Public Expenditure as percentage of GDP	16.4%	17.0%	16.9%	16.6%	18.7%

Note: § The public expenditure comprises expenditure by the trading funds, the Housing Authority, the Urban Council, the Regional Council, expenditure financed by the Government's statutory funds and all expenditure charged to the General Revenue Account. Expenditure by institutions in the private or quasi-private sector is included to the extent of their subventions. The payments of Government departments which are wholly or partly financed by charges raised on a commercial basis are also included (e.g. airport, waterworks). But not included is expenditure by those organisations, including statutory organisations, in which the Government has only an equity position, such as the Mass Transit Railway Corporation and the Kowloon-Canton Railway Corporation. Similarly, equity payments are excluded as they do not reflect the actual consumption of resources by the Government.

* The estimates are subject to routine revisions later on as more data become available.

† Preliminary estimate.

APPENDIX 10

(Chapter 5: The Economy)

Total Government Revenue and Expenditure and Summary of Financial Position

$ Million

Revenue

	Actual 1991–92	*Actual 1992–93*	*Revised Estimate 1993–94*
Operating Revenue			
Direct taxes			
Earnings and profits tax	44,870	55,061	65,150
Indirect taxes			
Duties	6,844	7,216	7,154
General rates	3,494	4,423	4,425
Internal revenue§	18,406	23,012	29,335
Motor vehicle taxes	3,437	4,940	4,045
Royalties and concessions	886	1,136	1,366
Other revenue			
Fines, forfeitures and penalties	885	892	1,073
Properties and investments	1,572	1,821	2,027
Reimbursements and contributions	2,777	3,798	3,765
Utilities—			
Airport and air services	2,106	2,373	2,770
Ferry terminals	218	251	288
Government quarries	1	—	—
Postal services	2,198	2,428	2,557
Tunnels	302	211	—
Water	1,825	1,911	2,257
Fees and charges	7,170	8,015	8,534
Interest	2,982	1,767	3,280
Total Operating Revenue	**99,973**	**119,255**	**138,026**
Capital Revenue			
Direct taxes			
Estate duty	683	1,025	1,000
Indirect taxes			
Taxi concessions	302	—	—
Other revenue			
Land transactions	412	267	242
Miscellaneous	86	234	2,702
Funds			
Capital Works Reserve Fund (Land sales and interest)	9,074	8,957	19,072
Capital Investment Fund	2,468	2,368	2,577
Loan Fund	603	686	793
Total Capital Revenue	**13,628**	**13,537**	**26,386**
Net borrowing	1,098	2,519	—
Total Government Revenue	**114,699**	**135,311**	**164,412**

Note: § Including bets and sweeps tax, entertainment tax, hotel accommodation tax, air passenger departure tax, Cross Harbour Tunnel passage tax and stamp duties.

$ Million

Expenditure

	Actual 1991–92	*Actual 1992–93*	*Revised Estimate 1993–94*
Operating Expenditure			
Recurrent expenditure			
Personal emoluments	25,286	25,852	28,892
Personnel related expenses	3,183	3,275	3,522
Pensions	3,401	4,436	5,416
Departmental expenses	4,782	4,438	5,148
Other charges	10,939	11,770	14,264
Subventions—			
Education	9,728	10,921	12,313
Medical	5,452	11,181	13,309
Social welfare	1,587	1,824	2,016
University and Polytechnic	4,357	5,614	6,824
Vocational Training Council	814	901	1,128
Miscellaneous	1,244	1,381	1,472
Other non-recurrent	904	3,431	3,516
Total Operating Expenditure	**71,677**	**85,024**	**97,820**
Capital Expenditure			
General Revenue Account			
Plant, equipment and works	758	641	552
Capital subventions	416	822	1,116
Funds			
Capital Works Reserve Fund	16,405	19,676	35,694
Loan Fund	1,141	1,108	1,850
Total Capital Expenditure	**18,720**	**22,247**	**39,212**
Total Government Expenditure	**90,397**	**107,271**	**137,032**
Equity Investments (Capital Investment Fund)	1,794	6,061	12,275
Total Government Expenditure and Equity Investments	**92,191**	**113,332**	**149,307**

$ Million

Summary of Financial Position

	Actual 1991–92	*Actual 1992–93*	*Revised Estimate 1993–94*
Total Government Revenue	**114,699**	**135,311**	**164,412**
Less: Total Government Expenditure and Equity Investments	**92,191**	**113,332**	**149,307**
Consolidated cash surplus	**22,508**	**21,979**	**15,105**
Reserve balance at April 1	**76,545**	**99,053**	**121,032**
Reserve balance at March 31	**99,053**	**121,032**	**136,137**

APPENDIX 10A

Total Government Revenue by Source

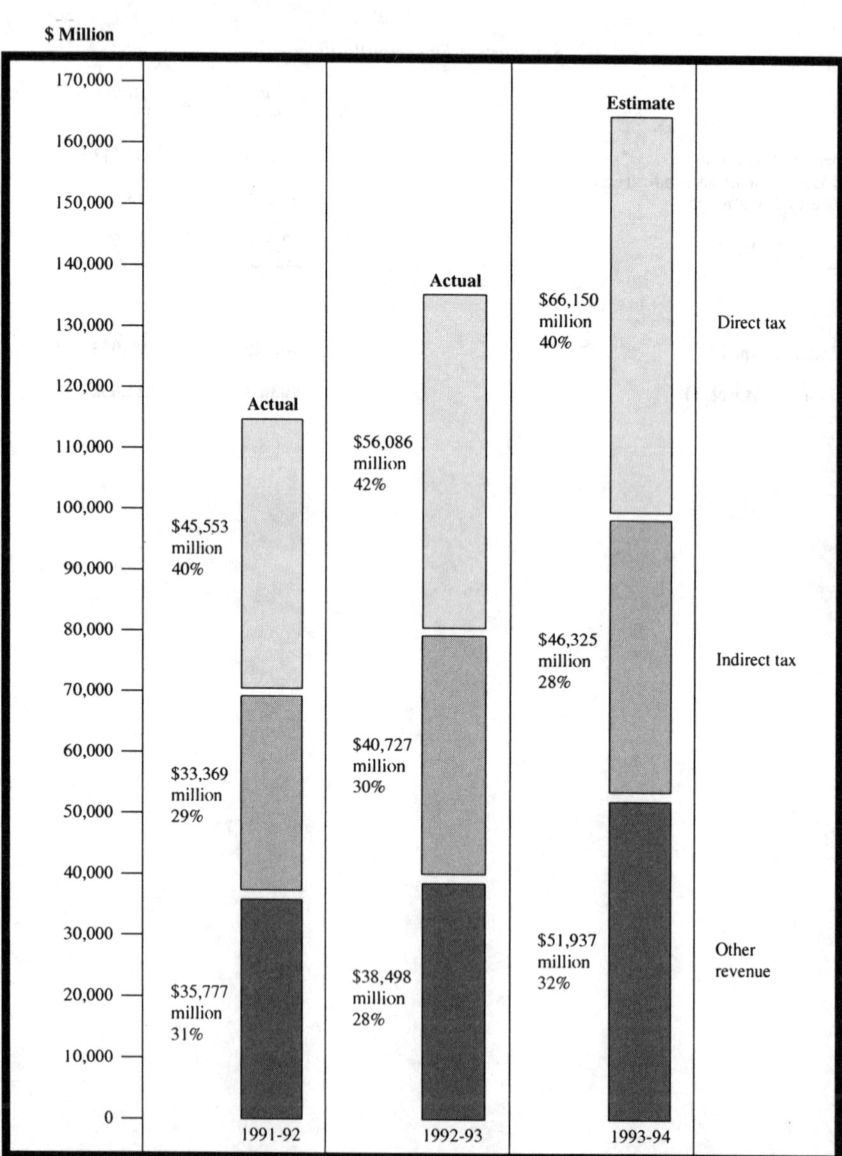

APPENDIX 11

Major Sources of Revenue
(1992-93)

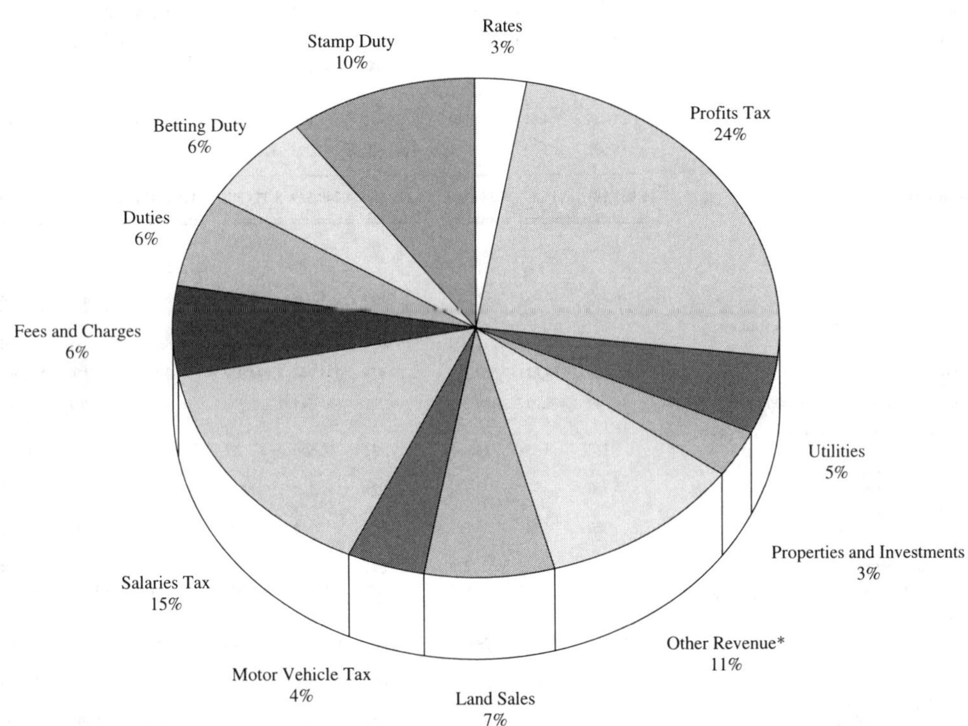

***Other Revenue Includes –**

Other Direct Tax:
1. Property Tax
2. Personal Assessment
3. Estate Duty

Other Indirect Tax:
4. Air Passenger Departure Tax
5. Hotel Accommodation Tax
6. Cross Harbour Tunnel Passenger Tax
7. Entertainment Tax

Others:
8. Royalties and Concessions
9. Fines, Forfeitures and Penalties
10. Loan Fund
11. Capital Investment Fund
12. Capital Works Reserve Fund (excluding suspense account)
13. Reimbursement and Others

APPENDIX 12

(Chapter 6: Financial and Monetary Affairs)

Liabilities and Assets: Licensed Banks

$ Million

	As at end of year								
	1991			*1992*			*1993*		
	HK$	*Foreign currency*	*Total*	*HK$*	*Foreign currency*	*Total*	*HK$*	*Foreign currency*	*Total*
Liabilities									
Amount due to authorised institutions in Hong Kong	228,267	224,906	453,173	210,689	215,352	426,041	236,195	182,463	418,658
Amount due to banks abroad	124,365	3,113,320	3,237,685	123,341	3,088,241	3,211,582	124,529	3,163,701	3,288,231
Deposits from customers§	540,193	771,239	1,311,432	602,773	846,616	1,449,390	770,865	905,079	1,675,944
Negotiable certificates of deposit outstanding	21,284	4,617	25,901	23,617	6,027	29,643	29,044	9,564	38,608
Other liabilities	118,072	103,725	221,797	143,623	93,293	236,916	195,403	94,728	290,131
Total liabilities	**1,032,181**	**4,217,807**	**5,249,988**	**1,104,043**	**4,249,529**	**5,353,572**	**1,356,036**	**4,355,535**	**5,711,571**
Assets									
Notes and coins	6,560	1,695	8,255	8,969	1,638	10,606	8,497	1,870	10,368
Amount due from authorised institutions in Hong Kong	265,963	249,829	515,792	263,057	243,870	506,928	298,144	224,959	523,103
Amount due from banks abroad	42,426	2,214,811	2,257,237	59,976	2,074,946	2,134,922	89,435	1,934,250	2,023,684
Loans and advances to customers	644,149	1,473,077	2,117,226	719,741	1,611,644	2,331,384	859,198	1,854,307	2,713,505
Negotiable certificates of deposit (NCD) held:	5,377	8,454	13,831	7,131	10,590	17,721	10,656	13,392	24,047
Issued by licensed banks in Hong Kong	4,550	377	4,927	5,877	1,369	7,247	8,479	2,148	10,627
Issued by restricted licence banks in Hong Kong	426	89	515	555	143	698	847	324	1,171
Issued by deposit-taking companies in Hong Kong	301	225	526	691	85	776	1,268	46	1,314
Issued by banks outside Hong Kong	100	7,763	7,863	8	8,993	9,001	62	10,873	10,935
Negotiable debt instrument held, other than NCDs	25,012	174,816	199,827	33,463	178,950	212,414	57,579	203,284	260,862
Acceptances and bills of exchange held	2,839	29,655	32,493	3,018	41,515	44,534	2,925	42,733	45,659
Floating rate notes and commercial paper held	4,937	49,608	54,546	3,528	45,814	49,342	3,796	53,295	57,091
Government bills, notes and bonds	15,117	52,813	67,929	25,545	45,959	71,505	48,843	62,358	111,201
Other debt instruments held	2,119	42,740	44,859	1,372	45,662	47,034	2,014	44,897	46,911
Investments in share-holdings	8,163	1,226	9,389	7,958	1,453	9,411	14,099	1,476	15,575
Interest in land and buildings	28,812	512	29,324	31,960	445	32,404	35,339	268	35,608
Other assets	27,329	71,778	99,107	29,389	68,392	97,782	37,882	66,936	104,818
Total assets	**1,053,791**	**4,196,197**	**5,249,988**	**1,161,644**	**4,191,928**	**5,353,572**	**1,410,828**	**4,300,743**	**5,711,571**
Number of licensed banks in operation			**160**			**161**			**168**

Notes: § Unadjusted for foreign currency swap deposits.

Liabilities and Assets: Restricted Licence Banks

$ Million

	1991 HK$	1991 Foreign currency	1991 Total	1992 HK$	1992 Foreign currency	1992 Total	1993 HK$	1993 Foreign currency	1993 Total
As at end of year									
Liabilities									
Amount due to authorised institutions in Hong Kong	36,963	23,447	60,410	43,187	24,198	67,385	45,556	25,194	70,750
Amount due to banks abroad	902	56,175	57,076	3,543	65,457	69,000	4,946	46,235	51,180
Deposits from customers§	10,234	29,393	39,627	11,640	22,971	34,611	6,161	23,318	29,479
Negotiable certificates of deposit outstanding	733	1,091	1,824	1,232	1,438	2,670	1,935	11,314	13,249
Other liabilities	10,378	25,314	35,692	13,386	29,525	42,910	16,173	17,102	33,275
Total liabilities	**59,210**	**135,419**	**194,629**	**72,988**	**143,589**	**216,576**	**74,771**	**123,162**	**197,933**
Assets									
Notes and coins	@	@	1	@	1	1	0	1	1
Amount due from authorised institutions in Hong Kong	14,229	19,558	33,787	12,760	17,856	30,616	5,715	13,372	19,087
Amount due from banks abroad	1,078	42,063	43,142	3,303	41,313	44,616	4,568	47,442	52,010
Loans and advances to customers	42,821	19,085	61,906	52,049	21,734	73,782	56,537	22,892	79,430
Negotiable certificates of deposit (NCD) held:	3,399	1,172	4,570	4,700	1,853	6,552	4,185	2,761	6,945
Issued by licensed banks in Hong Kong	2,641	23	2,664	3,451	438	3,889	3,399	794	4,193
Issued by restricted licence banks in Hong Kong	185	—	185	408	225	633	280	261	541
Issued by deposit-taking companies in Hong Kong	565	39	604	754	—	754	372	117	488
Issued by banks outside Hong Kong	8	1,110	1,118	87	1,190	1,277	135	1,588	1,723
Negotiable debt instrument held, other than NCDs	4,720	39,022	43,742	5,911	49,384	55,294	7,192	27,543	34,735
Acceptances and bills of exchange held	176	1,237	1,414	159	1,686	1,845	19	2,602	2,621
Floating rate notes and commercial paper held	1,666	19,497	21,162	1,583	16,852	18,435	719	13,577	14,296
Government bills, notes and bonds	2,661	7,924	10,585	3,799	19,718	23,517	6,146	5,592	11,738
Other debt instruments held	217	10,364	10,581	370	11,128	11,498	308	5,773	6,080
Investments in share-holdings	273	739	1,012	132	700	832	220	451	670
Interest in land and buildings	91	284	375	148	259	407	158	265	424
Other assets	1,145	4,948	6,093	1,186	3,288	4,474	1,417	3,213	4,631
Total assets	**67,757**	**126,872**	**194,629**	**80,189**	**136,388**	**216,576**	**79,993**	**117,940**	**197,933**
Number of restricted licence banks in operation			**52**			**55**			**57**

Notes: § Unadjusted for foreign currency swap deposits.
@Less than HK$ 0.5 million.

Liabilities and Assets: Deposit-taking Companies

$ Million

	As at end of year								
	1991			*1992*			*1993*		
	HK$	*Foreign currency*	*Total*	*HK$*	*Foreign currency*	*Total*	*HK$*	*Foreign currency*	*Total*
Liabilities									
Amount due to authorised institutions in Hong Kong	26,310	40,207	66,517	28,377	38,154	66,531	29,370	39,789	69,159
Amount due to banks abroad	429	23,880	24,309	400	22,478	22,879	418	19,181	19,599
Deposits from customers§	13,500	10,048	23,547	10,953	8,155	19,107	9,415	7,683	17,099
Negotiable certificates of deposit outstanding	1,215	2,383	3,598	2,016	388	2,405	2,472	387	2,859
Other liabilities	11,572	45,760	57,331	11,992	37,037	49,029	14,626	28,789	43,414
Total liabilities	**53,025**	**122,277**	**175,302**	**53,739**	**106,212**	**159,951**	**56,301**	**95,829**	**152,130**
Assets									
Notes and coins	8	6	14	16	6	22	22	5	28
Amount due from authorised institutions in Hong Kong	11,319	17,319	28,639	9,097	14,363	23,460	8,886	10,439	19,324
Amount due from banks abroad	211	35,323	35,534	93	30,677	30,770	320	21,448	21,768
Loans and advances to customers	36,862	27,778	64,640	40,298	24,094	64,392	41,588	22,367	63,955
Negotiable certificates of deposit (NCD) held:	1,251	2,621	3,871	1,088	1,678	2,765	934	2,939	3,872
Issued by licensed banks in Hong Kong	1,087	272	1,359	931	361	1,292	767	449	1,216
Issued by restricted licence banks in Hong Kong	56	78	133	79	105	184	58	265	323
Issued by deposit-taking companies in Hong Kong	75	206	282	70	191	261	86	70	156
Issued by banks outside Hong Kong	33	2,064	2,097	8	1,022	1,030	23	2,155	2,177
Negotiable debt instrument held, other than NCDs	897	33,612	34,509	952	30,792	31,745	2,176	34,926	37,102
Acceptances and bills of exchange held	56	2,207	2,263	63	2,798	2,862	94	2,940	3,033
Floating rate notes and commercial paper held	585	17,728	18,313	280	14,836	15,117	76	14,298	14,375
Government bills, notes and bonds	109	3,749	3,859	372	4,173	4,545	1,776	5,662	7,438
Other debt instruments held	147	9,927	10,074	236	8,985	9,221	230	12,026	12,256
Investments in share-holdings	191	635	826	168	512	681	196	611	807
Interest in land and buildings	222	150	372	235	87	322	380	112	493
Other assets	1,347	5,551	6,898	1,024	4,770	5,794	1,502	3,279	4,781
Total assets	**52,308**	**122,995**	**175,302**	**52,971**	**106,980**	**159,951**	**56,004**	**96,126**	**152,130**
Number of deposit-taking companies in operation			**157**			**146**			**140**

Notes: § Unadjusted for foreign currency swap deposits.

APPENDIX 13

(Chapter 6: Financial and Monetary Affairs)

Exchange Value of the Hong Kong Dollar

(A) Historical changes in the exchange rate system

	Par value of the HK$ in grams of fine gold	*£1 = HK$*	*US$1 = HK$*	*SDR1 = HK$*
December 18, 1946				
IMF parities established; Hong Kong dollar was pegged to sterling	0.223834	16.00	3.970	
September 18, 1949				
Hong Kong dollar devalued *pari passu* with sterling by 30.5%	0.155517	16.00	5.714	
November 20, 1967				
Hong Kong dollar devalued *pari passu* with sterling by 14.3%	0.133300	16.00	6.667	
November 23, 1967				
Hong Kong dollar revalued by 10%, including against sterling, but continues pegged to sterling, at new rate	0.146631	14.55	6.061	
December 18, 1971				
As part of the general currency realignment, Hong Kong dollar and sterling appreciated by 8.57% against US dollar. As a result of USA terminating, in August 1971, the convertibility of US dollar into gold, gold par value no longer had a practical meaning. IMF began to adopt the SDR as its accounting unit		14.55	5.582	6.061
July 6, 1972				
Hong Kong dollar pegged to US dollar following the floating of sterling			5.650	6.134
February 14, 1973				
US dollar devalued; Hong Kong dollar remains pegged, at new rate			5.085	6.134
November 26, 1974				
Hong Kong dollar allowed to float, *ie* the government no longer undertook to maintain a particular rate against any other currency				
October 17, 1983				
Hong Kong dollar was linked to US dollar, through a new arrangement in the note-issue mechanism, at a fixed exchange rate of HK$7.80 = US$1				

(B) Exchange rates of the Hong Kong dollar against several major currencies

	£	*US$*	*DM*	*¥*	*SDR*	*Effective exchange rate* (24–28 Oct 1983 = 100)*
End of period	*(HK dollars to one unit of foreign currency)*					
1974	11.53	4.910	2.03	0.0164	6.012	150.7
1988	14.17	7.808	4.42	0.0626	10.507	100.6
1989	12.60	7.807	4.63	0.0544	10.261	109.3
1990	14.95	7.801	5.20	0.0576	11.098	109.3
1991	14.53	7.781	5.13	0.0622	11.130	109.2
1992	11.77	7.741	4.80	0.0623	10.644	114.2
1993	11.45	7.726	4.46	0.0690	10.612	114.3

Note: * The effective exchange rate index is derived from a weighted average of nominal exchange rates of the Hong Kong dollar against the currencies of 15 principal trading partners.

APPENDIX 14

(Chapter 6: Financial and Monetary Affairs)

Money Supply

$ Million

	As at end of year								
	1991			*1992*			*1993*		
	HK$	*Foreign currency*	*Total*	*HK$*	*Foreign currency*	*Total*	*HK$*	*Foreign currency*	*Total*
Legal tender coins and notes in circulation									
Commercial bank issues (A)	46,506	—	46,506	58,226	—	58,226	68,896	—	68,896
The Hongkong and Shanghai Banking Corporation Limited	40,194	—	40,194	50,644	—	50,644	58,914	—	58,914
Standard Chartered Bank	6,312	—	6,312	7,582	—	7,582	9,982	—	9,982
Government issues (B)	2,671	—	2,671	2,931	—	2,931	2,978	—	2,978
One thousand-dollar gold coins	372	—	372	372	—	372	372	—	372
Ten-dollar coins							1	—	1
Five-dollar coins	790	—	790	866	—	866	873	—	873
Two-dollar coins	589	—	589	695	—	695	718	—	718
One-dollar coins	495	—	495	543	—	543	538	—	538
Subsidiary coins	424	—	424	454	—	454	475	—	475
One-cent notes	1	—	1	1	—	1	1	—	1
Authorised institutions' holdings of legal tender coins and notes (C)	6,569	—	6,569	8,985	—	8,985	8,520	—	8,520
Legal tender coins and notes in hands of public (A+B−C)=(D)	42,608	—	42,608	52,172	—	52,172	63,354	—	63,354
Demand deposits with licensed banks (E)	69,161	16,728	85,889	87,307	16,078	103,385	105,086	19,168	124,255
Time deposits with licensed banks (F)§	281,979 (241,744)	629,512 (669,747)	911,491	329,363 (270,673)	662,763 (721,453)	992,126	455,834 (384,034)	673,573 (745,373)	1,129,408
Negotiable certificates of deposit issued by licensed banks (other than those held by authorised institutions) (G)	13,006	3,944	16,950	13,357	3,859	17,216	16,399	6,173	22,572
Savings deposits with licensed banks (H)	229,287	84,764	314,052	244,792	109,085	353,878	281,744	140,538	422,282
Deposits with restricted licence banks and deposit-taking companies (I)	23,734	39,440	63,174	22,592	31,125	53,718	15,576	31,001	46,578
Negotiable certificates of deposit issued by restricted licence banks and deposit-taking companies (other than those held by authorised institutions) (J)	341	2,837	3,178	692	1,078	1,770	1,498	10,617	12,115
Money supply									
Definition 1 (D+E)	111,769	16,728	128,497	139,479	16,078	155,557	168,440	19,168	187,608
Definition 2 (D+E+F+G+H)§	636,042 (595,808)	734,948 (775,182)	1,370,990	726,992 (668,302)	791,785 (850,475)	1,518,777	922,417 (850,618)	839,452 (911,252)	1,761,870
Definition 3 (D+E+F+G+H+I+J)§	660,117 (619,882)	777,225 (817,460)	1,437,342	750,276 (691,586)	823,989 (882,679)	1,574,265	939,491 (867,692)	881,071 (952,871)	1,820,562

Note: § Adjusted for foreign currency swap deposits. Unadjusted figures are shown in brackets. Foreign currency swap deposits are deposits involving customers buying foreign currencies in the spot market and placing them as deposits with authorised institutions, while at the same time entering into a forward contract to sell such foreign currencies (principal plus interest) upon maturity of such deposits. For most analytical purposes, they should be regarded as Hong Kong dollar deposits.

APPENDIX 14A
(Chapter 6: Financial and Monetary Affairs)

EXCHANGE FUND BALANCE SHEET

$ Million

	Note	As at end of: 1987	1988	1989	1990	1991	1992
ASSETS							
Foreign Currency Assets	1	113,089	127,089	149,152	192,323	225,333	274,948
Hong Kong Dollar Assets	1	5,746	5,962	9,625	3,874	10,788	12,546
		118,835	133,051	158,777	196,197	236,121	287,494
LIABILITIES							
Certificates of Indebtedness	2	26,831	31,731	37,191	40,791	46,410	58,130
Transfers of Fiscal Reserves	3	32,557	38,269	52,546	63,226	69,802	96,145
Coins in Circulation		1,470	1,890	2,012	2,003	2,299	2,559
Exchange Fund Bills		—	—	—	6,671	13,624	19,324
Other Liabilities	4	4,453	2,554	1,603	391	4,834	3,220
Balance of Banking System	5	—	860	978	480	500	1,480
		65,311	75,304	94,330	113,562	137,469	180,858
ACCUMULATED EARNINGS		53,524	57,747	64,447	82,635	98,652	106,636

NOTES ON THE ACCOUNTS

1. (*a*) **Investments**
The fund is invested in interest bearing deposits with banks in Hong Kong and overseas and in a variety of financial instruments, including bonds, notes and treasury bills. Only instruments which have good marketability and which are issued by or guaranteed by governments with high credit standing are acquired.

(*b*) **Foreign currency assets distribution**
A large proportion of the Fund's foreign currency assets are held in US dollars because this is the intervention currency and there is no exchange risk involved, given that the Hong Kong dollar is linked to the US dollar. Apart from the US dollar, the Fund also holds assets denominated in other major foreign currencies. They are the Canadian dollar, deutschemark, Japanese yen, pound sterling, Swiss franc, Dutch guilder, French franc and the ECU.

(*c*) **Location of assets**
The assets are held in deposit, trustee and safe-keeping accounts with banks, central banks and custodial organisations situated in Hong Kong and other major financial centres.

(*d*) **Valuation of assets**
Short-term money market instruments are valued at cost. Bonds, notes and treasury bills are valued at mid-market prices as at the close of business on the last business day of each accounting period.

(*e*) **Translation of foreign currency assets**
US dollar (USD) assets are translated into Hong Kong dollars (HKD) at an exchange rate of USD 1=HKD 7.80. Assets in other foreign currencies are translated into Hong Kong dollars based on US dollar middle market cross rates in New York at the close of business on the last business day of the accounting period.

2. As backing for their bank note issues, the two note-issuing banks are required to hold non-interest bearing certificates of indebtedness issued by the Exchange Fund. Since 17 October 1983 these certificates have been issued to or redeemed from the two banks against payment in US dollars at a fixed rate of HKD 7.80=USD 1.00.

3. This is that proportion of the fiscal reserves which has been transferred from the General Revenue Account, Capital Investment Fund, Loan Fund and Capital Works Reserve Fund to the Exchange Fund on an interest earning basis.

4. Other liabilities comprise expenses accrued at the year end, in the main interest due on fiscal reserve transfers, contingency reserves for bank rescue operations and any other borrowings.

5. In accordance with the Accounting Arrangements introduced in July 1988, The Hongkong and Shanghai Banking Corporation Ltd., as the Managemnet Bank of the Clearing House of the Hong Kong Association of Banks, is required to maintain a Clearing Account with the Exchange Fund. The balance in the Account, which represents the level of liquidity in the interbank market, can only be altered by the Fund. The Accounting Arrangements enable the Fund to maintain exchange rate stability more effectively by influencing the level of interbank liquidity through money market operations.

APPENDIX 15

(Chapter 7: Industry and Trade)

Hong Kong's External Trade by Major Trading Partners

Imports

	1991		*1992*		*1993*		*1992–93*
	$ Million	*Per cent*	*$ Million*	*Per cent*	*$ Million*	*Per cent*	*Change in per cent*
Supplier							
China	293,356	37.7	354,348	37.1	402,161	37.5	+13.5
Japan	127,402	16.4	166,191	17.4	178,034	16.6	+7.1
Taiwan	74,591	9.6	87,019	9.1	93,968	8.8	+8.0
United States	58,837	7.6	70,594	7.4	79,419	7.4	+12.5
Republic of Korea	34,944	4.5	44,155	4.6	48,220	4.5	+9.2
Singapore	31,525	4.0	39,087	4.1	47,835	4.5	+22.4
Federal Republic of Germany	16,641	2.1	21,911	2.3	24,918	2.3	+13.7
United Kingdom	16,545	2.1	19,221	2.0	21,438	2.0	+11.5
Italy	11,729	1.5	14,825	1.6	17,880	1.7	+20.6
Malaysia	9,859	1.3	12,825	1.3	15,855	1.5	+23.6
Others	103,553	13.3	125,118	13.1	142,869	13.3	+14.2
Merchandise total	**778,982**	**100.0**	**955,295**	**100.0**	**1,072,597**	**100.0**	**+12.3**

Domestic Exports

	1991		*1992*		*1993*		*1992–93*
	$ Million	*Per cent*	*$ Million*	*Per cent*	*$ Million*	*Per cent*	*Change in per cent*
Destination							
China	54,404	23.5	61,959	26.5	63,367	28.4	+2.3
United States	62,870	27.2	64,600	27.6	60,292	27.0	−6.7
Federal Republic of Germany	19,318	8.4	15,956	6.8	13,969	6.3	−12.5
Singapore	8,794	3.8	10,360	4.4	11,344	5.1	+9.5
United Kingdom	13,706	5.9	12,541	5.4	10,771	4.8	−14.1
Japan	11,666	5.0	10,997	4.7	9,677	4.3	−12.0
Taiwan	6,066	2.6	6,500	2.8	6,261	2.8	−3.7
Canada	5,014	2.2	5,018	2.1	4,734	2.1	−5.7
Netherlands	5,238	2.3	4,878	2.1	4,520	2.0	−7.3
France	3,710	1.6	3,164	1.4	2,707	1.2	−14.4
Others	40,260	17.4	38,151	16.3	35,385	15.9	−7.3
Merchandise total	**231,045**	**100.0**	**234,123**	**100.0**	**223,027**	**100.0**	**−4.7**

Re-exports

	1991		*1992*		*1993*		*1992–93*
	$ Million	*Per cent*	*$ Million*	*Per cent*	*$ Million*	*Per cent*	*Change in per cent*
Destination							
China	153,318	28.7	212,105	30.7	274,561	33.4	+29.4
United States	110,802	20.7	148,500	21.5	180,349	21.9	+21.4
Japan	29,574	5.5	37,465	5.4	44,156	5.4	+17.9
Federal Republic of Germany	32,073	6.0	33,103	4.8	40,798	5.0	+23.2
United Kingdom	14,663	2.7	20,591	3.0	24,536	3.0	+19.2
Taiwan	24,765	4.6	26,156	3.8	21,910	2.7	−16.2
Singapore	12,094	2.3	13,866	2.0	17,143	2.1	+23.6
Republic of Korea	14,631	2.7	13,588	2.0	15,538	1.9	+14.3
France	9,038	1.7	11,039	1.6	12,864	1.6	+16.5
Canada	8,498	1.6	11,101	1.6	12,656	1.5	+14.0
Others	125,385	23.4	163,315	23.6	178,713	21.7	+9.4
Merchandise total	**534,841**	**100.0**	**690,829**	**100.0**	**823,224**	**100.0**	**+19.2**

APPENDIX 16A

(Chapter 7: Industry and Trade)

Hong Kong's External Trade Analysed by Standard International Trade Classification Revision 3 (SITC Rev. 3)

Imports

$ Million

Section/division	*1991*	*1992*	*1993*
Food and live animals			
Live animals	2,924	3,441	3,248
Meat and meat preparations	5,055	5,394	5,689
Fish, crustaceans, molluscs and aquatic invertebrates, and preparations thereof	9,398	10,728	10,597
Vegetables and fruit	10,175	11,040	11,000
Miscellaneous edible products and preparations	3,013	3,040	3,338
Others	8,931	9,827	9,363
Sub-total	**39,496**	**43,469**	**43,235**
Beverages and tobacco			
Beverages	5,050	5,814	6,270
Tobacco and tobacco manufactures	11,102	13,388	11,838
Sub-total	**16,152**	**19,203**	**18,108**
Crude materials, inedible, except fuels			
Hides, skins and furskins, raw	1,659	1,920	2,281
Cork and wood	1,396	1,382	1,870
Textile fibres (other than wool tops and other combed wool) and their wastes (not manufactured into yarn or fabric)	7,735	6,898	5,654
Crude animal and vegetable materials, n e s	5,329	5,472	4,408
Others	3,599	4,779	4,713
Sub-total	**19,718**	**20,450**	**18,926**
Mineral fuels, lubricants and related materials			
Petroleum, petroleum products and related materials	12,966	15,312	15,806
Others	3,366	3,618	3,687
Sub-total	**16,331**	**18,930**	**19,493**
Animal and vegetable oils, fats and waxes			
Fixed vegetable fats and oils, crude, refined or fractionated	1,130	1,026	1,094
Others	97	107	150
Sub-total	**1,228**	**1,133**	**1,244**
Chemicals and related products, n e s			
Dyeing, tanning and colouring materials	6,907	7,844	7,759
Plastics in primary forms	18,629	21,119	20,563
Plastics in non-primary forms	6,842	8,161	8,716
Chemical materials and products, n e s	5,952	6,850	6,979
Others	22,477	23,653	22,818
Sub-total	**60,806**	**67,627**	**66,836**
Manufactured goods classified chiefly by material			
Textile yarn, fabrics, made-up articles, n e s and related products	93,678	101,322	98,895
Non-metallic mineral manufactures, n e s	24,561	29,335	33,431
Iron and steel	14,226	15,439	21,246
Manufactures of metals, n e s	11,600	14,295	16,834
Others	38,379	47,388	49,847
Sub-total	**182,443**	**207,778**	**220,253**
Machinery and transport equipment			
Telecommunications and sound recording and reproducing apparatus and equipment	60,094	75,629	93,346
Electrical machinery, apparatus and appliances, n e s, and electrical parts thereof	77,791	95,434	116,357
Road vehicles (including air-cushion vehicles)	17,000	33,653	50,466
Others	72,556	102,285	117,314
Sub-total	**227,440**	**307,002**	**377,482**
Miscellaneous manufactured articles			
Articles of apparel and clothing accessories	66,507	80,078	91,325
Footwear	22,338	31,689	41,668
Photographic apparatus, equipment and supplies and optical goods, n e s; watches and clocks	39,233	45,860	48,661
Miscellaneous manufactured articles, n e s	55,694	71,924	79,460
Others	28,696	36,049	41,944
Sub-total	**212,468**	**265,599**	**303,058**
Commodities and transactions not classified elsewhere in the SITC	**2,899**	**4,103**	**3,961**
Total merchandise	**778,982**	**955,295**	**1,072,597**
Gold and specie	**28,692**	**30,774**	**21,001**
Grand total	**807,674**	**986,069**	**1,093,598**

Note: n e s = not elsewhere specified.

Domestic Exports

Section/division	*1991*	*1992*	*$ Million* *1993*
Food and live animals			
Fish, crustaceans, molluscs and aquatic invertebrates, and preparations thereof	773	731	783
Cereals and cereal preparations	267	342	252
Miscellaneous edible products and preparations	871	975	1,004
Others	618	592	460
Sub-total	**2,530**	**2,640**	**2,498**
Beverages and tobacco			
Beverages	377	405	473
Tobacco and tobacco manufactures	2,613	2,610	2,423
Sub-total	**2,990**	**3,016**	**2,897**
Crude materials, inedible, except fuels			
Pulp and waste paper	442	372	248
Textile fibres (other than wool tops and other combed wool) and their wastes (not manufactured into yarn or fabric)	119	105	82
Metalliferous ores and metal scrap	1,295	1,341	1,262
Others	103	101	82
Sub-total	**1,958**	**1,919**	**1,674**
Mineral fuels, lubricants and related materials	**1,277**	**2,091**	**1,941**
Animal and vegetable oils, fats and waxes	**76**	**113**	**113**
Chemicals and related products, n e s			
Dyeing, tanning and colouring materials	688	942	1,011
Essential oils and resinoids and perfume materials; toilet, polishing and cleansing preparations	750	882	875
Plastics in primary forms	3,576	3,367	3,441
Plastics in non-primary forms	1,352	1,292	1,161
Chemical materials and products, n e s	731	697	728
Others	384	506	548
Sub-total	**7,482**	**7,686**	**7,765**
Manufactured goods classified chiefly by material			
Paper, paperboard, and articles of paper pulp, of paper or of paperboard	2,369	2,841	2,980
Textile yarn, fabrics, made-up articles, n e s and related products	17,595	17,226	16,180
Non-ferrous metals	1,035	1,237	1,410
Manufactures of metals, n e s	4,902	4,788	4,639
Others	1,957	2,224	2,800
Sub-total	**27,859**	**28,316**	**28,009**
Machinery and transport equipment			
Office machines and automatic data processing machines	18,292	20,530	17,247
Telecommunications and sound recording and reproducing apparatus and equipment	15,168	12,983	13,278
Electrical machinery, apparatus and appliances, n e s, and electrical parts thereof	19,251	20,138	22,668
Others	6,839	7,786	8,504
Sub-total	**59,550**	**61,437**	**61,697**
Miscellaneous manufactured articles			
Prefabricated buildings; sanitary, plumbing, heating and lighting fixtures and fittings, n e s	965	861	630
Furniture and parts there of; bedding; mattresses, mattress supports, cushions and similar stuffed furnishings	461	430	411
Travel goods, handbags and similar containers	1,045	1,020	803
Articles of apparel and clothing accessories	75,525	77,156	71,857
Footwear	721	548	300
Professional, scientific and controlling instruments and apparatus, n e s	1,332	1,480	1,720
Photographic apparatus, equipment and supplies and optical goods, n e s; watches and clocks	20,259	18,879	16,053
Miscellaneous manufactured articles, n e s	23,576	22,152	20,568
Sub-total	**123,883**	**122,526**	**112,342**
Commodities and transactions not classified elsewhere in the SITC	**3,440**	**4,381**	**4,090**
Total merchandise	**231,045**	**234,123**	**223,027**
Gold and specie	—	—	—
Grand total	**231,045**	**234,123**	**223,027**

Note: n e s = not elsewhere specified.

Re-exports

Section/division	*1991*	*1992*	*$ Million* *1993*
Food and live animals			
Meat and meat preparations	943	1,038	1,442
Fish, crustaceans, molluscs and aquatic invertebrates, and preparations thereof	3,615	3,565	3,089
Vegetables and fruit	4,040	4,412	4,186
Coffee, tea, cocoa, spices and manufactures thereof	1,034	1,224	1,109
Others	2,898	3,417	3,346
Sub-total	**12,529**	**13,656**	**13,172**
Beverages and tobacco			
Beverages	2,493	3,000	3,432
Tobacco and tobacco manufactures	8,240	9,999	9,168
Sub-total	**10,733**	**12,999**	**12,600**
Crude materials, inedible, except fuels			
Cork and wood	743	813	1,075
Textile fibres (other than wool tops and other combed wool) and their wastes (not manufactured into yarn or fabric)	4,654	4,618	4,231
Metalliferous ores and metal scrap	759	1,308	1,078
Crude animal and vegetable materials, n e s	4,658	4,589	3,764
Others	2,346	2,464	2,963
Sub-total	**13,160**	**13,792**	**13,111**
Mineral fuels, lubricants and related materials			
Petroleum, petroleum products and related materials	4,249	5,261	7,370
Others	128	181	180
Sub-total	**4,377**	**5,442**	**7,550**
Animal and vegetable oils, fats and waxes	**489**	**529**	**559**
Chemicals and related products, n e s			
Dyeing, tunning and colouring materials	4,376	4,970	5,286
Plastics in primary forms	11,344	14,218	14,845
Plastic in non-primary forms	3,418	4,544	5,487
Chemical materials and products, n e s	4,355	5,249	5,502
Others	14,533	14,879	14,211
Sub-total	**38,026**	**43,860**	**45,330**
Manufactured goods classified chiefly by material			
Textile yarn, fabrics, made-up articles, n e s and related products	58,159	67,744	70,556
Non-metallic mineral manufactures, n e s	13,175	14,440	16,127
Iron and steel	6,073	8,448	12,830
Manufactures of metals, n e s	9,642	12,694	15,517
Others	18,450	25,797	28,291
Sub-total	**105,499**	**129,123**	**143,321**
Machinery and transport equipment			
Office machines and automatic data processing machines	15,588	21,994	28,756
Telecommunications and sound recording and reproducing apparatus and equipment	45,079	55,763	74,082
Electrical machinery, apparatus and appliances, n e s, and electrical parts thereof	41,065	53,746	69,141
Road vehicles (including air-cushion vehicles)	8,468	17,186	32,747
Others	27,055	42,936	53,729
Sub-total	**137,255**	**191,624**	**258,455**
Miscellaneous manufactured articles			
Articles of apparel and clothing accessories	63,577	78,095	90,574
Foot wear	24,951	35,327	47,226
Photographic apparatus, equipment and supplies and optical goods, n e s; watches and clocks	21,765	29,651	36,498
Miscellaneous manufactured articles, n e s	71,918	97,316	108,036
Others	29,118	37,038	44,322
Sub-total	**211,329**	**277,427**	**326,656**
Commodities and transactions not classified elsewhere in the SITC	**1,444**	**2,378**	**2,469**
Total merchandise	**534,841**	**690,829**	**823,224**
Gold and specie	**845**	**635**	**1,118**
Grand total	**535,686**	**691,464**	**824,342**

Note: n e s = not elsewhere specified.

APPENDIX 16B

(Chapter 7: Industry and Trade)

Hong Kong's Domestic Exports of Principal Commodity Groups

Commodity groups [1]	*1991 $ Million*	*1992 $ Million*	*1993 $ Million*	*Percentage Change 1993 Over 1992*
Textiles and clothing	93,120	94,383	88,037	−7
Electronic products [2]	58,617	60,291	57,333	−5
Watches and clocks [2]	17,037	15,476	13,161	−15
Plastic products [2]	7,027	7,196	5,869	−18
Jewellery, goldsmiths' and silversmiths' wares	5,668	5,047	5,303	+5
Manufactures of metals	4,902	4,788	4,639	−3
Printed matter	3,937	4,414	4,447	+1
Toys and dolls [2]	4,431	3,724	3,036	−18
Electrical appliances	3,231	2,028	1,608	−21
Total domestic exports[2] of the above 9 groups	183,113	183,044	172,267	−6
As a % of all domestic exports	79%	78%	77%	

Notes: (1) For a breakdown of Hong Kong's external trade by the Standard International Trade Classification (SITC) Revision 3, readers should refer to Appendix 16A. The statistics there are presented according to the classification of commodities by SITC Section, and within each Section, by major SITC Division. The table presented here is based on the Harmonized System and compiled for the convenience of those readers who may be more interested in domestic exports of certain commodity groups which are commonly referred to but which may not be readily derived from Appendix 16A.

(2) There is some overlapping in the commodity coverage of 'electronic products' and 'watches and clocks'. Some commodity items, such as digital electronic watches, are included in both groups. There is also overlapping between 'electronic products' and 'toys and dolls' (items such as radio controlled toys, T.V. games and electronic games), and between 'plastic products' and 'toys and dolls' (item such as plastic toys). However, the values of these items are counted only once in the value of 'Total domestic exports of the above 9 groups'.

APPENDIX 17

(Chapter 8: Employment)

Number of Establishments in Private Sector by Industry

Industry Group	*1991*	*1992*	*1993*
Mining and quarrying	**7**	**9**	**9**
Manufacturing	**46 276**	**41 937**	**39 238**
Food product, beverage and tobacco manufactures	884	789	812
Wearing apparel	7 336	5 840	5 656
Leather and leather products and footwear	831	694	557
Textiles	5 055	4 422	4 136
Wood and cork products, furniture and fixture	1 530	1 347	1 083
Paper and paper products	1 460	1 295	1 187
Printing, publishing and allied industries	4 569	4 394	4 820
Chemicals and chemical products, products of petroleum and coal	772	741	698
Rubber and plastic products	4 539	4 239	3 312
Non-metallic mineral products	385	351	322
Basic metal	219	211	177
Fabricated metal products	6 092	5 621	5 134
Office, accounting and computing machines	220	160	189
Radio, television & communication equipment	283	284	183
Electronic parts and components	430	368	410
Electrical appliances & houseware	296	302	259
Other machinery and equipments	5 922	5 831	5 408
Transport equipment	589	541	574
Professional instrument and optical goods	1 624	1 479	1 374
Other manufacturing industries	3 244	3 030	2 947
Electricity, gas and water	**21**	**22**	**31**
Wholesale, retail and import/export trades, restaurants and hotels	**151 648**	**160 446**	**170 085**
Wholesale	16 533	17 088	17 154
Retail	54 162	54 694	51 726
Import/Export	70 159	77 907	91 262
Restaurants	9 102	9 473	8 897
Hotels and boarding houses	1 693	1 284	1 047
Transport, storage and communication	**6 288**	**6 904**	**7 923**
Land passenger transport	8	8	9
Water and air transport	571	546	733
Supporting services to transport	1 604	2 019	2 275
Services incidental to transport	3 334	3 489	3 996
Storage	322	353	370
Communications	449	489	540
Financing, insurance, real estate and business services	**33 749**	**36 411**	**41 307**
Financial institutions	4 891	5 507	6 503
Stock, commodity and bullion brokers	1 048	953	973
Insurance	4 795	4 474	5 104
Real estate	9 569	10 545	11 133
Business services	13 445	14 932	17 594
Community, social and personal services	**23 861**	**23 626**	**23 988**
Sanitary and similar services	934	992	985
Education and related services	2 165	2 041	2 067
Medical and health services	4 082	3 970	4 234
Other community and social services	2 437	2 333	2 308
Amusement and recreational services	2 786	2 717	3 141
Personal services	11 457	11 573	11 253
Total	**261 850**	**269 355**	**282 581**

Notes:
(1) Figures refer to September of the year.
(2) Data are based on the Survey of Employment, Vacancies and Payroll conducted by the Census and Statistics Department.
(3) This appendix does not cover activities of the following industries:
  (i) Agriculture, hunting, forestry and fishing.
  (ii) Construction.
  (iii) Hawkers and retail pitches (other than market stalls).
  (iv) Taxis, public light buses, marine cargo handling services and tow boats.
  (v) Veterinary services, religious organizations, authors and other independent artists, domestic servants and miscellaneous recreational and personal services.
(4) As from March 1991, the Hong Kong Standard Industrial Classification (HSIC) is adopted for the classification of economic activities in place of International Standard Industrial Classification (ISIC). Figures from March 1991 onwards are therefore available only in HSIC and are not strictly comparable to those in the past series which are in ISIC.
(5) Comparing with Chapters 7 and 8, the textiles industry in this Appendix includes 'knit outerwear and underwear', however, the textiles industry quoted in Chapters 7 and 8 does not cover the 'knit outerwear and underwear' as they have been included in the 'clothing industry'.

APPENDIX 18

(Chapter 8: Employment)

Number of Persons engaged in Private Sector Establishments and Number of Manual Workers Engaged at Construction Sites

Industry Group	*1991*	*1992*	*1993*
Mining and quarrying	**436**	**564**	**427**
Manufacturing	**654 662**	**571 181**	**508 133**
Food product, beverage and tobacco manufactures	24 008	24 731	23 470
Wearing apparel	187 554	154 975	134 841
Leather and leather products and footwear	8 307	6 551	4 395
Textiles	98 724	84 972	75 742
Wood and cork products, furniture and fixture	7 386	6 253	4 654
Paper and paper products	13 866	12 754	10 358
Printing, publishing and allied industries	39 118	38 497	40 918
Chemicals and chemical products, products of petroleum and coal	8 291	8 007	7 771
Rubber and plastic products	42 733	36 480	28 251
Non-metallic mineral products	3 655	3 286	3 062
Basic metal	2 620	2 810	2 309
Fabricated metal products	46 000	39 881	34 626
Office, accounting and computing machines	17 337	13 508	11 761
Radio, television & communication equipment	10 129	8 487	5 654
Electronic parts and components	25 702	24 141	21 792
Electrical appliances & houseware	10 318	7 963	5 970
Other machinery and equipments	41 028	37 548	35 813
Transport equipment	13 269	13 134	14 010
Professional instrument and optical goods	29 120	24 188	21 311
Other manufacturing industries	25 500	23 014	21 425
Electricity, gas and water	**11 771**	**11 763**	**11 989**
Wholesale, retail and import/export trades, restaurants and hotels	**880 293**	**906 859**	**958 042**
Wholesale	75 923	78 296	79 518
Retail	205 461	203 745	198 199
Import/Export	375 245	391 457	452 262
Restaurants	186 046	194 454	187 655
Hotels and boarding houses	37 618	38 907	40 408
Transport, storage and communication	**131 403**	**144 158**	**153 325**
Land passenger transport	22 782	23 558	23 925
Water and air transport	26 642	30 696	33 873
Supporting services to transport	14 397	16 312	17 337
Services incidental to transport	37 883	38 503	41 347
Storage	4 956	5 655	5 742
Communications	24 742	29 435	31 102
Financing, insurance, real estate and business services	**289 121**	**307 538**	**336 026**
Financial institutions	100 794	103 469	112 149
Stock, commodity and bullion brokers	11 005	11 325	12 699
Insurance	19 095	19 995	20 019
Real estate	52 864	55 672	63 365
Business services	105 363	117 076	127 793
Community, social and personal services	**262 133**	**263 274**	**275 480**
Sanitary and similar services	31 273	27 108	27 823
Education and related services	83 903	84 427	89 877
Medical and health services	32 928	41 838	46 394
Other community and social services	30 291	27 569	28 023
Amusement and recreational services	27 944	27 337	31 220
Personal services	55 792	54 995	52 143
Total	**2 229 819**	**2 205 337**	**2 243 422**
Manual workers at construction sites	**63 873**	**63 384**	**52 179**

Notes:
(1) Figures refer to September of the year.
(2) Data are based on the Survey of Employment, Vacancies and Payroll conducted by the Census and Statistics Department.
(3) This appendix does not cover activities of the following industries:
  (i) Agriculture, hunting, forestry and fishing.
  (ii) Construction (persons other than manual worker at sites).
  (iii) Hawkers and retail pitches (other than market stalls).
  (iv) Taxis, public light buses, marine cargo handling services and tow boats.
  (v) Veterinary services, religious organizations, authors and other independent artists; domestic servants and miscellaneous recreational and personal services.
(4) As from March 1991, the Hong Kong Standard Industrial Classification (HSIC) is adopted for the classification of economic activities in place of International Standard Industrial Classification (ISIC). Figures from March 1991 onwards are therefore available only in HSIC and are not strictly comparable to those in the past series which are in ISIC.
(5) Comparing with Chapters 7 and 8, the textiles industry in this Appendix includes 'knit outerwear and underwear', however, the textiles industry quoted in Chapters 7 and 8 does not cover the 'knit outerwear and underwear' as they have been included in the 'clothing industry'.

APPENDIX 19
(Chapter 8: Employment)
Reported Occupational Accidents

Cause	1991			1992			1993*		
	Fatal	*Non-fatal*	*Total*	*Fatal*	*Non-fatal*	*Total*	*Fatal*	*Non-fatal*	*Total*
Machinery: power driven	20	6 436	6 456	13	4 442	4 455	23	2 164	2 187
Machinery: non power driven	1	114	115	1	77	78	—	25	25
Transport	56	3 196	3 252	75	2 629	2 704	87	1 559	1 646
Explosion or fire	12	482	494	7	519	526	7	311	318
Hot or corrosive substance	—	5 373	5 373	—	4 614	4 614	—	2 335	2 335
Gassing, poisoning and other toxic substances	—	61	61	4	41	45	4	34	38
Electricity	7	117	124	10	61	71	8	48	56
Fall of person	45	11 155	11 200	43	10 790	10 833	43	6 298	6 341
Stepping on, striking against or struck by objects	10	25 390	25 400	14	19 229	19 243	16	13 038	13 054
Falling object	8	3 603	3 611	4	2 873	2 877	9	1 528	1 537
Fall of ground	1	16	17	1	24	25	3	6	9
Handling without machinery	—	12 376	12 376	1	13 122	13 123	1	7 694	7 695
Hand tool	—	9 223	9 223	—	8 223	8 223	—	3 831	3 831
Miscellaneous	85	5 234	5 319	99	4 855	4 954	84	1 671	1 755
Causes not yet ascertained	—	4 824	4 824	—	3 848	3 848	19	26 831	26 850 #
Total	**245§**	**87 600**	**87 845**	**272§**	**75 347**	**75 619**	**304§**	**67 373**	**67 677**

Note: * Figures for 1993 are subject to amendment.
§ Including 18 (in 1991) and 26 (in 1992) and 17 (in 1993) which were subsequently verified to be outside the scope of the Employees' Compensation Ordinance because the employees concerned died of natural causes unrelated to work.
# Including 23 941 cases known to involve nil permanent disability and days lost of 7 days or less.

APPENDIX 20

(Chapter 8: Employment)

Consumer Price Index (A)

(October 1989–September 1990 = 100)

Section	Weight	*Annual average* 1991	1992	1993	*Index for December* 1991	1992	1993
All items	**100.00**	**114.5**	**125.2**	**135.9**	**118.1**	**129.3**	**140.4**
Food	41.20	114.1	124.1	133.1	116.5	124.9	135.7
Meals away from home	(20.52)	117.0	129.4	140.7	121.1	133.0	144.0
Food, excluding meals away from home	(20.68)	111.2	118.9	125.5	112.0	116.8	127.4
Housing	20.56	116.6	131.7	148.3	122.0	141.3	155.3
Fuel and light	3.18	110.0	115.7	120.1	111.1	118.1	121.4
Alcoholic drinks and tobacco	2.45	145.5	159.6	176.3	145.6	166.6	181.5
Clothing and footwear	4.56	108.4	117.6	126.5	114.9	125.1	133.3
Durable goods	4.92	104.6	107.0	109.4	105.4	107.7	111.4
Miscellaneous goods	5.88	108.6	116.0	123.9	113.0	120.0	128.1
Transport	7.20	116.1	124.5	134.8	119.5	126.9	140.4
Miscellaneous services	10.05	116.0	129.7	142.1	122.1	136.6	149.8

Note: The CPI(A) covers about 50% of urban households with a monthly expenditure of between $2,500 and $9,999 in the base period 1989–90.

Consumer Price Index (B)

(October 1989–September 1990 = 100)

Section	Weight	*Annual average* 1991	1992	1993	*Index for December* 1991	1992	1993
All items	**100.00**	**114.1**	**125.1**	**136.0**	**118.3**	**129.8**	**140.9**
Food	35.34	114.7	125.1	134.4	117.7	126.7	137.3
Meals away from home	(20.51)	117.0	129.3	140.6	121.2	133.1	144.0
Food, excluding meals away from home	(14.83)	111.6	119.2	125.9	113.0	117.8	128.1
Housing	23.77	116.2	132.0	149.2	122.5	141.8	156.5
Fuel and light	2.36	109.6	115.0	119.5	110.7	117.3	120.7
Alcoholic drinks and tobacco	1.64	138.0	151.8	166.4	139.4	157.7	170.8
Clothing and footwear	7.23	109.4	118.5	127.7	116.1	126.3	134.7
Durable goods	5.12	104.2	106.6	108.9	105.2	107.4	111.1
Miscellaneous goods	5.89	107.7	114.6	121.8	111.4	117.9	125.1
Transport	7.57	116.1	124.5	134.2	118.9	127.1	139.8
Miscellaneous services	11.08	114.8	127.4	138.6	120.5	133.3	145.4

Note: The CPI(B) covers about 30% of urban households with a monthly expenditure of between $10,000 and $17,499 in the base period 1989–90.

Hang Seng Consumer Price Index
(October 1989–September 1990 = 100)

Section	Weight	Annual average 1991	Annual average 1992	Annual average 1993	Index for December 1991	Index for December 1992	Index for December 1993
All items	**100.00**	**114.0**	**125.1**	**137.0**	**118.5**	**130.0**	**143.3**
Food	25.95	113.3	123.9	134.2	117.4	126.7	138.9
Meals away from home	(16.37)	113.8	126.0	138.4	119.2	130.8	144.6
Food, excluding meals away from home	(9.58)	112.5	120.4	127.2	114.3	119.6	129.2
Housing	29.48	118.1	132.3	150.4	123.5	140.5	159.3
Fuel and light	1.76	110.0	115.0	119.5	111.2	117.2	120.8
Alcoholic drinks and tobacco	0.88	134.6	148.3	162.1	136.7	153.5	166.2
Clothing and footwear	8.81	110.5	125.0	136.6	117.8	130.5	147.1
Durable goods	5.86	105.1	109.9	114.1	107.1	112.6	116.9
Miscellaneous goods	5.64	107.7	113.8	120.7	111.2	116.7	123.5
Transport	7.89	117.3	125.5	134.5	119.8	128.4	139.2
Miscellaneous services	13.73	112.2	123.0	132.4	117.4	127.6	138.1

Note: The Hang Seng CPI covers about 10% of urban households, living in private dwellings or Home Ownership Scheme flats and with a monthly expenditure of between $17,500 and $37,499 in the base period 1989–90.

Composite Consumer Price Index
(October 1989–September 1990 = 100)

Section	Weight	Annual average 1991	Annual average 1992	Annual average 1993	Index for December 1991	Index for December 1992	Index for December 1993
All items	**100.00**	**114.2**	**125.2**	**136.2**	**118.3**	**129.7**	**141.3**
Food	35.07	114.2	124.4	133.8	117.2	125.9	136.9
Meals away from home	(19.45)	116.3	128.6	140.1	120.7	132.5	144.1
Food, excluding meals away from home	(15.62)	111.6	119.2	126.0	112.7	117.6	128.0
Housing	24.06	116.9	132.0	149.3	122.6	141.2	157.0
Fuel and light	2.51	109.9	115.3	119.8	111.0	117.7	121.0
Alcoholic drinks and tobacco	1.74	141.3	155.3	170.8	142.1	161.7	175.6
Clothing and footwear	6.66	109.5	120.5	130.4	116.4	127.4	138.6
Durable goods	5.24	104.6	107.7	110.6	105.8	109.0	112.9
Miscellaneous goods	5.82	108.0	114.9	122.3	111.9	118.3	125.8
Transport	7.52	116.4	124.8	134.5	119.3	127.4	139.9
Miscellaneous services	11.38	114.4	126.8	137.8	120.1	132.6	144.6

Note: The Composite CPI covers all households of the CPI(A), CPI(B) and the Hang Seng CPI.

APPENDIX 21

(Chapter 9: Primary Production)

Imports of Crops, Livestock, Poultry and Fish

Item	*Unit*	*1991*	*1992*	*1993*
Crops				
Rice (unhusked)	tonne	391 644	400 165	372 725
Wheat	tonne	133 250	144 887	84 842
Other cereals and cereal preparations	tonne	378 738	373 006	315 189
Other field crops	tonne	88 760	75 209	78 385
Vegetables (fresh, frozen or simply preserved)	tonne	427 335	414 367	400 892
Vegetables (preserved or prepared), fruit and nuts (fresh, dried, preserved or prepared)	tonne	973 305	1 034 559	1 112 020
Flowers	$ thousand	156,153	177,821	178,366
Sugar and honey	tonne	216 589	193 169	188 469
Coffee	tonne	5 998	6 760	6 063
Cocoa	tonne	1 572	536	1 570
Tea and mate	tonne	24 274	31 229	25 747
Livestock and poultry				
Cattle	head	156 731	149 505	134 780
Sheep, lambs and goats	head	16 819	15 441	12 848
Swine	thousand head	2 821	2 792	2 605
Chicken	tonne	48 414	50 988	50 591
Other poultry	tonne	20 499	22 178	20 162
Live animals	tonne	3 572	3 090	4 729
Meat and meat preparations	tonne	404 517	470 841	535 014
Dairy products and eggs				
Milk (fresh)	tonne	42 290	49 344	48 683
Cream (fresh)	tonne	384	354	940
Milk and cream (evaporated, condensed, powdered, *etc*)	tonne	74 754	80 448	81 808
Butter, cheese and curd	tonne	11 203	13 739	15 695
Eggs (fresh)	thousand	1 451 307	1 518 307	1 406 947
Eggs (preserved)	thousand	188 063	207 781	193 987
Fish and fish preparations				
Fish (fresh, chilled or frozen)	tonne	162 621	188 865	169 143
Fish (dried, salted or smoked)	tonne	10 436	13 322	12 715
Crustaceans and molluscs (fresh, frozen, dried, salted, *etc*)	tonne	116 257	114 023	107 227
Fish products and preparations	tonne	10 272	7 103	6 793
Crustacean and mollusc products and preparations	tonne	4 782	5 562	5 437
Oil and fats (crude or refined)	tonne	90	191	205
Fish meals (animals feeding stuffs)	tonne	43 601	23 971	14 679

APPENDIX 22
(Chapter 9: Primary Production)
Estimated Local Production of Crops, Livestock, Poultry and Fish

Item	*Unit*	*1991*	*1992*	*1993*
Crops				
Vegetables (fresh, frozen or simply preserved)	tonne	105 000	95 000	91 000
Fresh fruit and nuts	tonne	3 950	2 730	4 150
Flowers	$ thousand	134,000	157,000	117,000
Other field crops*	tonne	1 260	540	670
Livestock and poultry				
Cattle	head	820	490	410
Swine‡	thousand head	314	182	169
Chicken	tonne	23 500	21 200	20 700
Other poultry	tonne	9 900	5 900	5 600
Dairy products and eggs				
Milk (fresh)	tonne	1 670	1 180	520
Eggs (fresh)	thousand	84 500	52 600	47 800
Fish and fish preparations				
Fish (fresh, chilled or frozen)				
Marine fish§	tonne	167 500	160 990	158 990
Freshwater fish	tonne	5 900	5 400	5 760
Fish (dried, salted or smoked)				
Marine fish	tonne	1 140	480	320
Crustaceans and molluscs (fresh, frozen, dried, salted, *etc*)	tonne	21 840	27 400	26 630
Fish products and preparations	tonne	330	370	380
Crustacean and mollusc products and preparations	tonne	240	180	220
Fish meals (animal feeding stuffs)	tonne	33 280	30 550	31 390

Note: * Other field crops include yam, millet, peanut, soybean, sugar cane, sweet potato and water chestnut.
‡ Including local swine not slaughtered in abattoirs.
§ Including cultured marine fish.

APPENDIX 23
(Chapter 9: Primary Production)
Local Production and Imports of Ores and Minerals

Tonnes

Item	*Production 1991*	*Production 1992*	*Production 1993*	*Imports 1991*	*Imports 1992*	*Imports 1993*
Quartz	—	—	—	1 235	1 937	1 302
Feldspar	—	—	—	185 599	205 310	344 551
Graphite	—	—	—	2 546	1 569	9 492
Kaolin/feldspar sand	—	—	—	480 678	477 896	659 241

APPENDIX 24

(Chapter 10: Education)

Number of Educational Institutions by Type*

	1991	As of September 1992	1993
Kindergarten	767	743	730
Primary Schools	671	652	633
Secondary Schools	487	494	489
Special Schools	74	74	72
Technical Institutes	8	7	7
Technical College	—	—	2
Colleges of Education	4	4	4
Approved Post Secondary Colleges	1	1	1
Tertiary (UPGC-funded) Institutions	7	7	7
Open Learning Institute	1	1	1
Total	**2 020**	**1 983**	**1 946**

Note: * Including evening schools.

Student Numbers by Type of Educational Institutions§

	1991	1992	1993
Schools			
Kindergarten	193 658	189 730	187 549
Primary	517 137	501 625	485 061
Secondary	454 372	461 460	472 200
Special education	8 224	8 257	8 279
Sub-total	**1 173 391**	**1 161 072**	**1 153 089**
Technical Institutes #			
Craft courses	28 173	23 503	22 376
Technician courses	28 245	27 279	26 284
Sub-total	**56 418**	**50 782**	**48 660**
Technical Colleges	—	—	**4 944**
Colleges of Education #	**4 891**	**4 355**	**4 225**
Approved Post Secondary Colleges #	**3 373**	**3 070**	**2 787**
Tertiary (UPGC-funded) Institutions†			
Subdegree	25 832	23 251	19 179
First Degree	32 138	36 057	40 848
Postgraduate	6 960	8 781	10 399
Sub-total	**64 930**	**68 089**	**70 426**
Open Learning Institute‡	**17 535**	**14 462**	**14 979**
Total	**1 320 538**	**1 301 830**	**1 299 110**

Note: § Student numbers refer to students in day and evening schools, and full time and part time students in other educational institutions.
Figures are as of October.
† Figures are as of December.
‡ No. of active students for October Semesters.

APPENDIX 25

(Chapter 10: Education)

Overseas Examinations

Examinations conducted by Hong Kong Examinations Authority		*Candidate Entries*	
	1991	*1992*	*1993*
London Chamber of Commerce and Industry	66 300	65 900	62 500
Test of English as a Foreign Language (TOEFL)	33 200	27 000	21 100
Associated Board of the Royal Schools of Music	42 800	45 100	45 100
Pitman Examinations Institute	24 200	21 400	17 900
Chartered Association of Certified Accountants	16 400	19 400	20 700
University of London – General Certificate of Education	9 200	6 500	4 600
Royal Academy of Dancing	5 900	6 100	6 400
Chartered Institute of Bankers	3 200	2 500	2 100
Associated Examining Board – General Certificate of Education	3 300	2 100	1 400
Institute of Chartered Secretaries and Administrators	3 700	3 700	3 500
Test of Spoken English	1 400	800	400
City and Guilds of London Institute	2 300	2 100	1 900
University of London – External Degree	1 700	1 900	2 100
Association of Accounting Technicians	1 700	1 800	2 400
University College of Southern Queensland	1 700	1 400	1 000
Australian Insurance Institute	1 300	1 300	1 300
Trinity College of Music	800	800	900
Others	12 200	9 200	8 700
Total	**231 300**	**219 000**	**204 000**

Note: Figures are rounded to the nearest hundred.

Conducted by Hong Kong Polytechnic:			
The Engineering Council Examination	804	955	837
Total	**804**	**955**	**837**

APPENDIX 26

(Chapter 10: Education)

Students Leaving Hong Kong for Overseas Studies§

Country	*1991*	*1992*	*1993*
Britain	4 428#	4 408#	3 477#
United States	5 866	5 410	5 025
Canada	4 541	3 583	2 828
Australia	3 590	2 866	3 153

Note: § Figures are based on the number of student visas issued as supplied by visa-issuing authorities.
Excluding returned students, students on short courses and Government servants on training courses.

APPENDIX 27

(Chapter 10: Education)

Expenditure on Education

$ Thousand

		School year Aug–July	
	1990–91	*1991–92*	*1992–93*
Recurrent expenditure	1,533,854	1,674,343	1,876,084
Capital expenditure	436,545	492,993	364,557
Grants and subsidies	9,571,778	10,287,429	11,580,316
Grants to Universities and Polytechnic (including rates)	4,228,110	5,991,029	7,413,072
University and Polytechnic Grants Committee (including university student grants)	115,071	121,464	162,567
Total	**15,885,358**	**18,567,258**	**21,396,596**
Education expenditure by other departments	1,442,391	1,835,277	2,455,577

APPENDIX 28

(Chapter 11: Health)

Vital Statistics

	1991	*1992*	*1993*
Estimated mid-year population	5 754 800	5 811 500	5 919 000
Births:			
Known live births	68 281	70 949‡	70 476
Crude birth rate (per 1 000 population)	12.0	12.3	12.0
Deaths:			
Known deaths	28 429	30 550‡	30 247
Crude death rate (per 1 000 population)	5.0	5.3	5.1
Infant mortality rate* (per 1 000 live births)	6.5	4.9	4.7
Neo-natal mortality rate* (per 1 000 live births)	4.0	2.9	2.8
Maternal mortality rate* (per 1 000 total births)	0.06	0.06	0.04
Life expectancy at birth (years)			
Male	75.1‡	74.8‡	75.1
Female	80.6‡	80.5‡	80.8

Note: * Based on registered deaths.
‡ Revised figures.

APPENDIX 29

(Chapter 11: Health)

Causes of Death*

	1991	*1992*	*1993†*
Infective and parasitic	**950**	**926**	**944**
Tuberculosis, all forms	409	410	396
Neoplasms	**8 861**	**9 107**	**9 304**
Malignant, including neoplasms of lymphatic and haematopoietic tissues	8 832	9 021	9 212
Endocrine, nutritional, metabolic and blood	**324**	**522**	**562**
Diabetes mellitus	271	413	451
Nervous system, sense organs and mental disorders	**213**	**324**	**272**
Circulatory system	**8 132**	**8 789**	**8 377**
Heart diseases, including hypertensive diseases	4 858	5 359	4 852
Cerebrovascular diseases	3 009	3 067	3 128
Respiratory system	**4 746**	**5 605**	**5 557**
Pneumonia, all forms	1 819	2 002	2 165
Bronchitis, emphysema and asthma	431	490	469
Digestive system	**1 201**	**1 254**	**1 337**
Peptic ulcer	34	36	33
Chronic liver disease and cirrhosis	375	444	495
Genito-urinary system	**1 292**	**1 108**	**1 065**
Complications of pregnancy, childbirth and the puerperium	**4**	**4**	**3**
Skin, subcutaneous tissues, musculoskeletal system and connective tissues	**37**	**60**	**84**
Congenital anomalies	**179**	**143**	**146**
Certain conditions originating in the perinatal period	**218**	**178**	**160**
Symptoms, signs and ill-defined conditions	**715**	**813**	**687**
Injury and poisoning	**1 810**	**1 693**	**1 727**
All accidents	868	747	787
Suicide and self-inflicted injuries	748	732	672
Unknown	—	—	—
Total deaths	**28 682**	**30 526**	**30 225**

Note: * Based on registered deaths.
† Provisional figures.

APPENDIX 30
(Chapter 11: Health)

Hospital Beds

	As at end of year		
Type of institutions	*1991*	*1992*	*1993†*
Hospital Authority hospitals	21 684	22 437	23 471
Correctional Institutions	776	847	816
Government clinics/maternity homes	173	164	131
Private institutions	2 951	2 999	2 971
Total	**25 584**	**26 447**	**27 389**

Note: † Provisional figures.

APPENDIX 31
(Chapter 11: Health)

Registered Medical Personnel

	As at end of year								
	In Government service #			*Under Hospital Authority §*			*Total registered*		
	1991	*1992*	*1993*	*1991*	*1992*	*1993*	*1991*	*1992*	*1993*
Medical – Doctors	456@	447@	478@	2 218@	2 333@	2 502@	6 545‡	6 818‡	7 625‡
Interns on provisional register	—	—	—	234	254	282	232	272	257
Externs on provisional register	—	—	—	63	21	41	63	69	61
Dental – Dentists	181	182	192	5	4	4	1 526‡	1 565‡	1 575‡
Dental hygienists	3	4	7	—	—	—	98	108	111
Nursing – Registered nurses (general)	828	841	876	10 744	11 113	11 621	20 072	20 884	23 239
Registered nurses (psychiatric)	—	—	—	1 033	1 037	1 074	1 315	1 367	1 420
Registered nurses (mental subnormal)	—	—	—	—	—	—	13	16	17
Registered nurses (sick children)	—	—	—	—	—	—	4	6	8
Enrolled nurses (general)	329	325	321	3 064	3 219	3 221	7 047	7 451	7 926
Enrolled nurses (psychiatric)	—	—	—	640	661	630	611	689	751
Pharmacists	28	29	28	82	87	99	720	784	874
Medical Laboratory Technologists*	218	227	228	303	316	340	1 826	2 158	2 298
Occupational Therapist	4	3	4	213	213	247	438	499	559

Note: Annual re-registration is required for doctors, dentists, pharmacists, medical laboratory technologists and occupational therapists.
§ The management responsibility of all public hospitals was taken over by Hospital Authority on December 1, 1991.
# Figures were those working in the Department of Health.
@Including unregistrable medical officers.
‡ Referring to the professional medical/dental personnel on both the local and overseas lists.
* Referring to medical technologists and medical laboratory technicians.

APPENDIX 32

(Chapter 12: Social Welfare)

(A) The Hong Kong Council of Social Service

Member Agencies

Aberdeen Kaifong Welfare Association Social Service Centre
Action Group for Aid to the Mentally Retarded
Against Child Abuse
Agency for Volunteer Service
American Women's Association of Hong Kong Limited
Arts with Disabled Association Hong Kong
Asbury Village Community Centre of the Methodist Church, Hong Kong
Association for Engineering and Medical Volunteer Services
Association for the Advancement of Feminism
Association of Evangelical Free Churches of Hong Kong

Baptist Assembly
Baptist Oi Kwan Social Service
Barnabas Charitable Service Association Limited
Birthright Society Limited
Board of Studies in Social Work, The Chinese University of Hong Kong
Boys' and Girls' Clubs Association of Hong Kong
Boys' Brigade, Hong Kong
Breakthrough Counselling Centre

Caritas – Hong Kong
Catholic Women's League
Causeway Bay Kaifong Welfare Advancement Association
Chai Wan Areas Kaifong Welfare Advancement Association (HK) Limited
Chai Wan Baptist Church – Social Service Centre
Chain of Charity Movement
China Coast Community Limited
Chinese Evangelical Zion Church Limited Tze Wan Shan Zion Youth Centre
Chinese Young Men's Christian Association of Hong Kong
Ching Chung Taoist Association of Hong Kong Limited
Christian Concern for the Homeless Association
Christian Family Service Centre
Christian and Missionary Alliance Church Union Hong Kong Limited – C & M A Social Service of Hong Kong
Chung Shek Hei (Cheung Chau) Home for the Aged, Limited
Church of Christ in China, Hong Kong Council, Social Welfare Department
Church of United Brethen in Christ Hong Kong Ltd – Social Service Division
Community Drug Advisory Council
Conservancy Association

DACARS, Limited
Department of Applied Social Studies, City Polytechnic of Hong Kong
Department of Applied Social Studies, Hong Kong Polytechnic
Department of Public and Social Administration, City Polytechnic of Hong Kong
Department of Social Work and Social Administration, University of Hong Kong
Duke of Edinburgh's Award

Ebenezer School and Home for the Blind
Evangel Children's Home
Evangelical Lutheran Church Social Service – Hong Kong

Family Planning Association of Hong Kong
Finnish Missionary Society
Five Districts Business Welfare Association
Foreign Mission Board, Southern Baptist Convention, Hong Kong – Macau Baptist Mission
Free Methodist Church (Hong Kong)

Girls' Brigade (Hong Kong)

Hans Andersen Club Limited
Harmony House Limited
Haven of Hope Christian Service
Heep Hong Society for Handicapped Children
Helping Hand Limited
Heung Hoi Ching Kok Lin Association

Holy Carpenter Church and Community Centre
Hong Kong Association for the Mentally Handicapped
Hong Kong Association of Occupational Therapists
Hong Kong Association of Speech Therapists
Hong Kong Association of the Blind
Hong Kong Association of the Deaf
Hong Kong Association of Workers Serving the Mentally Handicapped
Hong Kong Baptist College, Department of Social Work
Hong Kong Baptist Hospital, Au Shue Hung Health Centre
Hong Kong Baptist Theological Seminary
Hong Kong Cancer Fund – Friends of EORTC
Hong Kong Catholic Marriage Advisory Council
Hong Kong Catholic Youth Council
Hong Kong Children and Youth Services
Hong Kong Chinese Women's Club
Hong Kong Christian Mutual Improvement Society
Hong Kong Christian Service
Hong Kong Council of Early Childhood Education and Services
Hong Kong Council of Women
Hong Kong Down Syndrome Association
Hong Kong Emotion and Health Association Limited
Hong Kong Eye Bank and Research Foundation
Hong Kong Family Welfare Society
Hong Kong Federation of Handicapped Youth
Hong Kong Federation of Societies for Prevention of Blindness
Hong Kong Federation of the Blind
Hong Kong Federation of Youth Groups
Hong Kong Girl Guides Association
Hong Kong Housing Affairs Association
Hong Kong Housing Society
Hong Kong Joint Council of Parents of the Mentally Handicapped
Hong Kong Juvenile Care Centre
Hong Kong Life Guard Club
Hong Kong Lutheran Handicrafts Society
Hong Kong Lutheran Social Service, Lutheran Church – Hong Kong Synod
Hong Kong Macau Conference of Seventh-Day Adventist Church
Hong Kong People's Council on Public Housing Policy
Hong Kong PHAB Association
Hong Kong Playground Association
Hong Kong Recreation and Sports Association
Hong Kong Red Cross
Hong Kong School for the Deaf
Hong Kong Shue Yan College
Hong Kong Social Workers Association Limited
Hong Kong Society for the Aged
Hong Kong Society for the Blind
Hong Kong Society for the Deaf
Hong Kong Society for the Protection of Children
Hong Kong Society for Rehabilitation
Hong Kong Sports Association for the Mentally Handicapped
Hong Kong Sports Association for the Physically Disabled (SAP)
Hong Kong Student Aid Society
Hong Kong Student Services Association
Hong Kong Tuberculosis, Chest and Heart Diseases Association
Hong Kong Workers' Health Centre
Hong Kong Young Women's Christian Association

Industrial Evangelistic Fellowship
Industrial Relations Institute
Institute of Cultural Affairs Limited
Intellectually Disabled Education and Advocacy League
International Baptist Church (Hong Kong) Limited
International Church of the Foursquare Gospel – Hong Kong Districts Limited
International Social Service Hong Kong Branch

Jane Shu Tsao Social Centre for the Elderly, Hong Kong Mutual Encouragement Association

Keswick Foundation Limited
Kowloon Union Church Wai Ji Training Centre

Kowloon Women's Welfare Club
Kwai Shing Christian Social Service Centre
Kwai Shing Estate Residents' Association
Kwun Tong Methodist Centre

Lai King Estate Tenants' Association
Lai Tak Youth Centre
Link Association
Lok Sin Tong Chu Ting Cheong Home for the Aged
Lutheran School for the Deaf

Mary Rose School
Maryknoll Sisters
Matilda Child Development Centre
Mental Health Association of Hong Kong
Methodist Ap Lei Chau Centre
Methodist Centre
Methodist Epworth Village Community Centre
Mission Covenant Church Limited
Mother's Choice Limited

Neighbourhood Advice-Action Council
New Life Psychiatric Rehabilitation Association
New Territories Women and Juvenile Welfare Association Limited
New Voice Club of Hong Kong
North Point Kaifong Welfare Advancement Association

O.M.S. 'St Simon' Home for Fishermen's and Workmen's Children

Parents' Association of the Mentally Handicapped Limited
Parents' Association of Pre-School Handicapped Children
Pentecostal Church of Hong Kong Limited
Pentecostal Holiness Church Ling Kwong Bradbury Centre for the Blind
Playright Children's Playground Association Limited
Po Leung Kuk
Pok Oi Hospital
Pre-School Playgroups Association
Project Concern Hong Kong
Pui Hong Self-Help Association

Rehabilitation Alliance Hong Kong
Richmond Fellowship of Hong Kong

Salesian Society
Salvation Army
Samaritan Befrienders Hong Kong
Samaritans (English Speaking Service)
Save the Children Fund – Hong Kong
Scout Association of Hong Kong
Sheng Kung Hui Diocesan Welfare Council
Sheng Kung Hui Kei Oi Social Service Centre
Sheng Kung Hui Lady MacLehose Centre
Sheng Kung Hui St Christopher's Home
Shun Tin Christian Children's and Youth Centre
Sik Sik Yuen – Social Services Unit
Sisters of the Good Shepherd – Marycove Centre
Sisters of the Good Shepherd – Pelletier Hall
Sisters of the Precious Blood – Precious Blood Children Village
Social Service Group, Hong Kong University Students' Union
Society for Community Organisation
Society for the Aid and Rehabilitation of Drug Abusers
Society for the Rehabilitation of Offenders, Hong Kong
Society for the Relief of Disabled Children
Society of Boys' Centres
Society of Homes for the Handicapped
Society of St Vincent de Paul
Spastics Association of Hong Kong
St James' Settlement
St John Ambulance Association and Brigade
St Stephen's Society
Stewards' Company (Hong Kong) Limited
Street Sleepers' Shelter Society Trustees Incorporated
Suen Mei Speech and Hearing Centre for the Deaf

Tai Hang Tung and Nam Shan Estate Residents' Association Limited
Tai Wo Hau Residents' Association
TREATS
Tsuen Wan Ecumenical Social Service Centre
Tsung Tsin Mission Social Service Division
Tung Lum Buddhist Aged Home
Tung Sin Tan Home for the Aged
Tung Wah Group of Hospitals

United Christian Medical Service

Victoria Park School for the Deaf

Watchdog Limited
Wong Tai Sin District Federation of Welfare Services for the Aged
World Vision of Hong Kong
Wu Oi Christian Centre

Yan Chai Hospital
Yan Oi Tong Community and Indoor Sports Centre
Yang Memorial Social Service Centre
Young Men's Christian Association of Hong Kong

Zion Youth Service Centre

(B) The Community Chest of Hong Kong

Member Agencies

Aberdeen Kaifong Welfare Association Social Service Centre
Action Group for Aid to the Mentally Retarded
Adventure Ship Limited
Against Child Abuse
Agency for Volunteer Service
Asbury Village Community Centre of the Methodist Church
Association for Engineering and Medical Volunteer Services
Association of Baptists for World Evangelism Incorporated
Association of Evangelical Free Churches of Hong Kong

Baptist Oi Kwan Social Service
Barnabas Charitable Service Association Limited
Boys' Brigade, Hong Kong
Buddhist Li Ka Shing Care and Attention Home for the Elderly
Buddhist Po Ching Home for the Aged Women
Butterfly Bay Baptist Church Social Centre for the Elderly

Canossian Missions
Caritas – Hong Kong
Chain of Charity Movement
Cheung Hong Baptist Church Social Centre for the Elderly
Chinese Young Men's Christian Association of Hong Kong
Christian & Missionary Alliance Church Union Hong Kong Limited
Christian Concern for the Homeless Association
Christian Family Service Centre
Christian Nationals' Evangelism Commission Aged People Centre
Christian Oi Hip Fellowship Limited
Church of God Limited
Community Drug Advisory Council

Duke of Edinburgh's Award

Ebenezer School and Home for the Blind
Evangel Children's Home
Evangelical Lutheran Church Social Service – Hong Kong

Family Planning Association of Hong Kong
Finnish Missionary Society

Girl's Brigade (Hong Kong)

Hans Andersen Club Limited
Harmony House Limited
Haven of Hope Christian Service
Heep Hong Society for Handicapped Children
Helping Hand
Holy Carpenter Church Multi-Service Centre for the Elderly

Holy Carpenter Church Social Centre for the Elderly
Holy Nativity Social Centre for the Elderly
Hong Kong Anti-Cancer Society
Hong Kong Association of the Deaf
Hong Kong Catholic Marriage Advisory Council
Hong Kong Children and Youth Services
Hong Kong Christian Aid to Refugees
Hong Kong Christian Industrial Committee
Hong Kong Christian Mutual Improvement Society
Hong Kong Christian Service
Hong Kong Council of Social Service
Hong Kong Down Syndrome Association
Hong Kong Evangelical Church Tai Hing Social Centre for the Elderly
Hong Kong Family Welfare Society
Hong Kong Federation of the Blind
Hong Kong Federation of Youth Groups
Hong Kong Federation of Women's Centres
Hong Kong Housing Authority North Point Estate Residents' Association
Hong Kong Life Guard Club
Hong Kong Lutheran Social Service Lutheran Church – Hong Kong Synod
Hong Kong Red Cross
Hong Kong School for the Deaf
Hong Kong Sea Cadet Corps
Hong Kong Sea School
Hong Kong Society for Rehabilitation
Hong Kong Society for the Aged
Hong Kong Society for the Blind
Hong Kong Society for the Deaf
Hong Kong Sports Association for Physically Disabled
Hong Kong Sports Association of the Deaf
Hong Kong Students Aid Society
Hong Kong Workers' Health Centre Limited

International Church of the Foursquare Gospel – Hong Kong District
International Social Service, Hong Kong Branch

Kei Oi Social Centre for the Elderly
Kowloon Union Church Wai Ji Training Centre
Kwun Tong Community Health Project

Lady MacLehose Centre
Lai King Baptist Church Bradbury Social Centre for the Elderly
Light and Love Home
Lok Wah Swatow Christian Church Social Centre for the Elderly

Marriage and Personal Counselling Service
Maryknoll Sisters Social Service
Mental Health Association of Hong Kong
Methodist Ap Lei Chau Centre
Methodist Church Hong Kong – Kwun Tong Methodist Centre
Methodist Epworth Village Community Centre
Mission Covenant Church, Yiu On Tong Social Centre for the Elderly
Mother's Choice Ltd

Neighbourhood Advice-Action Council
New Life Psychiatric Rehabilitation Association
New Voice Club of Hong Kong
North Point Kaifong Welfare Advancement Association

Pelletier Hall – Good Shepherd Sisters
Pentecostal Church of Hong Kong Limited – Ngau Tau Kok Social Centre for the Elderly
Pentecostal Holiness Church Ling Kwong Bradbury Centre for the Blind
Pinehill Village
Playright Children's Playground Association Limited
Project Care
Project Concern, Hong Kong

Rehabid Society Limited
Richmond Fellowship of Hong Kong

Salvation Army
Samaritan Befrienders Hong Kong
Samaritans (English Speaking Service)
Sheng Kung Hui Diocesan Welfare Council
Shun Tin Christian Children's and Youth Centre
Society for the Aid and Rehabilitation of Drug Abusers
Society for the Rehabilitation of Offenders, Hong Kong
Society of Boys' Centres

Society of St Vincent de Paul Central Council – Hong Kong
Spastics Association of Hong Kong
St Christopher's Home
St James' Settlement
St John Ambulance Association and Brigade
St Luke's Settlement
St Matthew's Church Senior Citizens' Club
Steward's Company (Hong Kong) Limited
Street Sleepers' Shelter Society Trustees Incorporated
Suen Mei Speech and Hearing Centre for the Deaf

Tai Hang Tung and Nam Shan Estate Residents' Association Limited
Tsuen Wan Ecumenical Social Service Centre

Watchdog Limited

Yang Memorial Methodist Social Service
Young Women's Christian Association, Hong Kong

APPENDIX 33

(Chapter 13: Housing)

Number of Quarters and Estimated Persons Accommodated as at March 31, 1993

Number of Quarters

Category	*Hong Kong Island*	*Kowloon and New Kowloon*	*New Territories*	*Total*
Government quarters	**8 100**	**8 800**	**12 100**	**29 000**
Public housing				
Housing Authority estates	64 200	250 300	322 800	637 300
Housing Authority cottage areas	500	400	1 900	2 800
Housing Society estates	10 700	12 800	9 600	33 100
Home Ownership Scheme Blocks*	17 000	35 600	104 100	156 700
Sub-total	**92 400**	**299 100**	**438 400**	**829 900**
Private housing	**314 700**	**325 300**	**344 800**	**984 800**
Total permanent	**415 200**	**633 200**	**795 300**	**1 843 700**

Estimated Persons Accommodated

Category	*Hong Kong Island*	*Kowloon and New Kowloon*	*New Territories*	*Total*
Government quarters	**20 600**	**20 100**	**22 500**	**63 200**
Public housing				
Housing Authority estates	226 600	809 400	1 193 200	2 229 200
Housing Authority cottage areas	1 400	700	3 700	5 800
Housing Society estates	38 300	42 000	35 800	116 100
Home Ownership Scheme Blocks*	48 400	120 900	351 500	520 800
Sub-total	**314 700**	**973 000**	**1 584 200**	**2 871 900**
Private housing	**917 900**	**923 500**	**878 900**	**2 720 300**
Total permanent	**1 253 200**	**1 916 600**	**2 485 600**	**5 655 400**
Temporary				**170 300**
Marine				**19 300**
Total population				**5 845 000**

Note: * Includes private sector participation scheme and middle income housing.

APPENDIX 34

(Chapter 14: Land, Public Works and Utilities)

The Land Registry

Item	*1991*	*1992*	*1993*
Instruments registered			
Assignments of whole buildings or sites	6 704	10 249	8 017
Assignments of flats or other units	182 997	157 920	151 501
Agreements for sale and purchase of flats or other units	180 964	139 927	136 915
Building mortgages/building legal charges	156	117	100
Other mortgages/legal charges	213 081	168 478	155 652
Reassignments/receipts/discharges/releases and certificates of satisfaction	137 030	123 921	100 478
Exclusion orders	51	6	56
Re-development orders	3	8	36
Miscellaneous	102 856	84 510	79 094
Total	**823 842**	**685 136**	**631 849**
Conditions of sale, grant, exchange, *etc* registered	588	691	710
Government leases registered	21	20	26
Multi-storey building owners corporations registered	163	202	281
Public searches in Land Registry records	3 168 942	3 207 280	3 328 390

Considerations in Instruments Registered in The Land Registry

			$ Thousand
Assignments of whole buildings or sites	41,071,778	58,225,310	81,791,479
Assignments of flats or other units	227,014,978	296,063,889	326,701,518
Agreements for sale and purchase of flats or other units	318,537,996	385,384,460	424,328,826
Building mortgages/building legal charges	8,955,048	5,791,832	10,507,929
Other mortgages/legal charges	92,107,888	88,538,235	104,032,779
Reassignments/receipts/discharges/releases and certificates of satisfaction	40,473,520	45,163,161	41,611,802
Miscellaneous instruments	10,769,070	267,949	—
Total	**738,930,278**	**879,434,836**	**988,974,333**

APPENDIX 35
(Chapter 14: Land, Public Works and Utilities)
Land Usage

Class	*Approximate area (km²)*	*Percentage of whole*	*Remarks*
A. Developed Lands			
i. Commercial	2	0.2	
ii. Residential	41	3.8	Including all residential areas except public rental housing estates, HOS/PSPS and temporary housing areas
iii. Public Rental Housing	10	0.9	Including HOS/PSPS
iv. Industrial	10	0.9	Including warehouse and storage
v. Open Space	15	1.4	
vi. Government, Institution and Community Facilities	17	1.6	
vii. Vacant Development Land	36	3.3	Including land with construction in progress
viii. Roads/Railways	23	2.1	Including flyovers and railway lands
ix. Temporary Housing Areas	1	0.1	
B. Non-built-up Lands*			
i. Woodlands	220	20.4	Natural and established woodlands
ii. Grass and scrub	519	48.2	Natural grass and scrubland
iii. Badlands, swamp and mangrove	44	4.1	Land stripped of cover, or denuded granite country including coastal brackish swamp and mangrove
iv. Arable	65	6.0	Cultivable lands, including orchards and market gardens, under cultivation and fallow
v. Fish ponds	16	1.5	Fresh and brackish water fish farming excluding coastal marine fish farms
vi. Temporary structures/livestock farms	12	1.1	
vii. Reservoir	26	2.4	
viii. Other uses	21	2.0	Including cemetery, crematorium, mine and quarry etc.
Total	**1 078**	**100.0**	

Note: * Within these are 413 km² of country parks and special areas designated under the Country Parks Ordinance for protection of vegetation and wild life and for recreation.

APPENDIX 36

(Chapter 14: Land, Public Works and Utilities)

Electricity Consumption, 1993

	Maximum demand	*Sales*	*Consumers*
	megawatts	*million megajoules*	*hundreds*
China Light and Power Company	5 244	88 109	16 186
	(5 289)	(86 042)*	(15 643)
The Hongkong Electric Company	1 890	27 902	4 715
	(1 819)	(25 975)*	(4 562)
Total		**116 012**	**20 901**

Note: Figures in brackets refer to 1992.
* Excluding inter-connection sales.

Electricity Distribution

million megajoules

	1991	*1992*	*1993*
Domestic	20 586	21 716	24 092
Industrial	25 051	24 194	22 309*
Commercial	45 245	47 971	53 131*
Street lighting	259	271	278
Export to China	11 019	17 866	16 201
Total	**102 159**	**112 017**	**116 012**

Note: * The classification of commerical and industrial customers has been changed in 1993.

Gas Consumption and Distribution (Towngas)

million megajoules

	1991	*1992*	*1993*
Domestic	8 133	9 152	9 657
Industrial	701	823	889
Commercial	7 404	8 232	8 652
Total	**16 238**	**18 207**	**19 198**

Local Sales of Liquefied Petroleum Gas (LPG)

tonnes

	1991	*1992*	*1993†*
Total	**202 580**	**213 845**	**199 130**

Note: † Estimated figure.

Water Consumption

million cubic metres

	1991	*1992*	*1993*
Fresh water	884	889	915
Salt water (flushing purposes)	123	127	129

APPENDIX 37

(Chapter 15: Transport)

International Movements of Aircraft and Vessels

	1991	1992	1993
Aircraft			
Arrivals	54 863	60 483	67 500†
Departures	54 855	60 485	67 500†
Total	**109 718**	**120 968**	**135 000**†
Ocean-going vessels@			
Arrivals	21 178	26 052(27 812)	32 972†
Departures	21 217	25 939(28 716)	33 524†
Total	**42 395**	**51 991(56 528)**	**66 496**†
River steamers, hydrofoils, hoverferries, catamarans and river trading vessels@			
Arrivals	106 672	123 289(120 906)	132 511†
Departures	106 266	123 766(120 430)	131 752†
Total	**212 938**	**247 055(241 336)**	**264 263**†

Note: † Provisional figures.

International Movements of Passengers (Immigration figures)

	1991	1992	*Thousands* 1993
Arrivals			
Air	7 412	8 451	9 339
Sea	8 984	9 621	9 905
Land	18 167	20 453	21 937
Total	**34 563**	**38 525**	**41 181**
Departures			
Air	7 602	8 636	9 492
Sea	9 235	9 904	10 222
Land	17 737	19 960	21 338
Total	**34 574**	**38 500**	**41 052**

Note: All figures quoted here exclude:
i. Passengers in transit.
ii. Passengers refused permission to land.
iii. Military passengers.

International Movements of Commercial Cargo by Different Means of Transport

	1991	1992	*Tonnes* 1993
Air			
Discharged	372 126	422 621	520 000†
Loaded	477 660	534 286	620 000†
Total	**849 786**	**956 907**	**1 140 000**†
Ocean-going vessels # @Ω			
Discharged	52 898 899	58 423 474(58 882 000)	69 932 000†
Loaded	23 546 272	25 798 891(24 500 000)	27 987 000†
Total	**76 445 171**	**84 222 365(83 383 000)**	**97 919 000**†
River vessels@			
Discharged	6 722 342	11 991 721(11 627 332)	10 600 000†
Loaded	4 424 955	5 385 260(7 705 829)	10 100 000†
Total	**11 147 297**	**17 376 981(19 333 161)**	**20 700 000**†
Rail			
Discharged§	1 742 697	1 542 556	1 247 331
Loaded	338 735	368 992	365 489
Total	**2 081 433**	**1 911 548**	**1 612 820**
*Road**			
Discharged	5 503 363	6 417 657	7 312 457
Loaded	5 492 133	5 736 338	5 688 877
Total	**10 995 496**	**12 153 995**	**13 001 334**

Note: # Figures on cargo movement by ocean-going vessels are based on the Shipping Statistics System set up by the Census and Statistics Department and are estimated from a sample of consignments on ocean cargo manifests. Figures on cargo movement by river vessels are provided by the Marine Department. The totals of these figures differ from those provided by the Marine Department and used elsewhere in this publication.
@ Starting from 1993, ocean-going vessels have been redefined as all vessels operating beyond the river trade limits whereas river vessels have been redefined as all vessels operating exclusively within the river trade limits. To facilitate comparison with 1993, statistics for 1992 compiled according to the new definition are presented in brackets ( ).
Ω All figures compiled under the new definition are published in the nearest thousand.
§ Excluding livestock totalling 1 875 272 heads in 1991, 1 907 675 heads in 1992 and 1 798 166 heads in 1993.
* Road transport refers to cross frontier traffic through Man Kam To, Sha Tau Kok and Lok Ma Chau to and from China.
† Provisional figures.

APPENDIX 38

(Chapter 15: Transport)

Registered/Licensed Motor Vehicles

	As at end of year					
	1991		*1992*		*1993*	
Public service vehicles	*Registered*	*Licensed*	*Registered*	*Licensed*	*Registered*	*Licensed*
Public buses						
China Motor Bus Company	1 015	948	1 011	999	1 014	959
Kowloon Motor Bus Company	3 038	3 022	3 109	3 097	3 197	3 144
New Lantao Bus Company	70	65	76	64	56	56
Citibus Company‡	0	0	0	0	207	200
Others	3 780	3 582	4 011	3 743	4 144	3 835
Public light buses	4 350	4 336	4 349	4 336	4 350	4 327
Taxis	17 529	17 308	17 720	17 537	17 758	17 639
Private vehicles						
Motor cycles	22 961	17 762	24 871	18 667	26 768	19 199
Motor tricycles	25	15	19	11	24	20
Private cars	236 747	212 017	265 755	237 035	291 913	259 874
Private buses	201	197	240	231	266	263
Private light buses	2 561	2 384	2 525	2 348	2 564	2 387
Goods vehicles	134 285	118 061	140 755	119 790	144 093	120 661
Crown vehicles (excluding vehicles of HM Forces)						
Motor cycles	1 287	1 287	1 198	1 198	1 274	1 274
Other motor vehicles	5 920	5 920	5 582	5 582	5 881	5 881
Total	**433 769**	**386 904**	**471 221**	**414 638**	**503 509**	**439 719**
Tramcars						
Hongkong Tramways	163	163	163	163	163	163
Peak Tramways Company	2	2	2	2	2	2
Light Rail Transit	70	70	82	82	100	100
Total	**235**	**235**	**247**	**247**	**265**	**265**

Public Transport: Passengers Carried by Undertaking

			Thousand journeys
	1991	*1992*	*1993*†
Kowloon Motor Bus Company	968 082	970 653	961 544
China Motor Bus Company	267 145	262 430	242 458
New Lantao Bus Company	4 286	3 989	4 087
City Bus§	182	957	14 060
Kowloon-Canton Railway Bus	33 984	33 933	32 041
Mass Transit Railway Corporation	725 966	751 005	775 118
Kowloon-Canton Railway Corporation	190 668	199 905	207 855
Light Rail Transit	82 061	92 273	106 884
Hongkong Tramways	123 247	124 087	125 708
Peak Tramways Company	3 132	3 267	3 437
Green Minibus	250 634	259 128	265 592
Residential Coach Services	23 342	25 638	30 916
Hongkong and Yaumati Ferry Company	50 960	44 368	40 783
'Star' Ferry Company	36 602	35 844	34 791
Minor Ferries	7 517	8 730	8 741
Public Light Buses #	378 746	371 905	368 139
Taxi #	455 825	463 595	471 580
Total @	**3 602 377**	**3 651 707**	**3 693 734**

Public Transport: Passengers Carried by Area (excluding passengers of public light buses and taxis)

Thousand journeys

	1991	*1992*	*1993*†
Hong Kong Island	489 575	495 920	498 196
Kowloon	764 478	757 687	747 147
Cross Harbour			
Ferry	63 410	56 275	52 514
Tunnels	415 278	424 292	430 301
New Territories	1 035 065	1 082 431	1 109 552
Total @	**2 767 807**	**2 816 605**	**2 837 710**

Public Transport: Daily Average Number of Passengers Carried by Different Modes of Transport

Thousand journeys

	1991	*1992*	*1993*†
Bus	3 489	3 475	3 436
Red Minibus # and Green Minibus	1 724	1 729	1 736
Taxi #	1 249	1 267	1 292
Ferry	260	239	233
Tram	346	348	354
Railway*	2 736	2 850	2 986
Residential coach	64	70	85
Total @	**9 870**	**9 978**	**10 122**

Note: † Provisional figures.
§ City Bus Ltd. started operating a franchised bus route No. 12A from September 12, 1991 and the network 26 from 1.9.1993.
# Estimate.
* Includes Mass Transit Railway and Light Rail Transit.
@ Figures may not add up to total due to rounding.
‡ Citibus included as others in 1991 and 1992.

APPENDIX 39
(Chapter 18: Public Order)
Traffic Accidents

	1991	*1992*	*1993†*
Hong Kong Island	3 748	3 644	3 729
Kowloon	7 923	7 766	7 452
New Territories	3 619	3 886	4 239
Marine	37	30	8
Total	**15 327**	**15 326**	**15 428**

Traffic Casualties

	1991	*1992*	*1993†*
Hong Kong Island			
Fatal	51	50	60
Serious	838	786	781
Slight	3 936	3 960	4 022
Kowloon			
Fatal	136	155	156
Serious	1 834	1 704	1 730
Slight	8 152	8 182	7 713
New Territories			
Fatal	127	123	129
Serious	1 272	1 294	1 314
Slight	4 226	4 446	4 929
Marine			
Fatal	1	—	2
Serious	18	23	4
Slight	46	64	2
Total	**20 637**	**20 787**	**20 842**

Note: † Provisional figures.

APPENDIX 40

(Chapter 18: Public Order)

Crime

Police Cases

	Number of cases reported			Number of persons arrested		
	1991	*1992*	*1993*	*1991*	*1992*	*1993*
Type of offence						
Violent Crime						
Rape	114	116	103	86	86	97
Indecent assault	1 101	1 099	1 030	655	611	607
Murder and manslaughter	92	108	86	136	138	96
Attempted murder	12	17	6	14	8	6
Wounding	1 398	1 170	1 216	1 166	1 008	1 051
Serious assault	4 983	4 600	4 857	3 389	3 157	3 620
Assault on police	953	1 018	888	609	707	585
Kidnapping and child stealing	8	12	10	24	29	24
Cruelty to child	73	82	80	69	82	75
Criminal intimidation	410	519	653	343	400	551
Robbery with firearms	46	46	22	33	17	24
Robbery with pistol like object	501	372	269	101	64	96
Other robberies	8 591	7 976	6 746	2 378	2 342	2 370
Aggravated burglary	4	1	0	4	1	0
Blackmail	719	883	859	761	938	888
Arson	553	548	629	92	94	129
Total	**19 558**	**18 567**	**17 454**	**9 860**	**9 682**	**10 219**
Non-Violent Crime						
Burglary	13 894	13 595	13 711	1 563	1 626	1 758
Snatching	1 995	1 685	1 528	277	272	280
Pickpocketing	779	675	687	373	281	383
Shop theft	6 008	6 362	6 497	5 462	6 008	6 220
Theft from vehicle	4 007	3 497	3 555	757	854	1 041
Taking conveyance without authority	6 475	7 046	4 698	431	454	444
Other thefts	12 324	11 810	11 872	4 591	4 535	4 791
Handling stolen goods	230	235	231	300	312	290
Deception, fraud and forgery	2 128	2 080	2 483	1 265	1 266	1 373
Sexual offences other than rape and indecent assault	1 052	948	917	989	851	787
Manufacturing and trafficking of dangerous drugs	2 998	1 803	3 506	3 720	2 192	4 155
Serious immigration offences	4 042	4 452	4 038	4 113	4 473	4 018
Criminal damage	4 422	4 298	4 303	1 307	1 507	1 616
Unlawful society offences	1 096	1 466	1 308	699	755	705
Possession of offensive weapon	1 007	791	779	1 335	916	891
Other crimes	6 644	4 746	4 997	7 017	5 796	6 071
Total	**69 101**	**65 489**	**65 110**	**34 199**	**32 098**	**34 823**
Grand Total	**88 659**	**84 056**	**82 564**	**44 059**	**41 780**	**45 042**

Overall detection rate 1991 = 45.2 per cent 1992 = 45.2 per cent 1993 = 48.7 per cent

Narcotic Offence Cases

	Number of cases reported			Number of persons arrested		
	1991	*1992*	*1993*	*1991*	*1992*	*1993*
Type of offence						
Serious offences						
Manufacturing of dangerous drugs	5	10	32	12	17	46
Trafficking in dangerous drugs	171	421	673	228	538	909
Possession of dangerous drugs (indictable offence)	2 821	1 372	2 798	3 477	1 637	3 196
Other serious narcotic offences	1	—	3	3	—	4
Sub-total	**2 998**	**1 803**	**3 506**	**3 720**	**2 192**	**4 155**
Minor offences – Opium						
Simple possession of opium	35	29	50	19	18	47
Possession of equipment	39	10	20	12	—	3
Keeping a divan	9	7	3	4	9	3
Consuming opium	21	12	7	11	2	5
Other opium offences	1	—	—	—	—	—
Sub-total	**105**	**58**	**80**	**46**	**29**	**58**
Minor offences – Heroin						
Simple possession of heroin	2 776	5 963	6 094	2 698	5 886	6 387
Possession of equipment	489	545	455	200	240	395
Keeping a divan	2	1	3	5	1	8
Consuming heroin	196	171	114	101	149	115
Other heroin offences	23	35	6	9	16	—
Sub-total	**3 486**	**6 715**	**6 672**	**3 013**	**6 292**	**6 905**
Minor offences – Other dangerous drugs						
Simple possession	823	1 023	1 456	760	989	1 560
Consuming	—	1	9	—	2	7
Other offences	34	40	10	25	22	6
Sub-total	**857**	**1 064**	**1 475**	**785**	**1 013**	**1 573**
Total	**7 446**	**9 640**	**11 733**	**7 564**	**9 526**	**12 691**

Note: Serious narcotics offences include police cases only.

ICAC Cases

	1991	1992	1993				
			Number of persons prosecuted				
			Pending	Convicted	Acquitted	Nolle Prosequi	Total
Involving individuals employed in government departments							
Architectural Services	—	1	—	—	—	—	—
Buildings and Lands	3	—	1	—	—	—	1
Correctional Services	1	4	1	5	1	—	7
Customs & Excise	8	—	6	2	—	—	8
Drainage Services	1	—	—	—	—	—	—
Environmental Protection	1	—	—	—	—	—	—
Fire Services	1	—	—	—	—	—	—
Highways	—	1	—	—	—	—	—
Housing	—	1	—	1	—	—	1
Immigration	—	3	3	2	—	—	5
Hospital Services	1	—	—	1	—	—	1
Post Office	1	1	—	—	—	—	—
Regional Services	1	—	—	—	—	—	—
Royal Hong Kong Police	8	9	9	5	1	—	15
Transport	1	1	—	—	—	—	—
Urban Services	6	4	—	4	—	—	4
Water Supplies	—	1	—	—	—	—	—
Sub-total	**33**	**26**	**20**	**20**	**2**	—	**42**
Others							
Crown servants/private individuals ‡	47	13	20	8	7	—	35
Public bodies #	21	9	1	4	—	—	5
Public bodies/private individuals ‡	4	2	—	2	1	—	3
Private sector **	209	253	80	420	34	—	534
Sub-total	**281**	**277**	**101**	**434**	**42**	—	**577**
Total	**314**	**303**	**121**	**454**	**44**	—	**619**

Note: ‡ These are cases in which Crown/public servants and private individuals were involved.
As defined in the Prevention of Bribery Ordinance, Cap. 201.
**These are cases in which only private individuals were involved.

APPENDIX 41

(Chapter 18: Public Order)

Judiciary Statistics

	1991	1992	1993
Supreme Court			
(i) Court of Appeal			
Civil appeals	206	211	218
Criminal appeals	588	548	738
Total	**794**	**759**	**956**
(ii) High Court			
Criminal jurisdiction			
Criminal cases	419	424	478
Appeals from Magistrates	1 190	1 112	1 072
Total	**1 609**	**1 536**	**1 550**
Civil Jurisdiction			
High Court actions	10 020	9 305	11 863
Commercial cases	205	152	213
Construction cases	20	13	24
Miscellaneous proceedings	3 997	4 206	4 438
Adoptions	10	8	2
Divorce	6	1	4
Admiralty jurisdiction	421	335	365
Bankruptcy	859	887	915
Company winding-up	422	423	539
Appeals from Small Claims and Labour Tribunals	98	84	145
Total	**16 058**	**15 414**	**18 508**
District Court			
Criminal cases	1 235	1 316	1 328
Other cases			
Civil actions	26 369	34 927	21 638
Stamp Appeals	55	37	88
Employee's compensation	784	693	689
Distress for rent	4 557	4 381	5 038
Divorce	7 287	8 067	8 626
Adoptions	341	319	332
Lands	4 875	5 373	4 724
Total	**45 503**	**55 113**	**42 463**
Small Claims Tribunal			
Number of cases filed	**38 756**	**38 930**	**39 380**
Labour Tribunal			
Number of cases filed	**4 964**	**5 199**	**5 194**
Obscene Articles Tribunal			
Number of cases filed	**1 211**	**849**	**1 459**
Coroner's Court			
Number of death inquiries made	**270**	**257**	**267**
Magistracies			
Charge sheets issued	111 834	122 111	128 388
Summonses issued	345 977	360 536	414 037
Miscellaneous proceedings issued	16 753	17 131	17 898
Anti-litter notices issued	40 011	38 459	40 174
Total	**514 575**	**538 237**	**600 497**
Defendants charged			
Adults	520 803	551 113	591 610
Juveniles	2 858	2 541	3 446
Total	**523 661**	**553 654**	**595 056**
Defendants convicted			
Adults	479 607	469 245	539 720
Juveniles	2 135	1 782	1 961
Total	**481 742**	**471 027**	**541 681**

APPENDIX 42

(Chapter 18: Public Order)

Correctional Services

	As at end of year		
	1991	*1992*	*1993*
Population of			
Prisons	8 972	9 035	8 517
Training centres	722	576	593
Detention centres	319	271	242
Treatment centres	1 018	1 067	1 200
Vietnamese migrants/Illegal immigrants	34 778	33 004	22 886
Number Discharged under aftercare	3 121	3 256	3 346

APPENDIX 43

(Chapter 21: Communications and the Media)

Communications

	1991	*1992*	*1993 Estimate*
Postal traffic:			
Letter mail (million articles)			
Posted to destinations abroad	142.1	142.2	151.5
Posted for local delivery	711.2	742.7	782.6
Received from abroad for local delivery	87.5	91.0	96.6
In transit	3.8	3.0	2.3
Parcels (thousands)			
Posted to destinations abroad	1 347	1 257	1 145
Posted for local delivery	51	46	53
Received from abroad for local delivery	508	507	497
In transit	37	40	47
Telecommunications traffic:			
Telegrams (thousand messages)			
Accepted for transmission	344	280	223
Received	425	362	303
In transit	137	121	108
Telex calls (thousand minutes)			
Outward	23 907	20 322	18 502
Inward	27 345	22 627	20 626
International telephone calls (thousand minutes)			
Outward (voice)	731 343	918 822	1 132 671
Outward (fax and data)	135 255	160 667	190 458
Inward (voice, fax and data)	742 617†	955 726†	1 198 451
Radio pictures			
Transmitted	—	—	—
Received	157	99	120
Broadcast and reception services (thousand hours)			
Press	0.6	0.4*	—
Meteorological	108.5	106.5	104.5
International telephone circuits	14 732	17 641	24 207
International telegraph circuits	3 070	2 844	2 657
Telex trunks	2 373	2 259	2 187
International leased circuits	1 637	1 610	1 586
Telephone exchanges	75	76	79
Exchange capacity (thousand lines)	2 850	3 004	3 138
Keylines and PABX lines (thousands)	372	407	442
Fax lines (thousands)	137	183	228
Telephone lines (thousands)	2 596	2 777	2 957
Telephones (thousands)	3 455†	3 649†	3 856
Telephones per 100 population	60.0†	62.8†	65.1
Outgoing international calls (million)	264.56	335.85	373.8
Telecommunications licences (all types)	80 249	83 983	89 861

Note: † Estimate.
* Customer terminated its service with effect from August 1992.

APPENDIX 44

(Chapter 23: Recreation, Sports and the Arts)

Recreational Facilities

	Urban Council			Regional Council		
Facilities	*1991*	*1992*	*1993*	*1991*	*1992*	*1993*
Indoor games halls/Indoor recreation centres	34	34	34	25	27	29
Squash courts	121	131	131	86	100	105
Tennis courts	112	122	130	68	89	97
Fitness centres/Sports centres	10	10	—	4	4	3
Stadia (outdoor)	2	2	2	—	—	—
Grass pitches	39	40	38	14	17	17
Hard surfaced pitches	123	127	130	76	78	84
Athletic grounds	9	8	8	10	12	12
Bowling greens	2	2	2	—	—	—
Obstacle golf courses	2	2	2	—	—	—
Roller skating rinks	18	17	17	24	24	22
Jogging tracks/Fitness trails	23	24	28	1	1	13
Cycling tracks	3	3	4	2	2	2
Boating parks	1	1	1	1	1	1
Beaches	12	12	12	30	30	30
Swimming pool complexes	14	14	14	10	13	13
Water sports centres	—	—	—	3	3	3
Holiday camps	1	1	1	3	3	3
Gardens/Sitting-out area	777	794	797	430	487	506
Children's playgrounds	258	265	270	224	247	263
Zoos/aviaries	4	4	1	1	1	1
Total area of public open space administered (hectares)*	**513**	**518**	**535**	**633**	**651**	**693**

Note: * Open space on beaches are excluded.

APPENDIX 45

(Chapter 24: The Environment)

Climatological Summary, 1993

Month	*Mean pressure at mean sea level*	*Maxi-mum air tem-perature*	*Mean air tem-perature*	*Mini-mum air tem-perature*	*Mean dew point*	*Mean relative humidity*	*Mean amount of cloud*	*Total bright sunshine*	*Total rainfall*	*Prevailing wind direction*	*Mean wind speed*
	hectopascals	*°C*	*°C*	*°C*	*°C*	*per cent*	*per cent*	*hours*	*mm*	*degrees*	*km/h*
January	1 021.3	23.7	14.6	5.4	9.6	74	61	132.8	33.5	030	25.9
February	1 019.1	23.4	18.0	12.8	13.9	78	60	126.7	1.0	090	24.6
March	1 016.8	28.1	19.4	11.3	16.2	82	87	77.3	49.0	090	23.5
April	1 013.9	29.8	21.8	14.6	19.3	86	85	81.3	136.3	090	23.4
May	1 010.3	31.7	26.0	20.6	23.0	84	73	162.8	338.4	090	16.7
June	1 006.2	33.0	28.3	23.6	25.2	84	84	139.5	485.2	200	20.6
July	1 005.9	33.5	29.4	24.3	25.3	79	75	259.8	213.7	240	24.0
August	1 006.1	33.4	28.6	25.0	25.1	82	63	211.5	182.8	100	21.7
September	1 009.4	32.1	27.5	22.6	23.5	79	59	172.8	655.9	090	24.6
October	1 016.2	29.0	24.6	17.2	18.3	69	49	198.4	87.8	080	28.4
November	1 016.9	27.8	21.7	11.9	16.9	76	66	131.2	144.6	080	31.1
December	1 021.5	25.3	17.1	9.2	10.5	67	53	165.8	15.7	020	30.0
Year	**1 013.6**	**33.5**	**23.1**	**5.4**	**18.9**	**78**	**68**	**1 859.9**	**2 343.9**	**090**	**24.5**

Climatological Normals (1961–1990)

Month	*hectopascals*	*°C**	*°C*	*°C**	*°C*	*per cent*	*per cent*	*hours*	*mm*	*degrees*	*km/h*
January	1 020.2	26.9	15.8	0.0	10.2	71	58	152.4	23.4	070	24.0
February	1 018.7	27.8	15.9	2.4	11.8	78	73	97.7	48.0	070	23.8
March	1 016.2	30.1	18.5	4.8	15.0	81	76	96.4	66.9	070	22.1
April	1 013.1	33.4	22.2	9.9	19.0	83	78	108.9	161.5	080	19.7
May	1 009.1	35.5	25.9	15.4	22.6	83	74	153.8	316.7	090	19.2
June	1 006.0	35.6	27.8	19.2	24.4	82	75	161.1	376.0	090	21.6
July	1 005.3	35.7	28.8	21.7	24.9	80	65	231.1	323.5	230	20.0
August	1 005.1	36.1	28.4	21.6	24.8	81	66	207.0	391.4	090	18.5
September	1 008.8	35.2	27.6	18.4	23.3	78	63	181.7	299.7	090	21.9
October	1 014.0	34.3	25.2	13.5	19.8	73	56	195.0	144.8	090	27.6
November	1 017.9	31.8	21.4	6.5	15.2	69	53	181.5	35.1	080	27.2
December	1 020.2	28.7	17.6	4.3	11.2	68	49	181.5	27.3	080	25.5
Year	**1 012.9**	**36.1**	**23.0**	**0.0**	**18.6**	**77**	**65**	**1 948.1**	**2 214.3**	**080**	**22.6**

Note: * These extreme values are for the period 1884–1939; 1947–1993.

APPENDIX 46
(Chapter 26: History)

Governors of Hong Kong

The Right Honourable Sir Henry POTTINGER, Bt, GCB	June 26, 1843
Sir John Francis DAVIS, Bt, KCB	May 8, 1844
Sir Samuel George BONHAM, Bt, KCB	March 21, 1848
Sir John BOWRING	April 13, 1854
The Right Honourable the Lord ROSMEAD, GCMG, PC (formerly the Right Honourable Sir Hercules ROBINSON, Bt)	September 9, 1859
Sir Richard Graves MACDONNELL, KCMG, CB	March 11, 1866
Sir Arthur Edward KENNEDY, GCMG, CB	April 16, 1872
Sir John Pope HENNESSY, KCMG	April 22, 1877
The Right Honourable Sir George Ferguson BOWEN, GCMG	March 30, 1883
Sir George William DES VOEUX, GCMG	October 6, 1887
Sir William ROBINSON, GCMG	December 10, 1891
Sir Henry Arthur BLAKE, GCMG	November 25, 1898
The Right Honourable Sir Matthew NATHAN, GCMG	July 29, 1904
The Right Honourable the Lord LUGARD, GCMG, CB, DSO, PC	July 29, 1907
Sir Francis Henry MAY, GCMG	July 24, 1912
Sir Reginald Edward STUBBS, GCMG	September 30, 1919
Sir Cecil CLEMENTI, GCMG	November 1, 1925
Sir William PEEL, KCMG, KBE	May 9, 1930
Sir Andrew CALDECOTT, GCMG, CBE	December 12, 1935
Sir Geoffry Alexander Stafford NORTHCOTE, KCMG	October 28, 1937
Sir Mark Aitchison YOUNG, GCMG	September 10, 1941
Sir Alexander William George Herder GRANTHAM, GCMG	July 25, 1947
Sir Robert Brown BLACK, GCMG, OBE	January 23, 1958
Sir David Clive Crosbie TRENCH, GCMG, MC	April 14, 1964
The Right Honourable the Lord MACLEHOSE of Beoch, KT, GBE, KCMG, KCVO (formerly Sir Crawford Murray MACLEHOSE)	November 19, 1971
Sir Edward YOUDE, GCMG, GCVO, MBE	May 20, 1982
Lord WILSON of Tillyorn, GCMG (formerly Sir David Clive WILSON)	April 9, 1987
The Right Honourable Christopher Francis PATTEN	July 9, 1992

INDEX

Printed and Published by H. Myers, Government Printer
at the Government Printing Department, Hong Kong

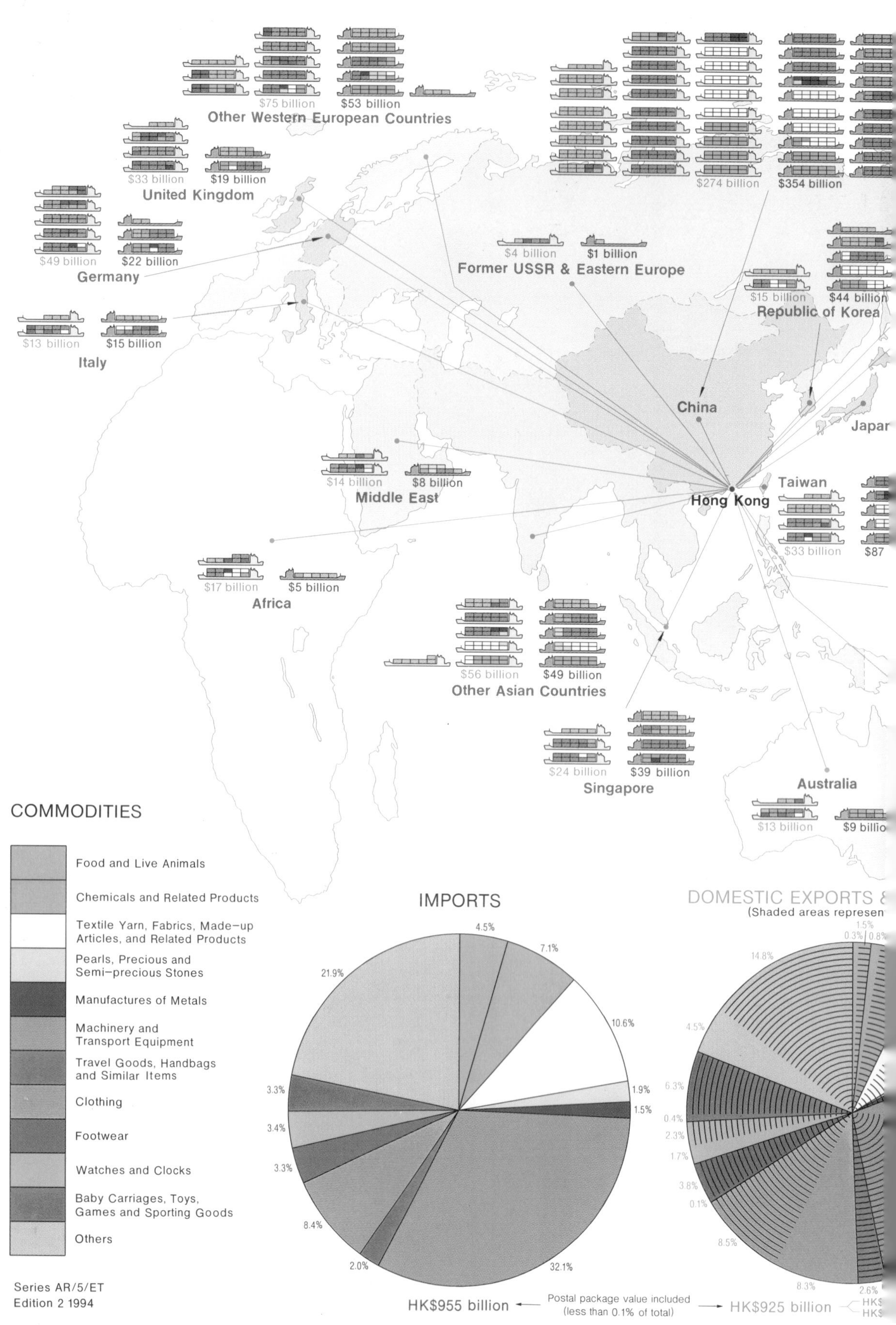

Series AR/5/ET
Edition 2 1994